THE INSIDERS' GUIDE® TO

Bermuda

THE INSIDERS'® GUIDE TO

Bermuda

by
James Ziral
and
Liz Jones

The Insiders' Guide®
An imprint of Falcon® Publishing Inc.
A Landmark Communications Company
P.O. Box 1718
Helena, MT 59624
(800) 582-2665
www.insiders.com

Co-published and marketed by:
The Royal Gazette Ltd.
2 Par-La-Ville Road
Hamilton, Bermuda
(441) 295-5881
manager@circ.newsmedia.bm

Sales and Marketing: Falcon Publishing, Inc.
P.O. Box 1718
Helena, MT 59624
(800) 582-2665
www.falcon.com

Advertising: Falcon Publishing, Inc.
150 W. Brambleton Ave.
Norfolk, VA 23510
(757) 446-2933
rwalsh@falcon.com

•

SECOND EDITION
1st printing

•

©1999 by The Royal Gazette Ltd.

•

Printed in the United States
of America

•

Publications from *The Insiders' Guide®* series are available at special discounts for bulk purchases for sales promotions, premiums or fundraisings. Special editions, including personalized covers, can be created in large quantities for special needs. For more information, please contact Falcon Publishing.

ISBN 1-57380-108-9

Preface

Viewed from several thousand feet, on the glide path into its airport, Bermuda appears a flat green carpet dropped in a pale blue puddle. Its mainland, seven islands joined by bridges tiny enough to thread the eye of a needle, is dotted by jellybean-colored houses topped by white roofs. They hug the landscape like candies in an emerald jar.

Outlying barrier reefs, burnished deep brown and black by wind and waves, are reminders that beneath a sea warmed by the gulf stream lie the bones of hundreds of once-proud ships. In this silent aquatic world, these skeletons have become an abode for sea fans, delicate sea anemones, purple sponges and parrot fish. As magnets for divers hopeful of retrieving some overlooked memento from another age, some of these vessels have yielded genuine treasures.

One of the most expensive pieces of beachfront in the world, Bermuda has an undeniable beauty. But it is more than just a pretty face. Scratch the surface and just beneath what Mark Twain called its "tranquil and contenting" skin is a country that within 25 years has evolved from an almost mythical sleepy hollow into a dynamic international business hub. Tourism and international business now compose a duality that gives Bermudians a standard of living ranked among the highest in the world.

Certainly the country easily attracts pretty words, and always has. Like fragrant scents of delicate evening blossoms, they float effortlessly, all too often spilling into vivid imagery. Early in the 1930s, with tourism the only economic pillar of any consequence, a writer for the Trade Development Board — the precursor of today's Department of Tourism — penned a description that captured several colors of the rainbow.

"The road to yesterday," he wrote, "will take you far from the chill, bleak cities of here and now. It will lead you to a gleaming group of coral isles, riotous with tropical color, set in an azure sea, warmed by a golden sun that will flood your veins with youth. It is a soft road, paved with cushions of green, spume-flecked velvet, bordered with white flowers of healthy salt-spray."

We don't usually (well, sometimes we succumb) get quite so "purple" with our tourist promotions today. But there is no doubt that once here, whether your intention is to have your veins flooded with youth or not, you will find us a blend of delightful ironies and exquisite eccentricities.

Actually, as far back as 1663, the Reverend Michael Wigglesworth, a rhyming divine from Malden, Massachusetts, chose to visit Bermuda to improve his failing health. "It was a full month ere we got thither," he would later write, "by which long and tedious voyage no doubt I received much hurt." But despite the pain and discomfort of an arduous journey, he safely arrived, and remained here for seven months, his spirits and body rejuvenated by what he described as the island's "sweet and temperate air."

The good reverend is generally acknowledged as Bermuda's first bona fide tourist. Today visitors find it easier and considerably more comfortable and quicker to travel to our shores.

Bermuda, a neat country, is shy, even coy. While some destinations entice with brashness, bright lights and revelry until dawn, Bermuda prefers to seduce with gentle caresses.

And our national quirks — difficult to explain quickly — are probably better understood when one remembers that we're a British colony steeped in ancient traditions, yet influenced by American habits that have penetrated almost every nook and cranny. We live a sweet mystery. Perhaps that's why Twain, one of our most famous repeat visitors, loved us so much. That and the fact he found us "tidy, the right place for a jaded man to loaf in."

But we're not just for loafing. We're a land of festivals, holidays and events that embrace theatre, jazz and reggae, classical concerts, cricket and jet-skiing, soccer and scuba-diving, golf and tennis, snorkeling, sailing and rugby, motocross and bicycle races, bridge and chess competitions, and...well, you see the point. And we're also a land with a fascinating history, our cool and quaint museums revealing another side of our character and personality.

But the best way to begin to know us is to visit. We won't greet you with garlands of flowers; you'll find natural floral arrangements throughout our countryside, some dripping from our walls and hedges. And there are genuine welcomes in our smiles. After all, we've been called some of the friendliest people on earth. After that first visit, you'll want to return as you discover that Bermuda is more than festivals, storied street names and vanilla crème beaches tinged with pink. It is a mood, a promise, a pastel book of colors edged in sunlight and bright blue sky.

About the Authors

James Ziral

James Ziral was 15 when he sold his first article to the *Bermuda Sun*, a local newspaper. Seventeen years later he would become an investigative reporter and columnist at the same paper. Although writing always sat on his shoulder and thumped him between the shoulder blades, he ignored it in pursuit of making what he thought was *real* money. But in 1977 he realized that working for a real estate agency, an insurance company and a radio and television station were not career choices that truly satisfied him. In a moment of complete clarity, James wrapped up his business in Bermuda and boarded a plane to New York where he lived and worked for six years before returning to his island home.

Despite having graduated years earlier from the local Cable & Wireless Training School, and having studied business in New York, James remained intimate with the manual typewriter, finally committing to writing for the newspaper where he had sold his first story — it had something to do with Christmas, he recalls.

As an investigative journalist and columnist, he learned much about Bermuda behind the scenes. However, a travel bug that had been with him since his teens bit down hard — in 1985 he resigned from the *Sun* and flew off to London, where he lived for four years. It was, he admits, just another step in learning more about the world through being there. Travel to the Bahamas, Martinique, Canada and a number of American cities helped broaden that experience, as did living in Michigan for a while.

Returning to Bermuda in 1989, James continued to write for publications both here and abroad, among them *Civil War Times Illustrated*, *Destination Bermuda* and *Bermuda Cruise*; he eventually became an associate editor for *The Bermudian* magazine until leaving in 1994. It was during this period that he authored the text for *Emeralds On A Silver Zone*, a coffee-table book on early color photography in Bermuda. In 1992 he was voted the island's Journalist of the Year.

After a subsequent stint as editor of the *Bermuda Times,* James became fascinated with television; he soon produced and directed the television news magazine *64 West*, his own concept that took its title from Bermuda's longitudinal position. Also during this time James accepted an invitation to become a member of the Bermuda Arts Council and wrote ad copy for local and international company brochures and annual reports.

Since 1995, after recovering from a stroke, James has been a full-time freelance writer, writing regularly for the *Mid-Ocean News*, *Bermuda*, *The Bermudian*, *Caribbean Week*, *American Visions* and other publications. In 1997 he wrote, produced and directed a half-hour television documentary on tourism for the Ministry of Community and Cultural Affairs. It was his second television project for that ministry.

Restless, curious, and hard to satisfy, when James is not at the computer keyboard, he collects rare books, Haitian paintings, ancient maps, Bermuda cedar sculpture, African sculpture and 18th- and 19th-century original lithographs of botanicals. The house he shares with his wife, Helen, has been described as a museum and art gallery.

"Bermuda is one of the most complex little places on the planet," James says, "and treat with caution anyone who tells you they really understand it."

Liz Jones

In 1970, Liz Jones was studying literature at the University of East Anglia, England. In a bar one evening, she met Mike, who explained he was from Bermuda. She did not have the slightest idea where Bermuda was. Being more interested in the Romantic poets than in the intricacies of geography, she decided not to pursue the topic. Three years later, Liz married Mike and met Bermuda, where she has lived happily ever since. In 1977, Liz felt the family name was in serious danger of dying out. Douglas Dewar Jones duly arrived. The other three important people in her life are all called William: William Shakespeare, William Blake and William Butler Yeats.

Having grown up in English villages and the Scottish Highlands, Liz has always had the good fortune to live in beautiful surroundings. Bermuda is, of course, stunningly beautiful, but there is more to it than that. Teaching English language and literature at Bermuda's Berkeley Institute and at the Bermuda College gave Liz the opportunity to enjoy the island's great asset — the diversity of its people. Compiling an anthology of oral history for Bermuda's Ministry of Community, Culture & Information gave her additional exposure to senior citizens whose memories of Bermuda stretched back to the early 1900s. Liz is also passionate about creative writing. In the past, she conducted creative writing workshops for the Bermuda College, but these days she would rather practice than preach. As a member of Bermuda Writers' Collective, she enjoyed contributing a story to *An Isle So Long Unknown*, an anthology of Bermudian short stories.

Currently, Liz is enjoying the freedom of freelance writing for a variety of Bermudian and British publications including *Bermuda Magazine*, *The Bermudian* and the *Guardian Weekly*. She also has fun writing a lighthearted "That's Life" column for the *Mid-Ocean News*. One day, she hopes, she might create a decent novel. Where will it be set? In Bermuda. Of course.

 **Bermuda**
Department of Tourism

9th March 1999.

On the 9th November 1998, Bermuda effectively witnessed the first real change in Government in nearly 400 years of history, an historic event which altered the way in which Bermudians viewed themselves, and indeed the way they are viewed by others in the outside world.

The Government of Bermuda sees the Insiders' Guide as a most appropriate communications tool for sharing with our visitor that this destination is culturally dynamic and exciting, offering a far greater dimension in this regard than many other island experiences. We further believe that the content of the contributions in this edition of the Insiders' Guide, more than adequately captures what is quintessentially Bermudian.

As we approach the threshold of the new millennium, it is critically important that first-time visitors and frequent repeaters have a permanent reminder of all that Bermuda has to offer — both from a leisure perspective and for business and corporate meetings.

In congratulating the publishers and contributing editors for this brilliant glossary and smorgasbord of uniquely Bermudian experiences, I wish, at the same time, to extend a very cordial welcome to all our visitors to the NEW BERMUDA.

With sincere and warm regards,

The Hon. David H. Allen, JP, MP
Minister of Tourism.

Dear Insider,

Having published one *Insiders' Guide to Bermuda* and receiving many very encouraging comments — some almost embarrassingly so — we thought, let's do it again.

So here it is. And again, it's a team effort.

If your plans will bring you to Bermuda in six months or if you are already here, either way, this book is definitely for you. Our two authors, Liz Jones and James Ziral, have gone the length and breadth of our island to research all the essentials required to assist you with your plans.

Quite naturally we'd like to believe that we have succeeded and that this is an improved version over the first. Additional restaurants are included in the Restaurant chapter with greater detail devoted to them. Other chapters including Attractions, Annual Events and Festivals, Kidstuff, Worship, and International Business and Shopping — all have been improved or expanded.

Getting about the Island and locating various facilities and key sights is now easier with new maps located near the front of the book.

Enjoy this guide at home, in the office, in the air, on Front Street or Featherbed Alley. Please take it everywhere and join the many others...mark the pages, make notes in the margins, bend back the pages special to you. Most of all, let us know what you feel and how the *Insiders' Guide to Bermuda* can be even better.

delMonte Davis
Circulation Manager
The Royal Gazette
manager@circ.newsmedia.bm

Acknowledgments

James Ziral

This has been both an intense and an interesting ride. During the journey several people provided information and assistance. But thanks must first go to Helen, my wife, who provided the encouragement, love and support needed when the sheer volume of work and tight deadlines threatened to send me to the funny farm with a glazed and strange expression.

And thanks must go to those persons who went the extra mile with no self-interest involved. Many of them actually wish to remain in the background without their names mentioned in print. So to everyone who showed me new ways of appreciating this tiny little corner of the world, I say thanks with all my heart.

I also want to extend my appreciation and gratitude to Kelly Phillips at the Special Services Division of the Bermuda Monetary Authority and Vernee Fullerton at the Bermuda Maritime Museum. Special thanks go to those cedar sculptors who taught me much about their medium, among them Chesley Trott, the dean of cedar carvers, and Roy Boyer, both of whom have helped in this project without realizing it. Thanks also to Dennis Eldridge, the computer guy who came to the rescue of Liz and me when seemingly perverse technology tried its best to be uncooperative. Thanks also to Nancy Acton, Tom Butterfield and Louise Jackson.

Thanks must also go to regular visitors Don and Marilyn Diloreto, dear friends from Virginia, and Ruth and Basil Mott, from New Hampshire, who visit the island regularly. Their opinions and observations have been priceless.

I cannot ignore delMonte Davis, who as always was a complete gentleman throughout the project, and most definitely I must say thanks to Erin, my editor, who patience was remarkable and very much welcomed.

She doesn't read English, but I must thank Girlie, my calico cat, who seemed to know when her affection was needed and found a home on my lap as I labored at the keyboard.

And last but not least there is Liz, my co-author, who knows what it is like to be in the trenches. Thanks Liz, your support was invaluable.

Liz Jones

As Molière said, often "Books and marriage go ill together." My greatest thanks, then, go to Mike who definitely proved Molière wrong. I want to thank him for dealing with bouts of penicillin appearing on our walls, for cooking eggs when they were urgently required, for keeping me in socks and for generally being entirely understanding about my nine-month retreat from normal living. Thanks also go to our son Doug for providing me with useful bits of information on all sorts of topics, including watering holes and watery excursions.

Where writing for Insiders' Guide is concerned, ignorance is most certainly not bliss. I must therefore thank a vast number of people who helped to fill gaps in my knowledge. Millard Beach has to be one of the most tactful people in Bermuda since he didn't laugh once when I got confused about what constitutes a golf hole and what does not. The same cannot be said of Claire Rushe or of Brian and Kim Webb who did laugh. (But they also helped to improve my golf vocabulary.) Brian and Kim's help on international business and on Bermuda's real estate is also much appreciated, as is Wayne Jackson's. George Rushe's help on a whole range of Bermuda topics was invaluable as is his book, *Your Bermuda*. And Nathalie and Philip Rushe's help on insurance and soccer has been immensely helpful, too. I must also thank Adrian Robson and Dexter Smith for help with Bermuda's sports. Thanks also go to Derek and Sally Singleton for their tennis information and to Randy Benjamin and Richard Tucker for more help with cricket and sports. Juliet Jackson and William and Joyce Zuill added to my knowledge of Bermuda's wedding traditions while Wayne Augustus helped me identify trees. Thanks also to William H. Cook for helping me with parks information and to John Barnes for info on flora and fauna. I'd also like to thank Anne-Marie Gosling for accompanying me on a park exploration and for showing me that there are 13 ways of looking at a grain of sand as well as at a blackbird.

Thanks to Jeremy Hindle, I was able to understand the principles of weather prediction so important to insurance business. Ronald Lightbourne, Bermuda's Renaissance man, helped me enormously with music, nightlife, history and cricket. Ianthe Wade gave up time to supply me with information about Summerhaven and Peter Frith explained with great patience and clarity the hotels' different rate systems. Thanks also to Charles Barclay and Emma Mitchell for their massive funds of information and useful contacts, to Terri Greenslade for answering myriad questions and to Pam Shailer and Lyn Brady. A special thank you must go to my young friend and neighbor, Sarah Fletcher, who made all sorts of useful suggestions about sports and recreations.

Many thanks go to delMonte Davis who kept me calm and well supplied with ideas Last but by no means least, I want to thank my coauthor, James Ziral. It's not that we met very often; for obvious reasons, we were far too busy. However, our regular telephone communication kept my brain alive and my spirits cheered.

Table of Contents

Directory of Maps

The Bermuda Islands

The West End

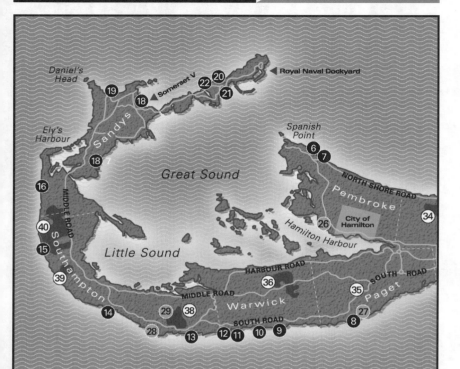

Places of Interest

BEACHES AND PARKS

1. Clearwater Beach
2. Tobacco Bay
3. Ferry Point Park & Whale Bone Bay
4. Shelly Bay Beach
5. John Smith's Bay
6. Admiralty House Park
7. Clarence Cove
8. Elbow Beach
9. Astwood Park & Beach
10. Warwick Long Bay
11. Jobson's Cove
12. Stonehole Bay
13. Horseshoe Bay
14. Church Bay
15. West Whale Bay
16. Hog Bay Park
17. Scaur Hill Fort Park
18. Mangrove Bay
19. Somerset Long Bay
20. Lagoon Park
21. Parson's Bay
22. Black Bay Park & Beach

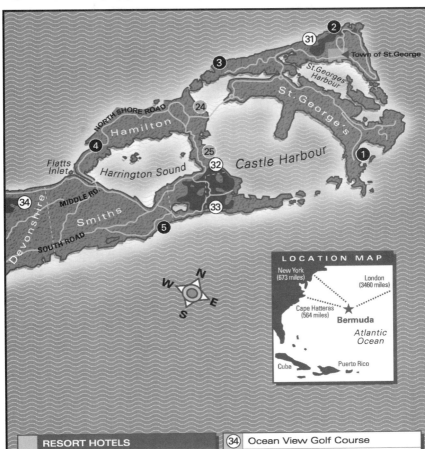

LOCATION MAP

New York
(673 miles)

London
(3460 miles)

Cape Hatteras
(564 miles)

Bermuda

*Atlantic
Ocean*

Cuba

Puerto Rico

	RESORT HOTELS
24	Grotto Bay Beach
25	Marriott's Castle Harbour Resort
26	The Hamilton Princess
27	Elbow Beach Bermuda
28	Sonesta Beach Hotel & Spa
29	The Southampton Princess

	GOLF COURSES
31	St. George's Golf Club
32	Castle Harbour Golf Club
33	Mid Ocean Golf Club

34	Ocean View Golf Course
35	Horizons & Cottages Golf Course
36	Riddells Bay Golf & Country Club
37	The Southampton Princess
	Golf Course
38	Bermuda Golf Academy &
	Driving Range
39	Port Royal Golf Course

City of Hamilton

Pembroke Parish

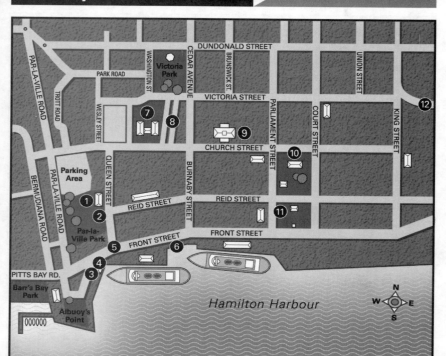

Places of Interest

1. Library & Historical Society Museum
2. Perot Post Office
3. Visitor's Service Bureau
4. Ferry Terminal
5. Bird Cage
6. Horse & Carriage Stand
7. City Hall
8. Bus Terminal
9. Cathedral
10. Sessions House
11. The Cabinet Building
12. Fort Hamilton

Town of St.George

St. George's Parish

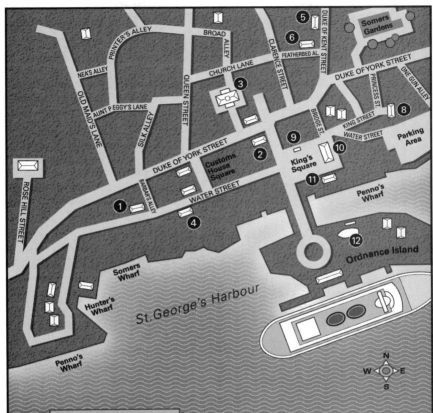

Places of Interest

1. Tucker House Museum
2. Bermuda National Trust Museum
3. St.Peter's Church
4. Carriage Museum
5. St.George's Historical Society Museum
6. Featherbed Alley Printery
7. Bridge House and Gallery
8. State House
9. Stocks
10. Town Hall
11. Visitor's Service Bureau
12. The *Deliverance*

Royal Naval Dockyard ▶ Sandys Parish

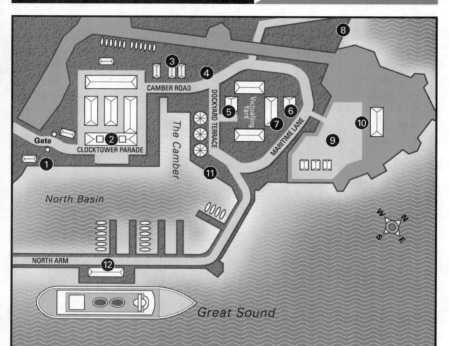

Places of Interest

1. Watersports Centre
2. Clocktower Shopping Mall
3. Bermuda Clayworks
4. Moped Rental
5. Masterworks Foundation Gallery
6. Bermuda Arts Centre
7. Bermuda Craft Market
8. Snorkel Park
9. Bermuda Maritime Museum
10. Commissioner's House
11. Ferry Stop
12. Cruise Ship Terminal

Somerset Village

Sandys Parish

Mangrove Bay

MANGROVE BAY ROAD

SOMERSET ROAD

MANGROVE BAY RO

EAST SHORE ROAD

MANGROVE LANE

LOYALTY ESTATE

N
W E
S

Places of Interest

1	Springfield (National Trust Property)
2	Police Station
3	Watersports Centre
4	Public Dock
5	Post Office
6	Mangrove Bay Beach
7	Sandy's Boat Club
8	Village Shopping Area

Our American visitors tend to think that Bermuda is like a small version of England, while our British visitors think that the island is a minuscule America. We know better, on both accounts. Bermuda is, quite simply, Bermuda. It's unique.

How to Use This Book

Emily Dickinson once wrote, "There is no Frigate like a Book/To take us Lands away." The book you hold in your hands is designed take you to Bermuda and let you sail easily through myriad facts and details about our small but complex island. We'll tell you where to stay, eat and shop, of course. And we'll tell you about our beaches, parks, recreations, attractions and a multitude of other features.

But perhaps most important of all, we'll identify and try to explain our idiosyncrasies that may at first puzzle those with an American mindset. Strangely enough, our American visitors tend to think that Bermuda is like a small version of England, while our British visitors think that the island is a minuscule America. We know better, on both accounts. Bermuda is, quite simply, Bermuda. It's unique. Our History, Let's Explain Bermuda and Area Overview chapters will give an insight as to what makes us different. Read our History chapter, for instance, and you'll understand why we add an extra layer to the meaning of "onion." Let's Explain Bermuda will give you the long and short of it regarding our famous Bermuda shorts.

Organization is key for any travel guide. How have we organized this book? Well, chapter titles should tell you where to dip for the specific information you want. In terms of style and format, our chapters fall into two categories: those that are written in a narrative voice, and those that contain individual listings of businesses, events, beaches, services or what have you. All our chapters, of course, begin with introductions that will alert you as to what to expect.

With the chapters that use individual listings, we have maintained a consistent geographical order. Bear in mind that Bermuda does not have states or provinces or even counties (although counties do count where cricket's concerned; see our Spectator Sports chapter for an explanation). Instead our island is divided into nine parishes (see our Area Overviews chapter for more on the origin of our parishes), and it is their names we use as major headings.

When you arrive at Kindley Airport, you will have landed in St. George's Parish, at the eastern end of Bermuda. It's only logical then that in every chapter with listings, we start with St. George's and then take you parish by parish east to west — Hamilton Parish, Smiths Parish, Devonshire Parish, Pembroke Parish (where the City of Hamilton is located), Paget Parish, Warwick Parish, Southampton Parish and, lastly, Sandys Parish, where Somerset Village and the Royal Naval Dockyard are situated. Listings in each parish are generally placed thereafter in alphabetical order. However, there are some exceptions. For example, in our Beaches chapter we use a geographical rather than alphabetical order for those beaches that are part of our South Shore Park description. And in our Attractions, Restaurants and Shopping chapters, listings for the Town of St. George are grouped together, as are those for the City of Hamilton.

Most listing headers include a street number address. However, we confess that finding street numbers to go with names has often been a challenge. Another of our Bermudian idiosyncrasies is that we're not too keen on street numbers, preferring instead to identify buildings by their color and their relationship with each other, as in: "You know, the pink building with white trim, next to the church." If there's no street number in a header, well, there was none to be found. The good thing is that most anyone you might ask for assistance likely wouldn't know the location you're looking for by number anyway.

Interspersed at the bottom of various pages throughout the chapters, you'll find several Insiders' tips, offering advice or nifty pieces of information. In addition, some chapters have Close-ups — feature stories that offer in-depth information on a number of topics including Bermudian coinage and wedding traditions. Our international telephone area code is 441, important to know only if you're telephoning a destination outside Bermuda. Inside Bermuda you won't have to dial it.

If you're the sort of reader who has to start at page one and keep going until the end, you'll probably notice we frequently make use of cross-references. Let's give you some examples. Without a doubt, you'll find historical information in our History chapter, but you'll also find nuggets of it in others, such as the Resort Hotels or Area Overviews chapters. We both love our history. Should you be interested in flowers and animals, you'll naturally head for the Flora and Fauna chapter, but there is valuable information on these topics in other chapters as well. How could we describe our parks, for instance, without pointing out some trees, or birds, flowers and weeds? And how could we take you snorkeling or diving in our Watersports chapter without showing you fish and marine life? So watch out for those cross-references. The index should prove extremely valuable as well.

You may be surprised that for such a small island we have produced such a fat book. When we started on this project, even we underestimated just exactly how much Bermuda has to offer. Bermuda *is* small and yet . . . and

Photo: GIS

Gibb's Hill Lighthouse is one of Bermuda's most famous landmarks.

yet. . . . We could agree with Mark Twain, who once reputedly said: "Bermuda is the largest small place in the world."

Lastly, we in the Insiders' Publishing family value feedback from our readers. After all, you're the only ones who can tell us if we are giving you what you need. To that end, if you spot an error or an omission that you feel should be brought to our attention (remem-ber, virtually all Insiders' Guides® are updated annually), we encourage you to contact us. Visit us online at www.insiders.com, or write to us at:

The Insiders' Guide® to Bermuda
Falcon® Publishing Inc.
P.O. Box 1718
Helena, MT 59624

While we appear on any map as a dot in the Atlantic Ocean, our land mass is really a cluster of 180 small islands, islets and rocks.

Let's Explain Bermuda

Can thousands of our repeat visitors be on to something? We think so and apparently so do they, or they wouldn't return to Bermuda time after time, confirming that our unique characteristics put us pretty close to a sunlit fairy tale. But our allure is not simply one of picture-postcard vistas and colorful snapshots for the photo album. . . . It is a state of mind, a sense of history, a moped-ride through a mid-ocean Arcadia transformed over the last 20 years into a modern and sophisticated Shangri-La.

We have some of the friendliest people you'll ever meet, no income tax, a low unemployment rate, comparatively little crime, a fine education system, excellent and up-to-date healthcare, and a stable government, all nestled within a pollution-free environment.

Although millions have visited Bermuda over the years, many travelers still don't quite know where we are. This is not new. In the sixteenth century some maps put us off the Florida coast; in this century some folks have put us off the west coast of Africa, or placed us in the Pacific. Actually, we're a group of bite-sized islands in the Atlantic, nearly 800 miles north of the Bahamas.

In this chapter we've provided some Insiders' tips and tidbits that will prove helpful in understanding what makes Bermuda and Bermudians tick. For example, we often refer to our corner of paradise as the "Rock," and a trip to the United States is a "jump across the pond."

Now there's no hard and fast pattern to our explaining a land where many of our older citizens grew up riding Shank's Mare (traveling on foot) and rumbled through the countryside as passengers on the old Rattle and Shake

(the train) before it finally rattled off into oblivion. This, after all, is a place where no sidewalk shoeshine men exist, and when it rains during bright sunshine we know the devil is abusing his wife.

Our snapshots will introduce some useful guidelines, which are expanded upon at greater length elsewhere in the book, while also clueing you in on a few governmental rules and special gems. We also include a few quirks, tales, habits and customs so you'll know us better when we meet. This, we believe, could be the beginning of a beautiful friendship.

Wedded to the Sea

While we appear on any map as a dot in the Atlantic Ocean, our land mass is really a cluster of 180 small islands, islets and rocks, situated a two-hour flight and 673 miles southeast of New York City or 564 miles dues east of Cape Hatteras on North Carolina's Outer Banks. And although we're not in the Caribbean, many of our ancestors came from various Caribbean islands and their cultural influence is a part of our rich heritage.

You may be interested in knowing we are at the northern apex of the infamous Bermuda Triangle (the other vertices are generally considered to be San Juan, Puerto Rico, and Miami).

The Triangle and other Sargasso Sea anomalies notwithstanding, most local fishermen simply won't go to sea on Good Friday. "Those who have gone out," says an experienced fisherman who has been pulling a living from Bermuda's waters for almost a half-century, "simply don't come back." Superstition? Perhaps. But most of these chaps would rather do something else, even engage in marble competitions on Good Friday, or fly wood-framed, colored tissue-paper kites, a tradition with an elusive beginning.

But for those of us who own pleasure craft and don't fly kites or "nick" marbles almost any day is a good day to go to sea. You'll find every bay and cove dotted with our boats and it is highly unlikely you'll find a sail or motor-cruise charter captain who'll refuse to take you a-cruising. If he does refuse, he probably was once a fisherman.

www.insiders.com

See this and many other **Insiders' Guide®** destinations online.

Visit us today!

Tied to the Land

Bermuda is 21.6 square miles of parks, beaches, farms, private estates and open spaces zealously watched by environmental groups. We have more forts and churches per square mile than any other place — cannon and canon juxtaposed, both rimmed by aqueous borders.

We're passionate campers who, during the summer and on holidays like Cup Match (see our Annual Events and Festivals chapter), take to the beaches and designated camping areas like mature turtles staking out a patch of ground during breeding season. Some of us, for a week or two, even travel to work and back from tents pitched less than 100 yards from sand and surf.

Our population, hovering around 60,000, is comprised of 58.6 percent black and 36.4 percent white citizens. Ethnically, we're a soup bowl of British, West Indian, Portuguese, Philippine, American, African, Canadian, European and Asian seasonings.

Bermuda's climate is the envy of most areas, with temperatures heating up in April, then leveling off to the high 80s or low 90s until the end of September. High humidity is a frequent feature of the local climate and can make for some bad hair days. Many folks believe it can be just as bad when the wind is from the south. But you're in paradise, so who cares about hair? When bitter winter winds bite elsewhere, we enjoy temperatures that generally remain in the mid-60s. Occasionally, but not too often, the mercury will fall into the 50s, particularly during the first three months of the year. This gives us the best of both worlds — superb in the summer and splendid during the winter.

A few years ago, and probably only about a handful of people believe it really happened, it was rumored that there were a few snow flurries at our airport. And in March 1784, the *Bermuda Gazette* reported that snow had fallen overnight. But don't bother to pack your skis, they'd really be quite useless.

While arrival protocol is not quite as simple as grabbing your bag and hailing a cab, immigration and customs officials have made getting into Bermuda relatively painless. All visitors who arrive by air will need to present a valid passport, return airline ticket and completed Bermuda Immigration Visitor Arrival Card. There are other requirements depending on where you're coming from, how long you plan to stay and when you are leaving. See our Getting Here, Around and Home chapter for the complete rundown.

Leave the Driving to Us

You won't find Avis trying harder and Hertz offering discounts in Bermuda. Car rental services simply are not allowed. But fear not, we wouldn't invite you without ensuring you'll be able to get around quickly and easily. And we offer a very popular mode of visitor transportation for the more daring — mopeds. You'll find a number of moped rental firms that will deliver the bikes to your guest house or hotel door if desired. Well, not exactly your hotel door, but you get the point.

However, never forget that here we drive on the left, and our speed limit is only 20 mph. Sure, you'll see locals whizzing past faster than that on occasion, but we advise that you be very careful and observant on local roads. For those accustomed to straight, several-laned freeways, our narrow, winding roads can be a challenge.

If you decide to forgo zipping smartly along on a rented moped (helmets are compulsory, by the way), our taxi services are excellent, with our cab drivers generally considered our frontline ambassadors. You cannot be gouged — all rates are fixed and fares are shown on taxi meters.

An efficient bus system also makes it easy to get around; you can't miss the busses' pink and blue profiles. The bus-stop poles are color-coordinated as well: Pink on top means the bus is inbound, headed for the City of Hamilton; blue on top means the bus is heading away from the city. Keep in mind that bus travel will be a great deal less stressful, and ultimately cheaper, if you purchase transportation passes obtained at the central bus terminal in Hamilton and at hotels, guest houses, post offices and the visitors service bureaus. Bus operators are not supposed to accept paper money and are not allowed to make change. But don't be bashful about asking fellow passengers if they can change a couple of notes.

Bermuda Shorts (Or, Parade of Knees)

Before we go any further, we have to tell you: Bermuda is essentially a conservative country with flamboyant ironies. Our ad campaign invites you to "Let Yourself Go," but don't go too far and shed everything on our beaches. Nudity is a no-no. We deal with specific dress requirements and expectations in several different chapters, but be aware that you might need to upgrade your usual loafing wardrobe to feel at home on Bermuda's streets. Men should never go shirtless, and short-shorts, tank tops and scanty cover-ups should be replaced by more genteel leisure threads.

And then there are our Bermuda shorts, those colorful Irish linen or tropical worsted wear items that are standard attire for an army of local businessmen. Hanging a couple of inches above the knee, the shorts originated in India around the turn of the century. Baggy British Army khaki trousers were chopped off below the knees and eventually incorporated into accepted military wear.

Our men have developed a sartorial rule that insists they be worn with blazer, tie and knee socks. Whatever color the blazer, do not attract the fashion police by wearing similar colored shorts. Egad! And the color of your knee socks should match either blazer or shorts.

Now we mentioned fashion police somewhat tongue-in-cheek, but in the 1950s, when shorts began inching indiscreetly upwards, our actual police politely ticketed wearers with a "green card" as an admonition against wearing them higher than two inches above the knee. It was all very proper, complete with the application of a six-inch ruler to ascertain the number of inches of offense. Today no tickets will be issued, this style of business attire having entered the establishment with no apologies for exposed knees.

Oh, lest we forget: Although accepted as our national dress, parliamentarians, judges and lawyers are forbidden to wear Bermuda shorts within our House of Assembly and courts of law. The conservatives have had the last word on that. But having made that admission, our judges can be (and have in the past been) much less conservative in other areas, and we must tell you one of our favorite stories. In the 1930s the case of a man charged with stealing a turkey was made difficult by defense and prosecution witnesses who appeared so obviously to be lying that the judge dismissed the case in disgust and confiscated the turkey for his own Christmas dinner.

The Price of Paradise

You'll quickly notice that Bermuda is not a cheap thrill. Depending on what other destinations you compare us with, you will probably find things more expensive here. But be mindful that everything we supply in our restaurants, shops and grocery stores has to be imported, and because we have no income tax, our customs duties and the subsequent increased business overhead impact pricing.

Visiting us during winter can be a bonus, as you'll find various discount packages available for travel, dining and accommodations. Some hotels and cottage colonies offer discounts for honeymooners and families with children, often providing a variety of meal plans.

As for lodging, Bermuda can fill the bill, regardless of your 'druthers. There are all-inclusive resort hotels where many folks find they can have a fine vacation without ever leaving the property (but get out and see us if you want a really great vacation); old-fashioned guest houses and cottage colonies showcasing traditional architecture; housekeeping cottages (which could be considered Bermuda's version of America's efficiencies) where families on a tight budget can save a few dollars by cooking in; and small, traditional hotels and motels. Take a spin through our five chapters of accommodation offerings, and you'll get a sense of the variety.

What's in a Name?

Bermuda has a thing going with names — first names, nicknames, names of boats, names of homes, names of roads, names of cars, names of you-name-it.

With first names, changes began within the past 20 or so years, particularly in the black community. Susan and John and Peter and the like have been replaced by Malikah, Tioniea, Jelani and the like. Many first names are creative mergers of fathers' and mothers' first names, and African names are often borrowed unchanged or borrowed and modified.

Nicknames often provide a source of fascination and humour. In fact, for men not to have a nickname is perhaps more uncommon than having one. You'll find all sorts — Big Lunch, Gatepost, Peapost, Old Hell, Eager Toes, Greedy Guts — and there are those that sail so close to the shores of the risqué that we dare not mention them here.

It's not odd to name your boat. In fact, everybody does it all over the world. But we also name our homes and our cars. If you look carefully at the rear of many of our cars — and we admit that it's not as common today as it

was a decade ago — you'll see monikers like "Woman of Substance," "High on the Hog," "Bad Man" and "The Good Twin."

Just imagine Big Lunch leaving a house called Spoon Fed and climbing behind the wheel of a car dubbed High on the Hog. Bermuda is, as the calypso song says, "Another World."

Greetings and Grapevine

So now that you've learned about a few of our peculiarities, you'll find Bermudians some of the most amiable folks you're likely to encounter. However, there is a caveat. If you want to make friends and curb some stony looks, please follow the niceties. Some of us do get a little nonplussed and downright resentful at visitors who barge right up to us without so much as an "excuse me" or "good morning" preamble before asking a question.

One of our friendliest Insiders, Johnny Barnes, may very likely be more forgiving. He has become Bermuda's literal poster-man of good wishes and blessings and can be found between 5 and 10 AM at the Crow Lane entrance to the City of Hamilton. Standing on his chosen patch of grass on the roundabout every day except Sunday, rain or shine, he waves, blows kisses and greets pedestrians and motorists alike, his "I love you" rising over the hum of traffic.

But don't err in thinking Johnny is a six-pack shy of a full case. A local television interview with him a few years back by one of this book's coauthors, revealed a smart, likeable and deeply religious man who genuinely cares about people. A former train and bus mechanic, he has claimed his spot at the Crow Lane spot for 15 years (there is now a statue of Johnny at the entrance to the city) and has also been interviewed for German television. Now that's some distance for a good reputation to travel.

And speaking of traveling, news moves pretty quickly via the local grapevine. It used to be joked that if something happened in St. George's in the morning it would reach Somerset before lunch, and that was in the days of the horse and buggy. Today news

travels even faster, the grapevine now aided by, among other things, cellular phones. But just as in the old days, the truth tends to get somewhat massaged during its journey, and the story often arrives a little worse for wear.

One of the Safest Places in the World

We pride ourselves on living in one of the safest places in the world, yet there is no room for complacency. We are finding it necessary to take continuing bites out of crimes driven mostly by an illegal drug scourge. As anywhere else, caution and good sense will take you a long way and prevent any sort of bad experience.

When going about the island, keep all personal belongings in a safe place, and never leave anything unlocked, be it your moped, hotel room or guest cottage. When dining out in the evening or checking out the nightlife, it's always a good idea to ask a friend to join you.

Also be aware that handbag snatching has become an irritating problem, and when renting a moped be careful of riding with camera and bags resting unsecured and exposed in a basket; another rider can simply come alongside, reach into the basket and speed off with your property.

Although we emphasize that you are safer in Bermuda than just about anywhere, we do

caution that when swimming or snorkeling at any of our beaches, do not leave your camera and other valuables unattended on your beach blanket as you dip into our delightful emerald waters.

A Tale of Warmth, Nourishment and Luck

In Flatts Village in Hamilton Parish is a delightful eighteenth-century home known as Wistowe. At one time a roadhouse, theater and bakery, it was bought early this century by Professor Reginald Fessenden, a Canadian-born inventor and radio pioneer. The property was known for its row of coconut trees, reputed at the time to be among the tallest in Bermuda.

According to William Zuill in *Bermuda Journey* (published 1946), Professor Fessenden, who many years before had been headmaster of local Whitney Institute, then a private school, believed the trees should have been yielding a more plentiful crop of coconuts. Employing a West Indian fellow who was a self-styled "coconut tree doctor," Fessenden watched as the man climbed to the tops of each tree and applied a generous serving of salt to the young fruit. Surprising to everyone except perhaps the "doctor," a bountiful crop resulted.

Later, when planting a new row of coconut palms, Fessenden followed an old Bermudian custom of placing in the holes a lump of charcoal for warmth, a pound of ship biscuit for nourishment and a horseshoe for luck!

Grave Matters

On more than one bus ride we have overheard visitors exclaim that Bermudians bury their deceased above ground! This observation is apt to occur during the journey from the city of Hamilton to Somerset or Dockyard. This western route, on bus number 8, takes the traveler past St. Paul's Anglican Church in Paget — on Middle Road near the traffic lights. On passing by this church and seeing the gravesite next to the road, those unfamiliar with our customs see a striking similarity with the "Cities of the Dead" in New Orleans. However, we do bury below ground, as in most of North America. In Bermuda, tomb-like structures can be quite large and deceiving. Most families have a plot wherein departed members are laid atop those who have gone before. It is said that at one burial a heavy iron casket was lowered onto a Bermuda cedar coffin. You can imagine the dismay of those present as the sound of fracturing wood splintered the air. Although some morticians have tried to introduce a crematorium, that idea has been shot down in flames.

Bucks and Banks

Unless your luck is soaring, it is unlikely you'll find any examples of Hog Money, Bermuda's first coinage dated 1616 to 1624 (see the Close-up on Hog Money in our History chapter). Find one of these ancient coins, and the Bermuda Monetary Authority will beat a path to your door.

However, our coinage and notes are still distinctive. Visitors are quick to notice our $2 bill, and tourists often comment on the variety of colors of our paper money. Our coins are also thumbnail historical, environmental and cultural sketches — with the hog on the cent, angelfish on the five-cent, longtail on the quarter and the Bermuda Fitted Dinghy (see the Close-up in our Yachting and Marinas chapter) on the dollar.

Although our money looks different, it is worth the same as the U.S. dollar, which is readily accepted here. In fact, you can request that the shops you buy goods from give you change in American currency; if they can at the time, most will be quite happy to do so. But remember that shops don't purposely keep American dollars on hand. We suggest that you exchange any Bermudian money for your own currency before leaving the island, unless you want to keep a few coins and bills for keepsakes.

It is unlikely that you will need their services, but if so our three banks — the Bank of Bermuda Limited, the Bank of N.T. Butterfield and Son Limited and the Bermuda Commercial Bank Limited (which primarily handles private corporate accounts) — are more than capable of handling any requirements. You will find bank reception staff most helpful.

Run out of cash? All you need is your Visa, MasterCard or any bank card connected to the Cirrus or Plus systems. Between them the banks have 13 branch offices and 40 Easylink and BankCardPlus ATM machines at various points throughout the island; a few are just outside or inside some supermarkets and pharmacies. You can withdraw up to your credit limit through the Cirrus network or up to $500 a day through the Plus system.

The Bank of Bermuda, 6 Front Street, Hamilton, (441) 295-4000, and the Bank of N.T. Butterfield and Son Limited, 65 Front Street, Hamilton, (441) 295-1111, both offer assistance with travelers' checks and wire transfers.

By the People and for the People

A British-dependent territory, Bermuda has a parliamentary system dating from August 1, 1620, when the first colonial parliament was held in St. George's. Queen Elizabeth II is the head of all governmental power, and a governor — always a British civil servant appointed for a minimum of three years — represents her in Bermuda, aided by a deputy who is also appointed in London.

The Bermuda constitution gives the governor responsibility for Bermuda's defense, police and internal and external security. However, he generally takes his cues from the premier and elected government before exercis-

The Majesty and Mystery of the Gombeys

The pulsing cadence of the drum reaches out and grabs you as it rushes out of the hinterland to run unfettered through the streets. And from around the bend, appearing as suddenly as midday apparitions, come the Gombeys, leaping flashes of color and pulse-pounding agility, with their peacock-feathered headdresses waving in counterpoint to the drumbeat, always the drumbeat . . . its passionate and staccato tempo igniting some secret place deep in the soul.

Then the drum changes voice, its command subtle, and the Wild Indian (bow and arrow at the side), the Trapper and chiefs and warriors obey, slipping easily into the "snake dance." Shrieks from the Captain's whistle **Close-up**
pierce the air, punctuating the throb of the drum, and he high-steps and turns and bends and sunlight bounces from 100 or more bits of broken mirror sewn into his cape.

Shuffling behind the masked dancers are the drummers, faces exposed, nimble fingers rapping drumsticks against the tight face of the snare drums, the deep-throated kettle drum joining in thumping chorus. Bringing up the rear of the Gombey "crowd" are men, women and children, hips rocking and swaying, shoes clapping on the hard street, responding to the language, the symbolism, the artistry of a dance cultivated from native soil, nurtured through slavery and celebrated in freedom.

Yet most visitors rarely see them.

No one is certain when the Gombeys first appeared. We do know they were active around the end of the eighteenth century and into the nineteenth century, their name derived from the African *gumba*, a word for drum. Had some inhabitants had their way, the dance would have been outlawed.

"The savage and nonsensical exhibition of the Gomba, practiced here by the idle, should be done away with, as a thing not suited to a civilized community, and highly dangerous to passengers on horses or in carriages," complained a letter writer to the *Bermuda Gazette* in 1837.

The appearance of the Gombeys on Boxing Day — a local holiday celebrated the day after Christmas — was one of the season's anticipated highlights. It was then, as now, a pastiche of dancers leaping, doing splits and pirouettes. Men and women daubed their faces red and yellow, their scarlet dress enhanced by ribbons and flowers. As they

Photo: GIS

The Gombeys appear at many Bermudian festivals throughout the year.

— continued on next page

danced and sang from house to house, they were accompanied by the hypnotic tempo of the drum, its distinctive beat confirmed in 1970 at a UNESCO Cultural and Conservation Conference as entirely unique.

There have been several influences on the development of the Gombey tradition over the past hundred or more years, chief among them some Native American adaptations. Tomahawks, bow and arrow and feathers are readily evident. The "Wild Indian" is an obvious borrowing, and the dance ritual itself, while essentially African, has some aspects of Indian tribal dancing.

But perhaps the most significant factor lies in its family traditions. Each of the five or six separate troupes or crowds is generally composed of males (and recently one or two females) from one family who maintain and pass on traditional dance techniques from generation to generation. This makes the survival of the Gombey both a family and cultural tradition.

Apart from a few holidays and an annual competition when they appear in their vibrant costumes that are sewn by female family members, the Gombeys will take to the streets without costume at odd times through the year, attract eager crowds and then disperse quickly.

They are, for many, Bermuda's most powerful cultural tradition.

ing these powers. Our parliament, or House of Assembly, consists of 40 representatives elected from 40 constituencies or electoral districts within our nine parishes. Three parties vie for government's reins during a general election — the United Bermuda Party (UBP), the Progressive Labour Party (PLP) and the National Liberal Party (NLP).

The winning party's leader, confirmed by the governor as premier, then chooses a cabinet comprised of ministers, each of whom is responsible for a particular portfolio or ministry. However, with 12 ministries, some ministers may hold more than one portfolio.

Our bicameral system includes an 11-member senate, with five senators selected by the governor, premier and leader of the opposition party. But the senate has no legislative powers and serves as a debating and moderating influence. Both the senate and cabinet meet at the Cabinet Building on Front Street, where the premier's office is also found. See the map on page xvi.

Most visitors won't likely need the services of a particular ministry, but there are a few instances that require contact. These include obtaining a marriage license, extending your stay, taking up residence and obtaining a work permit or driver's license.

If you are pierced by Cupid's irrepressible arrow and plan on "jumping the broom" or tying the knot while here, you will need to contact the Registrar General (see our chapter on Weddings). The Department of Immigration, 30 Parliament Street, Hamilton, (441) 297-7941, can assist with issues relating to length of stay or obtaining a work permit, and the Department of Transport Control's Examination Centre, 11 North Street, Hamilton, (441) 292-2255, can help regarding a driver's license.

Phone and Post

Public pay phones are conveniently located throughout the island. A local call costs 20 cents — if you don't have two dimes you can use a quarter, but don't expect a nickel in return. Cash calling cards can be purchased at the Bermuda Telephone Company (BTC), 30 Victoria Street, Hamilton, (441) 292-5272, or at any of its satellite offices in St. George's and Sandys parishes. BTC also has a card dispenser at the Clocktower at the Royal Navy Dockyard.

TeleBermuda International Ltd., Mintflower Place, 8 Par-la-Ville Road, Hamilton, (441) 296-9000, is Bermuda's newest licensed long-distance carrier, providing a full range of telephone, fax and data services. In order to take advantage of TeleBermuda rates, which are generally cheaper, visitors can obtain prepaid calling cards directly from them. Call (441) 292-SAVE for commercial locations carrying the cards.

Should you need cellular service during your visit, call (441) 292-6032 to arrange advanced registration with Telco Mobility prior to arrival. Once here, you can acquire service by dialing the same number. Billing can be credited to your American Express, Visa or MasterCard. For the yacht skipper wanting to use a cell phone, call (441) 292-6032 when within 50 miles of the island. Cellular visitor rates are currently as follows: service activation charge, $10; daily access charge, $5; peak minute charge (7 AM to 7 PM), 60 cents per minute; off-peak charges (7 PM to 7 AM), 35 cents per minute.

Mail in Bermuda is delivered quickly and efficiently. We've moved quite a long way since the eighteenth century, when the blowing of a horn by a letter carrier, a slave on horseback, announced that post was near. The General Post Office, 56 Church Street, Hamilton, (441) 297-7893, is open from 8 AM to 5 PM weekdays and until noon on Saturdays. There is one sub-post office in each parish, and you can find addresses and phone numbers in the blue pages of the telephone directory.

At 11 Queen Street, Hamilton, you'll find the Perot Post Office (no, there's no relation to Ross; the pronunciation is "Pea-Rut"). This post office, also a part of the government-run system, was used in 1848 by William B. Perot, who owned the building and was the post-master at Hamilton. During the years before the mid-nineteenth century, some postmasters in the United States, on their own authority, issued "postmaster stamps." Perot, aware of this, imitated the experiment, and in so doing created what is now known as the Perot Stamp, of which only about a dozen specimens remain. There are two varieties, one blue-black, the other red, and both are among the more valuable stamps in the philatelic world.

You will notice as you travel about the island that we have bright-red pillar letter boxes at various locations. Secure from theft, mail is collected from them daily.

Incidentally, if your visit lasts through December, and you want to mail a letter from Bermuda to arrive before Christmas in the United States, your correspondence should be sent on or before the established deadline of 9:30 AM on December 12.

Water, Water, Use It with Care

There are times when rain pours out of the clouds with a vengeance, slashing straight down onto our roofs as though bent on piercing them. That is the kind of rain we like — "tank rain," for there are few things as critical to Bermuda as its water supplies. The island does not have the luxury of streams, rivers or freshwater lakes. However, we do have an underground "lens" or aquifer system — caves of water lying deep below ground.

Bermuda has four major lens areas: St. George's, Somerset, Southampton, and the Central lens (which covers nearly 1,700 acres and sprawls under much of Pembroke, Devonshire and Smiths parishes). The full potential of these lens areas has only been tapped within the last couple of decades; monitored by the hydrogeology section of the Department of Works and Engineering, their total capacity is in the billions of gallons.

Approximately 30 percent of the island's annual rainfall permeates the ground to re-

INSIDERS' TIP

If it rains during a funeral it means the person being buried has led a good Christian life.

Photo: GIS

Bermuda is the perfect place to get lost and find yourself at the same time.

plenish these lenses from which around 1.5 million gallons are extracted daily. The water is treated and chlorinated to health department standards and delivered by private water truckers to homeowners (who pay $55 to $65 per 900- or 1,000-gallon load) when tanks run dry, a not uncommon occurrence during summers when rainfall is below normal. But dry conditions have rarely been cause for a national crisis — except 50 years ago.

In 1949 and into 1950, a drought so devastated the island that tens of thousands of gallons of water had to be imported from overseas. Henry Gross, a dowser from the United States (that's someone skilled in locating underground water sources, by the way), was eventually brought in under the auspices of a leading politician to locate underground water supplies. Gross was successful in St. George's, dowsing a subterranean spring that yielded what was described as "the freshest water ever produced out of the ground in Bermuda."

When bathing at home, we do not fill the tub to the brim, but we joyfully and shame-lessly indulge ourselves when we travel. When you visit the Rock, be clean, but be water-conscious when taking a shower or luxuriating in that bubble bath.

Bermudian Alps

We have referred to "tank rain," and that directly relates to our unique home construction. Our houses are a delightful marriage of several borrowed features — aspects of the British farmhouse, West-Indian styled shutters, and the Oriental moongate, among others — all adapted to subtropical island living. Our white, "stepped" roofs are eye-catching. Sometimes called Bermuda's version of the Alps, our roofs are constructed of quarried limestone slabs sawed into one-inch thick, 18 inch by 12 inch slates. Placed in an overlap pattern on a wood-beamed structure, the slabs are cemented together and to the beams. And that "tank rain" mentioned above is channeled via gutters and "down pipes" into concrete cisterns built beneath the house. When you walk across a local porch, or kitchen, or living room, you won't be walking *on* water, but you will more than likely be walking *above* water.

Bermuda's Work Force

The latest 1997 employment survey showed our economic engine is maintained by a labor force of 35,296 persons. When analyzed, the working population is 77 percent Bermudian and 23 percent non-Bermudian. Factor in gender, and women make up 50 percent of workers.

Leading employers continue to be government and the hotel industry, closely followed by the retail sector. Although far less labor-intensive, Bermuda's collection of international companies, represented by more than 11,000 registered corporations, accounts for an average of 2,420 positions held by Bermudians. These businesses engage in varied enterprises, including insurance and reinsurance, investment holdings, commercial trading, shipping and chemical trade.

We must point out that of these thousands of corporations registered here and known locally as "exempt" companies, less than 300 have an actual physical presence. (See our International Business chapter for more details.)

Keep Bermuda Beautiful

We try to keep our face clean and well-scrubbed by placing public trash receptacles throughout the City of Hamilton and the outlying parishes. Keep Bermuda Beautiful, (441) 295-5142, is a volunteer organization that relies on contributions from individuals, small businesses and corporations to promote a national "Keep Bermuda Beautiful" message.

A government recycling program begun six years ago has received tremendous support. Since 1993 we have recycled in excess of 5,000 tons of glass, aluminum and steel. Up to the beginning of last year we disposed of more than 35,000 pounds of household batteries, 48,663 lead acid batteries, 154,000 fluorescent tubes and 231,000 gallons of used motor oil. Most of our recyclable materials go to New Jersey and Pennsylvania for reprocessing.

Our Rock Watcher program is directed at individuals and groups, encouraging responsibility for keeping a particular area clean. Every May, hundreds of Bermudians engage in island-wide neighborhood tidying, and every two years scuba divers and snorkelers slip beneath the surface to haul up stuff carelessly dumped in Neptune's locker.

It Takes a Whole Island

But our concern is not only about refuse and recyclables, oceans and open spaces; we're also a place where people really do reach out to help other people, both at home and abroad. We have always responded when disasters strike areas overseas, such as in the mid-'90s, when Eleuthera in the Bahamas suffered severe hurricane damage. Through the past several decades, in the face of various crises, we have made financial contributions, donated clothing and blankets, sent troops from our Bermuda Regiment to help in rebuilding efforts and, in some cases, provided all three services simultaneously. BELCO, our utility company, has also sent out personnel and equipment during emergencies.

The element of caring extends into every facet of our community life. It's a force that helps link our multicultural society. We have approximately 182 registered charities, excluding church- and government-operated organizations. There are Rotarians and Lions' clubs, banks and businesses, and health and community organizations staffed and supported almost entirely by volunteers (among them our "Pink Ladies"; see our Healthcare chapter), all of which get into the act. Add to that mix the

INSIDERS' TIP

Many of our museums, attractions and restaurants close for renovation or reduce their hours during our slow season from November through February. Call ahead to confirm operating hours. Most places are closed on public holidays.

Photo: GIS

Most of Bermuda's beaches are found within beautiful park settings.

Salvation Army and a host of other individuals and groups that support and promote existing programs and help structure new ones. On many Fridays and Saturdays throughout the year, you will find men and women stationed outside several of our supermarkets, banks and malls to collect charitable donations from passersby to support any number of worthy causes.

Since 1991 the Centre on Philanthropy, 7 Par-la-Ville Road, Hamilton, (441) 292-5320, has been one of the key players in Bermuda's charitable community. It offers support, information and assistance to charitable concerns through educational workshops, publications, a lending library, an inquiry service, development of a directory of registered charities and much more. The Centre is integral in bringing together donors, charities and the public. If while visiting Bermuda you want to locate a branch of a charity you're involved with or interested in, the Centre will be happy to assist you.

Healthcare

We're proud of a lot of things here in Bermuda, and tops on the list is our healthcare system. Visitors who have had the misfortune of needing emergency medical care offer high praise for the facilities, staff and treatment at King Edward VII Memorial Hospital, 7 Point Finger Road, Paget, (441) 236-2345. To reach the hospital emergency room directly, call (441) 239-2009. And, as in the United States, dial 911 for immediate ambulance, fire department or police response.

In emergency situations, a patient not needing admittance to the hospital must pay for treatment at the time it is received. Payment for outpatient care can be made with cash, check or credit card. No overseas medical insurance is accepted for outpatient treatment. However, should medical treatment require admittance to the hospital, Blue Cross and Blue Shield insurance is accepted. (For much more information, see our Healthcare chapter.)

When You Leave Us

If you are departing by air, check in at Bermuda International Airport at least an hour or more before your scheduled departure. The Bermuda immigration form and other documentation received at the time of your arrival should be attached to your ticket. All passengers pay a departure tax of $20, which is included in airline fares.

Logistical details regarding departure can be found in the Getting Here, Around and Home chapter. Check to see what the limitations are for taking various plants or foods off the island. Certainly the U.S. Department of Agriculture representative may want to know what you have in your possession. You are not allowed to carry indigenous flowers or greenery or sea life (such as sea cucumbers, urchins and brain coral). Soil and seedlings are a major no-no as well. But you can take items such as flowers bought from a florist, seashells that don't have any critters growing inside them, frozen seafood, Portuguese sausage in plastic store wrapping or cassava pie, if it's filled with no other meat but poultry.

Should you return home with one of these pies — a big part of most Bermudian Christmas dinners along with turkey — then you will be carrying across the pond a genuine taste of Bermuda, an echo of a unique experience and a personal invitation to return.

Bermuda's physical beauty was, and remains, undeniable, making it one of the most expensive pieces of beachfront in the world.

Area Overviews

Seventy years ago Bermuda was considerably more tranquil. Uncluttered shorelines swept inland and vanished into cedar-dominated landscapes; bicycles and horse-drawn carriages left their marks along dusty roadways; and the island, rich with the scent of poinsettias, lillies and morning-glories, was often called a "playground for the rich." (Bermuda still isn't a cheap thrill.) Its fabled beauty was legendary, leading one frequent visitor to enthuse: "One's first visit to Bermuda is, indeed, an enchanted holiday! But one's second, or third or fourth! With what breathless eagerness one peers from the ship's porthole on the early morning of one's subsequent arrival, incredulously questioning, 'Is it still there, that Lilliputian miracle of beauty?' "

Mrs. George Draper's personal observation in 1930 was a common reaction to an uncommon land. Bermuda's physical beauty was, and remains, undeniable, making it one of the most expensive pieces of beachfront in the world. And it would be wrong to conclude that serenity is a thing of the past. Within the city itself there are parks like Par-la-Ville and Victoria. Beyond Hamilton's borders, beaches and quiet coves may have only a few couples taking the sun or swimming languidly in the island's fabled waters. But the island is more than just a pretty face. Scratch the surface, and just beneath the "tranquil and contenting" skin is a country that over the last twenty years has evolved from an almost mythical sleepy hollow into a dynamic international business hub.

The effect of this growth is reflected to varying degrees in all of the island's nine parishes, each named after a prominent shareholder in the Bermuda Company. The only exception is St. George's Parish, which was named after England's patron saint. Our parishes, originally called "tribes," were surveyed and divided by English mapmaker Richard Norwood, who began traversing the island in 1615, finishing the following year. However, the designation "tribe roads" (and not "parish roads") remains.

With the exception of St. George's, Hamilton and Smiths, every parish has them. Running north to south, they are public rights of way, and several are tiny, quiet lanes opening onto major arteries like South Road and Middle Road. Others are little more than footpaths.

In 1913 a Tribe Road Commission was appointed to look into these off-roads that often meander through the most unlikely places, some sliding past homes nestled behind stone walls deep in the heart of rural Bermuda. Their origin is not quite clear, though in 1620 the first government created specific pathways to deter persons from trespassing through corn patches and tobacco fields. Interestingly, the locations of these roads were never recorded on any map, and the commission identified 31 such roads surviving out of an estimated 46. Today most serve as shortcuts to somewhere else.

East End

The Town of St. George, on the cusp of a new makeover, is redefining its economic and physical terrain. Here, street names like Blockade Alley and Petticoat Lane have a quaint, colorful and sometimes lurid history. Blockade Alley, for example, is named in recollection of the Blockade Runners who operated out of St. George's and its harbor during the American Civil War.

Cultural tourism has become the password in an impetus by St. Georgians to preserve, develop and promote a lingering Old World ambiance. A $20 million-plus, five-year project begun in 1997 is motoring through the green light. Town plans include construction of a waterfront boardwalk beginning near the Ordnance Island cruise ship terminal, to run west along the harbor's edge and end at Penno's Wharf. This is one of the principal features of a scheme that includes perking up the streets with the installation of antique-style lamps.

The planting of additional trees is directed toward an image-softening of King's Square, an ancient venue for floggings, executions, and disciplining of gossiping women via a "Ducking Stool." The overall facelift has an ultimate goal: The St. George's Foundation, overseeing the project, seeks recognition of the town as a United Nations International Heritage Site. In 1999 the realization of this goal inched closer when Britain's Minister for Culture nominated the ancient town to the United Nations Educational, Scientific and Cultural Organization (UNESCO) as a World Heritage site. St. George's was one of only two sites selected from a shortlist of 25 that included the UK and its colonies.

This small community, an enclave with minimal population growth since 1960, has taken some enervating economic body blows over the past decade or so, precipitated in 1987 by the then temporary closure of the area's largest hotel (it was originally the St. George's Hotel, then a Holiday Inn, then a Club Med) following a particularly nasty hurricane. Temporary has ultimately become permanent. Atop a hill overlooking Fort St. Catherine (see

www.insiders.com
See this and many other **Insiders' Guide®** destinations online.
Visit us today!

Attractions), the once-popular landmark now begs conversion to something other than a vacant multimillion-dollar pink elephant.

But the town, once a mecca attracting adventurers and poets, clerics and pirates, has never lost its personality. Neither have its people. Many former St. Georgians have moved back to the area, buying and restoring old homes. Reserved but friendly, the people are fiercely loyal to their patch of turf. And it takes time for "outsiders" to grow on them. As one old St. Georgian said recently to a "newcomer" who had been living there for more than 15 years, "You better say nice things about St. George's because the ink on your passport is not yet dry." That newcomer was at the time a representative for a St. George's constituency in the local Parliament!

Just as loyal about their community are the residents of St. David's, a part of St. George's Parish sitting across the harbor south of the town. A short bus ride away, this area could be the poster community for quiet, rural contemplation. Many of its original inhabitants claim Native American ancestry, their Pequot forebears renowned as intrepid whalers and superb boat builders. It was from St. David's that shark hash, turtle soup and fish chowder meandered across the island, establishing reputations for seducing the palate.

The former US Naval Air Station, renamed Southside, is undergoing major revitalization, exhibited in part by name changes of roads, buildings and facilities — Corregidor Avenue is now Southside Road, and Marginal Wharf has become Ships Wharf, named in reference to nearby Ships Point from which in the early 1900s St. David's farmers loaded produce onto St. George's-bound boats.

The siting of the US bases in this area came during the Second World War, when Britain offered the United States air base facilities on

INSIDERS' TIP

Courtesy is very important to Bermudians. We mind our p's and q's, and we also like our "Good mornings," "Good afternoons" and "Good evenings."

Bermuda with a 99-year lease. On 27 March 1941 a Lend-Lease agreement was signed by President Roosevelt and Prime Minister Churchill, an agreement to ten percent of the island being turned over to the United States. St. David's, hitherto a small community of 500 acres, was literally divided into half.

Now, with the return of these lands to Bermuda, a St. David's Islander tradition of naming bays and islands after women is being resurrected — Aunt Jinny's Lane, named after a former slave who farmed arrowroot and lived in a cottage below Longfield House, and Miss Vicky's Lane, after writer Victoria Hayward (1876-1958) being just two examples.

Tommy Fox, called the "uncrowned king" of St. David's Island until his death in 1945, and after whom a road on the US Base was named, was a veteran whale hunter who once crawled into the belly of a beached whale to convince doubters about the biblical story of Jonah. Tommy Fox Road will now designate a more central thoroughfare running close to property he once owned.

While the St. David's community has retained much of its traditional flavor, most other neighborhoods throughout the island have not, with two main factors contributing to a seemingly unavoidable, certainly sobering, impact.

The increased migration of people from parish to parish over the past 25 years has seen new local and non-local faces reshaping neighborhoods and ultimately parish characters. Once considerably more distinct, with easily defined personalities, most parishes have succumbed to almost cookie-cutter profiles.

Although reflecting diversity through expanded populations, several have lost the intimacy once common within neighborhoods where everyone knew everyone else. Among them, Southampton has recorded the largest influx (26 percent) of people since 1980. And while housing developments in Warwick,

Photo: GIS

This aerial view features the revitalized Royal Naval Dockyard area.

Devonshire, Hamilton and Smiths parishes have stimulated the economy, they have also redefined much of those parishes' ambient characteristics. Yet, some things do remain.

As we travel through the parishes during the summer months, we find temporary stands where snowballs — crushed-and-flavored ices — are sold to thirsty motorists and curious visitors. This is the local cousin to the sidewalk lemonade stand, and Bermudians are just wild about the simple sweet treat.

Farmers selling produce and fishermen selling the day's catch in island neighborhoods and at roadside locations are as indelible a part of local life as are the longtails, Bermuda's unofficial harbingers of spring (see our Flora and Fauna chapter). Returning from their sea journey, the longtails can be seen cavorting around shorelines between March and October, soaring on air currents, sweeping in graceful aerial courtships. Later they will lay their eggs in holes and crevices along the island's rugged cliffs.

But courtship is not just for the birds. Bermuda's own courtship of international businesses continues to attract more and more Fortune 500 companies to the island's economic nest. Their presence has made Bermuda the world's leading domicile for the insurance and reinsurance industries (see our International Business chapter).

Flatts Village

The development of Flatts began simply in the early 1600s, before colonization in 1612. The Somers Chart of 1610 shows a small house at the entrance of Flatts Inlet, a house believed to have belonged to one of the men who chose to remain in Bermuda following the wreck of the Sea Venture (see History chapter). At the mouth of the inlet, sits Gibbet Island, used in the late 1600s for hangings and for burning witches at the stake. You can still see a pole — now with a navigation light attached — that marks where gallows once stood.

Following colonization, as more settlers arrived, several small communities sprang up throughout the island, most of them centered around various bays and inlets — particularly around Riddell's Bay in Southampton and Crow Lane in Pembroke. These tiny villages, as with Flatts, quickly became homeports as Bermudians turned increasingly to shipbuilding and overseas trade. Their locations provided opportunity for ship captains to engage in activities that often included smuggling of contraband and slaves.

During the 1700s, Flatts emerged as a port second only to St. George's, and continued to expand throughout the 1800s, the island's shipping industry a driving economic force. Late historian and author William E.S. Zuill, in Bermuda Journey (1946), captures the flavor of life in Flatts during its early years: "Here at Flatts let us picture a sloop, homeward bound from the West Indies, silently creeping in through the inlet on a rising tide of a moonless night. As she enters the channel the men begin to hail to rouse the village, so that by the time she is ready to drop anchor there are many willing hands on shore to catch a hawser and wrap her in. Candles are now being lit in many houses, and soon the narrow road, deserted only a quarter of an hour ago, is bustling with activity as women and children follow the men to the waterfront. Greetings are brief and the night's work commences."

That work often included offloading rum from Barbados, bales of silk from wrecking operations in the Caribbean, and other cargo quickly spirited ashore and hidden from authorities. But with the dominance of Hamilton and St. George's as official ports of entry, Flatts began to decline, and by the middle of the 1850s its glory years had vanished.

INSIDERS' TIP

It would be easy to conclude from our graveyards that Bermuda buries its dead above ground. Nothing could be further from the truth. The depth of graves varies on average of 6 to 8 feet. Beneath the whitewashed lids of our stone-covered graves are departed family members whose coffins are interred atop each other. It makes for a quaint reunion.

Photo: GIS

The beaches in Bermuda are always nearby and almost never crowded.

Today, however, Flatts has begun a resurgence, a dozen or so businesses along with the Bermuda Aquarium, Museum & Zoo (see Attractions) taking center stage.

City of Hamilton

Hamilton, Bermuda's capital, is the nucleus for the country's emergence onto the global economic stage, firmly putting the lie to the island's motto: *Quo Fata Ferunt* or, "whither the fates carry us," adapted from Virgil's Aenid...(and so we set sail, though none could say where fate may take or settle us). Bermuda has indeed hoisted sails, but its fate is manipulated not by chance but by determined political and economic policies.

The city's skyline stretches higher even as Hamilton itself inches outward, absorbing every potential chunk of commercial and industrial real estate. The wrecker's ball has claimed many old buildings — to the consternation of preservationists — that were architectural remnants from an era when horse, buggy, bicycle and train were common modes of transportation.

Commensurate with this brisk development has been a marked population exodus from within the city, hastened by increased commercial use of existing and new buildings. An efficient public bus system has also aided expansion. But transportation has bred another array of issues. If there's a leading vote-getter in the grab bag of Bermudian dichotomies, it is in the number of motor vehicles whose wheels daily hit the island's 1,346 named roads.

When cars were introduced for private use in 1946, the prediction was that they would never exceed 1,000. It was a charming but wishful peek into the future and deserves a blue-ribbon prize for optimism. The leap from horse power to horsepower has resulted in the current number of motorized vehicles (including auxiliary cycles, private cars and other commercial vehicles) exploding to more than 49,000, slightly less than half of which jostle through and into Hamilton each morning, and limp out every evening.

Yet, while Hamilton is by turns both brash and coy, with surrounding parishes stepping firmly to the cadence of economic progress, golden arches have been rejected and neon glitz spurned. And you won't find billboards cluttering our highways. This may seem surprising, for this colony has embraced North American habits with unbridled passion. Yet the British and Caribbean flavor is maintained. Overall, it's an intriguing mix and quaintly eccentric. And the island does attempt to hold on to its homegrown traditions — like "lunch wagons."

These wagons are specially-converted vans, their owners having attracted a dedicated clientele. However, only three of these mobile dispensers of fast food survive. Each proprietor is confined to operating his business from set locations within the city limits. Businessmen in Bermuda shorts rub elbows with construction workers in overalls, and secretaries and government workers line up to be served homemade hamburgers and beef pies washed down with soda pop. These wagons are, in cultural ethos, somewhat reminiscent of the heyday of the North American diner.

But even as Bermuda celebrates a high standard of living fueled in great measure by North American and European visitors, it is plowing through the middle, or sometimes the muddle of coming to grips with changed and changing population and business dynamics.

Significant numbers of the workforce have been caught flat-footed and unprepared for the 21st-century workplace. Global corporate giants, more than 11,000 of which are registered here to take advantage of tax breaks (see our International Business chapter), have generated a rapid social and financial metamorphosis that has yanked the island, in some instances kicking and screaming, toward the next millennium.

The construction industry, which toppled from '80s boom to a pronounced early '90s bust, gathered a second wind in 1997 with some $70 million spent in the year's first nine months on private and public sector expansion and renovation. As we prepare to enter the 21st century, Hamilton has once again begun to boom. The character of the city has changed, the pace more dynamic as Hamilton has become the touchstone for a symbiotic relationship between billion-dollar corporations and a country ranking among the top half-dozen wealthiest per capita in the world. It is a match made in boardroom paradise, scripted by political and economic bedfellows. And Bermudians, both passive and active players on the gameboard, are harvesting the benefits.

West End

Whatever the vagaries of the weather — and local weather can at times be remarkably capricious — there are no signs of the island experiencing an economic drought. Even as Hamilton and St. George's repaint the signposts to prosperity, the West End municipalities have not been couch potatoes.

Among anticipated changes in Southampton is the re-development of the former US Naval Air Annex. Once completed, the revamp is expected to have a positive impact on Bermuda's tourism industry. Plans, many yet to receive a firm starting flag, involve building a luxury hotel, a championship golf course, a 400-berth marina, and a residential village on the 250-acre site.

INSIDERS' TIP

The average tides in Bermuda rise and fall between three and four feet.

Somerset Village, through which buses en route to the Royal Naval Dockyard must travel, has asserted itself. (The name Somerset is derived from Sir George Somers, who during the months he was shipwrecked on Bermuda, particularly enjoyed this part of the island. His crewmen called the area "Somers-seate".) Unlike many other parishes, Somerset, like St. David's, has retained a genuine country charm. It is a rural area with small farms and open spaces, old homes and craggy coastlines, parks and nature reserves. For many Bermudians Somerset is the birthplace of their grandparents and great grandparents. It is, as any Somerset resident will tell you, "God's Country."

Dockyard

There is big sky and open spaces at the Dockyard or "Yard," a place from which men once set to sea to do battle. An hour away from Hamilton by bus, or a direct 30 to 40 minute ferry ride past sheltered bays and inlets (some rides are longer, depending on the stops along the way), this westernmost area has been sculpted from its original architectural shell. The construction of the Dockyard had generated the largest military defense utilization of money, manpower and materials in 19th century Bermuda. With bases already established at Antigua (1743) and Halifax (1749), the building of the Yard provided a critical third prong to British naval power in the North Atlantic. In fact, it was from here during the War of 1812 that Rear Admiral Sir George Cockburn (a road in the area is named after him) sailed in the summer of 1813 to harass the Delaware and Chesapeake bays. The following year, Admiral Sir Alexander F. Cochrane (yes, he has a road, too) set out with a task force to subdue Washington. Although the 20th century brought a new focus, and although the Yard proved valuable to America and its allies during both World Wars, after 1950 it fell into disuse, becoming a grungy group of deserted and crumbling buildings.

Rising from the ashes of neglect more than 15 years ago like a mid-Atlantic phoenix, the Dockyard has been transformed from a tarnished Victorian eyesore into a charming waterfront village. More than 50 businesses are located within and around the solid, thick-walled, renovated buildings that are a legacy of British sea power in the Atlantic. Dilapidated storehouses, foundries, power plants and timber yards have been replaced by restaurants, a Maritime Museum (see Attractions), an Arts Centre, a movie theater and a score of other amenities.

Enter the Dockyard between the two stone pillars topped with antique lanterns, and you'll find a large complex with well-marked signposts. While the ambience is relaxing — there are park benches, green lawns, picnic tables — there is much to see and do here, beginning with an amble through the quaint Clocktower Mall, once called the Great Eastern Storehouse. Within the mall you will find a number of small shops offering everything from clothing, books, paintings, perfumes and prints to ice cream and artifacts (see Shopping chapter).

Environment

The pecking away at open spaces and green belts on the island has alarmed environmentalists. During the past 15 years farmers have taken some serious hits. The long-term future of their industry is inextricably linked to the extent of the protection of Bermuda's arable land. Between 1981 and 1991 the distribution of farmlands — and their sizes — throughout the nine parishes declined. This contraction continued in 1997 when 40 acres of arable land succumbed to housing development, leaving little more than 800 acres of farmland.

While there are more than 1,500 individual fields, only two exceed 5 acres, and the overwhelming majority are a half-acre or less. Although the Department of Agriculture, Fisheries and Parks plays a critical role in promoting the farming industry, housing developments have taken an irreversible toll. Subdivision has fragmented many neighboring fields and ruptured the integrity of several farm units. This situation is aptly illustrated by one of Bermuda's major farmers having to cultivate 25 acres broken up over seven parishes.

If there is a leading environmental beacon, it is not found in tracts of farmland, but on Nonsuch Island, a 14.5-acre preserve of native and endemic plant and animal species. Sited southeast of Castle Harbour, and privately owned until purchased by government in the late 19th century, it is frequently referred to as a living museum.

On this patch of ground, Dr. David Wingate, the chief conservation officer, has carved a vivid recreation of "Las Bermudas," prior to man cutting a swath through pristine forests. A virtual Eden has been forged, with land and sea birds, native crabs and the Bermuda skink (related to the lizard) living among cedars and other tree species.

Wingate, who lives on Nonsuch, has also played the key role in saving Bermuda's oldest bird species, the cahow (pronounced KA-how) from extinction. Believed to have gone the way of the Dodo before the turn of the century, the cahow's ultimate survival is a story of a man who has dedicated himself to saving it, and of a creature that has refused to die.

However, with just over a few dozen nesting pairs — a far cry from its estimated population approaching one million when the island was discovered — the cahow, roughly the size of a pigeon but with a larger wingspan, has been seen by few. It spends most of its life floating low over ocean waves, coming ashore only to breed. (See our Flora and Fauna chapter for much more on the birds and animals of Bermuda.)

Cave Systems

Among the unique and attractive aspects of the local environment are the natural caves. The eastern end of Harrington Sound, a virtually landlocked body of water bordered by Hamilton and Smiths parishes, is where the concentration of caves is highest. Formed thousands of years ago when the island perched much higher above sea level, today many of these caves are underwater. Created by acidic rainwater filtering through soft limestone, several of them interconnect below ground to form extensive and far-reaching systems. Crystal Cave, said to have been discovered by two black boys looking for their lost cricket ball, is the best known (see our Attractions chapter), drawing thousands annually to its cool and quiet beauty.

But Bermuda's caves have an added ecological importance. Several species of shrimp unique to the island live in the marine caves, and endemic Bermuda cave ferns have been discovered just within and close to above-water entrances.

Sadly, many cave systems have been compromised or destroyed by careless disposal of garbage and the encroachments of stone quarrying and housing construction. Toward the end of 1997, battle lines were drawn when environmentalists challenged the proposal of a private company seeking to build a $65 million housing development above a Hamilton Parish cave system that contained 11 endangered species of microscopic shrimp-like creatures.

Studies commissioned by each side proved contradictory. However, what generally emerged was that chlorine from pools and pesticides from gardens could threaten the delicate ecology of the cave system if allowed to permeate the soil and seep through natural fissures above the cave.

Water Resources

Few things are as critical to Bermuda as its water supplies. The island does not have the luxury of streams, rivers or freshwater lakes. We rely instead on water caught via roofs or drawn from government-controlled underground "lenses" — caves of water lying deep below ground.

The full potential of the four major supply areas — St. George's, Somerset, Southampton and the Central Lens, which covers nearly 1,700 acres and sprawls under much of Pembroke, Devonshire and Smiths parishes — has been tapped only within the last couple of decades. Monitored by the hydrogeology section of the Department of Works and Engineering, their total capacity is in the billions of gallons.

Approximately 30 percent of the island's annual rainfall permeates the ground to replenish these lenses, from which an average 1.5 million gallons is extracted daily. The water is treated and chlorinated to health department standards, purchased by homeowners, and delivered by private water truckers when tanks under houses run dry, a not uncommon occurrence during summers when rainfall is below normal, precipitating near drought-like conditions.

Race and Immigration

Sustaining an upward economic curve has required the immigration via work permits of non-Bermudians into the local workplace. The physical presence of hundreds of international corporations, and particularly those in the brokerage, chemical and insurance fields, has resulted in growing numbers of professional guest workers moving here with their families for varying periods of time. And in the service sectors of tourism, foreign workers are filling gaps. The most recent census (1991) of population and housing reveals that non-Bermudians comprise 19.1 percent of a total population of 58,460. These numbers have sparked some local feelings of resentment toward the foreign-born worker.

This side of the socioeconomic coin is generally kept fairly well hidden, and relationships for the most part are conducive to good business.

An insight into our society may be gleaned through a perusal of the *Royal Gazette*'s letters to the editor, through not only their content, but the large percentage written by persons lobbing ideas, opinion and biases from behind the net of the pseudonym. To use a real name seems almost a badge of courage. But perhaps we exaggerate slightly. Bear in mind though that Bermudians traditionally don't believe in airing soiled linen in public, especially to guests. As perfect hosts, we prefer to kick these things around in our own backyard. Taking up the cudgels against racism is a case in point.

Five years ago, in bringing the subject to the social front burner, *RG* Magazine conducted a series of monitored interviews of blacks and whites drawn from almost every financial and social strata. The results indicated that many, perhaps most, black and white respondents recognized the lingering problem, and expressed disgust with prevailing racial divisions.

These and other challenges notwithstanding, Bermuda is facing the better of times, has largely sidestepped the worst and is gradually coping with social and technological change. Future shock may be here, but is losing some of its sting under bright blue skies and determined educational policies that are equipping more of the local workforce to compete in the world of international business, particularly regarding insurance and reinsurance. Well-oiled and constantly monitored, the island seems set to finish the decade with gears meshed and running pretty smoothly. At the end of the day, our report card says we are doing well, but can do better.

Once here you'll discover an excellent public transportation system and a way of life typified by gracious Bermudian hospitality.

Getting Here, Around and Home

Whether traveling to Bermuda by major airline, cruise ship, corporate jet or private yacht, one thing is certain: once here you'll discover an excellent public transportation system and a way of life typified by gracious Bermudian hospitality.

Centuries ago referred to as the "Isle of Devils," and shunned by intrepid but superstitious mariners, our 21-mile-long island has evolved into a cosmopolitan destination with a coy charm, attracting tourists and corporate clientele from around the globe. As a leading world insurance and reinsurance centre (see International Business chapter) Bermuda has become home to a delightful mix of cultures. Our pace may appear a bit slower than that to which you are accustomed. However, appearances can be misleading. We're very much acquainted with the cut and thrust of making a dollar; after all, many of our ancestors were pirates and privateers, so profit is in our blood. We simply smile a little more than most along the way. Whether you're discussing business between holes on any of our excellent golf courses, or are inking a multimillion-dollar deal, you'll quickly appreciate that things get done timely and effectively — no matter how laid back our image.

In tandem with the aim of maintaining efficient public transport, the new government (see History chapter) is developing a National Transport Management Plan. Part of this plan will include expansion of existing minibus services to neighborhoods currently under-serviced. There is also some consideration of introducing high-speed ferry services (hydro-foil) between the Dockyard, Somerset and Hamilton, particularly with an eye on increased cruise ship visits to the Dockyard.

Private sector initiatives have also gained impetus. Travel by trolley will be a pleasant experience for visitors and commuters when the Bermuda Train Company (no, Bermuda does not have a train) launches a trolley train service sometime in '99. This service is expected to run through the heart of Hamilton, picking up tourists and stopping at places of historical interest. At this stage — and there may be changes — the route will include Albuoy's Point near the Ferry Terminal, and run through various city areas and down to the city's eastern boundary as far as the Bermuda Underwater Exploration Institute. (See Attractions and Education and Child Care chapters for more information on BUEI.) The trolley, powered by a locomotive engine, is expected to have three carriages capable of carrying up to 72 passengers.

Getting Here by Air

According to Department of Tourism figures, our annual average is just under 400,000 tourists arriving by air from the US, Canada, the United Kingdom and Europe. The majority of North American visitors find the island's proximity to the Eastern Seaboard — roughly two hours away by air — a plus. Although today visitors jet in and land at Bermuda's East End, in the 1930s the sea towards our western end was Bermuda's landing strip, with passengers requiring a short boat ride to reach the city of Hamilton.

On 12 June 1937, Darrell's Island Marine

Airport in the Great Sound was formally opened, and four days later an Imperial Airways (the precursor of today's British Airways) Cavalier flying boat dropped out of the skies to herald the beginning of commercial air travel to and from Bermuda.

World War II saw Darrell's Island play a critical role as a mid-Atlantic refueling stop for military aircraft. But with the construction and development of the American bases in Bermuda subsequent to the war, the importance of this marine airport quickly diminished, and it ceased operations in 1946.

An interesting legacy surrounds the old seaplane terminal at Darrell's Island. Architect John Gardner, writing in Bermuda's 1988 Heritage Magazine, described it as "an example of the Bermuda-Industrial-Art-Deco style. It is a hybrid structure reflecting many influences. It is not the most beautiful of buildings but it is fascinating and architecturally significant."

Bermuda's civilian air terminal — at the western end of the American air base at St George's — developed after World War II. Known as Kindley Field, after American Captain, Field E. Kindley, a distinguished World War I Flight Commander, it had one short and three long runways. Commercial air traffic began 3 January 1946 with the touch down of the first regularly scheduled PAA aircraft. And 11 days later, a PAA "Constellation" arrived from La Guardia after flying for two hours and 22 minutes, setting a New York-Bermuda air record. Ensuing decades witnessed tremendous improvements and expansion. In 1970 the base was renamed the United States Naval Air Station (USNAS). But a quarter-century later, USNAS joined the list of closures of many US bases worldwide.

With this closure, air traffic control services that had served the island for 50 years departed, and Bermuda assumed total responsibility for the operation of the newly named Bermuda International Airport. Changing from a military- to a civilian-run air facility has involved major alterations and upgrades to meet international civil aviation standards.

Bermuda International Airport

2 Kindley Field Rd., St. George's Parish • (441) 293-2470

On 1 June 1995, USAirways Flight 599 was the first to land following Bermuda's takeover of the airport. It has been business as usual, with hardly a glitch. Canadian-based Serco Aviation Service, which has trained a number of Bermudians, provides infrastructure maintenance and runs ground operations: air traffic control, meteorological services, crash, fire and rescue services, and ground electronics systems.

Bermuda International Airport's facilities continue to be enhanced to better serve arriving and departing visitors. With the 1998 completion of a refurbishing project, almost $20 million has been spent on improvements to the departure and arrival area and baggage hall; resurfacing the runway cost around $5 million.

A new $17.5 million blueprint containing more than two dozen fresh projects was launched toward the end of 1998. Included in its plans for continual upgrading of airport facilities is a longer-term goal to introduce "air bridge" tubes for taking passengers directly onto planes. The cargo terminal is also targeted for rehabilitation. However, the long-term nature of many aspects of the blueprint will see improvements occurring at staggered periods over the next 20 years.

Some anticipated improvements will be the reinstatement of the Visitor Information Desk in the arrivals area. It will be open and staffed

INSIDERS' TIP

Visitors already in Bermuda are not permitted to have their prescription drugs and medications mailed to them. Nor can prescriptions be refilled unless prescribed under an emergency condition.

for all arriving flights. Visitors will in the near future find the works of Bermudian artists exhibited in the arrival and departure areas.

Commercial Flights

Eight commercial airlines fly the Bermuda route. Except for British Airways, which operates on a three-day schedule, all provide daily service. During the March to November peak season, most of the airlines increase their number of daily flights. It is best to verify flight information with your travel agent, wholesaler, or call the airline services directly.

The following commercial airlines fly to Bermuda.

From the U.S.

American Airlines, (800) 433-7300, offers daily nonstop service from New York City (JFK) and Boston. The number of flights increases during peak season. **Continental Airlines**, (800) 231-0856, has nonstop service from Newark, New Jersey. This flight is also subject to change without notice. **Delta Airlines**, (800) 221-1212, flies nonstop from Boston and Atlanta. **USAirways**, (800) 622-1015, offers nonstop flights from Baltimore/Washington, Charlotte, Philadelphia and New York (La Guardia).

Outside the U.S.

Air Canada, (800) 776-3000, offers nonstop service from Toronto and Halifax, with connecting services throughout Canada and Europe. The flights from Halifax are seasonal. Continental Airlines and United Airlines are Air Canada's U.S. partners. From the U.K., **British Airways**, (800) 354-8722, has nonstop service from London's Gatwick Airport on Tuesdays, Thursdays and Saturdays. For those persons traveling from Europe, British Airways provides connecting flights. Contact your travel agent or call the airline directly.

Private and Leased Aircraft

Bermuda International Airport serves as a base for private and commercial aircraft.

From April through October, anywhere from 25 to 60 private aircraft fly here within any given five-day period. December, January and February are the slack months for this type of air traffic.

The Bermuda government requires that owners or pilots of all private and commercially leased aircraft arrange to be ground-handled by an approved agency. Two authorized independent handling agencies in Bermuda reserve the right to accept or reject any service request: **Bermuda Aviation Service Ltd.**, P.O. Box HM 719, Hamilton HM CX, (441) 293-2500; VHF frequency: 131.6 MHz; and **Mid-Atlantic Aviation Ltd.**, Suite 43, P.O. Box 11 GE CX, Bermuda Air Terminal, (441) 293-4622; VHF frequency: 131.65 MHz.

These agencies act as island-based representatives for the crew and passengers aboard private or leased aircraft. They handle all customs and immigration procedures, ensuring that documentation is in order. Additionally, they oversee aircraft-related services, coordinate hangar services, and arrange crew and passenger transportation.

An Executive Aircraft Handling Facility is due to open at the airport in the near future. It will serve as a lounge and communication center for business executives, private aircraft passengers and crews.

Immigration Procedures

After leaving your airline you will enter the arrivals/departures walkway and the recently refurbished Immigration Hall. Once inside, you'll see separate lines for Bermuda residents and for visitors, who may again be divided as U.S. residents and residents of other foreign countries. An immigration officer will quickly verify your documentation for entry.

While aboard the plane, flight attendants should have provided you an opportunity to fill in a Bermuda Immigration Visitor Arrival Card. This must be completed, and along with valid ID, presented to Immigration officers. You will be asked to verify whether this is your first visit and where you will be staying while on the island. As in most countries, the immigration area is a no-nonsense place. If you do not have the forms completed or do not have proper identification, you will be asked to leave the Immigrations Air Arrival Facility, and an officer will assist you into an office to help expedite your processing.

Once you've received your valid stamp to enter Bermuda, you will be able to pick up your luggage in the baggage area.

Customs

Inside the baggage hall, Skycap Porter Service workers can assist with your luggage and guide you to the Customs Hall. Or, you may choose one of the easily visible baggage carts for a dollar. Be prepared to have the contents of your luggage examined. How extensive this will be depends on the customs officer. Remember, possessing illegal drugs invites possible incarceration. Some visitors enter the country believing that marijuana is legal here — it is not! Once customs has finished, the same Skycap will meet you on the other side of the line, reload your luggage and walk you out to where you will be able to find a taxi.

Her Majesty's Customs Regulations

Visitors may bring their personal clothing and valuables with them duty-free. This includes items such as sports equipment, cameras, hair dryers, portable TV or radio, small computer, travel iron, etc., provided these items accompany the visitor on departing. Liquor, wine and tobacco are also duty-free,

Coming and Going

To enter Bermuda you must present the following documents to the Immigration Office.

All Arriving Passengers (visitors)
- Valid passport
- Return airline ticket
- Completed Bermuda Immigration Visitor Arrival Card

U.S. Citizens (visitors)
- Return airline ticket
- Completed Bermuda Immigration Visitor Arrival Card
- One of the following:
—Valid passport
—U.S. birth certificate and photo ID
—U.S. Naturalization Certificate and photo ID
—Voter registration card and photo ID

U.S. Residents (visitors)
- Valid passport
- Return airline ticket
- Completed Bermuda Immigration Visitor Arrival Card

Returning Bermuda Residents
- Valid passport
- Completed Bermuda Immigration Residents Arrival Card
- Entry or Re-entry permit (where applicable)

Arrive by Air, Leave by Ship
- Proof of citizenship
- Cruise ship ticket
- Completed Bermuda Immigration Visitor Arrival Card

but strict measures are enforced. No more than one quart of wine or other spirits, 200 cigarettes, one pound of tobacco, and 50 cigars are allowed. A reasonable amount of beer may be brought in for personal consumption, but a duty must be paid — about 30¢ per can or bottle.

Visitors may bring in gifts, which if not intended for resale are duty-free. However, any gift worth more than $30 will be subject to customs duty. Some foods are dutiable between 5 percent and 22.25 percent of value.

There is no quarantine facility in Bermuda; hence, customs will not allow plants, fruits, vegetables or pets without an import permit from the Department of Agriculture and Fisheries, 169 South Shore Road, Paget Parish, (441) 236-4201. All plants, fruits and vegetables will be held for inspection. Any animal must be certified by a general health certificate issued by a licensed veterinarian within 10 days prior to its arrival. Pets that are allowed in and that leave with visitors are duty-free. Animals arriving without proper documentation will be refused entry and returned to the point of origin.

All prescription medications must be declared to the customs officer, and the quantity should be sufficient only for the duration of your stay.

Strict regulations and penalties apply to firearms. You cannot import guns, rifles or ammunition into Bermuda without a license granted by the Commissioner of Police. Normally, such licenses will be issued only to visiting rifle club members attending a meet in Bermuda. Spear guns and similar weapons are treated as firearms, but antique weapons — determined as weapons more than 100 years old — can be brought in if the importer proves the item's antique value. For yacht captains, be advised that Verey pistols or signal guns are classified as firearms.

Leaving the Airport

Your documentation is in order, you've cleared customs, and unless someone is picking you up, you'll need transportation.

Once you leave the customs clearance hall, don't expect signs advertising Hertz or Avis. There are no rental cars in Bermuda. But don't fret. Transportation is readily available and quite efficient. Exploring the island by taxi, bus, moped and ferry can be fun.

Taxi Service

Some Insiders maintain our taxi drivers are Bermuda's best ambassadors. They're brimming with information about the island. Many are qualified tour guides and enjoy sharing local facts and folklore.

Using a taxi is one of the easiest ways to get around (but depending on your destination, can be costly). From the airport, expect the odd occasion — particularly if two couples are going to the same hotel or guest house — to share a ride, depending on the total amount of luggage. It costs about 25¢ for each piece of luggage carried in the boot (trunk) of a cab.

All taxi services, independent or incorporated, must meet professional standards set and controlled by the Bermuda Transport Control Department, the sole authority for issuing taxi licenses.

Some of the frequently used taxi operators in Bermuda include:

Bermuda Taxi Radio Cabs Ltd.
Trott Road, Hamilton • (441) 295-4141

B.I.U. Taxi Co-op Transportation
40 Union Street, Hamilton • (441) 292-4476

Bermuda Taxi Operators Company Ltd.
P.O. Box HM 1433, Hamilton HM FX
• (441) 292-4175

Bermuda Taxi Services Ltd.
P.O. Box HM 2252, Hamilton HM JX,
• (441) 295-8294

Trott Travel Ltd.
P. O. Box HM 721, Hamilton HM CX
• (441) 295-0041

Taxi rates are metered, and tariffs are fixed by law. Fares are based on taxi hire only and not on the number of individual passengers. However, more than six passengers per taxi is illegal. For tours, you may hire a taxi by the hour or the day; all are equipped with two-way radios and meters.

There are no reduced tour fares for children, but two children under 12 years count as one passenger. Note that once you're seated in the taxi, the meter is set at $3.12 for one to four passengers and $3.90 for five to six passengers. There are five rates of fare (including surcharge rates) that apply to both four- and six-seated taxis. The following rates were effective as of January 1997 and are subject to change.

Rate 1: per mile from 6 AM to midnight for one to four passengers is $4.80 for the first mile. Each additional mile is $1.68.

Rate 3: per mile from 6 AM to midnight for five to six passengers is $6 for the first mile. Each additional mile is $2.10.

Surcharge rates add additional charges at various times. Surcharges apply to Rate 1 at 25 percent of the regular fare from midnight to 6 AM for one to four passengers and all day Sunday and on public holidays for one to four passengers.

Surcharge rates (**Rate 4**) apply on Rate 1 at 50 percent from midnight to 6 AM for five or six passengers, and all day on Sunday and public holidays for five or six passengers.

Taking a sightseeing tour by taxi is a comfortable way to observe some of the more remote locations on the island. Tour rates are set by the hour starting at $30 (**Rate 2**) for one to four passengers and $42 (**Rate 5**) for five to six passengers.

Should you have any concerns regarding taxi service, contact the Bermuda Transport Control Department on weekdays between the hours of 8:30 AM and 4:45 PM at 292-1271. When filing a complaint, you must be able to supply the taxi license number, date, time and journey.

Airport Coaches

When planning transportation from the airport, you can hire one of two airport coach services. The limousine-bus services seat 20 to 26 passengers, with one company also offering six-seater vans. These air-conditioned vehicles travel between the airport and the hotels. Bookings must be made in advance — either by a travel agent or by directly contacting the companies: **Bee-Line Transportation (Bda) Ltd.**, P.O. Box HM 2270, Hamilton HM JX, (441) 293-0303, and **Bermuda Hosts Ltd.**, P.O. Box CR 46, Hamilton Parish CR BX, (441) 293-1334.

You will be charged individually when riding an airport coach. The zone you are bound for determines the rate, with prices increasing the farther you travel from the airport. You can arrange to ride one way or purchase a round-trip fare to return to the airport when leaving the island. Rates include baggage but do not include gratuities for the driver.

Getting Here by Water

Cruise Ships

Cruising to Bermuda aboard a luxury ocean liner is popular. From April through December, as many as 180,000 visitors travel to Bermuda by cruise ship, with close to 35,000 arriving and disembarking during July, a peak month.

Liners destined for Bermuda depart from Baltimore, Boston, Florida, Philadelphia and New York. One-and-a-half to two days later they enter Bermuda's waters. More than 60 years ago the experience of cruising to Bermuda prompted one frequent visitor to enthuse: "One's first visit to Bermuda is, indeed, an enchanted holiday! But one's second, or third, or fourth! With what breathless eagerness one peers from the ship's porthole on the early morning of one's subsequent arrival, incredulously questioning, "Is it still there, that Lilliputian miracle or beauty?" So wrote Mrs. George Draper in *Vogue* magazine those many decades ago. That same excitement still exists.

INSIDERS' TIP

Illicit drugs and firearms are strictly prohibited in Bermuda. Importation of these items can lead to imprisonment and heavy fines.

If you are planning to cruise to Bermuda, there are as many packages available to suit your budget as there are ways to enjoy yourself once your ship berths in either Hamilton, St. George's or Dockyard. Note that a few of the cruise ships that come to Bermuda are too large to berth at any of our docks. For these liners, a specially arranged ferry, organized by the Marine and Ports Department, provides transport to and from.

Bermuda on Cruise Control

In 1874 the Bermuda government and the Quebec Steamship Company signed a contract establishing a regular steamship service between New York and Bermuda, marking the beginning of a concerted effort to develop tourism as a viable industry. For more than a century Bermuda has welcomed cruise passengers to its shores, among them many writers who found rest, inspiration or both: Eugene O'Neill, Sinclair Lewis and John O'Hara are but a few.

Although today the island's tourism relies largely on commercial airline flights from the U.S., several cruise liners service Bermuda regularly, with various other liners paying occasional visits throughout our cruise ship 'season' which runs from April through October.

We suggest you contact a travel agent to arrange your cruise ship itinerary. We have provided keys to abbreviations that help provide information about visiting ships.

Key:

NCL...Norwegian Cruise Line
CH.....Celebrity Cruises
RCL...Royal Caribbean Cruises
CU...Cunard Line

Origin and Destination code.

(NY/BDA/NY) – New York/Bermuda/ New York
(BOS/BDA/BOS) – Boston/Bermuda/ Boston

Bermuda Ports

Ham 1....Berth in dynamic (and laid-back, a splendid dichotomy) Hamilton at No. 1 Shed, near the horse and buggy stand, where drivers offer evening rides through a lovely residential area lying a few minutes west of the city boundaries.

Ham 5/6 ...Berth in Hamilton, No. 5/6 shed (Immediately east of No.1).

Pennos....Berth at Penno's Wharf, St. George's, a mere stone's throw from the center of the old Town.

OI...Berth at Ordnance Island, St. George's, overlooking the Town's hub: King's Square.

WE...Berth in the West End at delightful Dockyard (see Area Overviews).

Hint: When you read, for example (Penno's/Hamilton 5/6), this simply means the ship berths first at Penno's Wharf in St. George's for a couple of days then sails to Hamilton's No.5/6 shed. Both of Hamilton's cruise ship berths lay alongside Front Street, the island's main shopping thoroughfare.

Regular Cruise Ships

Norwegian Crown (NCL) (NY/BDA/NY) arrives (Pennos/Hamilton 5/6) on Mondays and departs the island Thursdays.

Norwegian Majesty (NCL) (BOS/BDA/BOS), specifically serving St. George's, arrives (OI) on Tuesdays and departs Fridays.

Zenith (CH) (NY/BDA/NY) arrives (Ham 1/Penno's) on Mondays and departs Thursdays.

Horizon (CH) (NY/BDA/NY) arrives (WE/Ham 5/6) on Tuesdays and departs Fridays.

Nordic Empress (RCL) (NY/BDA/NY) arrives (Penno's/Ham 1) on Tuesdays and departs Fridays.

Other cruise ships that occasionally visit are the **QE2, the Inspiration, Seven Seas Navigator** and the **Royal Viking Sun.**

The same travel documentation is needed when traveling aboard a cruise ship as when traveling by air. (see the Coming and Going section earlier in this chapter). Visas are not required of passengers from the United States and most other countries. Exceptions are nationals from the following countries: Albania, Algeria, Armenia, Azerbaijan, Belarus, Bosnia-Hercegovina, Bulgaria, China, Croatia, Cuba, the former Czechoslovakia, Georgia, Haiti, Iran, Iraq, Jordan, Kampuchea (Cambodia), Kazakhstan, Kirgizstan, Lebanon, Libya, Macedonia, Mongolia, Morocco, Nigeria, North Korea, Romania, Russian Federation, Slovakia, Slovenia, the former Soviet Union, Sri Lanka, Syria, Tajikstan, Tunisia, Turkmenistan Ukraine, Uzbekistan, Vietnam (North and South) and Yugoslavia (Federal Republic of Serbia).

All cruise ship passengers pay a $60 tax, collected in advance by the shipping line. Currently, children younger than 2 years are exempt

Sailing to Bermuda

Many a skipper enjoys the thrill of sailing from the East Coast to Bermuda, a journey of some 640 nautical miles from Norfolk, Virginia, and 687 nautical miles from Boston.

Although various types of small craft successfully complete passage to Bermuda, it is suggested that a boat be at least 30 feet long to avoid excessive risk and discomfort. A well-equipped vessel of 35 feet with a seasoned crew of at least four or five should be satisfactory for a normal ocean passage.

Bermuda is not in a trade wind zone, and the northeasterly flow of weather systems over the Eastern Seaboard of the United States continues over the island. According to the Bermuda Department of Tourism, private yachts sailing to Bermuda during the summer months will find a high-pressure cell between the Azores and Bermuda that usually produces a wind speed averaging 15 knots. Referred to as a Bermuda-Azores High, it is the predominant meteorological factor for sailors. The Gulf Stream also has an effect on our weather. Its northward flow between the United States and Bermuda warms the island's waters and stabilizes the climate.

If you are considering piloting a boat to Bermuda, note that there is much more weather information in our Flora and Fauna chapter, including a Close-up on hurricanes. Our Yachting and Marinas chapter provides comprehensive information on sailing to and from the island.

Getting Around Bermuda

When tourists first started coming to Bermuda more than a century ago, bicycles and horse-drawn carriages were the only modes of travel. Things changed on 31 October 1931 when the Bermuda Railroad Company opened for business. Operating for 17 years — at a loss — the Bermuda Railway (known fondly as the old Rattle and Shake; see our Let's Explain Bermuda chapter for more) transported 14 million passengers over millions of miles. On 1 May 1948, the train chugged to a halt, and when the tracks were dismantled, both train and tracks were sold to British Guyana.

The old train route — now the Bermuda Railway Trail (called the Tracks by Bermudians) — is accessible, its 18 miles (30 kilometres) offering some of the most revealing and enchanting views of the island. (See our Area Overviews and Recreations chapters for more on the Railway Trail.)

For those who enjoy a traditional horse and buggy ride, a carriage stand is located on Front Street in Hamilton close to the No. 1 shed, about a half-block away from the corner of Queen Street, directly across from Trimingham's department store. See the map page xvi.

Mopeds and scooters are incredibly popular and are arguably the most desired modes of visitor transportation after the buses. Riding them can be exciting, allowing the freedom to come and go as you please. But he cautioned! Unless you are familiar with riding motorcycles, traveling by moped can be dangerous. You will be confronted with riding on the (left) side of narrow, winding roads, and rush hour traffic can be unnerving. Although a moped can be incredibly liberating, please think carefully before renting one. Many a visitor has had a close up and personal encounter with road rash. We cannot overstate it: If unfamiliar with motorcycles, use the buses and ferry.

There are more than 25 cycle liveries that rent motor bikes, pedal bikes and equipment. Rates are competitive, and are on a sliding scale that makes each day of use cheaper. (For complete information on cycle liveries, see our Recreations chapter.)

No matter how you decide to tour the island — whether by bike, bus, ferry, moped, taxi or on foot — it is easy and safe once you understand a few basic rules of the road, keep your wits about you, and always err on the side of caution and common sense.

Road Rules, Bermuda Style

1. It is imperative to remember that in Bermuda one drives on the left side of the road. This is the most significant difference for North American visitors. Be careful at spots where you may instinctively want to veer to your right. The island's major roadways are easy to remember — North Shore Road, Middle Road and South Road.

2. Generally speaking, no one is in a hurry, but we do, as elsewhere, have our speeders and road idiots. There are no expressways. The speed limit is 35 kilometers per hour (about 21 mph). However, in the Town of St. George the limit is reduced to 25 kph, and it is even lower — 24 kph, or 15 mph — in the City of Hamilton and other congested areas. Note that our roads can be very slippery when wet, and visitors are advised not to ride during rainy weather, or to be extra careful.

3. With no expressways, there are few traditional intersections. Traffic circles are called roundabouts. Vehicles already on a roundabout have the right-of-way over vehicles attempting to enter. The rule is to always give way to roundabout traffic coming from the right. Once you are on the roundabout, you have the right-of-way. Never stop on a roundabout or at road intersections to study maps or wait for friends to catch up. Always pull off the roadway to be safe.

4. It is illegal to ride a motorized cycle without wearing a safety helmet. This cannot be overemphasized. Your helmet is your best friend should you have a nasty spill. When you rent a moped or scooter, the cycle livery should go over the rules of the road and provide a lesson or two. Although mopeds are fairly simple to manage, do not attempt to ride one until you are completely certain that you are familiar with the controls. It is best to practice in a safe area before riding in traffic.

5. Always wear the proper clothing when riding. Bathing suits and abbreviated clothing are not permitted. Men, do not ride without a shirt. Do not attempt to maneuver your moped when wearing flip-flops, clogs, or with your feet bare; it is dangerous and against the law.

6. Pedestrians have the right-of-way on a crosswalk. If a pedestrian is already on the crosswalk, or looks as if they may step onto it, you must stop. Also do not jaywalk — use the pedestrian crossings where they are available. Slow down at Zebra (striped) crosswalks and Pelican crosswalks, which are found in the City of Hamilton at various junctions, including those with traffic lights. At these intersections you'll find buttons allowing pedestrians to stop the flow of traffic.

7. When strolling along our outlying country roads — many of which do not have sidewalks or pavements — walk facing oncoming traffic; it is safer. Also, if walking or jogging before sunrise or at dusk, wear light-colored or reflective garments and carry a flashlight if possible. This will help motorists see you more clearly. Avoid walking two abreast.

Riding the Buses

Traveling on our pink and blue buses is guaranteed to be a most pleasant adventure.

Beginning in 1946 with six used yellow buses purchased from Newark, New Jersey, Bermuda's bus fleet has grown to 106, providing islandwide transportation.

Busstops along main thoroughfares are designated by pink and blue poles: pink on top indicates service inbound to the City of Hamilton; blue on top indicates service outbound from Hamilton.

Bus schedules are available in a number of places around the island, including the airport. You will find them at the Visitors Service Bureau (Front Street, Hamilton, near the ferry terminal), at your hotel or guest house information desk, and at the central bus terminal just off Church Street, a few steps east of City Hall in Hamilton. See map page xvi.

The bus schedule includes a table of the most frequently visited attractions on the island and displays the numbers of the routes serving each destination. The schedule also provides a map showing the 14 bus route zones — each about 2 miles in length — and the location of the main attractions within each zone.

Bus Fares

You are required to have a day or weekly pass, a 3- or 14-zone ticket or token, or exact change in coins (drivers are not permitted to make change). Paper currency is not accepted (although, depending on the kindness of the driver, you may be forgiven for proffering notes and allowed on the bus with the stern reminder to obtain a token or pass for future travel).

Bus tokens are sold at the main post office and branches, the central bus terminal in Hamilton, Public Transportation Board (PTB) headquarters on Palmetto Road in Devonshire and at hotels.

One-, three- and seven-day transportation passes may be obtained at the Visitors Service Bureau, the central terminal in Hamilton, PTB headquarters and many hotels and guest houses. Valid passes are good for unlimited trips through all zones on buses, and can also be used for traveling by ferry.

INSIDERS' TIP

Should you lose an item while traveling on the bus, call the Bermuda Public Transportation Board, 292-3851, and they will gladly help you locate anything you've lost.

Photo: GIS

Recent expansion and improvements bring greater comfort and efficiency to Bermuda's International Airport.

Bus tickets are also sold in books of 15 and can be used only on the buses. These tickets are sold at the central terminal in Hamilton and many of the branch post offices. Children younger than 5 currently ride free, as do Bermuda seniors who are 65 or older.

Adult Bus Fares

Cash fares:
$2.50 for 3 zone and $4 for 14 zone
Tokens:
$2.25 for 3 zone and $3.75 for 14 zone
Tickets (15 per book):
$15 for 3 zone and $24 for 14 zone
1-Day Transportation Pass
(All zones): $10
3-Day Transportation Pass
(All zones): $21
7-day Transportation Pass
(All zones): $34
Monthly Pass (All zones): $40
3-Month Pass (All zones): $105

Student-Child Bus Fares (Ages 5 through 16)

Cash fares (All zones): $1
Tickets (15 per booklet, all zones): $6
Visitor 3-Day Transportation Pass: $10.00
Visitor 7-Day Transportation Pass: $15.00
Term Pass (for student usage; all zones): $38.00

The Wheels Go Round and Round

Before boarding the bus, wait a moment to see if someone is getting off; the driver will not allow you to get on before he checks for and allows departing passengers off.

Remember that between 7:30 and 9 AM and 3:30 to 5:30 PM, the buses are generally crowded and hectic with schoolchildren and individuals traveling to work. You may want to consider avoiding these rush hours, or you may see it as an excellent occasion to mingle with locals.

If you need a transfer, you must request it when you first board. Transfers are free where appropriate, but you cannot get off the bus in Hamilton, shop, and reboard a bus to your next destination using the same transfer. Transfers must be used for connecting to the next scheduled bus along your route.

If you have any doubt about the correct stop at which to get off, when you board tell the bus driver of your uncertainty and he or she will gladly announce your stop as it is approached.

Buses are not accessible by wheelchair; none have the necessary hydraulic lifts or storage space. However, persons with limited mobility may be able to enter with some help. Also, remember that buses don't run after midnight on most routes. Should you need transportation after the witching hour, call for or hail a taxi (see previous listings in this chapter).

Taking the Ferries

The Ferry Terminal, (441) 295-4506, is next to the Visitors Service Bureau on Front Street in the City of Hamilton between Point Pleasant Road and Heyl's Corner. See map page xvi. The service offers travel to Paget, Warwick and Somerset. Some residential islands are also accessed. From April through October, and only on Wednesdays and Thursdays, ferries take a triangular round-trip route — Hamilton, Dockyard, St. George's.

The ferry system — a timetable is included on the bus schedule — is an economical and terrific way to thread the exceptionally beautiful waters around many of Bermuda's tinier islands.

Getting to the Dockyard from Hamilton by a direct, 30-minute ride, takes you past small sheltered inlets and bays where sailboats rock gently at anchor. White, pink, blue and green homes seem only an arm's length away as they perch on lush hillsides that slope to the water's edge.

Incidentally, rental cycles can be taken on the West End ferry for an additional $3.75.

Optional Methods of Transportation

There are other ways to get around Bermuda.

Mini Buses

There are two mini-shuttle bus companies servicing the East and West ends of the island.

St. George's Mini-Bus
St. George Square, Town of St. George • (441) 297-8492

This service is located next to Town Hall on King's Square. These blue buses (which carry up to 22 passengers) travel to the outlying beaches — at Fort St. Catherine and Tobacco Bay — the Town of St. George, St. George's Parish and St. David's.

St. George's service operates every day from May through September and is available Monday through Friday from 7 AM until 11 PM, Saturday from 8:30 AM to 11 PM, and Sunday from 9 AM to 6 PM. During the winter season, buses operate Monday through Friday from 7 AM until 8 PM, Saturday from 8:30 AM to 8 PM, and Sunday from 9 AM to 6 PM. Fares vary between $2 and $5 per person traveling one way. For information on reduced rates for seniors, children and frequent riders, contact the office.

INSIDERS' TIP

If you are staying in a private home, ask your friend or host how he or she describes where the house is located if you need at any time to call for a taxi. Although each house is numbered, taxi service despatchers will want a description of how to reach the house and your name. Example description: I'm at the third house on the right after you turn on to Cedar Lane. It's blue with white blinds. My name is Smith.

West End Mini-Bus
Hook and Ladder Ln., Somerset Village
• (441) 234-2344

West End provides shuttle service for the area between Somerset Bridge and the Royal Naval Dockyard. Two buses carry 14 passengers each. They are operated Monday through Saturday from 8:30 AM to 5 PM, and on Sunday from 8:30 AM to 1 PM, from April to November. From December to March, buses are available from 8:30 AM to 5 PM on Wednesday and Friday and from 8:30 AM to 1 PM on Monday, Tuesday, Thursday, Saturday and Sunday. The highest fare is $3 one-way; senior citizens living in Bermuda pay $1. Call ahead to arrange advance bookings.

Getting Back Home

Your vacation has come to an end, and you're ready (reluctantly?) to return home. Departing Bermuda is a simple procedure.

All airline passengers should check in at Bermuda International Airport at least an hour-and-a-half before scheduled departure. When arranging transportation to the airport, allow for travel time based on where you are staying, time of day, and traffic flow. If staying at the West End for example, allow at least 50 minutes traveling time to the airport. If in the City of Hamilton, allow a half-hour.

The Bermuda immigration form and other documentation received at the time of your arrival should be attached to your ticket. All passengers traveling to the United States are required to pay a departure tax of $20, which should have been included in your fare. You're exempt from this tax if you are flying directly to your destination; children 2 years or younger are also exempt.

Clearing U.S. Customs

Pre-clearance at U.S. customs is available in Bermuda for all scheduled flights. It's a simple, time-saving procedure. All passengers leaving for the United States must fill out a declaration form before clearing customs in Bermuda. Once you've checked in at the airline reservation counter, you will enter the U.S. Customs Terminal. A representative from the U.S. Department of Agriculture will question you regarding the types of souvenirs you have, particularly plants and foods. This is usually a formality, as inspectors are looking for insects, pests or anything that may carry infectious germs into the States. It is important to remember that you cannot take back any indigenous flowers or plants (such as hibiscus, pine and Bermuda cedar) or sea life (such as sea cucumbers, urchins, brain coral and soil). You may leave with flowers bought from a florist, seashells that don't have anything growing inside them, frozen seafood, cassava pies filled with poultry (but not beef or pork), and Portuguese sausage in plastic store wrapping. A list of fruits allowed into the United States may be obtained from the United States Department of Agriculture's International Services offices in Bermuda, (441) 293-2752.

U.S. residents who have been out of their country for 48 hours or more may take back (once every 30 days) articles valued up to a total of $400. Anyone entering Canada must now make written declarations regardless of whether they have something to declare or not. If you have been absent from Canada for 24 hours or more, you can claim exemption on $50 worth of goods (not including alcohol or tobacco); if you have been out of the country 48 hours, the exemption limit is $200, which rises to $500 if you have been away seven days. United Kingdom citizens are allowed up to £136.

A duty-free shop at the airport, located upstairs, allows passengers to purchase last-minute gifts before departing. A small food court is nearby.

As you leave us, plan to come back and see us again. We'll be waiting.

Coughed from the belly of the Atlantic a hundred millennia ago, this fishhook-shaped coral archipelago perched at the summit of an extinct submarine volcano was once avoided like the plague.

History

Prologue

Coughed from the belly of the Atlantic a hundred millennia ago, this fishhook-shaped coral archipelago perched at the summit of an extinct submarine volcano was once avoided like the plague. Discovered in 1503 by Spaniard Juan Bermudez, a mariner from Palos, Spain, the islands were throughout the sixteenth century believed to be inhabited by demons.

This superstition had a simple origin. The trills of hundreds of thousands of cahows (also known as the Bermuda Petrel), floating on the wind to the ears of passing seafarers, were oddly interpreted as the cries of devils. Appearing early in the century on many manuscripts and printed maps as Las Bermudas, Bermuda was quickly dubbed Ya de Demonios by Spanish mariners. And yet, despite its unalluring reputation, some historians believe a small number of French privateers became familiar with the safe passages through the surrounding treacherous reefs and occasionally used the island as a base.

French explorer Samuel de Champlain, returning from the West Indies in 1600, described this "Isle of Devils" as a place where, "It almost always rains, and thunder is so frequent that it seems as if heaven and earth must come together. The sea is very tempestuous about the said island and the waves as high as mountains." Nine years later, heaven and earth did come together violently, conspiring in a scenario that led to near death, and subsequent habitation.

Shipwreck and Settlement

By 1609, Jamestown, founded two years earlier on the banks of the James River in Virginia, was slipping into oblivion. Backed by a syndicate of influential London merchants operating as the Virginia Company, the young settlement was decimated by disease, starvation and Indian raids.

During trade development with the lands bordering the eastern Mediterranean Sea and the East Indies, company stakeholders had gained considerable experience in financing far-flung commercial enterprises. Moving quickly to save their Virginian investment, in June 1609 they dispatched Admiral Sir George Somers as commander of a fleet of nine ships. The mission set off from Plymouth, England, to rescue settlers who were still many weeks and an ocean away.

All went well until the fleet neared the dreaded Las Bermudas. The ships were within seven or eight days of making Cape Henry on the Virginia coast when they sailed bow first into disaster. "A dreadful storme and hideous began to blow from out the Northeast, swelling and roaring as it were by fits and at length did beate all the light from Heaven; which, like an hell of darkenesse turned blacke upon us," wrote Silvanus Jourdan and William Strachey, passengers on board Somers's 300-ton flagship *Sea Venture*.

The ship was battered for a day and a half by hurricane winds and pounding seas that broke open the seams of its hull. "Windes and seas were as mad as fury and rage could make them," Jourdan and Strachey wrote. As water rushed in, the passengers and crew threw weapons and chests overboard to lighten the load. And just as it seemed that passengers' prayers would go unanswered, the ship was edged between reefs at the eastern end of the islands and wrecked within sight and striking distance of shore.

Fortuitously, there was no loss of life as the exhausted settlers struggled ashore. Somers promptly claimed the land for England, and Bermuda's opening chapter of permanent settlement had begun, not with a placid landfall but with a preface of howling winds, angry seas, and personal possessions hurled into a summer maelstrom.

The 150 men and women found a chain of islands heavily forested with cedars and palmettos and populated with birds and wild hogs. But while the tiny isles proved more hospitable than the haunted lands of seafarers' superstitious tales, Jamestown was not forgotten. The settlers there were still expecting the cavalry. In little more than nine months, two new ships, *Deliverance* and *Patience*, were built from local cedars and salvaged *Sea Venture* timbers.

However, even as the new vessels took shape during those months of sojourn, this island that would inspire Shakespeare to pen *The Tempest* was the setting for one murder, an execution, five deaths from natural causes, a marriage, two births and three mutinies. When the admiral and the ships finally departed a land that, though it had proved challenging, was essentially tranquil, they left two men behind. One of them, Christopher Carter, was Bermuda's first permanent inhabitant, remaining here until he died.

News of the shipwreck intrigued the Virginia Company. In 1612 a subsidiary known as the Bermuda Company was formed to finance and manage colonization. That same year the first wave of 60 white settlers, led by company-appointed Governor Richard Moore, a carpenter, left England for Bermuda. On July 11 the pioneers arrived in St. George's Harbour, eager to carve a prosperous life from an isolated wilderness.

Early Years

Survival on a group of tiny islands almost 600 miles from the nearest land and with no freshwater rivers or streams was difficult but possible. Rainwater was caught in wooden barrels, "cabbens" were erected using cedar and palmetto thatching, and within a decade a fleet of small fishing boats had been built.

In 1616 the first black man and first Indian were brought from the West Indies to dive for

pearls. The company had grandiose dreams of realizing profits from cargoes of pearls, rare spices, whale oil and ambergris, but time yielded few profits. Investors were disappointed, but men continued to arrive from England and to explore many of the smaller islands. Women, however, remained scarce.

The arrival in 1621 of "certaine younge maydes" from England created excitement. However, it was an arrangement with a price attached. Those single men who could scrape together 100 pounds of tobacco secured themselves wives. How many women arrived and how many men came up with the price is unclear. But at the latter part of the century, several communities grew up around Flatts, Crow Lane, Riddell's Bay and Mangrove Bay. Each of these pocket-sized settlements boasted a small inlet that served as a haven for privateers and smugglers. In these sheltered bays, cargo was unloaded far from the prying eyes of inspectors based in St. George's, Bermuda's political center, commercial hub and first capital.

Tobacco, whaling, cedar and salt were critical to the infant economy. Cedar forests were cleared for the cultivation of potatoes, cabbages, onions and tobacco, which emerged as a principal commodity grown only for export to England. As early as 1626, "triers and tasters" were sent out to ensure that the quality of tobacco was acceptable; quantities judged unfit were burned, sometimes at the grower's doorstep. By 1687, Bermuda and Virginia shared a monopoly on the tobacco trade; yet the quality of the Bermuda variety was poor, as local tobacco farmers battled worms, ants and wireweed. Tobacco production was banned at home, and the British government taxed tobacco grown in the colonies. Bermuda's farmers refused to pay, insisting that to do so would destroy an industry already in decline, a decline so rapid that by 1712 a reversal of fortunes saw Bermuda importing, not exporting, tobacco.

An agricultural-based economy didn't appeal as much to Bermudians as did the call of the horizon. From the beginning, they regarded the ocean as the ultimate road to prosperity, and whenever possible pursued lucrative opportunities through a trading triangle — Bermuda, the West Indies and the continental colonies.

Much of the work during those early years, whether it was on land or ocean, was carried out by indentured white servants and black slaves. Ultimately, indentured workers were completely replaced by slaves. Although slavery here never descended to the brutal levels common elsewhere in the New World, local slaves struggled against the wretched institution. Prior to emancipation, three major rebellions were planned and thwarted, and the ringleaders were executed.

Yet the Bermudian dichotomy in the early years of development saw a handful of free blacks in the community who overcame various restrictions to pursue various occupations as fishermen and blacksmiths. Some had been released from indentured servitude to become free men during the early years of the island's development, Others were granted freedom through stipulations in slaveholders' wills. But by the end of the seventeenth century, the three classes of blacks — indentured servants, slaves, and free men — were replaced by one dominant class, that of slave.

The Wood of Prosperity

As owners and slaves strengthened their ties to the sea, reliance on cedar was crucial. The richly scented wood rather quickly evolved from mere practical resource into the sinew of economic and cultural prosperity.

The importance of juniperus bermudiana prompted one nineteenth century naturalist to write that "in olden times the native squires of Bermuda calculated their wealth by the numbers and growth of the cedars on their estates, and tradition has it that the fair 'Mudian damsel who possessed a right and title to a thousand goodly cedars was in a certain way of possessing a husband, should she feel so inclined."

A superb asset for squires and damsels, cedar was used to build homes and make furniture, farm implements, window frames, rolling pins, cradles, altars, coffins and even fish pots. But its most significant contribution was to the success of the shipbuilding industry. Maritime activities encouraged the establishment of several shipyards that were kept busy throughout the eighteenth century. As many as 30 sloops were built annually, several of which were destined for New York merchants.

As Bermuda-built vessels achieved a reputation for durability and speed, it was inevitable that shipbuilders would not only receive contracts from clients engaged in legitimate commerce, but also from merchants with eyes on a different prize.

Privateering

As early as the sixteenth century, piracy and privateering had flourished in the Caribbean. Following Bermuda's settlement, a few local merchants and officials became closely acquainted with privateering captains who occasionally brought their brigs into St. George's Harbour to stock up on supplies.

The hazardous, yet frequently rewarding, forays against north bound ships returning home to Spain or France from the Caribbean was too tempting to resist for Bermudians with a thirst for adventure and profit. Several merchants outfitted their own privateers and hired white captains, slave crews and black pilots to voyage in search of plunder. As a result of countless successful engagements, the fortunes of many prominent families were founded on profits from such raids.

In 1684, when the British government took over the charter of the Bermuda Company, the island's sailors of fortune had established a reputation where they "were feared by merchantmen more than those of any other nation." Between 1685 and the middle of the eighteenth century, hundreds of local seamen turned to this endeavor with gusto. Some became highly successful. One of them, Nathaniel North, retired to become a rajah in Madagascar.

During the American Revolution a score of swift, copper-keeled sloops were operated as privateers, and in one month alone, September 1782, captured 20 ships. But the island became even more directly involved. A trade embargo declared by the Continental Congress against Britain and her colonies put Bermuda in a tenuous position. Squeezed by the hostilities, well-established and viable trade contacts along the eastern United States were in danger of perishing. Inability to obtain food and other essentials put the islanders so near starvation that many considered deserting the country.

A small delegation journeyed to Philadelphia to plead for Bermuda's exclusion from the embargo. Appeals fell on stony ground. Dominant in the salt trade, the islanders offered to supply as much as the States wanted. The response was quick. There was no pressing need for salt, they were informed, but if, by some good fortune, arms or gunpowder were somehow substituted. . . .

The delegation returned home. On August 14, 1775, one of the largest gunpowder storehouses in St. George's was raided, virtually under the nose of the governor. A hundred barrels of powder were rolled down to Tobacco Bay and rowed out to two American ships anchored just offshore. When dawn broke over the town, the gunpowder was on its way to George Washington's men, who put it to good use in driving the British out of Boston. The unwritten deal of gunpowder for provisions was honored. The embargo on Bermuda was lifted.

The Salt Trade

The salt offered to the Americans by the delegation came from a thriving undertaking established a century earlier. Having claimed Turks Island in the Caribbean as a Bermudian possession, Bermuda then raked the salt from the cays (pronounced "keys") during the winter and stored it at home. In spring, supplies were taken to Virginia, Maryland, Pennsylvania, New York and Newfoundland to be traded

for corn, flour, beef, salt fish and other necessities. Prior to opening the trading season, bushels of cabbages and onions were taken to the West Indies in exchange for rum, molasses and cotton.

In 1710, wanting to hone in on this enterprise, the Spanish attacked and captured the salt ponds. This audacious seizure of the salt piles did not go unchallenged. A retaliatory expedition under Capt. Lewis Middleton routed the Spaniards and restored possession of a profitable business.

The Dockyard

Early in the 1800s British naval power in the North Atlantic was consolidated by the construction of the Royal Naval Dockyard (often simply called the Yard) at Bermuda's most western end. With two bases already established at Antigua and Halifax, the Yard provided a valuable third prong. The construction of storehouses, repair slips, timber yards, foundries, fuel tanks, engineering shops, boat sheds, living quarters for men and officers and, later, a school and hospital, generated the largest military defense utilization of money, manpower and materials in nineteenth-century Bermuda.

The strategic value of this mid-Atlantic naval post was immediately evident during the War of 1812, when Rear Admiral Sir George Cockburn sailed from here in the summer of 1813 to harass the Delaware and Chesapeake bays. The following year Admiral Sir Alexander Cochrane set out with a task force to help in the attack on Washington.

At the beginning of the war, the Yard was still relatively embryonic, with work carried out by slaves, free blacks and craftsmen from England. During this war, large numbers of American slaves, including entire families fleeing bondage, sought help from British sea captains. Given refuge on British ships, significant numbers of escaping blacks were brought to Bermuda.

Restricted to Dockyard confines, the men were employed in direct construction while the women and children were put to work picking oakum, a fiber often treated with tar and used chiefly for caulking seams in wooden ships. While the majority of local and Ameri-

Hog Money Discovery at Castle Island

In summer 1994, employees from the Bermuda Monetary Authority led by Dr. Edward Harris, director of the Bermuda Maritime Museum, and Professor Norman Barka from the College of William and Mary in Williamsburg, Virginia, headed up two volunteer teams in an archaeological dig on Castle Island.

This 3-acre island near the entrance of Castle Harbour, barren except for a few stunted cedars and tricky to get onto, is the site of the ruins of King's Castle, once the main fortification of 17th-century Bermuda.

The focus of the excavations was a defensive ditch cut between 1612 and 1620. Appearing to have been used as a trash dump following its initial construction, the ditch yielded substantial amounts of bird, fish and animal bones. After sifting through the soil and detritus  of almost 400 years, the diggers were elated on discovering 13 pieces of "Hogge Money" (usually referred to as Hog money). These ancient, rare coins are believed to be among the earliest such coinage in the British colonies.

Excavations undertaken a year earlier by the William and Mary team had unearthed a sixpence and a twelvepence. The sixpence, a remarkably fine specimen, showed surprisingly little wear from either handling or contact with other coins. The twelvepence, however, typical of many pieces of this type, was considerably debased.

Numismatist E. Rodovan Bell, writing a half-century ago on Hog money, speculated that the coins were probably first minted in London. Presumably struck in a short period of time and perhaps by more than one mint, the quantity produced is unknown, as are the designer and engraver. It appears that the number of coins minted was never large and there was the problem, noted by historian Henry Wilkinson, that, "Coin had always been scarce and the little there had been had nearly all gone to passing ships for aqua vitae (whisky, brandy or other strong liquor)."

Photo: The Royal Gazette

Nineteen Hog money coins have been unearthed at King's Castle on Castle Island.

Photo: The Royal Gazette

11311

This Hog money sixpence (circa 1616)
features a wild boar.

The earliest reference to a coinage for Bermuda is found in the commission granted by the Virginia Company to Governor Moore in 1612. After stipulating the amount of wages for skilled and common laborers, the company promised to "speedily" send out a special coin for the purpose.

It is believed the first minted coins were sent to the island in February 1616 with a proscription that their use be restricted to Bermuda. The denominations are generally supposed to have been in the values of twelvepence, sixpence, threepence and twopence. Of similar design, they varied in size and weight and were made of a mixed metal termed "brasse." The ship design on one side probably represents the *Sea Venture*, with the obverse showing a wild boar.

There is some speculation as to the origin of the term Hog money, but most believe it derived from the abundance of wild pigs found on Bermuda in the early days of habitation. Although there have been suggestions purporting the existence of a fourpence and a one-penny denomination, neither has ever been found. The most common is the shilling or twelvepence, the rarest the threepence.

In 1996 four more coins were found at Castle Island. As far as is currently known, these 19 coins are the only pieces of Hog money found in an archaeological context. With all the coins authenticated by the Bermuda Monetary Authority, they comprise the Castle Island Collection, occasionally on display at the authority's headquarters on Burnaby Hill in Hamilton.

can blacks were unskilled laborers, an 1823 Dockyard Table of Wages shows that quite a few blacks were employed as shipwrights, caulkers, masons, blacksmiths, sawyers and sailmakers.

On a number of occasions, captured American merchant and war vessels were brought into Bermuda with onboard slaves who voluntarily offered their services as laborers and craftsmen. They became known as the "King's Blacks." Eight years or so after the end of the war, most of these refugees were sent to Trinidad.

The arrival in 1824 of the *Antelope*, which carried 300 convicts from England, marked an escalation of manpower and opened an entirely new chapter in the Yard's construction. From then until 1863, housed on filthy

prison ships called "convict hulks," thousands of prisoners were put to forcible labor, a development that ironically coincided with the slowly dying institution of slavery. Writing about that era, historian Roger Willock stated that "perhaps the most pleasant thing that can be said of, or written about, the convict establishment at Bermuda was that it was brought to a close in 1863."

Emancipation

Ten years after the first shipload of English convicts arrived in these waters, slavery was abolished in the British colonies. But the months leading up to August 1, 1834, the Day of Emancipation, were filled with contradictions, greed and great sadness.

During that summer, the Emancipation Proclamation appearing in the local newspaper shared space with advertised slave auctions. And as slaves anticipated release from bondage, many slave owners noticed that impending abolition in the colonies had driven up prices of slaves sold in the United States. Although the British government had set aside 20 million pounds for distribution to its colonies as compensation for freed slaves, local owners shipped their slaves out of Bermuda, destined for American auction blocks, often in groups of a dozen comprising "various shapes and sizes."

This continued up to the day before emancipation. Even during those final hours, slaves were marched to the Devonshire Dock and Flatts Inlet where, wrote historian Nellie E. Musson, "rowboats carried them to the slave ships. Those who refused to walk were put in chains and carried away."

When August 1 did arrive, celebrations were joyous but muted as families attended various church services to pray for friends and family members transported from the island and sold overseas.

The Century Closes

It is said that the first genuine tourist to Bermuda was the Rev. Michael Wigglesworth, who arrived in 1663 from Malden, Massachusetts, after a long and unpleasant voyage. Be that as it may, Bermuda did not begin to get a glimpse of its tourism possibilities until 1852, when a 36-room hotel was built in Hamilton.

Located in Pembroke Parish, Hamilton had replaced the Town of St. George as the island's capital in 1815 over the strenuous and bitter objections of that town's citizens. Centrally located with an excellent harbor, Hamilton was a logical choice. However, when the American Civil War broke out in 1861, St. George hosted all the action despite Hamilton's title as capital.

When the Union-imposed blockade on southern ports made direct shipments from abroad impossible, it was no surprise that Bermuda would once again become involved in matters affecting its closest neighbor. Strong family and commercial ties between prominent Bermudians and their counterparts in Virginia and other southern states guaranteed the island would become one of the focal points of trade between Europe and the Confederacy. From headquarters in the old Globe Hotel on King's Square in St. George's, the Confederacy's chief political agent negotiated with shipping suppliers and agents, arranged payment for goods and secured the shipment of food, arms and ammunition destined for the South.

Blockade runners — shrewd seamen who could slip through the sea lanes past Union ships — crowded the alleys and byways of the small town. Money flowed freely. The town's merchants pocketed more gold and silver in one year than they had in any 10 previously. The economic bonanza lasted until its decline was sealed in January 1865, when Fort Fisher in North Carolina fell to a combined land and sea assault by the Union. The fort's 12-pounder Whitworths had protected blockade runners as they ran along the coast of the Carolinas and into the entrance of the Cape Fear River. The news dismayed merchants in Bermuda, who were left holding surplus goods when the dust finally cleared. Within a year, St. George's ancient alleys were once again tranquil and sedate.

Ten miles away, Hamilton seemed to have ignored the intrigue that marked activities at the East End. The city's business leaders were more concerned with promoting Bermuda as a welcoming place to visit for a restoration to good health.

In 1874 the Bermuda government and the Quebec Steamship Company signed a contract establishing regular steamship service between New York and Bermuda. It was the beginning of a concerted thrust to develop tourism. When Princess Louise, daughter of Queen Victoria, visited the island in the winter of 1883, the owners of the Pembroke Hotel renamed it The Princess in her honor (see our Resort Hotels chapter).

But whether royalty or commoner, few visitors were as entranced as Mark Twain, who described Bermuda as "an earth-bound heaven." Twain's heaven, while starting to market itself overseas, still depended on an economy bolstered by agricultural exports to the United States and Canada. Steamship services subsidized by the government carried potatoes, arrowroot and onions to those markets.

This development and expansion of the agricultural trade had necessitated the importation of additional laborers several years earlier. In 1849, Bermuda had invited Portuguese agricultural workers from Madeira to come to the island on contract. The invitation was quickly accepted; the first dozen men and their families arrived in November on the ship *Golden Rule*. Throughout the rest of the century the Portuguese population grew, with the overwhelming majority continuing to be engaged in farming. Onions were the staple produce.

In fact, so critical was the onion that Twain observed during one of his visits, "The onion is the pride and joy of Bermuda. In her conversation, her pulpit, her literature, it is her most eloquent figure. In Bermuda metaphor, it stands for perfection."

In other words, an Englishman might be a Limey, but a Bermudian was an Onion and remains one to this day.

The 20th Century

As the doors to a new century flew open, Bermuda's economy pivoted on tourism development and maintenance of the agricultural trade. With export as a major economic player, bringing visitors to these shores did not get into full swing until 1912, when a syndicate of merchants backed an advertising promotion in Atlantic City, New Jersey, that included an exhibit of live Bermuda fish. A year later, this was followed up with a display at the Grand Central Palace in New York.

Tourism slowly began to achieve greater importance as Bermuda became increasingly popular as a winter resort. Yet, while spoken of as a place of legendary beauty and serenity, many simply did not know where it was. Its location was variously cited off the coast of Africa, Florida or in the West Indies. During a conversation between two elderly gentlemen watching a cricket match in London, one was heard to remark, "Bermuda is our stronghold in the Pacific!"

Early in the 1930s, a writer for the Bermuda Trade Development Board (the precursor of today's Department of Tourism) penned a vivid portrait that tried to capture every color of the rainbow. "The road to yesterday will take you far from the chill bleak cities of here and now," he wrote. "It will lead you to a gleaming group of coral isles, riotous with tropical colour, set in an azure sea, warmed by a golden sun that will flood your veins with youth. It is a soft road, paved with cushions of green, spume-flecked velvet, bordered with white flowers of healthy salt-spray."

On June 12, 1937, Darrell's Island Marine Airport, in the Great Sound, was opened, and the first commercial flight, a seaplane, touched down six days later. Jaded Americans tired of noise and nasty winters could now have their veins flooded with youth faster than voyaging here by sea. As tourism ascended, agriculture faced decline. Throughout the 1930s it was hit by American protective tariffs. By the 1940s, domestic sales were more profitable. And as mid-century dawned, agricultural exports virtually died. Bermuda's economy now turned exclusively to tourism.

The '30s also brought the rumblings of social and political change. Blacks were becoming increasingly restless about discrimination and prejudice, and women began a long fight for voting rights. Despite being taxed equally with men, they were denied the vote. In 1923 the Bermuda Woman Suffrage Society had been founded, but after several years of trying and failing to be taken seriously, the society drew up a document and sent it to the Secretary of State for Colonies in London.

The 1929 petition, spearheaded by Mrs. Gladys Missick Morrell and a core of other determined women, requested that a Royal Commission examine the subject of women's suffrage. The petition was returned to local governing politicians for them to handle. They refused to budge. One stated reason was that women were "unduly dominated by clergy"

INSIDERS' TIP

The Hon. Premier Pamela Gordon was the first woman to hold the office of premier of Bermuda.

Photo: GIS

Bermuda's parliament or House of Assembly is a major landmark in the capital city of Hamilton.

and giving them the vote would lead to a "priest-ridden Bermuda." Indignant, Mrs. Morrell traveled to London in 1931 for a face-to-face confrontation with Lord Passing, the Secretary of State, but her efforts were fruitless.

The suffrage struggle, initially an effort by white upper-class women, changed complexion as it entered the 1940s. Black women, hitherto written out of the scenario, were courted by Mrs. Morrell when she addressed a forum at a black club. By 1944, with the support of black women, the fight prevailed. The House of Assembly passed the voting measure by a 20 to 13 margin. That same year, the first woman to cast her vote was Edna Williams Tucker, a black landowner. Mrs. Morrell saw out the end of 1944 and the beginning of 1945 as Bermuda's first elected vestrywoman. And in the 1948 general election, two women were elected to the House.

Railroad, Automobiles and Turtles in the Net

For many years the debate on the intro-duction of the motor car had been lobbed back and forth around the community. Bermudians in general were aghast at the thought of such contraptions spluttering and wheezing along peaceful country lanes, and a law prohibiting its importation brought sighs, perhaps even neighs, of relief. Horsepower had served the island faithfully for centuries, but transportation could not remain forever dependent on dobbin (work horses). The decision to establish a railway was believed a suitable compromise as well as a deterrent to the automobile. Property was purchased by the Bermuda Railway Company, a syndicate of private investors, bridges were built, with trestles erected along coastlines, tunnels cut and tracks laid from Somerset to St. George's.

When the first train ran on October 31, 1931, its presence was generally welcomed. But some visitors were appalled. The editor of *Harper's Bazaar* castigated it as "an iron serpent in the Garden of Eden." Although the railway proved a boon for those living at opposite ends of the island — scores of folk had never ventured out of Somerset or St. George's until the railway — the Garden of Eden was soon rid of its iron serpent. Costly to run, it was a financial disaster. In 1946 the government surprisingly purchased this losing enterprise, even as new legislation allowed the import of the motor car. By 1948 the train had become a snake needing only to be put out of its misery. A deal with British Guiana resulted in the sale of the train and its tracks to that country.

However, even as Bermuda continued to debate the relative merits of horse, road and rail throughout the life of the railway, a sea-related incident occurred five years after the train's introduction. Bermuda's waters were known for claiming vessels run aground on outlying reefs. In the 19th century, wreckers would row out to plunder these helpless "turtles in the net." In 1936 the Spanish ship *Cristobal Colon* joined the roster of turtles. Despite their best efforts, local authorities were unable to prevent the ship from being boarded and looted. For several months afterward, scores of homes were searched and the stolen goods were retrieved. One man, accused of having a radio taken from the wreck, protested indignantly, "Why would I steal a Spanish radio? I can't speak Spanish!"

American Bases

World War II brought in the American military. Britain appealed for help from the United States in the first year of the war, and in 1941 a House of Commons announcement by Sir Winston Churchill offered the Americans air base facilities on Bermuda for 99 years. It was a land-for-ships trade, with Britain receiving 50 U.S. destroyers.

On March 27, 1941, President Roosevelt and Prime Minister Churchill signed the Lend-Lease Agreement. As a result of this agreement, St. David's, a 500-acre island at the eastern end, was divided, with 250 acres taken over by the American military. Construction began quickly as a massive landfill project got underway with soil dredged from nearby Castle Harbour. When completed in 1943, homes and even graveyards had been buried forever.

During these war years, the island also hosted more than 100 British censors. The British government requisitioned the Princess and Bermudiana hotels, closed at the outbreak of war. The Princess became the focal point,

where all mail between Europe and the United States was opened and the contents studied for microdots and coded messages. A few spies were indeed unmasked during this imperial censorship.

With the construction of Kindley Air Force Base and the building of the Naval Air Station in Southampton completed by war's end, the economy was energized by the spending power of American personnel. Another distinct advantage was that the Kindley base was constructed in tandem with the Bermuda Civil Air Terminal, located at the base's west end.

In January 1946, Pan American airways began regularly scheduled flights from La Guardia in New York City to Kindley Field. Darrell's Island, which for nine years had been the entry point for visitors arriving by seaplane, was closed down.

Parties, Protest and Confrontation

Postwar resurrection of a stalled tourist trade gathered momentum in the '50s, but in this vital effort color prejudice dictated that the thrust be divided along black and white lines. While the white-controlled Bermuda Trade Development Board embarked on major promotions, black-owned hotels, guest houses, restaurants and clubs formed their own organizations to promote penetration of the black American market. These efforts were effective, and black tourist dollars directly benefited the local black community. Equally successful were the separate white promotions. Bermuda cashed in, but race problems lurked in the wings.

In 1959 NASA established a tracking station on Coopers Island, part of the East End base. The station participated in tracking the orbital flights of John Glenn and Walter Schirra and provided a crucial communications link when Apollo 11 made the first manned lunar landing in July 1969.

The same summer of the lunar landing and "one giant step for mankind," racial tensions that had been simmering finally bubbled to the surface. A peaceful boycott against segregated seating in cinemas continued until the color bar was dropped. White-owned hotels abandoned discrimination in their restaurants and nightclubs. The black community became more active in challenging racial frictions in the workplace. In 1963 the Progressive Labour Party (PLP) was founded to promote interests of the predominantly black working class. The following year the predominantly white United Bermuda Party (UBP), headed by Henry Tucker (later Sir Henry), was formed, and Bermudian politics entered an entirely new arena.

In 1966 a Bermuda Constitutional Conference attended by representatives from both parties was held in London. At the beginning of 1967, a new Parliamentary Election Act became law, granting "one man, one vote" to every British subject older than 21 and resident in Bermuda for three or more years. That summer a new Bermuda Boundaries Commission approved the division of the nine parishes into 40 voting constituencies.

On February 6, 1970, the Bermuda pound was scrapped and the island went decimal, welcoming dollars and cents. In August 1971 a dollar crisis that temporarily closed foreign exchanges saw Bermuda's banks refusing to accept U.S. currency and traveler's checks. The local government, in the interests of preserving a smooth-running tourist trade, then pegged the local currency to the American dollar.

The '70s were dominated by strikes and dissension, and by the decade's close, a police commissioner had been killed, a governor and his aide assassinated and their two killers executed. The violence and retribution that had claimed the lives of victims and perpetrators came as startling by-products of a violent element in the thrust for civil rights. But while the decade was marked by volatility, the island rejoiced in 1979 when Miss Bermuda, Gina Swainson, was crowned Miss World in London.

Toward the 21st Century

When Bermudians awoke on January 1, 1983, they found that whatever benefits they had received from carrying a British passport had been unceremoniously eliminated. As a result of a new British nationality law, they had become British Dependent Territory Citizens, and the old passport was invalid. Prior to this development, the original Bermudian passport allowed an almost automatic option of living and working in England without much of a problem. The new passport nullified that.

While tourism, once the island's unquestioned mainstay, vacillated, the construction industry found the 1980s an unequaled golden egg. By 1990 Hamilton literally doubled its commercial office space in the past decade, while home building also recorded significant gains.

It was a period of unbridled expansion. The resident population increased, employment grew 34 percent, and more cars cluttered the roads. The domestic economy was buoyant. Bermuda was ranked fourth in the world in per capita income and loving it. The economic surge did not last, however. Development reached a plateau and tapered off as the country entered the '90s. Jobs in the construction trades declined. Bermuda began to experience the pains of unemployment in a way it never had before. And tourism, which had always led the economic charge, was trembling with a bad cold.

Concern over the state of the economy and the environment took center stage along with the issue of independence. The idea had bounced back and forth since the late '70s, when it was the subject of a 1978 Royal Commission. It emerged again as an issue in the mid-1990s, brought to the political front-burner by Bermuda's premier, Sir John Swan, the second black UBP leader. The majority of his party was set firmly against Bermuda's severing ties with Britain. The country was bitterly divided.

On August 16, 1995, an Independence Referendum, failing to gain support from the PLP (who advised its members to abstain), was shot down in flames by voters. Only 58 percent of the electorate went to the polls, among them 18-year-olds who voted for the first time as a result of 1990 legislation. With the defeat of his initiative, Premier Swan resigned. He was replaced, very briefly, by David Saul, the UBP finance minister.

Although the original Lend-Lease Agreement called for both American bases to revert to Bermudian ownership on March 27, 2040, on September 1, 1995, the Bermuda government took possession of the base properties

after the Americans ceased operations. With some 10 percent of Bermuda's total land mass returned, the government has embarked on a 20-year redevelopment plan involving both areas.

In March 1997, as the UBP regrouped, Pamela Gordon, daughter of legendary black Labor leader Dr. E. F. Gordon — a thorn in the side of the white establishment in the '40s and '50s — was voted Premier by her party, making her the first woman to hold the position. The previous year, Jennifer Smith was elected as the new leader of her party, the PLP.

The political duel between these determined and capable party leaders heightened during the lead-up to the November 9 general election. While the thrust and parry of campaign elements had been ongoing for most of the year, the final weeks before voting day marked the most intense period of political activity in the history of local politics. It was a financial boon for the media, with an unprecedented avalanche of radio, print and television advertisements vying for voter allegiance. The election result: a PLP triumph with the capture of 26 out of 40 House of Assembly seats, making Ms Jennifer Smith the first woman to lead her party to victory. With 80 percent of registered voters participating, the PLP had received a decisive 54-percent mandate.

In celebration of its first victory since the advent of party politics in the middle 60s, the PLP designated January 4, 1999, as a one-off holiday. This decision annoyed many businesses, but the holiday was celebrated with activities including a parade and evening fireworks. However, although political matters dominated throughout 1998, there were lighter moments.

In late summer the *Royal Gazette* newspaper mailed a pair of Bermuda shorts to Iraqi president Saddam Hussein, following a report that he had banned shorts because they "inflamed the passions of women." The newspaper was unable to confirm whether Hussein had received the gift. If he did, one might safely presume he hasn't worn them, certainly not in public.

On the tourism front, two of the island's largest and best known hotels — the Southampton Princess and Hamilton Princess — were sold to Canadian Pacific in a $540 million deal that included five other international hotels.

As the island counts down to the witching hour leading into the twenty-first century, Bermudians will probably enter the new millennium as full citizens of the UK, with the restoration of British citizen rights taken away in 1963. The latter months of 1998 and the early months of 1999 witnessed the UK Foreign Office working on details necessary for granting full rights to the less than 200,000 citizens of the remaining British colonies, including Bermuda.

By and large, the island has maintained a strong economy and a low unemployment rate. However, there are areas of concern: drug-related crime (although Bermuda remains one of the safest destinations on the planet),

preserving the environment while facilitating infrastructure development, educational restructuring (see our chapter on Education and Child Care), and stalled tourism.

But Bermudians have always faced challenges and emerged stronger and revitalized. It is in the national genes — a grit that turns adversity into an enviable prosperity.

While Bermuda is more urban, it definitely still feels rural. Gardens may be smaller and patios may be larger, but we do want to plant, as our gardening centers will testify.

Flora and Fauna

"Wherefore my opinion sincerely of this land is that it is in truth the richest, healthfullest, and pleasing land — and meerley natural as ever man sat foote upon."
—Sylvester Jourdain, 1610

Jourdain surely knew what he was talking about since he was one of the crew who survived the wreck of the *Sea Venture* in the hurricane of July 1609. (See our History chapter for more details.)

Once the passengers and crew had reached the safety of Bermuda and the winds had dropped, it must have been a case of "summertime, and the living is easy." The island during that time was covered with cedars and palmettos. Birds, particularly the cahow, were abundant and so tame they were just asking to be eaten. And the fish were certainly jumping. As for meat lovers, well, they could depend on the wild hogs left by an earlier visitor for a feast of roast pork. A "meerely natural" paradise indeed. However, humanity being what it is, the island did not stay "natural" for long.

When the first settlers looked at the cedars, they immediately thought "ships." In fact, the first thing Sir George Somers, admiral of the *Sea Venture*, did was build the *Patience* entirely out of cedar. And when the settlers looked at the landscape, they thought, "What can we plant?" In a short period of time, they planted wheat, beans, "cowcumbers" and other seeds they had brought with them from England. Naturally, they also had an eye on profit. As Jourdain put it, "they have made a greate deale of Tobacco and if some would come that have skill in making it it would be

very commodious both to the Merchant and to the maker of it." And so they started the trend of introducing new plants to Bermuda.

Biologists will tell you Bermuda's flora and fauna consist of what is endemic — that is, unique to Bermuda — and what is not. It is noteworthy that just 17 endemic plants, including our Bermuda cedar, exist today in contrast to the other species that number more than 3,000. It is more difficult to assess how many animals are endemic. Apparently, there are dozens of unnamed small moths and even smaller insects that may be endemic. However, one bird species and one lizard species are definitely individual to Bermuda. When we mention specific plants and animals, we will tell you if they are endemic. If we don't mention their status, so to speak, you may take it they are not unique to our island but have been introduced, either by natural phenomena or by humankind.

Until fairly recently, Bermuda's environment was primarily rural. Agriculture took an upturn in the nineteenth century with the coming of the New York steamers, and Bermudians became well-known for their export of agricultural produce to the New York markets. They exported tomatoes, celery, potatoes and arrowroot, but were particularly famous for their Bermuda onions and beautiful Bermuda Easter lilies. Indeed, so famous was the Bermuda onion, the colony became known as "The Onion Patch," and true Bermudians still refer to themselves as "Onions." Visitors in those days would have seen large areas of arable land — large, that is, considering the island is only about 21 square miles. In addition, many Bermudians had access to fairly spacious pieces of land where they planted vegetables, herbs and fruits for personal consumption.

After World War II, the picture changed with the growth of our two main industries, tourism and international business. Instead of "plant," "build" became the key word. Tourists needed hotels, and exempt companies (see our International Business chapter) needed office space. Moreover, the growing population and increase of foreign workers meant a need for more houses and apartments. Building was especially intense during the '70s, and since that time Bermuda has become more and more urban. As a result, concern about dwindling natural space has led to some legislation for the protection of land and species (see our Parks and Conservation and Fishing chapters for details) and the careful landscaping of new buildings.

While Bermuda is more urban, it definitely still feels rural. Gardens may be smaller and patios may be larger, but we do want to plant, as our gardening centers will testify. When you arrive, you will immediately notice a plethora of trees, foliage and flowers on the roads and hillsides. This chapter will help you identify a sampling of them. It will also alert you to other living things in the sky, the sea and the land, although not necessarily in that order. Much of our flora and fauna is contained in parks and nature reserves, so look in the Parks and Conservation chapter for additional information, particularly for information about exotic trees and plants.

Climate

Because climatic conditions shape the environment, we will start by explaining our weather. Bermuda is situated near 32 degrees north latitude, 65 degrees west longitude. Our location means we are more subtropical than tropical, but our proximity to the Gulf Stream guarantees a White Christmas is most definitely a dream. Though we may occasionally see hail, there is absolutely no snow.

However, we do have seasons: winter, spring and summer. During the first three months of the year, our temperatures can drop below 60 degrees Fahrenheit, but they tend to stay in the mid-60s. While visitors appear comfortable in shorts and tops, we wrap up in woollies and scarves. Our blood is thin, you see. Besides, we get to enjoy a change of wardrobe.

Spring can lead to clothing confusion. Mornings tend to be chilly and call for sweaters, but by the middle of the day we eagerly shed them. Sometimes spring is not necessarily much warmer than winter, but it is always marked by the coming of the longtails, the blooming of our freesias and lilies and the appearance of abundant fruit on the loquat trees.

Temperatures start to heat up in April and in July. In August and September the temperature can reach the high 80s or low 90s. High humidity is a feature of our climate and often affects our energy levels. It may explain why we walk so slowly. Sea breezes and a dip in the ocean can help reduce lethargy. Humidity also creates mildew problems, so we have to be particularly careful about how we store our food and our clothes. Bread, for example, belongs in the refrigerator — otherwise it rapidly grows penicillin — and a closet heater helps to protect our wardrobe, particularly our shoes.

"Hey," you might say, "What about the fall? Don't you have autumn?" Well, yes and no. At precisely the time people in more northerly climates are harvesting, we are planting. In late September and October we grow vegetables and flowers that will arrive in time for Christmas. In November we plant our bulbs. Nonetheless, we do have our fair share of autumnal colors, but sometimes they appear in April rather than the traditional fall months, as you will discover when we subsequently discuss hedges and trees. And we don't experience that autumnal chill in the air in September and October. So for us, these months count as an extension of summertime.

As for rainfall, it is usually spread over the year. At least that is what we hope. When it rains, often we are split between sympathy for our visitors — who, after all, have come for sun — and relief that our water tanks are being replenished. Our water supply, you see, depends on how much rain we can catch from our roofs. True, we can buy water, but who needs the expense? In addition, we value the lush greenness of our surroundings. A prolonged period without rain means brown grass.

Because we have such a small land mass, you would think that rains must cover the whole island. However, this isn't necessarily so. It's perfectly possible for St. George's to be drowned out in a deluge, while the western end of the island remains dry as a bone. In fact, sometimes you can walk on one side of the road in clear sunshine and watch rain fall on the other side. This phenomenal localization of rainfall may explain why we often have amazing rainbows.

Insiders distinguish between rain and "good tank rain." A drizzle may relieve plants but is not much use to our catchments. Actually, it rarely drizzles in Bermuda. Usually the rain comes in torrents. Torrential rain is good tank rain, provided it falls straight down. The horizontal rain that comes with high winds is no good at all.

"Winds?" you might ask. Yes, we have them. Winter winds are common, and in the summer hurricanes sometimes happen. The optimistic side to winds is that they make for spectacular seascapes. (See this chapter's Close-up on When the Wind Blows... for more information.)

Trees, Plants and Flowers

Hedging Our Bets

Face it, we in Bermuda love to hedge, and we love to stonewall. When you explore, whether by taxi, bike, bus or on foot, you will see that most of our roads are lined with foliage and flowers. Hedges rise up behind limestone walls of varying heights. If you like uniform hedges, fair enough, you will see them. Many consist entirely of oleander, which flowers continuously most of the year but thrives on brilliant sunshine. It has thin, pointed leaves and clusters of flowers that are most commonly pink. However, there are hedges of white and red oleander dotted around the island.

The other common hedge is hibiscus that flowers in a variety of colors — pink, red, white, peach and yellow. Sizes vary, but some flowers are 4 or 5 inches in diameter. The flowers have long, protruding pistils: Brush against them, and you will be dusted with bright yellow pollen. Hibiscus flowers for much of the year.

Another hedging plant is pittosporum of the Victoria box variety. With its dense, dark green leaves and small but fragrant white flowers, it is popular because it can survive well in windy, exposed areas. "Match me if you can," a copper-colored hedge, gives us a touch of autumn year-round. Its name sounds like a tease, doesn't it? If you have children to distract, ask them to find two identical leaves on this plant. They won't be able to manage it. The plant's variegated leaves range in color from green to copper to pink. To this day, Bermudians use them to make poultices.

Many of our hedges, however, are more mixed than uniform. The pale blue flowers of the plumbago, a plant that can be hedge or vine, tumble with the orange of the honeysuckle and the pinks and purples of the bougainvillea. Incidentally, the vibrant colors of bougainvillea are thanks to its "bracts" — modified leaves — not to its flowers, which are tiny and white. This plant can also be trained as a vine.

Vines are very common in Bermuda, and it would be impossible to mention all of them. Watch out for the bright yellow trumpet flowers of the allamanda vines that scramble down walls. Blue cascades of morning glory are common, although gardeners aren't too keen on them. If allowed, morning glory takes over. Should you explore in the evening during the summer months, you might be lucky enough to see the night-blooming cereus, which has exquisite, white flowers that come out one hour after sunset and smell of vanilla ice cream. By morning, the flowers are shriveled.

Hedges also incorporate a huge variety of grasses and ferns. These have a more subtle beauty and perhaps can best be appreciated first thing in the morning, when drops of dew touched with sunlight hang from the feathered grasses. Asparagus fern, so useful for wedding decorations, looks even spikier and greener in the early morning light. Wildflowers are also part of the mélange. In springtime, look for the little purple Bermudiana flower (endemic) and for riotous tumblings of nasturtium flowers, which, from a practical point of view, are excellent in a salad.

Branching Out to Trees and Shrubs

Trees and shrubs, of course, can be classified in many ways: deciduous and evergreen, tropical and subtropical, small and large and so on. We have decided to classify them into two very practical categories — those you can eat from and those you cannot. The trees we describe in this section can easily be seen on the roadsides. However, check the Bermudian Gardens section below for more information about some of our exotic and ornamental trees. We must mention here that some of the plants mentioned above, such as hibiscus and oleander, can also be grown as trees. Where hedges and trees are concerned, we have to confess we sometimes beat around the bush.

Incredible Edibles

Come late February and March, many children disappear into the loquat trees that are then weighed down with their yellow to orange, pear-shaped fruits. Introduced from China, this small tree can be found throughout the island. The fruit makes for delicious jams, chutneys and pie fillings. Some of us also like to soak the loquats, together with rock candy, in rum or gin so that six months later we can enjoy a tot of loquat liqueur after dinner.

The Surinam cherry tree is another favorite. Twice a year, it produces clusters of red, ridged fruits that have a distinctively tart tang and can be cooked to make jam and jellies. Sometimes the taste of the fruit varies in sweetness from tree to tree. By the way, we often use the cherry tree as hedging, because it is hardy and easy to grow. And while we're talking jams and jellies, we must mention the guava, a tree that grows up to 30 feet and produces round yellow fruits. Guava jelly goes excellently with roast lamb.

Citrus trees have a long history here. They are not endemic but go back to 1616, when seeds were sent to Gov. Daniel Tucker. In that century, rents were sometimes paid in fruit. Our oranges, to quote Andrew Marvell, are like "golden lamps in a green night." In addition, we have lemons, limes and grapefruit. They mostly grow in private orchards that you may glimpse as you ride or walk by. You will also be able to see small plantations of banana trees that were also introduced here in 1616. Their sweet, almost nutty flavor is quite different than that of the ones we occasionally import. And when dried, their tattered leaves come in very useful for making our traditional banana-leaf dolls. Historically, the leaves were also used for stuffing mattresses and as a remedy for burns.

Paw-paw trees, originally from Colombia, are extremely popular in Bermuda. They appear in pairs (male and female) and have succulent trunks. Their fingerlike leaves have seven lobes, and their oval fruits serve as both

INSIDERS' TIP

Bermuda has a unique collection of old established roses. The Bermuda Rose Society has published a book called *Roses in Bermuda* that includes a guide to roses you can see in the public gardens, parks and hotel grounds of the island. You can buy it at any of Bermuda's bookstores.

savory and dessert. When green, the fruits are tasty in a stew and are an effective meat tenderizer. When yellow, they can contribute to a fruit salad. The paw-paw has medicinal properties — according to our senior citizens, its juice helps to reduce high blood pressure. Another local fruit-vegetable is the avocado pear. Salad is just not salad without the nutty taste of the avocado. One problem with the avocado pear tree has to do with its complex cross-fertilizing system. Apparently, the tree changes gender once a day — difficult for us and for it. Growing an avocado tree is easy. Getting it to bear fruit is a trickier matter.

One more fruit must be mentioned, although it does not grow on trees. Locust and wild honey are extraordinary vines with large leaves that have slits and holes in them. It's as if someone has attacked them with a pair of scissors to create interesting patterns. A white flower spath encloses the fruit, which is scaled. Imagine a furry version of the pineapple, and you will have some idea of the taste.

Look but Don't Cook

No book on Bermuda could be complete without mention of our beloved, endemic cedar tree, the *Juniperus Bermudiana*. In a way, we are incorrect to put it in the "inedible" category, since once upon a time Bermudians fed themselves and their animals on cedar berries. The berries were also fermented to make a cough syrup. But these days, those practices have died out. The Bermuda cedar has had a rather bumpy ride of it throughout history. When the first settlers arrived, cedars were plentiful, but so many were felled to make boats, houses and furniture that in the 1600s the Bermuda Company tried to enforce orders against cutting them down.

In the eighteenth century, the landscape was once again filled with cedars, though they were still highly prized. One John Crevecoeur wrote in 1784: "A girl's fortune is counted by the number of cedars — that of my hostess has been two thousand, seven hundred." Disaster struck in the mid-1940s when a blight caused by an insect destroyed approximately 80 percent of the trees. No longer could we go out and cut a cedar for our Christmas tree. Since then, thanks to the Department of Agriculture, Fisheries and Parks' reforestation program, cedars have made a comeback, although they do not dominate the landscape to the extent that they did in 1609. Watch out for them behind hedges and on our hillsides.

Why do we love our cedars so much? Well, the older trees (some did survive the blight) have a dusty but evergreen appearance. They add a biblical effect to our landscape and gardens. And the wood appeals to at least two of our senses: It has a pink, warm glow and smells delicious. Sachets of cedar shavings put in closets and chests give a fragrant smell to our clothes. It smells even better when it is burning, but these days using cedar for firewood seems sacrilegious. Incidentally, Spanish moss loves cedars too. Very often you will see masses of its long, silver-gray threads growing and hanging from cedar branches.

Many of our hillsides, once dominated by the cedars, are now covered with casuarinas, deliberately planted in the '50s and '60s to reforest the island. Casuarinas, also known as Australian pines, are evergreens and have small fruits grouped in woody, conelike structures. These cones are useful for making Christmas decorations. Because these trees are resilient to wind and salt, many gardeners like to grow and cut them as hedges.

Yikes! Fronds and Spikes

Palmetto is also endemic, and, like the cedar, was once the source of food and drink. Both people and animals fed on the black berries. Some people made an alcoholic drink called "bibby" out of the liquid drawn from the trunk. No doubt the drink was ample compensation for the lack of British ale. The crown was eaten instead of cabbage.

Palmettos, with curved, green fronds whose leaf blades are touched with yellow, had other practical uses as well. Its leaves were used to thatch houses and to plait baskets, ropes, bonnets and hats for export. Today craft makers use the leaves to create dolls or Christmas ornaments. You will see palmettos of varying sizes all over the island. Often they intermingle with our hedges or stand alone on hillsides. In gardens they can give shade to other plants that find the sun too fierce.

Numerous palms of other kinds lend our island a tropical look. Some are aristocratic,

When the Wind Blows . . .

"It's an ill wind that blows nobody any good," the saying goes. While it is true that a hurricane in 1609 fortuitously started Bermuda's first settlement, most of us would rather do without hurricanes altogether. However, whether we like it or not, we do have a hurricane season. Officially, it starts June 1 and ends November 30, but the following old Bermudian doggerel, found in Terry Tucker's *Beware the Hurricane!*, is often apposite:

June. Too soon.
July. Stand by!
August. One must.
September. Remember?
October. All over!

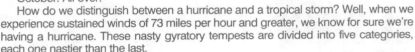

How do we distinguish between a hurricane and a tropical storm? Well, when we experience sustained winds of 73 miles per hour and greater, we know for sure we're having a hurricane. These nasty gyratory tempests are divided into five categories, each one nastier than the last.

Category 1 has winds of 73 to 95 mph; Category 2, 96 to 110; Category 3, 111 to 130; Category 4, 131 to 155; and Category 5 ... We won't even think about Category 5. Winds stronger than 156 mph are just too horrendous to contemplate.

Of course, weather satellites are extremely useful in that they do give us some warning, and we do have a hurricane watch system. However, there are oldtimers who feel their own methods of hurricane prediction are far more reliable than those of meteorologists. St. David islanders, in particular, swear by shark oil. After hanging a shark's liver in the sun so that the oil can drip, they pour about a cup of the liquid into a clear glass bottle, which they then cork and hang outside in a shady place. Clear oil means sunny skies. Churned, cloudy oil means trouble is coming.

Bermudians have other predictors too. "Listen to the South Shore roaring!" is one piece of advice. When a storm starts 500 or 600 miles to our south, our waters react long before we experience a breath of wind. Tides rise higher than usual, and huge swells pound onto the rocks and beaches. The longer the interval between the swells, the more severe the storm will be.

Silk spiders warn us as well. If they weave their webs close to the ground then, the argument goes, they know we're in for trouble and therefore so do we. A leaden atmosphere is another sign. Sometimes the air is so heavy with humidity that we have to fight lethargy in order to prepare for the brewing storm.

A day or so before the storm arrives, our birds fall ominously silent. They know there's nothing to sing about. Preparing for a hurricane is tedious but essential. This is the time when some of us wish we had not bought so many planters or so many items of outdoor furniture that we must now put away. Others fret over their boats. And "battening down" becomes our stock phrase as we close our shutters or hammer boards over the windows of our houses and shops.

Candles become vital articles of equipment, as are batteries for radios and lamps. As for fresh water, we store it in as many containers as possible. The bathtub is the most capacious one. And all the while, we tend to think uncharitable thoughts: "The hurricane can hit anywhere else it likes, but please let it not come to Bermuda."

Sometimes we're extremely lucky, and the hurricane, changing its mind at the last moment, bypasses Bermuda altogether. Other times it plays cat and mouse, teasing us with gale-force winds, loving us and then mercifully leaving us without directly hitting us.

— continued on next page

Photo: The Royal Gazette

Bermuda has seen its share of hurricanes.

In August 1995, Hurricane Felix indulged in such a flirtation. It caused enough havoc to cause a one-day postponement of our Independence referendum. Once the island voted against saying goodbye to dependency, Felix had the nerve to return, as if showing disapproval of our decision.

Because of our tiny land mass, we tend not to suffer direct hits that often. Nevertheless, Hurricane Emily of 1987 taught us never to be smug. She came literally out of the blue one morning in September. Short, sharp and vicious, she destroyed one-third of our trees, blocked many of our roads and left us without electricity for weeks after she had gone. Lack of light and running water made us feel utterly powerless (pun intended). And many of us realized that although suffragettes Susan Anthony in the United States, Emily Pankhurst in Britain and Gladys Morrell in Bermuda had a lot to do with women's liberation, the most powerful factor was electricity.

Ten percent of our roofs went sky high, although no houses were totally destroyed and no people were killed. The sturdiness of our architecture stood us in good stead. Though Emily was a very ill wind indeed, some good did come out of it. The community came together in a way it had not for years. Those who regained electricity gave new meaning to "shower parties" by opening up their houses to people desperate for flowing water, and people rallied to help those whose houses were badly damaged. Still, Hurricane Emily is not an experience we'd like to repeat.

to say the least. We have the Cuban royal, the queen and the princess palms, together with the more plebeian spindle, date and coconut trees. The coconuts, by the way, are not too good to eat. They take 12 months to mature and though it's possible to have flesh and milk neither is as sweet as you find in coconuts further south.

Watch out for our spiky plants. Their sharp edges give spunk to the landscape, but a close encounter with Spanish bayonet, for example, can be very painful. Its leaves are sharp enough to use as fencing foils. Century plants, a variety of aloes and cacti all add a tropical touch.

Spice and All That's Nice

Mexican pepper trees are abundant, and their small red berries come in very handy at Christmas for decorations. The allspice tree is feathery and its tiny white flowers are exquisitely fragrant — scrunch a leaf in your hand, and you will smell the spice.

The Pride of India tree is also prevalent. Although deciduous, it offers shade in the summer. Don't eat its yellow berries, though — they are poisonous. Remember we promised you autumnal visual effects? The fiddlewood splashes the island with the reds and oranges associated with the fall. But unlike the maple tree, for example, it drops its leaves twice a year: once when it "should" and once in springtime. Similarly, the bay grape tree, which has round, shiny leaves and withstands wind and salt spray well, also has the eccentric habit of turning red in April.

Bermudian Gardens

Very often our hedges, walls and trees serve to screen both public and private gardens. Public gardens will be discussed in our Parks and Conservation and Attractions chapters. Remember that public landscaping in Bermuda is a priority. Roundabouts, for example, are not just for vehicles. Very often, their centers are covered with flowers. And restaurant owners or managers take just as much pride in their gardens as they do in their menus.

Where private gardens are concerned, don't be afraid to be discreetly pokey (Bermudian for "inquisitive"). If you can look over or through a hedge, by all means do so. In spring you will see banks of creamy white freesias, subtly streaked with purple and gold. But we also like more vividly colored freesias as well. Pinks, purples, yellows, reds — we like them all. Other popular bulbs are paper whites (which we plant in November in time for Christmas), the dramatically striped amaryllis and lilies, including, of course, our Easter lily.

Come October, we flock to the garden centers to buy our annuals. Impatiens (sometimes known as "busy lizzies"), petunias, pansies and snapdragons give a medley of color to

our gardens, patios and pots from Christmas through early summer. Geraniums are popular too and in the past were also grown as hedges. In July, August and September, begonias and periwinkles take a more prominent place because they can cope with fierce sun.

Of course, private gardens vary according to the owners' tastes. Some are formal and carefully manicured while others have more of a wilderness effect. Ambitious gardeners often go for the exotic. The bird of paradise plant is a favorite. Named for its appearance, it has stiff, bright orange flowers and blue stamens. Bottlebrush is another favorite, and, yes, its vibrant, scarlet flowers do resemble a baby's bottlebrush.

Exotic trees are loved by serious gardeners and include the gigantic Indian rubber tree, the equally huge Indian laurel and the banyan tree. These will be described more fully in our Parks and Conservation and Attractions chapters. However, we must mention the tall, graceful jacaranda, which has lilac-colored flowers, and the frangipani tree, which comes with either white or pink fragrant flowers. Deciduous, the budding of the frangipani marks the coming of spring. Also deciduous is the glorious royal poinciana tree that graces so many gardens. The poinciana starts to bud in April, then for some weeks the leaves bunch at the end of the branches. By June, the tree looks like a massive leafy parasol, and by the end of the month, it is covered with fiery red blossoms. Come July and August, it offers respite against the blazing sun. Sit under the poinciana, gaze up into the intricate design of its lacy leaves and you may understand the infinite geometry of fractals.

Arable Fields

Although we are no longer the farming community we once were, we still have acres of land devoted to the planting of vegetables and flowers. People of Portuguese descent mostly tend these areas. Look out for plots of reddish-brown earth planted with Bermuda onions, potatoes, cabbages, carrots and broccoli, to name just a few of our vegetables. At Easter you will see our beautiful Bermuda lilies (a selection of which, by the way, we annually send to Her Majesty, Queen Elizabeth) and other flowers, such as chrysanthemums and snapdragons. These flowers, along with the vegetables mentioned, are sold in our stores and in stands along the roadsides.

Birds, Fish
and Other Animals

In Bermuda, animals can be bright and beautiful, but they are definitely small rather than great. We don't have deer or foxes or elk, for example. True, whales sometimes visit us in April and true, some exotic larger animals can be seen at our Aquarium (see our Attractions and Kidstuff chapters). But the largest wild animals you will see on the island are feral cats, chickens and rabbits. Even these are not wild in the true sense of the word. They originated from abandoned pets or animals kept for domestic use. Much as we like to visit the bigger wild animals when we travel to larger countries, we're, on the whole, happy not to have them here. Given the size of our island, our vegetation could not support them. As for the rabbits, we are keeping an eye on them. They may be cute, but they can over populate. Where our gardens are concerned, too many a bunny isn't funny.

Fine, Feathered Friends

When Bermuda was a peaceful, rural community, our birds were probably much happier. Horse-drawn traffic, once our chief means of transportation, was far less threatening to them than the motorized kind, introduced in 1946. And the reduction of open spaces, together with the destruction of trees, has led to a decline in some of our species. Domestic and feral cats don't help either.

Nevertheless, we are still lucky in that on average, some 200 species seen in Bermuda are recorded each year. Many of our migrating birds come from North America, but sometimes gulls and ducks can arrive from the Old World, from the West Indies, from Greenland and from South America. We have 22 nesting species, and it is a small sampling from this category that we will describe in this chapter. (See our Recreations, Beaches, and Parks and Conservation chapters for more information about woodland, sea, pond and marshland birds.)

The Bermuda petrel, or cahow, was the bird that the first settlers saw in such vast numbers. Within 20 years they managed to eat most of them. So cahows were almost — but not quite — wiped out. Some 300 years later, in 1951, cahows were miraculously rediscovered. Thanks to the work of David Wingate, ornithologist and Conservation Officer at the Department of Agriculture and Fisheries, they are continuing to survive. In 1998 the numbers of breeding pairs and chicks were approximately 53 and 30 respectively. (See Parks and Conservation and Area Overview chapters.)

White-tailed Tropic Bird or Longtail

Though longtails are here for just eight months of the year, we have claimed them as our own. Almost a Bermudian emblem, they decorate our pottery, glass and jewelry. Sometimes these pelagic birds can be seen in late February, but the majority of them arrive in March, bringing with them the promise of spring.

Be sure to take a walk on the South Shore cliffs for a Bermuda longtail experience. Gaze across the sea and up into sky. At first, the sky may seem empty, but eventually you will be able to just make out a flash of white separate from the whiteness of the waves breaking on the reef. The flash will rise into the air and then swoop towards the cliff, the black markings on its wings and sleek tail clearly identifiable now. Seconds later, its mate will follow and together they will tilt and swerve along the coast in an aerial dance. Sometimes the birds will veer towards each other; sometimes they diverge so that once again it can be difficult to distinguish them from the spray. But back they will come, plunging and soaring — their curved wings hammering the air, their twin tail feathers bending gracefully into the breeze. The gilded version of the longtail, so popular in Bermuda as a pendant or brooch, seems a mockery when we witness the elegant vibrancy of the true longtails' flying courtship.

Eastern Bluebird

The male bird's back feathers are as blue as its name. Its chest is a warm, pinkish brown. Once plentiful, our lovely bluebirds suffered from the introduction of the house sparrow and the kiskadee. However, the Department of Agriculture, Fisheries and Parks and the Audubon Society have encouraged the setup of special nesting boxes, and as a result, in recent years, more of these birds have been mating. Whether bluebirds enjoy watching golf is uncertain, but they certainly haunt our golf courses. Look out for them there (see our Golf chapter). You might be interested to know that ornithologists are debating the possibility that our bluebirds may be a subspecies endemic to Bermuda.

Great Kiskadee

You will see this flamboyant bird all over the island. It is predominantly bright yellow with some brown and rufous (that's tinged with red) feathers. You will hear it as it literally calls "kiskadee." Some Insiders claim it is calling in French — asking the question, "Qu'est-ce-qu'il dit?" (Translation: "What is he saying?") Our visitors love this bird, but we are more cautious in our affection for it. It is rough and rude, you see, and it terrorizes the bluebirds. Introduced in 1951 to control our lizards, it must have changed its mind about its meal preferences. We still have plenty of lizards.

Northern Cardinal or Redbird

We love our cardinals, especially the male ones, which are definitely very red. In the morning they like to perch on trees or telephone wires and serenade you. Their song is pure and true, in contrast to their comically pompous appearance. They also like to show off their own importance by puffing out their chests.

Chick-of-the-Village

This yellow, white and black bird is also called a white-eyed vireo. It sings merry notes and is partial to fruits and berries. Always known to be native to Bermuda, it's now thought to be possibly an endemic subspecies. You also will see migrant white-eyed vireos whose plumage is similar but brighter and whose songs and calls are more nervous than our own chick-of-the-village.

Fish Are Jumpin'

Surrounded as we are by ocean and reefs, we obviously have fish. And it's not just two little fishes and a mama fish too. We have a wonderful variety of species, ranging from the massive marlin to the diminutive sergeant major. Since scuba diving and snorkeling are the best means of observing our fish, we will give you more detailed information in our Watersports and Beaches chapters. The former is also where to look if you are more interested in catching than observing — in Watersports, we cover all aspects of fishing and our fish conservation laws. In our Attractions chapter we will alert you to the aquarium where visitors may see many species. Here, we want to introduce you to just a few of our more ornamental fish and some of their behavior and habits that can only be described as, well, fishy.

Parrotfish

These are perhaps our favorite. They come in all colors, the most common being blue-green. Parrotfish are not shy at all, and often they swim so close to shore that you can see them from your window or the water's edge. What you probably won't notice is that the male parrotfish is apt to change sex. Let us explain this extraordinary phenomenon. You

---

INSIDERS' TIP

When you go for a walk, do yourself a favor and leave your Walkman behind. That way you won't miss the busy call of the "chick of the village" or the melodious song of the redbird. Be sure to appreciate Bermuda's sweet sounds.

Photo: GIS

Easter lilies grown in Bermuda are presented annually to
Queen Elizabeth II of England on her birthday.

see, parrotfish swim in groups with one dominant female. When that female dies, the next
most dominant male in the group changes
sex and takes over. Apparently the sex change
takes about two weeks to complete.

Angelfish

Angelfish are multicolored but predominantly blue with yellow markings. They are
very pretty, and, where mating is concerned,
they do behave like angels. They mate for life.
When one dies, the other pines until it dies.
Who says that monogamy is against nature?

Four-eyed Butterfly Fish

This tiny fish is most commonly pale yellow. However, it doesn't really have four eyes.
It just pretends to have them. A conspicuous
black spot that resembles an eye is positioned
on each side of its tail, but its real eyes are
cunningly concealed by two black stripes,
each running from the fish's nape to its gill
cover. Result? Predators get tricked because
they can't see eye to eye.

Sergeant Major

Like human sergeant majors, this tiny fish

can be aggressive. It is usually yellow but changes to a dark blue or olive gray when in captivity or when attacked. It always has distinctive black stripes as befits its rank.

Frogs and Other Fauna

Tree Frogs

In the summer months, come evening and nighttime, you may well be reminded of Caliban's lines in Shakespeare's *The Tempest*: "Be not afear'd. The isle is full of noises/ Sounds and sweet airs, that give delight and hurt not." Our diminutive tree frogs, hiding in trees and shrubbery, love to sing in the dark. Their favorite tune ought to be "Singing in the Rain," because it is after rainfall that they are particularly loud. But "sing" perhaps is not accurate. "Whistle" is better.

Don't let anyone tell you they produce their sound by rubbing their back legs together. That simply isn't true. The sound very definitely comes from their little throats. Tree frogs are easy to hear but hard to see. They are greenish brown with protruding eyes that are large in proportion to their body size.

Giant Toads

These are much more visible. You will often find a giant toad sitting in contemplative silence next to a puddle. Female toads are brown and black; males are brown and yellow. Both types have very wise expressions although where traffic is concerned, they are, unfortunately, not wise at all. They particularly like to sit in the middle of roads after a rain shower. Perhaps that is why their numbers are depleting.

Deliberately brought to Bermuda in 1885 from what was then British Guiana, the toads were, and still are, useful consumers of cockroaches and other pests. However, dogs must watch out. Biting toads is not a good idea

because they have poison glands that secrete a deadly mucous. If your dog is silly enough to attack a toad, wash its mouth out immediately with vinegar and take it to a vet for an antidote.

Lizards

All over Bermuda you will see lizards scuttling on walls, trees and hedges. They are cold-blooded creatures and descendants of the large vertebrate class of reptiles that dominated the earth 70 to 200 million years ago. Indeed, our lizards have the look of miniature dinosaurs — that is their chief charm.

We actually have one endemic lizard, known as the Bermuda rock lizard, or skink. It is 6 to 7 inches long and when it is young it has black, tan and white stripes and a brilliant blue tail. Unfortunately, it is only abundant in protected areas (see our Parks and Conservation chapter), but if you are lucky, you might see some in the quieter areas of Castle Harbour, North Shore and Somerset.

Our other lizards are of the anolis family. While it is true that they change color, it is not true that they are chameleons. Introduced to us from the West Indies at the beginning of the century, they have settled down nicely. The Jamaican anolis is the most common. It changes its brownish black color to bright or gray green, and the male has a throat pouch that flashes orange to attract the ladies. The Warwick lizard is larger and is distinguishable by its lime green color and the yellow rings around its eyes. Sometimes lizards like to live in our houses. Don't be too horrified. They don't make a mess, and they do eat our flies. Hence, lounge lizards can be useful.

Butterflies, Bugs, Creepy-Crawlers and Pests

Let us start with the good news. We have beautiful butterflies. We have the Gulf fritillary, which has orange and black markings and silver underneath its wings. We have the cloudless sulfur, which, as you might guess, is bright yellow. But above all, we have the Monarch butterfly. It is large with glorious white and tortoiseshell markings. For some years we were worried it might disappear from Bermuda, and for that reason, during the '80s and early '90s, the Department of Agriculture, Fisheries and Parks annually offered free milkweed seeds to grow in our gardens. Monarchs dine on milkweed. As of now, our schools have taken over the project, planting milkweed in student gardens. So far, the numbers of monarchs seem to be increasing.

We also have silk spiders. If you are frightened of spiders, at least appreciate their large, intricate webs that are so exquisite in the early morning dew.

Now for the bad news. We have cockroaches. And though the toads are doing their best, they are just not eating enough of these hideous insects. Our roaches are large — some can be more than 2 inches long. What's worse is that sometimes they are indecent enough to fly. However, do not mistake our hard-back beetles for cockroaches. Beetles do not deserve to be swatted or sprayed. They can be distinguished by their black, shiny backs and the clicking noise they make with their wings. Frequently, the beetles land on their backs, their legs waving helplessly in the air. When that happens, be kind to them, please, and turn them the right way up.

Other less-than-pleasant bugs include horseflies, mosquitoes that bite but don't spread disease and termites that are very partial to munching our wooden furniture. Land crabs can be pests because they love to burrow holes in our gardens, particularly in properties close to the ocean. Sometimes they scuttle into our houses. (See the Beaches chapter for a description of their breeding habits and their lamentable lack of parenting skills.) Perhaps the worst news of all is that we have rats, which are often attracted to banana plantations. At night they can be seen running down cable lines. Yuck. What more can we say? Cats and Bermuda's pest control companies help to make them keep their distance. Besides, Bermuda cannot be perfect. And at least we have absolutely no snakes.

For two-and-a-half centuries, Bermudians were too busy earning their living at sea or on land to worry much about providing luxury accommodations for visitors.

Resort Hotels

For two-and-a-half centuries, Bermudians were too busy earning their living at sea or on land to worry much about providing luxury accommodations for visitors. Tourism had modest beginnings in 1850 when trickles of visitors were brave enough to come here in small sailing boats from the United States and Canada.

Past and Present

In 1851 the Corporation of Hamilton decided it might be a good idea to open a hotel to suit these visitors' needs. After much procrastination, disagreement and delay, the Hamilton Hotel opened in 1863. Unfortunately, the United States was suffering its Civil War at the time. Since tourism and war do not usually go hand in hand, business for the Hamilton Hotel during the 1860s was not too good. However, by the early 1870s the picture changed as steamships regularly visited Bermuda from New York. For many years the Hamilton Hotel prospered, and tourism grew to the extent that in 1884 another hotel was built in the city of Hamilton. (See The Princess listing in this chapter.)

In those days, incidentally, our high season was during the winter months to suit the many North Americans who wanted to escape the rigor of their climate. But according to William Zuill in his *Bermuda Journey*, in 1910 the Bermuda-Atlantic Steamship Company enticed visitors to come in the summer by offering them a round trip on the *Oceana* for just $10. Unfortunately, many of the passengers did not realize how distant Bermuda was, so when they arrived, they had no money for lodging. Locals saw a great deal of them sleeping out in Victoria Park and in other open spaces in Hamilton. Bermuda's first hippies, perhaps?

World War I put a temporary stop to Bermuda's tourism, but after 1918 the island took the hospitality industry even more seri-

ously. Many Bermudians still remember the London-based Furness Withy and Company shipping line. Its ships, *Monarch of Bermuda* and *Queen of Bermuda*, were regular visitors to Hamilton. The growth of our luxury hotels was largely financed by that company during the '20s and '30s.

Once again tourism came to a halt at the outbreak of World War II, but some of the hotels were put to use. Bermuda became the base for Imperial Censorship, and the censors worked from the Princess Hotel and from the Bermudiana (now destroyed, it was on Bermudiana Road in Hamilton). After 1945, tourism again became vitally important, and, indeed, at present it is our key industry, matched only by international business.

Today, Bermuda has a huge range of accommodations, but in this chapter we will concentrate on our larger, more luxurious hotels. (See our Cottage Colonies chapter for a different luxury option and the Small Hotels chapter for less expensive lodging choices.) Bermuda currently has five resort hotels, each in a prime location and offering an extensive range of activities, entertainment and amenities. It would be a mistake, however, to view them as being identical. In our individual listings we explain the features and ambiance particular to each. First, we will discuss the policies and qualities they have in common.

Staff and Seasonality

Ask any of the resort managers what they are most proud of, and they will inevitably mention their staff. The word "resort" can connote impersonality, but in Bermuda hospitality staff are generally truly hospitable, so that even the larger resorts have more of a personal, family atmosphere.

Whereas in the past our peak season was in the winter, now it is most definitely summer. Typically the summer season begins April 1 and ends at the end of October, while the winter season begins November 1 and finishes at the end of March. However, season dates do vary from hotel to hotel, so we will specify any variations in each listing. Some hotels, for example, have a third shoulder season, which we will also specify when applicable. Seasonality affects availability of rooms, prices and services offered. We will explain these effects when we discuss each topic.

Reservations and Cancellations

Make reservations either by calling the hotel directly or by calling a travel agency. All the resort hotels require a two-night room deposit. Some stipulate a first and last night deposit. When this requirement applies, we will tell you so in the listings. In all cases, you may use major credit cards or pay with cash, traveler's checks or, in some cases, personal checks. Generally speaking, cancellations within 14 days prior to arrival result in loss of deposit.

Rooms tend to be heavily booked in the summer season, so we advise you to reserve at least 30 days in advance. Nevertheless, last-minute cancellations can make last-minute bookings possible. So if you are a spur-of-the-moment person, do give the hotel of your choice a call. Check-in and check-out times differ, so look for information about these in the listings.

Location, Amenities and Other Policies

Whether your hotel is in Hamilton Parish, Paget, Pembroke or Southampton — wherever it is — you are certain to have easy access to both sea and beach. Some of the resorts perch on hills, allowing stunning views of our island's most scenic ocean vistas; others almost hug the water so that you can reach the sea within two minutes of leaving your room. When beaches are not actually on the property, you will usually be able to take shuttles or golf carts to them. All the beaches are equipped with chairs, loungers and umbrellas. Changing and shower facilities are often right on the beach, as are food and beverage facilities. If not, they are within easy reach. However, there are no lifeguards.

If you want to explore our reefs and marine life, tour directors will help you make arrangements for snorkeling and scuba diving, fishing and trips in glass-bottom excursion boats. They will arrange other excursions too, such as a guided tour around St. George's or the botanical gardens (see our Attractions chapter for more details). If you want to explore Bermuda by moped or bicycle, you will find that cycle liveries are often on or near the hotel grounds. You'd rather have pool than sea? Then you'll be relieved that every resort has at least one swimming pool. Many have outdoor Jacuzzis as well. Be aware, though, that beach and pool facilities are sometimes reduced and beach bars and cafes generally close in the winter season.

For many tourists, Bermuda would be unimaginable without its golf and tennis. Some of the hotels have their own golf courses while others have arrangements with neighboring courses, some of which are world-famous (see our Golf chapter). All but one of the resorts, the Canadian Pacific's Hamilton Princess Hotel, have tennis courts you can enjoy free of charge or for a reasonable fee.

Perhaps you would rather exercise inside than out. Exercise rooms and fitness centers, equipped with weights, treadmills and other fitness machines, are available in several of the resorts. So are spas and hair and beauty salons where you will be pampered with massages, facials and hair styling.

Kids are very welcome at our luxury hotels and, in some cases, special kids' programs supervised by staff are available. We will alert you to these in the resort listings and in our Kidstuff chapter. In all cases, hotel staff can arrange baby-sitting for additional cost.

Not all our resorts are suitable for guests who are confined to wheelchairs. We give an assessment of room and beach accessibility for wheelchairs in each listing.

On the whole, the resorts have relaxed smoking policies. However, some do offer completely smoke free rooms. If the leftover smell of smoke bothers you, be sure to specifically request a nonsmoking room. Similarly if you wish to smoke, state that preference.

Generally smoking is allowed in lobbies, lounges and designated areas in the restaurants and dining rooms. When there are exceptions, we will tell you.

Pets, including dogs, are only allowed at one of the resorts, and this is explained in the write-up.

Eating, Drinking, Being Merry

"There is no love sincerer than the love of food." Well, that's what George Bernard Shaw said anyway. If food is your love, our resorts will not disappoint you. Many have several restaurants or dining rooms that specialize in all sorts of cuisine. In our listings, we will briefly mention the restaurants available, but they will be described more fully in the Restaurants chapter. Some have dine-around plans, which we will also explain in the listings. In the summer months, you will certainly be able to dine under the stars and by the sea. Bermudians love their evenings outdoors, so our hotels make full use of outside terraces for starry, starry night experiences.

Where rooms are concerned, our resorts' managers and staffs generally pride themselves on high standards. They therefore constantly refurbish and upgrade rooms and facilities. Most rooms are spacious and can easily accommodate a king bed as well as other bedroom and living area furniture. Frequently, the furniture includes pullout sofas that can sleep one or two extra persons. However, decoration and furnishings vary in style from resort to resort. Some are more classical and formal; others are more "island" and informal. But most are freshly painted and in excellent condition. Many have private balconies or patios. Amenities differ, but all rooms come with hair dryers in the bathrooms and ironing boards, irons and safes. By the way, televisions (satellite or cable) are in every room.

So you have a large family? You can reserve two rooms with connecting doors. On the other hand, a one- or two-bedroom suite may be for you. Most of the resorts offer suites that have separate living rooms as well as bedrooms. The larger suites also appeal to business travelers who may wish to entertain associates and guests. Some suites come with wet bars, refrigerators and small kitchen areas.

Recently, resorts have begun catering to the business traveler as well as the tourist. Many offer conference rooms, lecture rooms and all kinds of audiovisual equipment. However, we must stress that managers are well aware that visitors who are here for fun and relaxation do not want to feel they are in a fast-paced working environment. For that reason, very often business travelers check in and out in a different area of the hotel. And business packages tend to be offered during the winter season.

Room Rates

Room prices are typically based on water view, or on proximity to water, rather than on size. What does "water view" mean? Well, it can mean an uninterrupted view of the ocean, harbors or bays. It can also mean a partial view of water, interrupted by roofs or buildings. If a water view is important to you, be sure to be specific when you make your reservations. Actually, resort staffs are very up front about the room views available. They want you to be happy with what you see out of your window.

Pricing Key

The daily rates listed in the key below are based on room only for double occupancy during the peak season. They do not include the 7.25 percent Bermuda government hotel occupancy tax, the resort levy, gratuities or additional charges for meal plans, telephone calls or other expenses. They are also based on the rooms visitors would most typically reserve. As we have explained, many of our resorts have a variety of suites, but they are not included in the price ranges we quote. Call the hotel for information about suite prices. Bear in mind, too, that resort levies and gratuity policies can differ, so they will be stated in each listing. Rates during winter can be dramatically lower. Often the hotels offer special packages. Sometimes there is no extra room charge for children younger than 17. We will explain each resort's policy about charges for children in the individual listings.

$	Less than $225
$$	$226 to $260
$$$	$261 to $320
$$$$	$321 and higher

Meal Plans

Most resorts will ask you whether you want EP, BP or MAP. Baffled? Don't worry, we can explain. EP means European Plan, which offers room only and includes no meals. BP means Bermuda Plan and offers room and full breakfast. MAP means Modified American Plan and offers room, breakfast and dinner.

Our pricing key is based on the European Plan. Generally, the MAP plan costs approximately $50 per person per day, plus a fixed $14.15 gratuity that covers all meals and service. The BP plan costs about $15 per person per day plus $8.90 gratuity. Stay EP and you will pay a $6.65 gratuity. Room service is offered 7 AM to 11 PM.

Bermuda's Resorts

And now for the listings, which we present east to west, parish by parish, subset by subset and, thereafter, in alphabetical order.

Hamilton Parish

Grotto Bay Beach Hotel and Tennis Club
$ • 11 Blue Hole Hill, Bailey's Bay
• (441) 293-8333, (800) 582-3190

In the lower price range, this resort will suit you if you want leisure, relaxation and comfort in an intimate, island atmosphere. Managers mingle with the guests and solicitously ask if you're observing the 30/30 sun factor rule.

When you leave the airport and cross the Causeway, you will immediately see the white roofs of Grotto Bay on your right. See the map on page xv. Overlooking Ferry Reach, it has 11 lodges, many named after our parishes, with 18 rooms per lodge. A word here about the landscape: The property spreads over 21 beautifully landscaped acres that gently slope down to the water and the private beach. As you walk down, you will see on your left two natural grottoes. Descending a short broad flight of steps cut out of solid rock, you can enter Prospero's Cave, named after the central character in Shakespeare's The Tempest. Stalactites both fat and thin hang from the roof, and a deep lake fills part of the cave. Apparently many years ago, a carriage driver told a visitor: "Oh, that's where Mr. Shakespeare took shelter in a storm." A bust of the Bard is set in the rock near the entrance. If you've ever wanted the mystical, but cold, experience of swimming in an underground lake, you can do so in the second grotto, Cathedral Cave. In any case, now you know how Grotto Bay got its name. Palm trees, bay grapes and cedars surround the hotel, and the pathways have rustic, wooden fences. A moongate facing the ocean adds a romantic touch.

Guests can absolutely depend on enjoying a room with a water view and having their own private balcony or patio. Lodges can be two or three stories high. The more expensive rooms are directly on the water, whereas the less expensive ones on the hill overlook it. All of the rooms have bathrooms with full baths, showers and hair dryers. They also have telephones, refrigerators, coffee makers, clock-radios and televisions. They are tiled throughout and painted in soft Bermuda colors. Island-related pictures and photographs decorate the walls. King beds covered with floral spreads fit comfortably in the rooms as do tables and chairs. Up to two extra adults sharing the room can stay, but not eat, for free. Grotto Bay welcomes children. Children under 16 can stay for free in their parents' room, and children under 12 can eat for free if their parents are on the MAP plan. Cribs and babysitters are on hand for an extra charge. From June to Labor Day, trained counselors organize daily excursions to local attractions, games and swimming activities for children older than 4, but never on a Sunday. Times vary: They start at 9:45 AM and close anywhere from 1:30 to 10 PM depending on the activities planned.

A special room offers video games. Ground-level rooms are wheelchair-accessible as are many of the facilities. Be aware, though, that there is no room service. Incidentally, check-in time is 3 PM; check-out is noon. The resort levy is $3 per person per day.

Grotto Bay's MAP is a good value at $48 per person per day, plus a $12.80 gratuity. It includes full breakfast and a five-course din-

ner. BP costs $15 a day plus $6.40 gratuity. Both meals are served in the Hibiscus Dining Room (smoking permitted in designated areas), which you will find in the main building. Spacious and decorated in Bermuda pinks and greens, the dining room evokes the island's tranquil but bright atmosphere. You can also enjoy that British tradition, afternoon tea, for no extra charge. In summer, you will delight in eating around the outdoor pool. During the day, you may relax in loungers, dip in the pool when you are hot and order lunch from the pool bar when you are hungry. If you start to feel lazy, indulge in a little self-torture in the exercise room. The Jacuzzi will help you recover from it afterward. At night, you will enjoy Bermuda Island barbecue theme nights, swizzle parties and live entertainment featuring steel bands and island shows. Have you ever harbored a secret dream to be a famous singer? Then karaoke is on hand especially for you.

Watersports are easy with the Blue Hole Water Sports and Diving Shop right next door (see our Watersports chapter). The sunken barge in the water across from the beach marks a spot for excellent snorkeling, as does the private deep-water dock. Anyone for tennis? For $8 an hour, you can play at any of the four all-weather courts. Two courts are lit: If you fancy a midnight game, no problem. It will cost you an additional $4. Staff are happy to arrange golf for you, and if you feel adventurous enough to try riding a moped, you can go to the cycle livery that's right on the property.

Marriott's Castle Harbour Resort
$$$ • 2 Paynters Rd.
• (441) 293-2040

The chief feature at Marriott's Castle Harbour is its offer of traditional elegance with all the comfort of modern amenities. When you first approach the resort, you may well think, "Surprise, surprise! It really is a castle." The main building, built in 1931 by the Furness Withy Line, appropriately has stone walls that have been left unpainted to emphasize the castle effect. Multi-storied, it rises up from the surrounding golf course and semi-tropical gardens and overlooks the Harrington Sound on one side and Castle Harbour (naturally) on the other. See the map on page xv.

Additional wings have rooms with superb water views. The more expensive rooms, remember, are the ones that definitely directly overlook the ocean and offer private balconies. All rooms have telephones with data ports, clock radios and color TVs with remote control. Many also have shoe polishers, safes and mini bars that are stocked on request. Walls are tastefully decorated in restful, pastel shades. Floral bedspreads complement the dark wood of the tables and chairs. These rooms are spacious enough to accommodate a king bed or two oversized doubles. They also offer good closet space. The bathrooms, all with full bath and shower, are roomy and equipped with hair dryers.

Marriott's Castle Harbour also has a good selection of one- and two-bedroom suites that come with garden, pool or water views. These suites are ideal for larger families. In addition, there are suites for visitors here on business. Indeed, with 10,000 square feet of business space, the hotel can cater to groups of 10 to 900 people. There is a business center, together with the huge Harbour Ballroom that divides into five sections and the Conference Center that divides into three.

Do not make the mistake of thinking, however, that Marriott's Castle Harbour does not welcome families and children. For starters, children younger than 18 (yes, 18!) can stay free if they are in the same room as their parents. (Actually, there's no additional charge for any extra guest in the room.) Second, children younger than 13 enjoy, for free, the same meal plan as their parents. Kids older than 13 get the plan for $25 per person. The staff organizes activities for kids during summer (see our Kidstuff chapter), and baby-sitters will al-

ways look after your children should you want an evening alone. Cribs and pullout sofas are on hand. This hotel welcomes guests in wheelchairs. Many rooms are wheelchair-accessible, as are most of the facilities.

Marriott's MAP plan is an excellent value. For just $52 per person (plus gratuity), you can eat a full breakfast and a five- course dinner at a choice of restaurants. You can dine more formally in the elegant Windsor Restaurant or in Mikado's, Bermuda's only Japanese restaurant. These restaurants, by the way, are completely smoke free. (See Restaurants for details on menus and ambiance.) Other, less-formal eating venues include the View Restaurant, also smoke free, the Pub and several pool and beach snack bars. The BP plan is available for $16 a day plus gratuity. Be aware that during the winter season (November to the end of March) some of the restaurants may close and entertainment will be reduced.

The Bayview Lounge, located in the main building, has the sumptuous elegance of the 1930s. Every afternoon, the staff there serves a complimentary English tea. Don't worry about calories. Remember that the prestigious writer Henry James once described afternoon tea as "an innocent pastime." Sink into the comfortable armchairs, admire the wooden paneling and stone fireplace and then enjoy sandwiches and cake and tea. Monday evenings, managers meet guests during complimentary swizzle parties. And in the summer season, the Bayview offers live music every night. Steel drum bands, trios and the sounds of the 1970s and '80s characterize the entertainment (see our Nightlife chapter) You want to dance? Go for it. It's allowed. Enjoy, too, Blossoms, a lounge where you can sip cocktails in a Japanese atmosphere.

If you can't help thinking about calories, you can burn them off in a variety of ways. You can, for example, swim. Where? You have a choice of three freshwater swimming pools: two heated and one not. You can enjoy the

Luxurious accommodations are sprinkled along Bermuda's coasts.

Castle Harbour watersports beach or the hotel's very own South Shore Beach, a stroll away from your room. The hotel has a private dock, and staff are happy to make arrangements for deep-sea fishing, boat rides or watersports. Golfers will be in their seventh heaven. Castle Harbour golf course is on the edge of the property, and guests receive preferred tee times. On Mondays, Wednesdays and Fridays, guests can also play at the Mid-Ocean Club course next to Castle Harbour's course (see our Golf chapter). As for tennis players, they can use any of the six all-weather courts.

Not enough exercise? Then the health club is for you. A session on the treadmill will help, and there's nothing like a sauna to help you lose a few pounds. Use of exercise equipment is free. You can also enjoy beauty treatments at the beauty salon (see our Attractions chapter). Other services include laundry, valet and room service. A doctor is on call, and porters will greet you and help with luggage and golf clubs. Check-in is 3 PM and check-out at noon. The resort levy is $4 per person per day. The hotel will close at the end of October 1999 and will reopen under new management after remodelling.

Pembroke Parish

Canadian Pacific's Hamilton Princess Hotel
$$$ • 76 Pitts Bay Rd., Hamilton • (441) 295-3000

Once upon a time, a very long time ago, there was a princess. She was the daughter of a queen called Victoria, and her name was Princess Louise, Marchioness of Lorne. Her husband was the Governor General of Canada, so, naturally, she went to live there. Now Louise wasn't just any old princess — she was an artist as well. In 1883 she decided she needed a break from the bleak Canadian winter, and she came to Bermuda. Princess Louise drew lots of pictures while she was here, but she also explored the island and met lots of Bermudians. She had such a good time she recommended it as a vacation spot to all of her friends.

When Harley Trott built the first privately financed hotel in Bermuda, he thought of Princess Louise. And so in 1885, The Princess came to town. The first wooden building is gone, but The Princess that now stands is built on the original site. See map page xiv.

Today, The Princess treats you like royalty from the moment you meet the door persons at the front entrance. It's a question of noblesse oblige. The lobby gives you an immediate impression of Colonial warmth and graciousness with its carpets and dark, Queen Anne-style furniture. Lush plants hang from the staircase railings, and a waterfall, together with more plants, gently cascades down one of the walls. On this level you will find the Colony Pub, with its distinctive canopy of cedar shutters, and a shopping arcade that includes gift and clothing stores. There is also a beauty salon and exercise facility, complete with intimidating machines that you can use for free.

The cheaper guest rooms have a garden view, others look out onto Pitts Bay Inlet, and the more expensive ones offer a view of Hamilton Harbour and the Great Sound beyond. Not all the rooms come with balconies, but if you procure one you can sit on your private balcony and enjoy watching ships and boats cruise past. All rooms have king beds or two doubles. A pullout sofa allows for children or an extra guest. The traditional ambiance of the lobby continues in the bedrooms. Discreet regency wallpaper and Bermuda-related art decorate many of the walls and, again, the furniture is dark and elegant. All rooms come with safes, telephones, TVs and clock-radios, data port telephones, hair dryers, irons and ironing boards, and some also with mini bars. Bathrooms have full baths and showers. Two rooms are equipped for guests in wheelchairs.

The Princess also offers a variety of suites for families and business travelers. The hotel's city location makes it ideal for travelers wanting to do business or attend conferences in Hamilton. The Princess itself has all kinds of meeting space including the Princess Room, a huge banqueting room that is easily divided into three separate soundproof rooms. The Adam Lounge is another particularly stately space within the hotel and is ideal for social functions. Call for more details of business facilities.

As for meal plans, BP for adults is $15 per person per day, plus $8.65 gratuity. The Princess does have MAP but calls it DAP, short for Dine Around Plan. This package allows guests to use an ID card for dining at the Southampton Princess (see subsequent listing), a sister hotel acquired in the '70s. There is a choice of three restaurants at The Princess in Hamilton, all with designated smoking areas. Harley's offers continental cuisine, while the Colony Pub Steakhouse serves beef (but of course) and other delights. Every princess has to have a tiara, right? Hence, the graceful Tiara Room, which offers a formal, elegant atmosphere and a la carte fare. Be aware that some restaurants may close in winter.

Although The Princess tends to appeal to older guests, children are welcome. Those younger than 12 can stay in their parents' room free, but they are charged for food and pay $28 for MAP. Kids older than 12 and younger than 16 pay full price for meals but only a $6.40 gratuity.

Room service is available. Complimentary afternoon tea, so fitting in this royal atmosphere, is served twice a week in the Colony Pub. Monday nights, the managers will be available at the complimentary swizzle parties on the outdoor terraces, where you can gaze peacefully at the water and ponder Dinah Washington's "Harbor Lights." The landscaping has a Japanese touch. A small garden with water and tiny bridges exemplifies a Princess tradition of featuring water to unusual effect.

As for entertainment, excellent musicians and singers perform at the Colony Pub Steakhouse (see our Nightlife chapter). On Tuesdays, November through March, you can ballroom dance.

Overlooking the harbor are two outdoor swimming pools — one small with salt water;

the other large with heated fresh water. Fishing and watersports happen right off the hotel's private, deep-water dock on the harbor. There is a putting green as well. You want beach, tennis and golf? This is where a sister can be so useful. A ferry ride across the sound will take you to the other Princess hotel, and from there you can take the shuttle to the South Shore private beach and enjoy all the facilities (see our subsequent listing for Canadian Pacific's Southampton Princess). Guests at The Princess in Hamilton have full privileges at the Southampton Princess golf course and can use any of the 11 all-weather tennis courts, three of which are lighted.

Back to children. Baby-sitters are available, but kids' activities are not. However, at no charge youngsters can join in kids' programs offered at the Southampton sister hotel (see our Kidstuff chapter). Check-in time at The Princess is 2 PM; check-out is noon. The resort levy is $3 per person per day.

Paget Parish

Elbow Beach Bermuda
$$$$ • 60 South Rd.
• (441) 236-3535, (800) 223-7434

It's difficult to imagine this hotel having any other name since the long, sandy strand of Elbow Beach is directly below it. But once it was called the Elba Beach Hotel. All we can say is had Napoleon Bonaparte stayed here, instead of on Elba Island, he would never have bothered to escape. See the map on page xiv.

Built in 1908, the hotel has been through various stages of expansion. Always a long building echoing the length of the beach, it now has separate suites and lanais. When you walk through the recently added front porch, supported by four imposing pillars, you might think you are in the marbled hall of a prince instead of a hotel lobby. The floor is a rich, forest-green marble. Real Italian marble is a feature you will also notice in the Elbow Beach bathrooms.

Most rooms offer a view of the beach, the ocean and the South Shore reef and all are elegantly decorated. You have a choice of a king bed or two twin beds. Pullout sofas allow for extra people. All rooms have a balcony or patio, safes, umbrellas, mini bars, bedroom slippers and terry robes. Closets are spacious, and the bathrooms, as we have mentioned, have marble floors and tile, full baths and showers, hair dryers and scales. (You are not required to step on the scales . . . Who wants to face reality when on vacation?)

Separate from the main building, which is on top of a hill, there are rooms near the pool and terrace and others in the sloping gardens that lead to the beach. Some rooms offer both garden and ocean views. In addition to standard rooms, Elbow Beach Bermuda offers a variety of charming suites — ideal for larger families and business travelers. There are 10,000 square feet of meeting space and a number of rooms that are ideal for business functions and conventions.

While the hotel does have some wheelchair-accessible rooms, we do not recommend Elbow Beach for guests who are totally confined to wheelchairs. The terraced landscaping and the steps leading down to the beach make access to the ocean difficult although a train running every ten minutes or so does help out.

Children, up to 18 years, are welcome and stay for free in their parents' rooms. (Cribs and high chairs are also free.) Between June and October, the hotel offers plenty of kids' activities. Children go on treasure hunts and beachcombing sessions. Baby-sitters are on hand.

While the children are doing their own thing, you can enjoy golf, tennis or watersports. Staff can book tee times at most Bermuda courses and will make your watersports arrangements. You can play for reasonable cost at any of the hotel's tennis courts, two of which are lighted for night play. There is swimming in the sea (beach facilities available) or the pool, which is complete with a Jacuzzi. The

INSIDERS' TIP

In the interests of fire safety, Bermuda law states that no more than four guests can sleep in any one hotel room.

health club with whirlpool may appeal to you as well as the beauty salon. The lobby shops come in handy if you don't want to make a trip into town.

Be aware that Elbow Beach Bermuda offers no meal plans at all. All meals are à la carte. But the hotel does have an interesting choice of restaurants, all with designated smoking areas. The Seahorse Grill serves a daily buffet breakfast and excellent five-course dinners. For a light lunch you can drop by the poolside deck. Whatever you do, make sure you dine at Cafe Lido. It's right on the beach, so whether you dine inside or out, you will see stars and ocean glinting in the night light, discreetly provided by cunningly placed spotlights.

The Surf Club Pub offers live entertainment. However, if you want some quiet with your evening drink, try the Verandah Bar for the aperitifs and cigars. Entertainment and restaurant choices are reduced in the winter season. Room service, laundry and valet services are available. Check-in is 3 PM, and checkout is at 11 AM. The resort levy is $4.50 a day.

Southampton Parish

Sonesta Beach Resort Bermuda
$$$ • 5 South Rd. and Sonesta Dr. , Southhampton • (441) 238-8122

Of all the resorts in Bermuda, Sonesta is the only one to be bang on the beach. And so its slogan: "Best on the Beach in Bermuda." Sonesta actually has three beaches, all on the South Shore. See map page xiv. Sinky Bay is sheltered and quiet; and you will sink — into loungers under palmetto-thatched umbrellas. Boat Bay is ideal for families, and Cross Bay is the ocean beach. Cross Bay is usually good-tempered, but if you like surf, you'll get it here. It is also the hotel's center for activities and entertainment.

The hotel has one bay wing and a six-story main building that curves gently around the promontory on which it was built. The less

expensive rooms have a view of the hillside and roof or of the roof and pool. If a view of the South Shore or Boat Bay is important to you, be sure to ask for it. All rooms have private balconies or lanais. They are decorated island style with subdued color schemes of pink, turquoise or cream and accented with floral curtains and bedspreads. Unusual abstract paintings decorate the walls throughout the hotel. Rooms have one king or two queen beds. Each room has a clock-radio, mini bar, safe, ironing board and iron and phone with data port. Bathrooms have full baths, showers and hair dryers. If you smoke, be sure to request a smoking room.

The hotel also offers a variety of split-level suites ideal for business travelers and larger families. Some are equipped with wet bars, sinks, refrigerators and ice machines. Sonesta does cater to many business and conference guests, but if you don't want to feel as if you are in a working environment, fear not: Groups and conventions check in separately and have their own floor. Ramps allow easy access to the beach for guests in wheelchairs. All the rooms in the bay wing are wheelchair-accessible and have baths with rails, and the main building has one room that is completely equipped.

BP for adults is $15 per person per day, plus gratuity, while MAP runs $55 per person. Room service is available from 7 AM to midnight. Kids 6 and younger stay free in their parents' room. They can sleep in a connecting room with a 30 percent discount on the second-room price. Children within this age range get the same meal plan as their parents at no extra charge.

You can enjoy full or continental breakfast on your balcony, or you can let La Sirena entice you into her dining room for breakfast served buffet style. By the way, she doesn't like smoking — it isn't allowed in La Sirena. The Cafe, which serves light lunches and pastries, is also smoke free. You have more choice of restaurants in the evening. The Sea Grape outdoor restaurant lets you dine and stargaze

INSIDERS' TIP

If you want internal access to the room next to you, be sure to ask for connecting rooms, not adjoining rooms.

Some Bermuda resorts provide a range of activities without leaving the property.

at the same time; Lilians offers Italian cuisine; and the Boat Bay Club, a restaurant and lounge that overlooks the ocean, is another attractive alternative.

Local music groups entertain in the Boat Bay Club, with jazz, reggae and contemporary music every night of the summer season. The Palm Court Club is a sports bar with TV, billiards and other games. The Honeymoon Point, a terrace carved out of a rock, overlooks the ocean and a Sonesta-made waterfall. Ideal for weddings, it is also a venue for the cocktail party held every week to celebrate repeat visitors, honeymooners and other VIPs.

Sonesta has a full range of activities that include scuba diving, snorkeling, boating, mountain biking, bingo and dice games. Two climate-controlled pools — one outdoor, one inside — are close by, complete with changing facilities, loungers and chairs. A croquet lawn and putting green offer ball-hitting variations. Tennis is $8 an hour on any of the six Laycold courts, two of which are lighted. Want to improve your game? Book a place in the free tennis clinics given three mornings a week. Since the hotel is just 10 minutes away from four courses (including the one on the property), golf is no problem. The Sonesta tour director can arrange tee times for Riddell's Bay, Southampton Princess, and Port Royal (see our Golf chapter). The "Just Us Kids" program offers games, parties, excursions, bike rides and other fun things for children (see our Kidstuff chapter). Baby-sitting is available for additional charge.

One of those options might be useful if you want to luxuriate in the comfort of the spa after a workout in the exercise room. There is a Jacuzzi, sauna and shower, and masseuses and beauty therapists are on hand to give a variety of relaxing treatments. Nine of Bermuda's major shops are housed in the Sonesta's main building (see our Shopping chapter).

Check-in is at 3 PM, and check-out is 11 AM. However, a number of courtesy rooms with showers and lockers are available for early arrivals. They come in handy, too, if you want that last dip before leaving for the airport. The resort levy is $3.50 per person per day. Sonesta is the only resort hotel in Bermuda that accepts pets. Call for more details.

Canadian Pacific's Southampton Princess Hotel

$$$$ • 101 South Rd. • (441) 238-8000

This resort is the younger sister of the Hamilton Princess. Younger she may be, but little she is not. Built nine stories high atop a large hill, this hotel is as familiar a local landmark as the Gibbs Hill Lighthouse nearby. The Southampton Princess looks down on 100 acres of landscaped grounds, including an 18-hole, par 3 golf course, and out over the South Shore on one side and the Great Sound on the other. See map page xiv.

Typically, first-time visitors prefer the South Shore option, while repeat visitors often go for the Great Sound view, so they can watch ships that pass in the night. Some rooms actually have views of both. Since the rooms on the higher floors offer the more spectacular waterscapes, they are the more expensive options. With the less expensive rooms, water views can be partially obstructed by the roof of the restaurant. Given that proviso, be assured that all rooms have water views and private balconies. If you hate cigarette smoke, ask for a room on one of the two smoke-free floors. Six rooms are specially equipped for guests in wheelchairs.

Many of the rooms are decorated in aquamarine shades that are accented by floral spreads and curtains. They offer one king or two double beds. Cribs are available for children. The TV is in the armoire, and your terry robe is in the closet, with the ironing board and iron. Clock-radios, telephones with data ports, refreshment centers, safes and hair dryers are in every room. Refrigerators are no additional charge. Bathrooms are spacious, with a separate sink and vanity area.

The Southampton Princess has a large variety of luxurious suites, duplexes and Newport Club rooms (on a special concierge floor). The hotel has extensive space and facilities for visitors on business. It has the largest ballroom in Bermuda and boasts a state-of-the-art multimedia amphitheater.

For adults, the DAP (as the two Princess hotels prefer to call it) costs $55 a day, plus $14.90 gratuity. Again, the Dine Around Plan gives guests a choice of six restaurants at Southampton, plus the three eateries at The Princess in Hamilton (see previous listing). It's free for children younger than 16 if they share their parents' room. During the summer season (mid-April through mid-November), kids can also eat in some of the restaurants for free. However, they will be charged a $10.85 daily gratuity. During the winter season, children enjoy DAP for $28 or BP for $10.

Hotel restaurants include Wickets Brasserie, Windows on the Sound (yes, it does overlook the water) and the Newport Room. Fitted with mahogany and teak, the Newport Room will give you the illusion that you are dining aboard a luxurious yacht. Another option is to take the hotel trolley from the front entrance and visit the Waterlot Inn, which also overlooks the Great Sound. Originally built more than 300 years ago, this restaurant was rebuilt after a fire in 1975 and will tempt you with Mediterranean and traditional island dishes, all presented with silver service.

If you'd rather eat on the beach, take the trolley to the Whaler Inn, perched above the surf of the South Shore, where you can feast on exquisite seafood and enjoy the waters. If you're a meat lover, try barbecue beef ribs and chops at the Rib Room in the Golf Club House, a 4-minute stroll from the indoor pool. All restaurants have large nonsmoking areas. Room service is available from 7 AM to 1 AM for an extra charge.

For a casual drink or cocktails before dinner, the lobby lounge is ideal. It offers light evening entertainment. The Neptune Club has live entertainment and dancing.

Activities abound at the Southampton Princess. Let's start with the kids. Monday, Wednesday and Friday, the hotel offers a "Tiny Tots" sitting service from 9 AM to 1 PM, and older children and teens can enjoy free supervised activity programs from mid-June to September. These will allow them play all sorts of games, swim, go on excursions and enjoy many other activities. Perhaps most exciting of all, children can shake hands and swim with dolphins! (See Kidstuff for details of these programs.)

For adults, there is golf on the hotel's executive course. Play all day for $54, cart included. In addition, the tour director will be happy to make arrangements for you to play other island courses. There is croquet, and the Southampton Princess boasts 11 tennis courts, three of which are lighted. Rates for tennis are $10 an hour for daytime play, $14 at night. Two swimming pools — one indoors, one out — will let you improve your stroke, but if the sea calls, you can take a trolley to Princess Beach on the South Shore. There is a cabana that serves everything from a piña colada to a hamburger. The Beach Club and Nautilus Dive Shop are good stops to arrange scuba diving and snorkeling for a close encounter with the fish (see our Watersports chapter). The hotel's Secret Garden has beauty therapists and hair-care professionals and offers massages, facials and all kinds of treatments. There is a gym and sauna.

For more information about Bermuda, you might like to attend lectures. As for shopping, the hotel has a large selection of Hamilton branch shops. When you explore the hotel and the grounds, you will notice a variety of graceful bronze figures. These are the work of Desmond Fountain, whose gallery is also in the hotel (see our Arts and Culture chapter). Other artists and experts in crafts display and sell their work in the hotel.

The Southampton Princess has three seasons. Summer season starts in mid-April, the "shoulder season" runs from about September 7 to November 13 and the winter season is from mid-November to mid-April. In winter, some of the restaurants close. Entertainment is reduced but so are room rates. Check-in is 2:30 PM, and check-out is at noon. The resort levy is $3 per person per day.

Gaston Bachelard, a French philosopher, once wrote that "the house allows one to dream in peace." This is exactly what Bermuda's cottage colonies allow you to do.

Cottage Colonies

Gaston Bachelard, a French philosopher, once wrote that "the house allows one to dream in peace." That is exactly what Bermuda's cottage colonies allow you to do. Smaller, more intimate and definitely more Bermudian than the larger hotels, they offer a haven from the stresses of twentieth-century living. If your idea of bliss is the peace that "comes dropping slow," then the cottage colony experience may well be for you. Be assured, though, that you won't miss out on twentieth-century luxury.

What exactly is a cottage colony? As you might expect, it is a collection of cottages separate from a main building that often houses front desk, restaurants, bars and lounge areas. However, the word "cottage" needs explanation. It originally meant a very small, detached house, and indeed some of our older colonies do have old cottages that fit this description. But the newer buildings could be better described as cottages with anywhere from two to five units. Rooms can be offered as individual units for double occupancy rates, or they can be offered as suites. In some cases, then, you could have a cottage to yourself for suite rates. If you opt for an individual room, rest assured you will have a private balcony or terrace and a private bathroom.

The cottage colonies generally have some features of the traditional Bermudian house — a buttery, for example, and a white ridged roof — and they all offer comfort, graciousness and privacy. Some of the suites have separate living rooms. Bear in mind that the living and dining area is always spacious, and bathrooms, without exception, are roomy and luxurious.

Many cottages have stunning water views and beautiful garden settings. You can sit on your private terrace or balcony and savor the fragrance of the flowers and the blues, greens and pinks that are Bermuda's true colors. Above all, you will feel that you are in the house of your dreams and not in a hotel at all. In fact, the tranquillity they offer makes them ideal for honeymooners, so be sure to ask for information on honeymoon packages. There's just one problem. We have six cottage colonies. Which one will you choose? Just as dream houses vary in detail and ambiance, so do these properties. The individual listings describe these variances, but first we concentrate on the policies and features the properties share. Having said that, we must point out that some of the premises are wheelchair-accessible, and some are not. In the listings we will tell you which ones are suitable for guests in wheelchairs.

Even by Bermudian standards, the staffs at most of the cottage colonies are remarkable for their friendliness and helpfulness. Many have worked at one colony more than 25 years and feel a personal loyalty to their managers and guests. Take the time to talk to them. They will certainly give you information and insights that will enrich your experience in Bermuda. But please, remember the social niceties of civilized life. "Good mornings" are important, as are "please" and "thank you."

Kids, Pets, Smoking

If you want plenty of add-on entertainment and activities for children, then the cottage colony option may not be for you. The emphasis is generally on peace and tranquillity.

If, on the other hand, you want casual time with your family for talking and walking, sailing and swimming, then that is what you will have. Some cottage colonies are more family-oriented than others; for that reason, we will tell you in each listing whether the colony welcomes children.

On the whole, cottage colonies have a relaxed smoking policy. Without exception, you may smoke in your rooms, in the bars and in the lounges. In some dining rooms you can smoke in designated areas, while in others you cannot smoke at all. In the individual listings, we'll specify smoking policies where dining rooms are concerned.

We're afraid that dogs, cats and other animals must stay at home. No pets are allowed in any of the cottage colonies.

Seasonality, Reservations and Cancellation Policies

Cottage colonies are very popular, particularly in the summer season. There is also a high repeat visitor rate, so be sure to book as early as possible. We will give you the necessary lead time in each listing, since they range anywhere from 30 days to six months. Generally speaking, the colonies require a first and last night deposit, usually refundable if you cancel up to 21 days before your reservation date. Be aware that some do not accept credit cards; we will specify which ones do not in the listings. In all cases, you can pay by personal check, travelers' checks or by money order. Guests, by the way, usually reserve through a travel agent, or they call direct.

Typically, the summer season starts in April and ends October to November. We will again be specific in each listing, as season dates can vary from property to property. Do verify these dates because they can make an enormous difference in cost. A few properties close to refurbish for a short period in the winter. In all cases during the winter season, entertainment is reduced and beach facilities, such as beach clubs, close. Check for special packages (for golfers, for example) that are often offered during the winter season.

Rates of Rooms

Here we must confess that we have found it difficult to create a completely consistent pricing code. Nearly all the cottage colonies base their daily rates on MAP for two. MAP, you may recall from the Resort Hotels chapter, means Modified American Plan, and it offers room, breakfast and dinner. However, two of the listings in this chapter do not include MAP in the code that we quote. As it happens, both of these have been allocated one dollar sign. We explain what the rate covers in those individual listings. You may take it, then, that all cottage colonies showing two to four dollar signs include MAP in the daily rates.

Pricing Key

The daily rates listed in the pricing key are based on the rooms visitors would most typically reserve during the peak season. They do not include the 7.25 percent Bermuda hotel occupancy tax, gratuities or additional charges for telephone calls or other expenses. Bear in mind that gratuity policies can differ, so they will be stated in each listing. Rates are always subject to change.

$	$250 to $350
$$	$351 to $376
$$$	$377 to $407
$$$$	$408 and higher

Cottage Listings

We now go to our listings, presented east to west, parish by parish, subset by subset and thereafter in alphabetical order.

St. George's Parish
The St. George's Club
$ • Rose Hill
• (441) 297-1200

The St. George's Club is Bermuda's newest cottage colony, built in the early 1980s. In 1997, the property was completely refurbished, and 10 new luxury cottages were added to bring the total number of cottages to 71. An affiliate of Resort Condominiums International (RCI), The St. George's Club is also Bermuda's

Bermuda's finest cottage colony, Pink Beach overlooks two glarious pink sand beaches. Begin your day with breakfast on your private patio. Then it's tennis, superb swimming and snorkeling, and excellent golf nearby. Wind up with cocktails at sunset and dinner in our sea view Club House. For the most perfect vacation come to the Pink Beach Club in Bermuda.

Pink Beach Club

Tucker's Town   Bermuda
Tel: (441) 293-1666
Fax: (441) 293-8935
Toll Free Reservations: 1-800-422-1323
E-mail: pinkclub@ibl.bm
Internet: http//www.NetLink.com/PBClub/

first and premier timesharing resort. It has received the Gold Crown designation, the RCI's highest accolade, and many awards for design from the American Resort Development Association.

As explained in the introduction, the price code for The St. George's Club does not include MAP plan or any food plan. But luxury, fully equipped kitchens are provided as you will see. Thus, the code given refers to the price per night for a one-bedroom cottage that can house up to four guests with no meals included in the rate. As you will see, two-bedroom cottages are also available for about $100 a night extra. These can house up to six guests.

The clubhouse and cottages sit prettily on top of Rose Hill and overlook the old town of St. George's and St. George's Harbour on the one side and St. George's Golf Course on the other. In fact, proximity to Bermuda's old capital is what draws guests to visit again and again. While the property itself may be mod-

ern, it is surrounded by history. A short walk down steps in the grounds takes you to the town's many historic attractions.

Cottages are mostly double-storied, containing two bedrooms, two bathrooms, a kitchen and a living/dining room. (The second bedroom can be converted into a private studio if you want the one-bedroom option.) Stairs with attractive cedar railings lead up to the large master bedroom decorated in pastel shades and equipped with a double closet. A cedar chest adds a traditional Bermudian touch. Here you will also find a luxurious sunken tub. Sink in bubbles and watch palm trees outside your window sway in the breeze. You will find a separate shower in the bathroom and a double sink.

The living/dining area has a dining table, a pull-out sofa, comfortable chairs and a coffee table. There's also a television — the VCR you can rent. If you feel up to doing a little cooking, the kitchen will please you. It is equipped with microwave, electric stove, fridge, dishwasher, toaster, blender and coffee maker, together with all the china and glasses you might need. A convenience store on the property supplies the basics for breakfast and snacks. Each cottage has an iron and ironing board, and there's a laundry facility on the property.

All cottages have private balconies or terraces with garden views. Sit out and enjoy your breakfast to the music of Bermuda's sounds. Listen carefully and you will hear the church bells of St. George's. There's no room service, by the way, but there is maid service twice a week. Feel like some action? Three swimming pools (one heated) will let you cool off. The three tennis courts on the property, two of which are lighted for night play, offer a little more strenuous activity. Tennis, incidentally, is free. Golf? But of course — the St. George's Golf Course, designed by Robert Trent Jones, surrounds you (see our Golf chapter). The cottage colony itself has a putting green and a croquet lawn.

If the ocean calls you, no problem. The St. George's Club has its own private beach club that overlooks a beach shaped like a heel. Its name? Achilles Bay, naturally. But don't worry, it is neither sulky nor dangerous, unlike the ancient Greek hero it's named after. Achilles Bay offers some of the best snorkeling on the island. You can arrange watersports such as scuba diving, snorkeling and kayaking via the Front Desk. For evening romance, take a sunset cruise. As for Blackbeard's Hideout Beach club, it has a sun deck where you can enjoy lunch, snacks and cocktails from 11:30 AM to 10 PM. "Pirates" will serve you in best Bermudian courteous tradition. You can also enjoy watching glorious, simultaneous sunsets and moonrises. To reach Blackbeard's (and the golf clubhouse), you can take a shuttle that, in high season, runs every half-hour.

You will find a lounge and Tilly's, a bar and restaurant combined, in the clubhouse, owned and managed by Adrian and Patrick Jones as separate establishments. Come to the bar and restaurant area and you feel as if you're in a tropical rain forest. Ceiling murals, real bamboo on the walls and live lush foliage all add to the effect (see Restaurants chapter). Walk through the moongate and you'll find a smaller dining area overlooking St. George's Harbour. Entertainment includes a swizzle party held every Monday, a pool side barbecue on Wednesday and other theme shows, such as limbo dancers and steel bands. The Millionaire's Lounge also overlooks the harbor. However, the effect is not so much rain forest as that of the English Drawing Room. Colors are dark green and burgundy. Here you can watch sports on digital satellite television, play pool or a board game, or sink into an armchair and read one of the books provided in the bookshelves.

Kids are very welcome here. Cribs and high chairs are always on hand, and baby-sitters are $10 an hour. St. George's is not, however, a good option for guests in wheelchairs. The hilly setting makes wheelchair access difficult.

We mentioned timesharing, and it is the main thrust here. Every year 80 percent of the cottages are sold as timesharing units. Timesharing guests can buy anywhere from one week to 11 weeks of annual holiday over a period of 7 to 25 years of membership. On average, they tend to buy two. Because Bermuda is an extremely popular vacation destination, timeshares booked at this resort have very strong trading power with upgrades to larger accommodations in other resorts.

Remember that if you do book timesharing at The St. George's Club, you will reserve a particular cottage at a particular time or times of year. For more details on timesharing rates and conditions, call the membership office direct at (441) 297-1222 or (441) 297-1022.

The St. George's Club is unusual in that it has two shoulder seasons (March 1 through March 29 and November 8 through January 2). High season is March 31 through November 7. Check these dates with the hotel, as they are subject to change. For the summer season, book at least six months in advance to be sure of a cottage, although last-minute cancellations can make spur-of-the-moment reservations possible. You can use major credit cards to pay your first and last night deposit, which you lose should you cancel within 21 days of your arrival date. Check-in on Saturdays is at 4 PM, checkout at 10 AM. Other days, times are by arrangement. Courtesy rooms are available for early arrivals or late departures. In addition to the cottage rate, a $6.40 per person daily fee is charged for housekeeping gratuities.

Hamilton Parish

Pink Beach Club and Cottages
$$$ • 116 South Rd.
• (441) 293-1666

You can guess how this cottage colony got its name, can't you? Yes, it does have its own private beach — two, actually. And yes, the beaches are pink, thanks to the trillions of miniscule pink shells and skeletons that make up the sands of our South Shore.

Originally, Pink Beach's 16.5 acres were used for farming. Come the Depression in the '30s, an American family bought the land and built their own house on it. After World War II was over, Bermudian Harold Gibbons decided a cottage colony would be a good idea for people who wanted to travel again. He acquired the land and personally supervised the completion of the Club House and nine cottages. Michael J. Williams, Managing Director of Pink Beach, has some wonderful stories to tell about Mr. Gibbons.

Indeed, some of them are recorded in newsletters that he distributed to guests. Apparently Harold was a stickler for etiquette and for the work ethic. Even Gary Cooper, the film star, came under his watchful eye. When Cooper arrived late for dinner one evening, he received a strong reprimand for "upsetting the dining room." Staff today are convinced that Mr. Gibbons' ghost prowls the premises at night and that he is still enforcing the very high standards he always expected.

Since Mr. Gibbons' time, more cottage units and suites have been added, but they all retain the white ridged roofs of the traditional Bermudian cottage. You will also see buttery towers and long chimneys. The outer walls of the buildings are all painted pink — but naturally. As of 1999 two of the cottages have been converted into condominiums for sale to private owners, with extra suites being added to

the other guest cottages to compensate for loss of tourist accommodation.

The Club House, refurbished in 1999, is the focal part of the property. In it you will find the Bermudiana Dining Room and the small, but very comfortable, Hibiscus Lounge, complete with fireplace. Both have fantastic views of the South Shore reef. You will also find the Cedar Bar. Have a quiet drink here before dinner, and be sure to admire the Bermuda cedar that gives it its name. If you want a game of skittles or cards, find the games room that is also in the Club House. If you have to watch cable TV, you'll find it both in the lounge and the bar. Walk out of the bar to find the pool area, which was expanded and tiled in 1997. Here, during the summer months (May 1 to October 31) you can enjoy alfresco dining and barbecues. (You may use your MAP to dine here.) And children can eat here from 6 PM before the formal dining starts at 7 in the evening. Ideal for outdoor dining and management swizzle parties, it is also the venue for top local entertainment. Most nights in the summer season, Calypso and steel bands and pianists will serenade you. You want to "dance with the dancers and drink with the drinkers"? Feel free. There's plenty of floor space. During the day you can dip in the pool, then relax under an umbrella.

The cottage units and suites dot the landscape. All the ones within the price range we have quoted have close views of the ocean and reef. In fact, some are so close that you can actually see parrot fish from your patio or balcony. Early morning or evening you may see silver fish jumping right out of the water.

All the rooms are spacious, even if they have a combined living room and bedroom. They can accommodate a king-size bed or two doubles, and they are comfortably furnished with table and chairs, sofa, desk and plenty of drawer and closet space. Some have cathedral, beamed ceilings, while others have the Bermudian tray ceilings. All have sliding doors that open onto the patio or balcony. And all come with clock-radio, telephone with data port, safe, trouser press, ironing board and iron, hairdryer, and umbrella. Bermudian art decorates the walls. Note, however, that television is only available if you specifically request it. The idea, you see, is that for a little

Photo: GIS

Cottage colonies make for a uniquely Bermudian vacation experience.

space you enjoy quiet contemplation and gentle conversation without the rude interruption of the screen box. Bathrooms are spacious and often have double sinks. Bathrobes are provided.

Pink Beach is one of the two cottage colonies where a maid will deliver a full English breakfast to your room in the morning. She will make toast in your room and serve you inside or out on the patio. She'll also bring you a complimentary *Royal Gazette* and *New York Times* fax. Pink Beach's staff, by the way, have worked here for over 20 years. So they have a very special relationship with the guests. Repeat guests are always given extra tender loving care in the form of complimentary wine and cheese when they arrive.

So what leisure activities can you enjoy? Instead of watching television, you can rent snorkeling equipment and introduce yourself to the fish. If you are a strong swimmer, you can swim out to the reef and enjoy the glories of the marine world. Feel like exploring the island? Rent a motorized bike from a livery right on the property. Or you can have a gentle

game of tennis on one of the two courts. A tennis pro is on hand to help you improve your serve. As for golf, Pink Beach is right next door to Bermuda's famous Mid Ocean Club course. Mondays, Wednesdays and Fridays you can play on this exclusive club's layout. You can also play at Castle Harbour, another prestigious golf club nearby (see Golf chapter for details). The staff will be happy to make arrangements for you. You can practice at the net on the property. If you're into keeping fit, try out the Fitness Center, open 6 AM to midnight. There you'll find StairMaster, treadmill, weights and exercise cycle.

You might be wondering about children. They are very welcome, but they do stay at additional cost. Call direct for details of room rates. No activities are available specifically for children, but if you want to share leisure and activity time with your kids, Pink Beach is ideal. Baby-sitting can be arranged.

Pink Beach also welcomes business visitors, either local or from abroad. A meeting room holds up to 16 people. Swizzle receptions can be arranged.

Book at least 60 to 90 days in advance to be sure of a reservation. Public holidays are booked up particularly quickly. You may use major credit cards to pay the first and last night deposit and the bill. Cancel within 21 days of your arrival date, and you will lose your deposit. Gratuity is 10 percent of your room rate. Check-in is at 2 PM, check-out at noon. Courtesy rooms will let you have that extra swim if you want to arrive early or leave late.

Devonshire Parish

Ariel Sands Beach Club
$$$ • 34 South Rd.
• (441) 236-1010, (800) 468-6610

Ever since the Dill family converted this property into a cottage colony in 1952, Ariel Sands has had a distinctly theatrical flavor. This is hardly surprising, given that acting runs in the Dills' genes. When Matthew Dill starred in *The Tempest*, his grandmother decided to name the property after Shakespeare's sprite, Ariel, who is associated with magic, spirit and art. Besides, she thought the rock in the South Shore bay looked like him. In 1976, J. Seward Johnson sculpted Ariel out of 500 pounds of stainless steel. There he stands on that same rock as if poised for flight.

In 1995 the beach club underwent extensive expansion, and a new character appeared on the scene: Caliban's Seaside Restaurant and Bar, which offers even more spirit than Ariel. More exciting developments happened in 1997, when actor Michael Douglas (son of actress Diana Dill Darrid and Kirk Douglas) led a $5 million renovation of the property. In addition to completely refurbishing the cottages and the bar, Douglas also added The Ariel Sands Health Club & Nirvana Spa and Ariel's Seaside Conference Centre. (Call the

hotel for information about business and conference facilities.)

Ariel Sands makes full use of its hillside ocean setting. As soon as you arrive, you will notice the lush foliage of the landscaping and the tropical touch of the palm trees against the sky. You will also notice the traditional white-ridged roofs so loved by Bermudians. Front desk and lobby are in the one-story main building, as are the lounge and bar. A huge double fireplace, which can burn logs on both sides, divides the bar from the lounge. In the bar, the Bermuda cedar bar structure, canopy and mantle contrast strikingly with charcoal-gray painted walls. Photographs hanging in the bar allow you to become acquainted with Michael Douglas. The lounge, overlooking the pool and ocean, has white-paneled French doors that lead you into Caliban's. It also has comfortable chairs where you can curl up with a good book or chat with friends. A baby grand piano adds elegance and, in the evening, relaxing music.

Cottage units and suite names continue the Shakespearean theme. You could, for example, stay in Miranda's Cabana or in Prospero's Deluxe. It is difficult to describe a "typical" room or suite since, like most cottage colonies, Ariel deliberately adds individual touches to enhance the home-away-from-home effect. However, whether they have a separate living room or not, rooms are all spacious with plenty of vanity and living space. They tend to have Bermudian tray ceilings, and they are tiled throughout. Some have indoor shutters; others have natural fiber curtains. Walls are in vibrant, unusual colors, such as sea foam, periwinkle, lobster pink and melon sunburst. All units are fully equipped with cable television, refrigerator, coffee maker, iron, umbrella and safe. They also have telephones with data port, Internet access and voice mail. Bathrooms are tiled and come with

INSIDERS' TIP

Members of the Bermuda Collection dine-around plan are Ariel Sands, Cambridge Beaches, Pompano Beach, The Reefs and Stonington Beach Hotel. If you are staying at one of these properties, then on certain nights you can use your MAP to dine at any of the other hotels in the Collection.

hair dryers. Private patios give you your own little garden space. Relax in the Adirondack chairs you'll find there. All rooms have views of the South Shore and are within 100 yards of Ariel's beach. We should add that there are four rooms for guests who use wheelchairs. Please book these rooms well in advance.

Mornings, you can stroll down to Caliban's for your breakfast, or you can have it delivered to your cottage by one of the staff. (Staff at Ariel Sands are so friendly, by the way, that it is not unusual for them to pick up repeat visitors from the airport in their own cars on their own time.) Caliban's has an inside dining room, but it extends out to two wooden terraced decks — ideal for alfresco dining under the stars and for the outdoor bar (see our Restaurants chapter). A third outside dining area called the Baygrape Terrace lets you eat practically on the beach. If you want to catch a glimpse of Bermuda's politicians and civil servants, have lunch inside Caliban's. It's their favorite escape from the pressing problems of the day. The indoor restaurant has a strict no smoking policy — outdoors you may smoke. During the summer season, a steel band plays outside four nights a week. Other nights you can listen to the piano or guitar. Ariel has a dine-around plan, which means that you can use your MAP to dine at other restaurants that are members of the Bermuda Collection dine-around plan.

Relaxation is the name of the game at Ariel; even so, activities await you. You can swim in the heated freshwater pool or in one of two unusual, ocean-fed pools. Then there's the sea itself, of course. Snorkeling equipment, which is available for rent, will allow you to frolic with Ariel and also with the fishes. Or you can just relax under the palmetto umbrellas that dot the beach. Tennis is easy — you can play free of charge right on the property. A putting green will let you practice your golf before playing at any of Bermuda's famous golf courses (see our Golf chapter). The staff will happily make those arrangements for you. Mondays, Wednesdays and Fridays, you can play at the famous Mid Ocean Club. The new private spa offers a full gym with equipment for self-torture (open 24 hours a day), two massage rooms, a Jacuzzi and facilities for hydrotherapy (open until 7 PM). Expert therapists may look after your feet, face and hands while the stylists turn their attention to your hair.

Children are welcome at Ariel. Children under 12 sleep on rollaway beds and pay $35 MAP. Incidentally, for safety's sake, children of this age range must be supervised when they use the pool.

Book as soon as possible to be sure of a reservation. Public holidays are particularly booked up quickly. You may use major credit cards to pay the first and last day deposit. Cancel within 21 days of your arrival date, and you will lose your deposit. Gratuity is 10 percent of your room rate. Check-in is at 2 PM, check-out at noon.

Paget Parish

Horizons and Cottages
$$$$, no credit cards • 33 South Rd. • (441) 236-0048

On top of a hill, this cottage colony certainly does have horizons. Gazing across pool and tropical gardens, you can let your eyes concentrate on the blue of the Atlantic. Some days, however, you might ask yourself, "Now exactly where does the sky end and the ocean begin?"

Horizons' history goes back to 1710, when one of its owners, a Capt. Lewis Middleton, went off to the Turks Islands to squabble with the French and Spanish over a few salt beds. Nearly 200 years after that, an Alfred Blackburn Smith fell in love with it, expanded and renovated it and opened it as a guest house in 1928. If he were alive today, no doubt he would be gratified to know that Horizons is currently a member of Relais et Chateau. Membership depends on maintaining the five C's: calm, comfort, charm, cuisine and courtesy. Horizons achieves these qualities by blending the best of the old with the luxury of the new.

The historic atmosphere of the property is very apparent, especially in the main building, where the architecture is distinctively Bermudian. For starters, there's the white-ridged roof, which is charmingly bumpy in places, and the white painted chimneys. White keystone corners and "in and outs" edge the sides of pink outer walls. Dark green shutters emphasize the traditional look.

Walk into the drawing room, and you feel all the charm of an eighteenth-century country house. Alcoves and archways divide it so that you can enjoy a variety of seating areas. Armchairs and sofas are comfortable, while the dark wooden floors and occasional tables suggest the antique. The deep tray ceiling, cedar beams and cedar chest remind you that you are in Bermuda. Every afternoon from 4 to 5 PM you can enjoy complimentary afternoon tea in this enchanting room.

Books are an important feature at Horizons. In addition to the bookcases in the lounge, a well-stocked library will ensure that you're never short of a good read. While you're there, admire the dark oak Welsh hutch and the corner cabinet's display of beautiful china plates.

The pub, in the oldest part of the building, uses some of the original beams. Again, alcoves are a feature, dividing the room into different sections and giving the effect of nooks and crannies. Here you can have a drink before dinner or a game of skittles. If you are a golfer, you may well become a member of the Hole in One Club — a plaque displays all the names of players who have achieved this extraordinary feat. Bear in mind, though, that if you do get a hole in one, you are morally bound to buy everyone a drink! More on golf later.

Dining at Horizons means dressing up for the occasion, so jacket and tie are mandatory most nights. When you see the gracious formality of the dining room, you'll understand why informal wear would be unthinkable. However, from May to October, Friday nights are casual nights, when you can enjoy a barbecue on the terrace that overlooks the South Shore. Mondays, Thursdays, Fridays and Saturdays enjoy live entertainment that ranges from the melodious notes of the classical guitar to the traditional island music of the Bermuda Strollers. Dancing is definitely encouraged. Horizons, by the way, has a dine-around plan that enables guests to use their MAP for meals at Waterloo House in Hamilton (see our Small Hotels chapter). They are also given $25 per person credit for meals at Coral Beach and Tennis Club (a prestigious private club).

Horizons' 13 cottages, spread over 25 acres of beautifully landscaped gardens, offer 48 accommodations. For every five rooms there is a common room that, like the main drawing room, offers guests an opportunity to make friends with each other in comfortable, elegant surroundings. All rooms have private patios that allow guests peaceful contemplation of oleander, bamboo, palmetto and palm and sometimes of the ocean beyond. Again, it is difficult to describe a typical room, as Horizons prides itself on avoiding the boring and uniform. The rooms are decorated in a variety of colors, though fabrics for curtains and furnishings tend to be European. All the rooms have spacious living areas with comfortable chairs and sofas. Antique desks and chests add a traditional touch, and many units have working fireplaces. The private bathrooms are also spacious, as are the vanity areas, some of which sport charming kidney-shaped dressing tables that date to the 1930s. All are stocked with hair dryers and tissue boxes. Clock-radios and ice boxes are also provided. Television and VCR, by the way, are available if you request them. Room service is special at Horizons because this is the one cottage colony where a maid will follow the old Bermudian practice of preparing your breakfast in the kitchen area of the cottage. Yes, each cottage has a kitchen but worry not; only staff are allowed to cook there. The main building also has guest rooms, two of which are wheelchair-accessible and specially equipped with racks.

The swimming pool, together with the mashie nine-hole golf course and three tennis courts on the grounds, will prevent you from becoming lazy. Both golf and tennis cost $4 a round. If you want more recreational facilities and access to the sea, you will enjoy them across the road at Coral Beach and Tennis Club, which has a stunning beach with coral sands (comfortable loungers and towels are provided), plus excellent tennis and squash and an 18-hole putting green. You can also use the health club. On weekdays, Horizons' guests pay $6 a day for use of Coral Beach's facilities; on weekends, they pay $12 per person a day.

Children are very welcome. No kids' programs are available, but if you crave that precious, quality time with your family that is so difficult to find in these hectic times, you will have it at Horizons. Baby-sitting is available.

Book as early as possible, particularly for dates between March 15 and January 3 (high season). Be aware that Horizons does not accept any credit cards. A deposit for two nights is required. You can pay with personal or travelers' checks, cash or money order. If you cancel within 21 days of your arrival date, you will have a year in which to book another holiday at the property, otherwise you lose your deposit. Check-in time is flexible. Check-out is at noon. Horizons has a 10 percent service charge per room.

Warwick Parish

Fourways Inn
$ • 1 Middle Rd.
• (441) 236-6517, (800) 962-7654

Before we describe Fourways, we must remind you that the price code does not include MAP. However, it does include your room and continental breakfast for two. A MAP plan is available at $42.50 per person.

There are actually four ways to reach this inn. It stands at a four-way junction near Amen Corner that marks the boundary between Paget and Warwick Parishes. In fact, it has stood there ever since the early 1700s, when a certain John Harvey decided he wanted a Bermudian house made of coral limestone and native cedar. John, by the way, was a member of the Canadian Harvey family, famous for Harvey's Bristol sherry. In 1727 the house was duly built, and he sailed to Bermuda from Newfoundland to live in it. Its location was very important to him because it meant that his friends could easily reach him by horse and carriage. Apparently, they enjoyed his lavish parties so much, they ended up staying the night — no doubt they suffered from an excess of sherry and fine wine.

The house remained a private, albeit hospitable, residence until the 1950s when it became a guest house. Bermudian owner, Mr. Moss, advertised it as "Old England in a New World setting with an English Tap Room." Come the mid-1970s, a W. Sommer, together with a group of Bermudian entrepreneurs, bought it and converted it into one of the island's top restaurants. When Bermudians think of Fourways, they invariably think of Christmas dinner. The Old World charm of the dining room, which features stone walls and cedar, makes it an ideal setting for a Dickensian Christmas extravaganza. A favorite dining choice for locals, Fourways also caters to business travelers. Smaller dining areas off the main dining room and a banquet room are very suitable for business meetings and conventions. Smoking is allowed. In the summer months, dinner is served on the Palm Garden terrace. Every night, you can relax to the classical pianist's romantic music (see our Restaurants chapter for menu options). The Peg Leg Lounge and Bar also has a quaint atmosphere. The bar's old Bermuda fireplace and exposed beams in the ceiling remind us of the inn's history. To add to the atmosphere, the bar has a great selection of cigars. Lunch, high teas and cocktails are served in the lounge, where, in the evening, you can hear live guitar music.

Fourways is also famous locally for its pastry shop on the property. Many a dieter has been successfully tempted with fresh-baked croissants or almond Danishes. You can depend on your breakfast, which includes baked goodies straight from the oven. It's delivered to your room every morning, together with the *Royal Gazette*.

Which brings us to accommodation. Five separate cottages were added to the property in 1986. Double-storied, they surround a small, heated freshwater pool in the middle of a palm and oleander garden. Deluxe rooms with private bathrooms are on the top stories; one bedroom suites with private terraces are on the ground level. The price code covers the price of both. Rooms come with king-size bed, pull-out sofa, chairs and desk. Arrangements of cut flowers grace the table. All have double closets containing a safe, hairdryer, ironing board and iron, slippers and a bathrobe. Cable TV, telephone and clock-radio are all supplied. Bathrooms are spacious with marble double sinks. In addition, a small kitchenette area gives you a burner, fridge and sink. There's a coffee maker, together with a kettle and a toaster oven. The suites offer a microwave oven as well.

Fourways does not have its own beach. However, guests can obtain passes that allow them access to the private facilities on Stonington Beach (see our Beaches and Small Hotels chapters). The staff is happy to make arrangements for golf. If you are interested in watersports, they will arrange those too. You may want to rent bikes (staff will help you out there as well), but bear in mind that a bus stop is just around the corner, and a ferry stop is about a five-minute walk away.

Kids are welcome here. Those younger than age 11 stay with their parents for free. (This is where the pull-out sofa is useful.) Chil-

dren older than 11 are charged $40. We should tell you here that in the dining room, children under eight are encouraged to come at 6:30 PM. Fourways is probably not a good option for guests in wheelchairs. Access is not impossible, but it is difficult.

High season is April 1 to October 31. Low season is November 1 to March 31. You may pay your two-night deposit with major credit cards. Cancel within 21 days of your scheduled arrival, and you lose your deposit. There's a 10 percent service charge per room. Check-in is at 2:30 PM; check-out at 11:30 AM.

Cambridge Beaches
$$$$ • 30 King's Point Rd.
• (441) 234-0331, (800) 468-7300

You could be forgiven for thinking this cottage colony got its name from beaches called "Cambridge." True, it actually has five private beaches, but none of them has ever been called Cambridge. (More on the beaches later.) No, the name goes back more than 200 years, when a house called Cambridge was built close to the entrance of this property. You can still see it, though now it is called Torwood. During the late 1920s, Hugh Gray and his wife fixed it up as a guest accommodation for tourists visiting in the then-popular winter season. In the meantime, the Gilbert family ran "The Beaches" as a guest cottage. Mr. Gray eventually bought the property from the Gilberts to expand his business, and so the marriage of names. That cottage is now Cambridge Beaches' Main House. Over the years Mr. Gray gradually bought out other private homes, many of which are more than 150 years old. One, Pegem, was built by a seafaring entrepreneur more than 350 years ago. You can still see the original cedar beams in the ceilings.

And so Cambridge Beaches is the oldest cottage colony still in existence. Many of its cottages have a history behind them, and so does its location on the small peninsula off Somerset Island. Mangrove Bay, which it overlooks on one side, was a favorite anchorage

INSIDERS' TIP

If a close ocean view from your balcony or terrace is important to you, be sure to mention it when you make your reservation.

for Bermudian smugglers, who would unload their merchandise there to escape the watchful eye of officers at the St. George's Customs House. And families in Somerset, you may be interested to know, disobeyed the Bermuda government by supporting the rebels during the American Revolution (see our History chapter).

Today, Cambridge Beaches is the ultimate experience for those who seek romance. Michael Winfield, president of the colony, put it this way: "For many, relaxation is a forgotten art. We want our guests to rediscover it. . . . We offer a sophisticated but romantic environment in which guests can do nothing and do it well." What does "doing nothing" entail? Well, you can enjoy the 25 acres of beautifully landscaped grounds. You can swim in the outdoor pool or at any of the five aforementioned beaches that include Long Bay, Turtle Cove, Point Beach and numerous other coves. You can take a boat to the three islands off King's Point; if you fancy a picnic, staff will prepare you a lunch basket. A marina on the property offers sailing, kayaking, motor boats and fishing and snorkeling equipment. You can even go out for a cocktail or an after-dinner moon-

light sail. You can play tennis on any of the three all-weather outdoor courts (free during the day, $2.50 per token for a lit court), enjoy croquet on the lawn or practice on the putting green. Cambridge Beaches has membership at all of Bermuda's golf courses, including the Mid-Ocean Club, so games are easily arranged. Port Royal Golf Course is just 10 minutes away (see our Golf chapter).

If by any chance the elements are unkind to you, the new, spa will definitely cheer you up. A two-story, European health and beauty operation, the lower level houses the Ocean Spa with its six treatment rooms, sauna, steam, hair and beauty facilities. The upper level, the Seven Seas Solarium, has an indoor swimming pool under a retractable glass ceiling, exercise pool for lap swimming, a whirlpool and gym. In addition to the therapists on hand to pamper you with a myriad of treatments, there are counselors who can advise you on healthier lifestyles. Meanwhile, you needn't go hungry. After working out in the gym, you can always get refreshment at the cafe.

In fact, it would be entirely possible to stay on the property for the whole of your vacation. There's even a shop for that special gift you

Photo: GIS

This aerial shot offers a view of a section of Sandys Parish.

need to send to Uncle George or Auntie Agatha. However, if you feel like a more extensive shopping and/or sightseeing excursion, you can always take the complimentary ferry shuttle to Hamilton.

So what about the cottages? There are 38 in all and 81 units. As we mentioned, many are old, but several have been built much more recently. They are all traditional in design and modern in luxury. Of course they have the Bermudian white ridged roofs and shutters. Inside, fireplaces and antique furniture give them the country elegance of an eighteenth-century English house. Walls are pale; upholstery is fresh and bright. In most you will find an antique desk where you can practice the equally eighteenth-century art of writing letters. Bathrooms are magnificently marble and contain whirlpool tubs and bidets, double sinks and plenty of vanity space. Terry robes are on hand.

All rooms have safes, toasters, umbrellas, fridges, irons, and data port telephones with voice mail. And all have private terraces, where you can enjoy your full breakfast and views of coconut palms curving around the water's edge. Most rooms, incidentally, have a water view, but a few do not. If a water view is important, make sure you ask for one. Television? Only if you request it. The charge for television and VCR in your room is $15 for the first day and $5 a day thereafter.

Now to the Main House, which again evokes eighteenth-century elegance. Two fireplaces and a cathedral ceiling in the tea room area add to that effect. Feel like a leisurely read? Well-stocked bookcases will help you out. Here you will take morning coffee or complimentary afternoon tea at 4 PM. The Main House also contains the Port of Call Bar, where you can have lunch. In the evening enjoy a pre-dinner drink and then, on formal nights, proceed to the candlelit Tamarisk Dining Room for exquisite food prepared by award-winning chef Jean-Claude Garzia. You'll need to dress up for those occasions — jacket and tie are mandatory for men. Smoking is allowed in the dining rooms in designated areas. On alternate nights you can let down your hair by dining less formally out on Mangrove Bay Terrace. Gaze at the waters, the moon and the stars, and when the mood takes you, dance to the music played live every night. Also in the Main House, take the time to check out a plaque inscribed with the names of repeat visitors. The list is impressive. You might like to know that when we visited, one guest was enjoying his 74th stay. That speaks for itself. Many of Cambridge Beaches' repeat visitors originally came as honeymooners.

Kids are welcome, but those younger than 5 must be accompanied by a professional nanny or nurse. The idea, you see, is that you are meant to enjoy "emotion recollected in tranquillity." Colicky babies have a way of interfering with tranquillity. Check with the reservations staff for rates for kids. Generally speaking, an additional child in the room pays $120 a day MAP while an additional adult pays $170. Some of the rooms, including the spa and dining room, are definitely wheelchair-accessible. A variety of rooms also make it a good choice for business travelers. Call the cottage colony direct for details and rates of conventions.

Visitors typically reserve by calling the cottage colony direct. Book as early as possible. For the summer season (April 16 through October 31), we advise a six-month lead-in. Cambridge Beaches has two shoulder seasons between March 1 and April 15 and November 1 to November 30. Winter season is December 1 to February 28. First and last night deposit is required to reserve a room. Cancel within 28 days of your arrival date, and you lose your deposit. Check-in is at 2 PM; checkout at noon. Changing rooms around the pool and at the spa will allow you that last precious post-check-out swim before you take off for the airport. In addition to the $13.30 per person per day gratuity, there's a 4 percent energy charge.

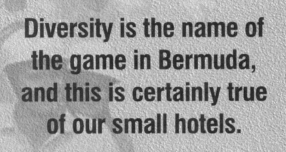

Diversity is the name of the game in Bermuda, and this is certainly true of our small hotels.

Small Hotels

Diversity is the name of the game in Bermuda, and this is certainly true of our small hotels. When tourism began to take off in the 1920s and '30s (see the introduction to our Resort Hotels chapter), our small hotels developed. Some, especially the ones closer to Hamilton, were originally gracious private homes converted, and sometimes structurally extended, into tourist accommodations.

After World War II, tourism again saw an upsurge, but during this time, summer became more the high season than winter, and visitors became increasingly interested in our beaches and water-related activities. Then, during the late '40s and the '50s, some custom-built hotels with close access to beaches were built. It would be a mistake, therefore, to see our hotels as being identical. They differ in location, ambiance and the facilities they offer. In this chapter, we describe the differences as well as the characteristics they share.

Rates of Rooms and Meal Plans

We have to confess that creating a consistent pricing key for our small hotels was just about impossible. Why? Because of the meal plans they may or may not offer. Let us remind you of the terms EP, BP and MAP that we introduced in our Resort Hotels chapter. EP means European Plan, which offers room only. BP means Bermuda Plan and offers room and full or continental breakfast. MAP means Modified American Plan and offers room, breakfast and dinner.

The daily rates listed in the pricing key below are based on double occupancy during peak season. They do not include the 7.25 percent per room hotel occupancy tax, gratuities or telephone calls or other expenses. Rates we use also are based on the rooms visitors would most typically reserve. So far, so good.

The majority of hotels, but not all of them, have quoted a BP rate. One has EP only, while offering BP and MAP for additional charge. Another offers only MAP, and yet another has an inclusive policy whereby the rate covers all meals, all drinks, all recreational activities and all gratuities. Gratuity policies also differ; some hotels charge no gratuity at all. Please read the individual listings very carefully to see exactly what the rates cover.

Pricing Key

Be aware that fewer dollar signs do not necessarily mean a lower standard of accommodation. For one thing, all hotels are licensed by the Bermuda government's Department of Tourism. To retain that license, they have to pass strict annual inspections by tourism, health and fire inspectors. A lower dollar sign doesn't necessarily mean fewer facilities or less personal service either.

Likewise, a higher dollar-sign code need not necessarily mean your stay at the hotel will be significantly more expensive since that rate may cover more than breakfast or breakfast and dinner. It can be confusing. It's best that you read our descriptions closely, and bear in mind that rates can be subject to change.

$	$150 to $206
$$	$207 to $258
$$$	$259 to $335
$$$$	$336 and higher

Seasonality, Reservation and Cancellation Policies

Typically, the summer season starts in April and ends October to November. However, some hotels charge high-season rates during Christmas and New Year holidays as well. We will be specific in each listing, as season dates can vary from property to property. Some hotels, for example, have a third "shoulder" season that we will specify when applicable. In any case, do verify these dates because they can make an enormous difference in cost.

Room rates in the low season can be considerably cheaper. Check the hotels for special packages they may offer during the winter season. For example, package rates are sometimes offered for golfing guests. A few hotels close to refurbish for a short period in the winter. In all cases, during the winter season entertainment is reduced and beach facilities, such as beach bars, close.

Visitors reserve usually by calling the hotel directly. Nearly all hotels require a two-night room deposit. Some stipulate a first- and last-night deposit. This means that if you cut short your holiday, you still lose the cost of the last night. When this requirement applies, we will tell you so in the listings. All properties listed accept major credit cards; alternatively, you may pay with cash, travelers' checks or, in some cases, personal checks. Generally speaking, guest cancellations within 14 to 21 days of arrival result in loss of deposit. How long should you book in advance? Most hotels are heavily booked during American public holidays — book as soon as possible for those. But we must tell you that while some hotels tend to be heavily booked in July and August, others are busier in May and June or September through November. Check the individual listings for recommended length of advance notice. Remember that last-minute cancellations can make last-minute bookings possible. If you are a spur-of-the-moment person, give the hotel of your choice a call. Check-in and check-out times differ, so look for those in the listings.

Policies on Kids and Other Issues

All but one of the properties listed accept children. But only two offer programs specifically for them. Room and meal rates for kids and extra persons in the rooms can vary enormously, so look closely at the individual listings for those costs. We will let you know which hotels are more family-oriented than others. Babysitting, by the way, can always be arranged.

Some hotels are wheelchair-accessible and have appropriately fitted bathrooms. When this is the case, we will tell you. The remaining hotels do not have facilities suitable for guests completely confined to wheelchairs. If you use a walker, however, some of the properties could work for you. Call the hotel directly to discuss details about steps, bathrooms and access so that you can be assured the accommodations will suit your needs.

Nearly all the hotels have a relaxed smoking policy. Some do not allow smoking in the dining rooms; we'll tell you when that is the case. All allow smoking in guest rooms. Some hotels accept pets on request, particularly small dogs that are participating in dog shows on the island. If we don't mention pets, assume they are not accepted. When they are, we'll tell you.

Location and Amenities

Basically, you have the choice between staying in a hotel very close to Hamilton or in one that has access to a private beach. Bear in mind that many of our small hotels have gorgeous private beaches on the South Shore that often allow easy access to the reefs. For kids, these can be ideal. Generally speaking, all hotels are a short distance from either a bus or ferry stop.

All the hotels we list have at least one lounge area. Most, but not all, have licensed bars and dining rooms. And every guest room has a private bathroom. Some hotels have a small number of suites or cottages suitable for larger families or groups. We'll mention them, but you should call the hotel directly for those rates. Every hotel has an outdoor swimming pool. Some also have facilities more often associated with resorts, such as tennis courts and fitness rooms. Where they do, we'll tell you in the individual listings. We cannot emphasize enough that all hotels have staff who will make your arrangements for golf, tennis, watersports, cycle rentals and any other activities or excursions you can think of. That you may take for granted. Hotel staff and management pride themselves on friendliness and

Photo: GIS

Bermuda's hotels and other accommodations are some of the finest to be found worldwide.

personal service. That's why many of the hotels enjoy a high repeat visitor rate.

And now for the listings, which, as usual, we will present east to west, parish by parish, subset by subset and thereafter in alphabetical order.

Smiths Parish

Palmetto Hotel and Cottages
$ • 1 Harrington Sound Rd., Flatts Inlet
• (441) 293-2323

Built more than 100 years ago and once a family mansion, Palmetto looks over Flatts Inlet on one side and the calm waters of Harrington Sound on the other. Inside the main building you'll find a reception area; the Ha'penny Pub, where you can have lunch and a drink; and the Inlet Restaurant, which actually overlooks the sound. If you opt for the MAP (it costs $32 per person per day), then you will enjoy your four-course dinner here.

You'll also find the lounge at Inlet Restaurant, and every afternoon you can indulge in complimentary tea. If you are musically inclined, try out the piano. Outside dining is on the front terrace, and from there you can see the Inlet. Smoking, by the way, is allowed everywhere on the property.

Guest rooms are in the main building and separate cottage units. Some rooms are very large and have two double beds; others have king-size or two twin beds. Rooms have closets, chairs and a dresser. All come with private balconies or patios, where you can have your complimentary continental breakfast or, for approximately $10, a full breakfast. While many rooms have gorgeous views of the water, an ocean view is not guaranteed. Be sure to request one if a water vista is important to you.

Rooms are equipped with telephones; ironing boards and irons are available on request. Coffee makers and clock-radios are in each room. There are no safes, so do leave your valuables in the front-office safe. Cottage units offer free cable TV. In rooms that are less expensive than the price range we quote, you can rent a television for $5 a day. Room service is available for breakfast, lunch and dinner; a $3 service charge is added to the cost of the meal. Most bathrooms have showers and tubs, but six have showers only.

Kids are welcome. Younger than 2, they stay for free; younger than 12, the charge is $24 (that includes breakfast) a day. Cribs are available for no extra charge. A small, artificial beach lets you swim in Harrington Sound. You can also swim in the saltwater pool. Loungers and towels are on hand.

Palmetto is just one minute's walk away from the Bermuda Aquarium (see our Kidstuff chapter) and from a bus route that will take you to Hamilton or to St. George's. Book at least two weeks ahead of your visit, especially in the high season between April 1 and October 31. A one-night deposit is required, which you will lose if you cancel within 14 days of your holiday. For BP, there's a $9.21 daily charge per person; for MAP it's $13.30 per person. Check-in is at 3 PM, check-out at noon.

Pembroke Parish

Rosedon
$$ • 61 Pitts Bay Rd.
• (441) 295-1640, (800) 367-0040

Rosedon was built in 1906 as a luxurious private home. In the years before electric light, Rosedon was famous because it was the only house in Bermuda to be lit by gas instead of by kerosene lamps. It became a guest house in the 1930s and then, after the war years, evolved into a small hotel.

As soon as you walk into the front entrance, complete with pillars and a gracious verandah, you will notice its elegant proportions and the archways and high ceilings so characteristic of its period. A separate office on the right is for friendly front-desk reception. On your left are two comfortable lounges, one of which has an honor bar and a VCR for nightly mov-

ies. You sign a voucher for each drink you take, and the price is added to your final bill. Complimentary afternoon tea is also served in this room. There's no smoking here, please. Everywhere else, it's OK.

There is no formal dining room at Rosedon, but some meals are offered. The price we quote includes a full breakfast, which is served in your room, by the pool or on the verandahs. For an extra charge, you can order a light à la carte lunch. You can order soup, salad and sandwiches for $10 a person in the evenings.

In addition to rooms in the main building, 38 double rooms have been added in the garden area. All but three have access to balconies that guests share. "The idea behind this design," says Ms. Muriel Richardson, manager, "was that guests could talk to each other." Before we talk about rooms, a quick word about the garden. Filled with huge shade trees, poinciana, palmetto and frangipani, and with lush subtropical and tropical plants, it offers a hidden haven from the busy city that's just minutes away. The large outdoor, freshwater swimming pool and terrace are probably its focal point. You can relax in loungers, and after dark, appreciate the lights that illuminate the garden. In the winter, the pool is heated.

All rooms in the price range we quote are air-conditioned and have ceiling fans. They are carpeted and painted in pastel shades. Rooms in the main house have the more traditional Queen Anne-style furniture while those around the pool have light, tropical furnishings. They all have spacious living areas and come equipped with telephones with dataports, clock-radios, mini fridges, safes, irons and ironing boards and hairdryers. Beds are either kings, doubles or twins.

Children are welcome. Younger than 18, they pay $20 per person for the BP plan. Having said that, Ms. Richardson confides that couples typically tend to come alone. The hotel's location makes it ideal for visitors coming on business who prefer the homey atmosphere of a smaller, less formal hotel. They also appreciate the fax service and the daily complimentary copy of *The Royal Gazette*.

Many of the staff members have worked at Rosedon for more than 20 years, and, to quote Ms. Richardson, "They have acquired the art of making our guests happy."

Ms. Richardson recommends that you book for summer season (April 1 until November 30 at Rosedon) at least two months ahead of time. A two-night deposit is required, and it is not refunded if you cancel within 14 days of your arrival. Service charge is 10 percent of your room rate. Check-in is flexible; check-out is at noon.

Royal Palms Hotel

$ • 24 Rosemont Ave.

• (441) 292-1854, (800) 678-0783

Until 1946, in the days before motorized traffic, Rosemont Avenue was a select part of Bermuda, containing gracious residences of manorial proportions. The avenue's proximity to Hamilton made for easy horse and carriage travel. Many of those residences are still there, including Royal Palms, which was built in 1903 as a private home. Between the world wars the owners started to take in guests, and eventually the property was converted into a hotel. Its location is still ideal for visitors who want easy access to the city and the tranquillity of a rural setting. And you can still hear the clip-clop of the horses and carriages that now take tourists around the neighborhood.

Richard Smith, who owns and manages the hotel with his sister, Susan Weare, takes pride in caring for the stunning gardens at Royal Palms. As well as palms, you'll see frangipani, a glorious poinciana, bananas (which you will have for breakfast in season) and superb purple bougainvillea. What might not interest you (but definitely interests us) is that the garden has an apple tree that actually bears fruit. Since apple trees need frost, which we never have, this is a remarkable gardening feat.

Outdoor terraces allow you to enjoy the gardens. See-through blinds and awnings mean you can stay outside even in cold or windy weather. An outdoor swimming pool will refresh you after your trip to town.

The price we quote in our key includes room and a generous breakfast that you can eat in a dining room with a fireplace (useful in winter) or outside on the terrace. You will have toast, fresh pastries and scones, fresh fruit and, if you wish, eggs. Susan and Richard will help you with the intricacies of eating boiled eggs in egg cups, typically used by the British (see the Insiders' Tip in our Guest Houses chapter). The two like to meet their guests in the mornings to discuss what recreational arrangements need to be made. Incidentally, Richard is a member of the Mid Ocean Golf Club. That means you can play there any day of the week, provided tee times are available.

Can you dine at this hotel? Absolutely. Ascot's Restaurant is within the hotel but is owned by Claudio Vigilante and Edmund Smith, who also run the lounge bar (open from noon to 3 PM and 6:30 PM to 1 AM). Your MAP rate costs an additional $42 per person per day and can be used as a dinner supplement for the à la carte menu offerings. We should tell you that Ascot's is a restaurant much loved by locals, particularly on special occasions (see our Restaurants chapter). Female guests needn't bother wearing fancy hats. Dining is the name of the game here, not horse racing, although the atmosphere is country British. Smoking is not encouraged in the dining room but is OK everywhere else. Room service, by the way, is available.

Rooms are all spacious, with living areas that are individually painted in pastel colors and furnished with bright fabrics. They are all light, thanks to large windows that sometimes have charming window seats, and they are all air-conditioned. Bed setups offer kings or two doubles, and all rooms come with ceiling fans, clock-radios, coffee makers, irons, telephones with dataports, Internet lines and cable television. Hairdryers and refrigerators are in most rooms. Bathrooms come with tubs and showers, and many have Corian (marble-like) vanity areas with sinks. For a higher price than the one in the code, mini-suites overlooking the pool are available with a kitchen area equipped with fridge, microwave and toaster-oven. Call the hotel for those rates and for those of a one-bedroom cottage with living room and kitchen. When you see the overall standard of accommodation, it will come as no surprise that in 1997 Susan and Richard won the Department of Tourism Buttery Award, for achieving a consistently high standard of accommodation during a four-year period.

Kids are welcome. Those younger than 3 stay free; for those between 3 and 16, the charge is $25 a day per child. Pets, such as small dogs, are allowed on request but guests must pay a fumigation fee.

Royal Palm's summer season runs from April 1 to November 15. For the busy months of May and June, book about two months ahead, although last-minute cancellations can make last-minute vacancies possible. A two-day deposit is required, and a 14-day cancellation policy applies. A 10 percent service charge is added to your room rate. Check-in is flexible; check-out is at noon.

Waterloo House
$$$$ • 100 Pitts Bay Rd.
• (441) 295-4480, (800) 468-4100

This hotel may have the name of a famous European battlefield, but when you meet your Waterloo here, you enter a haven just minutes away from the City of Hamilton. As soon as you walk through the road entrance, you can see the beautifully terraced grounds that lead right down to Hamilton Harbour.

Waterloo House is a sister hotel to Horizons and Cottages (see our Cottage Colonies chapter). Like Horizons, it is currently a member of Relais et Chateaux. Membership depends on maintaining the five C's: cuisine, calm, comfort, charm and courtesy.

Let us begin, then, with the dining room, where all these qualities are evident. Ragged-glazed, the walls are the color of crushed raspberries. The effect is stunning and contrasts strikingly with the cedar fireplace and the elegant, dark wood of antique dressers and cabinets. You will see on one of the walls a portrait of the Duke of Wellington, in whose honor the dining room is named. You can use your MAP ($40 per person per day) to dine in the Wellington Restaurant, where you will enjoy the exquisite creations of Steve Blumenthal, the award-winning executive chef (see our

Restaurants chapter for details). Dining is formal, so jacket and tie are mandatory. Smoking's OK here (except for cigars), as it is everywhere in the hotel.

While we're talking about food, we must tell you that in the summer months, dining also is offered outside on the Poinciana Terrace that overlooks Hamilton Harbour. Jacket is still required but no tie. Lunch is served there, much to the delight of locals who want an hour's respite from the city. In the unlikely event you want to try another restaurant, remember that you can use your MAP to dine at the sister properties, Horizons Cottages and Coral Beach and Tennis Club.

The main building has many other rooms where you can relax in aesthetically pleasant surroundings. There's the Long Room Bar, which is indeed long, and which, again, has an unusual wall finish. Walls are washed with yellow and have a clear gloss stripe that you only notice when the light falls on it. The bar is open from 11 AM to 1 AM. Want to catch up on international news? You'll find complimentary international newspapers in the drawing room, in addition to the free *Royal Gazette* and the *New York Times* fax each guest receives every morning. In the afternoons, you'll have complimentary tea. You won't find a television, though. Watching television in a drawing room is just not done. The sun lounge is light and airy with pastel washed walls, hanging baskets and light wicker furniture. Fancy a game of skittles or backgammon? A well-equipped game room is also in the main building, with an honor bar just outside it.

All the rooms in the price range we quote have harbor views. Rooms with garden views are less expensive. All rooms have private balconies or terraces where you may have your breakfast (full or continental) delivered in the mornings for no extra charge. (If you want company, breakfast is also served in the Wellington Restaurant. Breakfast is included in the rate

INSIDERS' TIP

Please read the individual listings very carefully to see what the quoted rates cover. Gratuity policies and meal plans can vary from listing to listing. Remember, the dollar-sign code does not necessarily reflect the standard of accommodation or the total expense of your stay in the hotel.

we quote.) Each room is individually decorated with all the tastefulness we have come to anticipate from Horizons Property Ltd. Seating areas are spacious. Beds are king-sized, or there are two twins. All rooms are air-conditioned and have ceiling fans. They come with clock-radio, cable TV, dataport telephone and Internet lines, safe, umbrella, trouser press and hairdryer. Fridges, irons and ironing boards are available on request. Naturally, all rooms have private bathrooms with tubs and showers. In fact, many of the bathrooms have Jacuzzi baths.

Kids are welcome at Waterloo House. If they are 12 or younger and stay in their parents' rooms, the charge is $45 per person for BP and an additional $18 for MAP. If they are older than 12, the charge is $90 and the full MAP rate. Kids sleep on pull-out sofas or extra beds. In addition, Waterloo House has a variety of delightful suites that are suitable for larger families. Call the hotel for those rates. Pets are accepted on request.

The grounds at Waterloo House are charming. All over the property you'll find shady nooks with garden or water views and plenty of verandah space. Split-level terraces are filled with flowers. The freshwater outdoor swimming pool will also keep you cool. If you want further recreation, remember that you can use all of the tennis and beach facilities at Coral Beach for no charge. Golf is easily arranged. Want to picnic at one of the islands in the harbor? No

problem. The hotel's private launch will take you there. On some enchanted evenings, it will take you for a Hamilton Harbour cocktail cruise as well. In the summer season at Waterloo, entertainment is offered every night and four lunch times a week. A three-piece band may well get you dancing. In addition, Calypso and soft piano music will relax you in the evening as you dine. In the winter entertainment is reduced to just three nights a week.

High season at Waterloo House runs from April 1 to November 30, then from December 20 until January 1. Low season is January 1 until March 31. Interestingly, the hotel can be busier in the winter months than in summer. For July and August, you may safely book a week or two in advance. For September to November, book three to four months ahead. You reserve with a two-night deposit that you will lose if you cancel within 21 days of your scheduled arrival. The service charge is 10 percent of your room rate. Check-in is at 2 PM, check-out at noon.

Paget Parish

Harmony Club
$$$$ • 109 South Rd.
• (441) 236-3500

The first thing we must tell you is that Harmony Club is Bermuda's first and only all-inclusive hotel. The rate for two in high season is $575. Don't be shocked. That rate includes a lot more than room and breakfast for two. In fact, it includes just about everything — even the government's 7.25 percent tax and all gratuities. From the moment you reach Bermuda, you'll scarcely need to open your wallet.

First, you will be met at the airport and taken to the hotel for free. Once at Harmony, you will discover that the only time you'll deal with money is when you pay your final bill. The rates include the following for two: room, breakfast, lunch, dinner (with house red or white wine) and an open bar serving complimentary soft drinks and alcoholic beverages from 11 AM to 11 PM. There is also free tennis on Harmony's two courts and staff will arrange golf. And you get free access to the Stonington Beach. (See listing below.) Anything else? After you pay the $15 nonrefundable insurance waiver required by the cycle shop, you get free use of a two-seat motor scooter for the duration of your stay. You also get free cover charges for admission to The Club and The Oasis, two nightclubs in Hamilton (see our Nightlife chapter). Drinks at the clubs you must pay for.

As William Griffiths, general manager, pointed out, "This inclusive policy means that the staff have more time to spend on the guests to create a friendly atmosphere. The bartender, for example, doesn't have to concentrate on dealing with cash." You'll find the barkeeper in the Tavern Bar, where lunches are served daily in addition to evening cocktails and hot hors d'oeuvres. Mornings, you'll find a full buffet breakfast in the Casuarina Restaurant, freshly decorated in green and white with hanging baskets of plants creating a garden effect. In the evenings, you'll dine there too (no smoking allowed at Casuarina, but it's OK everywhere else). On Sunday nights, a jacket is required. Other nights, smart casual dress is fine but no jeans, please . . . and no sneakers and T-shirts.

Six nights a week in summer you can dance the night away in the spacious Bay Grape Lounge to live pop, Calypso, reggae or jazz. Once a week in the summer, a poolside barbecue allows you to eat outside. You'll see the heated pool once you walk through the moongate in the beautiful garden grounds. In addition, a Jacuzzi, sauna and two tennis

courts are available. If you fancy an evening of games or television, try out the Gombey Lounge. Incidentally, in the 1940s and '50s, Nat King Cole and Eartha Kitt sang here. So if you start humming, "Chestnuts roasting round an open fire," or "I'm just an old-fashioned girl," you'll know why — you'll be picking up on the vibes. If you want an old-fashioned millionaire, dream on. But then again, in Bermuda, you never know.

The rooms are bright and cheerful, mostly in cabanas with garden and pool views. All but nine of the 68 rooms come with balconies. They are all furnished with king or twin beds and come with telephone, radio, satellite television and tea- and coffee-making facilities. All rooms have bathrooms equipped with tubs and showers, hairdryers and bathrobes plus in-room safes. Harmony does not allow extra guests in rooms, and all guests must be older than 18 years of age. So if you're looking for a respite from the children, this could be the place for you.

The architecture of the main house, Paget Manor, is interesting. Painted coral pink with a white ridged roof, its walls feature "in and outs" — white, decorative brickwork edgings. Some windows have around their arches similar brickwork known as "eyebrows."

Harmony Club's summer season runs from May 1 to October 31. Winter season starts December 19 and ends February 28. Two shoulder seasons run from March 1 to April 30 and November 1 to November 28. The hotel closes for refurbishing from November 29 to December 18. Rates vary during the shoulder seasons, so call the hotel directly for those rates and winter rates. For May and October (both very busy months) reserve at least six weeks in advance. Otherwise, a four-week lead-in on your reservation is recommended. A two-night deposit is required, which you will lose if you cancel within 14 days of your scheduled holiday. Check-in is at 2 PM, check-out at noon.

Stonington Beach Hotel
$$$$ • 8 College Dr. (off South Rd.) • (441) 236-5416

This hotel is unique to the island in the sense that it is owned and operated by the Bermuda College. Built in 1980, it was the first building to go up on the Stonington Bermuda College campus. Although the hotel is run by fully qualified staff, you may well meet student chefs, waiters, front-desk receptionists and others studying for associate degrees in hotel management. Under supervision, they work for a stipend during the holiday months as part of their training.

Stonington Beach Hotel overlooks the South Shore, and its private beach is (but of course) called Stonington. Located at the eastern end of Elbow Beach, the beach is small with pinkish sand. However, this part of the ocean is a prime spot for snorkeling since the potboilers are close enough to shore that at low tide you can wade out to them. On the beach, you will find a small bar for drinks and lunch. You may also rent a mask and snorkel for $7.50 per half-day, $15 for a full day. Flippers cost $10 a day. You might also like to buy a disposable underwater camera for $18. Use of umbrellas, loungers and beach chairs is complimentary. Two tennis courts and an outdoor freshwater pool (heated in winter) offer additional recreation.

Upon entering the main building, you will immediately find yourself in the lobby lounge, where complimentary tea is served every afternoon at 4 PM. Here, too, you will find the Overplus Bar open weekdays and Saturdays from 11 AM until 1 AM and from noon until 1 AM on Sundays. The Norwood Dining Room is also in this building, where you may enjoy the full or continental breakfast (your preference) that is included in the rate we quote. In the evening, The Norwood offers dinner, also included in the rate. There is no smoking in the dining room and no casual dress either. A jacket is required. In the summer months alfresco dining is also offered around the swimming pool. For an extra charge plus a 15 percent gratuity, you may also have lunch on the terrace. While you dine, you will appreciate the music of either a pianist or saxophonist. On Saturday nights, a small band will encourage you to dance. Incidentally, Stonington is a member of the Bermuda Collection, so you can use your MAP to dine at other restaurants that are also members.

Rooms in unit blocks all have close views of the South Shore, and all have terraces with outdoor furniture. If you can't face socializing first thing in the morning, you may have your breakfast delivered to these rooms for a $2 per person room-service charge. They are air-conditioned and come with ceiling fans, clock-radio, telephone with dataport, cable television, safes and mini fridges. Irons and ironing boards, hairdryers and umbrellas, bathrobes and coffee makers are also on hand. Rooms are uniformly decorated in pale beige and furnished with drapes and spreads of blue and yellow design. Seating areas have small tables, armchairs and a pull-out sofa. Bathrooms are marble and come with tubs and showers. One bathroom, incidentally, is spacious and fitted with railings designed for guests in wheelchairs. You may smoke in your rooms and everywhere else in the hotel except the dining room.

Kids are welcome. For ages 3 through 12, the charge is $52 per person per day for BP, and those older than 12 are charged $62 for BP. For rates for children younger than 3 and for MAP rates for children, call the hotel directly. An extra adult staying in the same room pays $82 a day for BP and an additional charge of $30 per person for MAP. Pets are permitted upon request. One honeymoon apartment is available. Overlooking the ocean, it has a kitchen with a refrigerator and microwave and a separate living room. Call the hotel for those rates. One other cottage is also available.

Stonington has three seasons. For the summer season (May 1 until October 31), book at least three months ahead. For American public holidays, book six months in advance. Winter season is November 1 until April 15, and the shoulder season is April 16 to April 30. Reserve with a two-night deposit, which you will lose if you cancel within five days of your expected arrival. Be aware that other than the 7.25 percent government tax and the 15 percent gratuity on lunch and extra drinks, there is no other service charge added to the room rate. Check-in is at 3 PM, check-out at noon.

The Newstead Hotel
$$$ • 27 Harbour Rd.
• (441) 236-6060, (800) 468-4111

Built in the nineteenth century as a private house, Newstead still has the ambiance of a Colonial manor house with beautifully land-

For some of the most spectacular sites, just look up.

Photo: Mark Emmerson

scaped gardens displaying the vibrant splendor of purple bougainvillea vines. It became a hotel in 1923, and guests then no doubt appreciated the tranquil view of Hamilton Harbour, just as they do today. During the late '60s and early '70s, the owners created two landscaped outdoor terraces on the harbor side so that guests could dine out and enjoy the sunset and night views.

Smoking is OK in the rooms and in designated areas of the lounge. No smoking is permitted in the dining room. Dress for dinner is formal except for Tuesday nights, when casual dress is encouraged. Throughout the hotel, antique and Oriental pieces contribute to the overall tastefulness of the decor.

All the rooms in our price range come with harbor views and balconies or terraces. They all have clock-radios, safes, telephones, cable television and coffee makers. Refrigerators are available on request, as are irons and ironing boards. Each room is individually decorated and furnished — one might have carpet while another has wooden flooring — but you can depend on exquisite taste. Bathrooms are spacious and come with tubs and showers. They are also equipped with hairdryers. Separate vanity areas have an additional sink.

Kids are welcome. Indeed, Newstead en-

courages them to take part in the Department of Tourism's Partaking Camp Bermuda for children (see our Kidstuff chapter). Cribs are free. Children younger than 13 pay $50 per person per day for an additional bed in their parents' rooms. Older than 13, they pay $75, which brings us to an explanation of the rate we quote. It's BP, but you can have MAP for an additional $40 per person per day.

For entertainment and recreation there is live music (a mixture of Calypso and jazz) every night except Thursday. Outside, a freshwater swimming pool (heated in winter) will let you cool down in summer. Complimentary afternoon tea is served daily in the dining room. Tennis is available on one of the two courts on the property. In addition, for $6 a day during the week or $12 a day on weekends, you can use the beach facilities at the Coral Beach and Tennis Club (see the Horizons and Cottages listing in our Cottage Colonies chapter).

Newstead's high seasons run from May 1 to November 30 and from December 15 to January 4. Low seasons are December 1 to December 14 and January 5 to March 15. March 16 to April 30 is the shoulder season. Call the hotel for winter and shoulder season rates. A two-night deposit is required, which you lose if you cancel within 21 days of your expected arrival. For a vacation here in May or October, book as early as possible. For other months, Newstead recommends booking a month in advance. A 10 percent service charge is added to your room rate. Check-in is at 2 PM, check-out at noon.

White Sands and Cottages
$$ • 55 White Sands Rd.
• (441) 236-2023, (800) 548-0547

This hotel has the advantage of close access to one of Bermuda's more secluded beaches, Grape Bay, and of being very close to Hamilton. For this reason, White Sands concentrates on affordable, relaxing accommodations rather than on a range of activities and entertainment. After all, stay here and you are just a 10-minute drive away from the city's nightclubs and attractions.

Having said that, the hotel does have two licensed bars and a dining room, called The Captain's Table. Except on designated casual nights, a jacket is required for dining. The price we quote includes a full American breakfast — sometimes kippers and Bermudian codfish cakes are offered to add variety. But for an extra $44 added to the room rate, (i.e., for two people, not per person) you can also have MAP. There is no smoking in the dining room, by the way, but you can indulge everywhere else.

The hotel also has a freshwater swimming pool with a partially covered terrace where lunch is served. You will find one of the bars there, open from noon until 6:30 PM. The other, The Sandbar Pub, is in the main building and is open from 6:30 PM until 1 AM. Thursdays and Sundays, there is live music to entertain you, and on Mondays, a managers' party will introduce you to the rum swizzle. A comfortable lounge with an area that overlooks the South Shore will make you feel at home rather than in a hotel lobby. That's why it's actually referred to as the living room. Here, you may enjoy complimentary afternoon tea.

Rooms are in the main house and in a terrace wing. All air-conditioned, they come with telephone, clock-radio, cable television, safe, mini refrigerator and coffee maker. Hairdryers, irons and ironing boards are available on request. Beds will be either one king or two doubles. Some of the rooms in the price range we quote have balconies with garden or South Shore ocean views. If an ocean view is important to you, tell the manager when you reserve. All have bathrooms with tubs and showers. Room service is available for breakfast and dinner and costs $3 per person.

Kids are welcome. Those younger than 6 stay free; ages 6 to 12 are charged $34 for BP and $45 for MAP. Cribs and rollaway beds are available. White Sands also has one two-bedroom and two three-bedroom cottages, all of which overlook the ocean. They can accommodate up to six persons each, have living rooms and kitchens and are ideal for families. Call the hotel for these rates — they can sometimes work out to be lower than the rate we quote. Guests in wheelchairs should call the hotel for details of access. Some rooms may be suitable. Pets are permitted on request.

Summer season is April 1 to November 15. For public holidays and the last two weeks of May and June, book as soon as possible. The rest of the season, you're advised to book four to six weeks in advance. A first- and last-night deposit is required, which you lose if you cancel within 21 days of your scheduled arrival. Check-in is at 2 PM, check-out at noon.

Warwick Parish

Mermaid Beach Club
$$ • 30 South Rd.
• (441) 236-5031, (800) 441-7087

"I have heard the mermaids singing each to each." So said T. S. Eliot's J. Alfred Prufrock. We can't promise that you'll hear them singing here, but we can tell you that just as mermaids have to swim, so will you when you see this hotel's private South Shore beach. In fact,

---

INSIDERS' TIP

If no safes are available in your rooms, leave valuables such as your passport, money and jewelry with the staff at the front desk. They will have either a safe or safety-deposit boxes available.

owner and manager Brian Alcon will probably swim with you. He swims approximately 2 miles a day and will tell (or show) you where the best snorkeling areas are on the reef. Parrotfish and angelfish, manta rays, octopi, crabs, lobsters and barracudas — he's seen them all around the part of the reef you can reach from Mermaid Beach. He's even seen an occasional moray eel. Snorkeling gear can be rented for a small charge. If you swim in the morning and return at noon, you'll be able to quench your thirst at the beach bar — it stays open from noon until 6 PM. Relax in a lounger, enjoy the shade of an umbrella and contemplate your next swim in the ocean or in the outdoor freshwater swimming pool. Or think about tennis — one court's available for a small charge.

The rate we quote here is for room only. BP and MAP rates are unavailable.

Rooms in the price range we quote all have seating areas and one double or two twin beds. They are all air-conditioned and come with refrigerator, clock-radio and telephone. You can request a television for a weekly charge of $25. All rooms have grass terraces or patios with good views of the ocean. For an extra $10 a day, you can get a kitchen equipped with refrigerator, electric cooker, china and utensils and microwave. The fee includes maid service.

Kids are very welcome. Cribs, high chairs and rollaways are available on request. Children 12 and younger stay free. Extra guests (kids included) older than 12 stay for $25 a day. However, extra guests are only allowed in suites. Call the hotel for suite rates. Be aware, too, that Mermaid offers family, golf and honeymoon packages; again, call for those rates. Incidentally, this is one of the few hotels that will take dogs on request, especially those taking their chances in local dog shows.

Mermaid recommends that you reserve at least two months in advance for the summer season. A first- and last-night deposit is required, and a 21-day cancellation policy applies. A $7 per person per day gratuity is added to the final bill. In addition, there's a 3 percent per person per day energy surcharge. Check-in is at 2 PM, check-out at 11 AM. Courtesy rooms are available, should these times prove inconvenient.

Surf Side Beach Club
$ • 90 South Rd.
• (441) 236-7100, (800) 553-9990

Until recently this charming property, situated on a hillside overlooking the South Shore, was in the Housekeeping, Cottages and Apartments category. But in 1997, the owners added a restaurant so it is now categorized as a small hotel. The result is that Surf Side now enjoys the advantages of both.

All rooms have fully equipped kitchens with coffee maker, full refrigerator and stove, gas or electric (state your preference when you book) and all the crockery and cutlery necessary for you to be self-sufficient. The rate we quote is for room only, but if you can't face preparing a meal first thing in the morning, then for an extra $10 you can have English or continental breakfast delivered to your room. (Room service is available from 8 to 10 AM.) Or you can have it served on the terrace around the swimming pool. MAP comes at $39 per person. Dining (and lunching) happens at the small, intimate PALMS restaurant, overlooking the pool and the ocean. Dress is smart casual and you can smoke. Every Tuesday staff will meet you at the complimentary swizzle party.

Kids are very welcome at Surf Side. They stay in suites or in the penthouse accommodations (call for those rates). Baby sitters are on hand for $10 an hour. All rooms have superb ocean views and have sliding glass doors leading to patios in garden settings where you can sit and linger over breakfast or take in the beauty of Bermuda's night skies. The rooms for the rate we quote have king-sized beds or two doubles. In addition to kitchens, they also come with cable television, telephones and data port, irons and ironing boards and safes.

INSIDERS' TIP

Many of our hotels have beautiful grounds and gardens. Take the time to explore them — they can be an excellent introduction to Bermuda's rich flora.

Hairdryers are available on request. All rooms have reverse-cycle air conditioning. No smoking restrictions apply. They are pleasantly decorated in pastel shades with floral curtains. Most of the bathrooms have tubs as well as showers but do tell the manager if a tub is important to you. A coin operated laundry is on the property.

The Fitness Centre, open from 6 to 1 AM and equipped with weights and bicycle walkers will let you work off extra calories. A sauna and Jacuzzi are on hand as well. And of course you can cool off in the pool or take the meandering path down to the dramatic shore line and enjoy the surf at the hotel's own beach. Beach loungers are always available on request. What other recreations are available? A cycle livery is on the property if you feel like exploring the island. And staff will be more than happy to arrange golf, tennis, watersports or any other recreation that might appeal to you. Bryony Harvey has been manager of Surf Side for over 27 years. Actually, it's a husband and wife team since Llewellyn Harvey is in charge of the restaurant. You'll most likely find

Bryony, together with the hotel cat, Smoky, in the reception area. Books and puzzles are on hand here and you can request board games.

Book as soon as possible for summer season, which runs from April 1 to 31 October. A two night deposit is required, which you will lose if you cancel within 14 days of your scheduled arrival. Bear in mind that there are extensive reductions in the winter season, November 1 to March 31. Check in is after 2 PM, check-out 11.30 AM.

Southampton Parish

Pompano Beach Club
$$$ • 36 Pompano Beach Rd.
• (441) 234-0222

Named after the many pompano fish that love to swim off the South Shore, this hotel opened in 1955 as Bermuda's first fishing club. Visitors used to go fishing on the club's deep-sea boat, and bring their spoils back to have them cooked for dinner the same day.

While that doesn't happen anymore, we

should tell you that Pompano's location still makes it an ideal resort for water-related activities. In fact, it has been described as Bermuda's best underwater beach. It faces a sand bar and the South Shore reef line. Dig in the sand bar with your feet, and you just might find a sand dollar shell. The sand bar means that at low tide you can wade out in waist-high water and become intimately acquainted with the reef's potboilers (see our Beaches chapter for an explanation of boilers) and the pompanos and other fish that hang out there.

If you don't fancy a watery walk, you can hire one of the many boats from the hotel's own watersports shop. Take a paddle boat or a windsurfer for $12 or a raft for $2 an hour. We particularly recommend a Sun Cat ($35 for one hour, $25 for a half-hour), which is like a motorized chaise lounge for two. The reef may well tempt you into snorkeling for a closer look at the fish. You can rent a mask, fins and snorkel for $7 a day. The hotel might not cook your catch anymore, but it will encourage you to go fishing. Light tackle and bait are complimentary. Yes, Pompano does have a private, sandy beach. It also has a 12 by 12-foot wading pool, filled with 18 inches of water. Children can play while their parents sit in it and read a good book. In addition, there's a freshwater swimming pool with plenty of poolside space and loungers for relaxing. Staff will serve you drinks, lunch and snacks there for additional charge. Two outdoor Jacuzzis will also help you relax. The Pool Bar is open from 2:30 to 5 PM. Here you can buy a drink or "light bites" such as nachos or deli-sandwiches.

While we're on the subject of activities, we must tell you this hotel is right next door to the No. 8 hole of Port Royal Golf Course. Of course, staff will happily book your tee times for you (see our Golf chapter). They will also provide a complimentary shuttle service, but it will be for your golf clubs only — Bermudian law prohibits these shuttles from carrying people. But golfers can easily walk to the first tee, which is about 500 yards away from No. 8. You can also play tennis free of charge on the hotel's clay tennis court or on the courts at Port Royal. Fitness rooms on the property give you complimentary access to a treadmill, Cross Trainer, Nordic Track, two exercise bikes, weights and a stair machine. Feel like

exploring Bermuda? Hire a moped or a scooter from the on-site rental center.

And now to the accommodations. The clubhouse, otherwise known as the main building, houses reception, the Cedar Room for dining (no smoking allowed here), delightful lounge areas and the Foc'sle Bar (smoking allowed but no cigars or pipes). All offer spectacular views of the ocean. Because Pompano is situated on a southwest peninsula, all offer terrific views of sunsets as well. Breakfast and a five-course dinner are served in the dining room (see our Restaurants chapter). During the summer months, weekly barbecues are held by the pool and swizzle parties are held in the lounge. Every night, you can depend on live music, which ranges from a five-piece band to a steel drum duo, from piano to Calypso guitar music. In winter, live entertainment depends on occupancy. Pompano Beach Club, by the way, is a member of the Bermuda Collection (see our Cottage Colonies chapter for more details of this dine-around plan), which means you can use your MAP to dine at any of the other four restaurant members. The rate we quote includes breakfast. MAP costs $20 a person — an excellent value.

Rooms are in double-storied pink buildings that are clustered on a hillside. With spacious living areas, they come with rattan furnishings, king-size bed, telephone with data port, Internet access and safe, clock-radio, refrigerator, coffee maker and cable television. Clothes are crumpled? Then the iron and ironing board will come in handy. Bathrooms have a shower and tub, hairdryer and bathrobe. All rooms have private patios or balconies, and all overlook the ocean. If you don't feel like being sociable first thing in the morning, have your continental breakfast there. Be aware, though — other than breakfast delivery, there is no room service. You can, incidentally, smoke in your rooms.

Kids are very welcome here. There are no organized activities, but the swimming and the sand bar are ideal for them. Babysitters can be arranged for an additional charge. Children younger than 4 are charged $30 per night MAP; younger than 12, they pay $50 MAP and older than 12, the charge is $70. Rollaway beds and cribs are complimentary.

Guests typically book by calling Pompano

directly. For high-season reservations, book at least three weeks in advance. You should know that for summer season and public holidays, the hotel sometimes requires a minimum stay of four nights. Because of local functions, the restaurant is closed to hotel guests from December 5 through Christmas Day. That date may change, so check with the hotel if you want to stay in December. Pompano's summer season is May 1 to November 14. Winter season is from November 15 to March 31. The shoulder season is during the month of April. A first- and last-night deposit is required, and it is non-refundable if you cancel within 21 days of your scheduled arrival. Gratuity is 10 percent of your room rate, and a 15 percent gratuity is added to extra drinks, snacks and lunch bills. Check-in is at 2 PM, check-out at noon. However, arrangements can always be made for guests who want to arrive earlier or leave later.

The Reefs
$$$$ • 56 South Rd.
• (441) 238-0222, (800) 742-2008

This hotel certainly lives up to its name. It stands on a cliff overlooking the South Shore reef line and its own private beach, Christian Bay. The clubhouse was originally built in the 1600s. At one point (no one knows when) it was a farmhouse belonging to a man with the illustrious name of Marmaduke Dando. In 1946, the clubhouse was extended and became the main building of a hotel. It still retains some of the original structure and, with its chimneys and white ridged roof, is traditionally Bermudian in appearance.

Inside, you will find friendly reception staff, an elegant, comfortable lounge and bar and a large dining room that stretches across the width of the building. On the south side, it overlooks the terrace and ocean; on the north side, it has a glass house or conservatory extension. Dining here is fairly formal. Except for Mondays and Thursdays, jackets are required in the evening. No smoking is allowed in the dining room, but it's fine in the lounge and bar. While we're talking about dining, we should tell you there are other eating options at The Reefs from May to early November. You can dine on the terrace in front of the clubhouse or at Coconuts, a delightful restaurant on a covered deck right on the beach. Coconuts is a favorite with locals, who often take a break from work and come for lunch. In addition, you can use your MAP to dine at any of the restaurants that are members of the Bermuda Collection (see our Cottage Colonies chapter). In summer, you are guaranteed entertainment every night. A three-piece band will get you dancing in the dining room or on the terrace. Sundays you can join the party on the beach and dance to live soca music. Mondays from 6.30 to 7.30 PM you can join the complimentary management swizzle party. Included in the rate is complimentary afternoon tea, served daily from 4 to 5 PM in the lounge.

Rooms are in double-storied buildings, and each has a balcony or patio overlooking the water and coastline. Staff will deliver full or continental breakfast to your room. If you want an ocean view that is completely unobstructed, be sure to ask for one. All rooms have king beds or two double beds, and all have spacious sitting areas with a pull-out loveseat, dresser and comfortable wicker chairs. Walls are moonstone in color; curtains and bedspreads are bright. Rooms come with safes, telephones and data port, ironing boards and irons, umbrellas, refrigerators and clock-radios. They do not, however, come with televisions. You can get a VCR on request. When you arrive, you'll find two little bottles of black rum, two ginger beers and an instructional leaflet on how to make your own dark and stormy. Alternatively, you can stick to Perrier. A separate vanity area with a sink leads into the bathroom, where there is a shower, tub and an additional sink. Hairdryers and bathrobes are supplied. Breakfast plus *The Royal Gazette* can be delivered to your room if you need time to ease into the day. No other room service is available.

Kids are welcome at The Reefs. If they stay in their parents' rooms and are younger than 5, they pay $36 a day MAP; those younger than 16 are charged $66; those 16 and older pay $86. In addition to the rooms we have described, there are some separate one-, two- and three-bedroom cottages. Call the hotel for those rates. Apart from breakfast, there is no other room service.

The beach means excellent swimming and snorkeling. Masks, flippers and snorkels you can borrow for free. Beach chairs and towels are also on hand. If you'd rather swim in fresh water, the heated swimming pool will be for you. And if you're into serious keep-fit routines, try out the exercise bikes, weights and exercise station in the fitness room. There's a jogging machine, but why jog on a machine when you can jog on a beach? You can play tennis free on the hotel's courts across South Road, directly opposite the property. A cycle livery is also there. Staff will happily help you with golf and watersports arrangements. From the hotel you can rent kayaks ($30 per boat) or for additional recreation try out the shuffleboard.

For summer season months, book at least six months ahead. A first- and last-night deposit is required, and the 21-day cancellation policy applies. Length of stay is a minimum of five nights. Summer season starts April 16 and ends November 7. Winter season goes from December 1 to March 31. There are two shoulder seasons: April 1 to April 16 and November 8 to 30. The price code denotes the MAP rate for two people. If you want breakfast only, deduct $25 per person from your bill. Gratuity is 10 percent of your room rate, and a 15 percent gratuity is added for extra drinks, snacks and lunch bills. Check-in is at 3 PM, check-out at noon. Changing rooms are available for late departures and early arrivals.

Sandys Parish

Willowbank
$$ • 126 Somerset Rd.
• (441) 234-1616, (800) 752-8493

We must tell you immediately that Willowbank is an entirely nonprofit organization. How can this be? Well, in 1960 it was created by a group of Christian trustees who wanted a hotel where people, to quote their motto, "in a hurried and anxious world might find rest, recreation and renewed purpose." Willowbank is, therefore, a nondenominational Christian charitable trust, which under British law cannot allow personal financial profit. Terri Allison, manager, explains it this way: "Profits go back into Willowbank's ministry and are used to maintain and refurbish the property. They are also used to help local charities."

Does religion play a part in your stay at Willowbank? The answer to that question is that it can if you want it to. Morning devotions and a 30-minute "Serendipity" Bible study happen every day in private rooms, but they are optional. "There's absolutely no proselytizing," said Terri, "and no campaigns either. But you know, tranquillity can lead to spiritual reflection. That's true for non-believers as well. Staff are here to talk and to listen, if that's what our guests want." She also made the point that "the personal touch" can be a buzz phrase. "At Willowbank we really do care. It's not just words to us. For example, Mrs. Morag Whitehead, our guest relations director, is a wonderful listener and helps people in all sorts of ways."

Before we describe Willowbank, know that the price we quote offers MAP. No other plan is offered. You'll be pleased to note that other than the 7.25 percent government tax, there are no extra gratuities or room-service charges. As for children, they are more than welcome. If they stay in their parents' rooms and are younger than 2, they stay for free; those younger than 12 are charged $21 per person per day for meals; and those younger than 17 pay $37 per person per day. An extra adult costs $70 a day. Some suites with adjoining rooms for older children are available; call the hotel for those rates.

Willowbank is the one small hotel that has a special program for children. The Willow Kids program operates during July and August for children ages 4 through 12 and offers a variety of activities such as tie-dyeing, fishing and sand-castle building. Children also go swimming and on excursions to places such as the Bermuda Aquarium (see our Kidstuff and Attractions chapters). In the evenings, supervisors are available to look after children who have finished their meals so that parents can enjoy dinner without interruption. Other than charges incurred for bus tickets, drinks or lunches, these supervised activities are free.

Perhaps the main source of recreation and tranquillity here is the beauty of Willowbank's two beaches. One is on Ely's Harbour; the other is on the South Shore, with easy access to the reefs that are close to the beach. Snorkeling is excellent here. (The hotel sells snorkeling equipment but does not rent it.) After breakfast and dinner, guests like to go on a walking tour to the dock and feed the fish with bread. Parrotfish, pompanos, angelfish, sergeant majors — you'll see them all. Early in the mornings, you'll even see green turtles. Birds like Willowbank too. Look out for longtails, bluebirds and yellow-crested night herons. A freshwater outdoor pool (heated in winter), two tennis courts, mallet pool and a ping-pong table offer additional fun.

In the main manor house, which is more than 200 years old, you will find the Loaves and Fishes Dining Room. A full breakfast is served every day except Sunday, when breakfast is continental. Dinner is served in the evenings. Meals are served at one sitting, family style. Guests are seated at round tables and, therefore, are encouraged to talk to one another. An ancient ship's bell announces when food is ready. A Christian grace, by the way, is said at the beginning of every meal. A jacket and tie are required every evening except Tuesday, Thursday and Sunday (except in the hotter months of July and August). No smoking is allowed. In fact, you cannot smoke in any public area of the hotel, including at the beaches and pool. You can smoke in your room. There is no licensed bar, and no liquor is served in the dining room. However, you may consume your own liquor in your room.

Lunch is available at very reasonable prices in the coffee shop for no extra gratuity.

The main house also houses two delightfully furnished lounges with open beams, tray ceilings and fireplaces, private meeting rooms and a library, where complimentary tea is served every afternoon. In addition, there's a video library. Verandahs and patios allow outdoor relaxation.

There's an unusual mixture of entertainment five nights a week in the summer. Along with Calypso music, you will have the opportunity to listen to school and local gospel choirs. Sometimes movies are shown. Entertainment is suitable for the whole family and lasts from about 8:30 to 9:30 PM.

Rooms are in unit blocks spread throughout the grounds. All the rooms in the price range we quote have beautiful ocean views and balconies or terraces. They are also air-conditioned and have ceiling fans. Rooms come with small water heaters for making hot drinks — coffee, tea, etc., are provided. Hairdryers, irons and ironing boards are also provided. There are no televisions in the rooms nor are there telephones. If you absolutely have to watch TV, there's one with local channels in the lounge. A panic alert button in each room will connect you with the office staff in case of an emergency. Some rooms are very wheelchair-accessible and equipped with rails in the bathrooms; call the hotel directly for details. Pets are accepted on request.

For the summer season (April 1 through November 15), book your room about two months in advance. A first- and last-night deposit is required, and the 21-day cancellation policy applies. Check-in is at 2 PM, check-out at noon.

So what do you prefer? The ambiance of a cottage, townhouse or mansion? All are available, so look carefully at our descriptions before making your choice.

Guest Houses

Only the very rich can afford to vacation in Bermuda, right? Wrong. True, we have a wide variety of hotels and cottage colonies for those guests who want luxury. But we also have choices that offer more affordable, comfortable accommodations. See our Housekeeping Cottages and Apartments chapter for one option. The guest house experience is the other.

So what can you expect from a guest house? In our listings we'll describe the features and atmosphere of each because, believe us, they do vary. Why? Because they so often reflect the personalities of the owners who typically live on or near the property and are responsible for running the business. Guest houses can also meet different needs. If you want easy access to shops and restaurants, choose one that is within walking distance of St. George's or Hamilton. If you want quiet and scenic views, opt for one well out of town. All, by the way, are close to bus and/or ferry stops.

So what do you prefer? The ambiance of a cottage, townhouse or mansion? All are available, so look carefully at our descriptions before making your choice. Whatever you choose, though, you will find a relaxed, informal atmosphere that allows easy social mingling with other guests. That's where the breakfast rooms and guest lounges come in. They are often common areas where guests can exchange sightseeing ideas and experiences. Spontaneous parties and singalongs sometimes happen. None of the listed guest houses has a licensed bar, but in all cases you may bring your own beer or liquor to your room or lounge. Some proprietors like to treat you to a complimentary rum swizzle or glass of wine. Smoking policies vary in common areas, but all guest houses except one allow you to smoke in your own rooms. Proprietors are, without exception, happy to help with arrangements for golf, tennis and other activities or to give helpful advice.

All guest houses offer full maid service, so your rooms will be tidied and your beds will be made. Children are welcome in nearly all the guest houses. Where they are not, we will tell you, and we give you rates for kids. Some guest houses take pets on request; some do not. We will specify the pet policies in the listings.

Facilities and Meals

Before we go to our listings, we should tell you that with one exception these accommodations do not have facilities suitable for guests completely confined to wheelchairs. (See our Close-up on Summerhaven in this chapter for an alternative.) If you use a walker, however, some of the listings could work for you. Call the guest house directly to discuss details about steps and access so that you can be assured the accommodation will suit your needs.

Typically, the room rate includes either a full breakfast or a generous continental one. When there's an exception, we'll tell you. Generally no other meal plan is offered. However, in most cases guests have access to a refrigerator, ice maker and coffeepot or kettle. In some cases they also have access to a kitchen or kitchenette. If kitchen facilities are important to you, check out our Housekeeping Cottages and Apartments chapter for more options. But if you'd rather eat out, ask the proprietor for information on affordable restaurants and, of course, explore our Restaurants chapter.

Most rooms come with private bathrooms. Where they do not, we will tell you. Some bathrooms may have showers only. Again, we will stipulate in each of the listings whether tubs are included or not. Hairdryers and ironing boards in every case are made available upon request.

Seasonality, Reservations and Cancellation Policy

Some guest houses have two seasons: summer and winter. Typically, the summer season runs from the beginning of April to the end of October, but dates can vary. We will be specific in the listings. Often, though not always, rates can be lower in the winter season. Other guest houses close for two months in the winter. Again, we will tell you if that is the policy.

Because of the personal atmosphere of these guest houses, the owners often have a loyal following of guests. Repeat business is very characteristic, and many visitors reserve for next year's vacation when they check out. Having said that, it is always worth calling on the spur of the moment since last-minute cancellations can happen. We will provide the suggested length of advance notice needed for reservations.

Generally speaking, proprietors require a two-night deposit; this deposit is usually refundable if you cancel up to 14 or 21 days, depending on the guest house's policy, before your reservation date. Be aware that some do not accept credit cards; we will specify this policy in the listings. In addition, some will accept personal checks for deposits only. Travelers' checks, cash or money orders are often preferred. Guests, by the way, usually reserve by calling direct.

Rates

With one exception, the rates provided include room and breakfast. We want to emphasize that a lower dollar-sign code for the price of a guest house does not necessarily mean a lower standard of accommodation. For one thing, all properties taking six or more guests are licensed by the Bermuda government's Department of Tourism. To retain that license, they have to pass strict annual inspections by tourism, health and fire inspectors. Winners of the government's annual Cedar Tree Award are recognized for achieving very high standards in these areas.

Pricing Key

The daily rates listed in the pricing key are based on the rooms visitors would most typically reserve during the summer season. Rates do not include the 7.25 percent per room Bermuda government hotel occupancy tax, gratuities or additional charges for telephone calls. Bear in mind that gratuity policies can differ, so they will be stated in each listing. Rates are always subject to change.

$	$90 to $111
$$	$112 to $120
$$$	$121 to $130
$$$$	$131 and higher

Guest House Listings

The accommodations included are listed in order from east to west, parish by parish, subset by subset and thereafter in alphabetical order.

St. George's Parish

Aunt Nea's Inn at Hillcrest
$$$ • 1 Nea's Alley, Old Maid's Ln., Town of St. George • (441) 297-1630

Before we describe this inn, you might like to be introduced to Nea. The alley where she lived may be off Old Maid's Lane, but there was nothing old-maidish about her at all. She was married to a William Tucker and had children by him. When Irish poet Thomas Moore arrived in 1803, she succumbed to his charms, much to the distress of her husband. It was probably just as well that Moore stayed in Bermuda just four months. Anyway, poor Nea died in 1817, at the young age of 31.

This gracious two-story house (probably built somewhere between 1750 and 1760, with additions in the nineteenth century) is steeped in history. The original owner was one Richard Pruden, a shipper and possibly a sea captain. He wasn't as prudent as his name suggests — he was probably involved in privateering.

Situated on a hill, the guest house has an upper and a lower verandah that both overlook St. George's Harbour. When it is busy, owner and manager Delaey Robinson likes to crack open a couple of complimentary bottles of wine and invite his guests to sit on the top verandah and exchange stories. Delaey has been involved in research covering all aspects of Bermuda. If the history of St. George's intrigues you, Delaey will most likely be able to tell you stories that will intrigue you still more, including the one about Nea.

All but two of the 10 rooms have bathrooms with tubs, showers and sinks. The remaining two have showers only. For an additional $10 per day, you can have one of the five bedrooms equipped with a Jacuzzi bath. The guest rooms all feature unusual four-poster beds. Some are handmade out of wrought iron while others are wooden with cotton canopies. In addition, there are sleigh beds that look like — well, let's say Santa Claus would find them comfortable, and so will you.

You'll enjoy the old paneling and staircase at Nea's and the interesting mixture of furniture styles, which includes the antique and the Oriental. Each room has a special name with ornaments or artwork that relate to it. You'll find a tree frog sculpture, for example, in the Tree Frog room. Rooms come with air conditioning, sets of drawers (often hand painted), a desk or vanity, rails for towels, clock-radios, bathrobes, shower caps and toiletries. No television, though. If you must, you can watch it in the downstairs lounge. One suite with a bedroom, upper lounge and bathroom is also available for $180.

The room price covers a continental breakfast (freshly baked goodies along with cereal, fruit and juice, coffee or tea), which you enjoy in the coffee nook off the downstairs lounge. During the day, tea and coffee (iced or hot) are always available for no extra charge. And you may use the refrigerator. You may not, by the way, smoke in any room in the building. However, you can smoke outside on the verandahs.

Kids are welcome, particularly older ones. Younger than 12, they stay for much lower rates. Call directly for information about ac-

commodating the kids. A 10 percent service charge is added to the room rate. Check-in is at 1 PM, check-out at 11 AM.

Aunt Nea's Inn is within easy reach of St. George's historic attractions, but it is also within reach of Tobacco Bay, St. Catherine's Beach and Achilles Beach. Book your room by calling the hotel directly. A two-night deposit is required, and you'll lose it if you cancel within 14 days of your arrival date. For public holidays, book at least two months ahead. Otherwise, reservations should be made one month in advance. Major credit cards are accepted.

Pembroke Parish

Edgehill Manor Guest House
$$$, no credit cards • 36 Rosemont Ave. • (441) 295-7124

Yes, Edgehill does have manorial proportions. Built more than 100 years ago, it was once a private mansion. The present owner, Bridget Marshall, runs it as a guest house, together with manager Julie Burford. The room rate used in our code covers continental breakfast, which is served in the dining room that's charmingly decorated with floral wallpaper — an amazing feat when you consider the humidity of Bermuda's climate. It contrasts nicely with the dark wood of the doors. Guests often use this room for playing games such as Monopoly or cards.

Guest rooms, located upstairs and downstairs, are as airy and spacious as you would expect to find in a manor house. All nine double rooms have extra beds or pull-out sofas for extra guests. Kids are welcome — those younger than 2 stay free; between ages 2 and 15, there is a $15 charge. An extra adult costs $20. All rooms covered by our pricing code have balconies or terraces with garden views. One on the lower level has its own private entrance. All these rooms have air conditioning and come with a ceiling fan, cable television and a clock-radio. Two have private telephones. (A pay telephone is available downstairs for guests without phones.) All rooms have private bathrooms with showers, and all but one have tubs.

Smoking is allowed everywhere, but Maria says smokers tend to go outside. Edgehill is ideally situated for easy access to Hamilton's shops and restaurants. But even though Hamilton is just a seven-minute walk away, the guest house has the secluded atmosphere of Bermuda's countryside. An outdoor fresh-water swimming pool by the side of the house will let you cool down after a busy day's shopping.

Summer season runs from April 15 through November 15. Book at least two weeks in advance. A two-night deposit is required within 10 days of making a reservation. You can pay your deposit with a personal check, but you should pay your final bill with travelers' checks, money orders or cash. A 10 percent service charge is added to your bill. Check-in and check-out times are at 11:30 AM.

Fordham Hall
$$ • 53 Pitts Bay Rd.
• (441) 295-1551, (800) 537-4163

Built in 1850, this guest house has the high ceilings and spaciousness of a comfortable nineteenth-century townhouse. In fact, in 1920 the Prince of Wales felt so comfortable that he apparently had lunch here. (That Prince of Wales, incidentally, became Edward VIII in 1936, abdicated in the same year and subsequently became the Duke of Windsor.) A 10-minute walk from Hamilton, Fordham Hall is ideal if you want easy access to the city's shops and restaurants.

The guest lounge is huge. With walls painted moonstone (off-white) and woodwork turquoise, it has a lovely bay window complete with a curved window seat. Chairs are comfortable, and there are plenty of books plus cable television. There is no smoking in the lounge or in the breakfast room, which gives you access to a fridge, ice maker, microwave and tea and coffee all day. Here you will enjoy continental breakfast as well as a clear view of Hamilton Harbour. You also may notice some hooks in the walls. While Admiralty House was being built in 1850 (see our Beaches chapter), British admirals used to sleep in hammocks in this room, hence the hooks.

The 12 guest rooms include one extremely large bedroom with a pull-out couch for an additional guest. Kids, by the way, are welcome. Call the guest house directly for rates. All rooms have either queen or double beds, private bathrooms (just one has no tub — only a shower) and air conditioning. They come with television, clock-radio and coffee maker. Some have a good view of the harbor.

For summer season and public holidays, try to book at least one month ahead. A two-night deposit (credit cards acceptable) is required, and a 14-day cancellation policy applies. Service charge is 10 percent per room. Check-in is flexible; check-out is 11 AM.

Hi-Roy Guest House
$$, no credit cards
• 22 Princess Estate Rd.
• (441) 292-0808

Why Hi-Roy? Everard Jones, owner and manager, will be happy to explain to you the reason for the name. He says, "'Hi' is for my wife, Hyacinth. When she was alive, she used to run the guest house. We ran it together. And people would call her Hi. For some reason, many people would call me Elroy instead of Everard. That's where the 'Roy' comes from."

So now you know. But what does he like to be called these days? Jonesy, and that's how we'll address him from now on. He has four loves: Bermuda, people, cooking and music. Jonesy makes no bones about it: "We live in the most beautiful place on this planet." By the end of their first stay, he has most of his guests convinced — that's why they tend to come back over and over again. When they arrive, he treats them to a complimentary rum swizzle or a dark and stormy (rum mixed with ginger beer); then he shows them the view.

Hi-Roy is on a hill overlooking the North Shore. Sit outside in the lawn seating areas or on the guest balcony, and you can watch the cruise ships gliding into Bermuda. You also can watch them while you're in the enclosed glass sun porch dining room, eating Jonesy's home-baked rolls for breakfast. Breakfast, by the way, is different every day. Sometimes you will be treated to salmon cooked with Bermuda onions and Bermuda tomatoes that he grows in his garden. "People get tired of eggs," he says. Breakfast is included in the price-code rate, but Hi-Roy is the only guest house in Bermuda that offers a MAP plan. If you've read the Resort Hotels chapter, you know that MAP means Modified American Plan and offers room, breakfast and dinner for one price. Jonesy's MAP costs $140 for two, and there is a different dinner every evening. Typically, the meal will include potatoes and two other fresh vegetables, often culled from his garden, and meat or Bermuda fish. Dessert could be homemade apple, lemon, blackberry or peach pie. Jonesy makes sure he finds out guests' special likes and dislikes where food is concerned. He also provides a complimentary glass of wine with dinner.

In addition to the sun porch, there's another dining room with a large table where guests like to play cards. There's a lounge with cable TV, a large curved sofa and comfortable chairs. Off the dining room, there's a "family bar" that guests can stock with their own alcohol. As well as being a teller of Bermuda stories, Jonesy is a serious jazz pundit. In fact, from time to time he has his own jazz program on local radio. The extremely good news is that he has a music room full of tapes and CDs. If you like jazz, he will invite you to listen to music here. Chances are you'll hear John Coltrane or Miles Davis — his favorites. And if you like boxing or basketball, you can watch them on the 60-inch TV in this room.

All five guest rooms have two twin beds and one double. They all have garden views and come with bathrooms (one has a tub — the others have showers only). They also have

clock-radios, cable television, ceiling fans and air conditioning. Children are welcome. There's one "family room" that actually consists of two rooms with an adjoining door. Kids younger than 2 stay for free; those 12 and younger stay for $28. Smoking is allowed outside and in the rooms but nowhere else.

The rates for Hi-Roy are the same year-round. Mid-November to mid-December, the guest house closes for refurbishing, but it is always open in time for Christmas. A two-night deposit is required, which you may pay with a personal check. However, you must pay your total bill with travelers' checks, cash or money order. Check-in is flexible. Check-out is at noon.

Oxford House
$$$$ • 20 Woodbourne Ave., Hamilton
• (441) 295-0503, (800) 548-7758

Winner of the Bermuda government's Cedar Tree merit award in 1996, 1997 and 1998, Mrs. Ann Smith prides herself on maintaining the high standards required by health, fire and tourism inspectors.

Built in 1938, Oxford House was apparently the first custom-designed guest house in Bermuda. Walk through the front entrance and you are in a lounge area that has comfortable chairs and round tables where you can enjoy continental breakfast, served buffet-style. It includes eggs that are boiled in a pan on the table. We mention this because you will be introduced to the curious British habit of eating an egg in a special egg cup. You will also be introduced to Staffordshire fine china. Ann makes sure your tea is served in thin china cups — it makes all the difference to the taste.

A curving staircase takes you up to an-

INSIDERS' TIP

If you choose a boiled egg for breakfast, you may well be presented with a special egg cup, used particularly by the British. Here's how to eat a boiled egg British style: Do not shell it first. Place the egg, pointed side up, in the cup. Holding the cup with one hand, take a teaspoon in the other and give the top of the egg a smart tap. You should then be able to easily slice off the top, which now resembles a small cap. Use your teaspoon to scoop and eat the white from the cap. Sprinkle salt and pepper on top of the yolk left in the shell in the cup. Scoop and eat again until you are left with an empty shell.

other charming seating area and to the bedrooms. The rate in our pricing code refers to a double room. However, rooms for three and four are available at approximately $40 extra per person. Children are welcome, and they stay for free if they are younger than 3. Cribs are supplied. Each room is individually furnished with bright English print drapes and bedspreads. English antique desks and chests add to the British ambiance. Beds are king-, queen- and twin-size — whichever you request. All rooms are air-conditioned and come with cable television, direct-dial phones, radios and tea and coffee makers. Each room also has a private bathroom supplied with soaps, tissues and face cloths. Hairdryers and irons are available on request. Freshly cut flowers greet you when you arrive, and honeymooners receive a free bottle of wine. Ann has a relaxed smoking policy throughout the guest house, but she says that so few people smoke these days, it's not really an issue.

Oxford is also popular because it is just a three-minute walk from Hamilton's shops and restaurants. It's the one guest house that is within the city's boundaries. The summer season starts March 16 and ends November 30. Book your room at least two months in advance. A two-night deposit is required, which you lose if you cancel within 14 days of your arrival date. A 10 percent service charge is added to your bill. Major credit cards are accepted. Check-in is at noon, check-out at 11:30 AM.

Paget Parish

Little Pomander Guest House
$$ • 16 Pomander Rd.
• (441) 236-7635

Little Pomander is a delightful house situated on a picturesque country road, one side of which overlooks Hamilton Harbour. Owner and manager Patricia Harvey says that it was built about 360 years ago. "It may have been one of the first houses to have been built this end of the island," she says. Its location means that you can enjoy seclusion while being just a five-minute drive away from Hamilton's restaurants and shops.

Walk through the entrance, and to your

left you'll find a charming guest lounge with sofas and chairs. An archway divides it from the dining room where you will enjoy a continental breakfast. You have access to the refrigerator here but not to the kitchen. Since all bedrooms are supplied with microwaves and refrigerators, this does not present a problem. While we're talking about rooms, we should mention that they all have private bathrooms with showers and tubs. They also come with telephones, cable television and a clock-radio. Some feature old fireplaces that, for now, are ornamental. "My dream," says Patricia, "is to get them working again."

Rooms are spotless and bright. One has an extra-large bathroom and is suitable for guests in wheelchairs. Another room can easily accommodate four people since it has two pull-out sofas and a king bed. Kids are welcome. Younger than 2, they stay for free; younger than 12, they stay for $15. An extra adult pays $30. Five of the six rooms have a view of the harbour. You may smoke anywhere on the property.

For at least one evening of your stay, make sure you sit out on the front lawn. Take in the harbour view and watch the sunset that bathes the water and boats with a pink glow. If you're a tennis fan, for just $10 you may join the Pomander Gate Tennis Club on the other side of the road. Membership lasts the duration of your stay. Once you've paid your membership, for $5 an hour you can play on one of their two courts.

Patricia recommends that you book a month in advance. A two-night deposit is required, which you will lose if you cancel within 21 days of your arrival. A 10 percent service charge is added to your bill. Her summer season starts April 1 and ends October 31. Credit cards are accepted. Check-in and check-out times are flexible.

Loughlands Guest House
$$$, no credit cards • 79 South Rd.
• (441) 236-1253

Mrs. Mary Pickles, owner and manager of this guest house, will tell you about one Mr. Lough (pronounced "Luff"). He was president of the savings bank in Staten Island, and he decided he wanted a private home in Bermuda. In 1920, he had this beautiful mansion built in the middle of 9 acres of grounds. Double-storied and stately, it has often been dubbed "The White House."

Walk into the gracious entrance hall, and you'll see a curving staircase that leads to the bedrooms. Look to the wall above the stairs, and you'll be confronted with a forbidding portrait of Queen Victoria. "We took it down for a while," Mrs. Pickles says, "but the guests wanted her back." She certainly does not cramp their style — an easy, relaxed atmosphere pervades the guest house. Perhaps it is Queen Victoria who influenced the style of the lounge. Located to the left of the staircase, the lounge is a large room with plenty of velvet chairs, books and a fireplace. The Oriental and Lladro figurines would have appeased Victoria's passion for ornamentation. We're not sure what she would have thought of the television, but she would definitely have approved of the no-smoking rule here. To the right of the stairs is the dining room (again, no smoking) where continental breakfast is served every morning. Off the main hall is a big refrigerator and ice maker, specifically for guests.

All 25 rooms are air-conditioned and come with private bathrooms, most of which have tubs (four have showers only). Beds are twin, double or queen. Rooms are equipped with coffee and tea makers and radios. There are no room telephones, but there is a pay phone. For $5 a day, you can have television in your room, where you are allowed to smoke. Kids are welcome, and cribs cost $5 a day. Call directly for details of room and breakfast rates for children. Mrs. Pickles will also accept dogs on request.

Loughlands has a tennis court where you can play for free, and an outdoor, freshwater, unheated swimming pool. Lounge chairs at pool side are good for relaxing, and this property is within easy access of the South Shore beaches (see our Beaches chapter). It also is close to a bus route that can take you to Hamilton or all the way to Dockyard in Sandys Parish.

As is often the case with guest houses, Loughlands has a high repeat-visitor rate. For summer season (April 1 through November 15), book at least three months ahead of time — preferably six months. Credit cards are not accepted here. Travelers' checks, cash or personal checks are fine. A two-night deposit is required, and a 14-day cancellation policy applies. You can check in whenever you arrive. Check-out is at 11 AM.

Que Sera
$, no credit cards • 28 Astwood Rd.
• (441) 236-1998

This little guest house has a garden setting on a quiet road that is opposite the King Edward VII Memorial Hospital. In fact, Mrs. Harriet Grimes started the business because hospital staff asked her to give accommodation either to convalescing patients or to patients' relatives who wanted to visit the ward.

The rate in our pricing code covers the cost of an apartment for two people. It can actually accommodate four people, so double the rate for an additional couple. The apartment has two bedrooms, each with a sitting area, private bathroom and a kitchen equipped with fridge and deep freeze, kettle, coffee maker, toaster and electric stove. Both rooms have cable television, telephones, irons and clock-radios, and both bathrooms have tubs and showers. Hairdryers are available on request. Smoking is allowed throughout the property.

INSIDERS' TIP

Our water supply depends on how much rain we can catch from our roofs. Particularly in the summer months, we try to conserve water. It's not that we run out — if there's a drought, we can buy it. Private water trucking companies deliver water taken from our network of "lens" or underground caves of water. Take showers and baths, by all means, but do be considerate about water. You can help by making sure that you do not leave taps or toilets running. If you notice that a tap drips, be sure to tell your host. A dripping tap can cost more than a drop in the bucket.

The rate does not include breakfast. However, guests can either prepare their own or walk over to the hospital coffee shop, a popular local meeting and eating spot, and enjoy breakfast for reasonable prices. Kids are welcome (check with Harriet for rates — they tend to be flexible), and they will no doubt enjoy the freshwater swimming pool at the back of the property. You can sit in lounge chairs around the pool and enjoy the fragrance of the oleander bushes and frangipanis in the garden. Pets are permitted on request.

The summer season starts at the beginning of March and runs until the end of December. January and February are generally put aside for refurbishing. If you want to stay in the winter months, call directly for room availability and rates. "Book," Harriet says, "as soon as you know." Two nights' deposit is required, which you lose if you cancel within 14 days of your arrival. Que Sera accepts personal checks and cash. Service charge per room is a mere 5 percent. Check-in and check-out times are flexible.

Salt Kettle Guest House and Cottages
$$, no credit cards • 10 Salt Kettle Rd.
• (441) 236-0407

As soon as they reach the arrival hall of the airport, guests of this establishment will see a local taxi driver, Mr. Harris, waiting for them with a Salt Kettle placard in his hand. Salt Kettle owner and manager Hazel Lowe likes to make sure that you are met at the airport. That is just one of the many personal touches that make this guest house so popular. When you arrive at Salt Kettle, Hazel will immediately take you into her inviting kitchen, complete with a large table, plants, family photographs and a gorgeous view of the harbor. There she'll sit you down with an orange juice or coffee and explain how to travel 'round the island (the ferry is a three-minute walk away from the property), where to swim and where to eat at reasonable prices. Within 10 minutes you will feel as if you've known Salt Kettle and Hazel all your life.

So what about the accommodations? The price we quote in our code covers a cottage for two with a spacious living area, bathroom and a kitchen that is fully equipped with stove,

coffee maker, kettle, toaster, blender and refrigerator. In addition, there's a cottage for four (five if you use the pull-out sofa in the living room) and an apartment for two with a separate living room and kitchen. For a lower rate, there are two double rooms with bathrooms in the main house. Guests in these rooms may use a courtesy kitchen that runs parallel to Hazel's. Call Salt Kettle directly for details of those rates.

All rooms are individually furnished and decorated, and with their floral curtains and bedspreads, pictures and cut flower arrangements, they have the charm of an English cottage. A word here about beds. As a former nurse, Hazel knows the importance of a comfortable bed, especially for people who have back problems. Every bed, therefore, has an orthopedic mattress. You can have a king or two twins, depending on your preference. Sheets are fresh and pretty. All rooms have air conditioning and ceiling fans, and two have fireplaces. Some bathrooms have tubs; some do not. If a bath is important, be sure to say so. There are no room telephones, but you can use a pay call box in the main house. Smoking in the rooms is allowed.

All cottages have a view of the harbor. And speaking of views, the property actually has two water views — the front of the guest house looks over picturesque Salt Kettle Bay. (The name "Salt Kettle," incidentally, goes back to the days when many Bermudians were involved with the salt trade — see our History chapter for details.) The grounds reflect Hazel's love of gardening. Throughout you will find vibrant vines (she loves the yellow allamanda most of all), trees and, on her front porch, pots and hanging baskets filled with annuals. There is also plenty of patio and terrace space with comfortable chairs, a hammock and outdoor tables. Fancy cooking a barbecue? Hibachis are on hand.

The rate includes a full breakfast, which is served on a huge antique cedar table at the end of the guest lounge. Beyond that is the enclosed sun porch with small tables and chairs. You can enjoy your breakfast there while gazing at the harbor. The lounge is spacious (you may smoke in it, but not on the porch) with a Bermudian tray ceiling, fireplace and comfortable chairs. Plenty of games and

A Special Place For A Special Event ...

Ascots

Nestled in an English garden setting, Ascots will delight you and your guests with inspiring cuisine which can be savoured under the stars, around the pool, on the verandah or amid the charming atmosphere of our antique-appointed rooms. Plan now for your special event at Ascots. Customised catering service available, on site, or at locations around the Island.

At the Royal Palms Hotel, Rosemont Avenue. Tel: 295-9644.

"A Place not to be missed"
USA Today Bermuda Restaurant Review

Ascots

RESTAURANT
AT
ROYAL PALMS

Located in the Heart of Hamilton

B·E·R·M·U·D·A

Waterloo House

**PITTS BAY ROAD, HAMILTON,
BERMUDA. 1-800-468-4100**

Just a short stroll from the heart of
Hamilton past the Royal Bermuda Yacht
Club stands this early 18th-Century
townhouse in an oasis of peace and tranquility.
Its terraced gardens stretch to the water's edge.
Lunch alfresco on the Poincianna Terrace
overlooking the water or dine in the beautifully
appointed Wellington Room. Sumptuous decor,
fine antiques, award winning gourmet dining, personal service, attention to detail and
Old World Bermudian charm are the hallmarks of this property, one of the Island's
most romantic and sophisticated establishments. (Front Street West on Pitts Bay Road).

Horizons & Cottages

**SOUTH SHORE ROAD, PAGET,
BERMUDA 1-800-468-0022**

Overlooking Coral Beach, this luxury
property embodies the '5 c's' of Relais
& Chateaux:
Character. Courtesy.
Charm. Calm.
Cuisine. Experience
'Old Bermuda'
without sacrificing
any of the amenities.
Enjoy attentive
service in a historic setting with exquisite cuisine.
Combine these creature comforts with the tennis,
squash, gym workouts and watersports of her
sister facility, the Coral Beach and Tennis Club,
and this is the ideal vacation destination.

We'll make you part of our family.

OR CALL YOUR TRAVEL AGENT

Meeting the Challenged

You may notice that opposite John Smith's Bay (see our Beaches chapter), next to Winterhaven Nature Reserve, there's a driveway off the South Road with the sign "Summerhaven" posted. Summerhaven is a first-class residence, specifically designed for the physically challenged.

As we explained in the introduction to this chapter, none of our guest houses have appropriate access and facilities for visitors in wheelchairs. But Summerhaven keeps aside one of its 14 self-contained studio apartments especially for guests from Bermuda and from abroad. That means it is possible for tourists in wheelchairs to vacation in Bermuda at an affordable cost.

Before we go on to describe the residence and facilities, you may like to know the story of Summerhaven. It's an inspiring one that illustrates how philanthropy, determination and courage can triumph over indifference and apathy. According to Mrs. Ianthia Wade, the present administrator, the story started in 1977 when Sir Peter Ramsbotham, together with his wife, arrived in Bermuda to take up his position as governor. Their daughter had been paralyzed in a diving accident, so Lady Ramsbotham took particular interest in the needs of the physically challenged. She quickly discovered that care and facilities for them at the time were woefully inadequate — those who were unable to live at home were forced to stay in the extended-care unit at King Edward VII Hospital. That meant that young people were spending most of their time with the elderly, and that brought about the idea for a specially designed residence to allow a home setting and as much independence as possible for the physically challenged.

Lady Ramsbotham met with Sir Richard Gorham, a Bermudian well-known for his philanthropic interests, and he subsequently took charge of fund-raising. Individual

Close-up

Photo: Liz Jones

Summerhaven is a great housing option for visitors with physical disabilities.

donors, such as impresario Robert Stigwood, and exempt companies generously contributed. So did the Bermuda government, which agreed to a 99-year lease of land for the project and a grant that provided and still provides 85 percent of the operating costs.

The next character to arrive on the scene, Margaret Carter, herself confined to a wheelchair, had founded, and was president of, the Bermuda Physically Handicapped Association. She was a woman of indomitable courage and fierce determination. Although she was financially independent and able to live in her own home, she was extremely sensitive to the needs of others less fortunate. Her suggestions and advice, together with those of the current president of the BPHA, Willard Fox, helped to ensure that Summerhaven was ergonomically designed. In 1983 the residence officially opened.

Enter the house and you will find yourself in a spacious hall that leads to a large, gracious lounge decorated in pastel shades. A fireplace, comfortable furniture and cut flower arrangements and plants help give it a pleasant atmosphere. Fittingly, a portrait of Lady Ramsbotham hangs on the wall. The front of the lounge has easy access to an outdoor patio overlooking the ocean. In addition, there's a kitchen and a dining room where supper is served five nights a week. No smoking is allowed in the dining area, but guests may smoke everywhere else. There are no alcohol restrictions either — residents can buy their own liquor at local stores.

Summerhaven residents live within the house in studio apartments — large living/bedrooms that are equipped with cooking facilities and decorated and furnished according to the individual taste of the occupants. Private telephones are available. Rooms come with large, well-designed bathrooms. Each studio has a patio overlooking the South Shore.

Summerhaven has a bus for residents, conveniently designed with a hydraulic lift and high windows that allow passengers a clear view. Tourists can make arrangements to have a Bermuda tour in this bus. In addition, the BPHA has a bus and a van (usually driven by volunteers) that are available for residents. As was noted, John Smith's Bay is a short distance away. The grounds of Summerhaven are ramped to the roadside and so is the entrance of the beach. Access to John Smith's is easy, and you can borrow a space buggy — a special beach chair that does not sink into the sand — that will let you reach the water. The lifeguard will let you borrow the chair for free. If no lifeguard is there, you can call the Department of Agriculture, Fisheries and Parks at (441) 236-4201. They will deliver a buggy to the beach.

Summerhaven is at 133 South Road in Smiths Parish. Should you be interested in vacationing at Summerhaven, make reservations by calling directly, (441) 293-2099, at least two months ahead of time. Priority, you see, is given to local guests. Be aware that you must be accompanied by an attendant so that staff at Summerhaven can feel assured your particular needs will be met. Although attendants are on hand for residents, there are not enough to assist extra persons. The rate per day for both guest and attendant is $100 total, and it includes supper. Reserve with a one-night deposit. No credit cards or personal checks are accepted, so pay with travelers' checks or cash.

books are on hand. If you have to, you can watch cable television there (just one cottage has its own television). As Hazel explained, the lounge is very important because it gives guests the opportunity to mingle and share their experiences of the day. Every morning, Hazel will greet you here to go over any arrangements you want her to make. You can, for example, join the private Pomander Tennis Club for a $10 fee, then play there for $5 an hour. Hazel loves to host children. Those younger than 1 stay free (a high chair and Victorian crib are available) and those younger than 12 are charged $35 per person.

Reserve by calling Hazel directly. Her summer season starts March 2 and lasts until December 1. Typically, first-time guests will immediately make reservations on departure for their next vacation at Salt Kettle — 95 percent of the visitors are repeat guests, so the earlier you book, the better. Hazel suggests reserving three months in advance. Of course, last minute cancellations make vacancies possible. A deposit of $200 may be paid with travelers' checks, personal checks or cash. There's a 21-day cancellation policy. In addition to your BP rate, there's a 10 percent service charge. Check-in and check-out times are flexible.

The White House
$$, no credit cards • 6 Southlyn Ln.
• (441) 236-4957

First, we must tell you that this listing is, strictly speaking, a bed and breakfast inn rather than a licensed guest house accommodation. Second, it is for adults and not children. Madame Odette Ramond, together with her husband, Monsieur Andre, owns and runs The White House because she enjoys making her guests feel comfortable and welcome. For this reason, she prefers to have no more than five guests at one time. "If I were to have more," she said, "I would have too little time to enjoy them."

With the official approval of the visitors' service bureau, there are three guest rooms, a guest lounge and dining room. The house is just as elegant as its name promises. The lounge features graceful archways and a fireplace that most definitely is used for log fires during the winter. Do take notice of the magnificent Swiss wall clock — 200 years old, its face is set in the middle of a bas-relief of deer carved out of wood. Odette's taste in antique tables and chests accentuates the pleasing proportions of the rooms. The rate includes continental breakfast, which is served in the dining room. Tea and coffee are available all day.

The guest rooms are upstairs. All light and airy with fresh floral curtains and bedspreads, they come with either one double or two twin beds, clock-radio and ceiling fan. They are not air-conditioned, but the thick Bermuda stone walls keep the whole house pleasantly cool. All rooms have private bathrooms with showers. Upstairs you will also find a handy ice maker. There is a freshwater pool outside. Stone walls surround it, giving you privacy.

The White House is ideal if you want an adult, relaxed, informal vacation. As Odette explained, flexibility is what she is about. That's why you can smoke if you wish. It's a three-minute walk to a bus stop, where you can catch a ride to Hamilton or to Dockyard in Sandys Parish. The Paraquet Restaurant is a short distance away and so is a grocery store.

A two-night deposit is required, and a 14-day cancellation policy applies. You may pay your deposit with a personal check, but the final bill must be handled with travelers' checks, a money order or cash. There is no additional service charge or gratuity. Check-in and check-out times are flexible. Madame says to book as soon as possible in advance — six months would be good — although last-minute cancellations can make last-minute vacancies

Southampton Parish

The Greenes' Guest House
$$, no credit cards • 71 Middle Rd.
• (441) 238-0834

Yes, this one is run by the Greene family: Jane and Walter, David and Lisa. Actually, Lisa helps out when she is not studying for her postgraduate degree in psychology. Jane says, "Our aim is to make our guests happy." That's why she often makes gingerbreads, loaves and cookies as extra treats for her visitors. Complimentary alcoholic drinks also are offered from time to time.

The guest house stands by the side of Middle Road, which means it is within easy reach of a bus route that can take you to Hamilton or to Dockyard in Sandys Parish. It is also within reach of Port Royal Golf Course (see our Golf chapter). However, once you walk through the reception area into the guest kitchen, dining and lounge areas, you will forget about the road. Look out the windows, and you'll see the waters of the Great Sound stretching out before you.

Mornings, you may have a full breakfast with eggs, pancakes, etc., in a dining area with attractive blue tablecloths and white Wedgwood china. The dining area, by the way,

Bermuda's frontline ambassadors.

is the only place where you can't smoke. Once breakfast is done you have full access to the kitchen, which is equipped with all the facilities you could possibly need. Coffee makers, stove, microwave, toasters, refrigerator, china, glasses, cutlery — they are all there. Downstairs, there's another large lounge. A dart board, chess boards and radios help to keep guests happy. They have been known to dance inside and also around the pool area. The pool is ideal for children. Half salt water, half fresh, it has a shallow end for nonswimmers. Walk through a moongate covered with bougainvillea, and you'll find a large field that offers plenty of space for ball games. Kids, obviously, are welcome. Call Jane directly for rates.

Three of the six bedrooms have water views; the other three look over the garden. All have private bathrooms with tubs and showers. Painted beige with blue floral drapes and bedspreads, the rooms are comfortable and equipped with an iron, a small fridge, tea and coffee maker and cable television. Honeymooners receive a complimentary bottle of wine on arrival. In addition, there's a two-bedroom, two-bath apartment, complete with living and dining room and kitchen. This apartment looks directly over the Great Sound. If two guests stay there, the rate is covered in the price code; double the rate for four.

Summer season starts April 1 and ends at the end of October. Call Jane directly for winter rates. Required deposit is two nights, payable by personal check. The total bill must be paid in cash, by money order or by travelers checks. A 10 percent service charge is added to your bill, and a 21-day cancellation policy applies. Check-in and check-out times are flexible.

Royal Heights Guest House
$$$ • 4 Crown Hill
• (441) 238-0043

This three-story guest house certainly has reached royal heights. Situated atop a rocky hill, it commands panoramic views of the Great Sound and the Little Sound. It also has reached lofty heights as a lodging option: In 1996 and '97, Royal Heights won the Department of Tourism Award for achieving a consistently high standard of accommodation over a four-year period.

Most owners of guest houses overlooking the ocean are convinced that their view is the best. Mrs. Jean Richardson, who, together with her husband, Russell, is owner and manager here, knows hers is the best. "It's both active and hypnotic," she says. "It's pure Bermuda. Islets, water, boats, rooftops — everything works together." As soon as you walk into the dining area and the guest lounges on the second floor, you will have to agree. Look to your left and you will see the curve of the coastline that stretches to Dockyard. Look to your right and you will see Hamilton Harbour.

You will take continental breakfast in the dining room in the morning. No doubt Jean's generous servings of muffins, pastries, cheese and fresh fruit will distract you for a while from the view. The lounge is spacious, with an oval ceiling and recessed lighting. Outdoor balconies surround it. A television? "No," says Jean very firmly. "A lounge is for chatting." It's also for the occasional impromptu rum swizzle party (complimentary, of course) and for playing the games and reading the books that are available. The other focal point for guests is around the outdoor, saltwater swimming pool. There you can relax on lounge chairs under umbrellas and still enjoy the view.

Two of the six rooms overlook greenery and Gibb's Hill Lighthouse, the remaining rooms have water views. All the rooms have balconies and separate entrances. Some guest rooms are on the first level and overlook the pool; others are on the third level. All rooms have private bathrooms, most of which have tubs and showers. A few rooms have showers only, so ask for a tub if you want one. If you have to watch television, you'll find one in your room (with cable) along with a clock-radio, coffee maker and refrigerator. There are no in-room telephones, but you'll find one in the lounge. Some rooms come with microwaves as well. All are painted moonstone and have floral curtains and spreads. Extra beds or pull-out sofas are available for additional guests. Extra persons are charged $50. One suite has an adjoining room and is ideal for families — call Jean for the suite rates. Kids are welcome (also $50 per person), but Jean says that on the whole her guests are romantic couples. Honeymooners, by the way, receive a complimentary bottle of wine, and seven-night honeymoon specials are available. Call for details. Smoking's fine in your room and the lounge, and Jean will take pets on request.

Royal Heights has just one season: April 1 to November 31. December to March, Jean closes the house. "When you know, let me know," she says of reservations—two months' notice is recommended. A two-night deposit is required, and you will lose it if you cancel within 21 days of your arrival. Major credit cards are accepted. There's a $10 service charge on returned deposits, and a 10 percent service charge is added to your bill.

This option is also ideal for families who prefer to do their own thing rather than being restricted by hotel meal programs.

Housekeeping Cottages and Apartments

So what do we mean by "housekeeping cottages and apartments?" As our Department of Tourism defines them, they are the Bermudian equivalent of "efficiency units." Typically, they offer cooking facilities in a kitchen or kitchenette as well as one or more bedrooms, a bathroom and, in some cases, a living room.

Cooking some meals for yourself means that you can reduce considerably the cost of your vacation, as eating out two or three times a day can get very expensive here. This option is also ideal for families who prefer to do their own thing rather than being restricted by hotel meal programs. Cribs, pullout sofas or extra beds are available for children, and proprietors can usually arrange babysitting. We'll state lodging rates for children in the individual listings, as they can vary enormously.

Since Bermuda has such a large selection of these types of units, we have chosen just a sampling for this chapter. All but one of those listed are licensed by the government's Department of Tourism. To retain the license, owners of these properties have to pass strict annual inspections by tourism, health and fire inspectors. Some accommodations consist of self-contained cottages or of units within cottages, some consist of upper and/or lower apartments in one- or two-story complexes, and others are in a main house that is occupied by the owner and/or manager. Whereas guest houses typically have lounge and dining areas, housekeeping accommodations often do not. However, they generally do have common outdoor areas where you can meet other visitors and perhaps arrange a barbecue together. We'll be very specific about communal areas in our listings.

Facilities and Meals

Some of these properties are suitable for guests in wheelchairs, particularly those visitors who are able to use walkers for a short period of time. However, we suggest you call the proprietor to discuss details of access and bathrooms.

Generally speaking, this category of accommodation offers an EP plan only — that is, room with no meals available at all. Nevertheless, there are exceptions to the rule. A few offer breakfast, and one offers dinner as well. When this is the case, we'll tell you and state the additional costs.

Part of the Department of Tourism's licensing criteria demands that proprietors supply their guests with dishes, pots and pans, cutlery and glassware, so you may assume that these are available, as well as barbecue equipment. Kitchen facilities do vary — some cooking stoves, for example, have top burners only, while others have ovens. Again we'll be specific about this in our listings. Most rooms come with private bathrooms. Where they do not, we will tell you. Some bathrooms may have showers only. Again, we will stipulate in each of the listings whether tubs are included or not.

All the properties have maid service. You may assume that maids will clean and tidy your rooms and make your beds either every day or every other day. However, the policy about washing dishes can vary. Some maids will wash breakfast dishes, some will wash all dishes and others will wash none at all.

You will find that owners and managers are very friendly and willing to advise you on transportation, recreation arrangements, grocery stores and affordable restaurants. Often they will help by driving you to a grocery store, particularly at the start of your stay.

Seasonality, Reservations and Cancellation Policy

Some housekeeping apartments have two seasons (summer and winter), and some have an additional, slower, shoulder season. Typically, the summer season runs from the beginning of April to the end of October, but dates can vary. We will specify them in the listings. Often, though not always, rates are lower in the winter. Other accommodations close from two to three months in the winter. Again, we will tell you if that is the policy.

Because of the personal atmosphere of these properties, owners frequently have a loyal following of guests. Repeat business is very characteristic, and, indeed, many visitors reserve next year's vacation while they are checking out. Having said that, it is still worth calling on the spur of the moment since last-minute cancellations can happen. We will also give you the lead-in reservation times suggested to us. Generally speaking, proprietors require a two-night advance deposit, usually refundable if you cancel more than 14 or 21 days before your reservation date. If credit cards are not accepted, we will tell you in the headings for the listings. Guests, by the way, usually reserve by calling direct.

Pricing Key

The daily rates listed in the pricing key are based on the rooms two adults would most typically reserve during the summer season. They do not include the 7.25 percent per room hotel occupancy tax, gratuities or additional charges for telephone calls. Bear in mind that gratuity policies can differ, so they will be stated in each listing. Rates are always subject to change.

$	$ 90 to $110
$$	$111 to $136
$$$	$137 to $182
$$$$	$183 and higher

Property Listings

As usual, our listings are presented east to west, parish by parish, subset by subset and thereafter in alphabetical order.

St. George's Parish

Taylor House
$ • Aunt Peggy's Ln., Town of St. George • (441) 297-1161

The house is on Aunt Peggy's Lane, which runs between Silk Alley and Old Maid's Lane. It's also closely bounded by Queen Street and Taylor's Alley. Who was Aunt Peggy? According to G. Daniel Blagg in his *Bermuda Atlas and Gazetteer*, Aunt Peggy was said to have been born a slave but eventually had her own house that was featured on turn-of-the-century Bermuda postcards. Apparently she lived to an old age and would sit by an open window so that she could chat with visitors and tell stories of what life was like in the old days. Present owner Mark Rowe is not sure about the origin of the name "Taylor." Early in

St. George's history, there was a postmaster called Taylor, but whether he owned or lived in the house is uncertain.

The outside of the house has white walls and pink trim. Mark, who lives at the east end of the property, has converted the west end into a self-contained guest apartment. Its charm is immediately apparent when you walk through the stable front door into the living room. The ceiling, equipped with fan, is wooden and painted white, while an inset alcove adds to the room's character. The living room, with white walls and pale green woodwork, is charmingly furnished with carpet, a sofa and two comfortable armchairs. Feel like reading? The bookcase will supply you with plenty of material.

A word about the windows: They're of seventeenth-century design and therefore have no counterweights. You can prop them up half open with the sticks provided or open them fully by using the "fish tails" that are screwed on the inside of the window frames. Rotate the fish tail toward you and rest the bottom corner of the sash in the notch. In case you think you're really going back in time, rest assured there's one anachronistic item in this room: the cable television.

A wooden staircase in the living room takes you up to the bedroom, where you'll find a queen-size bed plus one single bed. (However, Mark generally rents the apartment to no more than two guests.) You'll find two side tables, a chest of drawers and a roomy closet. If you're security-conscious, place your valuables in a lockable cupboard. If you like to watch TV in bed, a second television with cable will let you do so. A clock-radio, hairdryer and cordless telephone are on hand. The bedroom has air conditioning.

What about cooking and dining? Go back down to the living room, and on your left you'll see steps that lead down to the kitchen. Double chimneys at one end (they once served as baking ovens) and a single fireplace at the other will once again remind you of the house's age. The fireplace doesn't work because the chimney is blocked, but we're glad it remains since it adds to the charm. . . . So does the dresser where you'll find plates. A little door leads to the water tank where once upon a time you would have dipped water with a

bucket. You'll be glad to know that as much as Mark values the historic appearance of his house, he does believe in modern amenities: These days water runs from a tap. The kitchen is equipped with a full electric stove, microwave, coffee maker, fridge and freezer. There's also an ironing board. You can dine here at a small dining table that has two chairs. On this level you'll also find the bathroom with tub and shower.

Smoking is not permitted in the house, but you can smoke outdoors in the private garden. There you'll find poinsettia, prickly pear, lantana and, when in season, bananas that you're welcome to eat. A table, chairs and umbrella mean you can eat alfresco or simply relax. On Sundays you'll hear the bells of St. Peter's.

Taylor House is ideally located for easy access to golf and beaches, as well as to the restaurants and attractions of the town. Tobacco Bay and Achilles Bay are 15- to 20-minute walks away, while St. George's Golf Club is just a 10-minute walk (see our Beaches and Golf chapters). If you want to explore the rest of the island, you're within reach of a bus route to Hamilton. A grocery store is a five-minute walk away on York Street; if you don't feel like walking, the store offers free delivery.

At any time of the year, Mark's rates are extremely reasonable. They include water, electricity and laundering of linen. For an extra fee, maid service is available once a week. We suggest you call him directly to discuss rates, as they depend on the length of your stay. The daily rate is lower if you stay a minimum of one week. It's also lower in the winter season, which runs from November 1 to April 31. Call Mark to discuss deposits; they, too, depend on the length of your booked stay. A 21-day cancellation policy applies. Check-in and check-out are flexible.

Hamilton Parish

Clear View Suites and Villas
$$$ • Sandy Ln., Crawl Hill
• (441) 293-0484, (800) 468-9600

Come to Clear View and you'll be tempted not to bother visiting other parts of the island. The view of the North Shore is staggering —

even on hazy days you can see forever. Sit out on your private patio or terrace and gaze on nothing but the blues and greens of the ocean. Walk down to the sea and you'll find a small cove, ideal for children, inexperienced swimmers and snorkelers. On the grounds you will also find two swimming pools and a tennis court.

Rooms in the price range we quote all have this view. Some are studios with living areas; others have a separate living room. They all have clock-radios, cable television and private telephones, and they are all air-conditioned. Kitchenettes are supplied with a fridge, electric stove and oven, microwave on request, coffee maker and kettle. Private bathrooms have tubs and showers. Children are welcome at Clear View. If they are younger than 2, the charge is $12 per child per night; between 2 and 12, they pay $24. Extra adults staying in the rooms cost $40. You can, by the way, smoke in your rooms. Mrs. Paynter, owner and manager of the property, says that some of the rooms are accessible to wheelchairs. Call her directly to check that these rooms are suitable for your needs.

Unlike the operators at most of the housekeeping cottages and apartments, Mrs. Paynter offers eating plans. If you want BP (again, that stands for Bermuda Plan), you pay an additional $12 per person per night for full or continental breakfast, which you may have in your room or in the dining room. MAP (Modified American Plan), offering breakfast and dinner, costs $37 a person. Wine and beer are served. You will enjoy dinner in the elegant Landfall Restaurant, an eating venue also popular with locals. And on the property a conference room that has more of a lounge than business atmosphere is available for meetings.

Clear View is ideally located for access to either St. George or Hamilton. A bus route is a few minutes' walk away and will take you to either town. Rent a moped and you can reach Shelly Bay Beach in just two minutes (see our Beaches chapter). A grocery that delivers is nearby. If you're interested in art, you'll find the Clear View's Art Gallery interesting. It features the work of Otto Trott, Mrs. Paynter's son-in-law. He is happy to offer art workshops and individual lessons.

Mrs. Paynter recommends that you book as soon as you know you want to come to the island. She has a very high repeat visitor rate. Incidentally, her rates are the same year-round. "There's no such thing as winter in Bermuda," she says firmly. You'll pay two nights' deposit to reserve, and you will lose it if you cancel within 14 days of your scheduled arrival. Although there is maid service every day, Mrs. Paynter does not have a mandatory service charge. She says that tipping is at the guests' discretion. Check-in is flexible, check-out at 11 AM.

Angel's Grotto
$$$ • 83 Harrington Sound Rd.
• (441) 293-1986

The cottage units in the price range we quote all have water views of Harrington Sound. Guests share access to balconies and a patio, where they can enjoy the water view over breakfast. Can you swim in the sound? Absolutely. A private dock is handy for swimming, fishing and snorkeling. Daisy Hart, owner and manager, will advise you where to hire snorkeling equipment. If you prefer a beach, then John Smith's Bay is just a short walk away. Daisy will also direct you to a convenience store that's a three-minute walk away; another larger store will deliver groceries. The property is right next to a bus route to St. George or Hamilton.

Accommodations here are extremely spacious and well-maintained. Indeed, in 1996, 1997 and 1998 Angel's Grotto won the Department of Tourism's Hibiscus Award for excellent maintenance. The units include a double bedroom, a large living/dining area, a fully equipped kitchen and a private bathroom with a tub and shower. You'll have a queen-size bed or two twins. Sofa beds are available for extra persons. Rooms are all air-conditioned and come with clock-radio, cable television and private telephones. Hairdryers and ironing equipment are available on request. Kitchens have a full-size gas stove with oven, plus a fridge, microwave, coffee maker and toaster oven. Smoking is fine everywhere on the property.

In addition to the accommodations we describe, Daisy has an apartment that can take up to eight people; call for rates. Kids younger than 13 pay $15 dollars a night. Extra adults are $30 a night. Daisy recommends that you book about three months ahead for July and August. Her summer season, incidentally, starts April 1 and runs through November 16. Rates are lower in the winter season. Call direct for those prices. A two-night deposit is required, and you will lose it if you cancel within 21 days of your expected arrival. For service, add 10 percent of your room rate to the final bill. Maids clean guest rooms every day but will wash up only breakfast dishes. Check-in is at 1 PM, check-out at 11 AM.

Pembroke Parish

Robin's Nest
**$, no credit cards • 10 Vale Close
• (441) 292-4347**

First we must tell you that the rate we quote does not change according to season. Summer or winter, Robin's Nest is extremely reasonable considering you will have an apartment consisting of a bedroom, a living room with an adjacent area for extra beds, a kitchen and a bathroom. Three of the four apartments have air conditioning and ceiling fans. Bedrooms have queen, king or two twin beds, clock-radios and private telephones for local calls. (You may not smoke in your bedroom, but you may everywhere else.) Bathrooms all have tubs as well as showers, and hairdryers are available on request.

Kitchens are fully equipped, most of them with an electric stove (one has gas), fridge with large freezer, coffee maker, iron and ironing board and microwave (on request). Open the fridge when you arrive, and you'll see that owners and managers Milt and Reneé Robinson have left you a few complimentary drinks. Living rooms are spacious and come with wicker furniture and cable television. Each unit has a private outdoor seating area with table and chairs in a garden setting. Hibachis are available if you feel like a barbecue. A freshwater swimming pool in a separate garden area will cool you down after a trip to town. Robin's Nest is near a bus route that will take you to Hamilton. It's also close to a grocery store on the North Shore and to Clarence Cove Beach (see our Beaches chapter).

Kids are welcome at Robin's Nest. The charge if they are younger than 12 is $10 per person per night. Those older than 12 pay the extra adult rate of $30 per person per night. Three apartments, by the way, can accommodate two couples each. For four people, double the rate we quote. One apartment could be suitable for guests who use wheelchairs but can walk a little. Call Renée to make sure it suits your needs.

Renée recommends that you book about two months ahead, as she has a high repeat visitor rate. Cancel within two weeks of your expected visit, and you lose your two-night deposit. Add a service charge of 10 percent of your room rate to your final bill. Maid service, by the way, happens every other day, and the housekeepers will wash breakfast dishes. Check-in is flexible; check-out is at noon.

Rosemont Guest Apartments
**$$ • 41 Rosemont Ave.
• (411) 292-1055, (800) 367-0040**

If you're looking for easy access to Hamilton, an apartment at this property may well be for you. Before the days of motorized travel, Rosemont Avenue was a highly elite residential area, mostly because horses and carriages could easily get from there to the city. A five-minute walk will take you to town. Sisters Karen and Lorri Cooper, Rosemont's owners and managers, want you to enjoy the atmosphere of the traditional Bermudian family. They will be happy to make various recreational arrangements for you and to advise you on reasonable restaurants.

Air-conditioned rooms have seating areas and come with king or two twin beds, cable television, telephone with dataport and iron and ironing board. They are cheerfully deco-

---

INSIDERS' TIP

Electricity is very expensive in Bermuda. You can help keep costs down by making sure you close doors and windows when the air conditioner is running.

rated with white walls, floral curtains and blue bedspreads. Bathrooms have showers, tubs and hairdryers. In most cases, kitchens are separate and equipped with electric stove and oven, coffee maker, kettle, toaster and a small fridge with freezer. Need a microwave? You can use the one in the office. Maids visit daily and will wash dishes.

All rooms have private balconies overlooking the garden or the pool. In the garden you will see poinciana, citrus and banana trees. Naturally, Karen and Lorri will let you enjoy the fresh fruit when it's in season. The outdoor, unheated pool will cool you down after a shopping spree in Hamilton.

Kids are absolutely welcome. If they stay in their parents' rooms and are younger than 13, the charge is $20 a day. If they are 13 or older, they pay $25. The children sleep in cribs or on rollaway beds, or you may ask for adjoining rooms. We must tell you that this property has facilities for guests in wheelchairs. Bathrooms are specially equipped with railings and bench seats, and the garden is wheelchair accessible. The only drawback is that Rosemont is on top of a hill. We suggest you call the guest house for advice. Also, no smoking is allowed in the rooms or the lounge area.

For the summer season (April 1 until November 30), book at least one month ahead. A two-night deposit is required, which you will lose if you cancel within 14 days of your scheduled holiday. There is a service charge of $6 per person per day ($3 per extra person). Check-in is at 3 PM, check-out at noon.

Paget Parish

Barnsdale Guest Apartments
$$ • 2 Barnes Valley,
off Middle Rd.
• (441) 236-0164

This property is run by sisters Jane and Jennifer Conyers, winners of the 1998 Buttery Award from the Department of Tourism for a consistently high standard of accommodation. When you arrive, one of the sisters will take at least half an hour to introduce you to Barnsdale and to Bermuda's attractions.

Accommodations are studio apartments with an open-plan bed/sitting room, kitchenette and separate bathroom. Rooms are air-conditioned (with units that heat the rooms in winter) and have ceiling fans. They come with clock-radio, cable television, telephone, hairdryer and iron and ironing board. Beds are mostly queen-size, though two apartments have kings or two twins. Pull-out sofas in the seating area can also sleep two persons. Kids are welcome, and they stay free if they are younger than 4. If one parent and a child older than 4 come to stay, that counts as double-occupancy. Every extra person older than 4, in fact, costs $25 a night. Some rooms could be suitable for guests in wheelchairs; call Jane or Jennifer to discuss whether they are suitable for your needs. Smoking, by the way, is allowed everywhere.

Rooms are painted white, and windows have valences and venetian blinds that create a light and airy effect. Floors are mostly tiled. No studio, however, is decorated exactly the same. Some bathrooms have tubs; two out of the five studios do not. If you want a tub, be sure to ask for one. Kitchenettes have two-burner stove tops, large toasters, apartment fridges and, on request, microwaves. A few studios have full kitchens with ovens. Tell Jane or Jennifer if you want one. Need coffee first thing in the morning? The stove percolator will provide it. Meals are taken in a seating area with table and chairs in the kitchenette, or you can eat in the garden-view seating areas around the outdoor freshwater pool.

Barnsdale is centrally located. It's on a bus route that will take you to Hamilton or Sandys, and it's a 10-minute walk to a ferry stop. A five-minute walk will take you to the Modern Mart grocery store. More importantly, a 15-minute

INSIDERS' TIP

On Wednesdays, some of Bermuda's supermarkets have a 5 percent reduction on the price of goods (other than liquor and cigarettes). Check grocery store ads in *The Royal Gazette* for details.

Dawkins Manor You'll find Dawkins Manor to be the perfect vacation spot. Tucked away amidst the flowering rural lanes of Paget, yet minutes from South Shore beaches, restaurant shops and cycle liveries. The nearby bus stop will take you to the City of Hamilton in 10 minutes or 5 minutes by moped for shopping and entertainment. Guest rooms have private baths and kitchens. Family suites available. Patio & Pool.

Mrs. Celia Dawkins

Dawkins Manor, 29 St. Michael's Road Paget PG04 Tel: (441) 236-7419 Fax: 236-7088

walk will take you to Elbow Beach (see our Beaches chapter). If you're feeling adventurous, you can rent a moped from a cycle livery just down the road.

Summer season runs from April 1 until October 31. Be aware that if two or more guests stay in one studio for a week during the summer season, they get their seventh night free. During the winter season, visitors all get the fifth night free and can take advantage of long stay winter specials. Call to discuss winter rates. A two-night deposit is required, which you will lose if you cancel within 21 days of your expected arrival. Add 10 percent of the room rate to the final bill for service charge. Maids come every day, but they do not wash dishes. Check-in is at 2 PM; check-out is 11 AM. However, Barnsdale allows a 5:30 PM check-out for guests departing on the British Airways flight to London.

Dawkins Manor
$$$ • 29 St. Michael's Rd.
• (441) 236-7419

Dawkins Manor has two categories of accommodations. For the lower end of the price code we quote, you can stay in a spacious bed/sitting room with a separate bathroom that has a tub and shower. The room comes with air conditioning, king bed, coffee table and chairs, telephone, clock-radio, cable television, iron and ironing board. There's no kitchen,

but you will have a refrigerator, hot pot for making drinks and some dishes and cutlery, so homemade breakfast and snacks are possible. Some rooms may be suitable for guests in wheelchairs. Call Celia Dawkins, owner and manager, to check for details.

At the higher end of the rate range, you can get a suite consisting of a bedroom, separate kitchen with a sitting/dining area and a private bathroom with tub and shower. Again, the bed is a king. The kitchen is equipped with an electric stove and oven, microwave, coffee maker and toaster. A private patio overlooks the freshwater pool in a garden setting.

A guest lounge has cable television, a supply of books and, of course, plenty of comfortable chairs and sofas. A coin-operated laundry makes washing clothes easy. The property is centrally located. A two-minute walk will get you to the Modern Mart grocery store, and a five-minute one will get you to Elbow Beach (see our Beaches chapter). Work permitting, Celia will give you a ride in her car to Hamilton, particularly if it is raining. Children are welcome at Dawkins Manor. If they are ages 4 through 12, the charge is $25 a night. If they are younger than 4 and need a crib, the charge is $15 a night; otherwise, the very young ones stay for free.

Book for the off-season as soon as you know you're coming. For summer season (March 15 to November 30) Celia recommends booking three months in advance with a two-night deposit that you will lose if you cancel within 21 days of your arrival date. Add 10 percent of your room rate to your final bill for maid service. Maids come every day and are willing to wash dishes. Check-in is at 1 PM, check-out at 11 AM.

Grape Bay Cottages

$$$$ • Grape Bay Dr. (off Middle Rd.)
• (441) 236-1194

If your idea of bliss is to live in splendid isolation in a detached cottage right on the sea, then think about Grape Bay Cottages. There are two of them, each with a living/dining room, kitchen, two bedrooms, a private bathroom (with shower and tub) and a shady verandah overlooking the ocean. The first thing you will hear in the morning is the hushed song of the sea calling you to hurry up and have that pre-breakfast swim. Grape Bay is one of Bermuda's more secluded beaches, so you won't find yourself inadvertently sunbathing cheek to cheek with a perfect stranger. It can, however, have an undertow during windy weather. (Check the Beaches chapter for information about currents on the South Shore beaches.)

The cottages are spacious enough to comfortably accommodate two families of up to six adults. The rate for each cottage is $300 a night and covers up to four people. Extra adults cost $35 per person per night. Up to six persons can stay in a cottage. Of course, kids are welcome. If they are younger than 2, they stay free; younger than 12, the charge is $20 per night. Rooms are air-conditioned, have ceiling fans and come with a telephone, local television and clock-radio. Irons and ironing boards are available.

Kitchens are fully equipped with a four-burner electric stove and oven, big refrigerator, toaster, coffee maker and microwave. Incidentally, because Grape Bay Cottages is about a 15-minute walk away from a grocery store, staff will be happy to buy groceries for you in time for your arrival. Fax them at (441)

236-1662 with details of what you would like. You'll reimburse them for the groceries, of course, but you won't be charged extra for the service. They can also advise you on public transportation and will recommend hiring a moped for easier access to Hamilton and Bermuda's attractions.

What about maid service? You'll probably meet Gwen Saltus, who has been looking after the cottages for 28 years. As she says, "I've watched guests' children grow up and get married. Now they're back with their own kids." Gwen will tidy up every day except Sunday, but dishes are the guests' responsibility. Smoking, by the way, is fine.

Because these cottages are popular in winter and summer, the staff recommends that you book at least six months in advance. Summer season starts April 1 and extends to November 16. When you make your reservation, you'll be asked for a credit card number, which is held until your two-night deposit is received. You lose your deposit if you cancel within 21 days of your expected arrival date. Add 10 percent of the cottage rate for the service charge. Check-in is flexible; check-out is at 11 AM.

Greenbank and Cottages

$$ • Salt Kettle Rd.
• (441) 236-3615

A word about Salt Kettle before we describe this property. A peninsula protruding out into Hamilton Harbour, Salt Kettle was one of the first settlements on the harbor side. Its name goes back to the days when Bermudians involved with the salt trade made salt pans. Today it is a very quiet, picturesque part of Bermuda and an ideal location for a restful holiday.

Greenbank is a beautiful 200-year-old house. There you will find the office and a large guest lounge with tray ceilings, charmingly furnished in English country style. Guest singalongs sometimes happen 'round the piano here. Plenty of comfortable chairs and sofas will help you relax. If you must, you can

INSIDERS' TIP

Try not to leave dirty dishes overnight. They attract cockroaches, ants and other creepy-crawlies.

watch television there. For a lower rate than the one we quote in the price code, guests can stay in one of the two double rooms with private bathrooms in the main house. These rooms have refrigerators and coffeepots, but they do not have full kitchen facilities. For that reason, lower rates include continental breakfast. Accommodations in the range covered by the price code all have kitchens. With those units, breakfast is not included.

The accommodations represented in our price code consist of cottages with a bedroom/sitting room, a bathroom and kitchen. You'll have a king, queen or two twin beds, and living areas have a table and dining chairs plus two other comfortable chairs. All cottages have telephones and clock-radios; umbrellas, ironing boards and irons are available on request. Some bathrooms have tubs as well as showers; some do not. Be sure to request a tub if you want one. Kitchens are equipped with gas or electric stoves with ovens, plus a toaster, refrigerator and coffee maker. Loungers, chairs and tables on your patio will let you enjoy the view. Smoking is allowed throughout.

If a cruise in a yacht or motor cruiser appeals to you, take advantage of Salt Kettle Yacht Charters, which is right on the property (see our Yachting and Marinas and Watersports chapters). Or you can swim off Greenbank's private dock. Greenbank is not near a bus route, but it's just a minute's walk away from Salt Kettle ferry stop. When you take a ferry to Hamilton, you might like to consider that in 1867 Salt Kettle was the first place on the island to operate a steam ferry.

Kids are definitely welcome, and cribs are available. Call Greenbank for childrens' rates. An extra adult pays $25 a night. Note that, for very reasonable prices, Greenbank has waterside and garden apartments that can accommodate four people. Call directly for those rates. Also note that some apartments have large bathrooms that allow access for guests in wheelchairs. Again, call to ensure that they are suitable for your needs.

You should book as soon as you know you're coming to Bermuda; a two-night deposit is required, and you will lose it if you cancel within 21 days of your scheduled arrival. Add 10 percent of the room rate to your bill for maid service. Maids come every day. Check-in is at 1 PM, check-out at 11 AM.

SkyTop Cottages
$$ • 65 South Rd.
• (441) 236-7984

SkyTop is in an ideal location if you want reasonably priced accommodations offering easy access to both beach and city. Here, you're a five-minute walk away from Elbow Beach (see our Beaches chapter) and a 10-minute drive from the City of Hamilton. If you don't feel like cooking, you'll be within walking distance of a variety of restaurants. Owners John and Andrea Flood are happy to make recommendations. If you are in the mood to cook, the Modern Mart is five minutes away. On rainy days, John or Andrea will drive you there, and if you want groceries waiting for you on your arrival, they will arrange it. The Floods' aim is to make your vacation as relaxing and carefree as possible. If you are interested in golf, tennis, diving or snorkeling, they'll arrange the bookings for you.

So what are the accommodations like? As befits its name, SkyTop is on a hill and has a view of the South Shore. John and Andrea take obvious pride in their property's 2-acre garden setting. Frangipani and palmetto trees grace the lawns, and the bougainvillea, together with hibiscus, add splashes of color. In winter John and Andrea are happy to let you eat citrus from the garden. Throughout the year, Bermuda bananas grow here too. A large field allows space for a football or Frisbee game. Should you feel like a game of that genteel but vicious pastime — croquet — hoops and mallets can be supplied. Want a stroll in leafy shade? The Railway Trail runs on the edge of the grounds (see our Recreations chapter).

There are 11 units altogether; these include six studios, four one-bedroom and one two-bedroom units. All have patios, and all but one (a bedroom unit) have kitchens. Each kitchen has a four-burner stove with oven, plus a microwave, refrigerator with freezer compartment, toaster, coffee maker and ironing board. Barbecue facilities are available on request. You can eat inside — dining areas are comfortable with a dining table, dining chairs and armchairs — or you can dine Bermuda-style out on the patio. Bedrooms are air-conditioned and decorated in pale pastel shades with floral drapes. Closets are spacious. There is either a king bed or two twins, and a pullout or foldaway couch is on hand for an extra guest. (Kids, by the way, are welcome. Cribs can be supplied. If children are 12 or younger, the charge is $10 a day in summer. Those older than 12 pay $25.)

Four of the units have full bathrooms; the others have showers only. If you're a bubble bath enthusiast, make sure you ask for a bathroom with tub. Hairdryers are available on request. All units, incidentally, have cable television, and board games are on hand for extra amusement.

John and Andrea consider high season March 16 to November 15. The rest of the year counts as winter. During low season, they offer lower rates. Stay a week, and you get one night of the seven free. Call directly for winter rates. When you book, you'll pay a two-night deposit (first and last night) that you lose if you cancel within 21 days of your arrival. There's a 10 percent charge for daily maid service, and maids only wash up breakfast dishes. Check-in is at 2 PM, check-out at 11 AM.

Warwick Parish

Astwood Cove Apartment Resort
$$, no credit cards • 49 South Rd.
• (441) 236-0984

While most of these apartments are modern, the homestead actually dates back to about 1710. It belongs to Nicky and Gabrielle Lewin, and they also operate the business. The apartments are on the opposite side of the road from Astwood Cove Park, so some have a partial view of the ocean, which is visible over treetops.

Originally, both apartment resort and park were part of a dairy farm. In 1915, a whaler named Antonio Marshall lived there. He was the man who, together with his crew, took out a whaling boat in raging seas to rescue British SS *Pollockshields*. His son, Joseph Marshall, remembers how worried his mother was that her husband would drown. Everyone survived except the captain of the ship, who died trying to save some kittens on board (see Elbow Beach in our Beaches chapter).

Rooms in the price range we quote have bedroom/sitting areas, kitchenettes and bathrooms with showers only. Rooms come with private telephone (local calls are free), air conditioning and ceiling fans, and they have private balconies or terraces. Beds, either two twins or one king, are all Posturepedic. Children are very welcome. They sleep in cribs or in hideaway beds. If they are younger than 4, the charge is $20 per child per night; younger than 15, they pay $30. (Babysitting can be arranged.) Extra adults pay $35.

Kitchenettes are supplied with electric stove and oven, microwave, toaster, electric can opener, refrigerator, coffee maker and kettle. A coin-operated laundry is on the property — there you will also find an iron and ironing board. Maids come every day and will wash breakfast dishes. If you can't face washing up after supper, you are welcome to make financial arrangements with the maids for additional help. Smoking's allowed everywhere, by the way.

A large freshwater pool will help you to relax. Barbecues are easy at Astwood: You'll find barbecue stations outside, and a communal patio and pavilion allow you to meet other guests. Citrus, loquat and banana trees can often mean fresh fruit for breakfast, especially during winter when oranges and grapefruit ripen.

The Lewins have a high repeat visitor rate. They recommend that you book about six weeks ahead of time for the summer season (April 1 until November 15). You'll secure your room with a two-night deposit that you will lose if you cancel within 21 days of your arrival. Add a 10 percent room service charge to the price quoted in our key. Travelers' and personal checks are fine. Check-in is flexible; check-out is at noon.

Clairfont Apartments
$ • 6 Warwickshire Rd., off South Rd.
• (441) 238-0149

Mrs. Marilyn Simmons offers extremely reasonably priced accommodation with easy access to both city and beach. Directly opposite Warwick Long Bay, Clairfont is a five-minute walk from Jobson's Cove, an excellent beach for children (see our Beaches chapter), and a three-minute walk from a bus stop.

For the price we quote in our code, you'll stay in a very spacious, air-conditioned studio. There is a separate full kitchen and a bathroom with both a tub and shower. You'll have two twin beds or one king. Each studio is attractively furnished with a pine dining table and chairs, plus a pull-out sofa. Telephone, clock-radio, iron and ironing board and television (with local reception) are on hand. If you want cable TV, it's available on request for $2 a day. The kitchen comes with electric stove and oven, refrigerator/freezer, toaster and cof-

fee maker. All apartments have patios or balconies with outdoor table and chairs.

For a slightly higher rate, you can have an apartment with a separate living room — ideal for families. That should tell you that kids are very welcome. Those younger than 3 stay for $10 a night, while it's $15 for those younger than 12. Extra adults are $20 per person in a studio and $25 in a one-bedroom unit. Both kids and adults will enjoy the freshwater swimming pool, and children can have fun at the Warwick Long Bay children's playground. Smoking is fine in the apartments.

In 1997 Marilyn received the Department of Tourism's Buttery Award for exceeding their high standard of maintenance. Stay at Clairfont and you'll see why. You'll also meet Betty Hall, who has worked there for 23 years. Many adults remember Betty from their stays in the '70s, back when they were students enjoying a Bermuda College Week vacation at Clairfont. They still come back to visit her.

As a rule, you should reserve about three months ahead of time at Clairfont, although last-minute cancellations are always possible. Rates are the same year-round. Check-in is flexible; check-out is at 11 AM.

Marley Beach Cottages
$$$$, no credit cards • South Rd.
• (441) 236-1143

Have you ever seen the movie *The Deep*? The opening shot was taken at Marley Beach. Part of *Chapter 2* was also filmed here. So stay at Marley Beach, and you should feel like a star. The names of some of the accommodations will encourage you to feel that you're in heaven as well. The most expensive suite is called Heaven. Others are called Half Way to Heaven and A Bit of Heaven. Igon Jenson, manager, assures us that at Marley there's no such thing as The Other Place.

For the price we quote in our code you may well stay in Next to Heaven, a family suite consisting of a master bedroom, sitting room, kitchen and bathroom. Kids are welcome, but they are mostly treated as adults where cost is concerned. If they are younger than 2, there is a crib charge of $12 a night; older than 2, they pay the same rate as an extra adult: $35 a night.

Kitchens are equipped with electric stoves

for the most part (one is gas), plus microwaves, fridges, coffee makers and toasters. Bathrooms have tubs and showers. Bedrooms are all air-conditioned and have ceiling fans. They come with one king or two twin beds, local television, telephone, clock-radio and an iron and ironing board. Sitting rooms are furnished with wicker furniture and have two extra single beds made up as daybeds for extra guests. Each suite has an adjoining studio that can be rented separately or together with the suite. Suite and studio together are an ideal setup for a family of six. Call Marley directly for studio rates. All apartments and studios have private terraces overlooking the ocean. Hibachis are available, and a heated (in winter) freshwater pool with whirlpool offers an alternative to ocean swimming.

Marley Beach is very close to a bus route that will take you to Hamilton or to Sandys. The bus will also take you to the Modern Mart grocery store in Paget. Hayward's grocery store will deliver groceries. As for pets? "We love dogs," says Igon, but there is a fumigation charge of $35. Fleas can be problematic in Bermuda.

Igon recommends that for summer season, due to Marley's high repeat visitor rate, you book about five months in advance. Summer season goes from April 15 to October 31, winter season is from January 3 to March 14 and shoulder seasons are November 1 to January 2 and March 15 to April 14. Maids come every day but do not wash dishes unless you make special financial arrangements with them. Credit card numbers are used only to guarantee the necessary two-night deposit, which you will lose if you cancel within 21 days of your arrival. Check-in is flexible; checkout is at 10:30 AM.

Vienna Guest Apartments
$ • 63 Cedar Hill
• (441) 236-3300

Will you get to hear tales from Vienna Woods? There's a distinct possibility, as Vienna's owner and manager, Leopold Küchler, is originally from Austria and is our Austrian consul. He is actually fluent in English, French and Spanish as well as German. Guests from Europe really appreciate his proficiency in languages. Stay at Vienna and you may well have a cosmopolitan experience.

You'll probably meet Leo, as he likes to be called, the moment you're in the arrival hall at the airport. He'll pick you up, drive you to Vienna (so to speak) and show you your apartment. You'll see a fully equipped, separate kitchen with electric cooker, microwave, toaster and coffee maker. Open the refrigerator, and you'll find that Leo has stocked it up with complimentary wine, beer and soft drinks. There is no objection here to smoking, by the way. Accommodations consist of the kitchen, living/dining room, double bedroom and private bathroom (with tub and shower). All are air-conditioned and have ceiling fans, telephone, clock-radio and local television. Bedrooms have queen beds plus an extra twin to accommodate a child staying in the room. Children younger than 4 stay for free. Those younger than 12 pay $20 a night. Cribs are on hand for no extra charge.

All rooms have private terraces and views of either the Great Sound or Forest Hill. One suite used often by honeymooners was once the quarters of a dairy maid who worked for a farm called Longford. Its walls are charmingly "bumpy" because they are made of old Bermuda stone, and a small old alcove with red brick edging reminds us of the candlelight era. That's where the maid would rest her candles. While we're talking about maids — they will clean your rooms every day, but they don't do dishes. There's a coin-operated laundry on the premises.

There are two communal areas. One is around the unheated freshwater pool, where you can use the barbecue facilities, and the other is in the guest lounge that has a television and comfortable chairs and sofas. On Bermudian public holidays, Leo likes to orga-

INSIDERS' TIP

Be aware that hotel-owned or controlled private beaches have no lifeguards. Check the Beaches chapter for guidelines on safe swimming.

nize barbecue parties. He'll always be readily available to advise you on transportation, recreations and activities. He'll also rent you pedal bikes (with helmets) for $7 a day. If you want to snorkel, he has mask, snorkel and flippers available for $5 a day. As for shopping, Lindos grocery store is close by. When he's available, Leo will drive you there. Vienna is a two-minute walk away from a bus route into Hamilton or Sandys and a 15-minute walk away from a ferry stop.

Vienna has a high repeat visitor rate. For the summer season (April 1 through November 15), you should book at least two months ahead of time. You secure your room with two nights' deposit, which you'll lose if you cancel within 21 days of your arrival. Check-in is flexible; check-out is at 11 AM. But chances are that you won't say goodbye to Leo when you check out. He'll probably be taking you to the airport.

Southampton Parish

Munro Beach Cottages
$$$$ • 2 Port Royal Golf Course Rd.
• (441) 234-1175

These cottages, all overlooking the South Shore, have the advantage of facing southwest. So what? So in the evenings you'll be able to sit out on your terrace and watch the sun envelop the ocean in a swath of pink. Swimming and snorkeling are ideal at Munro. The property has its own beach, Whitney Bay, which is for guests only. The sandbar in this part of the ocean means that at low tide you can wade out to the reef and say hi to the fish. Relax on the beach in loungers. There's no need for umbrellas — the coconut palm trees will give you plenty of shade. If you like golf and tennis along with your beach activities, you'll be pleased to know that this property is surrounded by the Port Royal Golf Course (see our Golf chapter). Dawn Sharp, manager at Munro, will be happy to make golf and tennis arrangements there for you.

All accommodations have separate kitchens equipped with gas stove, oven/broiler, microwave, fridge and coffee maker. Large barbecues are on hand. Bedroom/sitting rooms overlook the ocean. All air-conditioned, they have ceiling fans, telephones, clock-radios and local television. You'll have one king or two twin beds; let Dawn know in advance which you prefer. Bathrooms have tubs and showers. Kids are welcome, but there are no reduced rates for them. Extra persons staying in the rooms pay $30 per person per night and sleep on pull-out couches. Cribs are available. You may, by the way, smoke in your rooms. Two non-smoking rooms are available.

Grocery shopping is easy here. For a $7.50 service charge and a minimum order of $30,

Photo: GIS

A couple roams the grounds at one of Bermuda's cottage colonies.

the Maximart grocery store will deliver groceries every day except Sundays and public holidays.

Dawn has three seasons. High season is from April 15 until November 14; shoulder season is from November 15 to January 14; and January 15 to April 14 is winter season. Book as soon as possible for summer. A two-night deposit is required, which you will lose if you cancel within 21 days of your arrival. Check-in is at 2 PM, check-out at noon.

Whale Bay Inn
$$, no credit cards • 34 Whaling Hill, Whale Bay Rd. • (441) 238-0469
This one overlooks Port Royal Golf Course and, of course, Whale Bay Beach. Will you

see whales? You will in April, if you're lucky. They'll be migrating northward to their summer feeding grounds. In any case this beach, just a few minutes walk away, is ideal for families, and you'll certainly encounter fish when you swim there.

Whale Bay Inn has five apartments, each with a private bathroom (with shower and tub), separate bedroom and kitchen/dining/living room area. Bedrooms have one double and one single bed and come with cable television, telephone and clock-radio. Like the blues? Then you'll appreciate the furnishings. Curtains are deep Wedgwood blue, walls are light blue and tile is white with streaks of blue. Pots, pans and some of the cutlery match the curtains. Wicker and pine furniture add to the light and airy effect. Kids are welcome. If they are younger than 12, the charge is $20 a night; those younger than 1 stay free. Extra persons older than 12 pay $40 a night. The kitchen is equipped with a two-burner electric stove, large refrigerator, microwave, toaster and coffee maker. All apartments have private patios overlooking the South Shore and the 14th hole of the golf course (see our Golf chapter). Hibachis are on hand for barbecues. Owner/manager Philippa Metschnabel says that while there are no communal areas, spontaneous parties sometimes happen. She has no objection to smoking, by the way. Note that Whale Bay Inn is a 20-minute walk from the Maximart grocery store (remember, they deliver) and minutes away from ferry and bus stops.

Philippa recommends that you book a month in advance. A first- and second-night deposit is required, and a 21-day cancellation policy applies. Her summer season runs from April 1 until November 15.

Sandys Parish

Garden House
$-$$$, no credit cards • 4 Middle Rd, Somerset Bridge • (441) 234-1435

When you arrive at Garden House, chances are you'll find owner/manager Rosanne Galloway wearing an extremely picturesque straw hat and driving her mini mowing tractor around the spacious lawns of her garden. On very hot days, she likes to wear her bikini and an elegant string of pearls. Of course, as soon as she sees you, she'll stop cutting the grass and personally introduce you to your apartment and Bermuda's attractions. She will also drive you to a grocery store if you need some provisions. It's very important to Rosanne that you feel Garden House is more like home than a tourist accommodation. That's why you'll find fresh flower arrangements in your room when you arrive.

You have a choice of three cottages on the Garden House property: a studio, a one-bedroom cottage with separate living room and kitchen, and a two-bedroom cottage with a huge, 37-foot living room that leads to a separate kitchen. Private bathrooms come with

each cottage. Beds tend to be single kings or two twins, but in the larger cottage you'll find a lovely Bermudian antique four-poster double bed. Bedrooms have fresh print curtains and sheets and are furnished with dressing tables. They have a private telephone and clock-radio. Bathrooms have a tub and shower and a spacious cupboard faced with a full-length mirror. You may have a hairdryer on request.

The kitchen is divided from the living room by a countertop that has bar chairs. The open-plan style gives a light and airy effect. Kitchens come with a freestanding gas stove, refrigerator/freezer, microwave, coffee maker, kettle and toaster. They also have a washing machine, iron and ironing board. Living rooms are furnished in British country house style with Bermudian touches of cedar. A generous supply of books and games is on hand, and cottages have VCRs. You may not, by the way, smoke anywhere inside the cottages, but you may smoke outside.

All cottages have patios where you can sit in a true Bermudian garden setting or barbecue on a hibachi. You can also enjoy the salt-water swimming pool. Although you cannot see the sea from the cottages, Rosanne's garden does extend down to Ely's Harbour, where she has a private dock for deep-water swimming.

Children younger than 12 stay free. If they are older than 12, the charge is $15 a night per person. Babysitting can be arranged. Rosanne recommends that you book as soon as you know you're going to visit the island. Garden House requires a $50 deposit, which you lose if you cancel within 14 days of your scheduled arrival. The prices denoted in our code are in effect from June 15 to September 15, and they apply because all cottages are air-conditioned during those months. Note that rates vary according to the size of the unit and the season; we strongly recommend you call Rosanne directly to discuss them. Be aware that Garden House is closed December through February. Service charge is 9 percent of your room rate. Maids come every day and will wash breakfast dishes. Check-in is flexible; check-out is at 11 AM. A courtesy room will let you have that last swim.

With our tourism mandarins inviting you to visit and "let yourself go," you'll find once you're here your dining options cover a wide range.

Restaurants

*"All human history attests
That happiness for man — the hungry sinner
— Since Eve ate apples, much depends on
dinner."*
— Lord Byron

It might be argued that Byron certainly knew a little something about sinning and equally as much about fine food and wine. With our tourism mandarins inviting you to visit and "let yourself go," you'll find once you're here your dining options cover a wide range. Thus, letting yourself go — from a dining perspective — includes choosing from an exciting array of dishes, among them Bermudian, French, Mexican, Italian, Indian, Continental, Thai, English and Irish pub-style cuisine. There are even a couple of lunch wagons for burgers and soft drinks — one of them is in the City Hall parking lot.

To aid you in selecting from the more than 100 restaurants, inns, pubs and taverns on our 21 square miles of landscaped oceanfront, we have listed more than half of the possible choices. We also include menu information to give you an indication of how each can satisfy your palate's desires.

However, there are a few things to keep in mind. Most of Bermuda's restaurants automatically add a 15 percent gratuity and will add the total on your charge card slip. If you're in doubt about the issue, ask. The majority of establishments accept "smart casual" dress for dinner. This description does not normally require a jacket, but some establishments prefer that men wear one. Also, while most of our restaurants are open for dinner every night including Sunday, public holidays can be another matter. Call ahead to be sure.

For those physically challenged and using a wheelchair, many of our restaurants are not readily accessible. However, you'll find restaurant staff willing to provide any assistance needed. During the summer months, when the temperature reaches into the high 80s, you can depend, except in a very few instances, on air conditioning and/or alfresco dining.

We're generally relaxed in Bermuda, and dining is a pleasure. As Virginia Woolf said, "One cannot think well, love well, sleep well, if one has not dined well." We want you to do them all well while you are here.

Price Code

The dollar-sign price code will aid you in gauging the cost of dinner entrees for two minus appetizers, beverages, dessert or gratuities. The majority of restaurants accept major credit cards and (of course) cash, but it's rare to find one that will take a personal check.

$	Less than $40
$$	$41 to $80
$$$	$81 to $100
$$$$	More than $100

St. George's Parish
Town of St. George

Bouchee
$$ • 36 Water St., Town of St. George
• (441) 297-2951

Word has it that this is one of the island's best restaurants. As waterfront bistros go, it is certainly one of the most delightful. Dine indoors or outside on the waterside terrace and choose from an intriguing menu. Among the taste-bud seducers is the pink peppercorn-crusted beef tenderloin with rosemary bordeaux sauce. One of our favorites is the cayenne-seasoned chicken and shrimp brochettes served with jalapeño mashed potatoes. But you'll discover your own. The chef welcomes any special requests. Also note that the menu is subject to change. Dress is smart casual.

Carriage House
$$$ • Water St., next to Carriage Museum, Town of St. George
• (441) 297-1270, (441) 297-1730

Once a warehouse for the Royal Engineers, the Carriage House's vaulted eighteenth-century brick-walled dining room, gazing out onto St. George's Harbour, creates a unique ambiance. During the evening, flickering candlelight enhances the grotto-like atmosphere. The dinner menu, a blend of continental, English and local dishes, includes prime rib served from the trolley and rack of English spring lamb carved at your table. The Bermuda Triangle, a combination of filet mignon, shrimp and chicken breast, is a favorite. Pasta specialties include linguine with julienne of chicken and green peppers flamed in cognac with shiitake mushrooms and spring onion cream sauce. The Sunday brunch is a smorgasbord of great choices. Dress is smart casual.

Freddie's Pub on the Square
$$ • King's Sq., Town of St. George
• (441) 297-1717

This pub is in a restored eighteenth-century building with a balcony overlooking King's Square, the town's hub. From this second-story perch, you can observe all the Square's comings and goings and even eavesdrop as a tour guide describes to visitors the ancient punishments doled out on the stocks and pillory almost directly below. From time to time, there is live music on the pub's ground floor, and a big-screen television should appeal to sports fans. English pub fare dominates, with fish & chips and Shepherd's pie the general favorites. Upstairs, dinner is served under the Bermuda cedar-beamed roof erected in the 1700s. The dinner menu is big on seafood, with tuna, grouper and snapper dishes featured along with the catch of the day. Reservations generally are not necessary. Dress is casual.

San Giorgio Ristorante
$$ • Water Street, Town of St. George
• (441) 297-1307

Just a few steps west of Tucker House (See Attractions chapter) and across from the Somers Wharf shopping complex, is this charming little bistro. Its menu is Italian, its décor continental, its service friendly. It has the obvious dishes one might expect, along with choices such as an antipasti of Squid tubes stuffed with herbs on grilled Italian bread; a scallop salad with walnut Pesto sauce; and Chicken Cacciatore, braised and with onions and mushrooms in a brown red-wine sauce made with beef stock. A nice feature of this bistro is its intimate atmosphere. Dinner is served every night except Sunday. Reservations are recommended and dress is smart casual

White Horse Tavern
$$ • King's Sq., Town of St. George
• (441) 297-1838

Many visitors find this a great place to take a break from their ambles through the old town. It has a waterside porch so close to the water that if you drop a morsel over the railing, you might attract curious fish. In the nineteenth century, the Tavern was the home of John Davenport, who amassed a fortune in gold and silver coins that he stored in his cellar in kegs. When he died and the stash was counted, his wealth amounted to hundreds of thousands of dollars. Today the Tavern is much more sedate, its dinner menu a cosmopolitan blend that includes duck liver pate with lychee and port sauce, chicken Tikka kebab and tenderloin steak. Fish and chips is a staple. Dress is casual.

St. David's

Blackhorse Tavern
$ • 101 St. David's Rd., St. David's
• (441) 293-9742

Informal and friendly, the Blackhorse experience is like dining at home with friends. This is one of the places locals go to get away from the rest of Bermuda. St. David's islanders are renowned for their affinity for the sea, in the 18th and 19th century establishing reputations as superb fishermen and whalers. Dine inside or eat outside on the grass (at a table, of course) under a big umbrella and blanket of stars. Listen to the gentle lapping of the water as you dig into conch stew, stuffed lobster or any choice of fresh seafood. No reservations are required, and dress is casual.

Dennis' Hideaway
$ — $$, no credit cards
• Cashew City Rd., St. David's
• (441) 297-0044

Former U.S. President Jimmy Carter has eaten here, and we've been told he absolutely loved this place. So saddle up your moped and head east for a happening you'll be telling your friends about for years to come. Genuinely charming and undeniably quaint, the Hideaway wins the gold medal for unique. It's the only restaurant in Bermuda where the owner — in this case Dennis Lamb, who also is the manager and chef — suggests you bring your own liquor, wine or soft drinks. Bring your own cake or pie too if you want. This hideaway is about marvelous seafood served without frills and fancies. It's a kick-your-shoes-off (literally, if that makes you comfortable) and let-your-hair-down experience.

Other notables have dined here, some so secretly that they don't want their identities revealed — and Dennis won't tell. From the exterior, the Hideaway is not much to look at; inside it is homey and clean. "Putty and paint only makes a ship what she ain't," says Lamb, "so don't be bothered by what she looks like." Always call ahead to let him know when you want to come and how many will be in your party.

Oh yes, it might be helpful if you didn't eat much at least a month before parking your feet under a Hideaway table, especially if you want to tuck into his "fish dinner with the works." Take a deep breath and loosen your belt; you'll be here awhile. What you get is eight to ten courses. Dennis starts you off with shark hash on toast, followed by conch fritters, mussel stew, fish chowder, fish, conch steak, shark steak and shrimp and scallops. Dress any way you like, but you must make reservations.

Hamilton Parish

Halfway House
$ • 8 North Shore Rd., Flatts Village
• (441) 295-5212, (441) 295-4608

Flatts Village has always had an aura of tranquility. And there seems to have always been a restaurant at Halfway House's location. Cozy and clean, it has become a favorite for locals. One visit will tell you why. The food is Bermudian, excellent, and the prices are superb. This is the place you always dream about finding when you travel — one that is friendly with homestyle meals cooked fresh daily. Errol Burgess, the owner and manager, welcomes you to visit the kitchen and watch the food being prepared; just ask. The varied menu encompasses specialties like lobster (in-season), T-bone steaks, filet mignon and fresh local fish. All soups, including the renowned fish chowder — some have even called it the best on the island — are homemade. "We don't use anything out of a can," says Errol. The experience is charming and delightful; savor it with wine or beer. By the way, the burgers are also homemade, with seasoning worked in before they hit the grill; no store-bought patties here, thank you. Stop in for breakfast, lunch or dinner. Dress is casual.

Landfall
$ • at Clearview Suites and Villas, Sandy Lane • (441) 293-1322

Eating at this charming Bermudian restaurant is rather like dining in an old cottage — because that's exactly what you'll be doing. Paintings by Clearview's resident artist Otto Trott (see Arts and Culture chapter) adorn the walls. Pleasant atmosphere, friendly service, brick floors and fireplace maintain that "at home" feeling. The food is good, nothing fancy, just like what grandmother used to prepare. Of course, Bermuda fish and chips heads the entrees, and dessert includes gingerbread and apple pie. Music, quaintly, is often via ra-

---

INSIDERS' TIP

On some of the menus you will see "lobster (in season)." In season locally refers to Bermuda lobster, which are very tasty too and are available September through March.

dio. Don't look for an extensive wine menu, although you will be able to have wine if you desire. Sunday brunch is highly popular with the local crowd who often flock here after church. Dress is smart casual and dinner reservations are not generally necessary.

Swizzle Inn
$ • 3 Blue Hole Hill, Bailey's Bay • (441) 293-9300

Swizzle Inn, named for the famous — perhaps infamous — Bermuda rum swizzle, has been catering to visitors and locals alike who relish its relaxed atmosphere and eclectic menu. You might begin with the escargot à la chinois, tender

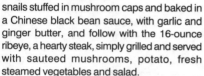

www.insiders.com
See this and many other
Insiders' Guide®
destinations online.
Visit us today!

snails stuffed in mushroom caps and baked in a Chinese black bean sauce, with garlic and ginger butter, and follow with the 16-ounce ribeye, a hearty steak, simply grilled and served with sauteed mushrooms, potato, fresh steamed vegetables and salad.

The upstairs dining room has been converted into a nonsmoking environment. For the youngsters, a special menu is available upon request. You can eat and tap your feet to live music May through September. The inn is open daily, including Sunday, and reservations are only necessary for five persons or more. However, the restaurant is closed on Christmas Day, Boxing Day (in Bermuda, Boxing Day is the day after Christmas Day and is a holiday) and a couple of other holidays; call ahead to be sure. Dress is casual.

Tom Moore's Tavern
$$ • Walsingham Ln. • (441) 293-8020

With elegant dining rooms, limestone walls, wood beams and fireplaces, this former seventeenth-century private residence owes its name to the poet Tom Moore who arrived in Bermuda in 1804 to take up the position of Registrar of the Court of the Vice Admiralty. He became a frequent guest at Walsingham House, then owned by Samuel Trott. This house, which has changed hands several times over the years, is now Tom Moore's Tavern, and the dining is superb. The cuisine is continental and includes duck, veal, fish, bone-

less quail in puff pastry and Bermuda lobster in-season (September through March). The tavern is closed mid-January to the end of February. Jacket-and-tie is the preferred dress.

Smiths Parish

Mikado
$$ • at Marriott's Castle Harbour Resort Hotel • (441) 293-2040 ext. 6751

If the mere idea of being in Seventh Heaven appeals, then you'll thrill to Mikado's "Seventh Heaven Menu" — seven courses of culinary elegance on Wednesday and Sunday evenings. On Wednesday, for example, among the courses are California Maki: crab meat with avocado and fish roe rolled with dried seaweed; Hibachi shrimp appetizer, prepared teppan-style with lemon butter; and Japonaise Geisha Tiramisu, geisha lady finger soaked in coffee liquor topped with mascarpone cheese and cocoa. Although the Japanese menu forms an impeccable experience, you'll enjoy the deft display by Teppanyaki Chefs. And if you love sushi, you'll be content, with sushi bar appetizers consisting of treats such as Mikado Avo: diced tuna and white fish served in avocado halves with the restaurant's special sauce. Dinner is served nightly except Monday. Reservations are highly recommended. Dress is smart casual, but remember, no jeans.

North Rock Brewing Co. Ltd
$ • 10 South Road • (441) 236-6633

This is a great watering hole for those traveling by moped to or from the East End. It is Bermuda's first brew pub, with draft beer brewed on the premises right before your eyes. In fact, as the name indicates, you'll find a varied selection of fresh ales on any given day, among them Whale of a Wheat, Somers Amber Ale, Old Colony Bitter and North Rock Porter. Lunch and dinner are served daily. The mahogany-trimmed dining room and outdoor roadside patio give this pub an authentic British flavor. And if you're really in the mood for a little British fare, try the Duck- and Goat's-

BERMUDA'S FIRST BREWPUB

BERMUDA

North Rock BREWING Co.

LUNCH
11:30 - 3 PM

DINNER
6-10 PM

HAND
CRAFTED
ALES

JNCT. SOUTH ROAD & COLLECTOR'S HILL
TELEPHONE 236-6633

cheese salad appetizer, roast barbary duck breast and goat's cheese dressed over arrugala salad with raspberry vinegar. Or the classic steak and ale pie, pub-style beef and mushrooms simmered in porter ale. An interesting salad choice is the Brewmaster's gingered duck breast atop mesclun greens with garden vegetables, fresh mozzarella, asparagus and pine nuts with a lemon-ginger dressing. Dress is casual. Reservations for dinner suggested.

Specialty Inn
$ • 4 South Road • (441) 236-3133

Open Monday to Saturday, this restaurant offers no frills, get to the point, tasty meals. Just across South Road from the bottom of Collector's Hill, and a mere 100 yards from a nearby gas station where you can top up your moped's tank, this home-style eatery is a favorite for cab drivers and locals for a quick and hearty breakfast and lunch. The dinner menu includes a Monday "Pasta Night" with popular dish Penne Hot & Spicy, tomato, green peppers, onion, hot peppers, garlic, mush-

rooms and pepperoni; and Spaghetti Puttanesca, black olives, capers, garlic, hot peppers, anchovies and tomato. Monday pasta dishes are served with tossed salad or soup of the day, homemade roll and foccaccia, tea or coffee. Dress is casual.

Devonshire Parish

Caliban's
**$$ • Ariel Sands Beach Club,
South Shore Rd. • (441) 236-1010**

This beach club has borrowed a couple of characters from Shakespeare's *Tempest*, hence the names Ariel and Caliban. At the restaurant, you can dine alfresco by the sea, hold hands across the table under a full moon, and have breakfast on the beach in the morning. Evenings here are magical as you dance under the stars to music provided by local entertainers.

The à la carte menu is international, and the food is expertly and elegantly prepared. The roast pork tenderloin stuffed with pecans and apples set on a Calvados sauce is one of the favored selections. Finish with a dessert of hot chocolate fondant set on a butterscotch sauce and served with vanilla ice cream. Dress is smart casual.

Pembroke Parish

City of Hamilton

Bombay Indian Restaurant
$$ • 75 Reid St. E., between Court and King Sts., Hamilton
• (441) 292-0048

Ah, for a taste of India, this is a secret visitors rarely ferret out. But if you want a genuine bite of New Delhi, this is it. Enter just right of Rego furniture store's main entrance and take the elevator to the third floor. Once here, you'll find it one of the most delightful restaurants in the city. Nicely decorated, the restaurant's ambiance is relaxing and its waiters are friendly. Most times the music is authentic Indian. The lunch buffet is reasonably priced and good. The dinner menu offers enough choices that, if unfamiliar with Indian dishes, you'll probably want to spend a while perusing it before deciding. Waiters are always willing to provide advice if you want a bit more information on some offerings. The favorites include Roganjosh, a popular lamb curry, and Murg Saagwala, chicken breast and spinach in a mild curry sauce. Choose Naan bread or Parantha as an accompaniment. Dress is smart casual, and reservations generally are not required. Now open Sundays.

Botanic Garden Tearoom
$ Triminghams, 37 Front Street, Hamilton
• (441) 295-1183

This is far from your cluttered, sidewalk café. Situated in Triminghams, one of the two largest department stores on the island, the Botanic Garden Tearoom offers Triminghams' shoppers the solitude to grab a small bite in a cool and comfortable niche on the shop's third floor. The choices are simple: sandwiches, coffee, tea, soft drinks and such. Don't look for hamburgers and fries.

Café Acoreana
$ • 21 Church St., opposite the bus terminal, Hamilton
• (441) 296-0402

For a morning snack or lunch while waiting for the bus, or if you just feel like relaxing in a bright, airy and clean cafe, here you'll find a variety of fresh pastries guaranteed to break down any resistance. Indulge now, diet later. Pastry favorites include malacadas, Portuguese doughnuts that seem to disappear as quickly as they appear, and custard tarts, which vanish just as rapidly. Sandwiches include ham, turkey, tuna and egg. There is also peito de gallina (chicken breast) and bolos de arroz, a plain but delicious muffin. Add some cakes and puddings, and your sweet tooth will e-mail a letter of appreciation. Dress is casual.

Chit Chat
$ • Queen Street, Hamilton
• (441) 292-3400

One of the interesting features of this charming restaurant is its daily specials, marketed as "great tastes from around the world." Each day from Monday to Saturday, a special dish from a different country — Asia, the Caribbean, Italy, India, America, Mexico — is featured, and on Sunday they offer Chef Doris' international buffet (11 AM — 4 PM) along with the Bermuda Breakfast of codfish and potatoes. And if you crave pizza, try their British Bombshell: chunks of ham, green pepper, mushroom, onion and sweet corn.

Chopsticks
$ • 88 Reid St. E., Hamilton
• (441) 292-0791

Whether you've mastered Oriental chopsticks or prefer an Occidental fork, the regional Chinese and Thai dishes taste equally intriguing. The decor is flavored with rice paper fans hanging from the ceiling and large open fans and attractive Oriental-flavored paintings on the walls — nothing elaborate, but it works splendidly. The tables are well-spaced, and service is quick and friendly. The lunch menu includes a wealth of main courses, and the dinner menu features a wide range of regional dishes, among them Thai chicken with sweet basil, and Evil Jungle Prince, a vegetarian alternative. Beef and vegetable Szechuan is popular. For dessert you can choose, among other things, a slice of Snickers bar pie. Uh huh. Visit in February and join in the celebration of the Chinese New Year; the multi-course banquet is magical. Dress is smart casual. Reservations are not generally necessary.

Flanagan's Irish Pub & Restaurant
$ • Emporium Bldg., 69 Front St.,
Hamilton • (441) 295-8299

For a taste of Ireland in the Atlantic, Flanagan's serves up Irish fare for lunch or dinner. Dine on the balcony overlooking Front Street and Hamilton Harbour beyond, or eat inside in an atmosphere that captures the essence of the shamrock.

This pub won the prize for Bermuda's Best Fish Chowder in 1995 and 1996. One of the menu favorites is the 8-ounce Gaelic Sirloin, a choice certified Angus strip steak, grilled or charbroiled, topped with sauteed mushrooms, served with an Irish whisky sauce and accompanied with your choice of potatoes, pasta or rice. Flanagan's is a great place for those who relish Murphy's stout or Gallagher's Irish Ale. Dress is casual, and reservations are not needed.

Four Star Pizza
$ • 6 North Shore Rd, Flatts
• (441) 292-9111
$ • 10 Angle Street, Hamilton
• (441) 295-5555
$ • 55 Middle Rd, Warwick
• (441) 232-0123
$ • 65 Somerset Rd, Somerset
• (441) 234-2626

Open every day, this chain of pizza restaurants — owned by the same folks who own Chit Chat — allows the options of dining in or carrying out. For locals and visitors living or staying within prescribed areas, there is free delivery.

Fresco's Restaurant & Wine Bar
$$ • Chancery Lane, Hamilton
• (441) 295-5058

Patio dining under a glass-roofed pergola, a focus on wine, and local art (that diners can purchase) hanging on the walls help season this restaurant's captivating ambiance. The menu is Mediterranean, but often with a touch of local flavors like pawpaw, cassava, and loquats. Their "wine flights" allow diners to buy five ounce-and-a-half tasters of different wines for around $10. Among the menu selections is pork filet mignon, rolled in ginger, eggplant and starfruit julienne, roasted and accompanied with raisin and pineapple polenta, waffle potato and Caribbean salsa. This dish won the Best Pork dish in a 1998 Caribbean competition in Miami. Dress is smart casual. Reservations are advised.

The Harbourfront
$$$ • 21 Front St. W., Hamilton
• (441) 295-4207

On the second floor and accessed through the cool, tunnel-like entrance just off Front Street, opposite the visitor's service bureau, this restaurant is a popular spot. Relax on its covered upstairs porch and absorb island life as it unfolds under balmy skies and languid breezes. From here, as you sip a cappuccino and contemplate a ferry ride to Dockyard, you get a sense of the dichotomy of Bermuda —

the hectic hustle in the street below juxtaposed with sailboats gliding sedately in placid Hamilton Harbour.

The sushi bar has tasty sashimi, nigiri, norimaki and temaki with sake and Sapporo beer. If sushi is not your pleasure, dip into a pasta specialty, or perhaps duck Curacao — tender breasts of duck, sliced and napped with an orange Curacao-and-cumin-scented sauce, garnished with glazed red cabbage. The service is friendly and efficient. Jackets are preferred for dinner.

The Hog Penny Restaurant and Pub
$$ • 5 Burnaby Hill, Hamilton
• (441) 292-2534

For more than 30 years, this restaurant has been a local favorite. Visitors love it too. The name (see our History chapter) is derived from the Hog money issued in 1615 to provide coinage for early settlers. This is the pub where you can raise a toast in a pewter jug, shimmy up to the dark wood bar or sit at one of the tables and drink in the authentic British ambiance. Order classics like bangers and mash (traditional plump beef sausages served with fresh mashed potatoes, fresh vegetables and onion gravy), fish and chips, or go for the day's dinner special. Among the house specialties is the chicken and shrimp brochette — plump juicy shrimp and tender morsels of chicken together on a skewer with bell peppers and onions, marinated in lemon and lime juice, then broiled and served over rice with an orange and ginger sauce. Finish with a dessert of banana fritters — bananas coated in a light batter, fried and tossed in cinnamon sugar and flamed at your table with Bermuda Black Seal Rum. Entertainment, often a guitar-strumming singer, is usually on hand. Dress is casual.

The Hungry Bear
$ • Chancery Ln., Hamilton
• (441) 292-2353

This bear is a honey, and it sure has some great coffees. Step off the lane and into a cool, neat atmosphere where flavored herbal teas, sandwiches, Italian pastries and chocolates, cinnamon and almond biscotti, pizzas and a few salads are available for a relaxing mid-morning snack or lunch. Seven different coffees are offered daily to go with the fresh pastries. The owner and manager emphasizes that The Hungry Bear serves real cappuccino, not pretenders to the throne. Although it's only open during the day, it's worth keeping in mind as a good place to take a breather from shopping. Note: You'll find some maps and visitor information here. Dress is casual.

La Trattoria
$$ • 22 Washington Ln., Hamilton
• (441) 295-1877

Relaxed, informal and in the heart of Hamilton, this is a great place for casual dining. The atmosphere is warm, accented by a wood-beamed ceiling from which a couple of plants hang. Copper utensils are displayed along a far wall. Add red and white checkered tablecloths and the picture is complete. This is home away from home. Pastas, pizza and regional Italian specialties compete to tempt a hungry palate. Fresh fillet of fish simmered in tomato sauce with garlic, white wine, olives, oregano and parsley, or sirloin steak served in a sauce of onions, fresh mushrooms and Barolo wine are two of the many choices. The convenient location (it's hard to stroll around Hamilton without noticing it) makes it ideal for lunch and a favored dinner destination. Dress is smart casual.

Le Figaro
$ • 63 Reid St., Hamilton
• (441) 296-4991

If you've never been to France, this will be your first trip. From the meals prepared by a chef who hails from Bordeaux, France, to the music that accompanies your dinner, this intimate little bistro is the real thing. One of the newest on the restaurant circuit, it has quickly become a hit. If you want a special wine, you need only to accompany the waiter across the entry way to Bacchus, the restaurant's wine shop, and select your own. Yes, the wine list is extensive. Two dinner favorites: coq au vin, rustic chicken marinated in Beaujolais and onions, braised in a rich red wine sauce and served with mashed potatoes; and steak frites, a hearty rib-eye steak, perfectly grilled and

PIZZA

FOUR STAR PIZZA®

★★★★

Dine-In • Carry-Out • FREE Delivery • Open 7 Days

Hamilton 295-5555 • Warwick 232-0123 • Flatts 292-9111 • Somerset 234-2626

Warwick Location Now Serving: Chicken, Fish, Pasta, Ribs, & Indian

served with Maitre d' Hôtel butter and home-made pommes frites. Top it off with the favorite dessert — chocolate crème brulée. Reservations are necessary. Dress is smart casual.

Little Venice
$$ • 32 Bermudiana Rd., Hamilton • (441) 295-3503

This restaurant has been around for several decades, and many regard it as one of the best of Italian-food choices. It is certainly a hit with the business lunch crowd. A convivial atmosphere is augmented by fun-loving waiters. Although the tables may seem rather close together, there is a sense of privacy.

Classic Italian cuisine is showcased in an array of tempting dinner choices. The scampi alla Mediterranea — jumbo shrimp sauteed with white wine and garlic and served with a caponata-like concoction of eggplant, fresh tomatoes and zucchini (flavored with basil vinaigrette) — is one of several "lighter fare" dishes. And for dessert, crostata di frutta — crispy sugar pastry filled with vanilla cream, topped with mixed berries, finished with apricot glaze and served with mango coulis — is positively sinful. Dress is smart casual, and reservations are necessary. One of the pluses here is that, after spoiling yourself at dinner, you can burn off a few calories by taking advantage of free admission to The Club (see

our Nightlife chapter) upstairs for music and dancing.

The Lobster Pot
$$ • 6 Bermudiana Rd., Hamilton • (441) 292-6898

Live Maine lobsters are available year-round; Bermuda spiny lobsters, only in-season. But this restaurant is not simply for lovers of either the local or imported crustacean; some fish, chicken and meat dishes also are served. Appetizers include curried Bermuda fish rolled in thin crepe glazed with Hollandaise sauce and mango chutney. The coconut shrimp — gulf shrimp rolled in coconut, fried golden brown and served with sweet Oriental sauce — is a tasty alternative. Dinner entrees include Creole shrimp pasta — shrimp sauteed with spicy sausage, fresh mozzarella, roasted peppers and basil served over angel hair pasta. The atmosphere is somewhat like being on board a comfortable wooden sailing vessel. Dress is casual.

Monte Carlo
$$ • 9 Victoria St., Hamilton • (441) 295-5443

Behind City Hall, this attractive restaurant, complete with murals, serves up Mediterranean cuisine amid a cozy French ambiance. Appetizers such as mushroom terrine — as-

There are over 100 restaurants and eateries in Bermuda to delight any palate.

sorted shiitake, oyster and cremini mushrooms served with a walnut sauce — enchant the palate. Entrees are equally delightful and include Veal Monaco: rolls of veal with Parma ham and Provolone cheese served with roasted garlic and tomato sauce. Monte Carlo's Tagliolini St. Tropez (angel hair pasta with roasted peppers, black olives and sun-dried tomatoes) is another favorite. Dress is smart casual.

M.R. Onions
$$ • 11 Par-la-Ville Rd., Hamilton • (441) 292-5012

Take a family-style approach to dining, season it with a singles-type bar where folks simply love to have a good time, add healthy portions of Internet and e-mail services so that it is Bermuda's first cyber cafe, give it a name that reminds you of the onion's importance in the island's early agricultural history, and you serve up a restaurant with upbeat character and personality that makes it downright popular. The menu crosses all culinary boundaries, from vegetarian and pasta, chicken and ribs,

beef and roasted meats to fish, seafood and surf-and-turf combinations. Two favorites are the barbecued chicken and ribs, and the Ménage à Trois, an adventurous pan-fried rockfish, Cajun mahi mahi and grilled wahoo served with lemon butter sauce. With a dinner selection so dubbed, it is almost predictable that this restaurant would win the Best of Bermuda Award for the Most Decadent Dessert, the Double Fudgie Wudgie — a rich chocolate brownie topped with vanilla ice cream and layered with hot chocolate sauce. Dress is smart casual.

Paradiso Café
$ • Washington Mall, 7 Reid St., Hamilton • (441) 295-3263

Paradiso, another recently opened café, is a convenient place to pop into when taking a breather from shopping. With a décor augmented by a tiny moongate, it offers a modest selection of dishes. Apart from sandwiches, there is a satisfying choice of salads. Paradiso Salad, mesclun served with shrimp, artichoke hearts and bean sprouts in tomato vinaigrette, is but one of several. Dessert includes Tiramisu, Paradiso chocolate mousse cake and mille feuille. They do not open for dinner and close at 5 PM. Dress is casual.

Pickled Onion Bar & Restaurant
$ • 53 Front St., Hamilton
• (441) 295-2263

Housed in a building believed to be at least two centuries old, with open cedar beams running straight and strong across the ceiling, this restaurant has an enchanting ambiance. An open-air balcony overlooks Front Street and the harbor. Live music (there is no cover charge) from 9.30 PM to 1 AM accompanies dining enjoyment. The varied menu features local as well as international dishes and it will be easy to find satisfying choices. Appetizers include Caribbean seafood salad, comprised of fresh mussels, calamari, shrimps and local fish tossed in a basil vinaigrette. The main course covers pasta, meat and seafood choices as well as pizza. They are particularly proud of their Angus beef that is cut and trimmed in-house, and served with their signature steak-cut potatoes and what they call their Whisky Warehouse Peppercorn sauce. For those who want a taste of the Azores, there is Azore Islands: Portuguese sausage, smoked ham, bell peppers, roast garlic and mushrooms with bowtie pasta. Dress is casual.

The Porch
$ • 93 Front St., Hamilton
• (441) 292-4737

Its terrace looks out over Front Street, the harbor beyond and cruise ships docked wharfside. A big plus here: the vegetarian and fat-free dishes added to the regular menu. Pub fare includes the Ploughman's Lunch — pork pie, cheddar and Swiss cheese wedges, a tomato, pickled onion, Branston pickle and stick bread. The dinner menu takes you on a whirlwind journey, from boneless breast of duckling grilled with a citrus-rum sauce to Rendang Daging, a dried fried beef curry in coconut milk with onions, garlic and chiles. Pasta specials include capellini tossed with sun-dried tomatoes, peppers, onions and Parma ham in a creamy tomato sauce. Your intimate dining pleasure is accented by nightly entertainment featuring jazz or blues. Dress is smart casual.

Port O' Call
$$ • 87 Front St., Hamilton
• (441) 295-5373

For landlubbers craving a dapper, slightly nautical theme, check out this Port on Front Street. It's a smart restaurant that caters to the Hamilton business and political crowd. Local seafood, continental and American dishes, augmented by a comprehensive wine list, make this an oft-chosen spot. Management is always happy to welcome you on board and cater to your lunch or dinner desires. Seafood choices include tandoori roasted red snapper topped with cucumber relish and served on cilantro mashed potatoes. When in season, fresh Bermuda lobster broiled with shrimp and herb stuffing is served. However, be advised that the seafood menu changes every 10 days or so depending on the availability of local fish. Among turf selections is roasted rack of New Zealand lamb with an herb crust and thyme-roasted potatoes. Dress is smart casual.

Portofino
$ — $$ • Bermudiana Rd., Hamilton
• (441) 292-2375

This popular restaurant has a relaxed atmosphere that captivates locals and visitors alike. Its specialty is Italian cuisine for lunch or dinner; call ahead if you want to place a take-out order. Apart from pasta dishes like Ravioli Bolognese (ravioli stuffed with ricotta cheese simmered in a Bolognese sauce with a touch of cream), there are specials such as Scaloppine Parmigiana — escallop of veal, sauteed in butter and topped with mozzarella cheese and tomato sauce. Seafood fanciers will enjoy the Calamari Fra Diavola — calamari sauteed in a spicy tomato sauce served over linguine. Dress is casual, and reservations are advised.

Red Carpet
$$ • Armoury Bldg., 37 Reid St., Hamilton • (441) 292-6195

You may bump into some of Bermuda's who's who here. In the Armoury Building opposite the Bank of Butterfield, this is their popular lunch spot. Red is the dominant color of the dining room. The ambiance at dinner is intimate, and if you have any special requests, put them to the maitre d'. The folks here will try, within reason, to accommodate your particular wishes. Appetizers include Mussels Red Carpet (mussels simmered in Chablis, garlic, herb sauce and laced with cream) and Scottish smoked salmon garnished with onions, capers and horseradish. Entrees include Rockfish Mangrove Bay, served with bananas and almonds; and Seafood Kettle St. David's, a combination of lobster, clams, mussels, shrimp and fish stewed in Chablis, sherry peppers, Gosling's black rum and tomatoes. Top off a romantic evening with Coup Red Carpet; try it and be wonderfully surprised. Dress is smart casual.

Rock Island Coffee
$ • 48 Reid St., Hamilton
• (441) 296-2347

This is a diminutive roasting house; laid-back and trendy are the key attributes. You won't find dinner here, but you will find a selection of lovely coffees, caffe latte, cappuccino and nice teas. Muffins and biscotti are available. Inside are a couple of local paintings hanging on the walls; outside, near the entrance as you step off the pavement, are tables where you can kick back if you wish. Dress, as you would expect, is casual.

Rosa's Cantina
$ • 121 Front St., 2nd Floor, Hamilton
• (441) 295-1912

Put on your 10-gallon hat or sombrero and saunter down to Bermuda's only Southwestern/Tex-Mex restaurant. The decor captures a spicy southwestern flavor, and so do many of the food choices. Thus it is appropriate that they have a broad selection of beer as well as wine, which you imbibe either by the bottle or glass to soothe your spice-tinged palate. Lunch or dinner can be had for a reasonable price,

and portions are substantial. The menu includes selections ranging from Iguana eggs (cream cheese-stuffed deep-fried jalapeños) and fajitas, to chimichangas and quesadillas. The crowd here tends to be young, and it is a great place for family and kids (if they can't handle the spicy dishes, there are also burgers and pizza). Dress is casual.

Spot Restaurant
$ • Burnaby St., Hamilton
• (441) 692-6293

Although the Spot does not serve dinner, there is probably no restaurant in Bermuda that has achieved equal name recognition. Ask any cabbie, or any local strolling or hurrying through the city, and they will be able to tell you how to get to the Spot. The food here is basic and unadorned — scrambled eggs, bacon, sausages, fries and toast, pancakes, hamburgers and so forth, quickly prepared and served by friendly waitresses. And just like the locals, visitors find it an ideal place for breakfast and lunch. Dress is casual.

Spring Garden
$ • Washington Lane, Hamilton
• (441) 295-7416

Although this highly popular restaurant, named after an area in Barbados, specializes in Bajan cuisine, its menu has been described by one of the owners as "flexible." You'll find West Indian favorites such as flying fish, and Bermudian staples like fish cakes, fish chowder and ox-tail soup. But varieties of fish, beef, chicken and lamb have certainly not been ignored. Opened in 1998, and thus one of our newest restaurants, Spring Garden has become one of the preferred lunch spots in the city. Visitors have discovered its good food, reasonable prices and comfortable atmo-

---

INSIDERS' TIP

As early as 1616 the cassava plant was brought from the West Indies. The root is starchy and edible, and pie made from it has become a favorite Bermudian dish. In fact, Christmas wouldn't be the same without it. Each cook has his or her own preference in how it is made. Eggs, milk and sugar are standard ingredients, but depending on who is preparing it, the pie can be made with a middle layer filling of chicken, pork or beef.

sphere. Dress is casual for lunch and smart casual for dinner. Reservations for dinner are advised.

Sung Sing Take Out

$ • Corner Victoria & Court Streets, Hamilton • (441) 296-8758

This little take out spot just three blocks up Court Street from Front Street should be able to satisfy whatever craving you have for Chinese food. You will find a plethora of available dishes — more than 140 — embracing fish, shrimp, beef, lamb, chicken, pork and vegetarian. Examples of choices include: Fish in blackbean sauce; beef with snowpeas; curry lamb; crabmeat foo young; and roast duck with white rice. Open until midnight, they also offer free delivery.

Tuscany

$ • Bermuda House Ln., 95 Front St., Hamilton • (441) 292-4507

The allure of the Tuscan countryside is reflected in this restaurant's murals, and it is easy to imagine that you are dining at an elegant restaurant in the heart of Florence. Bermuda beam-and-slate ceilings fit in well as do the handsome frescoes. A pleasant balcony for dining alfresco adds to its atmosphere. The strictly Italian menu enchants with offerings such as petto di pollo alla Dante, boneless chicken breast sauteed with sherry and tomato and topped with eggplant and mozzarella. Dress is smart casual.

The Wok

$ • 10 Bermudiana Rd., Hamilton • (441) 295-7789

Staying at a hotel or guesthouse in the city and want Chinese take out? You can expect to find just about every quick dish here, from sweet and sour pork, and chicken foo yung, to beef chop suey and fish in plum sauce. But staples for the western palate have not been forgotten. There are the ubiquitous cheeseburger and fries, a variety of sandwiches and salads, and a breakfast menu with the usual suspects. Although there is a counter and a few stools where you can sit and grab a quick bite, this is a definite take-out place. Open until midnight, they also provide free delivery within the immediate area.

Other Parish Areas

Ascot's

$$ • 24 Rosemount Ave. • (441) 295-9644

Escape the city for tranquil surroundings mere minutes away. *USA Today* has called Ascot's a "place not to be missed." This elegant nineteenth-century former home, nestled in an idyllic setting, now houses an award-winning restaurant that captures the ambiance of a fine English country inn. Dine indoors or outside in a secluded and quiet garden setting where bougainvilleas and other flowers entertain the eyes. The dining emphasis is on provincial European cuisine and fresh local fish. Try the vegetarian mushroom Diane, char-grilled Portobello mushrooms with spinach and Taleggio cheese, all resting on a bed of grilled vegetables drizzled with rosemary-infused olive oil and accompanied by grilled polenta. A non-vegetarian favorite is fresh Bermuda wahoo gravlax — home-cured, then served with a red onion and roasted tomato balsamic confit garnished with an array of salad greens. drizzled with a lemongrass-infused vinegar. Stop by for the Sunday carvery where you'll find offerings such as Chicken Royal Palms — chicken stuffed with sun-dried tomatoes, black olives and camborzola cheese on a bed of roasted pepper oregano cream sauce. Dress is smart casual.

Colony Pub Steakhouse

$$ • Princess Hotel, Pitts Bay Rd. • (441) 295-3000

Walk through the main hotel doors, keep straight ahead, turn left and step into a cozy dining room accented by a cedar-paneled bar. You're in a steakhouse where the aged Angus beef steaks are like Texas — big. The shrimp and lamb chops are pretty generous too. Even the salmon are Goliath-size. You know what kind of appetite to bring to the table, and we're not kidding. During the day the pub features a good-value buffet lunch, and during the evening . . . well, we're back to those big steaks and shrimp and chops. Chef Peter Evans absolutely thrives on preparing the succulent oversized meat entrees and other dishes. Dress is smart casual.

Fisch's Place

$ • 22 Richmond Road • (441) 296-7067

Located near the Esso Automart, this restaurant exudes a definite German culinary focus. Among the specialties are Bratwurst with mashed potatoes and sauerkraut; sauerbraten, braised beef marinated in vinegar served with homemade spatzle and red cabbage; and weinerschnitzel with french fries and salad. The dining room is comparatively small, and you can dine on their outdoor patio. Open daily. Dress is smart casual. Reservations required.

Green Lantern

$ • 9 Serpentine Rd. • (441) 295-6995

Outside city limits, just a couple of minutes from the center of Hamilton, locals go to this clean, tidy and friendly restaurant to find home-cooked meals without the fanfare. Green Lantern has been catering to Bermudians for many decades. Menu items include curried chicken served over white rice with the vegetable of the day. Fish & chips are also quite popular. Finish off with dessert — perhaps chocolate cake topped with fudge icing. The atmosphere is casual and relaxed. Reservations are not necessary. Dress is casual.

House of India

$• Park View Plaza, 57 North St.
• (441) 295-6450

This most recent Indian restaurant offers an Indian cuisine deli and specialty groceries. Serving lunch and dinner, and with an extensive menu, they are quick to point out that all dishes are gluten and wheat free except their breads and pastries. A buffet lunch is available each day with choices including vegetarian dishes. No two days are the same. Their à-la-carte menu includes a number of beef and lamb favorites, including lamb masala and beef roganjosh. Dress is casual.

Jamaican Grill

$ • Court St. • (441) 296-6577
$ • 40 Parson's Rd. • (441) 292-3269
$ • Paget • (441) 232-0420
$ • Somerset • (441) 234-4039

This popular chain of restaurants, as the name indicates, emphasizes Jamaican cuisine. Geared mostly toward the take-out crowd, they have become very popular with locals. Steamed vegetables, rice 'n peas, Spanish rice, pineapple glazed chicken, macaroni 'n cheese, roast beef in mushroom sauce and a host of other dishes are offered. They also have natural fruit juices.

La Coquille

$$ • Crow Ln. • (441) 292-6122

Located at the Bermuda Underwater Exploration Institute and situated overlooking the gentle waters of Hamilton Harbour, this fine restaurant allows you to arrive by boat if you wish. Tie up at the dock and dine on the waterfront terrace, or step inside and enjoy the local seafood dishes and French cuisine in air-conditioned comfort.

Appetizers include pan-sauteed duck liver foie gras with caramelized pears, port wine reduction and miniature brioche. Among the superb entrees are grilled semi-boneless quail and wild boar sausage, porcini mushrooms, risotto pancakes and roasted pearl onions. Another favorite is the seared rack of lamb with sun-dried tomato crust, roasted garlic whipped potatoes, sauteed baby artichokes and rosemary jus. Reservations are suggested, and dress is smart casual.

Monty's

$ • 75 Pitt's Bay Rd. • (441) 295-5759

Bright, cheerful and only a few minutes walk west along Front Street, this restaurant has in a short time become popular. Here you'll find Bermuda-styled food at reasonable prices. It is delightful for families. One of their signature dishes is Caribbean chicken, grilled chicken breast with a tasty papaya and mango topping, served with rice or baked potato and vegetable of the day. Another is Monty's Fish, grilled Bermuda fish topped with a flavorful champagne sauce and served with rice and vegetable. Their Friday night special is Beef Wellington. Contemporary light music often accompanies your dining. Dress is casual. Reservations not required.

Primavera Ristorante

$$ • 69 Pitts Bay Rd.
• (441) 295-2167

Near the center of the city and just a minute or so from the Hamilton Princess Hotel, this

Italian establishment offers what it calls the ultimate in Italian cuisine. The relaxed and intimate atmosphere is delightful. The selection of traditional dishes is wide-ranging. Choose from chicken specialties such as chicken alla Lariana (French-cut chicken breast stuffed with fresh vegetables and served with a raspberry and hazelnut sauce) and fish specialties such as zuppa di pesce alla Livornese (clams, mussels, jumbo shrimp, fish fillets, fresh tomato, wine and garlic sauce). Another favorite is saltimbocca alla Romana, veal escallop with a sage, prosciutto and Marsala sauce. Dress is smart casual.

Waterloo House
$$ • Pitts Bay Road
• (441) 295-4480

The restaurant located in this former eighteenth century town house, offers Bermudian and Continental cuisine within an easy walk from the city center. Waterloo (see Small Hotels chapter), charmingly ensconced on the harbor's edge, and with terraced gardens ambling to the waterside, is a tranquil oasis in an otherwise busy city. You can dine in the elegant Wellington Room — where a crackling fire may be going during cold or damp winters — or on the Poinciana Terrace overlooking the water. Romantic and charming, Waterloo captivates with an ambiance enhanced by exquisite antiques and plush décor. Among appetizers is ragout of escargots in a basil, lemon and garlic sauce, with spinach, sauteed mushrooms and herb brioche. Roasted carrot soup with ginger, caraway and almonds is another delight. As for entrees, selections include grilled wahoo with gremolata, purple whipped potatoes, carmelized butternut squash, charred tomato compote, and braised celery, red wine jus and curry oil. Gentlemen are requested to wear jacket and tie. Reservations are suggested.

Paget Parish

Crow Lane Bakery
$ • 35 Crow Ln.
• (441) 292-2220

We cannot fail to mention this little bakery at the entrance to the city, in the pink building where Hamilton's merchants and bigwigs gathered in the late eighteenth century to plan the transfer of capital status from the Town of St. George to Hamilton. This is a definite favorite spot for locals looking for superb pastries, cakes and breads for take-out. It's a great little place for picking up those sinful temptations you know you shouldn't eat but can't resist. So give your taste buds a treat. After all, you're on holiday!

Fourways Inn
$$$$ • 1 Middle Rd.
• (441) 236-6517

At Amen Corner (so-called because it's near the site of the Cobb's Hill Methodist Church built by slaves in the early nineteenth century) this restaurant has a sterling reputation. Built in 1727 of coral stone and cedar, this former private home was converted to a guesthouse and restaurant in the twentieth century. The original kitchen, notable for its large-stepped fireplace, is now the Peg Leg Bar, a quiet spot for meeting friends and acquaintances before or after dinner. Love them or not, Fourways' chefs have garnered high acclaim for their innovative and varied menu. Internationally favored for fine cuisine, the old-world decor charms and enchants. Seafood delights include pan-seared fillet of rockfish with a Louisiana crayfish sauce and fresh dill, and Atlantic salmon wrapped in rice paper, layered with leaf spinach and mushrooms and enhanced with black grape sauce. Add a bottle of great wine from the extensive list, and you have the ingredients to concoct a romantic evening. Gentlemen are asked to wear a jacket and tie. Reservations are necessary.

Café Lido
$$ • Elbow Beach Hotel, 60 South Shore Rd.
• (441) 236-9884

For dining by the sea, this on-the-beach restaurant has few peers. Enjoy lunch either alfresco or indoors in the glass-ceilinged dining room. Imagine dining beneath a full moon, its rays bouncing off the ocean. Ah, the romance of it all. Better still, don't just imagine — experience it. The menu is seasonal, but the typical fare includes roasted free-range Amish chicken with rosemary giblet sauce, mashed potatoes with roasted garlic and Mascarpone cheese, and swordfish Cartoccio, wrapped in parchment and served with baby clams, yellow and red tomatoes, white wine, garlic and fresh basil. A jacket is necessary for dinner.

The Paraquet
$ • South Shore Rd.
• (441) 236-5842

This restaurant attracts a very mixed clientele, and families find it one of the more relaxed places to bring children. The cooking is homestyle, and the dining room is modest and straightforward. Fish & chips are big here. Waitresses are friendly, and prices are reasonable. Should you want a magazine or newspaper, a newsstand is just to your left as you enter. Take-out service is also available for those on the run. Dress is casual.

Seahorse Grill
$$ • Elbow Beach Hotel,
60 South Shore Rd.
• (441) 236-3535

Named after the amazing little creatures found in many of our grassy-bottomed bays, this restaurant has taken Bermudian cuisine up market. Using locally harvested foods when available, Chef Neville King has created an imaginative and tantalizing menu. Starters include dusky shark-hash-stuffed spring rolls, loquat black rum barbeque sauce and pawpaw slaw. One of their soup choices is local white corn and lobster with cedar-smoked seafood. The entrees are equally tempting, among them: Bermuda bouillabaisse with scallops, guinea chick, local fish and shrimp in a chili tomato broth. For dessert, tickle your taste buds with sweet cassava pie stuffed with apples and pears, island coulis and Bermuda Gold scented whipped cream. Dress is smart casual and reservations are advised.

Warwick Parish

Paw Paws
$ — $$ • 87 South Shore Rd.
• (441) 236-7459

Paw Paws offers a welcome respite when riding your moped along South Shore Road.

You'll find it about a mile west of Elbow Beach Hotel. While you can relax inside, one of the lovely features is the outdoor terrace dining. The menu has some interesting choices. A favorite here is broiled lobster on the half-shell served with a baked potato and fresh vegetables. Dress is casual.

Jolly Lobster
$$ • Mermaid Beach Club,
South Shore Rd.
• (441) 236-5031

On the scenic South Shore route, in what has been called a "Jolly Roger" setting, this restaurant is all about seafood, except for the rack of lamb, sirloin steak and chicken Rollotini — chicken stuffed with asparagus, goat cheese and Parma ham and served with baby vegetables and rosemary potatoes. The Seafood Potpourri — scallops, salmon, wahoo and fried lobster-shrimp wonton served with couscous and baby vegetables in a basil-tomato sauce — is a seafood lover's favorite. Of course, Bermuda lobster and whole Maine lobster are the headliners. Dress is smart casual.

Ms Softys
$ • 235 Middle Rd.
• (441) 238-0931

Found on your moped journey westward, located on your right between an Esso gas station and the Marketplace supermarket, this little eatery is a great place to tie up your moped and mosey in for a quick Bermudian-styled lunch or snack. Fish cakes, hamburgers, and roast beef or fish lunches are the general fare. This restaurant is clean, unpretentious and not open for dinner.

Southampton Parish

Henry VIII
$$ • near entrance to Sonesta Beach Hotel, South Shore Rd.
• (441) 238-1977

Named after the King of England who initiated the English Reformation — and who also is well-known for having two of his wives beheaded — this restaurant and pub has hosted many joyful ceremonies, parties, banquets and

romantic dinners. If you lose your head here, it will be over the atmosphere and food. The four dining rooms are accentuated by rich oak paneling of which Henry himself likely would have approved. The fare is sumptuous — it also would have had old Henry raising his pewter mug in endless toasts. The wine cellar is formidable, and you can guzzle any one of a selection of English ales in the Oak Room Pub.

Specialty Night is something to be experienced! A Medieval Feast (ahem, fit for a King) is laid on, and you are a welcome guest for the feasting and festing. Apart from Specialty Night, the dinner menu includes a delightful duck à l'orange — Royal Aylesbury duckling, flamed crisp with Grand Marnier and organge sauce — and Chateaubriand for two — a double filet steak, broiled complete with a generous variety of garden vegetables, potatoes and mushrooms and accompanied by béarnaise sauce.

Among the wide range of choices are low fat, low sodium, low calorie selections cooked in natural vegetable oil. A favorite from this lighter side of Henry's is the curried vegetable strudel, a creative and delicious offering of carrots, potatoes, cauliflower, onions and cilantro in a curry sauce, all wrapped in phyllo pastry with shredded coconut. However you slice it, Henry's is a great choice. Jackets are required for dinner.

Lighthouse Tearoom
$, no credit cards • Gibb's Hill
Lighthouse, 68 St. Anne's Rd.
• (441) 238-8679

This beacon is one of the oldest iron lighthouses still in existence. Those who climb the winding 185 steps to the top are treated to a view of Bermuda as a canvas of tranquil bays, lush hills and pastel houses. At the base is a lace-curtained tearoom where you can enjoy a full English breakfast or lunch and take in a splendid view of the Great Sound. The menu includes smoked salmon, pork pies, salads and sandwiches. And there's the tea, tea cakes, scones, Bermuda honey and Devon double cream. The cozy atmosphere is delightful, and after eating you can visit the adjacent little shop to purchase jams and preserves, cups and mugs. However, cash is necessary in both the tearoom and the shop. Dress is casual.

Lillians
$$ • at Sonesta Beach Resort Hotel,
South Shore Rd. • (441) 238-8122

If your palate craves Italian, this gem might very well have it singing an aria. You can choose from a "deluxe dinner" which includes antipasti and two courses, or you may opt for à-la-carte; the deluxe is more costly (our price is based on a-la-carte). The restaurant is roomy and the service is good. Entrée choices include vegetarian eggplant and spinach cannelloni, with ultra thin eggplant wrapped around fresh cheeses, tomatoes and herbs. Among non-vegetarian selections is veal loin chop with rosemary and glazed lemon, medium seared for moistness, and with mashed fennel potatoes and asparagus. Dress is smart casual and reservations are suggested.

Newport Room
$$ • Southampton Princess Hotel South Shore Rd. • (441) 239-6964

Think of a luxury salon on a private yacht, and you have an idea of the flavor and décor of the Newport Room. Dimmed but comfortable lighting, and booths with glass-covered insets exhibiting barometers, knots and such, provide a nautical-flavored inducement to romance. The food, which also has won the Four Diamond AAA award, is impeccably served, presented on Wedgwood china with wine in a crystal glass. Chef Thomas Frost takes pride in his creative French dishes. Appetizers include bouquet of baby field greens, tossed with avocado and orange fillets, dressed in native banana and scallion vinaigrette, topped with warm Bermuda fishcake croutons. Among the entrees you'll find mint-glazed crowned rack of lamb, reigning atop crisp croquettes of Yukon potato and Bermuda goat cheese, Pommery, herb and natural lamb jus. Gentlemen are required to wear jacket and tie. Reservations necessary. Remember though, the Newport Room is usually closed for much of the winter and during one or two local holidays; call ahead to be sure.

Mrs. Tea's Victorian Tearoom
$ • 25 Middle Rd. (opposite Port Royal Golf Course) • (441) 234-1374

The key word here is Victorian. From its dainty cups and plates to the pictures on the walls, the tearoom oozes Victorian niceties without pompous conservatism. In a seventeenth-century Bermuda National Trust property just off the Railway Trail in Somerset, Mrs. Tea's offers traditional English tea — pastries, scones, biscuits and an assortment of delicious teas. (Remember: In British vernacular, "tea" refers as much to the event as the drink.) Casual dress is acceptable.

Waterlot Inn
$$ • Middle Rd.
• (441) 239-6967 and (441) 238-2555

This lovingly restored dockside inn, once a seventeenth-century waterside private home, retains a captivating old-world charm. The food is enchanting, as is the piano music floating through the dining room. French and continental cuisine served in candlelit elegance guarantee a memorable experience. The wine list is impressive. Once you've dined here, you'll understand why this restaurant is so highly acclaimed. Dinner selections include roasted whole Maine lobster atop porcini mushroom risotto, garnished with fresh roasted corn and served with an asparagus sauce. There is also Chateaubriand (for two), a seared center-cut filet mignon (U.S. beef) served with sauteed Mediterranean vegetables and potatoes au gratin with Gorgonzola. Top your choice off with strawberries Romanoff (for two), flamed with Grand Marnier and brandy, enhanced by cracked green peppercorns and served over vanilla ice cream. A jacket and tie are required here. Reservations are necessary. The restaurant closes in winter (usually January and February), but call ahead to confirm.

Sandys Parish

Il Palio
$$ • 64 Somerset Rd. • (441) 234-1049

This Italian gem is intimate and delightful. Its entrees open a fascinating window onto the specialties of several Italian regions. The dish may be seafood, veal or beef, but the style of preparation may be a traditional Monte Amiata region recipe, Livorno specialty, Siena delicacy, Florence favorite, or . . . you get the idea. A specialty from the kitchens of Florence is Stracotto Toscano — loin of veal braised in a red sauce with bacon, vegetables and herbs. Another fine choice is filet of rockfish — broiled with boiled egg yolk and lemon sauce in the traditional style of the Viareggio region. Open every evening except Monday. Dress is smart casual and reservations are suggested.

Somerset Country Squire
$• Mangrove Bay Rd.• (441) 234-0105

The ambiance is that of a British pub, but

their specialties combine Bermudian and English dishes. Located within the hub of Somerset Village, and overlooking Mangrove Bay, this charming restaurant combines delightful outdoor and indoor dining. During the summer, the Sunday, Monday and Tuesday night barbecues are highly popular with both locals and visitors. Dress is smart casual.

Traditions
$ • 2 Middle Rd. • (441) 234-3770

This little restaurant is a great stop on the way into Somerset or the Dockyard. Apart from the usual breakfast offerings — eggs, pancakes, sausages, bacon, omlettes, etc. — they have a number of sandwich, hamburger, soup and salad choices. Some of the main courses include their Land & Sea —a 4oz steak with fish, shrimp and scallops. Dress is casual.

Freeport Seafood Restaurant and Bar
$ • 1 Freeport Rd., Royal Naval Dockyard • (441) 234-1692

Immediately inside the entrance to the historic former Royal Naval Dockyard, this restaurant emphasizes seafood, both local and imported. A casual and relaxed atmosphere makes dining a pleasure. Lobster and even seafood pizza are on the menu, and there are daily specials. Dress is casual.

Beethoven's Restaurant and Bar
$ • Clocktower Centre, Royal Naval Dockyard • (441) 234-5009

Two Swiss chefs own and operate this cozy restaurant, which has an easy, intimate atmosphere. The cuisine is sophisticated, delicious and well presented. There are also fondue and raclette nights. Dress is casual.

Our nightlife revolves mostly around restaurants, bars and some nightclubs. Check out our Resort Hotels, Small Hotels and Cottage Colonies chapters for detailed information on evening entertainment at vairous accommodations.

Nightlife

Perhaps you agree with Dr. Samuel Johnson that "whoever thinks of going to bed before twelve o'clock is a scoundrel." If you're of a like mind, this chapter will give you some fun options that are available in Bermuda at night.

Let's begin with what not to expect. Though they are the subject of debate right now, we offer absolutely no casinos. There are business people who think casinos would appeal to a younger market and inject new vigor into our tourist-oriented entertainment environment. Yet others are convinced casinos would go against the conservative tone of our island. Given the strong influence of religion in Bermuda, it's unlikely that casinos will come anytime soon. Don't expect the lure of huge billboards and neon lighting either. We have strict laws prohibiting large advertising signs from dominating the landscape.

Our nightlife revolves mostly around restaurants, bars and some nightclubs. You might also agree with Rupert Brooke that "cities, like cats, will reveal themselves at night." The only trouble is, we only have one city — Hamilton. While it's true that much of our nightlife (particularly the club scene) is in the capital, there are nightspots scattered all over the island, many of them in hotels. Check out our Resort Hotels, Small Hotels and Cottage Colonies chapters for detailed information on evening entertainment at various accommodations. For more on dining and menu options at nightspots that are also eateries, see our Restaurants chapter.

What to Wear

There was a time when gentlemen would not be welcome in restaurants or nightclubs without jacket and tie. During the last five years or so, we've loosened up a bit to get in tune with our North American visitors, so few places insist on tie torture for men. Jackets are still required in the more upscale restaurants and bars, particularly those operating in hotels, but in most places smart-casual dress is now the norm. Of course, being quite conservative, "smart-casual" needs definition. To be safe, avoid wearing sneakers or jeans. Some establishments will allow them, but others won't. If you're unsure about a club's dress policies, give them a call before you go out.

Drinking and Driving, Safety

Be aware that we have breathalyzer testing here, same as in the States. If your blood-alcohol content is .08 or higher, you are over the legal drinking limit to operate a vehicle, and you could be prosecuted for drunken driving. Should you be convicted, you pay a $450 fine and will not be allowed to drive in Bermuda for one year.

We'd prefer you not drive after even moderate drinking. Remember, we drive on the left side of the road here. Most likely you're used to driving on the right. Even one alcoholic drink can cause reduced concentration and a sudden fit of right/left confusion. We don't want you careening 'round a roundabout in the wrong direction. If you want to drink, we advise that you take a taxi or choose a designated driver. Around Christmas and on New Year's Eve, bars will very often give free soft drinks to designated drivers. We are proud of our relatively safe environment here. However, you should not be completely complacent when hitting the clubs. It's important to take the normal precautions dictated by common sense. Keep your handbags zipped or fastened, and avoid walking alone late at night.

Cover Charges and Happy Hours

Where nightclubs charge entrance fees, we'll tell you. If a listing does not mention prices, you can assume there is no cover charge. Alcoholic drinks can cost anywhere from $3.75 to $5.75 a glass. Many bars and nightclubs offer reduced prices during a happy hour. An hour, of course, usually consists of 60 minutes, but where happiness is concerned, time in Bermuda becomes elastic. A happy hour can be up to three hours. We'll be as specific as possible since policy differs from establishment to establishment and night to night. Also, please remember that the following quoted prices are subject to change.

Bars and Nightclubs

As usual, our listings start in St. George's Parish and move from east to west.

St. George's Parish

The Wharf Tavern
14 Water St., Town of St. George
• (441) 297-1515

This bar and restaurant is appropriately named because it sits right on St. George's Harbour. About 120 years old, the building originally had residential accommodations upstairs and warehousing downstairs. When Somers Wharf was developed for tourism about 20 years ago, the tavern came into being.

Come to the Wharf Tavern, and you'll get to hear all the discussions on local issues and politics and the other stories the local regulars love to tell. You can sit at the inside bar or, on warm nights, outside on the patio overlooking the harbor. Happy hour is 4 to 6 PM every night; you'll get 75¢ off drinks. Normal prices range from $3.25 to $5. Draft beers on tap are Fosters and Bass, Tennants and John Courage. From April through October, guitarists play live music and often involve customers in singalongs. The dress here is casual. The Wharf Tavern is open year-round (except

Christmas Day) from 10.30 AM to 11:30 PM Monday through Saturday and noon to 1 AM on Sundays.

Hamilton Parish

Swizzle Inn
3 Blue Hole Hill, Bailey's Bay
• (441) 293-9300

The Swizzle is the inn where you either celebrate your arrival in Bermuda or drink to your departure. It's just a five-minute drive from the airport, you see. For cigarette smokers coming from Hamilton, it's the last place they can indulge before arriving at the smoke-free departure lounge and bar.

You'll find the walls of the bar downstairs covered with business cards and stickers. Guests from America, Canada, Australia, Europe and Asia left these souvenirs as proof that they visited Bermuda. The Swizzle also caters to local regulars who have been coming for years. Tourists and locals often meet in the bar, chat over a game of pool in a room off the bar or sit outside on one of the two patios. Happy hour, offering $1 off drink prices, runs Monday through Friday from 5 to 7 PM. As you might expect, this inn is famous for its rum swizzles as well its dark and stormies (a delicious, but potent, Bermudian drink consisting of black rum and ginger beer). Normal drink prices are about $4.75. During the summer you can enjoy live blues, jazz, calypso and rock music on Thursday, Friday and Saturday. The bar is open from 11 AM to 1 AM in the high season. From November through April, it closes every Monday and at 10 PM nightly.

Smiths Parish

North Rock Brewing Company
10 South Rd.
• (441) 236-6633

Yes, it is a brewing company, but it's also a restaurant and bar. As soon as you walk in, you'll see copper tanks containing the beers North Rock has (since 1997) been fast becoming famous for. Brewing is done through the early hours of the morning, but at some

points during the day you'll experience a waft of barley and hops.

Home-brewed beers on tap include Old Colony Bitter, Somers Amber Ale (Sir George Somers would surely have approved of it; see our History chapter), Whale of a Week and North Rock Porter. A 22-ounce glass is $4.75. These beers, by the way, are for North Rock's supply only — they are not sold to other pubs. Happy hour runs from 5 to 7 PM Monday through Friday and gives you a reduction of roughly 75¢ on all drinks. You can dine in the restaurant, relax on the patio or sit in the bar and imbibe the friendly atmosphere as well as the beer. North Rock is open from 11 AM to 1 AM year-round, except for Christmas week, New Year's Eve and New Year's Day. It is completely wheelchair-accessible with a specially equipped bathroom.

Pembroke Parish

Chancery Wine Bar and Restaurant
2 Chancery Ln., Hamilton
• (441) 295-5058

The Wine Bar is a great venue for quiet conversation over an excellent glass of wine. That's why many business people like to take a break here after work. Staff will tell you about the featured wine of the week. It could be from France, Italy, Spain, South Africa, New Zealand or California. You can buy a bottle of any of

the wines, or you can choose to have just a glass. Prices obviously depend on the vintage you choose. Ask for a beer or a glass of house wine, and you'll pay about $3.50 and $5 respectively. Chancery has recently become unofficially known as "the Tapas Bar." That's because *tapas*, or special Spanish hors d'oeuvres, are served. The bar is open daily year-round. Monday through Friday hours are noon to 1 AM; on Saturdays it's 7 PM to 1 AM and Sundays, it's open from 7 PM to midnight. In the summer months we like to sit out on the patio European style and enjoy watching the passersby go up and down the narrow alley that is Chancery Lane. Dress is smart-casual. Yes, there is a happy hour. It's from 5 to 7 PM Monday through Friday and offers about $1 off drinks.

The Club
32 Bermudiana Rd., Hamilton
• (441) 295-9627

This club is above the Little Venice Restaurant (see our Restaurants chapter). Open 9 PM to 3 AM, it offers a bar, music and a relaxing, cozy atmosphere. Occasionally there's live music, but on the whole it's DJ Ken Steede who'll get you dancing to rap, reggae, disco and soca (a Caribbean hybrid of calypso and American soul, served up with a heavy beat). The clientele tend to be in their 30s. The dress code is smart-casual; sneakers and cutoff jeans are not acceptable. Fridays and Saturdays are definitely the busy nights — that's when you'll meet lots of locals. Drinks cost $5, but there's no cover charge. Most of the year The Club closes only on Sunday, but in January it sometimes closes on Monday and Tuesday as well.

Coconut Rock
Williams House, 20 Reid St., Hamilton
• (441) 292-1043

Coconut Rock has a restaurant and two bars. The main bar is open year-round except Christmas and Boxing Day (that's December 26, by the way) from 11 AM to 1 AM. Happy hour runs from 5 to 7 PM, reducing drinks from $4 to $2.75. Up to about 10:30 PM, regulars like to meet for drinks, conversation and easy-listening music, and they often watch videotapes of Top 40 acts in America and the UK. After that, the Rock gets noisier, as people like to dance to European music.

Friday nights are particularly lively, and the increased party traffic leads management to open the second bar, the Bourbon Lounge, where you can listen to background jazz. Every other Sunday it's the venue for Flow Sundays, an evening featuring music and poetry. From 7 PM, DJ Beatnik plays all kinds of music: hip hop, Latin and jazz old and new. At 9 PM one featured poet and one musician give a performance. Open house starts at 10 PM: Twelve to 15 five-minute spots are given to musicians and poets in the audience. Emcee André Simons explains that this event offers an opportunity for free speech on any topic. "It's completely uncensored," he says. It also allows poets and musicians of all races and cultural backgrounds to meet and exchange ideas. Very often all performers are Bermudian, but artists from abroad are very welcome. Don't forget your sitar! Call (441) 296-3054 or (441) 293-1014 if you're interested in participating.

The Colony Pub
The Princess, 76 Pitts Bay Rd., Hamilton
• (441) 295-3000

Come to the Colony Pub during the summer months, and you'll get live entertainment

every night but Sunday. From 10 PM to 1 AM on Tuesdays and Fridays, you'll hear LeYoni Junos; the same hours on Thursdays and Saturdays, you'll hear Gita Blakeney. Both of these jazz and blues singers are famous in Bermuda for their superb voices and versatile repertoires. Jazz pianist Vic Lazer accompanies them. On Wednesdays, Vic joins the Jazztet for a night of . . . well, yes, jazz par excellence.

If assistant maitre d' Dean Hayward has his way, you'll be dancing. According to Duval Minors, the club manager, Dean is known as "Lean Dean, the Dancing Machine."

Drinks run from $4.90 to $5.75, depending on whether you have a beer or a highball. The atmosphere is upbeat and, as Duval puts it, "down-to-earth Bermuda." Dress is casual. Open year-round, the bar operates from 11 AM to 1 AM.

Flanagan's
Emporium Bldg., 69 Front St., Hamilton
• (441) 295-8299

This pub and restaurant is run by an Irishman — Thomas Gallagher. As he puts it, "Cead Mile Failte." That's Irish for "A Hundred Thousand Welcomes." On the second floor of the Emporium Building, Flanagan's is a favorite for people who like to dance as well as talk over drinks. Year-round, live music is played every night in one of the two bars. Usually about five acts play (one act per night) and offer rock, reggae, dance, soca and party music. These acts may vary from time to time but they are all local.

Happy hour is every day from 5 to 7 PM and offers anywhere from 50¢ to $1.50 off drinks that normally start at $4.25 for a glass of wine or beer. However, Flanagan's has an extensive drink menu that includes a variety of exotic drinks. Fancy a frozen mudslide? That concoction of vodka, kahlua, ice cream and milk will cost you $6. People of all ages like to visit, but around the holidays you'll see many students catching up on local news they missed while away. Sports fans will appreciate the sports bar, where they can watch live English, Scottish and other European soccer games on a 40-inch TV. Eight other 27-inch screens are available. A multi-channel satellite system means three different games can be played simultaneously. Worried about missing your favorite baseball, basketball and NFL games? Don't be; they are shown here every night during the season. The sports bar also offers a variety of games including table soccer (that's Foosball to Americans), interactive golf and touch-screen games. Flanagan's is open year-round (except for Christmas Day) from 10 AM to 1 AM.

The Hog Penny Restaurant and Pub
5 Burnaby Hill, Hamilton
• **(441) 292-2534**

The Hog Penny, named after our old hog money currency, is a tourist favorite. According to manager Andy Shirt, tourists come back year after year for the fun, friendly atmosphere that is reminiscent of a British pub. During summer, guitarists play soft rock music every night; for December, January and February, entertainment is cut down to weekends only. Happy hour runs from 5 to 7 PM Monday through Friday, offering $1 off each libation. Normal prices for drinks run about $4.25. Dress is smart-casual. Check the Restaurants chapter for dinner and lunch menus.

Hubie's Bar
Angle St., Hamilton
• **(441) 293-9287**

Hubie's is open Monday through Saturday from 10 AM to 10 PM, but the night to come is Friday. Between 7 and 10 PM that evening, it seems all of Bermuda comes together to hear local band Jaz play, yes, jazz. The bar is packed with people of all races, cultures and ages; by 7:30 PM, it's standing room only. OK, the place closes early; for some of us who are not night owls, that's an advantage. We don't have to wait until late for the live music to start. The rest of the week, you can come for a drink ($2.75 each) and play music on the jukebox. Hubie's does not accept credit cards.

Oasis Nite Life and Rockroom
Emporium Bldg., 69 Front St., Hamilton
• **(441) 292-4978**

Located on the third floor of the Emporium Building, which you reach by using a very snazzy, glass-enclosed elevator, Oasis offers both live and DJ-spun music. Call for information about live music, since it changes all the time.

DJs spin tracks in the main nightclub, which is equipped with mirrors and state-of-the-art lighting. What kind of music? As general manager Mark Osborne puts it, "Whatever's up to date. Music's got a life of about two weeks these days." You'll get a chance to hear music that's popular in Europe as well as the US. The cover charge during the summer season is $10 during the week, $15 on Fridays and Saturdays, and it gets you into both areas of the club. There's no charge at all on Sundays. During winter there's no cover charge during the week (although this policy is subject to change). Happy hour is 9 to 11 PM on Friday and means about a $2 reduction on drinks that are normally $5 to $5.50. Oasis closes at 3 AM.

The Pickled Onion
53 Front St., Hamilton
• **(441) 295-2263**

Repeat visitors to Bermuda will realize that until 1997 this pub and restaurant was for many years Ye Old Cock and Feather. Completely refurbished as well as renamed, The Pickled Onion is now "the hottest place in Bermuda" with walls painted in bright Bermuda yellows, pinks and greens. Guests sit at open tables or in booths covered with funky fabric. Live en-

---

INSIDERS' TIP

May to October is high season for our hotels. It's also high season for our summer night skies. Appreciate our smog-free atmosphere and take the time to stargaze. During summer months you can easily see the Milky Way and Scorpio. Stare at the same spot for five minutes, and we bet you'll see a shooting star.

tertainment happens from 10 PM on. Types of music range from blues to '80s and '90s favorites. Happy hour happens Monday through Saturday from 5 to 7 PM and means a $3 reduction on drinks. Open daily from 11:30 AM, The Pickled Onion closes only on Christmas Day and Cup Match. (See Annual Events chapter).

Robin Hood Pub and Restaurant
25 Richmond Rd.
• (441) 295-3314

Robin Hood has a variety of entertainment options, so chances are good that most nights you'll find lots of merry men and merry women here. During the high season (April through October), a DJ plays the latest reggae on Monday nights. Year-round on Tuesdays from 8 to 10:30 PM, you can take part in quizzes on general knowledge, movies, pop music, entertainment and live trivia. Wednesday nights during summer vacation, you get students (very merry ones indeed) participating in boat races. The winner of the race is the one who drinks a pint of ale in the fastest time. The prize? A bottle of champagne — just what they need. All contestants get their beer on the house. Fridays and Saturdays are jukebox nights for lovers of rock and reggae. Occasionally, local pop music entertainers will play.

OK, Robin Hood has no archery, but in the sports bar you can watch live coverage of various American and British league contests. Owners Shep and Chopper pride themselves on having Bermuda's premier sports bar. Happy hour is from 4 to 8 PM Monday through Friday and from 5 to 7 PM on Saturdays and Sundays. It'll save you 75¢ on drinks that normally cost about $4. Dress is casual. Robin Hood is open from 11 AM to 1 AM Monday through Saturday and noon to 1 AM on Sundays.

The Spinning Wheel
33 Court St., Hamilton
• (441) 292-7799

Named after an old song of the same name (it was The Fifth Dimension, if you can't think back that far), The Spinning Wheel has been a favorite for locals since 1970. Manager and part-owner Gladwyn Ming says, "Locals make up 95 percent of our business at the moment,

but we welcome tourists." You can relax in the outdoor pool area or the cocktail lounge, where plenty of dark and stormies are on hand, and you can dance in the disco area. Happy hour is 5 to 7 PM Monday through Friday; drinks that normally range from $4 to $5 per glass are about $1 off. The Spinning Wheel, by the way, takes no credit cards. The bar is open from noon to 3 AM year-round. Dress is casual in the summer. "In the winter," Ming says, "people like to dress up."

Surf Club
Number 6 Shed, Front St., Hamilton
• (441) 292-6566

Visitors disembarking the cruise ships docked by Number 6 Shed will find this club facing them once they reach the end of the gang plank. They can sit at tables outside on a terraced area or go to the bar, restaurant and dance floor areas inside. Happy hour runs from 5:30 to 7 PM daily and offers free hors d'oeuvres. This nightclub regularly features international bands including ones from the US and Europe. Tickets for band shows cost $10 per person. See Restaurants Chapter for info about menus. Monday through Sunday during the high season, the club opens from noon to 3 AM. It closes during January, February and March.

Sandys Parish

Freeport Seafood Restaurant and Bar
1 Freeport Rd., Royal Naval Dockyard
• (441) 234-1692

As soon as you enter Dockyard, you'll see this restaurant and bar on your left. It's famous for a drink it offers. Beer? Wine? No and no. It's the one place on the island where you can buy fresh mango juice. It's $3.50 for a 12-ounce glass. People who are seriously addicted to mangos after sampling them in the Caribbean islands feel that this elixir is cheap at that price.

Of course, alcoholic beverages are available too, ranging from $3.75 to $4.50 for a Fosters draft. There's no happy hour as such, but, as Valiero Ausenda told us, "That's because every hour here is a happy one." Valiero,

Photo: GIS

This is truly a dining room with a view.

who describes himself as "owner, manager, dishwasher and busboy," still has time to talk with his guests. Freeport is ideal for relaxing conversation since the background music is soft. You can sit inside or out in a garden patio area at the back. Dress is smart-casual.

The Frog and Onion
The Cooperage, 23 Freeport Rd., Royal Naval Dockyard
• (441) 234-2900

By now you're probably aware that we have whistling tree frogs and that "onion" is our substitute name for a Bermudian. And so, you have The Frog and Onion. The pub and restaurant's interior is evocative of the history of this former naval building. You'll see exposed stone walls and the old forge that now operates as a fireplace in the dining room. Old bottles, barrels, flasks and compasses currently act as decoration but were once utilitarian.

Opposite the Neptune Cinema, The Frog and Onion is ideal if you want a meal and a movie. Customers are both tourists and lo-

cals. A DJ offers a selection of popular music from the '60s to the '90s on Tuesdays and Wednesdays. Saturdays you'll hear the pianist; Fridays it's guitar music. English draft beers, such as Watneys, Flowers, Newcastle Brown and Guinness, are on tap for about $4.75 a pint. A separate game room offers pool and a variety of arcade games. The Frog and Onion is open 11:30 AM to 1 AM on Monday through Saturday and noon to 1 AM on Sundays. It's open year-round but closes on Mondays from December through February. Dress is casual.

Nightlife Afloat

Oscar Wilde once wrote: "Nobody of any real culture, for instance, ever talks nowadays about the beauty of sunsets. Sunsets are quite old-fashioned. . . . To admire them is a distinct sign of provincialism of temperament. Upon the other hand they go on." They certainly do go on. And we have to confess to being both old-fashioned and provincial in temperament, because we do admire our sunsets. Taking an evening cruise is a perfect way to experience the splendor. And after the spectacle is over? Then you can look at the stars and the lights of Hamilton Harbour and know that, yes, the night does have "a thousand eyes." Night cruises tend to be chartered, so check the Watersports and Yachting and Marinas chapters for information about boat charters. Here we offer you a declassé experience in the spirit of our less reputable ancestors.

Pembroke Parish

Bermuda Island Cruises
96 Pitts Bay Rd.
• **(441) 292-8652**

Actually BIC offers other cruises during the day (see our Watersports chapter). What they offer at night is a trip in the Great Sound to Hawkins Island, where you disembark to join the Pirates' Party. That means food, drink, and entertainment. A large barbecue is on hand for chicken and steak, or you can have fish cooked in lemon-butter sauce. You'll also get a variety of salads, rolls and (afterwards) your just desserts — cake. Sea Dog the pirate and his wenches will meet you and later will organize buck-off and wench-off limbo dancing competitions. Sounds sexist? Pirates were never known for being politically correct. And Sea Dog's gotten worse ever since he divorced his wife, but apparently he has become snazzily dressed: He favors bright orange. Tony Brannon's Island Fever calypso band plays the whole night long.

You can reserve tickets ($75 per person) by calling direct. You can board the boat at Albuoy's Point in Hamilton (arrive at 6:45 PM to board at 7 PM). You'll be back at Albuoy's at 10:30 PM. You can buy T-shirts and CDs for about $15 each from a small gift shop on Hawkins. The pirates hold their parties on Tuesdays, Wednesdays, Fridays and Saturdays from May 1 to October 31.

Movie Theaters

Worried that a vacation in Bermuda means you'll miss the latest hot movie in the States? Don't be. Very often, films open here on the same day they do in the US. In addition, films are sometimes offered that might not be huge box-office successes in America but that appeal to those who appreciate the British sense of humor. A Fish Called Wanda swims to mind.

Typically a movie runs from Thursday to Thursday. However, some movies run longer due to popular demand. Check The Royal Gazette for movie information and specific starting times. By the way, smoking's prohibited in all our theaters.

St. George's Parish

New Somers Playhouse
Duke of York St.,
Town of St. George
• **(441) 297-2821**

It's actually not so new. The building goes back to just after emancipation (1834), when it was headquarters for one of the local lodges, otherwise known as "friendly societies." It then became a movie theater, which was closed down until 1993, when St. Georgians could finally again watch a movie without having to tool into Hamilton.

The Playhouse is spacious and takes us back to the era when movie theaters were palatial rather than compact. Apart from the occasional Saturday matinee for children (cost $5), there are two showings a night, Monday through Friday. This theater is known for showing quality British films, such as Much Ado About Nothing and Secrets and Lies, that are seldom shown elsewhere on the island. Tickets cost $7 each.

Pembroke Parish

Little Theatre
30 Queen St., Hamilton
• **(441) 292-2135**

During school holidays this small, intimate theater offers two matinee shows (at 2:15 and 4:30 PM) for $5 a ticket on Fridays, Saturdays and Sundays. Usually, R-rated movies are not shown in the afternoon. In addition, films for nursery kids are sometimes shown at 10 AM. Check The Royal Gazette to see if and when they're offered and for information about matinees during the rest of the year. There are two evening shows at $7 a ticket. You can book advance tickets by calling directly and using your credit card number. Check www.Bermudamall.com for previews of movies that are playing.

Liberty Theatre
49 Union Sq., Hamilton
• (441) 292-7296

Owned by the Bermuda Industrial Union (BIU), you'll find this theater off Victoria Street, between Court and King Streets. Monday through Saturday it shows a matinee at 2:30 PM ($4 a ticket) and offers three evening showings at $7 a ticket. On Sunday there's a matinee at 2:30 PM and only one evening show at 7:30 PM.

On the whole, movies shown are ones that are popular in America, but occasionally manager Nelda Simons likes to pick quality movies from Europe and the Caribbean. You can pick up advance tickets from the Liberty on weekdays (with the exception of public holidays) from 11:30 AM to 5:30 PM.

Sandys Parish

Neptune Cinema
The Cooperage, 4 Freeport Rd., Royal Naval Dockyard • (441) 234-2923

Although this one is owned by Neptune Cinema Ltd., it's operated by the Liberty Theatre management (see previous listing). We mention this because, should you miss a movie in Hamilton, you can see it here instead. Occasionally the Neptune opens new films, but, on the whole, it's a "move over house." The same prices apply here as at the Liberty.

We love this cinema, as it means we can have a break from the city. It's also unusual in that the stone of its walls is left exposed, creating a castle effect. It's perfect, then, for watching Gothic horror movies. The Frog and Onion, located opposite, comes in very useful for a meal or a drink before or after the show (see previous listing in this chapter). There are two shows nightly, along with a 2:30 PM matinee on Sunday (and occasionally on Saturday). Pick up advance tickets from the Liberty Theatre between 11:30 AM and 5:30 PM, Monday through Friday.

Sixty years ago, visitors shopping in Bermuda (and this generally meant in the City of Hamilton) discovered English, Canadian and European goods priced well below prices in the United States. Today, savings on crystal, china, some jewelry, cashmere and lambswool can range between 30 and 40 percent lower than typical prices in America.

Shopping

Sixty years ago, visitors shopping in Bermuda (and this generally meant in the City of Hamilton) discovered English, Canadian and European goods priced well below prices in the United States. Today, savings on crystal, china, some jewelry, cashmere and lambswool can range between 30 and 40 percent lower than typical prices in America.

You may find a startling dichotomy between incredible bargains and steep prices, depending on the season, the item itself and the shop. But you will notice that we are rather laid-back; high-pressure sales tactics are absent. One guidebook published about a half-century ago pointed out that local merchants "do not tolerate sharp practices." Nothing has changed; you need not fear getting ripped off. On the other side of the coin, keep in mind that unlike some other destinations, you won't be able to strike deals with salespeople in Bermuda. Unless on sale, an item is sold as priced.

Duty-free purchases, allowed each resident of the United States who has been away from home for 48 hours or longer, apply to goods valued up to $400. These items must be declared on departure, and you will be taxed 10 percent on the first $1,000 worth of goods over the $400 limit. You are also allowed 100 cigars — no, don't even think Cuban . . . you can smoke them here, but you can't take them into the States — 200 cigarettes and one liter of booze. Remember to save your receipts for customs officials if you are near or over the duty-free limit. Antiques (defined as an item more than 100 years old) are also duty-free. For more information we suggest contacting a Visitors Service Bureau. Contact numbers are provided at the end of this chapter. Some regulations are also discussed in our Getting Here, Around and Home chapter.

You will quickly realize that with some of our listings, street numbers are absent. Locals do not get hung up on identifying locations by street number. It's not something we

worry about; taxi drivers don't request them, and 99 percent of the time the name of the shop and the name of the street is sufficient. Frankly, many store employees don't know the street number of the shop they're working in! And just as frequently it may not even be visible as you pass by. However this won't present a problem, as you will see when you start getting around.

And two other, very important things: The U.S. dollar is on par with the Bermuda dollar, and browsing through our shops in scanty attire or bathing suits is very much frowned upon.

St. George's Parish

Town of St. George

Early in 1999 this ancient town moved a step closer to being named a World Heritage site. It has been formally nominated to the United Nations Educational, Scientific and Cultural Organization (UNESCO) by Britain's Minister for Culture, Chris Smith. St. George was one of two sites selected from a shortlist of 25 that included the UK and its colonies.

There are two key shopping streets — York Street and Water Street — in this town that once hustled to the activities of Confederate blockade runners during the American Civil War. King's Square is the town's hub, around which you'll find the Bank of Butterfield to the north and the Town Hall to the east. Public restrooms, also east, are just a skip from the Visitors Service Bureau on the square's southern side. The Carole Holding Art Studio, the Bank of Bermuda, Paradise Gift Shop and the Confederate Museum sit along the west arm.

While the square was the site of 17th-century floggings and executions, today it is the center for various events like the Peppercorn Ceremony (see our Annual Events chapter).

In front of the sidewalk facing the Bank of Butterfield are cedar "stock and pillory" and whipping-post replicas — like the Ducking Stool that stands on nearby Ordnance Island — that re-create those used for those ancient punishments and humiliation. Most visitors get a kick out of photographing each other with their head and feet in the stocks, when they are not ambling through the shops of St. George's, most of which open at 9 AM and close at 5 PM.

Somers Wharf & Branch Stores
Water St., Town of St. George

This group of shops and restaurant includes branches of the island's "name" shops — A.S. Coopers, Trimingham's, Davison's of Bermuda, the English Sports Shop and the Crown Colony Shop, all of which have clothing for men and women. These shops have main stores in the city of Hamilton (see subsequent listings). An English pub-style restaurant, the Wharf Tavern sits on the waterside.

Book Cellar
Water St., Town of St. George
• (441) 297-0448

Just under the Tucker House Museum (see our Arts and Culture chapter), this small, cool and quaint bookstore carries both new and secondhand books.

Vera P. Card
Water St., Town of St. George
• (441) 297-1718

Sitting across from the Carriage Museum (see our Attractions chapter), this business has its main store at 11 Front Street in Hamilton and another branch store at Sonesta Beach Hotel (see our Resort Hotels chapter). The jewelry is sold at duty-free prices. Vera P. Card is the exclusive local distributor of Majorica pearl jewelry. They are so confident of their low prices that if your jewelry is examined by a licensed appraiser at another Majorica retailer overseas within 90 days of purchase, and the fair retail value is appraised lower, then Vera P. Card store will offer a full refund or pay you the difference.

Guerlain
Water St., Town of St. George
• (441) 297-1525

Exquisite ladies' and men's fragrances, including Gucci, Chanel, Fendi and Drakkar, give this store an international scent. Here too, lower-than-U.S. prices make for a welcome bargain.

Taylors
30 Water St., Town of St. George
• (441) 297-1626

Hear those bagpipes in your mind's ear? Well, if you can't play the pipes, you can dress the part. Kilts, skirts and other tartans for men, women and children will conjure up those high-pitched notes. Select a cashmere, Shetland, lambswool or mohair sweater for the feel and flavor of Scotland. There are often savings up to 50 percent over knitwear prices in the United States.

Frangipani
Water St., Town of St. George
• (441) 297-1357

Across from the post office (which used to be a jail), Frangipani, named after an island flower (see our Flora and Fauna chapter), has batiks, silks, casual wear, cotton sweaters and costume jewelry. It is a riot of color and fun fashions.

Bermuda Gombey Trader
13 York St., Town of St. George
• (441) 297-0399
Opus Encore 12 Reid Street, Hamilton
• (441) 295-8073

Here you'll find the Gombey rag doll, handcrafted straw hats, bags and baskets, and even some jams and marmalades along with other gift ideas. A branch — Opus Encore — carries similar items.

X-Pressions
26 York St., Town of St. George
• (441) 297-1173

Island pottery made in Bermuda is the focus of this intimate little shop found near St. Peter's Church, the oldest Anglican church in continuous use in the Western Hemisphere.

Robertson's Drug Store
York St., Town of St. George
• (441) 297-1828

One of the oldest stores in St. George, Robertson's is a veritable pirate's chest of odds, ends, bits and pieces, large and small. Although prescriptions can be filled here, you'll find toiletries, books, magazines, jewelry, local and foreign newspapers, sunglasses and myriad everyday items.

Havana Leaf & Bean and Caffe Latte
8 York St., Town of St. George
• (441) 296-1188

Take a break from your walking tour, ascend the steps opposite the Water Street entrance to Somers Wharf, and to your right is Havana Leaf & Bean and Caffe Latte. You can enjoy a gourmet cup of java, munch a tasty pastry and, if you wish, light up a genuine stogie from Cuba. This is a little spot of respite with a few outdoor tables and chairs, and it's just a few feet away an adjacent flight of steps will take you to the main bus stop.

Hamilton Parish

Flatts Village

Flatts Village (see Area Overviews), its homes spreading gently from the rim of a delightful sheltered inlet that leads into Harrington Sound, is one of the most charming and picturesque little spots in Bermuda. The origin of the name is uncertain, but this tiny village was one of the island's earliest settlements because of its small, fine harbor. Flatts Bridge, spanning the entrance to Harrington Sound, is believed to have been the first built in Bermuda, the builders being paid in tobacco. Quite often, in hoping to avoid the "searchers" in St. George's (comparable to today's customs officers), captains during the 17th century put into this gentle harbor and various goods and

contraband, including slaves, were off-loaded without discovery.

Today along with a Shell gas station that services boats as well as motor vehicles, are a cycle livery, pizza place, liquor store, and the Halfway House (see our Restaurants chapter) at Flatts. We have listed a few other shops.

Double Dip Too
12 North Shore Rd., Flatts
• (441) 292-5580
Double Dip 119 Front Street, Hamilton
• (441) 292-3503

Their claim is to be the "Home of the Double Dip" and to provide Bermuda's best quality ice cream. Both stores are quite popular throughout the year, but certainly more so during the hot summer months.

Link to Link Jewelry and Metal Studio
20 North Shore Rd., Flatts
• (441) 293-4401

The range here is not as extensive as some other places, but you will find interesting pieces created by Bermudian silversmith and goldsmith Shane Robinson. He specializes in homemade jewelry, and you'll find pendants, earrings and charms. If you have in mind a special design, Shane will be more than happy to create it and ship your order to you.

Flatts Gift Shop
13 North Shore Rd., Flatts
• (441) 292-0360

Menswear, along with some sports gear and souvenirs make up the bulk of items here.

Smiths Parish

Collector's Hill Apothecary
South Rd. • (441) 236-8664

About a half-mile east of Ariel Sands Club and Cottages (see our Cottage Colonies chapter), Collector's Hill fills prescriptions and of-

INSIDERS' TIP

One of the best times of year to grab a bargain is after Christmas when Hamilton's leading stores usually slash prices on fine quality European clothing.

fers a diverse range of items from colognes and gift items to cigarettes, books and magazines.

Devonshire Parish

Bermuda Florist
South Rd. • (441) 236-2333

The location less than a quarter-mile west of Ariel Sands Club and Cottages makes this florist convenient for guests seeking bouquets for that special anniversary or birthday occasion.

Pembroke Parish

City of Hamilton

Take all the superlatives and cliches, combine them, and you have Hamilton, an eclectic shopping experience. A city since 1897 and Bermuda's capital since 1815, it is the business heart of the island. Within little more than a square mile, hundreds of shops, restaurants, banks, supermarkets and international insurance and reinsurance companies abound, cheek-by-jowl. Clean and well-run, Hamilton has always prided itself on being able to offer a taste of the world through its many and diverse stores.

Late Night Shopping Festival

Make a note on your calendar that every Wednesday, May through October, there is a late-night shopping festival from 6 to 10 PM, sponsored by the Bank of Butterfield, the Bermuda Department of Tourism and the Bank of Bermuda. Hosted by the Bermuda Chamber of Commerce, this is an occasion when Front Street is closed to vehicular traffic, and many of the City's main shops remain open later than usual. You will meet a variety of artists exhibiting their creations (craft items, paintings, etc.), all set up on Front Street itself between Parliament and Queen streets. A few temporary food stalls are set up, and a band is usually on hand to keep your feet tapping as you eat, walk and explore.

City Malls and Shopping Centers

Washington Mall
Reid St., Hamilton
• (441) 295-4186

Entering the Washington Mall from Reid Street, you first encounter Herrington Fine Jewellers, and just opposite is the Body Shop with a wide range of natural hair and skin products. Go through the glass doors and you find Kodak Express, where film can be quickly developed and enlargements made if desired. Pop into The Deli for pastries, sandwiches, salads and more. And for having photographs taken there is the Mall Photographic Studio. An Easylink automatic teller (ATM), that takes Mastercard, Cirrus and Visa, is adjacent to Washington Mall Magazines, packed pretty tightly with a fair-sized book selection and a wide variety of magazines, many of which are unavailable elsewhere in Bermuda.

On this floor you'll also find the Quality Dry Cleaners and Shirt Launderers, Sportseller for sports clothing and footwear, and the Matchbox, a small kiosk that offers cigars, cigarettes, pipes and pipe tobacco. Adjacent to the Matchbox is the Harbourmaster, where leather bags, briefcases, wallets and other assorted leather goods tempt. Hang-it-All, immediately next door, has real and artificial plants for the plant lover. The adjacent Cotton Ginny has hip fashions and accessories for larger women.

Take the stairs above the cash machine and at the top you'll find Sound Stage for jazz, pop, country and western CDs, and Jeans Plus, where denim is the focus. Turn left at the top of the stairs to find Jazzy Boutique, which has fashions for the younger crowd. Bermuda Best Buys has typewriters, computers, fax and dictation machines, word processors and other great merchandise. Hungry? Pop into Take Five, a great place with local ambiance. The Accessory Box, another kiosk, has ties, hats and a few bags.

To the right at the top of the stairs is The Health Store. Its vitamin and mineral supplements, herbs and Bermuda honey might help you shop without dropping. Blades, a hair cutting salon, is nearby. Nature's Chi, another

health store offering a line of health-related products, books and magazines. Go through the glass doors and you face Church Street. On your left along the railed mall walkway, there is a Federal Express office, and Upper Deck, specializing in sports cards and other sports collectibles. Casual footwear for children and adults is at Locomotion, and M. Keyes & Co. Ltd. can test your eyes and fit you with sunglasses and eyeglass frames. Women can get well-coiffured at Headway Hair Centre, and Caffe Latte espresso bar is a good place to pause and sip fine gourmet coffees. Telecom has a range of pagers, cell phones, two-way radios and the like.

Washington Mall II

The front of the mall faces onto Church Street. A Crow Lane Bakery outlet (See Restaurants) has sandwiches and tempting pastries. Alongside is the London Shop for men's clothing. Turn the corner around London Shop and stroll the walkway overlooking Washington Lane below; you'll find Mr. C's Boutique, a division of London Shop, and Accents & Country Crafts, an interesting little place where craft items from cute plaques to candles, unique little lampshades and quizzical little dolls are displayed. Nicholas Lusher Fine Art always has an interesting selection of paintings, and Gorilla carries a selection of menswear geared more to the outdoorsy types. There is C.R.E. Properties Ltd., and the Hosiery Hut, which pretty much speaks for itself: hose and leggings for women.

Washington Mall West

If you enter this section of the mall from Reid Street — yes, there's the Washington Mall entrance and the Washington Mall West entrance, and both connect at the cash machine and stairs (see above). Paradiso Cafe is on your left as you enter from Reid Street, and just opposite is Sail On, its eclectic mix of items defying any single category. Pass through the

glass doors, and Secrets is on the left, with seductive lingerie. This Cotton Ginny mostly sells average and smaller sizes. The Source has casual loose-fitting shirts and some sportswear, and Treats of Bermuda has some children's books, candies and more candies. All Wrapped Up offers greeting cards and wrapping paper for special occasions, and the Colosseum sells men's and women's belts and shoes.

As you walk south along Washington Lane (which runs between Washington Mall and Washington Mall II), you'll find Panatel Ltd which specializes in video and multi-media production, Franklyn Travel Agency, the House of Flowers which has plants as well as flowers for that special occasion, La Trattoria restaurant (See Restaurants), Washington Lane Shoe Repair, and Spring Garden (see Restaurants).

Butterfield Place
67 Front St., Hamilton

Entered next to the Bank of Butterfield on Front Street, this set of shops features Voila, home of fine leather goods and accessories, including handcrafted Italian shoes for men. Just opposite is Louis Vuitton, displaying bags under the famous name. Michael Swan Gallery (see our Arts chapter), named after the artist and owner, features his own airbrush art, flameworked glass art, hand-crafted pottery and a myriad interesting items. Kirk's Jewelry design lies opposite. Lada Dana Mega Hair salon sits next to TeleBermuda Customer Care Centre (see Media and Communications). It is at this junction where Butterfield Place and the Emporium meet.

The Emporium
Front St., Hamilton

Pass through the entrance to The Emporium, a group of shops next to Butterfield Place, and you find Wine Rack (which accepts US checks), replete with a large selection of fine wines and accessories. Alongside is Person-

INSIDERS' TIP

When in St. George's, if you find you've run out of or forgotten bus tickets or lost your token, you can purchase tokens at St. George's Liquors, immediately next to the bus stop on York Street.

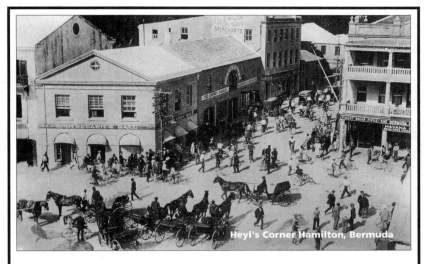
Heyl's Corner Hamilton, Bermuda

Located by the Birdcage at the corner of Front and Queen Streets, Hamilton.

Here you'll find exquisite hand-embroideries from the Island of Madeira, possibly one of the largest selections to be found anywhere. Table dimensions are never a problem, as they welcome the opportunity to do specially commissioned work. Amongst their extensive range of linens are Double Damask from Ireland, Le Jacquard Francais and Souleiado from France and beautiful laces from Belgium.

Upstairs is the Souleiado Shop where you'll find these colourful cotton prints from Provence by the yard and in an exclusive range of accessories.

Here you'll also find a new collection of luxurious European Bedlinens.

Children are not forgotten either as they carry a delightful selection of hand-embroidered clothes from Madeira and hand-smocked dresses from Brazil.

The Irish Linen Shop

HEYL'S CORNER, 31 FRONT STREET, HAMILTON HM 11, BERMUDA TEL: (441) 295-4089   FAX: (441) 295-6552

Shoppers will be pleasantly surprised by the bargains they will find in Bermuda.

alized Jewellery. To the left is Tienda de Tabacco, which sells cigars and touts itself as a great place to enjoy them. Descend the low flight of steps next to the bronze statue of a nude former Miss Bermuda and Miss World, and directly ahead is The Gallery, where Haitian and local paintings, African masks and various moderately sized sculptures make for a collector's delight. To the right is Portobello for old stamps, coins and antiques. Next to Portobello is Eve's Garden, with tempting lingerie that would make the modern Adam and Eve forget the apple. Kathy's Kaffee and Sushi Bar is at the rear — a little hideaway in which to relax for a daytime or evening snack.

Other City of Hamilton Shops

Pegasus Prints and Map Shop
63 Pitts Bay Rd. • (441) 295-2900

Although not strictly within the city limits, and located in an old Bermuda home just across from the Hamilton Princess Hotel, this is an enchanting place where prints, maps and original Curtis botanical lithographs form an eclectic delight. Engravings from Perry shells

and Denton fish help complete a fascinating mix.

Mailboxes Unlimited
48 Par-la-Ville Rd., Hamilton
• (441) 292-6563
Mechanics Bldg., 12 Church St.,
Hamilton • (441) 296-5656
122 Middle Rd., Warwick Parish
• (441) 236-4267

With the main store at Par-la-Ville Rd, and branches in Warwick and on Church Street, Mailboxes Unlimited is well-equipped to ship just about anything anywhere. They can handle all boxing, wrapping, airway bills, commercial invoicing and insurance. Photocopying is a cinch, and they sell boxes of all shapes and sizes along with bubble wrap, Styrofoam peanuts, brown paper and gift wrap.

The Bookmart
The Phoenix Centre, Reid St.
• (441) 295-1647

Containing Bermuda's largest selection of books, The Bookmart is accessed just off Reid Street via an escalator inside the Phoenix Cen-

tre. It is often overlooked by the visitor, but you should make the effort to drop by. It has a thorough collection of Bermuda books.

Stuart's
Reid St. • (441) 295-5496

Major name-brand cameras (including Canon, Olympus, Minolta, Fuji, Nikon and Pentax) along with televisions, tapes, film, tape recorders and other supplies make this Bermuda's leading center for photographic and electronic equipment.

True Reflections
53 Reid St. • (441) 295-9424

Right on the corner of Parliament and Reid streets, this shop has Bermuda's largest collection of books, puzzles and other items related to black Bermudian, African and Caribbean history. Afro-centered greeting cards, posters and lithographs are also available. True Reflections celebrates ethnic culture and art. Jewelry from the Ivory Coast, Kente cloth accessories and African print shirts are popular with visitors and locals. Various striking fabrics are available by the yard.

Twice Told Tales
34 Parliament St.
• (441) 296-1995

This is a secondhand bookstore with a difference. Those who gather here can sit at one of a few tables for coffee and conversation. The atmosphere is relaxed, and you are invited to tarry a while and meet the locals.

The Scottish Wool Shop
Queen St. • (441) 295-0967

Want to save up to 50 percent on U.S. prices for your memories of Scotland? Cashmere, lambswool and Shetland woolens are a bargain here. If you want to trace your ancestral Scottish clan, ask the staff; they may be able to help. Taylor's in St. George is an associated shop.

The Bermuda Book Store
Queen St. • (441) 295-3698

This modest bookstore has a comprehensive selection of new books. Every so often they offer selected books at bargain prices. Its collection of Bermuda books is quite good.

Just up the stairs is a selection of notebooks, paper and the like.

Riihiluoma's Flying Colours
5 Queen Street • (441) 295-0890

This store is indeed a colorful and delightful port at which to find tee-shirts with various Bermudian-related designs and logos. Sweatshirts, hats, and various other gift items and ideas celebrate a distinctly Bermudian flavor.

Trustworthy
19 Queen Street • (441) 295-5721

This lovely little shop is run by volunteers of the Bermuda National Trust. Here you'll find unique gift ideas, and several arts and crafts items. You will find interesting puzzles and selections of beautifully colored pottery.

The Card Cove
Queen Street • (441) 295-0727

Greeting cards for every occasion make this a neat little place to pop into when you want to find the right words for those Hallmark moments.

Rock On
23 Queen Street • (441) 295-3468

This Life Extension & Live Well Company provides a range of nutritional supplements, herb teas, and health-related books and magazines. You'll find anti-aging and weight-control products. Regular visitors might consider asking about the company's membership plan.

Everrich Jewellery
28 Queen Street • (441) 295-2010

Located near the Island Theatre cinema, Everrich offers fine jewelry for those occasions when you are looking for that special ring, necklace or gift for yourself or someone special.

W.J. Boyle & Son Ltd.
Queen Street • (441) 295-1887
Church St. East • (441) 292-6360
Water St., St. George's • (441) 297-1922
Mangrove Bay, Somerset
• (441) 234-0530

This chain of shoe stores offers quality men's, women's and children's footwear, along with several name brands of running shoes and cross trainers. Their Hamilton store is the more extensive.

H.S. & J.E. Crisson Ltd.
16 Queen St. • (441) 295-2351
71 Front St. • (441) 295-2351
55 Front St. • (441) 295-2351
20 Reid St. • (441) 295-2351
York & Kent Sts., Town of St. George
• (441) 297-0672
Water St., Town of St. George
• (441) 297-0107
Elbow Beach Hotel, 60 South Rd.
• (441) 236-9928
Sonesta Beach Hotel, 5 South Rd. and
Sonesta Dr. • (441) 238-0072
Southampton Princess Hotel,
101 South Rd. • (441) 238-3904

Started by Herbert and Jack Crisson in 1921, that single store has grown to include 11 stores islandwide. To shop at Crisson is to indulge in a friendly atmosphere where superior quality jewelry can be purchased at substantial savings over American prices. In addition to bracelets, brooches, necklaces and earrings, they are renowned for their quality watch selection, which features established names such as Rolex, Raymond Weil, Gucci, Seiko and Ebel at prices up to 30 percent below those in the United States. And don't overlook the special Bermudian jewelry designs, such as the keepsake collection of fabulous 14k and 18k-gold and sterling silver charms. These make ideal mementos of your sojourn in Bermuda.

Cecile
15 Front St. • (441) 295-1311
Southampton Princess Hotel,
101 South Rd. • (441) 238-1434

Fine designer clothing — Escada, Yves St. Laurent, La Perla and Louis Feraud are a few of the labels — is on display in what many locals consider Bermuda's leading ladies' boutique. Gottex swimwear is also available for those who take fashion to the beach.

Astwood-Dickinson Co.
83 Front St. • (441) 292-5805

Astwood-Dickinson has a reputation for providing jewelry and timepieces of excep-

tional quality. They have introduced a Bermuda Collection with unique Bermudian pieces — Cow Polly fish, Longtail and Sand Lantern, for example — created by their own staff. Having recently forged a partnership with Columbian Emeralds International, Astwood-Dickinson is poised to continue bringing in gems of superior quality.

The watches and timepieces include established names — Tiffany, Patek Philippe, Cartier and others. As in other major shops in Bermuda, items here are available at substantial savings on American prices. Branch stores are located at Walker Arcade on Reid Street in Hamilton and in H.A. & E Smith's in Hamilton.

The English Sports Shop
49 Front St. • (441) 295-2672
Aston & Gunn, Queen and Reid Sts.
• (441) 295-4866
The Scottish Wool Shop, 7 Queen St.
• (441) 295-0967
The Outlet, Queen St. • (441) 295-0084

Interested in trying out Bermuda shorts, finding superb sweaters, or menswear? Then pay a visit to these shops. Your Bermuda shorts come in several colors, including pink for men. Have a ball combining shorts and polo shirts! There is also a lovely selection of sweaters for those chilly evenings at home; styles include Shetland, lambswool and the soft and luxurious Glenagle cashmere.

Trimingham's
Front St. • (441) 295-1183
Somers Wharf, Town of St. George
• (441) 297-1726
Southampton Princess Hotel,
101 South Rd. • (441) 296-1648
South Shore Rd., Paget Parish
• (441) 292-3423
Sonesta Beach Hotel, 5 South Rd. and
Sonesta Dr. • (441) 296-1647
Somerset Village • (441) 296-1291

The Trimingham family, prominent in the shipping business during the nineteenth century, came to Bermuda with the first English settlers. In 1649, John Trimingham, was elected governor of Bermuda. Since 1844, when Trimingham Bros Ltd., was founded, family members have always been intimately involved in business operations.

With entrances on both Front and Reid streets, Trimingham's is one of Bermuda's largest stores. Men's and women's clothing and accessories, furniture, jewelry, shoes, etc., are tastefully displayed. Trimingham's claims to have Bermuda's largest collection of duty-free values, offering visitors up to 40 percent or more off U.S. prices on crystal, china and perfumes. You'll find Waterford, Portmeirion and Mikasa, plus fragrances from Estee Lauder to Christian Dior. Elevator service is provided to the three floors. Ladies swimwear fashion labels include Ralph Lauren, CK Calvin Klein, Karen Kane, and Tommy Hilfiger. You will also find 100-percent-cotton ladies and mens sweaters. They offer packing, shipping and mailing services.

H.A. & E Smith Ltd.
35 Front St. • (441) 295-2288
18 York St., Town of St. George
• (441) 297-1734
Southampton Princess Hotel,
101 South Rd. • (441) 238-0766
The Treasure Chest, Queen St.
• (441) 295-2288
Smith's Sampler, Royal Naval Dockyard
• (441) 234-2024

Founded in 1889 by Henry Archibald Smith and Edith Smith, H.A.&E Smith has been at its present location since 1934.

Simply called Smith's by locals, and with branch stores at York Street in St. George's, the Dockyard and the Southampton Princess hotels (see our Resort Hotels chapter), this establishment has been at the shopping vanguard since its inception. From English-tailored blazers to fine Italian silk ties and the traditional Bermuda shorts, Smith's is one of the island's largest clothing stores for men and women. Sitting across from the Birdcage on Front Street, it also carries fine leather handbags and lovely cashmere sweaters. There are hundreds of gift ideas, not the least of which is a Waterford crystal ship's decanter that is a reminder of Bermuda's nautical heritage. You can save 20 — 40 percent on many British and European products. It is exclusive retailer for a number of brands, including Church and Cheaney shoes for men, Burberry fragrances, fashions and accessories, and

Shiseido, Carita and Biotherm cosmetics. Smiths's also carries Liberty silk scarves, Kent and Mason Pearson Brushes for women.

Bluck's
Front St. • (441) 295-5367
Town of St. George • (441) 297-0476
Southampton Princess Hotel,
101 South Rd. • (441) 238-0992

Regarded as crystal and china specialists, Blucks has branch stores at the Southampton Princess Hotel and in the Town of St. George. A number of their designs have been specially commissioned from European masters including Staffordshire, Herend, Spode and Caithness. The Bermuda theme is prominent in the original flower and bird designs. You'll find Staffordshire enamel boxes with the Bermuda longtail, a Bermuda Regiment ice bucket and Herend Bermuda flower plates, to name a few. Here you'll also find Royal Grafton bone china.

Walker Christopher Goldsmiths
9 Front St. • (441) 295-1466

For some unique, unusual gold jewelry, this store fills the bill. The exquisite items will make you believe you've explored and found some ancient treasure chest. From South Sea pearls to a circa 2000 B.C. Babylonian cylinder seal carved from hematite, these folks have jewelry that fascinates. Their items are one of a kind. The ancient coins turned into striking and captivating jewelry are superb.

Solomon's
17 Front Street • (441) 292-4742

Opposite the Ferry Terminal on Front Street, Solomon's has become one of the island's leading jewelers, known for the quality of its gemstones and designs of its eclectic gold and silver jewelry. Winner of several "Best in Bermuda" Gold Awards, this store also features a boutique exhibiting an enchanting collection of engagement and wedding rings for bride and groom.

Wadson's Ltd.,
Front Street • (441) 295-3025

Across the street from the Ferry Terminal, this store specializes in t-shirts for both adults and children. You'll find a variety of souvenirs, sweatshirts, beach wear and some interesting items carried only by Wadsons. Generally, they have a buy-two, get-one-free t-shirt offer.

E.R. Aubrey Jewellers
19 Front St. • (441) 295-3826

Perhaps few other jewelry stores can offer the kind of low prices now synonymous with this shop. Diamonds, Colombian emeralds, sapphires and tanzanite are bought in bulk directly from the mines, and the jewelry is manufactured and designed by Aubrey's own designers. They create a complete range of jewelry including necklaces, bracelets, rings and bangles.

The Gem Cellar
Old Cellar Ln. • (441) 292-3042

Reached from Front Street through Old Cellar Lane, almost directly opposite the area where horse-and-buggy drivers cater to visitors, this store's location was the turn-of-the-century site of one of many stables along Hamilton's Front Street.

The Gem Cellar manufactures much of its own jewelry and has a selection of handmade Bermuda charms. These gemstone merchants and goldsmiths will also repair eyeglasses.

Swiss Timing
Chancery Lane
• (441) 295-1376

This watchmakers and jewelers has a complete selection of bracelets, gold chains, earrings, and semi-precious jewelry. You can save on watches (compared to US prices), as you choose from Certina, Michel Herbelin, Favre Leuba, Maurice Lacroix, and Jean D'Eve timepieces.

Jeweler's Warehouse
Walker's Arcade, Front Street
• (441) 292-4247

This store's concept in affordable jewelry has made it a favorite place for luxury jewelry at competitively-low prices. Visitors and locals have discovered that their dollar stretches farther here. Warm and friendly staff are happy

to show you fine selections from their diamond and gold rings, pendants and bracelets.

The Irish Linen Shop
Heyl's Corner • (441) 295-4089

Founded in 1949 by sisters Armine and Frances Gosling and located in a nineteenth century building on the corner of Front and Queen Streets, this shop is popular for those seeking superb linens. Co-managed by Jeremy Hartley, a grandson born the same year the shop opened, this treasure-trove yields Double Damask linen tablecloths and tea towels from Ireland, handmade embroideries from the Portuguese island of Madeira, and handmade laces from Belgium. The exclusively-designed Bermuda Cottage Collection will make setting the perfect table a delight. Souleiado cotton prints from France, and smock dresses from Brazil are among the shop's lovely selections. Equally charming is the eclectic music that greets you as you step into and explore this world of exquisite linens.

Gosling Black Seal Shop
97 Front Street
• (441) 298-7325

Here is where you'll find men's and women's gift accessories imprinted with the distinctive Black Seal logo. After World War I, because of problems obtaining suitable bottles for its locally made black rum (blended from a recipe more than a century old), the Gosling family, in Bermuda since 1806, found it necessary to use champagne bottles. The unlabeled rum was identified by the black sealing wax used to cover the cork. Labeling did not come until 1949 when the logo of a seal balancing a rum barrel on its nose was used. So this is a store where you'll find a plethora of gifts — ties, bags, hats, baseball caps and belts, mugs, pennants, boxer shorts and t-shirts — all with that historic logo.

Onion Jack's Trading Post
77 Front Street • (441) 295-1263

This theme store features the 'Onion Jack' logo on caps, golf towels, jackets, and a myriad of souvenir items — can/bottle holders, keychains, computer mousepads, shotglasses, mugs and more. They also carry

Bermuda souvenirs like the ubiquitous T-shirts, towels, and postcards. And you'll find gifts, confectionery and toiletries. Open 9AM - 10PM

A.S. Cooper & Son Ltd.
59 Front St. • (441) 295-3961
Reid St. • (441) 295-3961
Somers Wharf, Town of St. George
• (441) 297-0925
Southampton Princess Hotel,
101 South Rd. • (441) 295-3961
Clocktower, Royal Naval Dockyard
• (441) 234-4156
Elbow Beach Hotel, 60 South Rd.
• (441) 236-5046
Sonesta Beach Hotel, 5 South Rd. and
Sonesta Dr. • (441) 238-8357

This store, which had its centenary celebration in 1997, has produced several mementos on English teapots, bone china mugs and other items. Designer diamond and gemstone jewelry is available along with silver and gold Bermuda charms. Fragrances from Cartier and Givenchy to Tommy Hilfiger and Calvin Klein are sold at duty-free prices. Known for its crystal and china dinnerware — Swarovski, Wedgwood, Lladro and Royal Doulton — A. S. Cooper & Son is a must-stop for those planning nuptials. Have a look through the Garden Room on the ground floor.

Artcetera
Burnaby Hill • (441) 295-2787

Artcetera has a wide range of Windsor & Newton art products, and Caran d'Ache coloured pencils. This is the place for easels and sketchbooks, markers, pens, brushes and a host of other arts supplies. They also can help if you have something to e-mail or want to surf the Net. They have a copy service, take orders for business cards, and offer PC and Macintosh rentals on an hourly basis.

Christian Bookstore & Gift Centre
10 Burnaby St. • (441) 292-3257

This book and gift store offers a large se-

lection of religious-oriented books, T-shirts, puzzles, games, figurines and wall plaques. It's a delightful place for finding a devotional or inspirational gift for a loved one. Well worth the browsing, and selecting.

Heel, Sew Quik
34 Church St. • (441) 295-1559

Need quick shoe repair? These folks can often take care of the problem while you wait; in general they provide service within an hour or so. They also do clothing alterations, but that tends to take up to a couple of days.

TaMerry Offerings
43 Court Street
• (441) 292-7389

With its name taken from ancient Egyptian, and meaning "Happy Land", this shop is Bermuda's exclusive outlet for clothing and various other products made from hemp. The incredible range includes shoes, shirts, dresses, soap, shower gel, shampoos, body lotions, massage oil, bags and knapsacks. TaMerry also has a number of books on African culture and spirituality. There is also a modest selection of inexpensive jewelry. Well worth checking out. Open 11AM to 9PM.

Abyssian Imports
79 Court St. • (441) 292-3208

African garments, particularly Ethiopian, and incense, oils, silver and some leather bags are available at this store. You'll also find a limited number of carvings from the African west coast.

Dub City Records
46 Court St. • (441) 292-6775

At this shop the specialty is reggae; you'll find it has the island's largest selection. There are also some track suits and T-shirts.

The Metaphysical Book Shop
61 Reid Street • (441) 295-5683

This is the only book shop in Bermuda

INSIDERS' TIP

Many shoppers feel the best time to visit Bermuda is during the winter months — you'll be able to save on a bunch of things, not the least of which being your accommodations.

that specializes in books and various items of a spiritual and metaphysical nature — from Reiki (healing) to channeling, meditation, books by Deepak Chopra and so much more. Along with some specially-selected CD recordings, you'll also find various types of incense and oils.

Southampton Parish

Rising Sun Shop
Middle Rd. • (441) 238-2154

About a half-mile west of the Waterlot Inn, this treasure trove is filled to the rafters with diverse gift ideas and decorative pieces to suit just about any taste. Woodwork and crafts run the gamut from weather vanes to baskets and much else besides. This is one of the most interesting little places to stop on your journey.

Deja-Vu Flea Market
40 Middle Rd.
• (441) 238-8525

Looking for something different? Both the usual and the not so usual are packed into this shop, where secondhand items take on a new life. We have found everything from rare books on Bermuda to Tibetan rubbings and a complete dinner set used by the Carringtons on the television soap Dynasty. Rummage around, and there's no telling what you may come up with.

Sandys Parish

This parish, comprised of Somerset, Boaz, Watford and Ireland Islands, is named after Sir Edward Sandys, a major shareholder in the Bermuda Company. The place name for Sandys (pronounced "sands") was Mangrove Bay, with the attached rhyming couplet, "All the Way to Mangrove Bay, There the Old Maids go to stay."

It was at Sandys Wreck Hill — a site of early fortifications — where it is said that in 1775, on the day before the infamous gunpowder theft at St. George's (see our History chapter), Bermudians on the ships that eventually carried the stolen powder to Gen. George Washington's troops came ashore, dis-

mounted the 10 guns on Wreck Hill and rolled them into the sea. While such intrigue has found a place in the history books, this area is dubiously noted for the largest bank robbery in Bermuda's history — the culprit got away with more than a quarter-million dollars earlier this decade, and the caper has yet to be solved.

Dean's Bakery & Deli
Manchester St., Somerset Village
• (441) 234-2918

This family-owned bakery is one of the hot stops for a lunch-hour sandwich or a pastry to thrill your sweet tooth. The muffins, scones, coffee rolls and apple and lemon turnovers are a delight.

Caesar's Pharmacy
30 Somerset Road, Sandy's
• (441) 234-0851

One of the more recent additions to Somerset Village, the pharmacy dispenses not only prescription drugs, but some products (air purifiers, bedding, etc.) from the Asthma & Allergy Relief Centre on 61 Court Street in Hamilton. You'll find an extensive range of quality home health care items, from ambulatory aids like canes, crutches and walkers, to blood pressure monitors and diabetes test kits and supplies.

Frith's Liquors
Manchester St., Somerset Village
• (441) 234-1740

Staying in Somerset and needing a little aqua vitae for a celebration? Pop into Frith's on Manchester Street or make arrangements for duty-free delivery to the airport.

Dockyard Specialty Retail Centre
Clocktower, Royal Navy Dockyard

Filled with Victorian charm, this former 19th-century Royal Naval building — running alongside the upper front are a line of flags from many nations — is eminently browseable. Some have likened it to a combination Quincy Market and London's Burlington Arcade. However, considerably smaller than either, it is delightfully Bermudian and has a number of inviting shops selling paintings, linens, perfumes, jewelry, books and clothing. There is

Beethoven's Restaurant and Bar (see our Restaurants chapter) which is somewhat like a European bistro.

Within the thick walls of the Clocktower, which once throbbed to the "spit and polish" of British navy personnel, are more than a score of shops. Enter the main door, turn left and wander to the end, beginning your amble at Carole Holding (warehouse) Print and Craft Shop, owned and operated by watercolor artist Carole Holding. She has a studio on King's Square in St. George. Her paintings of Bermuda are available as originals as well as prints. At her Clocktower shop, you also will discover beautiful varieties of seashells as well as cedar handmade dolls and Banana Dolls (see our Arts and Culture chapter); for the doll collector, these are a must. Right next door is a branch of Smith's, where cotton knit shirts and a range of perfumes are displayed. The Dockyard Humidor has premium cigars and specializes in Havanas. There are a wide range of choices, among them Cohiba, Montecristo, Romeo & Julieta, Partagas, Bolivar and Hoyo de Monterrey. They also carry humidors, lighters, cigar cases and cutters. A sister store is at Water Street in St. George's. The Highlander, conjuring up images of Scotland, has a range of tartan fabrics and sweaters. And the Reef Gift Shop has a myriad of souvenir items.

Picturesque Bermuda, with its main store at 129 Front Street in Hamilton, is chock-full of photographic prints of Bermuda by photographer Roland Skinner, whose superb camera skills have captured Bermuda's famed land and seascapes. Burrows Lightbourn is great for picking up a soft drink, cold beer or something stronger, and nearby A.S. Cooper's Men's Shop has a modest selection of ties, and shirts by Polo and Ralph Lauren. Dockyard Linens has a collection of linens, including placemats and pot holders with a Bermuda theme.

Makin' Waves has gift items and t-shirts, hats and bags. Ripples Kids Wear, a 'little' division of Makin Waves, has, yes, clothing for the youngster. Dieters Fine Jewellers, just opposite, carries quality gemstones, gold jewelry and sterling silver. The lover of books may find an intriguing read at the Ship's Inn Book Gallery, where discovering a rare 19th-century book or a difficult-to-find first edition is not uncommon. (You might also check out Ship's Inn Book Gallery II, located above Pirate's Landing restaurant.) Next to and opposite the book gallery, are three shops associated with Trimbinghams (see previous listing under the City of Hamilton) called a Taste of Trims, with distinctive lines of casual clothing. There are gift items including the Outerbridge's line of products — sherry peppers, barbecue sauces and Bloody Mary mix.

Turn left at Beethoven's Restaurant and Bar, pass the visitor-interest stand where you can pick up all manner of helpful brochures on almost every nook and cranny in Bermuda, and discover Nannini Haagen-Dazs where you can subdue that compulsion for sweets with Perugina chocolate and Italian cookies. The Michael Swan Gallery not only has the artist's unique prints of various features of Bermuda architecture, but a melange of interesting items. Next door is Crisson, where you will find more selections of jewelry. There is A.S. Cooper's (see previous listing under the City of Hamilton) for a small selection of men's and women's clothing. Smuggler's Cove has gift items ranging from t-shirts and towels, to embroidered hats and stuffed monkeys. And there's Davison's for clothes to relax in and Calypso for casuals.

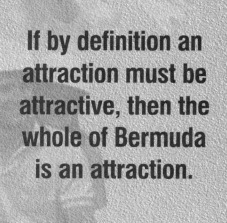

If by definition an attraction must be attractive, then the whole of Bermuda is an attraction.

Attractions

If by definition an attraction must be attractive, then the whole of Bermuda is an attraction. The only arguably unattractive area is the Bermuda Electric Light Company site in Pembroke. And given that BELCO empowers us with electricity, we shouldn't complain about that.

Our attractions, as you might suspect, have more to do with our environment, our history and our culture. Vast theme parks and fairgrounds you will not find here. With the return of the U. S. military base lands (see our History chapter), those may come in the future, but for now our attractions are small rather than large, soothing rather than sensational. Here we list the places that have traditionally proved popular with our visitors. Many are free. When there's a charge, we'll tell you. If we don't mention a senior citizen rate, then assume there is none. For more fun things to fill up your free time, check our chapters on Parks and Conservation, Recreations, Beaches, Kidstuff and Arts and Culture.

St. George's Parish

The Town of St. George

We must stress that our former capital is a major attraction in and of itself. Founded as a town in 1612 and as a corporation in 1797, St. George is our first and oldest town. (When we talk about a "corporation," by the way, we mean that St. George's status as town was formalized by an act of Bermuda's parliament.) Indeed, while Jamestown, Virginia, was the first English town to be founded in the New World, St. George was the second. Jamestown being long since abandoned, St. George is now the oldest English-speaking colonial town still in existence.

The corporation and people of St. George are determined to protect and enhance its his-

toric heritage. In 1995 they formed the St. George's Foundation, an organization designed to promote the town's tourist and cultural interests, which initiated a town plan. Eventually, many of the streets will be paved (currently, most of them are tarmac), and street lighting, together with shop signs, will evoke the town's seventeenth and eighteenth century past. The friendship that already exists between St. George's and Williamsburg, Virginia, the town that followed Jamestown, may well become cemented in an official twinship. Since 1996, St. George's has been the official twin of the ancient town of Lyme Regis, Dorset, UK. That connection goes back to Sir George Somers, who was born there. With England, Bermuda and Virginia involved as apexes, the Bermuda Triangle may soon have far friendlier connotations altogether.

Take the time to explore the narrow, topsy-turvy town streets with evocative names such as Old Maid's Lane, Petticoat Lane and Featherbed Alley, and enjoy the traditionally Bermudian houses that are not obliged to compete with towering skyscrapers. St. George's is, of course, rich in history. Look through the History and Arts and Culture chapters for more information about museums and development. Be sure to check the local options in the Restaurants, Nightlife and Shopping chapters as well.

All right, the letter K does not come first in the alphabet, but King's Square is the town center and the natural starting point for a walking tour. It's also one of our favorite locations for outdoor celebrations, such as Emancipation Day and New Year's Eve, when we like to go down for music and fireworks. And throughout the year, King's Square often resonates with the music of outdoor concerts (see the Annual Events and Festivals chapter).

As soon as you arrive in the square, you'll notice replicas of the stocks, pillories and whipping posts that were used as punishments during the seventeenth and eighteenth centuries. By Ordnance Island, you'll also see the ducking stool, used to dunk female gossips in the harbor. Most unfair, really, as it is a truth universally unacknowledged that men like to gossip as well. In the summer months particularly (actually, April through October), town crier Michael E. Jones arrives most days dressed in eighteenth century costume to announce re-enactment duckings. Some adults find these amusing, but be warned that younger kids may not. As they are perhaps more sensitive to the barbarism of such practices, they often become frightened.

And now let us start with attractions in King's Square. After that, we will resume alphabetical order for the rest of the parish's attractions.

Visitors Service Bureau
King's Sq.
• **(441) 297-1642**

This is not an attraction in itself, but it is the key to the rest of St. George's attractions. Friendly staff will inform and advise you about excursions, tours, events, sightseeing, shopping and transportation. They will also sell you bus tickets. Check the blackboard for daily information about tours. April through October, the bureau opens from 9 AM to 1 PM and 1:30 to 4 PM Monday through Saturday. During the winter, the hours are generally 9 AM to 2 PM, but they are subject to change. Call directly to verify. As you come out of the bureau you'll find Town Hall on your right. See map page xvii.

Town Hall
5 King's Sq.
• **(441) 297-1532**

This municipal center houses on its ground floor what is traditionally known as the Mayor's Parlour. It is the meeting place of the town's Corporation, which is headed by the mayor, currently Mayor Lois Perinchief. You're welcome to check out the cedar furnishings and the pictures of previous mayors Mondays through Saturdays from 10 AM to 4 PM. (It

closes for all public holidays.) See map page xvii.

Deliverance
Ordnance Island • (441) 297-1459

Stand in King's Square, and across the bridge you'll see a life-size replica of the original *Deliverance* that left Bermuda in 1610 to aid settlers in Virginia. For a small fee — adults and teens pay $3, children younger than 12, $1 — you can take a self-guided tour of the ship's interior. You'll see the small galley where the cook had to prepare food for 132 people. His equipment? One big pot. Explore the lower deck, where apparently a hundred people were huddled together at all times during the voyage, and be thankful Atlantic transportation is infinitely more comfortable these days. Mannequins representing passengers and an audio tape describing the wreck of the *Sea Venture* help to evoke the cramped and dangerous conditions of seventeenth century sea travel. The replica, by the way, is made of South American pine, teak and Bermuda cedar. However, the original was made out of the *Sea Venture's* wreckage, which was probably Irish oak. See map page xvii.

The Statue of Sir George Somers
Ordnance Island

Just across from the *Deliverance* is a likeness of Sir George Somers, cast in bronze by Desmond Fountain. The admiral of the *Sea Venture* holds up his arms in a gesture of incredulous wonderment that he is finally about to make it to land. He stands on a plinth set in a circular pool of water.

The Bermuda National Trust Museum
The Globe Hotel, King's Square
• **(441) 297-1423**

Was this property once a hotel? Yes. During the mid-nineteenth century the Globe Hotel was open for guests. However, its history goes back to 1699, when it was built as the Governor's house especially for Samuel Day, a governor who turned out to have a disrepu-

Possibly some of the most memorable view of Bermuda can be seen from atop the Bermuda Cathedral.

table character. Disagreeing that the house belonged to Bermuda and should continue to be used as a residence for future governors, Day secretly secured the title of the house unbeknownst to the next Governor until he turned up to move in.

Now a National Trust property, the museum houses exhibits featuring its own colorful history and the story of St. George. Downstairs you'll find a model of the *Sea Venture* and a video room showing the National Trust's 13-minute film, *Bermuda: Centre of the Atlantic*. Upstairs you can check out the exhibit, "Rogues and Runners: Bermuda and the American Civil War." If you've read our History chapter, you know that many Bermudians made their fortunes by supplying arms to the Confederates. A Confederate agent actually set up office here and was responsible for overseeing the transportation of supplies from Europe through the Union blockade to the southern states in America. So you see, this museum has had a somewhat checkered past. Apart from holidays, it's open year-round, Mon-

day through Saturday, from 10 AM to 4 PM and on Sundays from 1 to 4 PM. Admission rates are $4 per person for adults and $2 for children aged 5 to 16 years. See map page xvii.

Bermudian Heritage Museum 4 Duke of York St. and Water St.
• (441) 297-4126

Opened in March 1998 by the Bermudian Heritage Association, this museum is the first in Bermuda to focus on exhibits from our island's black history. It is appropriately located in the Samaritans Lodge on the corner of both streets listed in the heading above. We say "appropriately" because Bermuda's Friendly Societies, or Lodges, played a crucial role in providing practical and moral support to black Bermudians after Emancipation in 1834. Members would pool time and resources in order to assist with illness, education and funeral expenses. The Independent Order of Good Samaritans and its sister organization, the Daughters of Samaria, founded lodges in St. George in 1876. In 1900 they moved into this building, which is now a National Trust property and leased to the association. Upstairs you'll find the standing exhibit on the Friendly Societies that includes photographs, costume and regalia and the large bibles once used by the lodges. Downstairs you'll find beautiful cedar carvings by local carvers, Hubert Cookie Spence and David Ifor Nisbett, and a variety of old household objects such as an iron that was heated with coals and used for ironing clothes. The museum is open Tuesday through Saturday from 10 AM to 4 PM. Admission rates are $3 for adults and $2 for senior citizens, children and students. Children under 5 years of age can enter for free.

St. Peter's Church
Duke of York St.
• (441) 297-8359

This is our oldest church; it also stands on the site of the oldest Anglican church in the Western Hemisphere. Situated on a hill, it has a long flight of brick steps. Walk up them, and you'll appreciate the simplicity of this stone building with its cedar door and shuttered windows. But you might like to imagine the original cedar and palmetto church, which was blown down by a gale in 1612. In 1619, Governor Butler built another church, where, one year later, Bermuda held its first General Assembly. See map page xvii.

The present building was constructed in 1713, and a clock tower was added in 1814. Inside you'll find the font (possibly fifteenth century) that was brought to Bermuda in the 1700s and a three-decker cedar pulpit that dates back to the late seventeenth century. St. Peter's has two altars. The older one faces east, as is customary, and dates to 1612, when it was used in the original church. The other is freestanding and presently faces north. The cedar box pews and the gallery, where slaves once congregated, are visual reminders of the eighteenth century social hierarchy. So is the royal box, which is still reserved for the governor.

Other relics include a 1625 chalice, donated by the Bermuda Company (see our History chapter), and communion silver donated by King William III. Memorial tablets on the walls give historical information about local families and governors. Explore the churchyard, and you'll find the slave burial ground as well as the graves of governor Sir Richard Sharples and his aide-de-camp, Hugh Sayers, who were both assassinated in March 1973. You'll also find the "belfry tree," an old cedar that was there when members of the first General Assembly gathered together.

St. Peter's is open daily and for Sunday services. (See our Worship chapter for more information.)

Somers Gardens
Duke of York St.

Sir George Somers died in Bermuda in November 1610. His nephew, Matthew Somers, decided to take his body back to England. However, he had to be secretive about it since sailors were superstitious about corpses aboard ships. Apparently the body was embalmed and placed in a cedar chest that was shipped to Lyme Regis, UK, but the heart and entrails were cut out. So it wasn't just his heart Sir George left in Bermuda. All his organs were buried at this site, which eventually became a public park in 1920. A marble tablet in this walled garden commemorates him. A brass tablet inside the church in Whitchurch Canonicorum, a village just outside Lyme, is England's memorial to Sir George.

Gates Fort
Town Cut

To find this fort, head through St. George up Barrack Road and go to the end of Cut Road. Since there's no formal entrance, you can visit any time you wish. The fort has two King George III guns on the gun platform and a guardhouse at the entrance. It's worth climbing to the top of the keep for a view of the Town Cut Channel and the boats and liners that glide through it. Admission is free.

Fort St. Catherine
15 Coot Pond
• (441) 297-1920

Visit this intact fort — originally built in 1614, with extensions added during the eighteenth and nineteenth centuries — for historic information, a splendid ocean view and a bit

Slavery Left an Ugly Mark, Even Here in Paradise

It's true we have no snakes in Bermuda. It's a fact that is gleefully pointed out by those who argue that our island is paradise. You won't find a rattler or a cobra on our shores. But figurative snakes are a different matter. We certainly have not escaped the evils of the world, however much we'd like to think so.

The greatest evil of Bermudian history was slavery, which grew out of the early 17th-century practice of importing black and Indian indentured servants to work on the island. According to the late Cyril Packwood,  during the mid-1620s references to blacks and Indians changed from "indentured servants" to "life servitude" — in other words, their condition became slavery (see History). Go to the Bermuda Archives, and you will find chilling business documents and wills that almost casually refer to the buying, selling and bequesting of slaves.

For centuries those records, together with some accounts written by white historians, travel writers and letter writers, were the only written evidence of slavery. And while some of these writers might have deplored slavery and spoken against it, they mostly argued that, compared with plantation slaves elsewhere, Bermudian slaves were better off. Thus, there were virtually no books written on the subject that offered a slave's point of view.

One exception was *The History of Mary Prince, A West Indian Slave*, which was published in Britain in 1831. Mary Prince was actually Bermudian, having been born at Spittal Pond (or Brackish Pond, as she refers to it). She tells of the horrendous treatment she received in Bermuda, Turks Island and Antigua and of her eventual escape to London in 1831. However, few people had access to the book in Bermuda until 1993,

when it was republished in paperback form. Copies of Mary Prince's story are available in our bookstores (see our Shopping chapter).

The thin veil concealing the reality of slavery in Bermuda was finally removed in 1975 by Cyril Packwood's *Chained on the Rock,* a book that strenuously argues the malignancy of slavery in Bermuda. Packwood's archival evidence clearly shows the treatment of slaves was just as cruel here as anywhere else.

We have slave stories in Bermuda, although the few that have been recorded are striking for what is omitted. Under the Spittal Pond listing in the archives, you'll find a reference to a slave called Jeffrey. All we know so far is that, helped by a young female slave, he hid in a cave for a month and was dis-

— continued on next page

Photo: GIS

Legend has it that a purple Bermudiana flower bloomed from Sarah Bassett's ashes.

covered. Who did he "belong" to? What relationship did he have with the girl? What happened to them afterwards? And when was this escape? We don't know. And we can only guess at his feelings throughout and after the escapade.

Other stories do include details, often disturbing. Yet again, so much is left out. Take the story of Sarah Bassett for instance. Older Bermudians sometimes refer to an extremely hot and sultry day as "a regular Sally Bassett day." Why? The answer's horrific. William Zuill records in *Bermuda Journey* (first published in 1946) that Sarah was found guilty of compelling her granddaughter to poison slave owners Thomas Forster and his wife with "Rat's Bane and Manchineel Root." As a result, in June 1730 she was publicly burned at the Foot of the Lane or Crow Lane at the eastern end of Hamilton Harbour. The unusually high temperature that day, together with the fierce flames of the fire, gave rise to this old saying.

Who were the Forsters, and what happened to them? According to William Zuill, they "owned" Sarah as well as her granddaughter. They were still living, although ill at the time of the trial; their deaths were not recorded. Zuill also refers to the story in *The Story of Bermuda and Her People*, while Terry Tucker mentions Sarah Bassett in *Bermuda Today and Yesterday*. Both add that Sarah wanted a slave girl poisoned as well. Terry Tucker says the owners were actually called "Foster," not "Forster."

In *Chained on the Rock*, Cyril Packwood adds details that emphasize the horror of the incident. As he explains, from 1720 to 1730 slave conspiracies and poisoning plots against whites were common. Government reaction was to round up suspected poisoners and put them in jail in St. George's. Sarah Bassett, he argues, in fact "belonged" to Francis Dickinson, not the Fosters. He says that Sarah visited Beck, the granddaughter, who did "belong" to the Fosters. He confirms that she instructed Beck to administer the poisons to the Fosters, and that she wanted a slave girl called Nancy to be poisoned as well. What were Sarah's motives? Given that she had grandchildren, she was considered old and therefore without much "auction block value." According to Packwood's account, Sarah's actions were probably performed out of revenge for her own suffering.

He goes on to say that on June 2, 1730, she was indicted before the court in St. George's for poisoning several people. There were 10 witnesses for the king, including Mrs. Foster. (Mr. Foster and Nancy were too ill to attend.) When asked whether she was guilty or not guilty, Sarah answered, "Not guilty and for tryall put herself upon God and country." During the trial she was told that she could say what she liked, but court records show that "she made some slender denyall of the fact and said no more." The verdict as pronounced by the foreman was: "Guilty and we value her at one pound four shillings and six pence."

Three days later Sarah was brought back to hear the dreadful sentence: "It is the judgment and sentence of this court, that you, Sarah Bassett, the prisoner at the barr be return'd to the prison from whence you came and from thence you are to be conveyed to the place of execution where a pile of wood is to be made and provided, and you are there to be burnt with fire until your body be dead. And the Lord have mercy on your soul." Her response? "I never deserved it." Apparently she proclaimed that she was not guilty to the very end and was said to have cried out that God would prove her innocent. One legend has it that God did so — when her ashes were examined, a tiny purple iris appeared in full bloom. That iris is our endemic Bermudiana.

In *Bermuda Journey*, Zuill says: "It is curious that while so many punishments of bygone days should have been forgotten, the burning of Sally Bassett should have made such a deep impression that it became a Bermuda legend." But why is it so curious? While public executions were relatively common, burnings were not. Women accused of being witches during the 17th century were generally hanged. Horrendous as any execution is, a burning is particularly brutal.

And why was Sarah brought all the way from St. George's to Crow Lane to receive her punishment? Ordnance Island, minutes away from the jail, and Gibbet Islands in

— continued on next page

Smiths Parish were normally the sites of executions. Both Zuill and Packwood record that on her way to Crow Lane she was passed by many people, presumably in haste to get to the spectacle, and that she told them, "No use you hurrying, folks. There'll be no fun till I get there!" That she was made a public example, there's no doubt. Perhaps the site was chosen so that people from all over the island could reach it, and perhaps burning was chosen to dissuade others from poisoning.

But there are no easy answers to the other questions. When Sarah said, "I never deserved it," she was surely right. No human deserves to be a slave. But is that what she meant? Or did she mean that she did not poison the Fosters and Nancy? Was she sane or (as some people apparently argued) old and crazy? Insanity seems unlikely; her recorded words certainly reveal a shrewd understanding of the nastier side of human nature, as well as courage. And if she did want the Fosters poisoned, why implicate her granddaughter? Some of Sarah Bassett's descendants believe that Thomas Foster sexually abused his female slaves, including her granddaughter. And if Sarah was not a part of the Fosters' household, then it would be much easier for Beck to carry out the deed. But why poison a slave? Perhaps Nancy colluded with the Fosters or did nothing to help the other slaves. We can only speculate. We can also only guess what might have happened to Beck in the aftermath of the incident.

These days, younger Bermudians tend not to remark on hot weather with that grim old saying. Nevertheless the fate of Sarah Bassett should never be forgotten. It epitomizes the insidious effects of slavery, even on an island that many consider paradise.

of supernatural excitement. Dioramas in the magazine highlight events in Bermudian history. Check out the swords, muskets and pistols on display, plus the 18-ton rifled muzzle-loaders on the gun floor. Never had the chance to see the British Crown Jewels in the Tower of London? Never mind; you'll find replicas in the keep here.

At the top of the tower, an audiovisual presentation shows how Bermuda fortified itself.

St. Catherine's is open year-round from 10 AM to 4:30 PM Monday through Sunday. (No visitors after 4 PM, please. You need at least an hour to explore the fort.) Admission rates are $5 for adults and $2 for children under 12.

St. David's Lighthouse
Lighthouse Hill, St. David's

People first saw the light in St. David's on November 3, 1879, when Bermuda's second and last lighthouse was officially opened. It's not as elegant as Gibb's Hill (see subsequent listing under Southampton Parish), being rather squat in comparison. But with its red and white paint job, it is cute and cheerful. The lighthouse is 55 feet from base to light and 285 feet above sea. Climb the 87 steps,

and you'll reach the top for a great view of St. David's and St. George's. Mondays and Wednesdays it's open from 9 AM to noon; Tuesdays it stays open until 2:30 PM. The rest of the week it's closed. Admission is free. St. David's Lighthouse, by the way, was blown up in the movie *The Deep*. We were never worried. . . . The film crew had constructed a replica.

Hamilton Parish

The Bermuda Perfumery and Gardens
212 North Shore Rd., Bailey's Bay
• (441) 293-0627, (800) 527-8213

Read the Flora and Fauna chapter and you'll know that Easter lilies were once an important part of our economy. We used to ship the bulbs to the United States. However, the flowers themselves were often thrown out. Colin Curtis, president and manager of the Bermuda Perfumery, told us that one day in 1929 his grandfather (William Blackburn Smith) watched thousands of these flowers thrown into the sea. The waste was too much for him, so he hit on the idea of making perfume. A marine engineer, Smith designed and made the machinery necessary for the project. Visit the perfumery and you'll see that it's still in use.

Smith's daughter, Mrs. Madeline Scott, was an excellent floriculturist. She brought in a then-famous perfumer from France. Eventually, their combined expertise led to the production of Easter Lily Perfume, which they manufactured in a small wooden building. Sixty-nine years later, Bermuda's one perfumery is still flourishing in a charming Bermudian farmhouse that's some 250 years old.

It is well worth a visit (admission is free) for several reasons: First, you'll get to see how perfume is made now and how it was made in the past. A guide will show you around the plant and explain enfleurage, the ancient method of extracting fragrance from flowers. Second, you can buy perfumes, colognes, and moisturizing lotions all made right here in Bermuda under the name of LiLi. Bermudiana, Easter lily, frangipani and passion flower perfumes are for sale in the gift shop in a variety of sizes. A quarter-ounce bottle of each costs $25. The latest fragrance, Paradis, is a blend of floral notes and costs $38 for a quarter-ounce or $25 for eau de toilette.

Lastly, once you've finished your tour, you can explore the nature trail set in six acres of lush garden and jungle land. Admission to the trail is free. Depending on the season, you'll see passion flower, thumbergia and night-blooming cereus, old garden roses and orchids of all types. In fact, all the flowers, trees and shrubs we mention in our Flora and Fauna chapter are growing in these beautiful gardens. Rest areas will let you sit and peacefully appreciate them. You may catch sight of Mr. Curtis checking out his latest hibiscus hybrid or his gingers imported from Hawaii and Tahiti. Whenever he travels, he always has an eye open for what exotic plants he can try planting here.

If you're stuck for a gift to take back home, the Calabash Gift Shop, located on the prop-

erty, has a variety of gifts from all over the world. From April 1 to October 31, the perfumery and gardens are open Monday through Saturday from 9:15 AM to 5 PM; Sundays it opens from 10 AM to 4 PM. The rest of the year it closes on Sundays and public holidays, but it is open Monday through Saturday from 9:15 AM to 4:30 PM.

Caves

Hamilton Parish is known for its limestone cave formations. In the Resort Hotels chapter we've already mentioned the Prospero and Cathedral caves found on the grounds of Grotto Bay Beach Hotel. Here we list one more that is open to the public. Guides will escort you, mainly to ensure that you do not touch the formations. In the past, visitors would break off pieces for souvenirs. However, the slow growth of these formations of stalagmites and stalactites (1 cubic inch every 100 years) depends on the remorseless dripping of water on stone. Negative drip means negative growth. Take pictures, by all means, but please don't touch. Perhaps you are confused between stalactites and stalagmites? Remember, stalactites tumble (that is, grow down from the cave's ceiling), while stalagmites mount (that is, grow up from the cave floor). When they meet and grow together, they are known simply as columns.

Crystal Caves
Wilkinson Ave.
• **(441) 293-0640**

These caves are not named after crystal substances; rather they are named for their subterranean pools of incredibly clear water. Look approximately 55 feet down through turquoise depths, and you'll see the bottom. The water comes in from Castle Harbour, so the depth fluctuates according to the tides.

Crystal Caves' known history goes back to 1907, when two boys inadvertently discov-

Photo: GIS

Fine flippered friends are among the attractions in Bermuda.

ered the caves when playing cricket. They immediately took a lantern and a piece of rope to explore them. Since then, these stalagmite and stalactite formations have been open to the public. A guide will walk you along a pontoon bridge that crosses the pools. He or she will point out that the formations resemble fantastical creatures and the Manhattan skyline.

You can visit every day from 9:30 AM to 4:40 PM year-round. Admission rates are $6 for adults; $3 for children ages five to eleven. Children under 4 can visit for free. You can buy a souvenir from the gift shop. Prices start at about $2.50. Credit cards are not accepted for admission but are fine for gift buying.

Glass Blowing Studio and Show Room
16 Blue Hole Hill
• (441) 293-2234

OK, the Phoenicians started glass blowing in the first century BC. And the Venetians have been at it ever since the fifteenth century. Gail Cook, owner and manager here, brought glassblowing to Bermuda in 1986. We're so glad she did. For one thing, she and her staff of glassblowers make uniquely Bermudian objets d'art. Plates, bowls, glasses and vases come in the vibrant blues and greens and pinks that are Bermuda's true colors. Their exquisitely made longtails, bluebirds and angelfish will remind you of our fauna. For another, this ancient art is fascinating to watch. Visit the studio (entrance fee is $2 per person, children under twelve can visit for free), and you'll see the glassblowers in action. They'll show you the base material — a raw glass powder of sand, soda, lime and silica. It looks gritty and a bit dirty, to tell you the truth. Yet by the end of the melting, coloring and blowing processes it becomes "such stuff as dreams are made on."

During the summer, the studio is open from 9 AM to 5 PM Monday through Saturday and 10 AM to 5 PM on Sunday. The glassblowers take a lunch break from 12:30 to 1 PM, but the showroom remains open during this break. During the months of September through February, opening hours can be reduced, depending on the number of visitors. From November through February, the furnace closes and the staff concentrate on flame work instead. Generally, in the winter the studio opens at 10 AM and closes at 4 PM. Prices range from $11.75 for a Bermuda tree frog, to $80 and higher for larger pieces. Items made by apprentices can cost as little as $5.

Smiths Parish

Bermuda Aquarium, Museum & Zoo
North Shore Rd., Flatts
• (441) 293-2727

You're right, we listed the BAMZ in our Kidstuff chapter, but we urge adults to come here too. The aquarium has been a favorite attraction since its opening in 1928. If the weather happens to be unkind, then at least you'll have the chance to see the fish that live here. Tanks contain all kinds of marine life, including barracuda and a sinister moray eel that looks like a gigantic stuffed stocking. Less intimidating are the green turtles, puffer, trigger and angelfish, wrasses and sergeant majors. Tiny tanks show you tiny life, such as miniature crabs, bioluminescent corals and sea horses. Check out the North Rock exhibit— two giant tanks depicting the coral reef and its inhabitants. (See our Kidstuff chapter for more info.)

The Natural History Museum tells the story of Bermuda's environmental development; it also has an excellent exhibit on our whales and the part they played in our economy. In the outdoor zoo, you'll find the Islands of Australasia Exhibit, complete with real walla-bies, Australian bats, bearcats and three kangaroos. Look out for animals from other parts of the world: pink flamingos from the Caribbean and tortoises from the Galapagos. The Local Tails Exhibit focuses on animals endemic or native to Bermuda. Here you can see a cahow (albeit stuffed), that endangered, endemic bird we mentioned in our Flora and Fauna chapter. Small children will enjoy the touch pool that allows them to pick up sea urchins, sea puddings and starfish. If you get hungry or thirsty you can buy a burger at Peacock's Pantry, a concession on the grounds, which is open daily from 10 AM to 3 PM. The BAMZ itself opens from 9 AM to 4:30 PM, Mondays through Sundays, year-round except for Christmas Day. Admission rates are $8 for adults, $4 for children aged five to twelve, and children under 5 can visit for free. The Heritage Passport gives a 10 percent discount off these rates.

Devil's Hole Aquarium
Harrington Sound Rd.
• (441) 293-2072

Actually, there's nothing devilish about this natural aquarium. It offers a painless way of fishing — painless, that is, both for the fish and for you. A few seconds' walk away from the admissions office takes you to a deep lake in a cavern where you can stand on a small bridge and "fish" with line and bait, but no hooks. You'll see angelfish, snappers, moray eels and green parrotfish that are happy to take your bait and run. As Wendell Pond, owner and manager, puts it: "We may be skillful at one end of the line, but they're just as skillful on the other!" You'll also get to see Ninja, Stormy Eyes, Camouflage and Slow Poke. And who may they be? They are truly Bermudian green turtles. Born in captivity in 1988, they're still doing well.

Devil's Hole Aquarium was Bermuda's first

INSIDERS' TIP

Pick up the free guide, *This Week in Bermuda* from any Visitors Service Bureau and inside you will find the detachable Heritage Passport booklet. This booklet gives you discounts on admission to some of our attractions, including the Bermuda Aquarium, Museum & Zoo and the Bermuda Underwater Exploration Institute.

tourist attraction. In the early 1800s, Mr. Pond explains, the roof of the cavern collapsed as a result of water rushing in from the South Shore, approximately 1.5 miles away. In 1834 Mr. Trott, the owner at the time, decided to use it as a fish pond for the groupers he used to catch. Neighbors became curious and insisted on checking it out. Being a true entrepreneurial Bermudian, Mr. Trott decided to charge an entrance fee.

These days that fee is $5 for adults and teens, $3 for children ages 5 to 12, and 50¢ for children under 5. March 1 to November 30, Devil's Hole is open seven days a week from 9:30 AM to 4:30 PM. For winter times and days of operation, call Mr. Pond.

Paget Parish

Bermuda Botanical Gardens
Point Finger Rd. • (441) 236-5291

Actually, these gardens can be accessed from the South Road and from Berry Hill Road, but we give the above address since you can easily reach it by bus. Yes, these 36 acres of gardens are a tourist attraction, but we love them too. We come here with our children for family picnics and parties. We come early in the morning for a jog or a walk. We come on our lunch hour for a break from stress. And once a year, we flock here for our annual Agricultural Exhibition (see our Annual Events and Festivals chapter).

Ever since 1898, when they were officially opened as "The Public Garden," the Bermuda Botanical Gardens have been home to more than 1,000 varieties of plant life. You'll find all the flora we mention in our Flora and Fauna chapter and more, including exotic trees, shrubs and flowers that have been transported here during the last three centuries. Go down to the end of the park that faces the South Shore, and you'll find a wonderful banyan tree. This gigantic ficus tree originally came from Ceylon or India and is distinctive for its aerial roots that eventually reach the ground to form secondary trunks. Kids like to swing on the roots. Other exotic trees include an Indian rubber tree, an Indian laurel and an Australian banyan. Explore the gardens, and you'll come across a cacti and succulent collection, a plumeria collection (the trees here are more commonly known as frangipani), a palm garden and a rose garden. A small, walled garden for the blind specializes in fragrant flowers, herbs and shrubs.

Indoor collections include the Arrowroot Factory and Fern Collection, the Exotic House (where you'll find a fantastic display of orchids and bromeliads) and the Cacti and Succulent House, where you'll find that cacti are not always prickly. Many of them produce amazing flowers.

Tuesdays, Wednesdays and Fridays, you can meet guides outside the Visitors' Service Centre at 10:30 AM. They will take you for an informative hour-long tour of the gardens. Tuesdays and Fridays, from noon until 2 PM, you can also take a guided tour of elegant, eighteenth century Camden, the official residence of our premier. She doesn't live there, but she does hold receptions, parties and official functions when necessary. The Visitors' Service Centre is open Tuesday through Saturday from 9:30 AM to 3.30 PM year round, except on public holidays. Sundays and Mondays the centre closes. Go there for information, of course, and also for light snacks. The gift section specializes in English botanical items plus books on gardening, flora and fauna and plant-related subjects. Prices range from $10 to $40. The gardens are open from sunrise to sunset.

Pembroke Parish

Hamilton

Cathedral of the Most Holy Trinity (Bermuda Cathedral)
Church St., Hamilton • (441) 292-4033

Our cathedral is open daily from 8 AM to 5:45 PM. See the Worship chapter for information about its history and architecture.

Ocean Discovery Centre at the Bermuda Underwater Exploration Institute
40 Crow Lane, Hamilton
• (441) 292-7219

In 1870, Jules Verne's imagination took

readers 20,000 leagues under the sea. In 1997 this institute opened to let us explore at a more realistic 12,000 feet under the sea. Don't worry, you won't get wet. You sit in a capsule and let video, motion, light and sounds take you on a seven-minute simulated dive. But there is far more to see —the dive is just part of a self-guided audio tour. As you enter the building, you'll see a giant map of Bermuda on the lobby floor and three steel chandeliers (modeled after oceanographic instruments) that give introductory information about the sea and Bermuda's marine heritage. You'll then follow a path that takes you to the exhibits.

With lots of multimedia and interaction involved, the exhibits open your eyes to the revelations of the ocean, the history of underwater exploration, marine life living at different depths and Bermuda's shipwrecks. Imaginative use of lighting, video and touch-screen televisions all make the tour interesting. So do examples of underwater craft such as the full-scale bathysphere (a spherical, cable-lowered diving compartment), first used by American deep-water explorer Charles William Beebe in the world's first ever deep sea dive half a mile off Bermuda in 1934. He went down to a depth of 3,028 feet.

A room devoted to displaying about 3,000 seashells is particularly worth seeing. Bermudian Jack Lightbourn very generously donated his magnificent collection to the institute. Beautifully displayed, with special lighting emphasizing their delicate colors and sheen, these shells are a feast for the eyes. You'll see Bermuda shells that Lightbourn began collecting when he was just 11 years old. One tiny white shell with exquisite edging is actually named after him: the Murex Pternyotus Lightbourn. In addition, his collection includes a vast amount of foreign shells, many taken from the Pacific. Look out for the Australian trumpet that can hold up to three gallons of water.

The institute is open from 10 AM to 6 PM (last tickets are sold at 5 PM) Monday through Sunday, year-round except for Christmas Day. Admission rates are $9.75 for adults, $5 for children ages 7 to 16, and $7.80 for seniors over 65. Children 6 and younger may visit for free. If you have a Heritage Passport, you get a 20 percent reduction on all rates. Your ticket is good for the entire day. Given the detailed marine information you can find here, you'll definitely want to spend, at the very least, a couple of hours here. What's more, your ticket gives you access to the auditorium where you can watch movies about the ocean and marine conservation and exploration.

If you get hungry while exploring the museum, you can have a snack at the coffee bar, or you can visit La Coquille Restaurant for an excellent lunch, served between 11:30 AM and 2:45 PM. La Coquille is also open for dinner from 6:30 to 10:45 PM. (See our Restaurants chapter for further details.) Every month the institute hosts an Ocean Explorers' lecture series, followed by a buffet supper. Speakers tend to be internationally known scientists and explorers. Call for dates and price of lecture tickets. Two gift shops may solve Christmas shopping problems: The Logo Shop sells T-shirts and other items with the institute's logo; the Ocean's Gift Shop specializes in Bermudian items that are unavailable elsewhere. Prices range from about 95¢ to $1,500 for a handmade reproduction of an old Bermuda dinghy. We emphasize that the institute is completely wheelchair-accessible and has bathrooms equipped for visitors in wheelchairs.

House of Assembly (Sessions House)
21 Parliament St., Hamilton
• **(441) 292-7408**

We may be a colony, but we certainly have our own parliament. In fact, ours is the oldest in the Commonwealth outside the U.K. And yes, we do retain the British emphasis on pomp and ceremony. You can visit the House Monday through Friday from 9 AM to 12:30 PM and from 2 to 5 PM, but parliamentary debates happen on Fridays from 10 AM, October through June. You're welcome to sit in the visitors' gallery and experience debates between government leaders and the opposition. See map on page xvi. Do not be surprised to see one member wearing a full wig and flowing black robes. He is Mr. Speaker, and as arbitrator he has the unenviable task of maintaining order and decorum. Notice we do not give a finishing time — debates have been known to continue until the early hours of the following morning. By the way, it would be unheard of to turn up in jeans. Smart casual dress is required.

Supreme Court (Sessions House)
21 Parliament St., Hamilton
• **(441) 292-1350**

The chief justice presides over the Supreme Court, together with a number of puisne judges, who try the more serious criminal cases. The court is downstairs in the Sessions House. "How can this be an attraction?" Well, our lawyers wear gowns and short wigs; our judges wear full wigs and red robes. What for? Wigs were first introduced in the seventeenth century, when Louis XIV of France wore one to hide his baldness. In England, they reached the height of fashion in the eighteenth century. Judges and lawyers continue to wear them because of tradition, and because, they argue, the costume encourages a more formal and respectful atmosphere in court. Visitors are welcome, although space is limited. The court is open for the same hours as the House of Assembly. Again, smart casual dress is required.

Visitors' Service Bureau
Front St., Hamilton
• **(441) 295-1480**

Here friendly staff will give you all kinds of information about Hamilton in particular and Bermuda in general. Bulletin boards will keep you posted about entertainment, festivals and events. You can buy transportation passes here and pick up a free Bermuda map and numerous brochures. April through October, the bureau is open 9 AM to 1 PM and 1:30 to 4 PM Monday through Saturday. During winter, the hours are generally 9 AM to 2 PM, but they are subject to change. Call directly to verify them. See map page xvi.

Fort Hamilton
Happy Valley Rd.

Built in the 1860s, this polygonal fort is well worth a visit for its view of the city and Hamilton Harbour. See the map on page xvi. If forts interest you, then you'll appreciate the rare, 10-inch rifled muzzle-loader guns and emplacements for 60-pounder cannon on Moncrieff disappearing carriages. If you're into plants rather than military history, you'll enjoy the botanical gardens that have been planted in the dry moat. They contain a variety of tropical and subtropical ferns and plants.

Visit at noon on Mondays from November to March, and you might think you're in Scotland. The Bermuda Islands Pipe Band performs the Skirling Ceremony by the ramparts. You'll hear the haunting pipe music of Scotland and Ireland while you watch the Highland Dancers, who truly know what it is to have a fling. (See our Beaches and Parks chapters for information on other forts.)

Southampton Parish

Gibb's Hill Lighthouse
66 St. Anne's Rd.
• **(441) 238-8069, (441) 238-0524**

In 1846 we had a May Day with a difference. That's when Gibb's Hill Lighthouse, the first one to go up in Bermuda, beamed out upon the island. Since then it's been one of our most familiar landmarks. Ships 40 miles away can see it, and pilots flying at 10,000 feet can pick up its flash 120 miles away. Tall (117 feet from base to light, to be exact), elegant and graceful, it's well worth a visit if only for the view from the top.

For an admission rate of $2.50 you can climb the eight flights of stairs. The landings come in useful for rests (some of us need them) and for information about its construction. You'll learn that it's one of the few lighthouses in the world made of cast iron, and that its original light was a concentrated burner of four circular wicks. Count each step as you climb, and you should reach a total of 185. Once you reach the top, you can walk out onto a circular balcony enclosed by a railing. Warning: Do not look down, unless you are certain heights have no effect on you. Instead, look across, and you'll see the South Shore, Hamilton Harbour and the Great Sound.

Once you've hiked back down to the base again, for about $6 you can relax over a well-earned English cream tea in The Lighthouse Tearoom. Open 9 AM to 5 PM daily, the eatery offers breakfast and lunch as well. Sunday afternoons from 2 to 4:30 PM, Steve Crawford will serenade you with his classical guitar. Mementos of your visit are available at the Lighthouse Gift Shop, which sells collectors' lighthouse teaspoons, ceramic lamps and T-shirts.

Gibb's Hill Lighthouse itself is open seven days a week from 9 AM to 4:30 PM year-round. That said, it does close on Christmas and sometimes during January for maintenance. Kids younger than 5 can visit for free. A word about Christmas: The lighthouse reminds us that Christmas is coming by its windows, which are studded with colored lights in season.

Sandys Parish

Royal Naval Dockyard

Like St. George's, the entity of Dockyard is an attraction in itself. In our History chapter, you learned that its fortifications began in 1809 as compensation for British ports lost in the American Revolution. Bermudian slaves and convicts transported from Britain slowly and painfully created this naval base out of limestone, which they quarried out of land at the entrance. Until 1951 it was, according to Ed Harris, author of *Bermuda's Forts*, an "imperial fortress." It has also been described as "the Gibraltar of the West." For many Bermudians, though, it was known as "Little England" and the venue where local apprentices learned trades, such as masonry and building.

These days you'll see our tugs in dock, but the days of the British Navy have passed. Many of the limestone warehouses and buildings remain but have been imaginatively con-

verted into pubs, restaurants, shops and museums. We recommend that you visit by ferry (see our Getting Here, Around and Home chapter) — that way you'll enjoy seeing Bermuda from the water as well as the many attractions on hand here. See the map on page xviii.

The most important museum here is the Maritime Museum where you'll see the relics of our maritime heritage. Check our Arts and Culture chapter for details on the Maritime Museum, and for information about the Arts Centre, where exhibitions and workshops are held. For other attractions and businesses in the Dockyard area, check our Restaurants, Nightlife, Kidstuff and Watersports chapters.

Bermuda Craft Market at Dockyard
The Cooperage, 4 Freeport Rd.
• **(441) 234-3208**

We mention the Craft Market in this chapter because whether you are in the shopping mood or not, it's fun to visit.

Here you'll find many of our crafts experts at work — the majority of items on sale are locally handmade. You'll find seashell candles, stained-glass ornaments and lamps, quilts, hand-painted fabric designs and miniature cedar furniture. If you're into collecting Christmas tree ornaments, you're bound to find something Bermudian to hang on your tree, whether it's a tiny traditional cottage or a polished shell decorated with ribbon. Want to sample our loquat and Surinam cherry preserves? They're on sale here for $2 to $5.75 a pot. If you're interested in Bermuda-related books, an excellent range is available. Prices of gifts range from about $5 to $2,000. The Craft Market is open daily from 10 AM to 6 PM, April to November. During the winter it closes at 5 PM. It's also open for all special occasions and holidays, except Christmas and Good Friday. See map page xviii.

Bermuda Train Company Ltd.
No. 6 Valley Rd.
• **(441) 236-5972**

This is a brand-new train service offering a 20-minute loop from the Clock Tower in the Royal Naval Dockyard to the Cruise Terminal, with an additional five stops along its route. Built especially for Bermuda, the 60-foot, scaled-down train — a replica of a Baldwin Locomotive — seats 77 passengers in its airy coaches. The unique shuttle service is available from 8:30 AM to 5 PM daily for $2 per person. You can also participate in a fascinating train tour featuring the scenic and interesting attractions in the area. This one-hour daily tour and ride is $10 per person and starts at 11 AM.

The Snorkel Park at Dockyard
Freeport Rd.
• **(441) 234-1006**

Staff here definitely feel that they offer relaxation, rather than a watersport. They offer marked snorkel trails and floating rest stations where you can view the fish and corals of our ocean fauna. Bring your own equipment, and you pay $5 per person for up to a day's snorkeling. Rent equipment, and you'll pay $10 an hour or $17 for the whole day. Kids 12 and under pay $5 an hour (including rental equipment) Lifeguards are on hand, and they'll be happy to tell you whether you've seen a wrasse or a butterfly fish. See our Flora and Fauna and Watersports chapters for information about underwater life. Next door to the Maritime Museum, this park is open from 10:30 AM to 6 PM Mondays through Fridays. Saturdays and Sundays it is open from 11 AM to 5 PM. However, you can book earlier times on the weekends if you wish. During winter (November 1 to March 31) it's closed. After all, the fish like a vacation from being on show. See map page xviii.

Bermuda, then, offers the more old fashioned pleasures that children have enjoyed for centuries when life was a calmer, more leasurely business altogether.

Kidstuff

We have to start with a confession: we don't have theme parks, fun fairs or Disney glitter and glitz. (At least, not yet, though they may come in time when we develop our former base lands. See History chapter.) But that doesn't mean we don't like children. On the contrary, we welcome them. And we know that quality time with small children in these frenetic and sometimes stressful times is precious. Bermuda, then, offers the more old fashioned pleasures that children have enjoyed for centuries when life was a calmer, more leisurely business altogether. What, for example, can be better than a day spent on a safe, idyllic beach? Or a day in a boat exploring the fishy wonders of our reef and rocky promontories? A relaxing stroll in one of our many parks can expose children to the beauty of our flora and fauna and give them an understanding of why the natural environment is so vitally important. Recreations such as minigolf, junior golf, tennis and roller skating are also available, and attractions such as our aquarium and the Bermuda Underwater Exploration Institute can entertain kids on rainy days. Let's not forget the time-honored joy of reading a good book, either, or the fun of playing a board game. A vacation in Bermuda may be your chance to coax your children away from the television into more active pastimes.

In this chapter we will highlight venues and activities that are particularly suitable for kids up to 8 or 9 years old. We'll suggest options for rainy days. And we'll also mention hotels that have special kids' programs and babysitting services, plus restaurants and shops that are particularly children friendly. However, do bear in mind that children are all different and some may have more sophisticated tastes than others. Check out, then, our other chapters, especially Beaches, Parks, Attractions, Arts and Culture and Watersports, for more detailed information about fun things to do. For information about games such as tennis

and bowling, and other physical activities such as pedal biking and in-line skating, go to the Recreations chapters. If you have a young Tiger Woods in the family, then the Golf chapter will give you lots of information about our courses.

Beaching Out

We will start with our beaches because, for most children, Bermuda is synonymous with sea, sand and frolic. In fact, we have so many beaches that we have devoted a whole chapter to them. There you will find detailed physical descriptions and information such as address, telephone, lifeguard availability and, where applicable, prices of rentals. Here we will mention public beaches that are especially safe and ideal for kids. Typically, the water is calm and shallow, therefore perfect for tots with armbands and for snorkeling beginners. Remember, though, that young children should never be left unsupervised — just a few inches of water can kill. And older kids should not swim alone.

If you're at the eastern end of Bermuda, visits to Clearwater and to Tobacco Bay are a must; see the map on page xvi. Clearwater is a favorite with locals because, in addition to its two sandy beaches, it has lots of tarmac space for pedal bike riding. Small kids like to try out the new bikes with training wheels. And an equipped playground is there for those who've had enough of the water. Clearwater has a lifeguard during the summer season, by the way. Tobacco Bay is great for snorkeling and a franchise there sells snacks, drinks and lunches. It also offers watersports rentals. In Hamilton Parish, Shelley Bay Beach is a good choice, offering both restaurant and playground facilities. Move on to Smiths and you'll find John Smith's Bay that, on still days, is great for the whole family. However, watch out for riptides in windy weather. In the summer a lifeguard will advise you whether swimming is safe. After a morning in Hamilton, the kids might need a refreshing dip. Clarence Cove in Admiralty House Park, Pembroke Parish, is a magical spot; see the map on page xiv. It has two small sandy beaches and the water is more lagoon than ocean. Once you get to Warwick, you'll find a chain of beaches that extends into Southampton and that makes up South Shore Park. The one we particularly recommend for children is tiny Jobson's Cove, a wonderful choice for teaching kids how to swim and for fish exploring. Another similar beach is Port Royal Cove, farther along the coast and next to the western end of our famous Horseshoe Bay. At the Beach House in Port Royal Cove you can buy snacks and rent equipment. The western end of the island has several safe beaches. Try Somerset Long Bay (It is long and the water is extremely shallow), plus two beaches at Daniel's Head where there's also a playground and small restaurant. Enthusiastic snorkelers should try Snorkel Park in the Royal Naval Dockyard. (Check out the Attractions chapter for more information about it.)

Parks and Walks

Read our Parks and Conservation chapter and you'll see we have a variety of parkland areas. Although they are relatively small, they do offer you the opportunity to see our mêlée of flora and our striking rock formations. And remember small children love to linger over natural distractions, such as butterflies, trees with swinging roots (check out the Attractions chapter for a description of banyan and ficus trees in the Botanical Gardens.) They hate being rushed so that, in this regard, the size of our parks is ideal for them. A few, such as

Mullet Bay Park in St. George's, Pembroke Park and Warwick Children's Park, have playgrounds equipped with slides, swings and, in some cases, tree houses, climbing frames and static trains. So check out Parks for detailed descriptions. Check out Recreations and Attractions as well for walking the Bermuda Railway Trail and for exploring forts. (The two forts we most recommend for kids are St. Catherine's Fort in St. George's, home to a replica collection of the British Crown Jewels, and Fort Hamilton in Pembroke.) Here we'll tell you about guided walks and tours that are suitable for the whole family.

Older children interested in history should definitely visit the old Town of St. George. There, they can take a guided walking tour or a horse and carriage ride up and down, in and out of the narrow, twisting streets with quaint names, such as Featherbed Alley or Old Maid's Lane. Call the Visitors' Service Bureau at (441) 297-1642 for details. They could also visit Verdmont, located at Collector's Hill, Smiths Parish, (441) 236-7369, a historic house belonging to the National Trust. A collection of china faced dolls, a Bermuda doll's house and other toys of previous centuries may well appeal to them. And after checking out the samplers, girls can breathe a sigh of relief that these days they don't have to be perfect at needlework. Cost is $3 per person. Combination tickets to all three National Trust properties (see Arts and Culture and Attractions for information on Globe House and Tucker House) are $5 for adults and $2 for students with ID. For additional details on various other properties, contact the Bermuda National Trust Headquarters at Waterville, an eighteenth-century house in Paget, between 9 AM and 5 PM Monday through Friday. The number is (441) 236-6483.

For more rural walking tours, you can join Nature Walks, free outdoor excursions centered on specific nature themes, sponsored by the Department of Agriculture, Fisheries and Parks. Also, during spring break in February, the Bermuda National Trust, (441) 236-6483, has a children's walk at the Spittle Pond Nature Reserve and a Palm Sunday walk. For an ethnically different experience, kids may well be fascinated by the Gumba Trail and Outdoor Museum, (441) 293-7330, in the Royal Naval Dockyard in Sandys Parish. This seasonal one-hour walking exhibit runs every Wednesday from June 20 to July 30 from 11 AM and from 12:30 PM. It focuses on the magic of Jankanoo, a carnival or masquerade dance practiced throughout the Caribbean. Kids will learn about the different characters in this ancient African dance. They'll meet, for example, the Hobby Horse and they'll learn about the historical connections between our own Gombey dance and the Jankanoo. (See Gombey Close-up in Let's Explain Bermuda.) Led by the Gumba (the tour leader), kids will enjoy dressing up in the colorful dance costumes and going on a treasure hunt in the military graveyard nearby. Outdoor display cases will illustrate the historical and anthropological significance of the masquerade. Watch out for the Pitchy Patchy Devil! He may just be lurking round the graves, ready to do his dance. Tickets are $5 per person and the event is canceled on rainy days. (See our Recreations chapter for additional information about walking and our Flora and Fauna chapter.)

Three Family Favorites

Even kids who've never seen a golf club in their lives love the Bermuda Golf Academy in Southampton. For them the main attraction is the miniature golf course there, complete with pagodas, waterfalls and brilliantly blue waterways. They like to boast when they've successfully shot the 16th hole — that's because they hit the ball over a drawbridge. If the course doesn't appeal, then the jungle gym will. And if you need a snack or a drink you'll find it at the licensed restaurant, The Wedge and Divot. Check the Golf chapter's Academy listing for prices. Or call (441) 238-8800.

The Canadian Pacific Southampton Princess in Southampton knows that children and dolphins have a lot in common. They both like to play and they both like to frolic. That's why the hotel has the Dolphin Discovery Progamme so that kids and dolphins get to meet. On a 3-acre site at East Whale Bay, children aged 5 to 9 can enjoy a two-hour session. For 90 minutes they participate in a variety of learning and game activities that help them to learn more about these glorious mammals. And for 30 minutes they interact with dolphins. The cost is $85 for hotel guests and Bermuda residents and $95 for visitors. What about older kids? For the same rate kids aged 10 to 16 can pet and swim with the dolphins for a period of 30 minutes. Be sure to reserve at least four days in advance. Call (441) 239-6957 for times.

How about a trip to the lighthouse? Gibb's Hill Lighthouse, (441) 238-0524, can be found on Lighthouse Road between South Shore and Middle Roads, Southampton. Anytime between 9 AM and 4:30 PM, you can climb the 185 steps to one of the most spectacular views of the entire island. And yes, the lighthouse is still in operation. Visit after dark and you'll see its beam like a gigantic wheel of light against the night sky. Admission is $2.50, with children younger than 5 admitted free. (See our Attractions chapter for more information.)

It's Raining, It's Pouring — What Shall We Do?

Well all right, rain in Bermuda seems at best unfair and at worst immoral. Many of us feel very guilty when a wet spell occurs because we know that our visitors have come for blue skies and sun. But we also feel relieved since a heavy downpour means good tank rain (see Flora and Fauna chapter). If kids complain about the weather you could tell them that our water supply depends on how much water we can catch from our roofs. And after that you could divert them by suggesting any of the following excursions.

The Bermuda Aquar-ium Museum and Zoo in Flatts Village, Smiths Parish, is a great choice for a rainy day. There you can learn lots about Bermuda's environment and marine life as you visit visually appealing exhibits. Perhaps our favorite is the North Rock Exhibit, where you can gaze on sea creatures and plants from our reefs. Small children will love the Discovery Room or activity center. It features live animal specimens that are safe to touch, together with hands-on activities, books and wall displays all relating to animal themes. If you happen to be there on a Friday morning at 8:45 AM, you could go on the Curator's Behind-the-Scenes Tour that allows you to meet and chat with staff experts. Kids will love watching the animals being fed. Cost for that tour per person is $25.

Incidentally, there's also a host of summer programs for children at BAMZ, including the Aqua Camps Program, designed for school children up to primary 7 (equivalent to grade 6). The camps are held in July and August with a focus on the aquarium, museum and zoo facilities, the island in general and the environment. Camp sessions are for one week, and visitors who become members of the Friends of the Bermuda Aquarium may attend. Cost is $100, and camps run from 9 AM to 3 PM daily. Preschoolers may attend camp for a half-day for $50 per week. The Nature Encounter Program at BAMZ is held most weekends from September through July, usually early Saturday mornings. Here, groups of children between ages 5 and 12 meet at the facility to encounter nature during two-hour activity sessions. Kids can learn how animals move in different ways, have fun sorting animals into

groups or be the first to spy a whale during a whale-watching trip. For more extensive information about BAMZ, check the Attractions chapter or call (441) 293-2727.

Unless the sea is very rough, rain need not preclude a ferry ride. Why not pick up the ferry at Hamilton's Albuoy's Point and go to the Royal Naval Dockyard? Disembark and you'll find a number of interesting places to visit, including a craft market and a pottery. (See Attractions and Arts and Culture chapter.) But for children ages 2 through 12, we recommend a visit to the Children's Room, which is located in the Bermuda Maritime Museum. This fun room provides a hands-on environment for kids to explore. (However, an adult must accompany children.) The center's theme, "On Land and Sea," features a dress-up area with a naval motif for younger children. There are boats, cannons, a chest filled with a fantastic array of costumes, computers, quizzes and games in a variety of interactive areas. Admission to the Children's Room is included in the ticket price for entrance to the Maritime Museum. See Arts and Culture chapter for more information, or call (441) 234-1418.

A bus into Hamilton can drop you off by the Bermuda Underwater Exploration Institute, located at the foot of Crow Lane. Check out an underwater wonderland where history and science meet state-of-the-art technology. At the institute, you can explore the ocean depths, see shipwrecked treasures and even learn about marine environments at the same time. Kids will enjoy a simulated deep dive and the fantastically beautiful shell collection. See Attractions for more information or call (441) 292-7219.

You might like to get kids into the picture by taking them to an art gallery. In Hamilton, try the Bermuda National Gallery, City Hall and Arts Centre, Church Street, Hamilton, (441) 295-9428, together with the Bermuda Arts Society, Bermuda Society and Arts Gallery, (441) 292-3824, in the same location. Try also the Windjammer Art Galleries in one of their two locations: 95 Front Street, Hamilton, (441) 292-5878, and the corner of Reid and

A family builds an elaborate sandcastle.

King Streets, Hamilton, (441) 292-7861. The Masterworks Foundation, 97 Front Street, Bermuda House Lane, is especially geared towards children. In fact, during the summer it offers Artist Encounters for Children aged 8 to 13. Kids get to meet local artists who will introduce their personal style, media and philosophy to students as well as give hands-on demonstrations. Call (441) 295- 2379 for prices, dates and times. For more description of our art galleries, and opportunities to meet artists, check out the Arts and Culture chapter.

If all else fails, take the kids shopping. There's nothing so cheering for a child as a visit to a toy store. On the whole, toys on sale here are from the US and because of local mark ups, therefore are more expensive than ones in North America. However, go to Jack N' Jill's, 7, Park Lane, Hamilton (by Victoria Park) and you'll find many European items in an old-fashioned toy shop setting. You'll find a variety of toys and a good selection of games. European craft items such as plasticene (a modeling medium), clay, paper weaving and flower-drying kits could keep the family happy for a few rainy hours. The shop's also well known for its line of Bruunzeel color pencils from Holland. Kids need sweetening up? This is the one toy store on the island where you can buy unpackaged candy by the quarter, half and pound, or by the piece.

How about bookstores? We recommend the Children's Bookshop, (441) 292-9078, in the International Centre, 26 Bermudiana Road, Hamilton. It's very well stocked with a range of titles from the UK as well as the US. You're bound to find something there for every child in the family.

Bear in mind there's always the Bermuda Youth Library. Before visiting Bermuda, call to set the process in motion for obtaining a visitor's membership. The cost is $25 for the entire family. Each child will receive a borrower's card, and the $25 is refundable upon departure. To receive a card once you're in Bermuda, present your passport or other

INSIDERS' TIP

Kite-flying is not allowed around the vicinity of the airport. This includes Kindley Field Park, Clearwater Beach, areas of the former base lands and the area along Ferry Reach. Kites can be a safety hazard to aircraft taking off or landing.

means of identification with your return airline ticket or ship pass. There is no limit to the number of books you may borrow. Contact the Youth Library, 74 Church Street, Hamilton, at (441) 295-0487.

Eating Out with the Kids

Let's face it, eating out with small children can be sheer murder, especially if they are starving and impatient for food. Here we'll just mention a few restaurants whose staff go out of their way to welcome kids and who offer kids' menus and high chairs. In St. George's we recommend the White Horse Tavern, (441) 297-1838, on King's Square. The service here is fairly fast and kids are easily distracted by an active view of the harbor. If they sit out on the outdoor porch, they can feed the fish. In Hamilton, check out La Trattoria, (441) 295-1877, located in Washington Lane, Hamilton. Walk into the restaurant and you'll immediately notice children's paintings and drawings pinned on the wall by the cash counter. On request, kids can have paper and borrow crayons. Try also M.R. Onions, (441) 292-5012, on Par-la-Ville Road. Older kids can get on the Internet if grown ups want to linger over coffee. The Paraquet, (441) 236-5842, South Shore Road, in Paget is ideal for families. It's also unlicensed. And in Sandys Parish, the Frog and Onion is a good bet since it has a games room with pool and a variety of arcade games, which are loved by older kids.

Emperors of Ice Cream

On hot days kids scream for ice cream. We have ice cream shops and parlors scattered all over the island that boast some pretty tasty homemade ice cream, yogurts, sherbets and sorbets in many exotic flavors. Bailey's Ice Cream Parlour, Blue Hole Hill, Hamilton

Parish, (441) 293-8605, gets very busy when our temperature soars. It offers at least 20 flavors of homemade, all-natural ice creams, sherbets, low-fat yogurts and fat-free sorbets. At Double Dip Ice Cream Shop, 119 Front Street, Hamilton, (441) 292-3503, and Double Dip Too, 12 North Shore Road, Hamilton Parish, (441) 292-5580, you're certain to find a tasty flavor made just to your liking. Be warned you may have to stand in line with all the other ice cream lovers on the island. Visiting the West End? Stop by Nannini Häagen-Dazs at the Clock Tower, Dockyard, Sandys Parish, (441) 234-2474, for a refreshing sorbet or ice cream cone.

A Word about Ginger Beer

Why not try one of our local favorites — ginger beer?

This refreshing, nonalcoholic soft drink with a kick is actually made from ginger root concentrate. It's made by John Barritt and Sons, Ltd., (441) 236-7171, and Metro Mineral Water in Devonshire, (441) 236-6396, and is available anywhere on the island where sodas are sold (including many vending machines). Counting calories? It's also available without sugar and goes great with most tasty local cuisine.

Kid-Friendly Resorts

Read our Accommodations chapters and you'll see that most hotels offer special rates or plans to accommodate visitors with children. Many hotels allow up to two children 16 years of age to stay in the same room with the same meal plan as their parents for free. A few offer special kids' activities as well, which can give parents a much needed break. Here, we

Kites Make For An Especially Good Friday

Oh, go fly a kite!

On Good Friday, everyone in Bermuda seems to be doing just that. All eyes are focused on the balmy, clear blue skies, and the entire island shuts down for a day devoted to festive gaiety. There's kite-flying, shooting allies (a game of marbles) and plenty of plain good eating, with lots of hot cross buns and codfish cakes.

Good Friday, or Kite Day, is one of the great traditions of Bermuda and has been celebrated in this unusual way for more than a century. However, if you ask any of our senior citizens how it all got started, you'll hear a different oral account from virtually every one you question.

Many stories relating to kite-flying on Good Friday have religious significance. One story tells how a Sunday school teacher, trying to explain the ascension of Christ to her students, illustrated the story by flying a kite on Easter Sunday. When the kite went soaring into the heavens she cut the string, and the kite rose higher until it disappeared into the blue.

Although the exact origin is unknown, kite-flying is believed to have started in the Orient or Greece thousands of years ago. Kites have been used in the practice of religion, science and, of course, children's games throughout the course of history. It was just a matter of time before kites made it to Bermuda, but little was written on the topic before the 1940s. The sport of kite-flying did not really take off here (pun intended) until after World War II. Perhaps it was the lack of television in the '50s that caused just about everyone on the island to become involved in the Good Friday ritual, either as a spectator or participant. And now the sport is on the rise again with just as many "birdie kites" filling the skies as those crafted by the numerous talented kite builders on the island.

— continued on next page

Photo: GIS

Flying kites has been a Good Friday tradition in Bermuda for decades.

Kite-flying is enjoyed by entire families, and there are many Bermudian households that produce kites for retail sale as well as personal pleasure. The original Bermuda Boxy Kite is one of the first kites many Bermudian children have the opportunity to make. Constructed from dead, dry fennel sticks, brown paper bags or (nowadays) plastic trash bags, it is simple to make — the connecting strings of the kite are generally just pushed through holes in the paper covering the kite sticks.

Kite Day is not just an occasion to view some of the colorful and vivid displays of kite mastery. You can also hear the various sounds produced by the kites' "hummers." One kite famous for this is the Somerset Kite, or the Buzzer, which makes the loudest high-pitched humming sound of any of the kite designs on the island. Another of our favorite kite designs is the Three-headed Roundie, known for its splendid patterns, shape and many hummers. It is definitely a beautiful sight to behold soaring against azure blue skies.

For Kite Day, most Bermudians tote their carefully crafted, cherished kites to Horseshoe Bay Beach in Southampton for the annual Bermuda Kite Festival. Thousands gather for a festive outing that begins with an early morning church and song service, followed by a kite competition, organized games and entertainment and a performance by the Gombeys. Started some 13 years ago, this popular Good Friday beach party brings together families, friends and visitors to cheer on the pitching of some pretty fantastic kites. Prizes are given for kites ranging from a maximum of 6 feet wide to the smallest kite at the minimum of 4 inches.

And the kite-flying can bring on a pretty hearty appetite. Between all the events, festival patrons enjoy fresh-baked, moist hot cross buns and fish cakes fried to golden-brown perfection. It's a delectable, tasty treat that has become a big part of Good Friday.

So the next time you come across a sole kite flyer on a windy spring day in your neighborhood park, stop and say hello. It just might be a Bermudian homesick for Good Friday.

---

offer information on three of Bermuda's more kid-friendly resorts. Note that extensive information on each of these properties is at your disposal in the Resort Hotels chapter.

Sonesta Beach Hotel and Spa
5 South Rd. and Sonesta Dr.
• **(441) 238-8122**

So, you've brought along the novel you've been trying to read all year and booked a game of golf for later in the day. What to do with the kids? Don't worry.

Sonesta Beach Resort knows just what kids enjoy. The Just Us Kids program, from mid-June through the beginning of September for kids from ages 5 through 12, offers supervised activities in the morning or throughout the day. Day excursions around the island are planned, with only a small fee charged to cover transportation and entrance fees. Lunch can be arranged and charged to the parents' room. Kids' breakfasts and dinners are free for guests that have bought a meal plan. Children's menus are available in all restaurants. For smaller tots, aged 2 to 4, there is the Just Us Little Kids program on Monday, Wednesday and Friday from 1 to 4 PM. Activities for toddlers focus on arts and crafts, games, movies and "Computertots," a computer familiarization program for the tiny ones. Participating children must be potty trained.

Considering visiting during the Easter holiday? Sonesta Beach has an Easter Weekend program the kids won't soon forget. The Thursday before Good Friday there is a kite-making demonstration, and on Good Friday, kids will actually join in the tradition of kite flying in Bermuda. There are kites for all children, and refreshments are served. On Saturday morning, children are invited to gather on the Palm Court to decorate Easter eggs. Afterwards, prizes will be given out. Later that day, there's fun in the sun at the Boat Bay Beach, with activities including a sand sculpture contest. On Easter Sunday, the legendary Easter Bunny leads the children on an egg hunt. See the map on page xvi.

Southampton Princess
101 South Rd.
• **(441) 238-8000**

Camp Minor Manor at the Southampton Princess is geared specifically for children ages 5 through 16. Running from mid-June until the first of September, the activity program features Lenny's Loft game room from 8:30 to 11 AM, where children can participate in board or video games and play the jukebox or Ping-Pong. Children ages 2 to 4 may play in Lenny's Loft on Monday, Wednesday and Saturday from 9 AM to 2 PM. Infant and toddler sitting service is available at the resort at standard rates. See the map page xvi.

There is no charge for daytime activities (except lunch) conducted on premises. However, excursions away from the hotel require lunch and transportation fees. Should you need to have an escorted dinner for your children, this service is available at an extra charge in on-site restaurants only. Additional on-property activities at the Southampton Princess include pool sports and beach fun and games; a special "Mocktail Hour" every day from 4 to 5 PM, with pizza, popcorn and soft drinks; sand castle building, volleyball, badminton, tennis, table tennis and arts and crafts; movies on Tuesday and Friday evenings; karaoke on Thursday; a scavenger hunt and daily children's videos. Times and days are subject to change.

Grotto Bay Beach Hotel and Tennis Club
11 Blue Hole Hill
• **(441) 293-8333, (800) 582-3190**

The little ones will feel right at home when participating in Grotto Bay's summer children's program. Supervised by caring, qualified counselors, the Tree Frog Bunch is structured to help children enjoy Bermudian experiences.

For a minimal fee, children ages 4 and older can enjoy board games, swimming activities, treasure hunts, storytelling, beach fun, movie time, day excursions, fish feeding and more. Day activities are scheduled Monday through Saturday, starting at 9:45 AM and closing anywhere from 1:30 to 10 PM depending on the activities planned.

This children's program is not intended to be a baby-sitting service, although baby-sitting can be arranged through the resort's guest services desk for a fee. Baby-sitting rates range from $10.50 per hour for one child up to $13.50 per hour for four children. Add an additional 50 cents per hour for service provided after midnight. See the map on page xv.

At first glance it might appear the art world here is so small that the entire picture could be set in a modest frame. But several Bermudian artists have established reputations abroad, and their push for excellence and recognition serves as an inspiration to our dancers and musicians.

Arts and Culture

At first glance it might appear the art world here is so small that the entire picture could be set in a modest frame. But several Bermudian artists have established reputations abroad, and their push for excellence and recognition serves as an inspiration to our dancers and musicians. Almost quietly, many are carving local niches as a springboard for jumping "the pond" — local vernacular for the surrounding ocean.

The rivalry within the Bermuda art community is strong, creating both an upside and downside. Competition is keen, but, says one dance school head, the student community is often deprived of the kind of exchange that allows them to learn from each other.

Art galleries and studios are generally owned and run by artists who use them to promote their own works. Often the gallery or studio is a room or two in the artist's home. Three artists who have carved solid reputations with their art are Bruce Stuart, president of the Bermuda Society of Arts; Elizabeth Mulderig whose "onion" paintings of famous Bermudians are on exhibit at the Masterworks Gallery in Somerset; and Graham Foster whose interpretation of the ubiquitous Bermudian home is refreshingly unique. Each year most arts organizations have a major exhibition or performance, allowing established and new talent a showcase opportunity.

In this chapter we have organized local art and artists under the following categories: Music and Dance, Theater, Arts Centers and Museums, Galleries and Studios, Literary Arts and Arts Organizations. We'll bring you up to date with recent performances or exhibitions.

Please note that several theater groups and organizations do not have a formal location, and telephone numbers may sometimes be a home or office number for a contact person. There may be some difficulty in getting through to someone who may be able to immediately provide information. But don't despair.

We suggest several places to call or check for current information related to events, exhibitions, plays and so forth. These include the Visitors Service Bureau, with offices in Hamilton (441) 295-1480, St. George's (441) 297-1642, Dockyard 441) 234-3824 and Bermuda International Airport (441) 293-0736; the hospitality desk or management staff at your hotel, cottage or apartment facility; and *The Royal Gazette's* Bermuda Calendar, a listing of events, exhibitions, theatre productions and related happenings. Every Tuesday the calendar for the following week is published in the *Gazette's* Community section; on other days the information is broken down into a Today/Tomorrow format and published in the Today section.

Music and Dance

Bermuda Academy of Music
Astwood Hall, Church Street, Hamilton
• (441) 296-2289

Entering its 6th year, the academy offers instruction in conducting, composition, voice, and a wide range of instruments. Principal Graham Garton, GRSM, LRAM, ARCO, ARAM, also conducts the Bermuda Philharmonic Society and the Bermuda Chamber Choir.

Bermuda Conservatory of Music
Colony Club, Trott Rd., Hamilton
• (441) 296-5100

Formed by the 1997 merger of two leading music schools, the Bermuda Conservatory of Music is now the largest such school on the island. The union brought together a 12-member faculty that offers instruction in piano, violin, organ, viola and guitar. Accredited by the Associated Board of the Royal School of Music of London, and the Royal Conservatory of Music of Toronto, the school offers students access to further development in either the United Kingdom or North America.

Of several programs offered, one is directed at students as young as 9 months through a Mommy and Me program that owes much to the Suzuki method of immersion. This approach, developed by Japanese music educator Suzuki Shin'ichi, is based on his observations of young children's natural acquisition of language skills. Early musical training, without the use of written music, is supported by parental participation. This approach has achieved tremendous popularity and success and has been adopted in many locales worldwide.

The school's Kindermusik program for ages 4 to 8 allows a group experience to branch into individual preferences, as youngsters develop a leaning toward a favored instrument. However, the 800-strong student body is composed not only of youngsters, but also adults, a few of whom are at the so-called retirement age.

One notable 1998 chamber music concert was presented under the distinguished patronage of the Governor, His Excellency, Mr. John Thorold Masefield, CMG, Mrs Masefield, and deputy mayor of Hamilton, Mr. Lawson E. Mapp, JP, was entitled "Some Enchanted Evening." Held at St. John's Church in Pembroke, and sponsored by Partner Reinsurance Co. Ltd., it attracted an appreciative audience.

Bermuda Philharmonic Society
• (441) 291-6690

This choral society and orchestra, now in its 38th season, puts on four or more concerts each year, a couple of them open-air shows and exchange concerts. Their 1998 orchestral Spring Concert, splendidly conducted by Graham Garton, was held at the City Hall Theatre in Hamilton. In 1999 the Spring Concert program included "Gloria" by Vivaldi and piano Concerto No.2 in C minor by Rachmaninov. New members are always welcome. The contact person is Sue Blakely.

Bermuda School of Russian Ballet
Pembroke Sunday School Building, Pembroke • (441) 293-4147 or (441)295-8621

This school with an established reputation, was founded in the 1950s by Patricia Deane-Gray M.B.E., who had studied ballet and dance in England and Europe. Madame Gray had been a soloist with the National Theatre in Yugoslavia, and is past president of the Bermuda Ballet Association, among many other achievements.

The system taught at the school originated through M. Nicholas Legat who was premier dancer and teacher at the Maryinsky School and Company in Russia.

In 1998 the school, which also teaches modern dance, presented "The Captured Mermaid" and "Songs of a Distant Earth" at the City Hall Theatre. Annual summer school sessions generally include visiting teachers from abroad. Students have the opportunity to take part in 1999's Bermuda Civic Ballet production at Government House. Contact persons are Coral Waddell and Katina Woodley.

Gilbert and Sullivan Society
• (441) 236-6872, (441) 295-3218

Devoted to performing the works of Sir W. S. Gilbert and Sir Arthur Sullivan, those masters of political and social satire, the society began in 1972 as the Warwick Players before the name was changed. More than sixty devotees comprise current membership. Although Sullivan is perhaps best known for such works as "Onward Christian Soldiers" and "The Lost Chord," Gilbert's lyrics were less religious or conservative, taking clever potshots at the legal system, the naval hierarchy, class warfare and general snobbery.

During the past twenty-six years G&S has performed a variety of musical shows, including five Heritage concerts under the baton of local conductor Marjorie Pettit. Two of the musicals — *The Mikado* in 1992 and *A Little Night Music* in 1997 — were performed at the Bermuda Festival (see our Annual Events and Festivals chapter). In 1997, *Little Shop of Horrors*, originally an off-Broadway production set in an early 1960s New York florist shop, was performed at the City Hall. In the 1998 Bermuda Festival, the society's choral program was enriched by operatic highlights from Saint-Saens and Verdi and classical excerpts from Beethoven and Bach. Contact persons are Marjorie Stanton and Susan Bailey.

In Motion School of Dance
Chancery Ln., Hamilton
• **(441) 292-7615**

The Bermudian dance community received its most recent boost with the 1997 opening of In Motion School of Dance. The emphasis at In Motion is on providing a nurturing environment for young dancers to realize the fullest expression of their level of skill through both theory and practice. There is also a focus on guiding advanced students in understanding the business demands of actual production, from choreography to administration.

The school's 1998 first recital, "Expressions in Motion", was an up-beat and exciting high energy presentation of tap, modern, ballet, jazz and hip-hop dance styles. One performance, a "stepping" dance, is very popular in the southern US.

Elizabeth Pimental, the owner and director, is a member of the National Dance Company, has performed in the Premier's Concert, studied with the Alvin Ailey Dance Company and worked as a choreographer for the Miami Junior Orange Bowl.

Jackson School of Performing Arts
Arcade Bldg., Burnaby St., Hamilton
• **(441) 292-5815, (441) 292-2927**

Founded as a school of dance in 1953 by Louise Jackson, the school expanded in 1978 to include instruction in instruments, voice, gymnastics and theater. Enrollment has grown

from an inaugural 40 to more than 1,000 today. The gymnastics program, run as an after-school activity at several local schools, coaches kids from preschool age on up through higher grades, eventually leading to competitive levels.

The dance department, the backbone of the school, instructs in most disciplines, from ballet to modern dance, jazz and tap. Master classes tutored by guest teachers bring exposure to visiting professional dance companies. With an impressive list of performances, the school's students have strutted their stuff at the Columbus Celebration in New York with the National Dance Theatre of Bermuda, and in 1994 they danced before Queen Elizabeth and the Duke of Edinburgh during a royal visit.

Menuhin Foundation
• **(441) 295-2510**

Founded in 1975 through the inspiration of the late virtuoso Lord Yehudi Menuhin — the American-born violinist who moved to London in 1959, was knighted in 1965 and became a British subject in 1985 — the Menuhin Foundation is a charity funded by private and corporate patrons and the Ministry of Community Affairs.

Following initial funding in 1976, the Heller, Barbican, Guild and New London quartets of young teachers visited Bermuda to perform and teach, inspiring through their talent and enthusiasm for music. As noted by Lord Menuhin, a quartet is the requisite nucleus of a performing string ensemble and provides the ideal teaching unit for imparting the art of string playing. With this as a guiding principle, he auditioned the London-based Heller Quartet before sending them to the Menuhin Foundation in Bermuda as its first teaching quartet.

Through the years since, the Menuhin Foundation Youth Orchestra (open to any string instrumentalist on the island between ages 12 and 21 at grade 4 and above) has performed at the Bermuda Festival. The foundation's teachers, as a quartet, caressed the strings at a private dinner held for Queen Elizabeth and Prince Philip at Government House, the governor's official residence. Notably, all teachers play in the Bermuda Philharmonic Orchestra.

Each January the foundation's annual student concert at the Anglican Cathedral features more than 250 participants. Frequent workshops involving the Youth Orchestra are organized by the foundation, one of the latest given by the English Chamber Orchestra. A desire to spread a love of string music to Bermuda's schoolchildren takes the foundation to most island primary schools, where free instruction in violin, viola and cello is delivered.

For additional information, contact Alison Johnstone at the number listed or write foundation Chairman John D. Campbell, Appleby, Spurling & Kemp, P.O. Box HM 1179, Hamilton.

National Dance Theatre of Bermuda
P.O. Box 1759, Hamilton HMHX No phone

Leaping out of the hinterland in 1980, the National Dance Theatre of Bermuda (NDTB) has enjoyed success in Bermuda and abroad, most notably at the Quincentennial Celebrations in New York in 1992, the Carifesta in Trinidad that same year and the opening of the Gala Showcase of the International Association for Blacks in Dance Conference in Philadelphia in 1996, its second appearance at that event. The NDTB has built a nucleus of dancers trained in ballet, modern and jazz disciplines and now has a repertoire of more than 50 works. In 1997 it performed its first full-length classical ballet, *The Nutcracker*, with guest artists Elizabeth Dunn and Lorin Johnson, former members of the American Ballet Theater.

In 1998, professional dancers from the Alvin Ailey American Dance Center, the Philadelphia Dance Co., and the American Repertory Ballet conducted a two-week summer workshop in modern dance and ballet at the Bermuda College. Organized by the National Dance Theatre, the workshop attracted students 9 years and older to the junior, intermediate and advanced classes.

Somerset School of Dancing
135 Front Street, Hamilton
• (441) 292-0446
Somerset Masonic Lodge, Mangrove Bay
• (441) 234-2613

In response to requests for more artistic activity in the Somerset area, the Somerset School of Dancing was founded in 1970 by Sal Hodgson and Anne Cherry. Classes were held at the Somerset Brigade Band Hall on Scott's Hill Road. In 1971, under the auspices of the British Ballet Organization, a major examiner was sent to the school and ballet examinations were conducted for the first time in Bermuda.

Student enrollment is now 300, up from an inaugural 40. Students study all dance disciplines — classical ballet, tap, jazz and modern dance. In 1981 the school moved into the Armoury in Mangrove Bay.

In 1982 it switched its affiliation to the Royal Academy of Dancing, an organization universally recognized.

In 1990, responding to the need for larger premises in Hamilton, the school opened a studio at the corner of Front and King Streets. Instructors are registered teachers with the Royal Academy of Dancing in London, and keep abreast of modern teaching techniques through annual teaching courses with that Academy.

Early in 1999 the school completed its annual Royal Academy of Dancing examinations. Every student passed. Student ages range from 3 years to adult. Adults who want instruction in ballroom dancing, either privately or by group, can arrange classes by request.

Theater

Bermuda Musical and Dramatic Society
Daylesford Theatre, 11 Washington St., Hamilton • (441) 292-0848

Formed in 1944, this active theater society stages several major productions throughout the year. Very often it puts on workshops related to both acting and technical aspects of theater. While most productions are held in its Daylesford Theatre, larger performances such as its Christmas pantomime are staged at the City Hall theater in Hamilton.

Among 1998 productions was the "Art of Coarse Acting", (actually four one-act plays) that drew sell-out audiences. It humorously traced the trials and triumphs of amateur productions of Shakespeare's "All's Well that Ends

Photo: GIS

Ahh... the art and pleasure of sailing.

Well," "Moby Dick," "Stalag 69," and "Streuth," a murder mystery.

United Dance Productions
Court Street, Hamilton
• (441) 295-9933

This city dance school was founded in 1992 by dancer and teacher Suzette Harvey, an advocate for the arts, graduate of the Philadelphia College of Performing Arts (now the University of the Arts), and recipient of the Stella Moore Prize for outstanding achievement, among other awards. The school currently has eight teachers and more than 500 students. Although ballet, tap and hip-hop are taught, the school has a strong classical background. Ms Harvey herself specializes in modern dance. In 1998, the school's production "Chaos" was staged at City Hall. It was different to previous performances in that choreographers from abroad were invited to create works for the school's students.

Arts Centers and Museums

St. George's Parish

St. George's Historical Society Museum
Duke of Kent St. • (441) 297-0423

Collections of antiques, china, paintings, papers and documents related to Bermuda's history and development (and particularly that of St. George's) can be found in this storehouse of information. See map page xvii.

Tucker House
Water St., Town of St. George
• (441) 297-0545

This 18th-century home, built around 1712, became the Tucker home in 1775, when Henry

Bermuda's Cedar Carvers

For centuries, from the very beginning of Bermuda's colonization, craftsmen have been shaping *juniperus bermudiana* (the Bermuda cedar) to use as furniture. Even now there are exquisite tables and chairs, staircases and banisters, doors and moldings that can be traced back to the 19th century, and in some instances, the 1700s.

Close-up

What haven't come down through the centuries though, are artistic carvings, and it almost begs the question as to why not. Certainly the skill of the artisans could not have been directed only toward the functional. Surely there must have been a man or woman who took this most difficult of woods to work with and brought some artistic spirit to life. But there is nothing today to show that any such pieces have survived.

However, as we approach the end of the century, cedar carvers have and are continuing to leave a mark on Bermuda's cultural pages.

Interpretations of subject matter range from realism to abstraction. Some of the carvings are architectonic in nature and are not dissimilar to some African carvings. This is actually not too unusual. In the world of sculpture, wood is principally associated with African art and certain sculptures of the medieval period. In this century Henry Moore, who was fascinated with Mexican and African art, manipulated the special characteristics, its vertical graining and organic nature.

Similarly, a handful of local carvers have learned to manipulate the tricky and eccentric grain of the Bermuda cedar, creating splendid works of art. Leading the world of the cedar carver is Chesley Trott, who has a studio at the Dockyard. His works are frequently imitated by young carvers.

But cedar is a curious wood. The oils that impart its distinctive aroma can present difficulties. If wood that is too young is used, as the oils dry out (and some parts will dry faster than others) there may be splitting. The solution is to leave the wood in log form until it is seasoned and dry, then place it in a shady area and simply leave it. Sometimes for three years; often for more.

"Cedar is a funny wood," says carver David Nisbett, a furniture craftsman with few peers who began carving cedar under the guidance of Trott. "You must work with the grain, and the grain can vary from piece to piece, and often within the same piece."

Aromatic and eccentric, beautifully grained, Bermuda cedar is scarce. "By the end of the century," says Roy Boyer, "most of the available wood will be green and unsuitable for carving."

Ecological disaster in the form of insects struck the cedar in the mid-1940s, wiping out 90 percent of forests within a decade. Today's stock is beset by timber thieves, who have been recognized as a huge problem by the Department of Agriculture and Fisheries. It all combines to make cedar extremely costly.

Ten to 12 years ago, cedar wood cost $13 to $15 per foot. Thirty years ago an entire tree cost between $30 and $40. Today, according to one carver, a prime log can cost as much as $5,000.

The impact both on antique as well as contemporary cedar furniture is incredible. Many a credit card has been embarrassed, as the finest local sculptures can be quite costly. Yet even though the prices of some works easily exceed $1,000, only a rare one or two carvers are making any kind of a living through their work. It often takes months to finish a particular piece. Hundreds of hours go into the initial shape of the creation,

— continued on next page

and for one carver, Garen Simmons, scores more hours are used to simply finish a piece. Garen's finishing involves using finer and finer grains of sandpaper until the wood is sanded down to the heart of its inner beauty. His patience and technique have led Garen to be engaged by other carvers to "finish" their works.

But Garen's most outstanding and original work is in his masks. These masks, though reminiscent of an African influence, are unique in style and appearance.

Several local carvers quietly labor away in backyard sheds, small, cramped garages or in backyards in the shade. They work to create artistic pieces that are rarely, if ever, seen by the general public.

The works of one such artist, whose realistic carvings of animals are so exquisite that his carving of a dog terrified a young nephew, are comparable to that of any woodcarver working anywhere. But this fellow prefers anonymity, and his carvings are not for sale at any price. His zoo of animals, all created to scale, occupy his living room.

Photo: Mid Ocean News

"Marriage" is one of Chesley Trott's most popular pieces.

The future of the local cedar woodcarver is unclear. Only a few carvers have managed to put aside supplies that will last them for many more years. Others are turning to using imported Virginia cedar.

Tucker purchased it. For years the house, a legacy to generations of descendants, was at the center of 18th- and 19th-century political and social life. Of the family members who became notable abroad, one became a judge in Williamsburg, Virginia, and another a United States treasurer.

Tucker House, like Verdmont Museum (see subsequent listing), is run by the Bermuda National Trust. Architecturally, it is a good example of Bermuda's acquaintance with Colonial style. It is restored as faithfully as possible to the vanished era its furniture, china and silverware represent.

Displays include a tribute to Joseph Hayne Rainey, who fled to Bermuda with his wife, Susan, shortly after the outbreak of the American Civil War. He became a barber, operating out of Tucker House, and went on less than a decade later to be the first black man to be seated in the House of Representatives. A superb collection of 18th-century portraits and

silver and an archaeological exhibit showcasing the findings from an extensive three-year basement excavation are also displayed. Together, they open windows to an intriguing time. The house is open Monday through Saturday from 10 AM to 4 PM. Admission is $3. See the map on page xvii.

Smiths Parish

Verdmont Museum
Collectors Hill
• **(441) 236-7369**

Supposedly, many people have encountered a ghost in this 18th-century home. It is believed to have belonged to Capt. William Sayle, the leader of a band of Bermudian Puritans who fled to Eleuthera in the Bahamas in 1648. However, others believe that if a ghost does exist, it is virtually impossible that it is that of Sayle. The house and museum, with its collection of 18th- and 19th-century furniture arranged as if the home were still inhabited, is administered by the Bermuda National Trust. Verdmont is open Tuesday through Saturday from 10 AM to 4 PM.

Pembroke Parish

Bermuda Historical Society Museum
13 Queen St., Hamilton • (441) 295-2487

This little museum is a treasure trove of old Bermuda-made silver and antique cedar furniture. The history of the island and its various eras leaps off the page and takes on substance through the furniture and other artifacts displayed here. It all helps form a remarkable portrait of some aspects of Bermuda's past.

Sandys Parish

Bermuda Arts Centre
Royal Naval Dockyard • (441) 234-2809

Originals, prints and sculptures by a number of local artists grace the exhibition rooms of this fairly comprehensive center. Bermuda-made ceramics, jewelry and cedar work are also exhibited, along with a representative number of paintings. See map page xviii.

Exhibitions showcasing various artists are held frequently through the year. These often have a particular medium, like the recent one showcasing fiber art. Artists revealed their skills in quilting, needlepoint and collage; there was a feast of entries that were either twisted, woven, stretched or sewn. Toward the end of 1997, "All That Jazz," designed to coincide with Jazzscape 1997 (see our Annual Events and Festivals chapter), featured works inspired by music. The juried mixed-media show, with top artists Robert Bassett and Jonah Jones, included bronze sculptures, oils, and works rendered with wire and papier-mâché.

Their 1998 "Shades of Summer" exhibition included, among other fine entries, colored pencil studies of Bermudian plant and marine life by David S. Hill, and several watercolors by Christopher Marson. "Manchester," an exhibit of textile/embroidery art featuring

the work of internationally renowned artist and author Ann Morrell, was another of several fine exhibitions held last year. Perhaps one of the more intriguing exhibitions for 1999 could be late summer's "Up the Garden Path," with subject matter botanical in nature, or with the theme reflected using natural materials.

Bermuda Maritime Museum
Royal Navy Dockyard • (441) 234-1418

Housed in a 6-acre keep and officially opened by Queen Elizabeth II in 1975, the Maritime Museum is a testament to the once-powerful, 19th-century presence of the British Navy. The museum's exhibits are contained within six buildings with varying date stones (cornerstones, to you Americans) that indicate a span of construction between 1837 and 1852.

This is an exciting repository that vividly brings to life Bermuda's exciting and fascinating maritime past. The Queen's Exhibition Hall has exhibits and information on navigation, whaling, pilots, steamships and the renowned Bermuda sloops. The 1849 Shell House, found on the north side of Keep Pond, reveals to visitors the Age of Discovery through the "Isle of Devils" exhibit. Other buildings, like the 1837 Shifting House, a three-gabled structure and the earliest of the ordnance buildings completed, have exhibits that are intriguing guideposts to local seafaring history. The Boatloft, with its "Pillars of the Bridge" exhibit, even covers the 50 years of U.S. forces in Bermuda.

The museum is supported by admissions and privately donated funds. It is open every day except Christmas from 10 AM to 5 PM. See map page xviii.

Gumba Trail and Outdoor Museum
Cockburn Rd. • (441) 293-7330

Aspects of life in Bermuda between the 16th and 18th centuries is explored at this museum, owned and run by Juliette Duncan. Particular emphasis is placed on the Gombey, whose masks are seen as a key to ancient traditions and a connection to the Native American ancestors of Bermudians. The signs, symbols and secrets of the Bermuda Gombey were decoded in a special 1997 exhibition entitled "Hieroglyphics." (For more on the Gombey tradition, see the Close-up in our Let's Explain Bermuda chapter.)

In 1998, Ms Duncan's third exhibition was "Gombey Myths and Legends." The focus of the Gombey Trail, she has said, is to give Bermudians a sense of self through a greater understanding of the past.

The easiest way to get to the museum is to go into the Dockyard and catch a bus or minibus in front of the Clocktower. Tell the driver you want to get off at the stop nearest the turnoff to the Gumba Trail, which is near the T.S. Venture Sea Cadet building. The museum schedule is seasonal, so please call ahead. Admission is $5 per person.

Galleries and Studios

St. George's Parish

Bridge House Gallery
Bridge House, Town of St. George
• **(441) 297-8211**
This gallery of paintings and prints by a number of local artists is housed in Bridge

House, a fine example of late-17th-century Colonial-style architecture. It is also home of the studio for artist Jill Amos Raine, noted for her watercolor scenes that seem to have captured every nook and cranny of St. George's. Original oils and watercolors by several other local artists — among them Diana Amos and Eric Amos, Otto Trott, Jo Linberg, Helen Daniel and Mary Tucker — are found here, as are prints by Molly Smith, Joan Forbes and Sharon Wilson.

Hamilton Parish

Clearview Art Gallery
151 North Shore Rd., Bailey's Bay
• **(441) 293-4057 or (441) 293-0484**
With the work of artist Otto Trott as its core, this gallery, named after the guest house where Trott is resident artist, houses one of the island's largest collections of original oil paintings.

Otto, a graduate of the Maryland Institute College of Art, explores several aspects of

Bermudian life as well as the ubiquitous landscapes, seascapes and local flora.

"Builders," an oil painting rendered on linen, shows workmen building a traditional Bermudian roof and captures the mood and skill of the mason's art. It was featured in the 1993 month-long Carib Art Exhibition, a traveling exhibit of contemporary works by artists of the Dutch, English, French and Spanish Caribbean that was organized by the National Commission for UNESCO of the Netherlands Antilles. Otto also exhibits in member shows put on by the Bermuda Society of Arts.

Pembroke Parish

Bermuda National Gallery
City Hall and Arts Centre,
Church St., Hamilton • (441) 295-9428

The beginning of the gallery can be traced back to 1982 and the foundation of the Bermuda Fine Arts Trust. After four years of little activity, the trust created a committee to oversee the short-term development of a proposed institution for major works of art. In 1991 the gallery appointed its first director, Laura Gorham.

Located on the second floor of City Hall in Hamilton, the gallery has five spaces, each with its own character. The main gallery has a well-proportioned open space that is ideal for abstract exhibitions. Among permanent collections are paintings donated by the late Hereward Watlington. This collection of 18 oils called "Restoration — Hereward T. Watlington Collection" covers the 15th to 19th centuries and consists of works by Reynolds, Gainsborough, Romney, Murillo and others.

The first international exhibit at the gallery was the 1993 exhibition, "Secrecy: African Art that Conceals and Reveals." Since then there have been several major art shows and exhibitions. Generally, a variety of concurrent shows are presented to the public that include works from the Bermuda Archives, the Bermuda National Trust and the Masterworks Bermudiana Collection, the centerpiece of which is a Winslow Homer watercolor.

A revolving exhibition is "Celebration," a superb collection of 40 African artworks ranging from masks to Senufo shrine figures that open a window onto the creativity and resilience of various African cultures. Many of these pieces were formerly on loan to the High Museum in Atlanta. Others were generously donated by an anonymous collector. At any one time you will find a dozen or so pieces on show.

Exhibitions have also included "Pop/Op Art of the 1960s and 1970s," and a selection of Georgia O'Keeffe's Bermuda drawings painted on her island visits.

Toward the end of 1997, "Light, Air and Colour: American Impressionist Paintings from the Pennsylvania Academy of Fine Arts" featured 20 outstanding works by such artists as Daniel Garber, Birge Harrison and Cecilia Beaux. This exhibition was sponsored by American International Ltd. to celebrate a half-century in Bermuda.

Throughout 1998 the gallery's weekly "Lunchtime Series" covered a number of fascinating topics and artists. Its "Meet the Artists" included award-winning local photographer deForest Trimingham, artists Dr. Charles Zuill, Bruce Stuart and several others. An informative presentation on commercial and residential architecture in Bermuda by senior architect B. W. (Jordy) Walker, featured discussion on the late Wil Onions, the architect for City Hall. Equally interesting was the Gallery's International Film Series, held during the evening.

Heritage House Gallery
2 Front St., Hamilton • (441) 295-2615

The venue for several exhibitions throughout the year, Heritage House has shown the works of many of Bermuda's leading artists at one time or another. In 1997 it held its 10th annual Christmas Small Picture Exhibition. Of interest, among other exhibitions in 1998, was "Masters of the Sea," an exhibition of marine paintings by local and international artists. Fine paintings by popular artist Stephen J. Card, along with Jim Karvelas, Donald Stoltenberg and others, drew many aficionados of marine art. Apart from its frequent exhibitions, the gallery is a great place to find various antiques.

Masterworks Foundation
Bermuda House Ln., 97 Front St., Hamilton
• (441) 295-5580

From its inception, the Masterworks'

"Bermudiana" collection invited the entire community to participate in what has become a fascinating experience that has brought the island a permanent collection of paintings by well-known artists. Works by Andrew Wyeth, Albert Gleizes, Jack Bush and Georgia O'Keeffe indicate that American, French and Canadian artists are well-represented.

With Winslow Homer as the catalyst, the search for paintings (and the money to buy them) began seriously in 1987. A decade later, the list of painters whose palette and paints have shaped a historical and social pastiche of the island and its environment has grown. As perceived and interpreted by these visitors of the splendid brush stroke, images of West Indian immigrants, friendly societies, integration at fetes, landscapes and street scenes mix the expected with the unexpected. No medium has been ignored.

In spring 1997, Masterworks opened its artists-in-residence program at the Terrace in Dockyard. The vision is to recruit overseas artists and develop them to be ambassadors of Bermudian culture when they leave the island.

Exhibitions of paintings can be found at the Bermuda National Gallery, the Masterworks Gallery at 97 Front Street and the Colonial Insurance Company Gallery, which is in the foyer at Jardine House on Reid Street in Hamilton. See map page xviii.

Michael Swan Galleries
Butterfield Place, Front St., Hamilton • (441) 296-5650
Clocktower Mall, Dockyard • (441) 234-3128

Michael Swan is an artist who uses pastels to capture Bermuda's houses in a unique way. A graduate of the Nova Scotia College of Art and Design, his medium is acrylic, his tool an airbrush. Michael's two galleries feature his works, which use stark shadows and contrasting colors playing off each other. His fascination with local architecture is evident. Many of his originals hang in private collections, and he was one of four Bermudians whose paintings were exhibited in the Caribbean Art Exhibition in Bermuda in May 1995, then again in Paris in October 1995. He has also exhibited at the UNESCO International Art Exhibition.

Omax Ceramics Studio
Admiralty House • (441) 292-8478

First, let's explain the name. In our History chapter, we spoke a bit about the term "onion," as it relates to Bermudians. Well, "Omax" means, quite simply, "Onions to the max." Get it?

Found in an elongated building close to one of the scenic trails leading to a sheltered cove with a small beach at Admiralty House, ceramic pieces at Omax are wheel-thrown from low-fire white earthenware clay. Christine Wellman's pieces are decorated with any of 10 different designs, all of which (colors included) have a connection to something typically Bermudian. In 1996 the parrotfish joined existing designs; the following year brought a Cuppa Soup bowl with handle. Other designs are the popular hibiscus, morning glory, combo, fish and the classic lizard.

With collectors of her work established, each year Ms Wellman produces another form. In 1998, a vase and a rim bowl were released in limited quantities. Their popularity has encouraged complete editions of each for 1999.

Practicality, merged with decoration, is a key feature of these creations by Christine. The decoration is achieved through a combination of sponging and hand-painting techniques. Christine's background is in painting and printmaking, and she admits to not being a traditional potter, so that the shapes of her creations do not always conform to the expected. The results, however, are uniquely enchanting. Ceramics, she says, are her substitute canvas.

Regal Art Gallery
86 Reid St. E., Hamilton
• **(441) 295-7441**

Robert Bassett's paintings comprise the majority of the works featured at this gallery, which is owned and operated by him and his wife. Bassett's art offers a feast of brilliant, bold colors. Strongly influenced by the Bermuda Gombey as well as the universal jazz tradition, the works are impressionistic interpretations of the black experience.

Highly successful, Robert has exhibited at a one-man show at Howard University in Washington, D.C., at the Museum of African American Art in Los Angeles, at the prestigious Montauk Club in New York and at a number of other galleries in the United States. Permanently represented by the Apex Foundation Gallery in New Orleans, he has participated in the 1996 New York Art Expo. His creations are also found in the private collections of many notables, among them Coretta Scott King and Sir Lyndon Pindling, former Prime Minister of the Bahamas. A deeply religious man, Robert gives credit for his creativity to "the greatest artist of all, God Himself."

Windjammer Gallery
King and Reid Sts., Hamilton
• **(441) 292-7861**

A number of local artists have their works exhibited here, making it home to a large selection of artwork by both Bermudian and international artists working in varied media. Among the several artists represented are Diana and Eric Amos, Bruce Stuart, Michael Swan (who also has his own galleries) and Maria Smith.

Paget Parish

Art House Gallery
80 South Shore Rd.
• **(441) 236-6746**

Joan Forbes, one of the island's most successful artists, is as well-known on Canada's Pacific coast as she is in Bermuda. Noted for watercolors that capture the diversity and serenity of the island, she has been featured in exhibitions in New York and Boston as well as the East Coast of Canada.

While diversity marks her medium — she is comfortable with oils, acrylics, pastels or pen and ink — it is also present in her subject matter. Seascapes, landscapes, florals and portraits all display delightful color clarity and balance. Art House is filled with her original paintings, limited and open edition lithograph prints, and an array of her handmade craftwork. As a teacher, Joan is always happy to assist budding artists experiencing teething problems and firmly believes that everyone has artistic ability that can be brought to the surface with time and practice.

Mary Zuill Art Studio
10 Southlyn Ln.
• **(441) 236-2439**

"I've been painting since I could hold a brush," says 83-year-old watercolor artist, Mary Zuill, whose works have been purchased by visitors from a dozen countries including Switzerland, Germany, England, Scotland, Canada, Russia and the United States.

Yet despite her popularity, she does not enter exhibitions. Her landscapes and seascapes, along with gentle urban depictions (among them Hamilton, Flatts, Salt Kettle and Lower Ferry) have a warm simplicity, pastel-rendered in deft brush strokes. "I used to work in oils but find that medium too heavy," she admits, but emphasizes the permanence of her watercolors. In some paintings touches of black ink subtly highlight the trunks of palm trees, burnished cliffside rocks or sailboat masts. Her paintings occasionally reflect a simpler era; one has a homemaker on her porch talking with a door-to-door fisherman selling his catch from a wheelbarrow.

Working tranquil themes onto a big canvas appeals to this diminutive, spirited artist whose creations are surprisingly reasonable. A 24-by-18-inch painting can be bought for $300 to $400. And visitors who have photographed a favored Bermudian landscape and want a special painting reproduced from the photo will find this lady willing to consider doing it for them. She creates many of her works during December, January and February, when her home-based studio is closed. To get to it when it is open, turn onto Southlyn Lane, which lies opposite the entrance to Stonington Hotel. Follow the lane all the way to the top of the hill. A small sign indicates the way. The studio is open Tuesday to Friday from 10 AM to noon and from 2:30 to 5 PM.

Southampton Parish

Desmond Fountain
Sculpture Gallery
Southampton Princess Hotel,
South Shore Rd. • (441) 238-8840

Arguably one of the finest bronze sculptors in the world today, Desmond Fountain — whose life-size sculpture of Sir George Somers stands on Ordnance Island in St. George's — emphasizes that his sculptures are intended to seem natural and uncontrived. He has said his goal is to create works where "anybody viewing the sculptures might subconsciously expect one to move at any moment."

Located in the mezzanine of the Southampton Princess (see our Resort Hotels chapter), the gallery houses an extensive number of his bronzes. Desmond's sculptures have been sold to buyers all over the world (prices run well into four and sometimes five figures), and his works can be seen in galleries in the United States, England and the Channel Islands.

In 1998 his statue of John Barnes (see Let's Explain chapter) was unveiled at the Crow Lane entrance to Hamilton, a hundred yards or so from the Bermuda Underwater Exploration Institute.

Sharon Wilson Gallery
2 Turtle Pl. • (441) 238-2583

Within an easy three-minute walk west from the entrance to Horseshoe Beach, this gallery has been owned and operated since 1976 by Sharon Wilson, a graduate of the Massachusetts College of Art. She is a pastel artist who has become a major part of the local art scene since the late '70s. She has been a veteran public school art teacher and is now a full-time artist and illustrator of children's books.

Sharon's pastels are remarkably sensitive portrayals of relationships within the local black community — a grandfather with his granddaughter, schoolgirls whispering secrets to each other, a mother plaiting her daughter's hair. Admitting that the interplay between people fascinates her, providing an endless supply of ideas, she sees herself as a storyteller. "Bermuda is a complex environment. Here it is easy to miss the feel of the people and their fears amid the backdrop of hibiscus and frangipani," she says. Stepping within this complexity, she speaks from it through pastels that are brilliant narratives of local life.

Her first book, *The Day Gogo Went To Vote*, is a celebration of South Africa's first democratic elections. It drew critical acclaim when it received the distinction of "Notable Book" from the Smithsonian Institute, American Library Association and International Reading Association. The *London Financial Times* also responded with plaudits for her work. In 1997 Simon & Schuster released *Freedom's Gifts*, a second book which received rave reviews from the *New York Times*. This year she is completing a third book.

Twin Art Studio
70 Middle Rd.
• (441) 238-8364

Self-taught artist Joan Thompson always loved to draw. Although she began in the banking industry, the burning desire to paint was too difficult to ignore. She resigned from the bank and began painting full time.

Although Joan mainly paints landscapes, with most of her scenes focusing on the Somerset and Dockyard areas, she is turning her talent (and it is an extraordinary one) toward capturing even more of the island's heritage and culture. Her media are oil, pen and ink and charcoal, but she has a fondness for the gouache technique, where watercolors are mixed with gum arabic to make them opaque.

Joan stays busy with commissions from customers in the United States, Canada, Australia and, of course, Bermuda. Her studio, easily accessed from Middle Road in Southampton, can't be missed. Just look for the sign with the cow in the field eating grass. "I feel that the cow looks so peaceful," she says.

Warwick Parish

Amos Fine Art
"Corncrake," 28 Ord Road, Warwick
• **(441) 236 9056**
The Amos Studio
"Longhouse," 2 Water Street, St. George's
• **(441) 297 2354**

Both galleries are managed and owned by husband and wife artists, Eric J.R. Amos and Diana J. Amos. Eric Amos is a wildlife artist who has painted and studied Bermuda's birds for more than thirty years. His superb *Guide to the Birds of Bermuda* was published in 1991. Eric admits his passion for birds was fired in the late '60s and early '70s when he took part in a series of oceanographic research cruises exploring the waters around Antarctica. He has also painted numerous birds of Mexico, Australia, New Zealand, and several other countries including Canada and the United States. His paintings have been exhibited in London's 1972 *Bird Artists of the World* exhibition at the Tryon Gallery. The year before, he designed Bermuda's *Deliverance* commemorative stamp. And in 1994 was a Best of Bermuda "Gold Award" winner.

Dina Amos is well-known for her beautiful watercolor, oil and acrylic landscapes. A Fine Arts teacher at Bermuda College for more than 25 years, she recently gave up teaching to paint full time. Her work is included in many prestigious collections both at home and abroad. She and Eric have been commissioned to produce the Bermuda Colours 2000 Recipe Calendar, Diana's third calendar project.

The Amos Studio is open weekdays from May to the end of October. During the winter months it is advisable to telephone (441) 236 9056 to confirm opening times or make an appointment to visit.

Literary Arts

Bermuda Writers Collective
34 Long Ridge Pass, Devonshire
• **(441) 292-3999**

This is a mixed bag of multinational writers who meet periodically to share their work, mostly fiction in progress. No membership is required for participation in these readings, where incisive critiques are the usual format.

The collective has published the stories of members in three collections of short stories, *Palmetto Wine, The Vendor of Dreams* and *An Isle So Long Unknown*. The group meets intermittently throughout the year.

Arts Organizations

Bermuda Arts Council
• **(441) 236-9504**

This council, whose members are appointed by government, was formed in 1969. It receives an annual grant, which is directed toward assisting individuals and art and cultural groups who apply for help. Over the years it has helped scores of Bermudians pursue various artistic endeavors in every possible cultural direction. As a registered charity, and despite the government grant, it can accept bequests and donations from the public. Chairman Charles Zuill is the contact person for this group.

Bermuda Society of Arts
City Hall, West Exhibition Room, Hamilton
• **(441) 292-3824**

In 1952, an informal and friendly get-together for resident artists was the setting for the formation of the Society of Artists in Bermuda. Among this group were Donald

Kirkpatrick, Antoine Verpilleaux and Bermudian Charles Lloyd Tucker, who has been described as one of the few watercolorists who could capture the true blues and greens of Bermuda scenery. Four years later the original group became the Bermuda Society of Arts, a registered charity.

During the past 40-plus years, the society has grown into one of Bermuda's leading organizations directed to supporting art-oriented activities. Since 1987 it has blossomed to more than 600 members. The West Exhibition Room at City Hall in Hamilton is the venue for exhibits of members' works. Exhibits generally rotate every two to three weeks and feature new works. Each January the society's Annual Photographic Exhibition attracts entries from amateur photographers. During May, the Heritage Exhibition tells the story of some period or aspect of Bermuda's history through various visual media.

The West Exhibition Room is open daily, and there is always a current exhibit of members' works. Bronze or wood sculptures, portraits and paintings in oils or pastels or photographs focusing on a particular theme compose an ever-changing artistic landscape.

Bermuda's calendar is filled with all kinds of sporting, arts and holiday events that draw hundreds and even thousands of spectators.

Annual Events and Festivals

Bermuda's calendar is filled with all kinds of sporting, arts and holiday events that draw hundreds and even thousands of spectators. Major holidays like Bermuda Day and Cup Match bring together diverse ethnic groups — visitors and locals among them — to rub shoulders and chat and let their hair down. And almost every parade brings out the Gombeys and majorettes who dance and twirl and strut their stuff through Hamilton. Islanders are serious about work, and just as serious about their fun.

Cultural pursuits are not shunted into the back seat but are at the forefront, beginning early in the year with the Bermuda Festival. There are a number of arts events, from photographic exhibitions and competitions to classical concerts and jazz extravaganzas.

The following selection of events and festivals is just a sampling (broken down by month) of what we have to offer here where the sun caresses the sea and together with the land forms a blissful union. Where possible, we have included prices, but bear in mind that prices may change. Unless we have indicated otherwise after describing each event, admission is free. We list the events (and note that in some cases venues may vary from year to year) roughly in chronological order and provide an address and phone number when possible.

We do suggest popping into the Bermuda Department of Tourism, located on ground level in Global House at 43 Church Street in Hamilton, (441) 292-0023, and obtaining the latest booklets and pamphlets that are a guide to various events scheduled throughout the year.

January

Bermuda Festival of the Performing Arts
Various locations, Hamilton
• **(441) 292-8572, (441) 295-1291**

Having entered its 24th year in 1999, this has become a major showcase for the performing arts, attracting international and local artists. The dazzling displays of orchestral music and jazz, theater and ballet begin around the middle of the month and run until the last week in February. The usual venues are City Hall, St. Paul's Centennial Hall, both in Hamilton, and the Ruth Seaton James Auditorium at CedarBridge Academy, roughly five or six minutes away (by moped or taxi) from Front Street.

Supported by volunteers, benefactors, sponsors and patrons, this festival is a prestigious one on the cultural landscape. Performers in 1997 included American jazz saxophonist Joshua Redman, called the "Crown Prince of Jazz" by *Downbeat* magazine; the Vienna Boys' Choir; the English Chamber Orchestra;

and Tafelmusic Baroque Orchestra. The National Dance Theatre of Bermuda presented *The Nutcracker*.

The program for '98 was equally exciting, with performances from the National Black Touring Circuit, which staged the modern comedy "Checkmates," a play that explores the effect of the generation gap on two couples; the Royal Winnipeg Ballet, under the artistic direction of Andre Lewis; the American Boys Choir, which has sung at the Vatican, Westminster Abbey and the White House; and the Philadelphia Dance Company, or "Philadanco," as it is affectionately called. Comedy was not overlooked: Avner the Eccentric put on his mime, magic and clowning antics and thrilled Bermudian audiences the same way he has entertained crowds throughout the United States and as far afield as Tokyo and Tel Aviv.

In 1999, performing groups and individuals included a Swiss string ensemble, the Cannina Quartet; Romania's 'Black Sea" Philharmonic Orchestra; and jazz singer Ranee Lee, honored in 1994 and 1995 as the top Canadian female jazz vocalist.

If you want to attend any of the almost 50 shows put on by as many as 14 separate groups or individuals in 2000, take note of the phone numbers above. Tickets are $20, $25 or $30 for adults depending on the show; students pay $15. If ordering tickets from overseas, call for an order form, fill it out and return it with your check or credit card information at least 21 days before opening night. The mailing address is The Bermuda Festival Ltd., Suite 480, 48 Par-la-Ville Road, Hamilton HM 11, Bermuda.

A confirmation form will be mailed to you, but tickets will not be sent through the mail. Your tickets can be picked up at the festival box office near the Ferry Terminal in Hamilton after you arrive in Bermuda. Anyone with a hearing or other disability may request special seating, and organizers will attempt to facilitate specific needs.

Annual Photographic Exhibition
City Hall, Hamilton
• (441) 292-3824

Organized by the Bermuda Society of Arts and hung in the group's City Hall Gallery, this exhibition allows local amateur and professional photographers to showcase their best works. A number of the exhibitors are among the society's 700-strong membership (see our Arts and Culture chapter).

Entries span a number of classes, with cups given to each category's winner. Entrants can compete in as many classes as they wish. Among the various categories are Best in Show, Best Color Photograph and Best Black and White Photograph. Youngsters also get an opportunity to reveal their talents; the winner in this group skips happily away with the Best Junior Cup.

The Johnny Skinner Cup for photojournalism draws local magazine and newspaper photographers. Those who thrill to shooting fish and their environment through the lens get a crack at the cup for the Best Underwater Photograph. This class is usually strongly represented, with all entries bringing a new respect for the beauty of Bermuda's sea world.

This popular exhibition opens windows on Bermuda's natural and urban landscape, providing intimate glimpses of a cosmopolitan society in the Atlantic. There is no admission fee.

PBA Southern Regional Bowling Tournament
Warwick Lanes, 47 Middle Rd.,
Warwick Parish • (441) 236-5290

A bevy of professionals descend on Bermuda each year for this late-January tournament that puts $20,000 up for grabs. Experienced overseas professionals and hungry local bowlers meet in stiff competition. "This is a hot, happening event," says Mike McCallum, president of the Bermuda Bowling Association.

February

Bermuda Open Chess Tournament
Southampton Princess Hotel,
101 South Rd. • (441) 232-0528

This event is held at the prestigious Southampton Princess Hotel. In fact, competitors range from beginners to grand masters, with the winner receiving $1,000 and an expense-paid return trip to Bermuda.

Annual Bermuda Rendezvous Bowling Tournament
Warwick Lanes, 47 Middle Rd., Warwick Parish
• **(441) 236-5290, (441) 236-4373**

Open to all bowlers and sanctioned by the ABC and WIBC, the balls in this handicap tournament begin to thunder down the lanes around mid-February. Staged during four days at Warwick Lanes on Middle Road, this competition is sponsored by a number of local businesses, and there are many cash prizes. Bowlers' individual entry fee is $30.50; doubles team fee is $61.

Bermuda Musicians & Entertainers Charity Festival

Produced through the joint efforts of the Bermuda Musician & Entertainers Benevolent Fund, and Baha Productions, this year's charity festival was held in the Mid Ocean Amphitheatre of the Southampton Princess Hotel. Performers for the 3-hour event included students from several of the island's private and public schools, the Bermuda Conservatory of Music, the Jackson School of Dance, and top calypso singers as well as limbo dancers. No telephone number is available, and advertisements in the newspaper indicate where tickets — $20 advance, $30 at door — are available.

March

Spring Break Arts and Sports Program
Various venues • (800) 223-6106

In the 1950s and '60s, Bermuda threw open its doors to college students who flew down to lark it up in the sun while enjoying a host of college weeks programs put on by tourism officials. The introduction of this spring break event in 1997 marks an attempt to revive college kids' interest in Bermuda, and it aims at more artistic and sports-oriented activities.

The Bermuda Pipe Band participates in a skirling ceremony.

The arts program offers university- or college-credit lectures and workshops conducted by some of Bermuda's leading artists. Various tours, among them visits to the National Gallery, the Bermuda Society of Arts Gallery and National Trust properties are part of the cultural initiative.

But this is still very much about having a great time on an island noted for its incomparable beaches and delightful waters. Free beach parties, boat cruises and complimentary lunches are hosted by the Department of Tourism. Transportation and nighttime activities are also covered under the Spring Break program. Among participants in 1997 were students from Atlanta Metropolitan College and the Rhode Island School of Design. In 1998, studies in marine biology and the culinary arts were added to the ongoing workshops in glass blowing, architecture and furniture making.

But this is just half of the Spring Break experience. The other focuses on sports and runs concurrently with the arts offerings. Lacrosse, soccer, tennis and rugby are among the sports where participants can let themselves go. For detailed information about the Spring Break Arts and Sports Program, contact the Bermuda Department of Tourism at the listed number.

Bermuda Kite Festival
Horseshoe Bay

No one knows for certain exactly when or why Bermuda embraced kite-flying around the Easter season. The story goes that a Sunday school teacher used the flying of a kite to illustrate the way Christ ascended to the heavens. Once the kite was airborne at the full length of the string, the teacher is reputed to have cut the string, allowing the kite to be taken by the wind until it disappeared.

Whatever the original intent, kite flying on Good Friday has become as much a part of the day as codfish cakes and playing marbles. So popular are kites around this time that a small, seasonal cottage industry has emerged, with several entrepreneurs making scores of kites and selling them to shops and parents.

Good Friday at Horseshoe Bay in Southampton is a dazzling and exciting kick-a-ball-around, play-in-the-surf, listen-to-music, kite-flying festival. There are plenty of kites: colorful kites, small kites and big kites, such as the one entered in 1997 that secured the win for the Corporation of Hamilton in the "biggest kite" category. Almost two stories high (and proudly bearing the corporation's crest), it failed to rise to the heavens. "I'm not sure there's enough wind to get it up today," said one of the men who had taken three days to make, string and patch the 17-foot giant with blue and gold satin. More fortunate was a 10-year-old, whose 5-foot nylon parafoil kite took to the wind like a duck takes to water. And the smallest kite there? It could fit in the palm of your hand.

In 1999 the smallest kite, selected from three miniatures made by the same entrant, was possibly the tiniest kite ever entered in the competition. It is reputed to have been so tiny it was barely visible to the naked eye! Godfrey Smith took the prize for the most original. From a platform he explained his kite, cleverly designed with the colors of the Bermuda flag always visible through a "pop-up" technique. A young Saltus Grammar School student won the prize for the most original among the primary school entries. His "fish kite," complete with scales, took to the skies with ease. Amusingly, a high-tech entry didn't particularly excite the crowds of spectators, no matter how the creator tried to explain his complex entry. Incidentally, every year a few dozen kites become entangled in overhead electric wires. And 1999 was no different. Fifty-five kites became trapped, one of them causing a temporary power outage for residents in an area in Southampton.

Bermuda Spring Golf Festival
• (800) 999-7679 or (716) 586-8115

This Golf Festival is a packaged 5-day adventure on two courses that offer sensational views of the Bermudian landscape. The Festival is open to individual golfers and teams of two or four. The Port Royal Golf Course (Foursome Best Two Ball) and Castle Harbour Golf

Annual Bermuda Day parade attracts thousands of locals and visitors alike.

Club (Individual flights) are among the island's finest. For seniors (60 years and older) there is an optional division. Established United States Golfing Association (USGA) handicaps have maximums of 30 for men and 36 for women. For those with no established handicaps, the Calloway system is used. Net and gross prizes are awarded daily and on a festival basis. On the two days of foursome best ball competition, single players and two-person teams are paired with comparable competitors.

An Evening of Jazz
City Hall Theatre • (441) 292-2313

This jazz evening has been presented for eight years and has achieved a solid following of jazz aficionados. This year it featured pianist James Williams, Saxaphonist Andy McGee with John Lockwood on bass. Local favorites, singer LeYoni Junos and Charles Bascome on drums were superb. The event was hosted by popular M.C., Derrick "Juicy" Symonds. A reception is held after the concert and general admission is $35 with part proceeds donated to the Sunshine League Childrens Home.

Annual Quiz Contest for Schools

In 1999 the finals for this high-school contest, organized by the Ministry of Youth, Sport, Parks & Recreation, was held at Canadian Pacific's Hamilton Princess Hotel. The competition is sponsored by a number of private businesses including *The Royal Gazette*. Contest questions cover a wide range of subjects — history, music, arts, personalities, sports, current events. The 1998 winner was Warwick Academy. Top school for 1999 was Mt. St. Agnes. Donations, requested only at the finals, are given to a charity chosen by the contestants.

April

Peppercorn Ceremony
King's Square, Town of St. George • (441) 297-1532

Held on the Wednesday closest to April 23, this is a ceremony that, for all its color, pomp and pageantry, seems only to have real meaning to the governor and Freemasons of Lodge No. 200, a Scottish lodge established here in 1797. Of course, should you be on King's Square when the governor arrives in his landau (a four-wheeled, horse-pulled passenger carriage) wearing his ceremonial uniform, no doubt the pomp will fascinate you, even if the circumstance is somewhat obscure.

The governor is greeted by local dignitaries and members of the St. George's Lodge. The Bermuda Regiment provides a guard of honor, and lodge members are turned out in full regalia for the handing over of the annual symbolic rent for their use of the State House . . . a single peppercorn (the dried berry of the pepper plant). Lodge No. 200 is the oldest Scottish lodge outside Scotland; after its members pay up, and when all the speeches are finished, the governor and his escort depart.

Agricultural Exhibition
Bermuda Botanical Gardens,
Point Finger Rd., City of Hamilton
• (441) 236-4201

"The thrill and excitement of those occasions is still remembered by those who saw them as children. Bourne's ice-cream stall, gay with streamers; barking, yelping dogs so fierce and determined to consume small boys should they succeed in breaking their chains; awesome cows, safely viewed from a narrow gallery between their stalls along which one hurried to the far end and escaped; bandsmen, fascinating in their red coats, and a fine figure of a soldier standing on a box conducting the music with a long wand which he handled as easily as if it were a feather; cats, sad and uncomfortable in their cages and not a purr to be heard from any of them."

Thus was the agricultural exhibition as it was revived in the 1880s and described in *Bermuda Journey* by William Zuill. That late 19th-century exhibition of yelping dogs and sad-eyed cats took place near the western edge of the City of Hamilton. But an even earlier exhibition was staged in 1843 at Mount Langton, or Government House, the residence of the governor sited well north of the city limits. Then called the Agricultural and Horticultural Exhibition, it was described in the *Bermuda Gazette* as "the first exhibition of the kind ever got up in Bermuda, the specimens of the various productions were as the fancy or interests of the cultivator dictated."

It has been said that at one of those exhibitions, a black woman who was refused the opportunity of selling her coconut cakes near the entrance, placed a curse of rain on the entire exhibition and all those that followed down through the years. Whether anyone has actually compiled and compared rainfall data for the period in question is not known, but on those occasions when it does rain at any time during the three-day exhibition, many Bermudians remember the "curse."

Today the exhibition, with its festive atmosphere, is akin to a county or state fair. And once inside the "Ag Show," you are transported to a marvelous world where the sound of the Bermuda Regiment Band meets that of the Somers Isles Jazz Band, and the smell of hot dogs and vegetables and horses and fruit and fish cakes intermingle with myriad other scents. And then there are the colors — ribbons and bows and pretty cake sculptures, and the eye is bathed in everything from a marzipan longtail to an eggplant cockroach.

This is a high point on Bermuda's equestrian calendar. More than 6,000 people make their way to the Botanical Gardens annually to watch riders guide their sweating mounts in show-jumping displays, acrobats roll and leap and tumble, and majorettes smartly step and throw their batons spinning up into the sun, the return caught easily and smoothly.

It all kicks off toward the end of April and has been going strong now for more than 60 years. It is a reminder that, despite the precipitous decline in farmland over that period, farming and horticulture helped build Bermuda and have not completely surrendered to concrete and tarmac.

Buses are often rerouted to provide steady transportation to and from the main gate on Point Finger Road. It's only $5 to get you and a camera into the exhibition. (For more on the Bermuda Botanical Gardens, see our Attractions chapter.)

Spring Into the Arts Concerts
Department of Education
• (441) 236-6904
Contact: Shangri-la Durham-Thompson

Five special spring concerts showcasing the artistic talent of Bermuda's students take place toward the end of April. Ms Durham-

Thompson originated the idea in 1996 with the intent of encouraging greater participation by young persons in the arts. Although each year schools have made a 10-minute presentation in the areas of music, drama, poetry, storytelling and dance, in 1999 that has been reduced to seven minutes for each school so that the concerts finish by 9 PM. Also, several community artists and performers have been showcased, among them the United Production Dancers and the Portuguese Dancers. A couple of local arts organizations have also become involved

Schools that are geographically close join together to stage a "family of schools" concert for their locale. Each "family" has been organized into five neighborhoods.

April 26: Sandy's area schools concert at Sandy's Middle School at 42 Scott's Hill Road, Somerset.

April 27: Spice Valley concert at Spice Valley Middle School at 60 Middle Road, Warwick.

April 28: Dellwood "family" of schools concert at CedarBridge Academy in Devonshire.

April 29; Whitney concert at Whitney Middle School, 59 Middle Rd in Smith's.

April 29: The East End family of schools hold their concerts at Clearwater Middle School.

Note that dates do change each year.

May

Heritage Month Celebrations
Various locations • (441) 292-9447

May is Bermuda Heritage Month and features a host of cultural and commemorative activities sponsored by the Department of Community and Cultural Affairs. For 1998, the theme was "diversity," with the focus on contributions made by the island's different ethnic groups through their cultural traditions and activities — visual and performing arts, music

and food. Previous years have seen the spotlight trained on several historical as well as contemporary aspects of Bermuda, including an intimate look at Hamilton and its people, St. George's and Bermuda's environment. A display that illustrates the theme is set up at the Bermuda Society of Arts Gallery at Hamilton City Hall and runs throughout the month.

Young Artists Competition
Department of Cultural Affairs
• (441) 292-9447

Inaugurated in 1999, this competition covers a half-dozen categories – voice, strings, drama, piano, dance, and other instruments. It is open to entrants between 14 and 21 years. The venue for the competition is at the Ruth Seaton James Centre for the Performing Arts at CedarBridge Academy. (See more on CedarBridge in Education & Child Care chapter.)

Master Chef Cook-Off
Hamilton • (441) 295-1661

For three weeks in May, the Island's top chefs compete for Bermuda's "Master Chef" title. Spectators have an opportunity to not only watch as the chefs create original masterpieces, but to sample the results while sipping from a choice of specially selected wines. There is a price for all of this — $45 to attend the semi-finals and $60 for the finals (prices subject to change). Ticket proceeds go to a different local charity chosen each year.

Conyers, Dill and Pearman Cycling Grand Prix
Various locations,
ending in City of Hamilton
• (441) 295-6012

Named after the sponsoring law firm, this early May weekend cycling event, organized by the Bermuda Bicycle Association, is the biggest of its kind in Bermuda. Four days of

INSIDERS' TIP

November through March are great months for seasonal savings on sightseeing boat tours and moped rentals. Also, take advantage of discounted one-, three- and seven-day transportation passes on buses and ferries.

competition culminate in a Sunday criterion through Hamilton. Top cyclists from England, Ireland, the United States and Bermuda go head to head. The Saturday before the criterion features a 75-mile road race preceded by a 10-mile time trial. More than 40 riders compete for total prize money of $10,000. Contact the BBA at the number listed for more information.

Annual End-to-End Charity Walk
Town of St. George to Royal Naval Dockyard • (441) 299-8821

This scenic Railway Trail walk for charities (generally held the first Saturday of May) is one of the best ways to meet residents and see some of the most picturesque parts of the island. Beginning in King's Square in the Town of St. George and ending at the Dockyard, the 26-mile course can be daunting, even for those who walk quite a bit. Sore and blistered feet are common. Those who are wary of attempting the full distance can opt for a 15-mile alternate course that starts at Albuoy's Point in the City of Hamilton.

The walk, now in its 12th year, has during the past 11 years raised close to $1 million that has been distributed to 40 charities. More than 5,000 people have taken part over the years, and donations have been collected from many corporate sponsors. Beneficiaries in 1998 included the Bermuda Health Foundation, Parent Resource Institute for Drug Education (PRIDE), and the Conference on Deaf Awareness in Bermuda.

Youngsters can participate as well, and there is a mini-walk within the Dockyard for toddlers. For those braving either the end-to-end or middle-to-end, a pasta-loading banquet takes place the night before. Visitors can sign up at either King's Square or Albuoy's Point a half-hour before starting.

Samuel L. Jackson Celebrity Golf Classic
Port Royal Golf Course, Middle Rd., Southampton Parish
• **(441) 234-0974**

This classic draws celebrities from the United States to the Port Royal Golf Course for an event that is more about raising money for two charities — the local Council Partners Charitable Trust and the Catalog for Giving in New York — than about competition. Between the two organizations, some 20 separate programs are funded. At the conclusion of last year's classic, $242,700 had been raised and split evenly between the two organizational recipients.

Jackson, an Academy Award nominee known for his role in *Pulp Fiction* and other movies, has been joined by nearly 40 celebs for the tournament that bears his name. Among the visiting duffers have been Joshua Morrow from the daytime soap, "The Young and the Restless;" Alonso Ribeiro of "Fresh Prince of Bel-Air" fame; and Anna Maria Horsford, one of the stars of TV's "Amen" and the "Wayans Bros."

Golf at this classic is not taken that seriously, but the money that must be anted up by anyone wanting to play with the stars is: It costs $1,250 per day for the privilege. But it all goes to good causes. ACE Insurance Company Ltd., in association with Elbow Beach Hotel and Bank of Butterfield, is the presenting sponsor. Other corporate sponsors include the Bermuda Department of Tourism, Gosling Bros. Ltd. and Reebok.

The four-day early-May party is facilitated by 400 volunteers. Two other major events are the first night's black-tie opening gala, where cocktails, dinner and dancing to a couple of bands gets the classic off to a fun start, and a subsequent night of comedy. Tick-

INSIDERS' TIP

Visitors at participating hotels and guest houses can take advantage of an interesting November through March deal: On the day after the temperature falls below 68 degrees, admission is free for the Bermuda Aquarium, Fort St. Catherine and Bermuda National Trust properties. (See our Attractions chapter for more on these sites.)

This Cup Match Overflows With Bermudian Flavor

No other local event will give you a taste of Bermuda quite like this one. It is tradition seasoned with fun, daubed with color and molded like a cultural cassava pie. The biggest sporting event on the island (held the Thursday and Friday before the first Monday in August), it attracts up to 15,000 spectators. And why? Because this is the game of the year — a competition between St. George's Cricket Club and Somerset Cricket Club. It's East versus West. But this is not a field of dreams. This is hard ball. This is raw competition.

Die-hard cricket fans show up early, sporting their colors — dark and light blue for St. George's, red and dark blue for Somerset. They bring chairs, umbrellas and just about anything that will add to their comfort. Fashions depend on the mood of the wearer, but you  won't see jackets and ties. It is two consecutive days of revelry and socializing, and yet it is very much about cricket. The twain do meet, and link arms.

Cup Match has been played every year since 1902. Much has changed, however, since the early days. There was a time in 1916 when the match was almost cancelled because St. George's had difficulty in fielding a team. And in its struggling years, the match was not always a holiday, but this did not deter players or fans. They simply took time off from work and went to the game.

While the game is acknowledged as the crux around which the entire two days turn, the festival that surrounds the competition is also about food. Plenty of food. Curried mussels and mussel pies. Fish and chicken dinners. Peas and rice, codfish cakes and conch stew. Curried goat. Snowballs and soft drinks. Food stalls, as you will have by now imagined, abound. The area around the host club's field is ringed with them, music often emanating from within. So essential is the food that stall operators must apply for

— continued on next page

Photo: GIS

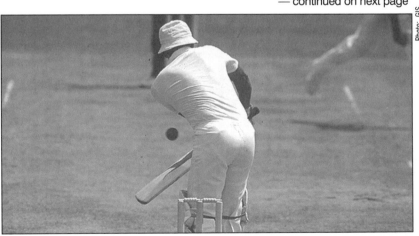

The annual Cup Match is a social and athletic tradition. It is our Fourth of July and World Series, all in one.

a plot to erect a temporary stall as early as January. Costs vary depending on size, but prices run up to $500 per day.

During these two days (timed to coincide with Bermuda's Emancipation Day celebration), all roads lead to either Somerset or St. George's, the venue alternating each year. And getting there is a great deal easier than in the days of the train, when on one occasion in 1933 the train conductor, with a full load of passengers bound for St. George's and the match . . . fell off the train! The old Rattle and Shake plodded on without him. Rushing to a nearby house, the conductor managed to convey by telephone the urgency of the situation. A replacement driver was immediately sent from St. George's to Mullet Bay where a fortuitous incline slowed the train enough to allow him to jump aboard. Most passengers had no clue of how close they were to possible disaster.

But there was always fun upon arrival — the atmosphere, the intense but friendly rivalries between spectators. Today this rivalry is backdropped by jazz, soca and reggae music mingling with the buzz of the crowds, the crack of the ball against the bat, the cheers and clapping and the smells of food wafting on the hot and languid air. There are youngsters with tired and perplexed faces. And the intent eyes of gamblers who hope their luck will change. Yes, Dorothy, here there be gambling, and many folks show up for that very purpose. In this instance the wagering is on Crown and Anchor, a dice game often called the "Stock Market."

This is a game where the operator of the "table" (and it really is a wooden table that is divided into six clearly marked squares containing each of the four card suits — hearts, diamonds, spades and clubs — and a square each for, yep, a crown and an anchor) does his best to separate players from their dollars. He places three dice into a rigid, felt-covered "cup," shakes them, then turns the cup over onto the table but does not raise it. At that time bettors place their stakes down on the square or squares of their choice.

The operator then lifts the cup and reveals the dice. Each of the six faces of the dice has either a crown, anchor, heart, diamond, spade or club. Bettors are paid off dollar for dollar on any of the suits that come up matching the appropriate square on the table where they have placed their money. If all dice show the same, the bet is tripled, and for each time the crown or anchor shows when you have money placed on those square, your stake can be doubled or tripled. Of course, every player has a system, but at the end of the day it is a matter of luck, and very few operators lose money. As many as two dozen tables can be kept busy by gamblers and tens of thousands of dollars change hands over the two days.

So the Cup Match is also about winners — the winning cricket team and the gambler who beats the odds. It is about parents and children, and visitors who come the first time out of curiosity and return whenever they can. It is a game, and it is life. It is Bermuda in microcosm: a pastiche of sight and sound and scents wrapped up in two days of pure fun and enjoyment. There really is no other local festival quite like it.

ets are $150 for the gala evening and $50 for the comedy night.

Bermuda International Film Festival (BIFF)
Various locations, Hamilton
• **(441) 293-FILM**

Launched in 1997 with a theme built around the concept of "firsts," this festival at-tracted submissions from first-time directors, producers, screenwriters and actors. The opening gala, sponsored by the Bermuda Telephone Company, was at Fort Hamilton, a fortification built in the late 1800s to protect the city and harbor beyond. The fort's lovely garden oasis was the setting for invitees to relax with good food and fine music provided by a local band.

The 1997 festival — with three categories and, consequently, three prizes — was juried by American actress, author and producer Jane Alexander, *Mid-Ocean News* editor Tim Hodgson and Tom Shoebridge, president of Ottawa's Summer Institute of Film and Technology.

The 14 entries, many submitted with the help of the New Producers Alliance in London, Independent Feature Film Market in New York and the Toronto International Film Festival, comprised a cross-section of independently produced drama and documentary films. Entrants from a number of countries — among them the United States, Canada, Russia, India and the United Kingdom — participated. The wide-ranging subject matter was assessed for effective storyline and development, excellence in direction and the impact of those intangible, often human qualities that make a film work.

The two cinema venues were both in Hamilton — the Liberty Theatre on Union Street and the Little Theatre on Queen Street. The winning documentary was *Family Name*, a true-to-life mystery wrapped around family secrets. It followed director Macky Alston's search for descendants of slave owners and slaves from plantations once owned by his family. Honorable mention was awarded to a joint American-Russian production called *The Riddle*. Directed by Evan Brenner, it was about a 10-year-old Russian youth obsessed with his past. The Audience Choice Award went to *Boston Kickout,* and Best Short Film was *Anna in the Sky.*

The closing gala, hosted by *Entertainment Weekly* magazine, was held at Ariel Sands Beach Club. The evening of music, barbecue, rustling palms and crashing surf capped a week of eclectic film enjoyment.

In 1998 cinema audiences were captivated by a number of fine entries, among them one by award-winning Bermudian director Alison Swan. Her film *Mixing Nia,* is a stylish, romantic comedy revolving around the story of a young woman who resigns her advertising job to write a novel. Other films were from France, UK, Canada, and the US, including the documentary *Green Chimneys* directed by Constance Marks. Widely praised at Sundance Film Festival '97, Marks' film was described by the *New York Times* as "intimate and affecting."

BIFF is held during the first week of May. A festival pass, at $100, provides a ticket to each film, including opening and closing films at the Liberty Theatre. Prices and some details are subject to change, but admission to individual films in this year's event should be in the $8 range. Film submission entry forms are available from the middle of September until January 31.

Although the festival was canceled in 1999, organizers anticipate that the competition will return to top gear in 2000.

Bermuda Day Parade
City of Hamilton

First staged May 24, 1979, this has become Bermuda's biggest parade, an exuberant celebration and display of local culture and heritage. A cycling race, a 13.3-mile half-marathon from Somerset Village to the City of Hamilton (for Bermuda residents only) and Bermuda dinghy races in St. George's Harbour head up the list of sporting events during the day.

The parade itself gets under way in the afternoon after Bermuda's premier officially launches proceedings at Bernard's Park, which is within easy walking distance of Front Street. Thousands line Hamilton's streets, in some places three and four persons deep, as the various floats, dancers, marching bands, majorettes and Gombeys go past. As many as 50

INSIDERS' TIP

From November through March, the Bermuda Department of Tourism offers a free evening lecture series on Bermuda. Scheduled topics for this year include Bermuda's Architecture, Culture and Traditions, Flora and Fauna, Marine Life, Fortifications, Art, Women in Bermuda's History and Bermuda's Prisoners of War.

groups have participated in the two-hour-plus parade, led by the Bermuda Regiment Band.

Many spectators stake out a favored spot, set up a chair, have a lunch basket at hand and just get comfortable. The decks of cruise ships overlooking Front Street are jammed with curious visitors who take in the color, music and jubilation of the carnival atmosphere. Bermuda's diverse culture is represented — among those participating are members of the Portuguese, Indian and Filipino communities. Special guests in 1997 included the Frederick Douglass High School Marching Band and Drill Team from Atlanta; it proved to be a big hit with the crowds.

With a number of prizes awarded for floats in various categories, the Best Parish Award in 1997 went to Warwick Parish Council for its "Bermuda Is Another World" entry.

Bermuda Open Karate Championships
Bermuda College, College Dr.
• **(441) 292-2157**

Now in its 16th year, this is the oldest continuously run karate event in Bermuda. Open to both juniors and adults, the event averages between 70 and 100 entrants. Participants at the May 24 championships have included competitors from England, the United States, Argentina, Germany and Canada. Judges are primarily instructors or senior-level students from the Bermuda Karate Institute, Zenji Ryu Bermuda and Bermuda Jujitsu Karate.

Spearheading the Bermuda Open Karate Championships is Skipper Ingham, the first person to establish and continue a martial arts school in Bermuda. Peter Urban, founder of American goju karate, has called him "Bermuda's Grand Patriarch of Karate." Together with his wife Kristina, Skipper has trained many students in goju karate during the 27 years since the Bermuda Karate Institute was founded. Among the most notable students is Gladwin "Roots" Phillips of Zenji Ryu Bermuda. He is the island's only international gold medalist in traditional karate sparring, winning his weight division in Buenos Aires in 1994.

Visiting judges for BOKC have included Chuck Merriman, former coach of the U.S. national karate team, and Joe Pina of Boston

Tae Kwon Do. Sponsors are the Marketplace supermarket chain, Colonial Insurance, Darrell Travel and Phoenix Stores. Admission for spectators is $10 for adults and $5 for children younger than 12.

June

Queen's Birthday Parade
City of Hamilton • (441) 292-2587, (441) 238-1045, (441) 295-0011

"At first I didn't know what was going on," said a visitor from Boston who was standing with more than 2,000 spectators amid last year's pageantry. What was going on was the Queen's Birthday Parade, held the third Monday in June as an official celebration of the birthday of England's Queen Elizabeth II (whose birthday is actually April 26).

This is one occasion when all the top political and civil service folks are in attendance. The premier, opposition party leader, chief fire officer, police commissioner and mayor of Hamilton (in top hat and chains of office) are all on hand. The governor, dressed in full ceremonial whites, plumed hat and blue sash, inspects the regiment troops. A feu de joie (a celebration involving the firing of rifles) 21-gun salute splits the air before the governor leads the crowd in three cheers for the queen.

"When you see something like this you know you're not in Boston," added the visitor. Indeed, old chap.

Ironkids Triathlon
Clearwater Beach, St. David's
Contact: Charles Duffy
• **(441) 236-3156**

This triathlon is open to boys and girls in two classes — ages 7 to 10 and 11 to 14. Seven to 10-year olds compete in a 100 metre swim, two-and-a-half mile bike ride, and half-mile run. Eleven to 14-year-olds compete in a 200-metre swim, 5-mile bike ride and 1-mile run.

Organized and sanctioned by the Bermuda Triathlon Association, and sponsored by Gibbons Deposit Company, the triathlon is in its 11th year and continues to increase in popularity. Entry fee is $8, and prizes include 2 bicycles courtesy of Winner's Edge Bike Shop.

Keep Bermuda Beautiful Annual Fun Barbecue
Contact: Lennox Boodram
• **(441) 295-5142**

This is definitely a fun day for the family. Face painting, petting zoo, fun castle, and sand castle competition are just some of the activities. There is a cash bar, raffle, and food covers surf and turf: wahoo, chicken and ribs, baked potato, assorted salads and corn on the cob. Last year the barbecue was held at Mid-Ocean Beach in Tuckers Town, Smiths, but this, say organizers, may change for 1999 and 2000. Up-to-date information is available on their website: www.kbb.bm. "Our web pages," says Lennox Boodram, executive director of KBB, "are very user friendly and our calendar of events should prove quite helpful." Tickets are available at the KBB office on Bermuda House Land, Front Street.

July

Atlantic International Junior Golf Championship
Various locations

This annual tournament is aimed at developing competition between junior golfers from countries bordering on or close to the Atlantic Ocean. Young golfers from Canada, America and the Bahamas normally attend, and the event tees off early in the month. A maximum of 175 golfers may enter the tournament, which is open to boys and girls in eight categories — from mini girls (12 and younger) and mini boys (aged 11 and 12), up to senior boys (aged 18 to 21).

Conceived in a spirit of goodwill and sportsmanship, the Atlantic International has during the past 21 years become a very popular event. The goodwill spirit is manifested islandwide, as visiting golfers get the opportunity to stay with local families and several social activities contribute to their enjoyment of Bermudian hospitality.

Emancipation Commemoration
King's Square, Town of St. George
• **(441) 292-9447**

On August 1, 1834, slavery was abolished in Bermuda. On that date nearly 5,000 slaves were freed. This historic event is commemorated toward the end of July in King's Square through dramatic readings, music and dance. Organized by the Ministry of Community and Cultural Affairs and the Corporation of St. George's, the evening event has had participants including the National Dance Theatre of Bermuda, the Mu-en Chorale and the Salvation Army Divisional Band. Various other groups and individuals also perform. Part of the commemoration is a visit to the burial ground for slaves and free blacks at St. Peter's Church on York Street.

September

Annual Sandcastle Competition
Horseshoe Bay, Southampton Parish
• **(441) 236-2930**

This is an Institute of Bermuda Architects (IBA) event that takes place at Horseshoe Bay around the middle of the month. There are several categories — children (12 years and younger), teenagers ages 13 to 19, adults, families, organizations/companies and tourists. The entry fee for "Castles in the Sand" is $20 for the use of an 8-foot-square plot. All proceeds go to the IBA Scholarship Fund. Entrants have four hours, beginning at noon, to erect their masterpieces. Judging is by an IBA council. Entry forms are available at the Planning Department, Government Administration Building, 30 Parliament Street, Hamilton. If inquiring about the event by phone, ask for Nicky Gurret.

October

Bermuda Jazzscape
Various venues in Hamilton, Town of St. George and Royal Naval Dockyard
• **(888) 4ESCAPE**

Jazz enthusiasts always bookmark a couple of great events on their happenings calendar, and this one, just a couple of years old, is fast gaining popularity. For five days beginning early in October, international and local artists deliver what have been called by local writers "some of the most captivating jazz performances this side of the Atlantic."

Presented by *Travel and Leisure* magazine, Jazzscape's past performers have included Nancy Wilson, whose vocal magic always captivates; David Sanborn, the veteran saxophonist and pop instrumentalist; and Arturo Sandoval, a premier trumpeter who crossed the pond to make great music under Bermuda's subtropical skies.

The festival kicks off with a giant jazz party along Front Street in Hamilton. While some details may change for 1998, last year the Sunset Swing at King's Square in St. George was a tribute to swing-era bands and had the old town rocking. The Warren Vache Quartet and local song stylist Gita Blakeney, among others, put on splendid performances.

An official Gala Opening Night Concert on the third night (reserved seats $55, general admission $45, with special VIP tickets available) featured performances by Wilson and by Sanborn's group. Ticket prices for the fourth day and evening, when the best of Bermudian cuisine, crafts and talent are presented, are the same as for the opening night concert.

Visiting aficionados will find shuttle buses to and from Dockyard, one of the three venues, available from all major hotels. For more information, you can also contact the Bermuda Department of Tourism.

November

Skippy Peanut Butter KICK
Pembroke Sunday School, Angle St.
• (441) 292-2157

Held November 1 at the Pembroke Sunday School, the Kids International Competition Karate (hence, KICK) event is solely sponsored by Skippy Peanut Butter through its local agent, Butterfield & Vallis. The event draws between 30 and 70 competitors, primarily from Bermuda but with a few from the United States. It is for karate students 17 years and younger. Admission for spectators is $10 for adults and $5 for children younger than 12.

The Bermuda Tattoo
National Stadium, 50 Frog Ln.
• (441) 238-1045, (441) 292-0023

For three nights in mid-November, the skies over Devonshire throb to the music of military bands . . . except when there is utter silence as drill squads are put through their paces. This tattoo (the name given to a performance by military bands) is the biggest event of its kind locally, and past performers, in addition to the Bermuda Regiment Band, have included the United States Marine Corps Band; the Celtic Cross Pipe & Drum Band; the Bermuda Regiment Silent Drill Team; the Lincoln & Welland Regiment Band from St. Catherine's, Ontario; the Bermuda Islands Pipe Band; and the Bermuda Regiment Attack Squad.

Tickets (prices, again, are subject to change) are $15 for adults and $5 for children and are available from the visitors service bureaus and Bermuda Regiment Headquarters in Warwick.

Annual Culture Shock
No. 1 Shed, Front St., Hamilton

Organized by Bermuda Tent Productions, this is the biggest reggae show in Bermuda, attracting between 4,000 and 5,000 people during its two-night run. Performed toward the end of the month, the event is two-tiered: There is Dancehall Night, its driving tempo and lyrics attracting a younger crowd, and Culture Night, which has a more adult following and music described as more rootsy.

Dancehall, originating in Jamaica, has become a major musical influence and has had an impact on many American rap artists and local reggae performers. The Bermuda event not only features top local reggae artists, but also top Jamaican singers. Past performers have included Judy Mowatt, Garnet Silk, Beres Hammond and Tony Rebel. Local acts include Bigga Dread, Ninja Cutty and Shorta Ranks, who has performed in New Jersey and The Reggae Lounge in Manhattan. In 1998 the Mighty Diamonds, Morgan Heritage and Sizzla were among the performers.

Advance tickets for both nights are $75. For individual nights, the advance price is $60, with tickets $70 at the door.

Jazz & Razzmatazz
The Princess, 76 Pitts Bay Rd., Hamilton
• (441) 296-3429

Sponsored by the local chapter of Amnesty International as a late-November fund-raising event, this is the jazz extravaganza that brings together the largest number of local jazz performers in a concert that has become one of the most popular for local enthusiasts. In the hotel's Princess Rooms, more than 30 artists and groups annually take the stage before sellout audiences. Popular local performers at the event have included the Ralph Ebbin Trio, Gita Blakeney, Legacy and the James Richardson Trio. Proceeds aid the Amnesty organization, which has more than a half-million members worldwide and has been credited with saving the lives of 50,000 prisoners of conscience and other oppressed peoples. Tickets are $20.

Women's Resource Centre Annual Flea & Craft Market
City of Hamilton • (441) 295-3882

First launched in 1997, this has become the island's largest flea and craft market. Held on the 2nd and 3rd floors of Bull's Head car park, the market — open from 10 AM to 4 PM — offers a melange of items including handmade ornaments, clothes, baked goods, old china, small appliances, pictures, books, African jewelry, fabrics, household items, and stocking stuffers. Admission is $2; seniors and children under 12 are admitted free.

Dockyard Illumination
Royal Naval Dockyard

This has been called Bermuda's newest Christmas tradition. In 1998, with a flick of the switch, the story of Robert Louis Stevenson's *Treasure Island* was brought to life in 12 spectacular illuminated tableaus. Beginning at the end of November, and running until the first week of January, the festival included puppet shows, storytelling, Ferris wheel and fun rides, Candlelight procession and the first Baptist Church choir. There was a magic show, tug of war and rides on the new Dockyard "train." The theme for 1999 is not certain, but may be some of the same, only greatly expanded.

December

Bermuda Underwater Exploration Institute (BUEI) Christmas Boat Parade
Hamilton Harbour • (441) 292-7219

On this island where during the Christmas season scores of homeowners compete for the best decorated house exterior, it was natural that a similar competition would entice boat owners. In 1998 the first Christmas Boat Parade, organized by the BUEI, added luster to an already bright season. More than 60 participants motored their decorated craft through and around Hamilton Harbour in a spectacular display of lights. Inspired by a similar parade in the annual Newport Beach event, the two-hour local inaugural attracted hundreds of spectators. The route began at the Royal Hamilton Dingy Club (see more on this club in the Yachting and Marinas chapter), passed through the harbor where Front Street spectators had a superb view, across the harbor, east along the Harbour Road shoreline, and back to the dinghy club.

Traditionally, our island has always been the place to honeymoon; these days it's rapidly becoming a favorite location for the ceremony and reception as well.

Weddings

So you've decided to get married. And you've decided you want a romantic but carefree wedding. It's at this point problems can occur. For starters, there's the sticky problem of relatives. We're not against relatives, rest assured, but we do realize that families of the bride and groom can have conflicting ideas on where and how the ceremony should be conducted. One family may be living in Washington, for example, while the other lives in Los Angeles. Meanwhile, the bride and groom are based in New England. How do you avoid pleasing one set of relatives at the expense of the other? The solution is easy: Come to Bermuda.

Traditionally, our island has always been the place to honeymoon; these days it's rapidly becoming a favorite location for the ceremony and reception as well. Approximately 480 overseas couples get married here every year. The majority are from the Eastern Seaboard, but some come from as far away as Japan and Australia.

Of course people don't choose to marry here just out of tact or to escape a potential family war zone. They come because of our scenery and because of our romantic atmosphere. And they come because they know we approve of weddings. We're good at them. Besides, they feel that combining wedding with honeymoon will make for a more relaxing experience.

But, isn't it difficult to make all the arrangements from overseas? Isn't it nerve wracking? One bride from the United States told us, "I couldn't believe how easy it was. I scarcely had to do a thing." She, like many of our visitors and, indeed, residents, used a wedding consultant to take charge of arrangements. These arrangements often include acquiring the license, arranging the ceremony and reception, advising on accommodations and coordinating the florists and the photographers. Consultants will also make hair and beauty appointments and make transport arrangements to and from the ceremony location. Of course, you can arrange your own wedding without incurring a consultant's fee. But if practical details stress you out, and if you're pushed for time, we strongly recommend that you do use their help, particularly if you have never been to Bermuda.

In this chapter, we'll talk about the legal requirements and about the ceremony and location choices available. We'll also list a sampling of well-established wedding consultants who are experienced in facilitating trouble-free weddings. And in our Close-up we'll tell you about our own wedding traditions, some of which you might like to adopt for a truly Bermudian celebration.

License to Thrill

Before you can marry in Bermuda, you have to fill out a Bermuda Government form or notice of your intended marriage and, together with a check for $176, send it to the Registry General (See Civil Ceremony heading below for address and telephone number). If you are younger than 21, you must send proof of parental consent. Where applicable, you should also send photocopies of divorce certificates.

Once the Registry General receives these papers, the registrar will put one announcement of your intended marriage in *The Royal Gazette* and one other in the *Bermuda Sun*.

Provided a Jane Eyre/Mr. Rochester situation doesn't happen (i.e., no one makes a valid objection), you will then receive your license. The procedure must be completed between 15 days and three months of your wedding date. The fee, by the way, includes your marriage certificate.

Where religious ceremonies are concerned, you also follow the above procedure. Wedding banns for overseas couples are not usually read unless some family members are living here and affiliated with a particular church.

A Civil Ceremony

The Registry General
Melbourne House, 30 Parliament St., Hamilton • (441) 297-7709

If you want a civil ceremony, you'll tie the knot, so to speak, in the Marriage Room of the Registry General. Now some people are worried that registry office marriages are too impersonal and cold altogether. However, the Registrar, Mrs. Christopher, and the Assistant Registrar, Mr. Dowling, genuinely care about each marriage they conduct. They combine formality and warmth in such a way that the significance of the event comes through. They want you to feel that your wedding is a very special occasion. The room itself is beautifully decorated with an ocean-view mural. Some couples like to add to the outdoor effect by having sand put on the floor. The staff are happy to comply and are unfazed by the sight of the bride and groom dressed in all their finery but in bare feet.

As soon as you acquire the license, you can make an appointment. Appointments can be any time between 10 AM and 3:45 PM Monday through Friday, and 10 AM to noon on Saturday. You will need two witnesses. They can be your relatives or friends, but staff will step in (except on Saturdays) if requested. The Registrar and the Assistant Registrar are not able to officiate at weddings outside or at any other location. The cost of the ceremony is $167.

Religious Ceremonies

Read our Worship chapter and you'll see that we have a diversity of religions and faiths. It is possible to have a religious wedding ceremony here if you come from overseas, but we must tell you that policies do differ from faith to faith. For example, although we have a Jewish community here, we do not have a resident rabbi. You are welcome to have a Jewish ceremony, provided your own rabbi is willing to come and conduct it. For a Muslim ceremony call Resident Imam-Ameer Shakir at either (441) 293-9108 or (441) 292-5986. He will be happy to help you. You can also have a Baha'i wedding ceremony in Bermuda. A Baha'i wedding officer will be happy to officiate either for an indoor or outdoor ceremony. Call (441) 292-2723 for information about arrangements.

Where Christian weddings are concerned, policies vary from denomination to denomination. If you're Roman Catholic, a priest will marry you here only if you have Catholic family living and practicing their religion in Bermuda or if you once lived on the island and were a member of one of our Catholic churches. All Catholic wedding ceremonies must be held in a church. Clergy of some Protestant denominations do perform weddings for overseas visitors, and some are willing to officiate at outdoor weddings. We recommend, however, that you call the church of your choice and receive information on policy.

Wedding consultants, by the way, can suggest ministers who they know are willing to conduct marriage services. The cost of the ceremony itself can vary. An outdoor wedding

---

INSIDERS' TIP

Don't be disappointed: To make all of the arrangements for your special day in Bermuda, book early. This is particularly true for Saturdays and Sundays. Whether you desire a traditional Bermudian wedding or something completely original, Bermuda is the ideal spot.

can be anywhere between $150 to $250, while a church wedding can cost between $300 and $500. Again, check with the church of your choice for information about costs.

Ceremony Locations

You can marry in the Registry General (see above), in a church or in a hotel. However, outdoor weddings have become a very popular option here. As one bride put it, "I wanted my wedding to be natural and romantic at the same time. So I really wanted to be near the ocean." She got her wish. Her wedding was held on the cliff top overlooking the South Shore at Astwood Park (see the Beaches chapter).

If you, too, long for an outdoor wedding, we can offer a wonderful choice of location. As we've already told you, we approve of weddings, so you are welcome to marry in our public areas. You can marry, for example, on a public beach, and have a paddle afterwards, or in a beautiful park. You can even marry on the *Deliverance* in St. George's. Our forts also come in handy — some couples have married, for instance, on the top of Fort St. Catherine, also in St. George's. (Perhaps they sensed a battle ahead of them? Let's hope not.)

However, if privacy is important to you, and you don't want to be distracted by members of the public, you should consider having the ceremony on the grounds of a hotel. Some of our hotels have outdoor areas specifically devoted to weddings. At this point, you might check out the Accommodations chapters for descriptions of their views and grounds. Check, too, our Attractions, Beaches and Parks and Conservation chapters for more outdoor locations. Believe it or not, there are couples who want the ceremony on a boat. Look at the Watersports and Yachting and Marinas chapters for boat charters.

Whatever venue you choose, you can make arrangements for seating, for champagne to celebrate the ceremony and for a focal point such as a moongate or a bridal arch to be set up. Go to a bridal consultant, and the staff will take care of these arrangements for you.

What about the winter? Outdoor weddings do happen in the winter. Remember our temperatures rarely fall lower than 68 degrees, and the sun doesn't usually desert us. Still, it's always a good idea to have a plan B in case the heavens decide to open. Marry at a hotel, for example, and you'll certainly be assured of an alternative indoor location.

What Happens After the Ceremony?

Sometimes the bride and groom hold a reception in the same outdoor location as the ceremony, but more commonly, after posing for photographs and relaxing with a glass of champagne, the party departs to a reception or a meal held at a hotel or a restaurant, or indeed on a boat. It's very difficult to generalize about receptions: They differ according to personal taste and to the size of the party. Some couples opt for a quiet meal either on their own or with family. Others have larger affairs altogether, and in the case of numerous guests — say more than a hundred — they may have buffet-style refreshments. Check our Restaurants chapter for menus. The Resort Hotels, Small Hotels and Cottage Colonies chapters will help too. Of course you can hire private caterers, but again this is probably easiest to do with the help of consultants. As for prices, again it's difficult to generalize. Once you know the kind of reception you would like and the number of guests, it's wise to call the hotel or restaurant direct to discuss prices.

Transportation

Car rentals are illegal in Bermuda, so for motorized transportation you will depend on taxis. If matching cars are important, you should book taxis in advance. Radio Cabs (see the Getting Here, Around and Home chapter) can provide uniform white Mitsubishi vans that comfortably take up to five people. They make sure that the cars are in tip-top condition and decorated with ribbons.

However, many couples like to follow the time-honored Bermudian tradition of a horse and buggy ride, usually from the church or the ceremony location to the reception. Typically, the driver will be formally dressed in navy blue Bermuda shorts, knee socks and a white hat. And his carriage will be decorated with flowers and ribbons. For romance there's nothing to beat this ride because, as we all know, love and marriage go together like a horse and . . . . Prices vary from about $180 to $400. Remember that you will be charged for the distance from the stable to the destination. It's wise, therefore, to choose a stable close to your ceremony location.

Accommodations

Read our Accommodation chapters and you'll see that we have a large range in terms of facilities and prices. If you want luxury then the Resort Hotels, Small Hotels and Cottage Colonies chapters will help you out. But if you're working with a tight budget, our Guest Houses and Housekeeping Cottages and Apartments chapters are the ones to check. One thing to consider is the distance between accommodations and ceremony location and between ceremony location and reception. The shorter the distance, the cheaper and more convenient the travel arrangements will be.

Of course, it's possible to hold the ceremony and reception in the hotel where you stay. If you use consultants, they will recommend that you make your own accommodation bookings, particularly if you are booking for a large group of guests. However, they will always give you advice on where to stay. Bear in mind that many of our hotels, even the most expensive ones, have wedding and/or honeymoon packages. These packages can offer special rates that can include the ceremony and reception as well as the accommodations. Call the hotel of your choice to see what packages they offer.

A Word About Showing Affection

"Let us be very strange and well bred: Let us be as strange as if we had been married a great while; and as well-bred as if we were not married at all." So said Mrs. Millamant in

Congreve's *Way of the World*. Bermudians could well agree with her where being physically demonstrative about love is concerned. Holding hands is OK but we don't tend to passionately kiss or embrace in public, even if we have just been married. In private, of course, it's a different matter.

Bermudian writer Dale Butler has written a book called *A Hundred Best Places to Kiss, Smooch and Snuggle in Bermuda*. According to him, Horseshoe Bay in Southampton is the favorite (see our Beaches chapter), but he also cites more unusual ones such as an elevator in a local company. You can buy his book for $10 at any bookstore.

Wedding Consultants

A successful wedding is always the result of attention to detail. Details can include hair and nails beauty, flowers, music, photographs and videos as well as ceremony, reception and accommodations. Look in the yellow pages of our telephone directory, and you'll see that we have a wide selection of businesses offering services in those areas. While they would be happy for you to deal with them directly, we highly recommend that you choose a wedding consultant instead. OK, you'll pay them a consulting fee, but consider the number of telephone calls and the time you'll save. You'll also benefit from the consultants' expertise and knowledge of Bermuda's idiosyncratic ways.

So given that you're going to use a consultant, what's your first step? It may sound obvious, but picking the wedding date is crucial. If you're planning a fairly complex wedding, do that as soon in advance as possible to avoid disappointment. Remember that ministers, photographers and musicians can be very heavily booked, as indeed can the consultants themselves. Six months to a year's advance notice is the norm, although if you want to marry almost on impulse, there may be last-minute cancellations.

So what will these consultants do for you? Let's start by explaining what they typically do not do. They don't usually take responsibility for the bride's dress. It's much safer and cheaper for the bride to bring her dress with her. However, it is possible to rent tuxedos

We're getting married in *Bermuda!!*

Romance ♥ Champagne ♥ Horse & Carriage
♥ Cliff Top & Tropical Beach Settings ♥
plus all the little extras that really count

"Weddings of a Lifetime"
The Bridal Suite

3 Park Road ● Suite 7 ● Hamilton HM 09 ● Bermuda
Toll Free: 1-(888) 253-5585 ● Tel: (441) 292-2025 ● Fax: (441) 296-2070
E-mail: wedding@ibl.bm ● Internet:http://www.bermuda.bm/wedding
Island Wedding Planners of Bermuda

here. As we've told you, they don't usually book accommodations either, but they will definitely describe and send pictures of hotels that might interest you (of course, this book does the best job of describing these properties that you'll find!). But they do everything else, including taking care of the marriage license and booking the person who will marry you.

Typically, they will start by discussing with you the level of formality you want, the number of guests and the kind of ceremony you require. They will be sensitive to budget and explain prices in relation to the size of your wedding. They will also arrange hair and beauty appointments (a hairdo starts at about $25), and make sure that photographers are on hand to take pictures and/or videos.

What about bouquets and corsages? If you have flower arrangements in mind, you can send them pictures and they will coordinate with the florists. Prices for flowers vary, but a bridal bouquet starts at about $75 while bridesmaids' bouquets are usually about $50. They will also send you pictures of possible locations and of wedding enhancements such as cake, marriage arch or moongate (for outdoor ceremonies). If you want the famous horse and buggy ride, they'll book that too.

Music? Ah, "If music be the food of love, play on . . . ." They will arrange anything from recorded music to a live jazz or island music band, from an organist to a string quartet or a choir. On the day itself, they will be on hand to set up equipment (for an outdoor ceremony) and to make sure that everything goes smoothly. In addition to arranging receptions, they will also organize rehearsal dinners should you require them.

In the following listings we'll include prices wedding consultants have quoted to us, but bear in mind that all are subject to change. Credit cards for these agencies are fine.

Pembroke Parish

The Bridal Suite
Parkside Bldg., 3 Park Rd., Hamilton
• (441) 292-2025

Allister and Carmen Simmons have owned and managed their bridal consultancy for the past ten years. In September 1997, one marriage they arranged was filmed and featured on a Learning Channel program called "The Wedding Story." That meant that close to 6 million viewers got to see a Bermuda wedding. The ceremony was held at Astwood Park, Paget, Mr. Simmons's favorite wedding location.

Judging from the number of happy bridal parties we see there most Saturdays, many people agree that the stunning views of the South Shore make it an ideal venue. Mr. Simmons can set up a portable moongate in the park. The diamond shape marked on the center of the arch represents, he says, the diamond in the engagement ring. Should the weather be indecent, you can have the ceremony at nearby St. Anne's Church or at a hotel. But if a different outdoor location appeals, he is happy to arrange it.

If good photographs are a priority, he will advise you on the best times of the day and the evening for good light. In fact, the Bridal Suite has in-house photographers. Photograph prices start at $350 for 48 photos, plus album. For extra photos the rate comes down. Order 96, for example, and you'll pay $600. Videos also start at $350, and you can have a deluxe package that includes great scenes of Bermuda, as well as your celebration, for $700.

In 1997, the Bridal Suite arranged 200 weddings for overseas couples. "We make sure there's never a mistake," he told us. "We want every bride to be very happy — that's what's important." Consulting fees range from $500

INSIDERS' TIP

Call Triple J's Products at (441) 238-2813 if you want the traditional silver and gold wedding cake. Mrs. Juliet Jackson makes and decorates all kinds of celebration cakes, but she specializes in creating ones for weddings. You don't happen to like fruit or pound cake? Then she will make and decorate whatever you like, whether it be rum, banana, strawberry mousse or carrot cake.

to $1,000, depending on the number of guests. Both Mr. and Mrs. Simmons are members of Bermuda's Chamber of Commerce.

Wed in Paradise
Fort House, 9 Fort Hamilton, Hamilton
• (441) 295-1968

Janet Le-Page, co-partner and manager of this consultancy, is certainly happy to tailor your wedding according to your specifications. But she also offers six different packages whose prices include all itemized services and items as well as the costs of her own administrative services.

Let's take her Paradise Lakes package, for example, that enables you to marry on a boat. She will arrange marriage license, marriage certificate and minister, plus two witnesses if required. She'll arrange for a hair stylist to come to the bride on the day of the wedding and will organize the bridal bouquet and groom's boutonnières. She'll hire a motorized yacht and order champagne, soft drinks, hors d'oeuvres and a two-tiered wedding cake for the bridal couple and four guests. How will she get you to Hamilton Dock? She'll get you to and from the dock in an open-topped car. And she'll arrange for a photographer to come as well. You'll exchange your vows while the yacht cruises gently around Paradise Lake, an area in the Great Sound known for its tranquillity and scenic beauty. How much? $2,600 for everything. Of course if you want extra guests there'll be additional charges.

This is the most expensive package. Others let you marry in St. Peter's Church (see the Worship and Attractions chapters) or under a moongate on a South Shore beach for between $1,684 to $2,339. Janet Le-Page is happy to arrange even more unusual ceremonies. You could, for example, marry on the seat of a bicycle made for two or at the bottom of the ocean floor. How would that be possible? You'd wear a helmet instead of a veil (see the Watersports chapter). To be honest, no-one has (up to the time of publication) chosen that option.

Tying the Knot in a Traditionally Bermudian Way

The first marriage recorded in Bermuda was on November 26, 1609, when Thomas Powell, Sir George Somers' cook, was married to Elizabeth Persons, the maidservant of Mistress Horton. No doubt they feasted on roast hog and cahow complemented by cedar berry wine.

Since that time weddings have become more complicated affairs altogether, and these days Bermudian weddings can be showy affairs with a large number of guests.

In fact, ironically, just as you may wish to marry here to avoid stress, many of us are tempted to marry off island to avoid the pressing problem of whom and whom not to invite. Hurt feelings on an island of this size are not a good idea.

But Mrs. Juliet Jackson, well-known on the island for her delicious and beautifully decorated celebration cakes (see Triple J's tip), laments the materialism of today's nuptial celebrations. Once upon a time, she says, weddings were primarily family occasions. There was no way receptions would be held in hotels; they would be held at the home of the bride's parents. Typically, the night before the wedding, the bride's and groom's mothers would take care of making the refreshments, usually, ham and egg sandwiches, and wedding cake, while the bride's and groom's fathers would take care of the liquor if it was served. Bridesmaids would serve the food and the groom's best man and friends would act as ushers. Usually, the brides wore long, white dresses with sweetheart necklines and veils while groom and the male members of the families wore black tuxedos.

Honeymoons? Well, up until the early 1970s, Thursday afternoons were half holidays and the traditional time for weddings. Once married, the couple was expected to attend their church on the following Sunday and then have the families back for lunch at their new home. So honeymoons did not mean vacations away from Bermuda; they meant setting up house. Families would help out by contributing furniture and items, such as table linen, for the bride's "hope" chest. Often the gifts were handmade — a far cry from the bridal registries in shops that guests use today.

Yes, things have changed. But some traditions we still follow. Brides' dresses may have changed in fashion, but they do tend to be white. We've already told you about the horse and buggy custom. Some of our other traditions focus on the wedding cake. In some ways we believe that it is possible to have your cake and eat it too. In fact, we have two cakes: one for the bride and one for the groom. The bride's is traditionally a three-tier fruit cake, signifying the fruitfulness of the marriage, while the groom's is a single-tier pound cake, signifying prosperity. From a practical point of view, fruit keeps, you see. The top tier is carefully put away until the christening of the first child.

What about the cake decoration? Well, there are two traditions here. First, let's talk about the silver and gold custom. The bride's cake is first covered with marzipan and royal white icing. After that it's covered with silver. How do you get the silver to stick? Well, you paint small areas of the cake at a time with slightly beaten egg white, which makes a good adhesive for the three-inch squares of silver leaf that you then carefully place on the cake. Exactly the same procedure happens with the groom's cake, except his is covered with gold leaf. Silver represents innocence and purity while gold of course represents wealth and prosperity. As you might imagine, this procedure is very exacting and time consuming. It has to be carried out in a completely airless room; otherwise the leaves will turn into blobs.

— continued on next page

Photo: GIS

New bride off on traditional horse and buggy ride.

On top of each cake is a cedar seedling placed in an appropriately sized vase. The bride's cedar should preferably have berries on it to symbolize fertility. On the day of the reception, the cakes, surrounded with ivy and/or fresh flowers, have a special table all to themselves. Once the cakes have been cut, the bride and groom plant the cedar seedlings. Bridal couples from overseas tend to have sprigs instead, since bringing seedlings back to their countries could contravene laws concerning the importation of plants.

The gold and silver tradition, probably dating back to the nineteenth century, was originally practiced by wealthy white families. However, these days it's more widely adopted. And yet, some of us wonder why it is that the groom is not expected to be innocent and pure? Eventually perhaps both cakes will have a mixture of silver and gold decoration, particularly since wives work these days and are just as responsible for their families' prosperity.

According to Mrs. Jackson, the second tradition also goes back to the nineteenth century. This one requires the bride's cake to be round and iced in white, with silver decorations added. These decorations are sometimes bay grape leaves sprayed with silver. The groom's cake, on the other hand should be square, two-tiered and trimmed with blue and silver. Again the cakes are surrounded with flowers.

What other traditions? Well, when you're safely married, you'll be safer still if you walk through a moongate. We borrowed this idea from the Orient, perhaps at the end of the nineteenth century. Walk through this moon-shaped archway, make a wish and you should have happiness and prosperity for the rest of your life. Don't worry; moongates are not hard to find. Architectural examples are everywhere on the island — on streets, in gardens both private and public, inside hotels and on their grounds. The older moongates were made of Bermuda stone and often covered with vines. A famous one is in Par-la-Ville Park (see the Parks and Conservation chapter), and another is next to the Bermuda Bakery on Pitts Bay Road, City of Hamilton. If a moongate is nowhere near your ceremony location or reception, worry not. Hotels or wedding consultants can usually rent portable wooden ones for you.

Another custom has to do with rice. Few people use confetti in Bermuda. Let's face it, it does cause unwanted litter. Traditionally, guests would sprinkle rice over the newlyweds, since rice also represents prosperity and fertility. These days we worry about the birds choking on it, so we tend to use birdseed instead.

So will you borrow some of our traditions, while perhaps including your own? If you do, you'll also be following the "something old, something new, something borrowed, something blue" tradition. The "blue," by the way, relates back to biblical days when that color, rather than white, represented purity. Whatever you choose to do, make sure that you let nothing to the marriage of true minds admit impediment.

Ms. Le-Page, by the way, is a member of the Association of Bridal Consultants in Connecticut.

Devonshire Parish

Bermuda Weddings Associates
Rapose Cottage, 47 Watlington Rd. E.
• **(441) 293-4033**

Shelly A. and Robin L. Hamill are co-owners of this consultancy. They started up in August 1994. Why? One reason was that they themselves had gotten married in Bermuda. "I didn't want other couples to make the mistakes we did," explained Shelly Hamill, the manager, who was originally from the United States. "For example, we decided on a DJ at 3:30 in the afternoon. A string quartet would have been much more appropriate."

She is willing to organize whatever wedding you require, but she specializes in large weddings. She does 10 large weddings a year — no more — so she can really pay attention to detail and not do a rushed job. She's happy to arrange golf tournaments, fireworks, brunches, rehearsal dinners and parties as well as the usual wedding arrangements. She can even arrange for flags from the countries of the bridal party to be flown. One of her Bermuda weddings for a couple from New York was featured in the March 1998 edition of *Modern Bride*.

Her charges? She basically charges $125 an hour for her administrative charges with a starting fee of $1,000. In addition to arranging weddings, she also publishes an 80-page annual magazine called *Bermuda Weddings and Setting Up Home*. Call her if you would like a copy. Cost is $3.95 plus shipping. She is a member of the Association of Bridal Consultants in Connecticut, of the Bermuda Chamber of Commerce and of the Bermuda Credit Association.

Photographic and Video Services

Pembroke Parish

Memory Bank Video Services
Cedarparkade, Washington St., Hamilton • (441) 236-3229, (441) 295-3378

Dennis Sherlock established this business in 1981. Ever since he has created all sorts of videos for the VSB television station (see our Media and Communications chapter) including The Curious Cook. He is also very experienced at creating wedding videos and offers a variety of packages that range from $350 to $1,000. For $350 he covers the ceremony (outdoors or indoors) and includes suitable graphics, together with panoramic shots of Bermuda at the beginning of the video. Dennis has plenty

of music to choose from but is happy to let you provide the music of your choice. An additional video copy costs $20. Memory Bank often has bookings a year or even two in advance, but Dennis can sometimes cover spur-of-the-moment weddings, particularly if they occur on weekdays. You should note that credit cards are not accepted.

Visual Impact Photography
63 King St., Hamilton • (441) 295-4755

Ernest McCreight has run his own photography business since 1988. He's experienced at covering weddings and, as he puts it, goes "beyond the expected" to make sure your special day is elegantly portrayed and beautifully documented on film.

Ernest offers three packages. "The Bermuda Getaway" costs $250 for one hour's work and a minimum of 30 4-by-6-inch prints plus negatives. This is a popular option for couples on a budget. "The Bermuda Dream" costs $520, again for one hour and 30 4-by-6-inch prints with negatives, but this package also offers 24 5-by-7-inch enlargements, displayed in a beautiful leather-bound album from the Renaissance Collection. "The Bermuda Fantasy" package is $1,300. It offers two hours' photo coverage and a leather-bound album from the Mario Acerboni Collection containing 29 8-by-10-inch prints of your favorite pictures. Ernest uses Hasselblad photographic equipment that ensures enlargements of the highest quality. After the ceremony he takes "Lovestory Portraits" of the bride and groom against a backdrop of Bermuda's most breathtaking scenery. Additional hours of coverage are $80 each.

Ernest has bookings a year in advance. However, last-minute coverage of weekday weddings can sometimes be arranged. It's important to book as far ahead as possible for weddings on Saturday or Sunday.

Our parks are small. But we're proud of them because they are protected from the onslaught of concrete and glass that the twentieth century has called "progress."

Parks and Conservation

So what are our parks like? Let's start by confessing that if you've got Yellowstone or Grand Canyon National Park in mind, forget it. Those, after all, are more vast than the whole of our island. Our parks are small. But we're proud of them because they are protected from the onslaught of concrete and glass that the twentieth century has called "progress."

Our largest park area is actually South Shore Park, the one that encompasses many of our South Shore beaches. It consists of 93 acres. Check our Beaches chapter for more information about it and about others that have beaches accessible to the public. And our smallest? Godet Rock is a tiny island in the Great Sound, consisting of 0.266 acre.

Some of our parks could best be described as our "green bits" or green open spaces where building is not allowed. Kindley Field Park in St. George's Parish, for example, is a grassy area edging Ferry Reach that is not particularly exciting. But it's important, nonetheless. We go there to watch speed boat racing or just to take a break from driving. We'd be horrified if someone were permitted to build on it.

Others are our conservation areas; they are examples of Bermuda's wildlife left in peace. Many of these parks are difficult to access because they have no trails. And some are deliberately restricted to visiting scientists or people who have a scholarly interest in the environment. Nonsuch Island, where cahows, skinks and other endemic wildlife still exist, is the best example (see our Area Overview chapter). Plans are afoot to make one of our conserved areas more accessible to the public. Paget Marsh on Lovers' Lane, Paget, will even-

tually have a boardwalk allowing visitors to explore the flora without damaging it.

But there are parks that do retain a wilderness effect while having pathways that make access easy. These, of course, we'll describe in our listings. Remember to think small while you're exploring them. Walk fast, and probably the longest time you'll take to get through them is at the most a half-hour.

So why not stroll instead? We recommend that you follow W. H. Davies' philosophy: "What is this life if full of care/We have no time to stand and stare?" There's certainly plenty to stare at: views of the ocean, Bermuda's lush foliage, birds, bees and butterflies. It's often a good idea to assume the eye level of a 4-year-old. Look down, then, as well as up, and watch out for our wild flowers, our feathered grasses and for birds and lizards that scuttle in the bushes. Look out also for the riotous tumble of our hedges. Our Flora and Fauna chapter will help you with identifying some of our plants and animals.

Not all of our parks are "wild," however. Some, particularly the ones belonging to the Corporation of Hamilton, could better be described as gardens. If you're into manicured lawns, exotic flowers and trees, then these are the ones to wander through. And if you're into military history, you'll appreciate the parks that feature forts. (Check our Attractions chapter for more gardens and forts.)

How about recreational facilities? At present two have swings, slides and play equipment for kids. Warwick Long Bay is described in the South Shore Park we describe in our Beaches chapter. See the Mullet Bay listing below for our other. Pembroke Dump, once an area as unsightly as its name suggests, is currently being turned into a park and will eventually also have recreational equipment. See the Pembroke Playground listing in our Kidstuff chapter.

Bear in mind that only three of the parks we describe in this chapter allow you to drive through. Usually you leave your car or bike in the parking lot nearby and trust to Shank's pony. So here we go: Let time stroll.

St. George's Parish

Ferry Point Park
Ferry Rd., St. David's

Ferry Point Park consists of an island and a promontory. (See map page xv.) If a blend of history and varied landscape appeals, make it a priority to explore the maze of hidden pathways and the railway trail that take you to hidden bays, thicket and rocky open spaces. In the wooded areas you'll find Natal plum bushes. Their white flowers are very fragrant, and their red fruits, some people say, are delicious. Imagine sweetened milk, and you have some idea of the taste. Slopes of spiky asparagus fern will give a spring to your step. The effects of light and shadow on them create infinite varieties of green, thus, as Andrew Marvell put it, "Annihilating all that's made/ To a green thought in a green shade."

Enjoy, too, the Mexican peppers, the bamboo, the buttonwood and the fiddlewood trees. Follow the coastline, and you'll hear nothing but the call of birds and the lapping water. Sorry, we must correct that. Occasionally, you'll hear and see a jet from North America flying into the airport. Look out for white egrets that, when observed from behind, look like animated, elongated spoons bouncing along. Once you reach Whalebone Bay, you may wonder why the sand on the bay looks darker

and grittier than sand found on our other beaches. You'll remember that Bermuda sits on top of an inactive (we promise) volcano? This is the only beach on our island where you can see traces of volcanic rock mixed with the minuscule shells of the sand.

"What about the history?" you might ask. Well, first of all, you'll find a cemetery with a large white marble cross commemorating British soldiers who lost their lives in the 1864 yellow fever epidemic. Second, in the woodland you may well come across the remains of an old lime kiln. Lime was once essential for maintaining our white roof tops and for building construction. Third, cross the bridge to Ferry Island, and you'll find the old St. George's terminus for the ferry. Before 1871, when the Causeway opened, a horse-drawn ferry was the main means of transportation connecting the mainland with St. George's Island. Look across the water, and you'll see the remains of a later form of transportation: the old railway.

And last, you'll find forts here. On Ferry Island you'll see one called Ferry Island Fort, but of course. First built in the 1790s and rebuilt in the 1870s, it offered protection against the dreaded American enemy. On Ferry Point you'll find two more. Governor Sir Robert Robinson built Burnt Point Fort in 1688 to prevent illegal trading by Bermudian vessels as well as enemy ships invading. It's actually St. George's oldest fort. Martello Tower is a more recent one altogether, having been built in 1823. An extremely deep ditch surrounds it. After crossing the narrow bridge, enter the tower and climb the steps that lead to the top. Circular in shape, the tower offers circular views. Look west, and you'll have a clear view of Dockyard in Sandys Parish. Paradoxically, these views fill one with a feeling of spaciousness on the one hand and a realization of Bermuda's smallness on the other.

---

www.insiders.com

See this and many other
Insiders' Guide
destinations online.

Visit us today!

INSIDERS' TIP

Dogs are welcome in Bermuda parks, but they must be on a leash.

There's plenty of parking space at the entrance. Restrooms are there too.

Great Head Park
Battery Rd., St. David's

Explore this park, and you will find St. David's Battery on top of the cliffs of St. David's Head. It features two British breech-loading guns that date back to the early 1900s and that are placed in batteries side by side. As Lance Furbert II points out in his leaflet "Forts of Bermuda in Bermuda's Parks," this battery "stands as a memorial to the men of the Bermuda Militia Artillery, the Bermuda Volunteer Engineers, the Bermuda Militia Infantry, and to all the Bermudian servicemen who served their country with honour at home and abroad." St. David's Battery, then, was manned during World War II.

In fact, the guns were never fired in anger, but they were fired to mark the death of King George V in 1936. William Zuill in his *Bermuda Journey* explains that Bermuda received the news of the king's death at night and that Government House ordered the customary 21-gun salute to be fired immediately. Although there was plenty of ammunition, there were no blanks available. Because the officers thought there was no shipping in the area, they decided that the salute should take place anyway. Unfortunately a small gun boat, which had been waiting for daylight, was directly in the line of fire. It turned out to be a Bolivian boat manned by British sailors. The good news is that they weren't hit and happily celebrated the fact over scotch and sodas with the officers.

Great Head is well worth a visit for its views and wildlife. Be warned, though, that the trail can be steep in places and is therefore not ideal for people who have difficulty walking. The trails lead you through areas of open field and fairly dense thicket. On hot days, the archways created by overhanging spice trees and fiddlewood offer welcome shade and dappled light. Look out for palmetto, allspice and bay grape trees.

But lower your eyes, too, because small wild flowers, herbs and feathered grasses are plentiful. You may notice small green plants with bright red bracts; these are Joseph's coat or tiny poinsettia. Tiny lilac flowers on a slen-

der stem are Jamaica vervain. Butterflies like this park and so do the birds. Listen carefully for bird song, including the cheerful call of the chick of the village.

Eventually, you will reach the top of the cliff. Rest for a view of the ocean, of St. David's Lighthouse and of the curving coastline. Then follow the cliff walk until you come to the battery. Great Head Park, by the way, has a small parking lot at its entrance and a portable toilet.

Littlehead Park
Cashew City Rd., St. David's

The entrance to this park overlooks picturesque Vaughan's Bay. Park in the small parking lot (a portable toilet is available) and follow the trail signs. For a few minutes you'll walk through woodland until you come to a cottage on your right and a yard. Don't worry; you're not trespassing. The land is definitely public. The small beach on your left is Gunner's Bay. Walk farther, and you'll see that the path hugs the coastline. That's why the land crabs like it, so watch out for their holes. Eventually you will come to Fort Popple where you'll have stunning views of the rocky coastline and, of course, of the fort.

"Why 'Popple?'" you might ask. It's named after Governor Popple who, fort passionate, built it in 1738. Once you've seen the fort, you can continue your walk until you come to the adjoining Great Head Park. See the listing above.

Mullet Bay Park
Mullet Bay Rd.

We list this one because it has recreational equipment for children. Located just outside the Town of St. George, it has swings, slides and climbing frames that should keep small children amused. While they release physical energy, you can sit on one of the benches and keep an eye on them.

Hamilton Parish

Blue Hole Park
Dolphin Dr., off Blue Hole Hill

This park is at the point where the Causeway meets Blue Hole Hill, opposite the Grotto

Bay Beach Hotel and Tennis Club. Drive in, and you'll see a parking area on your right with restrooms. Follow the trail signs, and you'll find yourself in a thicket carpeted with elephant ears foliage that also climbs trees. Surinam cherry trees act as thick hedges, and sago palms (actually cycads, not true palms) abound.

A five-minute walk will take you to a pond at the end of an open grassy area on the right of the trail. Artificially created, the pond fills what was once a garbage dump. On a hill there the Audubon Society has set up an observation hide complete with a bird blind. What's a bird blind? It's a small box with a slit that you can look through. That way you can see the birds, but they can't see you. Human faces can frighten them. The pond itself is often covered with algae, but look closely and you may notice herons. You'll certainly notice mangroves. And once in a while you might see a kingfisher fly across the pond in a streak of bluish gray and white.

Continue following the trail and you'll come to a break in the hedge on your right — walk through it and you'll have a surprise. There before you is one of Hamilton Parish's numerous caves. Look down and across to see the deep blue of this cave's pool. Look up to admire the stalactites that resemble small rhinoceroses on a downward flight.

Go back to the trail and walk for a few minutes until you come to a clearing and a small cove overlooking Castle Harbour. Sit on a bench here and gaze at the mangroves, or check out more caves by the edge of the water. Then pick up the trail again to find a large wooden deck. Stand on it and you can view a sunken cave filled with water, again of the deepest blue. Below the surface barracuda silently skulk. You'll see still more mangroves surrounding the pool plus the feathery tendrils of Spanish moss hanging from the trees. On clear days the trees and stalactites are perfectly mirrored in the pool. This park may be small, but there's magic to it.

Smiths Parish

Spittal Pond Nature Reserve
South Rd.

This reserve has two entrances: one at the eastern end of the property and one at the western end. Just for once, we want to reverse the spatial order we normally follow in this book and take you for a walk from west to east. As you drive through Smiths Parish with Hamilton behind you, you'll see on your left St. Mark's Church. The western entrance to Spittal Pond is just beyond it, on the opposite side of the road.

Drive in, and leave your bike or car in the parking lot. Most likely some feral or escaped chickens from the neighboring dairy farm will welcome you to the land of rural Bermuda. Go down some steps and follow the public footpath that slopes down into the woodland. Fiddle wood, Mexican pepper, cedars and allspice trees form a leafy tunnel. Interspersed with the trees are the vines of morning glory and elephant ears. Remember to look down as well as up, and look out for the wild flowers. Wire weed is common here. Actually, its name is most unfair to it; it has tiny apricot flowers that are delicate and pretty. If we have to discriminate between flower and weed, let's agree with Gerard Manley Hopkins: "Long live the weeds and the wilderness yet."

Come out of the tunnel and you'll see Spittal Pond on your left. The brackish pond with its surrounding marshland is a perfect sanctuary for herons, coots, ducks and geese. It's fenced, but as you continue along the footpath, you'll find plenty of areas where you can watch the birds without upsetting them. Look to your right, and you'll see the spectacular, craggy coastline of the South Shore.

INSIDERS' TIP

Most of our parks have portable or porto cabin toilets. They're reasonably clean but unfortunately don't have running water. Bring bottles of water and paper towels, particularly if you have kids.

Photo: GIS

A quiet walk through one of our many parks gives new meaning to the word solitude.

Ahead of you is a gate leading to the sanctuary and to Spanish Rock. However, before you enter, check out on the right an extraordinary geological formation locally known as "Chequerboard." It consists of a flat floor of rock scored into distinct squares, surrounded by crags of varying heights that overlook the ocean. To a geologist, the formation is interesting. For some years it was unclear as to whether the squared effect was artificial or natural. However, it is now agreed that the composition is indeed natural and that the lines or cracks happened as the marine limestone emerged from the sea. Ideally, you should visit Chequerboard in stormy weather. On any day the jagged effect of the rocks against sky and sea is dramatic but never more so than when the winds are high. Then the waves smash over the rocks, filling the squares with spray and pools of water. On calm, sunny days in spring and summer, it's a good vantage point for watching longtails swoop and soar.

Once through the gate, you have a short but steep climb up the cliff to Spanish Rock where you will find cast in bronze the initials of a sailor and the date 1543. These initials were once thought to be "TFC" and were attributed to a Spanish explorer named Theodore Fernando Camelo. These days perhaps we should call this area "Portuguese Rock" instead, since it's now believed that the inscriptions stand for Rex Portugaliae (King of Portugal) and for the Portuguese cross. No one is absolutely sure, but is seems likely that some shipwrecked survivor carved them while watching out for a sail from the cliff top.

Before you reach the bronze cast, notice a cavern on your right that is open to the sea. It's called Jeffrey's Hole. Why? Well, according to William Zuill in his *Bermuda Journey*, Jeffrey was a runaway slave who hid in this cave for a month. At first, his "master" thought that he had escaped by ship but eventually noticed that a 15-year-old female slave often disappeared at sunset with a package under her arm. He followed her and the next day found the cave with Jeffrey fast asleep inside. When did this happen? No one seems to know; the story is part of oral tradition.

Once you descend from Spanish Rock, you'll follow the path through more woodland. You'll notice in this area particularly lots of dead casuarinas and logs scattered throughout. Hurricane Emily in 1987 was mainly responsible for these, although subsequent storms have also left their effects. Why haven't we cleared them away? Well, dead trees also have their part to play in the ecological balance. Where there's natural decay, there's also compost, which will help to fertilize the soil.

Eventually, you'll come to an open area, with Spittal Pond still on your left and clumps of "Green Grow the Rushes O" on the edge of it. Take a moment to gaze at the pond and the bird life. A bright pink flamingo particularly likes this part of the reserve. Should it stretch its massive wings, you'll see that they're edged in dramatic black.

Cross the low wooden bridge across the water, and eventually you'll come to the eastern entrance that also has a car park. If you want to avoid returning by road, then turn left and left again. This time the pond will be on your left and you'll be following a pathway that runs parallel with South Road. You'll pass a fallow field. Look out for clumps of wire weed and wild lantana (sage). Walk fast and the whole excursion should take about a half-hour. But there's so much to appreciate in this 34-acre reserve, you'd be wise to allow at least a couple of hours.

Devonshire Parish

The Arboretum
Montpellier Rd., off Middle Rd.

Before 1987, the Arboretum had more of an overgrown, heavily wooded effect. However, in September of that year, Hurricane Emily hit and was particularly vicious in this park. Many of the trees were decimated. New trees and shrubs have been planted since, but today these 22 acres are more manicured park than conserved natural area. The grass is kept short, and the trees are carefully spaced. Ornamental and fan palms tend to grow in clusters, while ficus trees, poinciana

and golden shower trees are also featured. Look out for Bermuda olivewood and black ebony trees, too.

As you enter the park (there's a small parking lot), you'll see ahead of you a small wooden gazebo where you can sit and agree with Jane Austen that, "To sit in the shade on a fine day, and look upon verdure, is the most perfect refreshment." Explore further, and you'll find a small ornamental bridge with pools beneath it. We won't tell you exactly where; it's more fun to discover it for yourself.

Although there's plenty of open space, no games or sports are allowed in the Arboretum. Horse riding's OK, though, providing you stick to the pathways.

Palm Grove Gardens
South Rd.

"A garden is a lovesome thing, God wot!" Come to Palm Grove Gardens, and you'll know it too. They are actually the property of Sir David Gibbons who kindly allows visitors Monday through Thursday from 9 AM to 5 PM. (There's no entrance charge.) During those hours, he also allows wedding ceremonies to be held here, provided no more than nine people are present.

You will find palms — about 22 different species, some of which are rare in Bermuda. The Fiji and the European fan palms, for example, are growing here. But so are the endemic Bermuda palmettos together with the more common, albeit aristocratic, Cuban royal, queen and princess palms. Notice that the trunks of the Jamaican coconuts curve out from the ground in contrast to those of the spindle palms that stand straight and tall.

We love this property for its bower of gloriously yellow allamanda and its delightful garden ponds. You'll find two on the lower level. One has a Fiji palm set in the center while another has small stone ornaments and an ornamental bridge. You'll also find on this level a moongate and a little house, both covered with trimmed dark green foliage. Inside the house is a wishing well house where you can drop a penny and make a wish. Walk through the moongate and you get good fortune for free. But your penny will go to charity.

Walk up the hill and you'll see the pièce de résistance: a pond with a grassy Bermuda map

Photo: GIS

A view of the western end of the Island from Watford
Bridge in Somerset

set in the middle of it. Most of the year water lilies and hyacinths add vibrant blues and pinks to the overall effect. Interested in birds? At the top of the hill there are parrots in an aviary.

If you're driving from Hamilton you'll see Ariel Sands on the right side of South Road. Palm Grove is the next turning on the same side. Drive in and park your bike on the side of the narrow road. No restrooms are available.

Pembroke Parish

Par-la-Ville Park
Queen St., City of Hamilton

Parlez-vous Français? In case you don't, we'll translate this park's name as "By the Town." It actually was by the town in 1814, but these days it could more accurately be called "Through the Town," since it runs across from Queen Street to Par-la-Ville Road.

Adjacent to the park on Queen Street is the Bermuda National Library and, next to that, the Perot Post Office, which incidentally does not belong to Ross Perot, as some American visitors assume. Here's the deal: In the early

nineteenth century they were once the property of postmaster William Perot, famous for creating the first Bermudian postage stamp. We mention these buildings because Par-la-Ville Park was his back yard, so to speak. In fact, he infinitely preferred working in his garden to working at the post office. He tended his citrus groves and one year shipped as many as 40,000 boxes of oranges to Boston. But he also enjoyed planting the fruits, seeds and tropical plants that his sons sent him from foreign lands. In 1847, his son Adolphus sent him a seedling from Demarara. That seedling is now the mammoth rubber tree you can see just outside the library. Unfortunately the citrus trees disappeared.

These days Par-la-Ville is a favorite place of relaxation for locals. From your point of view, it's therefore an ideal place to people watch as well as to appreciate the flowers, vines and shrubs in the gardens. Lunch times, you'll see the business crowd take a break from their offices. Then you'll notice that business attire for men, in the summer, anyway, is often jacket, tie, Bermuda shorts and knee socks. And after 3 PM, you'll see schoolchildren, manifestly relieved to have escaped the classroom, dressed in neat school uniforms and making dramatic entrances. Boys and girls sit on low walls and indulge in gossipy conversations about who's going out with whom.

Other resting spots are benches set under tamarind trees and a bower in the center of the gardens. But sometimes it seems as if Par-la-Ville is on the move. People bustle along the pathways in a hurry to get to work. However, there's always time for the Bermudian greetings ritual: "Good morning, how are you doin'?"

Enter the park from Par-la-Ville Road and you'll go through the vine-covered moongate that was built in the 1920s. (See our Weddings chapter for information about moongates.) Restrooms (with running water) are next to the Queen Street entrance.

Pembroke Playground
Parson's Rd.

This is our most recently created park and we're very proud of it. That's because it's located in what used to be an unsightly dump. However, the playground is part of a larger park project yet to be completed. It has plenty of equipment for children. (See our Kidstuff chapter for more details.)

Spanish Point Park
Spanish Point Rd.

Why is this point called Spanish? Because according to William Zuill's *Bermuda Journey*, the *Sea Venture* settlers found evidence here of an encampment, probably used by Spanish survivors of a shipwreck.

It's well worth a visit because of the picturesque islets and bays that surround the headland. It's also worth it for the views. Look west and you can clearly see the curve of Southampton and Sandys Parishes and the Commissioner's House perched on a hill in Dockyard. Look east and you can see St. George's.

As you enter the park, you'll see Stovell

Bay on your left. New, smart boats are moored here, contrasting with the wreck of the old Floating Dock Bermuda that arrived in Bermuda in 1869 in all its glory. It was the largest floating dock in the world and the first to be towed across the Atlantic. Now the poor thing is rusting away. But the birds like it. Herons, kingfishers and gulls like to perch on the hulk.

Mangroves, by the way, surround this bay. Go farther into the park, and you'll see Nelson's Bay where the water is very blue and very shallow. The beach is rocky and ideal for children who like to clamber in the rock pools. Benches under casuarina trees overlook the water's expanse. Telephone, parking and restrooms are available at the entrance.

Victoria Park
Cedar Ave., City of Hamilton

This area did not always bear the illustrious name of Britain's monarch. Originally it was a playground for students of Mr. Deane's school nearby and so was called "Deane's Bottom." In the 1880s Hamilton Corporation turned it into a park, and in 1889 added an elegant bandstand to commemorate Queen Victoria's Jubilee that had happened two years before. The bandstand is still there, and we're all pleased about that.

Throughout the year, The Corporation and the Bank of N.T. Butterfield sponsor periodic outdoor concerts here. Usually each concert is dedicated to one type of music, such as jazz, rock 'n' roll or gospel. Weather allowing, a Christmas concert is also held, when the park rings out with carols and gospel music. The concerts usually start at about 6 PM and last for 2 hours. When dark falls, in the winter months, the bandstand and the trees are lit with white lights, adding magical ambiance to the festivities. We love these concerts because they give us an opportunity to come together as a community and to enjoy top entertainment from our local musicians. Local band, Legacy, is very popular, as is Shine Hayward, who plays a mean saxophone. Concerts are

INSIDERS' TIP

Most parks have trash cans. Please use them, and don't leave anything other than your footprint.

free. Check *The Royal Gazette* for notices of these concerts.

What can you see here during daylight? Victoria, as befits her namesake, has a more formal atmosphere than Par-la-Ville. A terrace leads down to a sunken garden where roses grow. A group of dwarf date palms stand together much like a family of kids posing awkwardly for a photograph. But there are tall palms, as well, and very royal they are too. Graceful mahogany trees add a touch of dark green to the landscape, while pink frangipani trees and plumbago bushes add pink, white and blue to the park's palette.

The tiny pink cottage at the edge of the park may make you think someone's living in it. Actually that's where the restrooms are, complete with sinks and running water. The main entrance to Victoria, by the way, is at the corner of Cedar Avenue and Victoria Street.

Sandys Parish

Heydon Trust
Heydon Drive (off Somerset Road)

If you want a bit of that peace, which passeth all understanding, we strongly recommend a visit to this 43-acre property that is a mixture of arable fields, citrus orchard and unspoiled woodland. During the 1970s it was donated to a Christian trust so that the land could be set aside for Christian purposes. As you drive towards Dockyard, you'll find Heydon Drive opposite Willowbank. (See Small Hotels chapter.) Go up it, noticing the copses, arable fields on your left, and continue until you see a chapel with a roughly hewn cedar cross hammered onto its western wall. Then you can park on the side of the road. The chapel is very small and very old. It dates back to at least 1620, if not earlier, and for centuries was a private home. It was consecrated as a chapel during the World War II but belongs to no particular denomination. Every day but Sunday, services are held at 7 AM and at 3 PM. Both services are sung in Gregorian chant. There are no Sunday services because the congregation does not want to compete with the parish churches. Outside on the south side of the chapel, you'll see another large cedar

cross overlooking the Great Sound. Set in a small rock garden planted with aloes, its situation is a little reminiscent of Calvary. If you're feeling contemplative, you can sit on the small stone bench behind it. Walk down the road, the cross on your right, and you'll come to a quarry garden framed by cedars, oleander and scrambling elephant ears. An empty cottage is there and also a royal poinciana which blossoms in June and early July. (See our Flora and Fauna Chapter for details of these plants and trees.) Follow the road to its end and you'll see it's a loop. You'll find yourself back on the road where you parked. With the western side of the church behind you, cross the road and you'll see a small area devoted to Bermuda roses. Behind that, a pathway edged with match-me-if-you-can, oleander and yellow lucky nut takes you to Heydon House, the property where the small community lives. They do not mind your visiting the citrus orchard and banana patch on your left. However, we do urge you to leave boom boxes behind and to respect Heydon's haven of tranquility.

Hog Bay Park
Middle Rd.

The Bermuda Government officially opened this park in March 1997. However, many of us have enjoyed exploring its pathways for years. So what will you find at Hog Bay? We think you'll experience Bermuda here as it used to be before the introduction of motorized traffic and technology. Here you'll find rocky slopes, thicket, hedgerows and irregular-shaped arable fields where potatoes and other vegetables are grown. You'll also find the remains of a lime kiln and of a buttery that, before the days of refrigeration, was essential for storing perishables. See the map on page xiv.

A number of different trails twist and turn around the fields, but if you keep southwest, eventually the ocean's expanse will appear magically before you. Climb the hill (known as Sugarloaf Hill), and you'll have magnificent views in all directions. Look west and across to the Lobster Flats and the outer reefs. You should be able to see the stakes and beacons marking the Hogfish Cut or channel. Look east

and northeast for a view of the Great Sound, the City of Hamilton and Spanish Point. Beyond are the North Shore and St. George's.

After you've taken in the vistas, clamber down the rocks to the water where you can enjoy rock pools and perhaps a swim at low tide. Most days the water's like glass. Walk in the evening, and you'll have a magnificent view of the sunset over the water. Hog Bay is Bermuda's third-largest park, and indeed, the mixture of landscape it provides gives us the illusion that it's larger than the 38 acres it actually contains. It's also a Mecca for bird watchers. More than 120 species have been recorded here, including orchard orioles, olive-sided flycatchers, purple finches and rough-legged hawks.

As you drive on Middle Road towards Dockyard, you'll find it on the left, just past the Maximart Supermarket. If you reach Somerset Bridge, you'll know you've gone too far. A small parking lot and portable toilets are available.

Scaur Hill Fort and Park
Somerset Rd.

If you're heading out to Dockyard, you'll see a steep turning to Scaur Hill on your right, a few minutes after you've driven over Somerset Bridge (the smallest drawbridge over the Atlantic, by the way). You'll find a parking lot at the top and the fort to your right. See the map on page xiv. This one was built by the British army in the 1860s, '70s and '80s to defend the Royal Naval Dockyard from possible American invasion. During the '80s, a deep ditch extending across Somerset Island was excavated and the fort was armed with 64-pounder guns on disappearing carriages.

In 1941, the enemy, of course, was not the United States at all. Indeed, the American 52nd Coast Artillery mounted two eight-inch railway guns here and, according to Lance Furbert II, nicknamed the fort "Cockroach Gulch." Let us not speculate why. Explore the top of the fort and you'll have wonderful views of the Great Sound. Look through the telescope (no charge) and you can see as far away as Fort St. Catherine and St. David's Lighthouse (see the Attractions chapter).

You'll also notice on the top of the fort a "Bermuda weather stone" that swings from a tripod and a notice with deep philosophical treatises. "If the stone's wet," it says, "it's raining. If it swings, it's windy." And so on. Believe it or not, some visitors actually read this notice and nod very wisely, especially when they get to the part: "When it jumps up and down there's an earthquake." Don't be one of them, will you? And bear in mind that if a blob of white appears on top of it, that does not mean it's snowing. It never snows in Bermuda. A bird is likely to be the culprit.

You can explore the moat, planted now with flowers and herbs, and walk down the ditch to the Great Sound. Parkland to the east of the fort is manicured — the grass is always kept short. It's rich in cedars both young and old, and palmettos, fiddlewood, loquat and cherry trees abound. As you follow the pathway, leaving the fort behind you, you'll see on your left a white stone construction that is a good example of one of our water catchments. And on your right, you'll see a turning off the pathway. Take it, and you'll find a bench where you can sit and muse on some of the Great Sound islands.

Continue along the pathway, and you come to an open field with a poinciana tree in the middle. Don't be surprised if you see a young child perching on one of its branches. Young children love that tree.

In this chapter we'll give you a potpourri of activities we've not mentioned elsewhere in our guide.

Recreations

To everything there is a season, and a time to every purpose. . . . Holiday season surely means a time to play. Of course for one person play can mean passive relaxation, while for another it can mean a strenuous workout.

In this chapter we'll give you a potpourri of activities we've not mentioned elsewhere in our guide. We'll categorize the recreations, and within each category we'll follow our usual geographical procedure for listings: east to west, parish by parish. However, be warned that some of the recreations we mention are centered in one or two parishes only. We'll be as specific as possible about prices, though they are all subject to change. Because of our island's size it's possible to explore the whole country within a couple of days, so we'll also include in this chapter information about hiring transport.

Cycle Liveries

If you've checked out our Let's Explain Bermuda and Getting Here, Around and Home chapters, you will already know that car rentals are illegal here. Motorcycle liveries, however, are not; it's perfectly possible to explore the island without being dependent on the buses. Actually, motorbikes are very important, even for those of us who may own a car. On the whole, men go to work on the bike while women lay claim to the car. As for our teenagers, acquiring a motorcycle is almost an initiation rite. Come that magic sixteenth birthday, the lucky among them will hit the road in a trail of glory, much to their parents' apprehension.

You can always distinguish between a tourist and a local rider. For one thing, the rented cycles always have red-lettered license plates. For another, local riders often manage to be ingenious about carrying enormous amounts of paraphernalia while driving: bags of groceries, bags of laundry and sometimes even the odd animal such as a dog or cat. At Christmas time you'll frequently see locals with Christmas trees precariously balanced over the bars. Please do not copy this behavior — unless you're very adroit it could lead to an accident. And for security reasons make sure your purse is zipped and not an easy target for snatchers. Bermuda is relatively crime-free, but we do have the occasional bag snatching. Also remember that in Bermuda it is mandatory to wear a helmet when riding on a motorcycle.

Normally, where driving is concerned, for many of our visitors right is right and left is wrong. Sorry, but in Bermuda left is definitely right (correct, that is). It's vital to remember that we drive on the left side of the road, and that at roundabouts we give way to the right. Actually when you hire a bike from one of our liveries, staff members will re-emphasize the rules of the road and make sure you are confident and stable on the bike. All the outlets we list have parking lots or training areas where you can practice before venturing out on our highways and byways. Staff will warn you not to drive too close to the curb and not to start your bike when facing a wall. They will also advise you not to try to walk your bike when the engine is running — bikes can have a nasty habit of running away from you.

All liveries will deliver bikes if you're staying near an area suitable for practicing. Pickup from your accommodation is always possible. What happens if your bike breaks down? Call the livery's number during operating hours, and the staff will arrange for a replacement to be delivered. If the breakdown happens at night, leave a message on the answering machine, then lock your bike securely and take a taxi. Frequently, liveries will reimburse taxi fares if a breakdown necessitates a cab ride.

Rates cover helmets, locks and third-party insurance. When we mention "daily rate," we mean the cost for 24 hours. Hire a bike at 10 AM, for example, and the daily rate lasts until 10 AM the following morning.

We give you a listing here of liveries that have locations other than in the hotels. Check out our various accommodations chapters for liveries operating at hotel sites; hotel staff will always be happy to make cycle arrangements for you. A few of these liveries also rent out pedal bikes. We strongly recommend you wear a helmet when riding a pedal bike, though they are not compulsory. The Railway Trail (see listing in this chapter) offers good places to pedal bike.

www.insiders.com

See this and many other **Insiders' Guide**° destinations online.

Visit us today!

St. George's Parish

Dowling's Cycles
26 Duke of York St., Town of St. George
• (441) 297-1614

In addition to this livery, Mr. Dowling also has one at St. George's Club and at Grotto Bay Beach Hotel and Tennis Club. He rents out a variety of bikes including Palio and Honda single and double scooters. Dowling's requires a refundable deposit of $20 plus a one-time payment of $15 for an insurance waiver. Rates are on a sliding scale: Hire a single-seat scooter, and you'll pay $38 (plus the insurance waiver and deposit) on the first day, and the rate will decrease day by day. By the sixth day your daily rate will be $12 from then on out. A double-seat scooter will cost $42 on the first day and from the sixth day will cost $14 a day.

St. George's Cycles
Water St., Town of St. George
• (441) 236-0839

For rates and information, check the Eve's Cycle's listing under Paget Parish.

Smiths Parish

Wheels Cycles (Devil's Hole) Ltd.
Harrington Sound • (441) 293-1280

For rates and information, check the Pembroke Wheels listing.

Pembroke Parish

Oleander Cycles Ltd.
15 Gorham Rd., Hamilton
• (441) 295-0919

Oleander is open 8:30 AM to 5 PM every day, including public holidays. See the Paget listing for rates and more information.

Wheels Cycles (Astwood) Ltd.
117 Front St., Hamilton
• (441) 292-2245

Wheels Cycles (Hamilton) Ltd.
13 Dundonald St., Hamilton
• (441) 295-0112

Actually Wheels, the island's largest livery, has rental shops all over the island. Wheels has liveries in Marriott Castle Harbour and the Southampton Princess Hotels (see our Resort Hotels chapter). This establishment uses Peugeot vehicles, so 90 percent of the bikes are scooters. In addition they have some Honda City Expresses. Wheels requires payment by credit card — that way you don't have to pay a deposit. For any bike you hire, on the first day you pay a one-time repair waiver of $15. Rates work on a sliding system. For a single-seat scooter you'll pay $33 (plus the repair waiver) on the first day, with the rate decreasing day by day. By the sixth day your daily rate will be $9 thereafter. Want a bicycle made for two? The starting rate for double-

INSIDERS' TIP

Pick up the free *Bermuda Railway Trail Walking Guide* **from your hotel or from the visitors service bureaus in St. George's or Hamilton. It has a map showing the different trail sections from Sandys to St. George's Parishes and includes some railway history and descriptions of points of interest.**

seaters is $42 plus the waiver. On day seven and thereafter, the daily rate is down to $17. Call for special group rates.

Wheels also rents mountain bikes for those who want a more energetic form of transportation. On day one you pay a one-time $10 repair waiver plus $10 rent. The daily rate is usually $10. However, rent the bike for more than two weeks, and Wheels will work out a special deal. These locations are open 8:30 AM to 5:30 PM every day, including public holidays.

Paget Parish

Eve Cycles Ltd.
114 Middle Rd.
• (441) 236-6247
Eve Cycles offers luxury double-seat Scarabeo scooters for hire. On day one, you pay a one-time third-party insurance rate of $15, plus $60. Rates decrease daily until the eighth day, when you pay a daily rate of $25 thereafter. Hire a Honda City Express (double-seat scooter), and the rates are cheaper. For the Honda, you'll pay $42 plus the $15 insurance on day one, then the rate decrease until the eighth day when you pay a daily rate of $14 thereafter. A single-seat electric moped starts at $33 plus insurance and by the eighth day costs $10 every day thereafter. Use your credit card, and you pay no deposit. Otherwise a $20 refundable deposit is required. Eve Cycles is open 8 AM to 5:30 PM every day, including public holidays.

Oleander Cycles Ltd.
6 Valley Rd.
• (441) 236-5235
Oleander Cycles offers Address and Palio scooters for hire. A refundable $20 deposit is required, plus a one-time repairs waiver payment of $15. For a single-seat scooter, on day one you pay $33; the rate decreases every day until the eighth day when you pay a rate of $12. For a double-seat scooter the daily rate starts at $42 and by the eighth day goes down to $15 a day. Credit cards are OK, and Oleander is open from 8:30 AM to 5:30 PM every day, including public holidays, except Christmas Day.

Southampton Parish

Oleander Cycles Ltd.
8 Middle Rd. • (441) 234-0629
See the previous Paget listing for rates and information about motorcycles. This Oleander branch also offers pedal bikes for hire. Rates? $10 a day. The livery is open 8:30 AM to 5:30 PM every day, including public holidays.

Sandys Parish

Oleander Cycles Ltd.
Bldg. 18, Royal Naval Dockyard
• (441) 234-2764
Again, refer to the Paget listing for rates and information about motorcycle rental. This branch of Oleander Cycles is open 8:30 AM to 5:30 PM every day from April to October, including public holidays, except Christmas Day.

Bermuda's End-to-End Railway Trail

As you read in our History chapter, Bermuda did have an active railway from 1931 to 1946. In 1984 the government decided to designate the old railway lands as a path and bridle way to be used mainly for walkers and pedal cyclists. As a result, it's possible to follow the old train line from St. George's to Somerset, with the exception of the 3-mile section in and around the City of Hamilton that was replaced by roads.

Annual Charity Walk

The first Saturday of every May, the Bermuda End-to-End Committee organizes a pre-pledged island end-to-end charity walk, with funds going to four local charities. What do we mean by "pre-pledged"? Walkers ask friends and admirers of their fortitude to pay them money for taking part. In 1997 the minimum pledge for entry was $20 — if your friends agreed to pay $5 each, you'd need four supporters.

The walk starts at 8 AM in King's Square in the Town of St. George and ends in Royal

Naval Dockyard in Sandys. How long does it take to walk the island end to end? Depending on your pace, anywhere between six and eight hours. Light refreshments at stops along the route will keep you energized. Overseas visitors are absolutely welcome. Call Karon Wolffe at (441) 299-8821 for information on the minimum pledge required and registration instruction. If a 26-mile walk intimidates you, then try the 15-mile alternative that starts at Albuoy's Point in the City of Hamilton at 11 AM and also ends at Dockyard. (For more information, see our Annual Events and Festivals chapter.)

Be a Trail Blazer

Of course, during the rest of the year you don't have to walk the whole Railway Trail. You can do as we often do: Drive to a small section, park your motorcycle and start your walk. Or alternatively, ride your pedal bike to and along the trail. You'll know you're on the right track, literally, when you notice brown "Railway Trail" signs. There are a few areas where riding a motorcycle on the trail is possible, but we don't advise it. Part of the Railway Trail's charm is the quiet. Motorized traffic blocks out the sounds of breezes, birds and insects. Besides, some of the pathways are so narrow that motorbikes could endanger those of us who want to stroll.

So what's the trail like? It offers a blend of Bermuda's scenery from ocean view to shady thicket; from arable fields to private gardens and properties; from open spaces to tunnels of greenery. The railway often hugged the shoreline and at various points crossed the ocean on trestle bridges. There were 33 bridges in all, 16 of which extended over water. Vestiges of those bridges can still be seen. If you notice concrete pillars emerging from the water, chances are they're old bridge supports. Pylons in Flat's Inlet in Smiths Parish are good examples.

If you're into flowers and birds, you'll see many of the ones we mention in our Parks and Conservation and Flora and Fauna chapters. By the way, the trail is not completely continuous; it's often interrupted by a main or tribe road. But the signs will show you how to

pick up the trail again. Also, the trail often criss-crosses paths that lead to attractions, such as the Martello Tower in St. George's Parish or Fort Scaur in Sandys. Be sure to check our Attractions chapter for more on these.

A word about safety. On the whole Bermuda is relatively crime-free, but we're not perfect. We advise women not to walk alone, particularly after dark, and to make sure their purses are securely zipped.

Guided Walking Tours

As of 1998 a number of escorted walking tours became available. They are ideal for people who like a blend of exercise plus cultural and or environmental information. Here we tell you about individuals or couples who will be happy to take you to places that you might not otherwise hear about. If you're interested in history, architecture and antiques then call Tim Rogers of Bermuda's Lectures and Tours at (441) 234-4082. He combines his 90-minute tour with a slide talk. He's willing to take you at anytime and charges $15 per person. Every Thursday from 8:45 to 11:30 AM, Marlee Robinson at (441) 295-9428 will escort you round the National Gallery in Hamilton and offer lots of info about Hamilton's art, architecture and galleries. Cost? $35 per person. If you're a keen photographer then calling Carla Bean and Tamell Simons of Native Adventures, (441)297-2957, is an absolute must. Mondays through Fridays from 7 AM to 1 PM they will take you on photographic nature walks to their own secret places. The excursions include a Bermuda-style lunch either on location or in a restaurant. They'll take a maximum of six and a minimum of two persons. Cost is $100 per person. Jo Cook of Out & About Bermuda also offers country walks. Call her at (441) 295-2595 and she'll arrange to meet you at any mutually convenient time. Her walks last about two and a half hours, and cost $20 per person, $30 per couple and $10 each for accompanied children between the ages of 6 and 16. As she puts it, she likes to share her knowledge of, and delight in, Bermuda's scenery. Check the Kidstuff chapter for info about the Gumba Trail and Outdoor Museum at (441) 293-7330.

Spas and Health and Fitness Centers

Worried that a holiday will relax you so much you'll wind up out of shape? Check out our Resort Hotels, Cottage Colonies and Small Hotels chapters, and you'll see that many lodging locations have exercise rooms for guests plus spa and beauty facilities. Here we'll give you a sampling of other health clubs that are used by locals but that also welcome visitors. Some offer exercise only, while others have massage and beauty facilities as well.

Pembroke Parish

The Athletic Club
Cedarparkade, Washington St., Hamilton
• **(441) 295-6140**

This facility offers full use of its gym, which is equipped with treadmills, StairMasters, free weights and other machines designed to bend you into shape. Locals pay a one-time fee of $175 plus $108 a month for use of facilities and aerobic classes. Overseas visitors are welcome. The cost is $17 a day for use of the gym plus $10 for an aerobics class. Facilities include whirlpools, saunas and a steam room. Feel like a massage? A one-hour session is $60; a half-hour costs $40. A personal physical assessment is $40. The Athletic Club is open 6 AM to 9 PM Monday to Friday, 8 AM to 4 PM on Saturdays and 8 AM to 2 PM Sundays.

Images Ltd.
Belvedere Bldg., 69 Pitts Bay Rd.
• **(441) 295-0615, (441) 295-0616**

Come to Images to enjoy a variety of hair and beauty treatments for very reasonable rates — reasonable for Bermuda, that is. A wash, haircut and blow-dry cost $44, a manicure costs $17 and a pedicure is $26. A full massage comes at $55 for an hour while a half-hour back massage is $35.

Facials, by the way, are a particularly good value ($65 for 75 to 90 minutes) since they involve massage of the hands and feet as well as the face, neck and shoulders. You bite your nails? Worry not. For $70 you can acquire a new set of acrylics. Tourists are welcome and spur-of-the-moment appointments are nearly always possible.

Magnum Power Force Gym
119 Front St., Hamilton
• **(441) 292-7007**

Believe it or not, owners and managers Ron and Karen really are called Magnum. Ron is Bermuda's only professional bodybuilder and wrestler. Locals pay a yearly membership of $700, or $340 for four months. Overseas visitors are welcome and pay $15 a day. If they come with a member, it's only $10. Certified trainers will help out with the cardio equipment, machines and weights. Magnum Power Force Gym is open 6 AM to 8:30 PM Monday to Friday and 9 AM to 3 PM on Saturdays and Sundays.

The Olympic Club
12 Dundonald St., Hamilton
• **(441) 292-4095**

This one is aptly named since it's said to be home to Bermuda's major athletes. Partners and managers are Nick Jones and Scott Stallard, a well-known local photographer. In addition to a wide range of equipment, including weights, life cycles, wind racers and StairMasters, the club offers aerobics classes. The Olympic is the only center offering Schwinn Spinning facilities and classes. Unfamiliar with Schwinn Spinning? It involves riding a stationary bicycle that simulates all the challenges you could face in the outdoors, including uphill climbs and jumps. Coaches at the club offer instruction, and you might find it to be an invigorating cardiovascular workout.

INSIDERS' TIP

Kindley Playing Fields, once operated by the base in St. David's, are now open to the public. Areas are suitable for in-line skating and bicycling.

Twenty-four-hour notice is required for Spinning. Saunas and showers are available. Visitors pay $12 a day; locals pay an initial fee of $90, then can pay $35 a week or $75 a month. The Olympic Club doesn't take credit cards. It is open 6 AM to 9 PM Monday to Thursday, 6 AM to 8 PM Friday, 9 AM to 6 PM Saturday and 9 AM to noon on Sunday.

Total Fitness Center
24 Brunswick St., Hamilton
• (441) 295-0087

This center offers an aerobics program as well as a wide range of equipment, including stair-climbers, Cybex cycles, treadmills and free weights. Overseas visitors are welcome and pay $15 per day. The fee includes aerobics, towel service and use of the whirlpool. Aerobics classes run Monday through Friday at the following times: 7 to 8 AM, 12:15 to 1 PM, 5:30 to 6:45 PM and 6:45 to 7:30 PM. On Saturday a class is held from 9:30 to 11 AM. On Sunday? Even the super healthy-minded deserve a lie-in. An hour-long class starts at 10:30 AM. Visitors can get a personal fitness assessment for $80.

Total Fitness can pamper as well. They offer all sorts of body treatments, facials and massages, together with beauty treatments such as manicures, pedicures and waxing. Costs vary, of course. An hour's aromatherapy face and body massage costs $70, while a pedicure costs $30. Call to make an appointment. The facility is open from 6 AM to 9 PM Monday to Friday and 8 AM to 4 PM Saturday and Sunday.

Healthy fat-free food is on hand at the Prince Deli (open Monday through Friday from 8 AM to 4 PM). Salads, burgers and soups are available, together with sodas, juices and sports drinks. You should be able to lunch for under $10.

Horseback Riding

Ian Fleming once said: "A horse is dangerous at both ends and uncomfortable in the middle." It's a good thing he didn't live in Bermuda before 1946, when horses were a vital means of transportation. These days horse riding, of course, is recreational rather than necessary. Here we list two stables that offer guided trail rides. Visitors can rest assured that the horses are not nearly as dangerous as Fleming might have feared. In addition, we include a listing for a wonderful facility that offers riding for adults and children confined to wheelchairs or who have special needs.

Warwick Parish

Spicelands Riding Centre Ltd.
50 Middle Rd. • (441) 238-8212

Spicelands is famous for its daily breakfast rides that take you along beach trails overlooking the South Shore beaches between Warwick Long Bay and Horseshoe Bay (see our Beaches chapter). The breakfast ride lasts 90 minutes and costs $50 per person. On your return you get a light continental breakfast. Starting time is 6:45 AM. A bit early for you? Well, early birds get to enjoy the coolest time of day, particularly in the summer months.

Monday through Friday the stable also offers one-hour rides, again on the South Shore, for $37.50 per person. Starting times are 10 and 11:30 AM and 3 PM. From May through September a ride is also offered from 6 to 7 PM. You should arrive at least a half-hour early so staff can instruct you. Children older than 10 are welcome, but those younger than 16 must be accompanied by an adult. Because tours involve as many as 16 horses, the rides are strictly walking only. Hats are available for everyone but mandatory only for riders younger than 18.

Bermuda Riding for the Disabled
WindReach Recreational Village, 5 Wind Reach Ln. (off Spice Hill)
• (441) 238-7433

Actually the telephone number above spells RIDE. This equestrian facility opened in December 1996, and we're so glad it did. It provides a permanent riding location for adults and children confined to wheelchairs or with other special needs. The stable has two paddocks where visitors can ride in a lesson format. Volunteers are on hand —sometimes as many as three per rider might be necessary. Bermuda residents have to have a certificate from a doctor saying that it's safe for them to ride. Overseas special-needs visitors are very

Photo: GIS

Plenty of opportunities to find some of the most breathtaking snorkeling anywhere.

welcome, if space permits. They should, however, have some prior riding experience. Call Moira Benbow, equestrian director, to discuss the requirements. There are just seven horses, so it's wise to book as soon as possible. Lessons take place Monday through Friday between 9:30 AM and 3 PM. On Saturday they're available from 9:30 AM to noon. Because WindReach is a registered charity, lessons are free. However, donations are always welcome. The facility is completely wheelchair-accessible. (See the subsequent WindReach listing in this chapter for information about other facilities in this village.)

Other Recreational Sports

Read our Spectator Sports chapter, and you'll see that Bermuda residents can enjoy a wide variety of games people play. Read our Golf chapter, and you'll see that we have more golf courses per square mile than any other country in the world. Here we will talk about sports and/or facilities that we haven't mentioned elsewhere.

Before we start, though, a word about swimming. At present we do not have a public swimming pool where swimmers can come for recreational purposes. True, there's a public swimming pool on the grounds of Saltus Grammar School, Pembroke, but this is used by schools and clubs for competitive swimming. Chances are if you're staying in a hotel, your accommodation will have its own pool (see our accommodations chapters). How do locals manage without a public pool? Well, many have private swimming pools, and the rest of us are happy to dip in the sea. Check our Beaches chapter for ocean swimming choices.

What a Racquet

Badminton

The Bermuda Athletic Association Gymnasium
Woodlands Rd., Pembroke Parish
• **(441) 236-7210**

You can play badminton here year-round on Tuesdays and Thursdays from 7:30 PM.

Visitors are welcome and pay a $5 per evening fee. The number above belongs to Junior Durrant, president of the badminton association. Call him for booking information. Shuttlecocks are provided, but only a limited number of racquets are available. There's no dress code, but you should wear rubber-soled shoes.

Squash

Bermuda Squash Racquets Association
Middle Rd., Devonshire Parish
• **(441) 292-6881**

Visitors are welcome to play as guests at this club. Fees are $10 per person for 40 minutes on a court. The staff is available to assist from 11 AM to 2 PM and from 4 to 10 PM Monday through Friday. Call at least a week in advance to book a court. This club holds a number of tournaments throughout the year for players of every level of ability.

Tennis

Check our Spectator Sports chapter for information on tournaments and tennis events to take in. Many hotels and all of the cottage colonies have tennis courts (see our accommodations chapters), and here are two public tennis facilities that welcome overseas visitors. Note that proper dress for the game in Bermuda consists of tops and shorts (or dresses or skirts) specifically designed for tennis. The all-white rule is not so rigidly enforced as it was in the past.

Kindley Tennis Courts
Clearwater Beach Rd., St. David's, St. George's Parish • **(441) 293-5791**

Originally these four courts belonged to the American military base. Now that the base has departed, residents and visitors can use the courts for $4 per person per hour (credit cards are not accepted). Call the above number for a court. You might want to combine a tennis game with a visit to Clearwater Beach (see our Beaches chapter). Changing rooms and showers are available. Tennis shoes and tennis dress code are mandatory. The courts are open from 10 AM to 7:30 PM Monday through Friday and 9 AM to 7:30 PM on Saturday and Sunday.

Tennis Stadium
2 Marsh Folly Rd., Pembroke Parish
• **(441) 292-0105**

Book one of the eight courts by calling two days in advance. During daylight, you pay $8 per person per hour; after dark, it's $16 an hour (no credit cards, please). Changing rooms and showers are available. Tennis shoes and tennis dress code are mandatory. The stadium is open 8 AM to 10 PM Monday through Friday and 8 AM to sunset on weekends and holidays.

Martial Arts

Martial Arts have become very popular in Bermuda among children and adults alike. They are seen not only as a means of self defense but also as a way of maintaining physical and mental health. Students generally pay a monthly fee instead of by the lesson. Here we give you a sampling of schools available and their fees. Prices are subject to change.

Bermuda Karate Institute
57 King Street, Hamilton
• **(441) 292-2157**

Skipper Ingham founded this institute in 1970. He focuses on Okinawan and Japanese Goju but also incorporates contemporary tournament fighting, ippon kumite (self-defense), judo, jujitsu and kibudo. O-Sensei Skipper received his rank from Grandpatriarch Peter Urban and in 1996, when he visited Okinawa, was certified 6 dan in Okinawan Goju by Grandmaster Eichi Miyazato. He was also assistant coach of the Trans World Oil Karate

---

INSIDERS' TIP

A sudden rain shower after a spell of dry weather can make roads very slippery. When coming to a halt on your motorcycle, be careful not to use right and left brakes simultaneously. That way you'll decrease your chances of skidding.

Team from 1987 to 1990. Classes are available throughout the year except on public holidays. Adults pay $65 a month, youth aged 12 to 16 pay $55 and children aged 5 to 11 pay $50. Private lessons are also available. Call for details.

Bermuda Sanuces and Harto Ryo Jiujitsu
Victor Scott Primary School, 4, Glebe Rd., Pembroke • (441) 292-4740

Arnold Allen was inducted into the Martial Arts Hall of Fame in March 1998 after nearly 30 years of experience and commitment. He offers classes in karate, jujitsu, personal self-defense and streetology. Adult classes run from 7:15 to 9 PM four times a week and cost $65 a month. On Saturdays from 12:15 to 2:15 PM, he offers classes for kids incorporating karate, judo and jiujitsu. Cost is $35 a month.

Bermuda Wing Chun Kung Fu Academy
St. Augustine Church, St. Augustine Hill, Pembroke • (441) 292-9827

Sifu Delroy Flood teaches students not to fight force to force. Instead they learn to use their opponents' strength against them. He offers practical and simple instruction that focuses on practicing direct economy of emotion. This art, he says was invented by a Buddhist nun some 300 years ago. He offers beginners' classes every Tuesday and Thursday from 6:30 to 7:40 PM and intermediate to advanced classes on the same days from 7:45 to 9:15 PM. In addition on Saturday, he offers a children's class from 10:30 to noon and a general class from noon to 1:15 PM. Cost is $60 a week.

Wing Lam Kung Fu School Bermuda
Corner of Robert's Ave. and Palmetto Rd., Pembroke
• (441) 236-6792

Trained instructors teach Northern Shaolin Kung Fu here. Classes for adults are held Mondays, Wednesdays and Fridays from 6:30 PM to 8:30 PM. Juniors can join adults every Monday from 6:30 PM to 7:30 PM only. Kids can attend classes on Wednesdays and Fridays from 5:30 PM to 6:30 PM. Cost is $50 per month. On Saturdays students can attend classes from 10:30 PM to noon for $40 a month. In Taichi Chaun, breathing and exercise are important for maintaining health as well as for practicing self-defense.

Bermuda Aikikai Aikido
Samaritans Hall, Cobb's Hill, Warwick
• (441) 236-2367

Collins Smith is a fourth degree teacher and is a black belt. Take Aikido, he says, and life changes for you. You suffer less stress and experience better coordination. He offers four adult classes on Monday, Tuesday, Wednesday and Thursday from 6:45 to 8 PM. Classes also run Saturdays from 9 to 10 AM (beginners), 10:15 to 11:15 AM (advanced) and 11:30 AM to 12:30 PM (intermediate). Students pay a one time initial fee of $100, and then $50 a month. Kids pay $40 a month.

Spring Break Sports

Check out our Annual Events and Festivals chapter for information about the Department of Tourism's sports program for college students on holiday here during March.

Bored? Try Board Games

Pembroke Parish

Bermuda Chess Association
Chamber of Commerce, Front St., Hamilton • (441) 238-2313

Visitors are welcome to play a game of chess here every Tuesday at 7:45 PM. Casual games are free; tournament play will cost you $5 per evening. In January or February, the Invitational Grand Master Tournament is held at Mermaid Beach. In addition, at the beginning of February, an international Swiss tournament is held at one of our major hotels. Regular grand master visitors are Julian Hodgson and Nick deFirmian.

Scrabble Club
Bermuda Public Services Association Headquarters, Cedar Ave.
• (441) 238-3727

From January to May and September to

November, you can play Scrabble at 8 PM on the last Saturday of each month. You need to be aware that British spelling is the official usage in Bermuda. We all know that Scrabble war can break out between American and British spellers, resulting in declarations of independence on both sides. In fact, in those situations Scrabble can more accurately be called "squabble." Mrs. Florenz Maxwell, president of the club, has resolved the problem diplomatically. Both spelling systems are allowed, and the Official Scrabble Words dictionary is always on hand. Visitors pay $3 per person per game. Call to confirm games.

Have a Ball Bowling

Warwick Parish

Warwick Lanes
47 Middle Rd. • (441) 236-5290

Why not get bowled over by a night of inexpensive fun for the family? Warwick Lanes is home to the Bermuda Bowling Club. Membership for adults is $45 a year, and it allows cheaper games. However, non-members are welcome. Adults pay $3.50 per person per game; children pay $2.25. Proper bowling shoes are a must — rent them for $1.25 a pair. While waiting on your pins you can have a chicken sandwich or hamburger in the restaurant or enjoy a drink from the bar. In September 1998, the club went wild because Bermudians Antoine Jones and Conrad Lister won silver medals at the Commonwealth Games in Kuala Lumpur. Warwick Lanes is open 6 PM to midnight Monday through Saturday and 3 PM to midnight Sunday. Call to book games.

Bridging the Gap

Paget Parish

Bermuda Bridge Club
7 Pomander Rd. • (441) 238-1332

Overseas visitors are welcome to play at this beautiful clubhouse. Open duplicate games are played Mondays at 7:30 PM, Wednesdays at 9:30 AM and Fridays at 8 PM. Novice (0-20 and 20-90) master points games

are held Wednesdays at 7 PM. And most afternoons, depending on demand, rubber bridge is played at 2 PM. Table fees are $8 a head. Visitors should call three or four days in advance to be sure of space. The clubhouse has a bar, and free coffee and tea are served.

You might like to know that the World Team Championship for the Bermuda Bowl, one of the most coveted prizes in international bridge, will be held in the year 2000 from January 8 to 22 at the Southampton Princess, Southampton Parish. Actually, this will be a 50th anniversary for the World Team of Four Bridge Championship, which was held in Bermuda in 1950. The silver jubilee was also held here in 1975.

Recreational Opportunities for the Physically Challenged

WindReach Recreational Village
5 Wind Reach Ln. (off Spice Hill)
• (441) 238-2469

This village was founded by Alexander Mitchell and is the second project he has undertaken for people with disabilities. In 1989 he opened a farm in Ontario, Canada, to allow people of all ages and with all sorts of special challenges to enjoy the satisfaction of farming and working with animals. Since Mitchell himself has cerebral palsy, he knows firsthand the frustration of being excluded from activities that can, in fact, be possible. Often, he says, participation simply depends on self-confidence.

The village is, at the time of writing, in a developmental stage. It will have a two-story activity center with an elevator and rooms for meetings, educational events and craft activities. It already has a petting zoo that is accessible to everyone. Meet the donkey, Eeyore, who's more stubborn than sulky; he's in no way been mistreated. Also meet Tilly and Annie, two miniature horses, and Magic, a very fetching gray-haired goat. Other animals include rabbits, rats (very small pretty rats, we promise, called Brie and Gouda) and a guinea pig.

A square-foot gardening project is under

way, which will allow both children and adults in wheelchairs as well as others to grow vegetables, herbs and flowers. On the roof of the petting zoo is a meeting area with a bench for picnics. Want to see whales in April? A telescope with views of the South and North shores will make it possible. Sensory trails, all wheelchair-accessible, will introduce visitors to Bermuda's sounds and smells as well as sights. You'll be able to smell the aromatic fragrance of our spice trees, for example, or the perfume of Bermuda's cedar. Benches at strategic points ensure that people can rest or picnic.

In addition, WindReach has a fantastic play center with a sandbox, swings, slides, hammocks and a seesaw and trampoline. A water pump makes for fun but also for arm-muscle toning. The pièce de resistance is a tree house.

Children in wheelchairs don't often get the opportunity to feel the sensation of being high up: This tree house is easily reached by wheelchair. Volunteers will be on hand to help.

A campsite allows visitors to have bonfires and singalongs. Eventually there will be "tebins" — a cross between a tent and a cabin — for overnight camping. All bathrooms, showers and telephones are easily accessible. There's no entrance fee, but since WindReach is a registered charity, donations, of course, are welcome. Overseas visitors with special needs are very welcome. Call Ann E. Lindroth, activity director, for information and to set a time to visit. See the previous listing in this chapter for the Bermuda Riding for the Disabled facility. It shares this location and works in partnership with WindReach, but the two establishments are autonomous.

Check out the sports section of *The Royal Gazette*, and you'll see the range of sports Bermuda has to offer. You'll also see that we're not only interested in the international sports scene, but we also contribute to it.

Spectator Sports

We may be a small country, but anyone with a mind to do so can certainly lead a sporting life. Check out the sports section of *The Royal Gazette*, and you'll see the range of sports Bermuda has to offer. You'll also see that we're not only interested in the international sports scene, but we also contribute to it. Bermudian soccer player Kyle Lightbourne, for instance, was the top goal scorer in 1997 for Walsall, a Second Division club in the U.K., and is now a prominent player for Stoke City.

The first Bermudian to play in a British league was Clyde Best, who played for West Ham (British First Division) in the early '70s. And since 1998 Shawn Goater has been playing for Manchester City (British Second Division). Bermudian triple jumper Brian Wellman, a former world indoor gold medalist, copped a silver medal at the World Outdoor Championships in 1995.

International events are sometimes hosted in Bermuda. In 1994, '95 and '96, the Mid Ocean Club (see our Golf chapter) hosted the Merrill Lynch Shoot-Out championship. In October 1997 and 1998 the club welcomed the Gillette Championship Challenge, an event that brings in 24 of the world's top golfers — eight are chosen from the PGA tour, eight from the LPGA tour and eight from the Senior PGA tour. Gillette champions for 1998 were Lee Trevino, Jim Furyk and Michelle McGann. The Gillette will also happen in 1999. Also in 1997 and 1998, the Southampton Princess Resort Hotel hosted the Davis Cup tennis matches for American Zones III and IV.

Dr. Gerard Bean, trustee in charge of sports and special events for the National Sports Centre, has high hopes that more international

events will be lured to Bermuda. Bean says by the year 2000 the Centre will have track and field facilities for a large range of sports, including cricket, soccer and hockey, and an Olympic-size swimming pool. Work on the facility is in progress.

In this chapter, we've chosen to document the spectator sports that we feel are the most popular. Having said that, we have, however, omitted sailing races that are very much part of our heritage. You'll find information about our yachting and fitted dinghy racing in the Yachting and Marinas chapter. Check our Annual Events and Festivals chapter for various golf tournaments. In some cases, we'll give a little of the history behind a sport, and, of course, we'll tell you what major events for each sport are held during the year. If we don't mention specific dates and months, it means they were not set in time for our publishing date. If there's an admission charge for watching, we'll note that as well. For information on sports not mentioned here, be sure to check our Recreations chapter.

Football

So what kind of football are we talking about? The kind that means players have to wear intergalactic headgear? No. In Bermuda, football definitely means soccer, the game where fancy footwork is essential and where, except for the goalkeeper, it's no hands allowed. Players do it for kicks.

Believe it or not, the first recorded game of football happened in England in the year 217 (at that time, however, the game consisted of about 300 players a side, and there were no rules). Approximately 17 centuries later, the British Army and Navy brought the game with them to Bermuda. In 1928 it became a fully organized sport and soon became very popular, with a variety of clubs being formed throughout the parishes.

Footnotes on Bermuda's Top Sport

David Sabir, general secretary of the Bermuda Football Association (BFA), says that football is without question the No. 1 sport on the island. He says more than 2,000 people play football weekly. Bermuda now has 22 clubs that are affiliated members of the BFA.

Do the clubs represent the parishes? Well, some of them include parish names in their titles. We have, for example, the Devonshire Colts (who, to complicate things further, do not play in Devonshire) and the Pembroke Hamilton Club. However, given that we have just nine parishes, you can see that each parish has more than one club. So, to give more examples, there's the Vasco de Gama Club in Pembroke and the Devonshire Recreation Club. Some teams are named after businesses who sponsor them; others take their titles from regional areas in Bermuda. There's the Robin Hood Team (Robin Hood being the name of a Pembroke pub), the Somerset Cricket Club (they play cricket and football) and the North Village Club. Schools are involved too — the Bermuda School Sports Federation is affiliated with the BFA.

There are several divisions: the First Senior Men's, the Alliance (with two subdivisions composed of reserve players for the First Senior Men's), the Second and the Commercial, which also has two subdivisions and is made up of veteran players. In addition, there's the Women's League and the Shell Youth League for players ages 8 through 21. There are at least five women's clubs such as the Rude Girls (of course they're not really rude) and the Dandy Stars.

Throughout the season, September to May, games are held every Saturday and Sunday at 12 venues across the island, such as White Hill in Somerset or St. John's Field in Pembroke. Cup games and finals tend to be held in the National Stadium at Prospect in Devonshire. Admission for regular games is $5, and it's $8 for cup games. Cup matches to watch for are the Charity Cup, which kicks off the season at the beginning of September; the Martonmere Cup, named after former governor Lord Martonmere; and the Dudley Eve Trophy, which is fought for during the Christmas break from December 15 until New Year's Day. All the teams have a go in the FA Cup. Games and venues are always announced in *The Royal Gazette*.

Supporters can get emotional, Sabir explains. "Agony when there's defeat; celebration when there's victory." You don't, however, get the singing and the chanting that you'd hear in other countries. No betting either. What makes spectators support one club over another? Sometimes the support is simply territorial — the fans live close to the club. But often support is born from family ties with one particular club that might go back for generations.

What about the international scene? "We really want to push that," Sabir says. Since 1962, the BFA has been a member of Concacaf (Confederation of North Central and Caribbean Football Association) and an affiliate of FIFA (the Federation of International Football Associations.) "These memberships put us in good stead for international games," Sabir says. Usually, Bermudians play in about six international games a year with three held in Bermuda. If you're interested in attending any of these games, check the *Gazette* sports pages or call the BFA at (441) 295-2199. In 1999 Bermuda played against Denmark and Antigua. How did we fare? In both countries we lost one game and won the other.

Sabir argues that football is important to the future of the island. "It acts as a stress-release valve for people who are maybe out of work during the winter months. We also want it to promote family values. We want a drug-free environment with plenty of respect for the players, the spectators and for the game."

Cricket

Cricket, of course, is a British and Commonwealth game par excellence. Keith Forbes, in *The Royal Gazette*'s "Bermuda Online," says it came to Bermuda via one Capt. J. Moresby in 1872. He introduced the game (before he became Captain-in-charge of the Royal Naval Dockyard) at a carnival held in Somerset, Sandys Parish, to celebrate "40 years since the unjust thralldom of slavery."

In 1902 three matches were held at the Royal Naval Field in Dockyard, once known as Moresby Plain. These were the forerunner games of our annual Cup Match — a two-day public holiday held on the Thursday and Friday before the last Monday in August. Officially, we celebrate Somers Day on Thursday (see "Shipwreck and Settlement" in our History chapter for more on Sir George Somers) and Emancipation Day on Friday. However, many Bermudians are more concerned about whether St. George's or Somerset's cricket team will win the cup.

Cup Match is well worth a visit to experience Bermudian tradition and culture. Supporters of each team go dressed in their new outfits (specially bought for the occasion), with the $10 entrance fee and extra cash on hand to spend on crown and anchor (a traditional betting game with dice). For more information, see the Cup Match Close-up in our Annual Events and Festivals chapter, which includes an explanation of how to play crown and anchor.

Stumped Over Cricket?

So you know all about Jiminy Cricket, but you haven't a clue about the game?

Cricket centers on two wickets — each made up of three wooden stumps topped with two crosspieces called bails. These wickets are placed 22 yards apart at opposite ends of a rectangular pitch (another name for the playing area) in the middle of a field. Two teams of 11 players take turns to bat and to field.

One batsman (OK, the term's not PC, but that's what the bat-wielder is called) stands at the far wicket facing the bowler (think "pitcher"). The batsman's partner stands at the opposite wicket. The bowler's aim is to knock off one, or both, bail. The batsman's aim is to prevent the bowler from doing so by hitting the ball as far as possible. If he fails, he's automatically out and another member of his team takes his place. If he succeeds and hits the ball far enough, he will attempt to gain a "run" by running in a straight line to the opposite wicket and exchanging places with his partner. If a fielder manages to catch the ball in midair, then the batsman is out.

During the two-day Cup Match event, this procedure can go on for hours. However, most matches are one-day events, with each team having one turn at bat. People who love cricket appreciate the leisurely pace of the game. British dramatist Tom Stoppard once said, "I don't think I can be expected to take seriously any game which takes less than three days to reach its conclusion."

If a batsman has "hit a six," it means he's scored six runs by hitting a ball over the field's boundaries without it touching the ground. (Runs, by the way, are not as hard to come by as they are in American baseball; a typical cricket score might include 200 runs in a one-day game.) If he's "bowled for a duck," he's out without scoring. And if he's "stumped"? Then the wicket-keeper (similar to a catcher in baseball) has knocked off a bail with the ball or his hand while holding a ball while he's out of the crease (the area immediately in front of the wicket) but not running. Clear as mud?

Cricketers can generally be recognized by their white peaked caps (some wear headgear), white open-necked shirts and white trousers. Cricket is the only sport in the world in which both sides are dressed identically. Batsmen and wicket-keepers wear white leg pads and white gloves. The bats have separate handles attached to elongated, oblong wooden pieces that constitute the hitting areas. One Bermuda club calls itself the Willow Cuts because bats are traditionally made of willow wood. Decorum is the name of the game. What if a player loses his temper? It can't happen; that just isn't cricket.

Cricket divisions in Bermuda are known as "counties," and there are three of them: Eastern, Central and Western. The Eastern County has a 90-year tradition behind it and is affectionately known as the counties' granddaddy. Clubs such as Bailey's Bay, St. David's and Flatts play for their regional areas. The same holds true for the Western County clubs but less so for the more recently formed Central County that includes, for example, the Police Recreational Club.

Other cup matches include the Central County's Cup Final in June. Eastern and Western Counties hold competitions in July and August. League cricket is played on fields all over the island, including the Wellington Oval in St. George's, the St. David's Oval, the Devonshire Recreation Club, Southampton Oval and White Hill in Sandys. For dates, times and venues of specific games check *The Royal Gazette* or phone the Bermuda Cricket Board of Control at (441) 292-8958. Admission to weekly league matches is free; for cup finals and counties cricket (special matches held on various designated weekends), the price is approximately $5.

Tennis

You might be interested to know that Bermuda feels responsible for introducing tennis to the United States. According to William Zuill

in *Bermuda Journey*, Bermudian merchant Thomas Middleton was first exposed to the game during a visit to England in 1871. He decided that this was an activity his wife would enjoy, so he brought tennis equipment back to Bermuda.

Whatever the reason (maybe she didn't enjoy it?), Thomas donated the equipment to Sir Brownlow Gray, who built the island's first private tennis court in the garden of his home, Clermont, in Paget. Mary, Gray's daughter, took advantage of the facility and eventually became Bermuda's first female tennis champion. Later, Mary Outerbridge, an American visitor from New York, played at Clermont and on returning to the States persuaded the Staten Island Cricket Club to create their own tennis court. Three years after Middleton's visit to England, tennis began in America.

www.insiders.com
See this and many other
Insiders' Guide
destinations online.
Visit us today!

Serving Up An International Mix

As Joseph Morley, administrator of the Bermuda Lawn Tennis Association (BLTA) explained, 1997 was a very good year for tennis in Bermuda.

For the first time ever, our country hosted the Davis Cup matches for American Zones III and IV (the Caribbean and Central American zones). Thirteen countries participated in this prestigious event, which was held at the Southampton Princess Hotel in April. During the same month in 1997 and 1998, the XL Bermuda Open Tennis Championship, an ATP Tour-sanctioned event, was held for the fourth and fifth consecutive year at the Coral Island Beach and Tennis Club in Paget (see the Horizons listing in our Cottage Colonies chapter for more information about Coral Beach). Will 1999 bring the same events to Bermuda? Defi-

INSIDERS' TIP

Spectator events are often held, subject to weather. Last-minute cancellations are announced on local television and radio stations.

nitely not the Davis Cup, but the XL will again take place here.

The XL Championship is an exciting event. Many of the games are held at night, which means locals can attend after they've finished work. No need to go home for dinner — hamburgers, chicken and salads are served under a marquee. Wine and beer are also served. And everyone enjoys the magic of Bermuda's balmy nights. As befits the traditional atmosphere of Coral Beach, male spectators usually wear jackets (actually, it's because many of them have come from the office).

The tournament, by the way, is for male players only. On the first Friday and Saturday of the event, spectators can attend qualifying rounds for free. Thirty-two players from all over the world participate in these rounds, out of whom four are picked to play in the tournament's main draw. Twenty-six players in the main draw are invited (based on the ATP ranking computer point system); two of these players are "wild cards" (usually players who have won international games some years ago but are not ranked highly at the time of the event); and the remaining four players are the winners from the qualifying round. Australian Pat Rafter, winner of the 1997 U.S. Open and a Bermuda resident, has won this championship in 1997 and 1998.

In 1998, tickets for main draw matches were $15 for day games, $20 for night matches and $25 for the final. (Rates for the 1999 XL are subject to change.) Spectators dress up for the final: Men wear suits; women don hats. About 2,000 spectators a day, many of whom come from abroad especially for the occasion, turn up for these games. Bermuda may be small, but it has the highest per capita attendance in the world for tennis. For more information, call Coral Beach at (441) 236-2233.

The Local Scene

What about local tennis? Bermuda has eight BLTA-affiliated tennis clubs, including Pomander Gate, Port Royal, The Reefs, All Bermuda Tennis and Coral Island Beach and Tennis. Players participate in Winter League tennis from October to March or April. Clubs host open tournaments throughout the year. For example, the Heineken Open is held at the end of May at the Tennis Stadium, 2 Marsh Folly Road, Pembroke, (441) 292-7146. Top local players participate in this one. November is invitation tennis month, when overseas club players from countries such as the United States, Canada and England participate in games hosted by our clubs. Spectators are welcome, and admission is free.

In addition to the Winter League, the Commercial League, consisting of players from local businesses and companies, plays games from April until September. For dates, times and venues of specific games check *The Royal Gazette* or phone the BLTA at (441) 296-0834.

Rugby

This game is named after Rugby School in England. One momentous day in 1823, a William Webb Ellis was playing soccer when he succumbed to an overwhelming urge to pick up the ball and run with it. That terrible infringement of soccer rules gave birth to a new game.

Interest in rugby spread to other countries. Feelings about it in America in the early days were mixed, however. The lack of precise rules, the ambiguities in the game and the complexity of the sport turned off U.S. players. In 1880 major rule changes were invoked, such as replacing the scrum with a line of scrimmage. But photographs of an apparently brutal game played between Swarthmore and Pennsylvania in 1905 drew the attention of President Theodore Roosevelt, who insisted on reform of the game to lower the level of brutality. He even threatened to use the big stick he wielded to abolish rugby by edict.

In 1906 the forward pass was introduced to the United States game. That meant that in the States, rugby, as the British defined it (no

For summer events, be sure to wear a hat. The sun can beat down heavily.

forward pass allowed), died out for a while and was replaced by American football. Since the 1960s, however, rugby has made a comeback across the pond.

Distant Cousins: Rugby and American Football

Rugby and football are similar, but there are major differences, particularly where equipment is concerned. Rugby players do not wear any padding or protection except for a mouth guard. The traditional uniform consists of a long-sleeved cotton shirt with a collar. Shorts are usually cotton and rise to about mid-thigh. Knee-length socks with turnover tops are worn along with boots similar to soccer cleats. Some forwards wear the optional scrum cap, which is made from leather or cloth and worn as protection for the ears.

The "pitch" is a grass field, but it nearly always features mud. (In fact, there should be a universal law compelling all rugby players to do their own laundry.) The goalposts are similar to those used in American football; they are shaped in the form of an H and stand on the goal lines at opposite ends of the field. With 15 players on each team, the objective of the game is to score more points than the opposing team during the two 40-minute halves. A "try" is scored when a player places the ball in the opposition's goal area. A try is good for five points, with two additional points awarded for a successful place kick. A three-point "goal" can be scored via a free penalty kick or a drop kick. Play pauses for penalties and scores and when the ball goes out of bounds; the game is not stopped for injuries until the ball is out of play. Unlike American football, play does not stop with a tackle.

The Local Scene

This rugged sport's most important annual event is Bermuda's World Rugby Clas-

sic, which in 1999 will be held from November 10 to November 16 at the National Sports Club on Middle Road in Devonshire. The tournament is for former international players who have represented their countries, and players must be at least 33 years old. In the past, players participating have included France's Philippe Sella, Ireland's Brendan Mullin, South Africa's Danie Gerber and England's Mike Harrison. The tourney will mark its 11th anniversary in 1999, and teams are expected from New Zealand, South Africa, Argentina, Ireland, Scotland, Wales, the United States and Canada.

Will any of Bermuda's rugby players take part? Absolutely. In the past, they have been added to the French, English and Argentinean teams. In 1999, they will have their own team. Daily admission will be $15, or you can pay $50 for a week pass. For $350, a silver pass will let you watch from a special tent and mingle with players, sponsors and special guests. A gold pass, costing $650, will give you the same privileges with the added advantage of free lunches and drinks. For more information, call John Kane, World Rugby Classic president, at (441) 291-1517 or (441) 236-9876.

The classic attracts about 2,500 visitors from overseas. It also involves five days of corporate hospitality. On the Friday before the final, an "Up-front Party" is held at Number One Shed, Front Street. (Admission is $20 a person.) There the teams perform (i.e., sing to extremely loud music). In addition, players participate in a golf tournament at the Riddells Bay Golf Club in Warwick. No doubt they have to resist the urge to pick up the ball and run with it.

This event, whose sponsors include the Department of Tourism, XL Insurance, ACE Insurance, Heinz and APT (see our International Business chapter), has international television coverage through ESPN and BBC "Rugby World."

If you fancy watching a local game, you can do so at the National Sports Club every

---

INSIDERS' TIP

If during a cricket match you hear the bowler shout "Howzat!" you'll know that his bowl has succeeded in knocking down the batsman's wicket bail.

Running sports are a major pastime for locals and visitors alike; the Boston Marathon — Bermuda Style.

Saturday and Sunday afternoon from October to April. Local teams are the Renegades, Teachers, Police and Mariners. Admission costs about $3.

Running

Bermudians love to run. You'll catch them at it first thing in the morning, last thing at night. Where? Everywhere. To quote Sir Winston Churchill, "on beaches, landing grounds, in fields, in streets and on the hills . . ." "Blood, toil, tears and sweat," might be apposite too. Sometimes you'll even see them out at lunchtime. To misquote Noel Coward: "Mad dogs and Bermudians run out in the midday sun."

Two key running events happen every year. The first is the Bank of Butterfield Bermuda International Race Weekend, held the third week of January. Where this set of races is concerned, "weekend" means three days, not two. The Bank of Butterfield Mile, held on Front Street and run by locals and top international runners, usually kicks off the occasion on Friday evening from 7:30 to 9:30 PM. On Saturday, there's the Bermuda International 10K and the Fitness Walk. Sunday, the Ber-

muda International Marathon (which negotiates the standard 26.2 miles) runs concurrently with a half-marathon.

Total prize money for the running weekend was $25,000 in 1996, with the male and female winners each pocketing $2,500. If you enter before December 17, the cost is $25 for the marathon and $15 for the half-marathon or 10K. (For more information, see our Annual Events and Festivals chapter.)

The second big event for runners is the Bermuda Day Half-Marathon, which is run on May 24 and restricted to Bermuda residents only. It starts in Somerset in Sandys Parish at 9:30 AM and ends in Bernard Park, Pembroke. Whether they run or not, Bermudians love to watch this race. It's a happening that lets all cross-sections of our community come together. It's also the one event each year where a very sunny day is not a good thing — from the runners' points of view, anyway. Some spectators choose to watch at spots where they know the runners are going to be particularly challenged, so that we can offer encouragement. On Burnt House Hill (Warwick Parish), for example, you'll find spectators yelling, "Way to go!" Or when runners stagger up the hill sweating and writhing and look in serious danger of dropping out, you'll hear, "You can do it; you can do it." Runners who contort their faces in hideous grimaces are greeted with affectionate laughter.

Winners of this race (male and female) get $300 or $400 and trophies. However, many of those on hand are more interested in cheering on friends and relations who have no hope of winning. These competitors want the satisfaction of having completed the run and improved their personal-best times. It is a point of honor to wait for the last stragglers — they need the most encouragement of all. Many participants run for charity; some run while pushing children in push chairs; others wear crazy costumes. In the past, Bermudian Tom Butterfield, founder of Masterworks Foundation and Gallery, often ran in a tutu. Locals all agreed his legs were lovely. Call Richard Tucker, (441) 292-4941, for more information. The entry fee is $10; late entries pay $25.

Cycling

Greg Hopkins, president of the Bermuda Bicycle Association, says there is an active competitive cycling calendar here from February to the end of October. The Grand Prix, an international racing event sponsored by the law firm of Conyers, Dill and Pearman, takes place every May over a four-day period. In 1997 and 1999 some 80 top professional riders from overseas participated, together with about 40 locals, including Bermuda's only professional cyclist, Elliot Hubbard, who came first in one section of the event, and who also, incidentally, competed in the 1998 Commonwealth Games in Malaysia. A staged race, the Grand Prix consists of two circuit races in the City of Hamilton, a 10-mile time trial and a 75-mile lap race held at South Side, the former U.S. Naval Base in St. George's Parish. A total of $15,000 is divided among the top three veterans, top three women, top three men and top three juniors. However, Hopkins says the atmosphere is more friendly than competitive.

(See our Annual Events and Festivals chapter for more information.)

The Heritage Day Classic, restricted to local cyclists only, is one of many Heritage Week activities. Starting around 8 or 8:30 AM, it precedes the Bermuda Day Half-Marathon on May 24. Cyclists ride from Sandys to Bernard Park in Pembroke Parish. Other races include the IBC Front Street Race, a local timed race held in Hamilton at the beginning of March, and the National Championships, which are held at the end of July at Clearwater, St. David's. At the end of the season, the Southampton Princess Hill Climb Championship in Southampton determines who can race up the hill in the fastest time. Spectators, of course, can watch all races for free. For more information call the Bermuda Bicycle Association's President, Greg Hopkins, at (441)297-7968.

Triathlon

By now you no doubt know that we have keen cyclists and runners. Well, we also have keen swimmers. Put the three sports together and you get, of course, a triathlon.

David Morrison, former president of the Bermuda Triathlon Association, says the sport is popular and the attitude of participants is upbeat. "It's drug-free, and there's tremendous camaraderie among the athletes." Bermudian Jim Butterfield started triathlon events some 20 years ago. From the mid-'80s on, Bermuda has taken part in the International Triathlon Union World Circuit (ITU). And in September, Bermuda hosts the ITU World Cup Championship, where some of the world's best triathlon athletes compete in swimming, cycling and running races. Total prize money is generous — $100,000. For more information, call Neil De Ste. Croix, president of the Bermuda Triathlon Association, at (441) 292-6528.

Another important two-day event is the Bank of Bermuda Triathlon, held either in August or September. The Individual Race takes place on the first day, usually with about 100 participants. These stalwart individuals swim

750 meters in Hamilton Harbour, get on their bikes for a 20-kilometer ride, then (as if that's not enough) proceed on a 5-kilometer run. The Team Race (about 100 to 150 teams of three participate) consists of a mile swim in the Harbour, a 15-mile bike ride and a 6-mile run. We're exhausted just writing about it. In 1997 American Karen Smyers, two-time winner of the World Cup Championship, came to Bermuda to support the Bank of Bermuda event, which attracts 400 to 500 participants and about 2,000 spectators. Both races start at 8 AM at Albuoy's Point, City of Hamilton. Call the Bank of Bermuda at (441) 299-5483 for more information.

Other triathlon events include the National Championships (dates depend on the dates for the World Championships), the National Duathlon and the National Sprint Championships, which are held in March.

We'd like to add that the Tri-Hedz Club offers a strong junior program. It paid off for 14-year-old Tyler Butterfield, Jim's son; he won the 14-year-old division of the American Championships held at Clairmont, Florida, in 1997.

Harness Racing and Horse Shows

Until cars were introduced to Bermuda in 1946, horses with carriages were among the chief means of getting around (along with the Bermuda Railway and the pedal bike). Today harness racing, revived in the early '90s, is a throwback to those days when horse-driving skills were important to daily living. It's also fun to watch.

Michael Cherry, president of the Bermuda Equestrian Federation, says the racing season starts in September and runs through March, with about 17 or 18 race meets during the year. In fact, harness racing is organized by the Bermuda Horse and Pony Driving Club, an affiliate of the Federation. The races usually take place on a Sunday afternoon at the National Equestrian Centre, on Vesey Street in Devonshire. Ponies harnessed to sulkies (small, two-wheeled frames with an unsprung seat) race against each other round a one-

fifth-mile track. Prizes are bales of hay and feed; the atmosphere is more friendly than competitive. Spectators are welcome. Admission is about $4. For dates of races, call Michael DeCosta, president of the Bermuda Horse and Pony Driving Club, at (441) 293-4964.

The Bermuda Equestrian Federation organizes horse shows that include jumping, dressage and equitation events. Other horse shows are held at local stables such as Hinson Hall in Smiths Parish and Spicelands in Warwick (see our Recreations chapter). For details of these shows, call the Equestrian Federation at (441) 295-4434. In fall and spring, a horse-driving show is held at the Botanical Gardens in Paget (see our Attractions chapter).

Golf

Bermuda currently has more golf courses per square mile than any other country in the world. Check our Golf chapter for detailed description of our nine courses and for booking information. Here we'll give you a sampling of tournaments held on the island. All entry fees mentioned were accurate in 1998. If you need more information about these events, Tom Smith at the Bermuda Golf Association (441) 238-1367) can likely help.

In addition to the Gillette Championship Challenge, mentioned in this chapter's introduction, the island also hosts the Bermuda International Open Golf Tournament for men. A four-day event, it's held in late October at Port Royal Golf Course and attracts many top players. Entry fees are $275 for professionals and $200 for amateurs. (The handicap limit is 6 for both professionals and amateurs.) In March the Bermuda Men's Amateur Championship is held at the Mid Ocean Club. This is a singles match-play event at scratch with a championship flight of 32 players and a handicap limit of 8. Entry fee is $225.

The Bermuda Ladies Amateur Championship is held in April at Riddells Bay Golf and Country Club. A four-day event, it is also a singles match-play event at scratch; the handicap limit is 24, the entry fee $200.

In the half-light of early mornings, for example, the sea can have more of an appearance of soft, gray silk that meets the horizon in a shroud of mist.

Beaches

Making Waves with Colors

Look at any travel article on Bermuda's ocean, and you will invariably find a reference to our "clear, sparkling turquoise waters."

What's the problem with that? Isn't it true? Put it this way: If Miles Davis had visited Bermuda for any length of time, he may well have played more than one kind of blue.

Yes, you will see that blue-green shade, but bear in mind that our part of the Atlantic Ocean is rarely just one color at any one time. The cloudscapes, the dark streaks of the reefs and the play of light and shadow make for a sea of contrasts. Sometimes the colors are as bright and dazzling as precious stones — sapphires and diamonds included. But let's not forget about the more subtle and muted shades either. In the half-light of early mornings, for example, the sea can have more of an appearance of soft, gray silk that meets the horizon in a shroud of mist.

There's a geographical factor that we should consider as well. It's true that some of our beaches are on the eastern and western tips of Bermuda, and others (mostly private) are around the Great Sound and Harrington Sound. But many of our popular public beaches can be geographically divided into roughly two categories: those situated on the North Shore and those situated on the South Shore.

Bermudians generally agree that the North Shore is different in scenery from the South. However, they often disagree about which is more beautiful. It's a question of loyalty, you see. Bermudians who live on the North Shore will extol the "activeness" of their views. By that, they mean that you can more frequently watch the cruise ships gliding to the islands as well as more boating activity. They also believe the scenery is more truly Bermudian

and less touristy because there are fewer hotels but lots of Bermudian cottages. South Shore residents, meanwhile, will claim that a) more beaches are on the south side, b) more longtails live there, and c) the reef line is closer.

We will not take either side in this argument. But we will tell you that the ocean on the north side does often appear expansively more green than blue, whereas on the South Shore it's a darker blue, especially beyond the reef line — definitely more teal than turquoise. Moreover, the water temperature on the North Shore, during the summer months anyway, is warmer, while on the South Shore it's always refreshing, even on the hottest of days. Though it is true that there are fewer beaches on the North Shore, you should know that some locals, particularly older children, like to swim directly off the rocks there.

Bermuda on the Rocks

As you probably know by now, Bermuda is surrounded by reefs. That's why Andrew Marvell referred to the island (or islands) as a "watery maze." On the South Shore, reefs are easily visible and, in many cases, easily accessible. They are known as potboiler reefs or, more technically, "serpuline atoll" or "algal-vermetid" reefs that protrude from the water. What do we mean by accessible? Well, sometimes the potboilers are so close to the beach that at low tide you can actually wade out to them and enjoy the deep, natural rock pools (see Stonington Beach Hotel, Pompano Beach and Willowbank listings in our Small Hotels chapter). If they are not that close, at some beaches you can swim out to the reefs (again, more easily at low tide) and join the fish. (For more details on the marine life on the outer reefs, check the Diving and Snorkeling section in our Watersports chapter.)

If you're after surf, you won't find it on the North Shore, where the waves get short and snappy during windy weather. When the wind blows southerly, you'll get rollers on the South Shore beaches. Be careful of the reefs then because salt spray can camouflage them, and bear in mind that because of our reefs, the waves are never as high as they are in Hawaii, for example, or California.

To See a World in a Grain of Sand

Impatient for sand? Here we worry about another cliche in travel literature: "the shimmering pink sands of Bermuda." Let's be more prosaic. Our sands actually consist of trillions of tiny skeletons. Are they all pink? In his book, *Bermuda's Marine Life*, Dr. Wolfgang Sterrer explains why our beaches appear pink. It's "because the Red Foram, a tiny, single-celled animal that grows in profusion on the underside of rocks, has a bright red skeleton. When the animal dies, the skeleton is eroded by the waves and gets mixed in with other such debris — broken clam and snail shells, sea urchin remains, pieces of coral — all of which are white. The Red Foram's remains give Bermuda's white sand its characteristic pink hue."

The name "foram," Dr. Sterrer explains, is short for foraminifer, which means "bearers of holes." Even so, our sand colors and textures do vary from beach to beach. Where they are particularly in the pink, we'll tell you.

Although our beaches are composed of shells, looking for larger ones on the shoreline is not particularly productive. It is possible to dive for shells, but we'd rather you refrain. See our Watersports chapter for details about protected species.

A Word on Land Crabs

Formally known as Red Land Crabs, these do generally prefer land. However, during the summer months the females have an overwhelming need to reproduce. They do this by making their way to the sea at least once a year, usually around midnight on the days following a full moon. Once they reach the sea, they shake themselves vigorously to release 100,000 larvae per female (yes, honestly!) into the shallows.

They then return to land, leaving their little ones to fend for themselves until they too reach land about a month later. Talk about family values. We mention this because a moonlight walk along the beach can mean a disconcerting meeting with these little creatures. In their haste to reach the water, they are not averse to pinching your toes.

Where to Go?

We have so many areas that can be described as beaches that we can't possibly report on them all. Actually, we can't visit them all either — about 80 percent of them are privately owned, either by individuals or by hotels. (See our Resort Hotels and Cottage Colonies chapters for more information on hotel-owned or controlled beaches.) True, it is legal to approach them by boat, provided you stay below the high-tide mark. But go above that mark, and you're definitely trespassing.

Our listings in this chapter will describe only the beaches that are available to the public. Some have lifeguards, changing facilities and beach cafes; most do not. We will specify when they do. If we do not mention one or more of these amenities, you may take it that they are not available. By the way, lifeguards here are fully qualified in swimming, advanced resuscitation and first-aid — indeed, they have to requalify every year. During the summer months they are on duty every day from 10 AM to 6 PM. No lifeguards are in service between November 1 and May 31.

A white flag posted means a lifeguard is on duty. A red flag means the currents are too dangerous for safe swimming. And a yellow one? That means you should be cautious and get advice on conditions from the lifeguard. If a beach has a reputation for riptides, we'll mention that too. As for parking, you may take it that, unless we mention otherwise, there is plenty of space for cars and motorcycles. The two beaches listed in St. George's Parish can be reached by taking a minibus from the Town of St. George's (see our Getting Here, Around and Home chapter). All but two of the other beaches discussed are near bus routes.

We'll also tell you which beaches are suitable for small children, and which are particularly good for snorkeling. Be aware in Bermuda that there are absolutely no beaches where nude bathing is allowed. W. B. Yeats once wrote, "There's more enterprise in walking naked." Bermudians do not agree. Swimming and/or sunbathing nude or semi-nude is an indictable offense.

As usual, we will start in the east and move westward, parish by parish. However, to avoid confusion, in this chapter we will not use alphabetical order within the parishes. Instead, we will use a geographical order. You see, all the public beaches are part of Bermuda's national park network, and some can be right next door to each other (so to speak) in the same park. The chains of public beaches in Warwick and Southampton Parishes, for example, are all part of the South Shore Park.

You'll find much more information about parks in our Parks and Conservation chapter. In this chapter, we will use the beaches' official names as headings and include the names of the parks in the address. If beach cafes and facilities are available, we will also include those phone numbers.

St. George's Parish

Clearwater Beach
Clearwater Beach Park, Mercury Rd., St. David's • (441) 293-5092

Once the Americans returned the military base lands to Bermuda in 1995, Clearwater for the first time became accessible to the public. It actually consists of two sandy beaches, both of which were artificially made for use by army personnel. They are now part of the

Clearwater Beach Park that overlooks the Cooper's Island Nature Reserve. See the map on page xv for the location.

The spaciousness of Clearwater makes it ideal for families, parties and functions. A large building left over from the base now houses Reid Clearwater Cafe, whose telephone number is listed above. You may buy the usual drinks, ice cream and hamburgers here, but you might also enjoy homemade mussel pies, fresh fish and other Bermudian specialties. You will definitely enjoy the friendliness of the staff.

Beach and swimming equipment are available for rent. Snorkeling gear costs $15 a day or $5 an hour. The rental prices we quote for the following are daily, rather than hourly, rates. Both beach mat and umbrella cost $5 each. A chair costs $10; a lounger costs $14. Towels are $3 each, and an inflatable raft/mattress (they are known as "lilos" in Bermuda) is $10. You can also rent a huge barbecue, suitable for large parties — call Reid's for prices. It opens at 7 AM and closes at 9 PM. The building also contains changing rooms, showers and bathrooms, which you can use free of charge.

Lifeguards are on duty daily here from May 24 through October 31. They say the beach is, on the whole, safe though in the winter, some strong currents occur farther out to sea between small rocky islands. Dark patches in the water here signify turtle grass, a species of underwater grass that appeals to fish and particularly to green turtles. The lifeguards also recommend Turtle Bay, just around the corner, for snorkeling. If you're extremely lucky, you might just see a green turtle. In any case, you'll see turbots and parrotfish, hogfish and trigger fish. Should a small family picnic appeal, you will find the two cabanas containing hibachis useful.

Tobacco Bay
Tobacco Bay Park, 1 Coot Pond Rd.
• (441) 297-2756

The telephone number belongs to Kenneth Bascome, who owns and manages the Tobacco Bay Beach Pavilion right on the beach. He serves drinks and fast food, such as burgers and ice cream, at very reasonable prices. He also rents out equipment. You can try a water bicycle (set on a pontoon) for $20 an hour. Snorkeling gear, including mask, snorkel and fins, costs $8 an hour or $12 for two hours. Lounge chairs cost $2 an hour, and an umbrella is a flat rate of $5. That means you can sit under it all day if you want. Mr. Bascome would hate for you to get sunburned. Fancy a tube float? Three dollars an hour. Changing rooms and public conveniences are available for free. From November 30 to April 1, the cafe closes. Summer months, it operates 9 AM to 6.30 PM. (For more on the Tobacco Bay Beach Pavilion, see our Kidstuff chapter.)

Tobacco Bay, on the North Shore (see the map on page xv), is perfect for families and inexperienced swimmers. Small children can stay in more shallow depths or make sand castles on the small beach. The sand here is more yellow than pink, incidentally. Sound too dull? The rocks surrounding the bay make for interesting snorkeling. Snorkel around Snapper's Rock, for example, and you may well see a snapper. Four-eyed butterfly fish, blue angels and wrasse, including pudding wives, like Tobacco Bay. So do barracudas. Don't worry — they may look threatening with their sharp teeth, but they don't attack humans; they have a more sinister interest in the other fish for a lunch munch.

Talk to Mr. Bascome, and he will tell you that this sheltered bay was the locale for the 1775 "Gunpowder Steal." Local conspirators stole gunpowder from the British magazine, then loaded it into whale boats for transport to American ships. The plot caused explosions in more ways than one. Americans used the gunpowder in their Revolutionary War against the British. Given that Bermuda was a British colony (right now it's a British dependent territory), you can see why sparks flew here as

well as in the United States (see our History chapter for more details).

Hamilton Parish

Shelly Bay Beach
Shelly Bay Park, 55 North Shore Rd., Shelly Bay • (441) 293-7208

The phone number we give here is for the Shelly Bay Beach House, where you may buy drinks, ice cream and fast food. Here, too, you will find bathrooms and changing rooms, but no showers are available. You can rent a locker for $1 an hour, snorkeling equipment costs $5 an hour, and umbrellas come at $1.50 an hour or $6 a day. Loungers and towels are $12 and $2.50 a day, respectively. See the map on page xv.

If you're feeling adventurous, either of two sailboats (Hobie Cats) are available for $40 an hour. A paddle boat can be fun too. You can rent one for $10 an hour. Remember that when you hire one of these boats, you must always keep within sight of the Beach House. In compliance with regulations, manager/owner Franz Egenolf is always on hand with his Jet Ski in case a rescue is necessary.

This North Shore beach and bay is absolutely perfect for children. The water is shallow (and yes, more often than not, it's blue-green), with no riptides to interfere with safe bathing. The sand on the beach and the sea floor is quite coarse. Pick up a handful, and you will find small white shells, many intact.

If your children get tired of sand and sea, they can try out the playground equipment in the park area. Swings, climbing frames and slides should keep them entertained. You

INSIDERS' TIP

Some of our beaches are ideal for small children. However, a foot of water can be just as deadly as 6 feet. Never leave your children in the water unsupervised. Where toddlers are concerned, keep your eyes on them at all times. A lot can happen in 30 seconds. Remember, too, that babies and young children can sunburn easily. A sun hat is a must.

might also like to check out the tidal pond, surrounded by mangroves and thickets. Here you may notice sora birds, warblers, herons and kingfishers.

Smiths Parish

John Smith's Bay
John Smith's Bay Park, South Rd.

This South Shore beach is an absolute favorite with locals. It's got sand — lots of it, with the pink bits included — and it's good for kids because they can easily keep in a shallow depth. More adventurous swimmers like to swim out to the reefs and meet with the fish. Snorkeling is certainly rewarding here. At the very least, you can introduce yourself to the parrotfish. See the map on page xv.

However, we must tell you that the water here is subject to riptides, although not as frequently as in some other South Shore beaches. (See the Warwick Long Bay listing below for a description of these currents.) It's just as well that lifeguards are on duty here during the summer. If the yellow flag is up, be sure to ask their advice on precautions.

There are public conveniences here but no other beach facilities. However, during the summer you can buy fast food and drinks from a mobile van restaurant. A pay phone is nearby and so is a bus stop. The grounds are shady, thanks to the Norfolk pine trees, cedars and the fronds of the palms. They are also ramped and completely accessible to guests in wheelchairs.

Pembroke Parish

Clarence Cove
Admiralty House Park, Spanish Point Rd., Spanish Point

Once you enter this park, follow the trail down the hillside until you reach the bottom. There you will find two magical little beaches tucked around a part of the North Shore, which is really more lagoon than cove. The swimming is so safe for children that during July and August holiday daytime camps are held here. The rest of the year it's fairly secluded.

Admiralty House, now a community center, was once what its name implies — a house for the British Royal Navy's admirals stationed here. In 1850 the Earl of Dundonald, commander-in-chief at the time, decided to excavate caves into the cliffs overlooking the sea. Or rather, he forced convicts to excavate them. Apparently the caves helped with the landing and storage of provisions. But in *Bermuda Journey*, William Zuill reckoned that the earl was satisfying his mole-like urge for tunneling and excavating.

According to "Bermuda Online's" Keith Forbes, "During World War II the property was at its busiest. It was crammed with the Royal Navy's intelligence staff. They encoded and decoded messages from convoys sailing between the United Kingdom and the USA, and from ships torpedoed at sea by German submarines and needing rescue services provided by the Royal Navy from Bermuda. They also sent signals directing attacking aircraft to pro-

INSIDERS' TIP

Watch out for the purple and blue Portuguese men-of-war, especially in spring after stormy weather when they tend to be blown onto the beach. This jellyfish has a balloon float structure of about 8 inches and a mass of tentacles that can be anywhere between 20 and 60 inches in length. It's the tentacles we worry about: They can seriously sting you. If you do get stung, rinse the affected area with salt water, then soak it with vinegar, alcohol or after shave. Immerse the wound for at least 30 minutes in water as hot as is tolerable. Shave the area with a razor and shaving cream to remove cysts, and do not dry it off with a towel. Remember, you can get reinfected. If a sting causes you or a companion to go into shock, or if the pain continues to be almost unbearable, call the hospital at (441) 236-2345.

Beautiful Horseshoe Beach is one of Bermuda's most popular destinations.

ceed to where U boats were sighted." Dances for officers were often held in the ballroom. Before the days of motorized traffic, women in long dresses would somehow manage to arrange their skirts so that they could get there by pedal bike.

Paget Parish

Elbow Beach
Elbow Beach Park, Tribe Rd. No. 4, off South Rd.

There are two sections to this magnificent stretch of South Shore beach. The eastern section is privately owned by the Elbow Beach Bermuda hotel and is accessed through the grounds (see our Resort Hotels chapter). The western one is open to the public — walk down to the end of the tribe road, and you'll see it immediately. See the map on page xiv.

We love the expanse of Elbow's sands and dunes; it allows us brisk walks or jogs for keep-fit routines. Actually, the fact that private Stonington Beach is on the one end and even-more-private Coral Beach on the other gives the illusion of even more length. And swimming is good, especially if you prefer swells to calm. It can be as smooth as glass, mind you, but on windy days, this is probably where you'll get surf.

The reef is visible and reminds us of the bravery of one Bermudian, Antonio Marshall. In 1915 he sailed his whale boat to save nearly all the crew on board the British S.S. *Pollockshields* that had crashed on the reef in violent seas. The wreck is still there and is a favorite diving location (see our Watersports chapter).

Warwick Parish

Astwood Cove
Astwood Park, South Rd.

This park has open fields, thickets and cliff walks. It is a perfect spot for watching the longtails' aerial courtships and for appreciating the sweep of the South Shore coastline. Tables and benches make picnics comfortable. In fact, it's a favorite location for wedding receptions. The cove between and below the field and the cliff thicket is tiny and rocky. Rocks do make for good snorkeling, but they also make for cut feet. For small children or people who lack confidence in the water, it may not be a good choice. And the water can be rough. See the map on page xiv.

Warwick Long Bay
South Shore Park, South Rd.

Yes, it's long. Very long and very spectacular. What's more, Warwick Long Bay has the advantage of being far less crowded than some of the other major South Shore beaches. Even in the peak season, you'll never find yourself just inches away from a perfect stranger. See the map on page xiv.

The swimming here, however, may not be ideal for inexperienced swimmers or small children. At high tide particularly, you'll encounter a sudden shelf on the sea floor that can quickly take you out of your depth. Also, we must mention rip currents here. They occasionally can be created by depressions or hollows on the sea floor that run perpendicular to the beach. Shallow water from the breaking waves flows out through the hollows, setting up a current. Because there is no lifeguard service here, it is even more important that you observe the never-swim-alone rule. And if the red flag is up, do stay out of the water.

Even if you don't swim here, you will enjoy the cliff trails, cedars and bay grape trees. It's a good venue for birds too. March to September, look out for the longtails. Year-round you'll see plenty of kiskadees (you'll certainly hear them even if you don't see them). On the beach itself, you may well see sanderling birds puttering along in twos and threes, together with ruddy turnstones that have small puffed-out chests. The sand? Yep. It's pink. And the water plays many an enigmatic variation on the blue and the green.

Kids can take advantage of the recently built playground in the park area. Lots of climbing and swinging equipment is there for them as well as a stationary train and a play house. Public conveniences are in the park area. If you're starving and thirsty, try the lunch wagon across the South Road opposite the beach for food and a snow cone.

Jobson's Cove
South Shore Park, South Rd.

OK, Warwick Long Bay is not ideal for kids, but Jobson's is. A tiny sheltered cove, it is surrounded by rocks. Very shallow steps are carved out of one of the rock-face backdrops. The water in most places is shallow and calm with a sandy bottom — perfect for kids who still depend on armbands to keep afloat. They can see, even without snorkeling equipment, parrotfish and sergeant-majors nudging around the rocks.

Our older local kids like to dive from the larger rocks into the few deep pools toward the back of the cove. We wish they wouldn't, though. A misplaced dive into shallow water can mean a serious accident; always go in feet-first. With that proviso, Jobson's is arguably the best beach on the South Shore for young families. It's a favorite setting for picnics. See the map on page xiv.

Stonehole Bay
South Shore Park, South Rd.

Right next to Jobson's, this bay is a stunning combination of water, sand and rock. See the map on page xiv. We all appreciate hearing the wind chimes of the Aeolian harp, right? Here we appreciate the swishing sound of salt spray against these dramatic Aeolian limestone rock formations. Swimming is generally safe, although on windy days, the sea can be choppy. Public conveniences are available. Walk along the trail that leads westward, and you can try out another similar beach. A listing for it follows.

Chaplin's Bay
South Shore Park, South Rd.

If it matters to you in what parish you're sunbathing, then we must tell you that if you pick a spot toward the western end of this beach, you've reached Southampton. Swim at the eastern end, and you're still in Warwick. Tides come in; tides go out — the sea cares nothing about geographical divisions. Right next to Stonehole Bay, Chaplin's also has Aeolian limestone formations, and the same swimming conditions apply.

Chaplin's Bay is a favorite with locals. It

INSIDERS' TIP

Even if you are a strong swimmer, our lifeguards recommend you never swim alone, particularly on South Shore beaches.

offers more seclusion in the summer months. However, in January the red flag often goes up because it is then the venue for the Bermuda Regiment's shooting practice.

Southampton Parish

Horseshoe Bay
South Shore Park, 94 South Rd.
• (441) 238-2651

The telephone number we give here belongs to the Horseshoe Bay Beach House, which has a large outdoor terrace where you may consume your drinks and snacks (mostly fast foods and ice cream) under umbrellas. The Beach House also rents snorkeling and beach equipment. Daily per person rates are as follows: Towels cost $3.50, beach mats cost $2.75, snorkels and masks cost $15, rubber rings, surfboards and lilos are $11. And noodles (no, not the edible kind — long, foam tubes for water frolic) go for $3. In addition, you may rent umbrellas to take on the beach for $4.50, sand chairs for $5.50 and loungers for $7.00. A $30 deposit is required for surfboards and a $40 deposit for surboards. For other equipment the deposit is $20. All deposits are refunded if you bring back the equipment by 5 PM.

Showers, foot bath with taps, bathrooms and changing rooms are available free of charge and two pay phones are on hand. The Beach House opens at 9 AM and closes at about 5:30 PM. It closes altogether from November 1 through the end of March. See the map on page xiv.

All that said, let us now describe what is probably the most photographed and definitely the most popular beach in Bermuda. Be warned, in the summer months from about 10:30 AM it does get very crowded, particularly in the area by the Beach House. Litter could be a serious problem were it not for the fact that the sands are cleaned and raked every morning at about 8:30 AM.

You reach the beach by walking or driving down a fairly steep hill that leads off the South Road. (A signpost marks the road clearly.) You will notice a mass of oleander on your left. Look out particularly for the deep red blossoms that are less common in Bermuda than the pink and the white. Listen for warblers that enjoy the oleander thicket. Once you reach the sands, you'll see the curve of the beach that extends for about a quarter-mile. (Yes, it does resemble a horseshoe.) You'll also see that it is enclosed on each end by cliffs of more Aeolian limestone.

As for the sand, it's pink all right. It's also very fine, which is why the beach is a favorite for locals who love jogging or walking in the early morning or the evening. Pick up a handful of sand, and you'll find the red foram and also minuscule snail shells. As you sunbathe, on less-crowded days, you'll notice sanderlings and ruddy turnstones enjoying the beach as well.

Swimming? We wouldn't recommend it for arm-banded tots except on the calmest days. Even then, there's usually a swell that keeps the water temperature gloriously cool when the sun is blazing. But the sea floor is sandy and its gradient is gentle — if you're older but inexperienced, you can easily stay in your depth. On the other hand, you can swim out to the rocks on the western side and snorkel. Parrotfish and sergeant-majors are especially fond of Horseshoe. Here again, some of our locals like to dive from the rocks here. At low tide, this can be dangerous. If you love to dive, check the depth of the water first.

We must also tell you that occasionally those rip currents happen here (see Warwick Long Bay listing for a description of rip currents). We are thankful two lifeguard stands are at this beach. Check the flags: If the red one is posted, give up that swim. At the western end of this beach, just in front of the cafe, walk up and then down a narrow cliff path, and you'll find the next beach, listed subsequently.

INSIDERS' TIP

Unfortunately, some of our beaches do occasionally have patches of tar, washed up from ships. Use a paper towel soaked in baby oil to remove tar from your feet.

Photo: GIS

The shoreline of Bermuda keeps pockets of pink sand ready for discovery in private bays all along the South Shore.

Port Royal Cove
South Shore Park, South Rd.

Most locals do not know the official title of this beach. It's commonly referred to as the Baby Beach. Many a parent has spent hours with toddlers here. Like Jobson's Cove, it's perfect for the very young. Slightly larger than Jobson's, with a larger expanse of sand, it can resemble a kindergarten in the peak season. Snorkelers like to explore the rocks, and children can easily see parrotfish even if they don't have a mask and snorkel. Again, older children like to dive from the larger rocks into the one small pool of deep water. And again, we wish they wouldn't. Jumping feet-first is far safer. See the map page xiv.

Church Bay
Church Bay Park, South Rd.

Now we come to the "religious" side of the South Shore (see the map on page xiv). It could be that this one is so named because of St. Anne's Church on the other side of the road. It is the next beach after The Reefs' private Christian Bay (see our Small Hotels chapter). Anyway, we must tell you that if you're a passionate snorkeler, this one's an absolute

must. It's arguably the best beach on the South Shore for fish visiting. The potboilers of the reefs are very close to the shore, you see. Swim out to them, and you'll see parrotfish, blue and yellow grunts, wrasse, trunk, angel and four-eyed butterfly fish.

One rock particularly protrudes from the potboilers. Locals refer to it affectionately as Poodle Rock because from certain angles that's what it looks like. There's plenty of sand down to the water's edge. However, once you enter the water you'll immediately find that you are standing on flat rock. We mention this because the floor can occasionally be very slippery — wearing flippers might be a good idea. Once you leave the rock, you'll find yourself very quickly out of your depth. For this reason, it's not a good choice for inexperienced swimmers or small children. In addition, the water can be very rough.

On the eastern side, you'll notice limestone formations that resemble chimneys or pillars. If you're interested in military history, check out the ruined fort on top of the cliff down from the parking lot. The site has a 1612 marker. Picnic tables and public conveniences are available in the park area.

West Whale Bay
Whale Bay Park, Whale Bay Rd. (off Middle Rd.)

The name is appropriate since in April, if you're lucky, you just might see whales migrating north to their summer feeding grounds. During the late-eighteenth and nineteenth centuries, Bermudian whalers set out in their whaling boats from this bay. They hoped for ambergris (an intestinal secretion of the whales that is used in perfume) and the other products, such as oil, that these massive mammals could provide.

Walk across a grassy field (with picnic tables and public conveniences), and you'll find this small beach tucked below a rocky cliff. See the map on page xiv. There is pink sand, but at high tide the beach tends to disappear. It's a favorite with local families since the swimming is safe and the water inland is shallow enough for small children.

On top of the cliff, to the west of the parking lot, you'll find a battery. Originally a fort was built in the 1620s. Now it's more or less buried under the sand below a second one (built in 1876) that still exists. By the way, the view at West Whale Bay is toward the southwest. We mention this because its position means terrific sunsets over the ocean.

Sandys Parish

Black Bay
Lagoon Park, Malabar Rd.

Be warned: This one is not posted with signs. Once you cross Grey's Bridge on your way to Dockyard, you will see Lagoon Park on your right. On your left, immediately off the roadside, you will see grassy areas with benches. Stop here. There's no parking lot, but you should have no problem parking your motor bike on the grass. You will see the unruffled waters of Black Bay that are very rarely

anything other than blue to green. About three tiny beaches come and go here with the tide. It's a perfect spot for picnicking and for children's swimming.

Daniel's Head Beach Park
Daniel's Head Rd. (Off Cambridge Rd.), Somerset Village

Between 1949 and 1994 the parkland and two coves here were closed to the public. That's because they were part of the land leased to the Canadian Forces Station. Now that the base has closed down, however, this park is a favorite with locals since it is ideal for family outings and for children. The deserted barracks are still there, with the old Recreation Hall overlooking the water. But the forces also left behind a patio area with a space for barbecues, together with a climbing frame, slide and variety of swings. On weekends particularly, families, school parties and church groups like to come here for cook outs and for swimming. The two beaches are ideal for children and for inexperienced swimmers because the water is always calm and shallow. On sunny days it's typically a deep peppermint green. Even so, it's not dull for the more adventurous because of the marine life around the rocks. Snorkelers love to come here for parrot and angel fish, sergeant majors and wrasse. But lie on the beach, gaze at the water and if you're lucky you'll see fish jumping in a shower of silver. Telephone, bathrooms and fresh water showers are available free of charge. There's plenty of parking space as well.

Mangrove Bay
Mangrove Bay Park, Mangrove Bay Rd.

This bay is a favorite for locals who like to fish and sail as well as swim. The mangroves, the boats in the water and the gentle curve of the shoreline give the bay a serene, picturesque quality. Swimming is safe. Look out for

---

INSIDERS' TIP

Even on hazy days, the sun can burn you. Start tanning for short periods of time, and use a lotion with a high sunblock factor. Remember that sunburn can cause considerable pain. Even if you tan easily, always use tanning lotion. Unprotected exposure to the sun can cause skin cancer in the long-term.

terns here, together with gulls and vagrant cormorants that come in the fall from North America. Christopher Isherwood, British playwright and novelist, once wrote: "The common cormorant (or shag)/Lays eggs inside a paper bag." A piece of nonsense, of course, except cormorants were really known as "shags" in the nineteenth century, and they do lay eggs inside a nest of seaweed. However, in Bermuda it doesn't nest at all. It just takes a break from the North American winter. What isn't nonsense is that Mangrove Bay was a favorite unloading anchorage for Bermudian smugglers in the eighteenth century.

No public conveniences are available at this site, but the Somerset Country Squire Inn is just minutes away, as are the shops in Somerset Village. See the map on page xiv.

Parson's Bay
Lagoon Park, Lagoon Rd.

Again, this one is not sign-posted, and it's not too close to a bus stop either. See the map on page xiv. But it is the only bay with a beach on the side of Lagoon Road, just before the road name changes to Craddock Road. It's sheltered, with white, coarse sand and shallow, calm water that's ideal for children. Families in small boats tend to stop here for a swimming break, while others prefer to set up canopies and picnic. Do not confuse this beach with the lagoon, however. The lagoon is almost completely enclosed in the middle of the park and is considered by some unsuitable for swimming, though in winter you might find herons and kingfishers there.

Somerset Long Bay
Somerset Long Bay Park, Daniel's Head Rd. (off Cambridge Rd.), Somerset Village

Enter the park, and you'll see a manicured grassy area much loved by locals for family cricket games and picnics. (See the map on page xiv.) Public conveniences are available here. To your right, you'll see a nature reserve edged with bamboo, wild fennel and grasses that contains a pond that was resurrected from an old garbage fill in 1975. According to Eric Amos in his *A Guide to the Birds of Bermuda*, this reserve "is one of the most versatile birding spots in Bermuda." Resident coots and moorhens live in the pond while visiting birds often drop in. One year, a fork-tailed flycatcher from South America and a Siberian flycatcher from northeast Russia apparently came here for a Bermudian vacation. Do, then, look out for the birds.

All right, all right, you want the beach. Walk over the grass, the reserve to your right, and you're there. The long strip of coarse, white sand is rarely very crowded, even in the summer months. The water is calm and very shallow. At low tide it is almost impossible for adults to swim out of their depth. It's perfect for children, but not so interesting for the potential Olympic swimmer. Turtle grass is responsible for the dark patches in the water.

Tool out into the sounds and harbors, and you immediately experience a sense of space and peace. Besides, seeing the island from the water lets you appreciate that Bermuda's beauty depends on a trinity of sky, sea and land.

Watersports

For centuries, Bermudians could hardly view the sea as a source of leisure-time activity. A source of excitement, probably. Of challenge and danger, most certainly. From its earliest days as a settlement, Bermuda depended on the sea for food, travel and trade both legitimate and illegitimate (see our History chapter).

But as tourism began to surface toward the end of the nineteenth century, so did water-related fun. Visitors, mostly from America, would charter boats so they could enjoy our islands from an ocean perspective. Indeed, senior citizen Edward DeShields remembers one Captain Joe Powell, who used to take Mark Twain out in his boat. The other literary celebrity that both Captain Joe and DeShields knew well was Eugene O'Neill, who lived on Harbour Road.

Today tourists can enjoy a large range of watersports. Even if you were not born a water baby, you should try at least once to see Bermuda from the water. Visitors sometimes ask, "Don't you ever get claustrophobic? Bermuda's so small." The simple answer to that is, "Yes." We do occasionally feel an overwhelming urge to get off the island — "Rock fever" is what we call it. The simple solution is to take out a boat for a day. Tool out into the sounds and harbors, and you immediately experience a sense of space and peace. Besides, seeing the island from the water lets you appreciate that Bermuda's beauty depends on a trinity of sky, sea and land.

In this chapter we'll introduce you to the variety of water activities you can enjoy here. The chapter is divided into sections so you can quickly find the water recreation that most appeals to you.

If it's fish you're after, then you must first decide what kind of relationship you want with these creatures. Do you want to gaze with wonder at the fish? Visit them in their own home, all the while being quiet, considerate and respectful? Then diving or snorkeling is for you. Where snorkeling is concerned, you can, of course, rent a small boat and go off on your own. See the Sailboat, Personal Watercraft and Motorboat Rentals section for information. However, for those who want some instruction on how to snorkel, together with information about our marine life, check out the Scuba Diving and Snorkeling and Motor Cruises sections. We tell you about our reefs, fish and shipwrecks. We also list the diving and snorkeling centers and tell you about prices, rules and regulations.

But you may want an unashamedly confrontational relationship with the fish. If you view them as potential lunch, then go to the Deep-sea and Reef Fishing section. There we discuss charters, catch policies and conservation regulations concerning protected species. So your dream is to catch a marlin? Many have done so here, so we'll talk about billfishing too.

Maybe you're more interested in water frolic. Again, check out the Sailboat, Personal Watercraft and Motorboat Rentals section, together with the Waterskiing and Parasailing section. For sailing yacht charters, turn to the Yachting and Marinas chapter. In all cases the rates we quote are subject to change.

A Word About Our Reef

By now, you likely know we have some 50 miles of barrier reef encircling our island. In fact, we have the most northerly coral building reefs known to exist in the Northern Hemisphere. We could never wish for a reef-free island, but we must admit our reefs were historically the curse of sailors attempting to reach our island. "Good grief, what a reef," they might have said while trying to negotiate through one of our channels.

Even today Bermuda is one of the most (if not the most) difficult areas to enter safely by sea. It's not surprising, then, that there are more than 450 shipwrecks (that we know about) off our coastline. Our pragmatic streak has allowed us to put some of them to good use. Because many of these ships went down on shallow reefs, divers can view them fairly easily. The Department of Tourism, together with Bermuda dive operators, has instituted the Bermuda Shipwreck Certificate Programme. This program focuses on 12 of the wrecks, chosen for their historical interest, accessibility and photogenic qualities. Dive at one of these sites and you will receive a Bermuda Shipwreck Certificate, printed on "parchment" paper. Each certificate names the shipwreck and gives a brief history of the ship and the circumstances of its sinking. See the Shipwreck heading in this chapter for descriptions of some of these wrecks.

Divers who are more interested in our marine life than the vestiges of past disasters will appreciate the natural beauty of our reefs and the rich ecosystem they support. Eventually, mind you, reef life will form around wrecks. If you are interested in learning more about the living organisms in our ocean, we urge you to read *Bermuda's Marine Life*, written by marine biologist Dr. Wolfgang Sterrer. Curator of the Bermuda Natural History Museum and former director of the Bermuda Biological Station for Research, he is somewhat of a present-day Renaissance man. His interests extend to poetry, history, science and jazz (he plays in a traditional jazz band). The book entertainingly describes in short paragraphs 225 of the 5,000 species that live in our waters. Only Dr. Sterrer could compare the bulbous lips of the bluebone porgy with those of the Austrian Hapsburg family. We mention *Bermuda's Marine Life* because it is the main source of the information we give you about our underwater fauna.

So what is our reef like? Dr. Sterrer compares it with an inner city that is "relentlessly being torn down and rebuilt, simultaneously decaying and being rehabilitated." Constructed mainly of stony corals, it's also composed of a multitude of living organisms such as coralline algae, coral anemones, sponges and soft corals. Yet all the while, boring sponges, clams and barnacles are undermining its foundations. When bits fall off in a hurricane, for example, new squatters arrive and set up house.

Dives close to the reefs reveal mysterious caverns, home to a myriad of living organisms. Actually, we were going to delineate between flora and fauna, but, as Dr. Sterrer points out, distinguishing between plant and animal in the underworld is often unbelievably difficult. A sea anemone is a flower, right? And a purple sea fan is a plant? Wrong. Both are animals. Does it matter? Yes, if you have the curiosity of a marine biologist. In the meantime, know that you will encounter corals (animals, too) of all shapes and sizes. There's hat coral and common brain coral and star coral. . . . We could go on for pages. You'll just have to come see for yourself.

Conservation Policies

"Is your reef healthy?" you might ask. Well, we have our fair share of worry about pollution, global warming and over-fishing. During the '80s there was excessive fishing, and certain species were seriously depleted. The large number of fish pots used by commercial fishermen certainly didn't help. Reef fish, particularly, got trapped in pots long after the fishermen had abandoned them. Numbers of grouper, red hind, rockfish and snapper all declined rapidly. People began to ask, "Where have all the fish gone?"

Shellfish such as clams and conchs suffered too — not because of pots, but because of an island wide addiction to clams casino (clams in a sauce topped with grilled bread crumbs and served in individual clam shells) and conch chowder. Harrington Sound, once the Mecca of Bermuda's calico clams and conchs, was almost completely depleted. Not only did we miss the fish, but we also worried about the effects this decline would have on the health of our reef. That's the bad news.

The good news is that the government woke up to the problem. Since 1990, fish pots have been completely banned in inshore and outside waters within and beyond the reef. And certain species have come under protection. All corals, sea rods and sea fans, calico clams, conchs and numerous other shellfish are protected. There are specific conservation rules, regulations and amendments that are so complicated they need a book in themselves. But in effect, our policy is that we treat our coral reef as a marine park. Bear in mind, too, that if you stand on or touch coral, you kill it. When you visit the reef, follow this maxim and you won't upset your guide or instructor: Leave everything you see untouched. The only thing you can take is a picture. What about shell collecting? Consider this: About 500,000 visitors come to Bermuda each year. Suppose each visitor were to take one shell? Our answer, then, is "Please don't do it." Other fishing restrictions also apply — check the Deep-sea and Reef Fishing and Charter Boats section for this information.

Scuba Diving and Snorkeling

At present there are six centers that specialize in diving and snorkeling. All dives are conducted by licensed scuba instructors. In addition, all the commercial dive operators we list are currently licensed by the Bermuda government and have their air tested annually. They operate daily, subject to weather conditions.

The diving season typically starts in mid-March and runs through November, although some operators operate year-round. We'll tell you which ones do. What about visibility? During summer months on the northern and eastern reefs, you can see about 100 feet. Because the southern and western reefs are closer, visibility there is 80 feet. Water temperature July to September is in the mid-80s, so a one-eighth-inch wetsuit should suffice. The rest of the year, when water temperatures can fall to the low 70s, wear a quarter-inch wetsuit. When in doubt, follow the advice of your instructor, or err on the side of warmth.

Shipwrecks

You will find a list of divers' favorite wrecks in the Department of Tourism's "Where to Dive" leaflet, available in most hotels and guest accommodations. Here we describe just a few that are frequently visited by our dive center operators.

Let's start with the *Mary Celestia*. A high-speed side paddle-wheel steamer, *Mary* was a Confederate blockade-runner. She sank in 1864 after a grim encounter with a reef close to the South Shore. Her paddle wheel stands upright in the water, and you can see her bow and anchor. *The Montana* was another paddle-wheeling steam Confederate runner, which also came to grief. She lies in 30 feet of water. Corals, both soft and hard, live on her.

Close to *The Montana* is *The Constellation*, a four-masted, American wooden-hulled schooner built in 1918. In 1943, on her way to Venezuela, she sank together with a cargo that included 700 cases of Scotch. You can see petrified sacks of cement as well as other salvage. The whisky? We're not sure. Perhaps there's a wee dram left. *The Constellation* was one of the wrecks featured in the book and the mid-'70s Nick Nolte movie *The Deep*.

Dive Centers

Our centers offer a variety of options — one-tank dives, two-tank dives or night dives. Generally, two-tank and night dives are for certified or experienced divers, but every center offers scuba training sessions for novices. Special packages and certification programs are available. Call directly for details and prices.

Rates usually include tanks and weights, with other equipment available for rent. Prices are explained in the individual listings. Snorkeling rates are cheaper, of course, and include equipment and instruction. It's important to reserve in advance as soon as possible. People who delay making reservations until the last couple of days of their holiday tend to be disappointed. In the summer months the operators are heavily booked. You may reserve through your guest accommodation or by calling directly. In any case, call the center to explain your level of expertise. And now, here are our dive and snorkeling centers listed east to west, parish by parish.

Hamilton Parish

Blue Water Divers and Watersports
Marriott's Castle Harbour Resort,
2 Paynters Rd. • (441) 232-2911
Blue Water Divers and Watersports actually has three operations: one at Marriott's

Castle Harbour, one at Elbow Beach Bermuda and one at Robinson's Marina in Sandy's Parish. Michael Burke is managing director of Blue Water and chairperson for the Watersports Division of the Bermuda Chamber of Commerce. He's a skilled underwater photographer as well, having published *Wonders of the Sea*, a book containing many of his photographs.

You can pick up a diving and/or snorkeling trip here, or you can rent a variety of water toys, including underwater scooters, Jet Skis and aqua bicycles. Please check the Blue Water listing under Sandy's Parish for diving and snorkeling rates and the Paget Parish listing for toy and kayak rental rates.

Scuba Look
Grotto Bay Beach Hotel and Tennis Club, 11 Blue Hole Hill
• **(441) 292-1717, (800) 582-3190**

Scuba Look is actually a division of Enterprise Submarine Ltd. But it's also the name of the 45-foot boat that will take you to dive on wrecks such as the *Rita Zovetto*, the *Cristobal Colon* and others that are seldom explored. A one-tank dive (check-in is at 8:15 AM or at 2 PM) costs $45, plus $35 for equipment rental (if necessary). A two-tank dive (check-in at 8:15 AM) costs $65, again with an additional $35 for equipment.

You've never been diving before? No problem. Check-in at 1:30 PM for instruction in a classroom and the pool, then go out for a dive where you will at all times be with a trained instructor. That costs $90, including equipment. PADI (The Professional Association of Dive Instructors) courses are also available. Call for more information. The Scuba Look staff is known for its friendliness.

If you don't fancy diving but want to snorkel instead, you'll go out on *Snorkel Look*, a fast, shallow boat that will cruise you through some of Bermuda's fishiest sites. A skipper will treat you to a lively and interesting historical narration on the East End of the island. Then the captain will anchor up in a couple of locations and let you float with the fish and maybe be touched by an angel. *Snorkel Look* departs at 10 AM and 2 PM daily. The cost is $35 for adults and teens and $18 for children 12 and younger. If you just want to go for a ride on one of the two boats, it costs $15.

The Scuba Look season begins March 16 and goes on to about the middle of November, weather permitting. Reserve as soon as possible by calling direct.

Pembroke Parish

Nautilus Instructor Development Centre
The Princess, 76 Pitts Bay Rd.
• **(441) 295-9485, (441) 238-2332**

Nautilus has been given five stars by PADI. In 1995 it was featured in the PADI wreck diver video. The 40-foot dive boat leaves from two locations: the Princess's private dock and the Southampton Beach Club's dock (see our Resort Hotels chapter). Every morning and afternoon, certified divers can take two-tank dives with instructors at two of Bermuda's shipwrecks. Which ones? That's up to you. If you prefer a reef-only dive, mention it when you reserve.

Dives cost $75, tank and weights included. If you're leaving from The Princess, for morning dives check in at 8 AM; you'll return at approximately 1 PM. Afternoons check in at noon to return at 4:30 PM. From the Beach Club, check in at 8:30 AM; you'll return at 11:30

INSIDERS' TIP

Make your reservations for water activities, especially diving, snorkeling and fishing, at the beginning of your vacation. If you can make the arrangements before you arrive in Bermuda, all the better. That way you won't be disappointed, and you'll have more leeway where weather is concerned.

AM. Afternoons check in at 12:30 PM to return at 3:30 PM. Puzzled by the time discrepancies? It's because Hamilton is much farther away from the South Shore. If you leave from Southampton, you can get to *The Marie Celestia*, for example, in just four minutes. Afternoon one-tank dives are available for $55, tank and weights included. Departure time from Hamilton is 1 PM; return is 4:30 PM. From Southampton it's out at 2 PM, back at 3:30 PM. So you're not a certified diver? No problem. For $99 you can have one hour of training in a pool, then go out on the afternoon dive. If you'd rather float than sink, for $40 (which includes snorkeling equipment) you can join the afternoon divers. While they are plumbing the depths, you can snorkel above.

Equipment rentals for divers are as follows: Mask, fins and snorkel are $8, a regulator is $15 and BC (buoyancy compensator) and wetsuit are $10 each. Advance reservations are essential. Reserve by calling direct. Nautilus is open year-round, though in December the Southampton Beach Club closes.

Paget Parish

Blue Water Divers and Watersports
Elbow Beach Bermuda, 60 South Rd.
• (441) 236-3535, (800) 223-7434

Read our Beaches chapter, and you'll see why Elbow Beach is so popular. Here, we'll just tell you that its stretch of sand and dune and its expanse of inviting ocean make watersports irresistible. Blue Water Divers and Watersports, located on the part of the beach owned by the resort hotel, is happy to supply you with a wide range of activities.

Into diving? If you're a novice, you can get diving instruction at the pool, where a one-hour lesson will cost $95. You also can take a certification course in the beach area; call to discuss rates, as they vary according to your needs and experience. Most exciting, you can go on a guided dive tour to the nearby reef, where you'll explore the wreck of *The Pollockshields*. Divers get to the reef in an underwater scooter. Driving at about 2 to 4 knots, the guide will speed the divers (who use their hands and hang on to the vehicle) along the breakers and through the caves and tunnels for half the dive. Then the guide will

anchor up at the wreck site for the latter part of the excursion. These battery-operated, electric underwater vehicles are entirely new to Bermuda. Only certified divers may take this trip, which costs $70 a person. Check Blue Water's listing under Sandys Parish for more information about diving facilities.

If snorkeling is more your idea of fun, you can rent equipment ($12 for two hours, $20 for eight hours) and check out the reef. For $34 per person, you can get instruction on snorkeling techniques and identifying flora and fauna, then take a guided snorkeling tour of the reef. Allowing for instruction, this program takes about two hours.

Feel like frolic? Elbow Beach can have that effect on you. For $19 an hour, try an aqua cycle (a water tricycle for two with giant wheels) and ride the waves. Kayaks, noodles, ball and paddle games and surfboards are available for rent. Call for prices.

Fantasea Diving
1 Darrell's Wharf • (441) 236-6339

A PADI five-star dive center, Fantasea offers a number of options. Mornings, for $70, certified divers can take a 4.5-hour trip to a reef and wreck site and enjoy a two-tank dive. Daily departure is 8 AM from the wharf. You can take a three-hour afternoon trip for a single-tank dive. Favorite locations during the afternoon are *The Constellation*, arguably one of the best shallow-water dive sites in the world, and the close-by *Montana*. Daily departure is 1 PM.

So you can't dive but want to learn? Then the three-stage Discover Scuba program is for you. First, your instructor will give a brief orientation to the world of diving. Next, you will have your first underwater experience in a swimming pool or at the beach. Finally, you will join the afternoon divers for your first wreck and reef dive. The program costs $91 per person. Call direct for lesson times.

Experienced divers can take a dive at night for $60; call to arrange time and location. Rates for diving include tanks and weights. Other equipment (such as BC) is available for $9 per unit. A credit card is required when you reserve. You can cancel without penalty if you do it by 5 PM the afternoon before your dive. You can buy a one-hour video record of your deep encounters for $60. An edited, cut version costs $75.

If a Jacques Cousteau experience does not appeal to you, try snorkeling instead. For $38, equipment included, you can float over the reefs while the divers view them from a lower perspective. Fantasea is open most of the year but does close for a couple of weeks in February or March. Incidentally, it has a concession at Sonesta Beach and Spa Hotel (see our Resort Hotels chapter). The telephone number at Sonesta is (441) 238-8122.

Sandys Parish

Blue Water Divers and Watersports
Robinson's Marina, Somerset Bridge
• (441) 234-1034

A Gold Palm five-star PADI resort, Blue Water Divers is Bermuda's oldest dive center. It caters to beginners and experienced divers. In the mornings, experienced divers can take a three-and-a-half-hour, two-tank dive for $70. They will explore one or two of the many wrecks that are just a 45-minute boat ride away from the marina. And, of course, they will explore the sea fans, huge finger corals and fish. Check-in at the marina at 8:15 AM for a 9 AM departure.

In the afternoons, certified divers, beginners and snorkelers get together for a two-and-a-half-hour trip that includes a one-tank dive out on the reef and a wreck. The cost for this dive and trip is $50. All rates quoted include tank, weights and belts. You can rent additional equipment, such as a wetsuit and regulator for between $6 and $9. Snorkelers can take the afternoon trip for $36, equipment included. Children 12 and younger can snorkel for $22. If you just want to go for the ride, you can do so for $14. Check in is at 12:45 PM for a 1:30 PM departure.

The uninitiated diver can take a three-hour resort lesson and dive for $91, equipment included. Videos of the trip cost $39.95. Certified divers can rent video cameras for $55 a trip. A credit card number is required when you reserve. You can cancel without penalty if you do so by 9 PM the evening before your dive. Call Blue Waters for information about group rates, special packages and certification programs. They are open year-round.

Helmet Diving

So you'd love to see fish in their own backyard but you object to getting your face wet? Furthermore, you believe in standing on your own two feet? In short, you can't swim? Helmet diving is the answer.

This is how it works. Dressed in swimming gear, you go out in a boat to a location where there's a sandy ocean bottom but plenty of fish. With the boat moored, you gingerly descend halfway down a ladder to the water. An operator will place a helmet over your head until it reaches your shoulders. You will then somewhat resemble a medieval knight, but you'll be able to look through glass, which is more than he could. Take a deep breath and you'll discover that, yes, breathing is possible. The helmet is filled with air. It may feel a bit heavy, but don't worry. Take another deep breath for courage and descend the ladder until you reach the sea floor, about 10 feet under.

Lo, the helmet will feel lighter, and you and the fish will meet each other on your own terms. Children ages 5 and older can do it, and so can 80-year-olds. You can even keep your glasses on. Don't jump up and down though. That's rude to the fish. The following two centers offer helmet diving service.

Smiths Parish

Bermuda Bell Diving
North Shore Rd., Flatts
• (441) 292-4434

You can join Carico, a recently refurbished, 50-foot motor yacht in Flatts Inlet, just across the water from the Bermuda Aquarium. Owners Paul Pike and James Outerbridge will take you to a location just 'round the corner of Shelly Bay (see our Beaches chapter). On the way, they'll explain the procedure and calm any trepidation you may be feeling.

When they moor the boat, you'll follow the procedure outlined above. Ten to 12 feet under water, you'll soon be on pally terms with sergeant-majors and slippery dicks. You'll also discover that some of James's and Paul's personal underwater regulars are suffering from identity problems. Helen's OK — she swims like the angel she is right through a hoop. But

Theodore's got a real identity crisis. She is a hogfish. James has named a recent newcomer Mortimer, but Paul doesn't approve. He wants Howard — the name goes so alliteratively with hogfish.

Daily departures are at 10 AM and 2 PM. The dive lasts approximately 25 minutes, but the whole trip is about three hours, depending on the number of people. No more than seven people dive at one time. While you're waiting your turn, you can watch on video as others dive; after you're through, you can watch yourself. The tape costs $25 if you want to keep it to show your grandchildren. Polaroid pictures are also available for $5 each. When the water's cooler than 80 degrees, you'll borrow a wetsuit and warm up with complimentary hot chocolate. The fun costs $48 for an adult, $36 for a child younger than 12. Call for reservations, and be aware that excursions are subject to weather.

Sandys Parish

Greg Hartley's Undersea Adventure
1 Mangrove Bay Rd. • (441) 234-2861

Climb aboard Greg's glass-bottomed boat, *Rainbow Runner*, at Watford Bridge dock in Somerset at 10 AM or 1:30 PM. Come dressed in swimming gear and bring a towel. You'll take a 25-minute boat ride to a reef about a mile off the western end of Bermuda, with Greg briefing you all the while. Once there, you'll follow the procedure outlined above, find your feet (so to speak) and meet Greg's fishy friends on an underwater walk. Say hi to Oliver, the snapper who keeps everyone firmly under control. He has a right — he's been around for about seven years.

The dive lasts approximately 25 minutes, and the whole trip is about three hours, depending on the number of people. No more than seven people dive at one time. You can have your picture taken for $6. On your return

you receive a complimentary fruit juice or, in the winter, a hot chocolate. When the water is cooler than 80 degrees, you wear a wetsuit for free. A changing room and shower facilities are on board. While you're waiting your turn or for the others to finish, you can gaze at the fish through the boat's glass bottom. The cost for adults is $48; for children younger than 12, it's $36. Call Lynda Hartley for reservations, and be aware that excursions are subject to weather.

Snorkeling and Sightseeing Motor Cruises

St. George's Parish

Coral Sea Cruises
Ordnance Island, Town of St. George • (441) 236-7637, (441) 235-2424

OK, you'd love to see the fish, but you're aquaphobic. Even floating face down on top of the water just isn't for you. No problem. Take a trip with Beau Evans and Stephen McKey on their *Coral Sea* glass-bottomed boat. They'll zip you to the barrier reef that is just 15 minutes away from St. George's Harbour. Once there, you'll spend an hour watching the multicolored fish float under the glass while Beau and Steve tell you all about life at the reef.

The trip costs $20 per person (half-price for kids younger than 12), and the ride out and back takes an hour. On Mondays, Tuesdays and Wednesdays, the *Coral Sea* leaves at 1:15 PM, on Thursdays it leaves at 10 AM and 1:15 PM, and on Saturdays it departs at 11:30 AM. Fancy a nature walk too? Then take the 2-hour eco-cruise for extra sightseeing at

---

INSIDERS' TIP

If you're cruising in Hamilton Harbour and the Great Sound, ask your skipper to point out Buck's Island and a house there with a tower. The captain will most likely tell you Denslow Homer, original illustrator of *The Wizard of Oz*, lived there and referred to himself as king of the island.

Paget Island. There you can amble on the island and enjoy the flora and fauna. The fish and reef viewing is also included in the $30 rate. Kids go for $15. This trip departs on Mondays and Tuesdays at 10 AM (on Tuesdays, there's a second trip that starts at 1 PM), Wednesdays at 9 AM and Thursdays at 2:30 PM. Call to make reservations.

Devonshire Parish

Bermuda Barefoot Cruise Ltd.
8 Kent Ave.
• (441) 236-3498, (441) 234-7609

Doug Shirley is skipper and owner of *Minnow*, a 32-foot custom-built picnic cruiser that has cover to chill out in the shade as well as plenty of space for sunbathing. You don't fancy cruising with strangers? Then charter Doug's boat, and he will take you anywhere you want (within reason, that is) for snorkeling and sightseeing by water. Ask any question, and he'll draw upon his huge amount of local information. He knows his fish (angels and parrots are his personal favorites), and he knows where to find them. We asked him where, but "off the West End" is all he would tell us. We can't blame Doug — he wants to make sure his secret spots stay secret. While we're talking about the West End, we should tell you the *Minnow* can cruise under Somerset Bridge, even when the tide is very low. Want a picnic? Bring your own food, and Doug will make sure you stop at a great spot. His price, by the way, includes free sodas and rum swizzles. Beer and wine are available for $3.50 a drink. He also carries snorkeling equipment and all sorts of beach toys for children and the young at heart.

Doug's season runs from mid-April until December 31. People typically charter his boat for a minimum of four hours. That will cost you $420 for the first eight people and $15 for each additional person. You should book as soon as possible with your credit card. If you cancel within 48 hours of your scheduled trip, you'll be charged half price; cancel within 24 hours, and you'll pay the whole fare. Departure times are flexible. Doug will pick you up at Darrell's Wharf or any of the hotel docks. Call for arrangements.

Pembroke Parish

Bermuda Water Tours
1 Fairyland Ln. • (441) 236-1500

Meet *Bottom Peeper*, a glass-bottomed boat with 150 square feet of viewing glass. For $25 you can take a two-hour sightseeing trip to the Sea Gardens off Somerset. Once you're there, you can view the reef and the wreck of the HMS *Vixen* through the glass. The skipper will fill you in on reef life and the fate of the *Vixen*, and he'll feed the fish so you can watch them jump. Weather permitting, he might also take you to the wrecks of the *Montana* and the *Constellation*. A washroom and bar are available on board.

All trips on the *Bottom Peeper* depart from the Hamilton Ferry Terminal. This sightseeing trip starts at 10 AM every morning. For $40 per person you can make it a four-hour trip — it's the same destination, but you will snorkel as well. On your way to the reef, Colin will brief you on snorkeling techniques, and, together with his instructors, he will snorkel with you. On the way back, you can relax over complimentary rum swizzles, beers or soft drinks. This cruise starts at 1:15 PM. Prices for kids ages 6 to 12 are 50 percent of those listed above. Those 5 years and younger go for free.

Underwater disposable cameras are available for $20. Call Susan Young to make reservations and for information about lunch and dinner cruises and charter rates. Susan and Bruce operate from the beginning of April until the end of November.

Jessie James Cruises
Old Cellar Ln. (Walker Arcade),
47 Front St., Hamilton • (441) 296-5801

Meet the friendly O'Connor family: There's husband and wife Jimmy and Jill, their son, Mark (cruise director), and husband and wife Ronnie and Dee. Next, meet their three boats: the *Rambler*, a 57-foot yacht; the *Consort*, a 48-foot motor cruiser, and their most recent acquisition, the *Looking Glass*, a 50-foot glass-bottomed motor cruiser.

During the summer season you can ride one of the boats for a four-hour "Snorkel Three Times" cruise that will take you to different locations. First you go to a beach with shallow water — novice snorkelers can learn the technique of breathing by mouth, while experienced ones can snorkel around a small island. Next, you cruise out to the *Constellation* and *Montana* for a guided snorkeling tour. Finally, you will explore the corals and sea fans in a sea garden. Instructors are on hand to help and inform.

The cost is $45 per person, $25 per child ages 5 to 12. Rates include all equipment, including snorkel vests and masks with individual prescription lenses if you need them. A full bar offering light snacks is on board. A changing room and shower facilities are also available. In addition, the *Looking Glass* goes out twice a day for a 2½-hour trip to the *Vixen* and the reef and then glides into Ely's Harbour. Costs are $25 per adult and $12.50 per child.

Departure points are Albuoy's Point, Hamilton, at 9:15 AM and 2:15 PM; Darrell's Wharf, Warwick, at 9:25 AM and 2:25 PM; and Belmont Wharf at 9:30 AM and 2:30 PM. In addition, the O'Connors also offer private charters. Call for details.

Paget Parish

Salt Kettle Yacht Charters
17 Salt Kettle Rd. • (441) 236-4863

David Ashton is owner and skipper of two yachts. Here, we'll tell you about *Magic Carpet*, his 35-foot Flybridge motor cruiser. David will take you on private snorkel trips to Bermuda's coves and bays, where you can leisurely check out the sea urchins, parrotfish and other underwater life. If you need snorkeling instruction, he'll provide it along with stories about the island's past. Since there are more coral fish (such as puffers and porcupine fish) on the outer reef, David will take you there too. Exactly where you go depends on your choice and the weather.

Starting times are also up to you; call David to arrange them. *Magic Carpet* can carry up to 18 people, but the rates we quote are for up to eight people. Additional riders cost an extra $22 per person for day or evening trips. During the day the base rates are as follows: $375 for three hours, $450 for four hours, $650 for six hours and $720 for eight hours. Call for evening rates.

In addition, there is a four-hour Snorkeling Adventure trip for groups only (minimum, 12 persons). The $45 per-person rate includes a snorkeling session on the reefs and around some of the wrecks, plus a complimentary soda or rum swizzle on the way home. Departure is usually from the dock at Salt Kettle, though he does sometimes pick up tourists from Cambridge Beaches in Sandys. Call directly for reservations, departure details and information on his sailing yacht, *Bright Star*.

Sandys Parish

Pitman's Snorkeling
12 Westside Rd.
• (441) 234-0700

Mr. Pitman is known by some locals as "The Old Man of the Sea," but he likes to be called by his first name, Joffre. Joffre offers "comprehensive and sensitive" snorkeling instruction. This is particularly important for people who really want to experience the fish but can't swim. "Sometimes," he says, "I feel like a psychologist because I know how to get people over their fear of water."

From June through October, Joffre offers a daily four-hour tour in his 44-foot glass bottom boat, the *Fathom*. He usually makes for the Eastern Blue Cut, where for 1.5 hours you can enjoy world-class snorkeling around underwater canyons with 60-foot drops. The trip is "aimed for the intellect," he says. On the way out and back, Joffre will share his extensive knowledge of the corals, the flora and fauna, the *Lartington* shipwreck and Bermudian architecture and culture. You'll soon realize he has a passionate feel for what created the environment.

A changing facility is on board. Bring your own lunch, snacks and soft drinks. No alcohol, please. The cost is $45 per person, and credit cards are not accepted. Departure time depends on tides, visibility and weather conditions. Joffre flatly refuses to take people out if he knows there's little chance of seeing much. He strongly recommends that you call as soon as you arrive in Bermuda to make reservations. Departure location is usually Robinson's Marina, but discuss it with him when you reserve.

Sailboat, Personal Watercraft and Motorboat Rentals

A few of the following listings rent out Jet Skis as well as a variety of boats. We must tell you here that Bermuda law does not allow the rental of Jet Skis unaccompanied by a safety instructor. And you have to be at least 18 years old to legally rent a ski, and at least 16 to drive one.

Hamilton Parish

Blue Hole Water Sports
11 Blue Hole Hill, Bailey's Bay
• **(441) 293-2915**

Want to cruise around Grotto Bay, explore Castle Harbour and see St. George's from the water? Blue Hole has a 13-foot Boston whaler, equipped with anchor and bimini, along with life jackets and whistle available for rent. Remember that before the days of cars and mopeds, East Enders mostly traveled by boat, so you will be following in their footsteps or, rather, in their wake.

Rates are per boat, not per person. They cost $65 for two hours, $110 for four hours and $165 for eight hours. Prices include snorkeling gear and a cooler. If you want to feel like a true St. David's islander, rent light fishing tackle for $5 an hour or $15 for all day. After all, boating means fishing, right? Friendly staff will give you a briefing on the rules of the sea. Other craft are available. You can go on a Sun Cat for $35 an hour or hire a single kayak for $15 an hour (double kayaks are $20). Each additional hour costs $10. Take out a Sunfish for $25 for the first hour, $10 for each additional one. Windsurfing appeals to you? The rate is the same as the rate for a Sunfish, and

Blue Hole has a large range of equipment suitable for the most experienced windsurfer, as well as for beginners. Newcomers to surfing the wind can have a two-hour lesson for $60. If you're not renting a whaler, snorkeling gear costs $18 for a 24-hour rental. Their season runs from April 1 to November 15.

Southampton Parish

Pompano Beach Club Water Sports Centre
36 Pompano Beach Rd.
• **(441) 234-0222**

This hotel's watersports shop has many options for wet fun, and you don't have to be a guest to give it a go. We recommend a Sun Cat ($35 for one hour, $25 for a half-hour), which is like a motorized armchair for two. If you are tempted to go snorkeling, you can rent a mask and snorkel for $7 a day. (For much more information on Pompano's offerings, see the hotel's listing in our Small Hotels chapter.)

Sandys Parish

Mangrove Marina
Robinson's Marina, Somerset Bridge
• **(441) 234-0914**

Rent one of Tony Roache's 14-foot Boston whalers, and the whole of the Great Sound, Hamilton Harbour, Ely's Harbour and the Sea Gardens off Daniel's Head will be yours to explore. You can sample the coves, the little islands and beaches, and snorkel to your heart's content. You can even zip over to Hamilton, tie up the boat and have lunch in town. Cruise under Somerset Bridge, and you're cruising under the smallest drawbridge over the Atlantic in the world.

These whalers are easy to operate and are equipped with an anchor, bimini and a map. They carry an extra jug of gas and life-saving equipment such as jackets, flares and a whistle. Friendly, experienced staff members with great senses of humor will brief you. In addition to telling you about the boat and rules of the sea, they'll also ask you not to go onto the North Shore or farther than Pompano Beach on the South Shore.

Rates are per boat, and credit cards are not accepted. Two hours will cost you $65, four hours are $100, and eight hours are $165. In addition, you'll pay for the gas you use, which averages between $10 and $20. The flat rate for snorkeling gear rental is $6, and it's $12 for light fishing tackle (including bait). A cooler can come in handy; it will cost you $4 to rent one. Boats can take up to four people, including children younger than 12. A 15-foot bow rider and a 15-foot whaler are also available. They can accommodate up to six adults. Rates for these are $20 an hour more than the ones previously quoted.

You'd rather paddle your own canoe? No problem. A single ocean kayak costs $15 for one hour, $25 for two hours and $40 for four hours. Add $5 an hour to those rates for a double canoe. The staff will give you instructions and, if you like, will take you on a banana boat ride. You'll sit in a "hydro sled" while they tow you around at whatever speed you like.

For kids, that usually means the faster, the better.

If adrenaline is more your style, then their escorted Jet Ski tours will be perfect for you. You'll be taken on a 75-minute speed tour, riding your own three-seater 700cc Wave Runner, capable of speeds in excess of 50 mph. Instructions on their operation and safety are provided before the tour, and the skis are easier to ride than a motor scooter. As there is a maximum of four skis on each tour, you're assured lots of personal attention. The guides are all informative, fun and humorous, as well as being qualified in emergency first aid. You will zip out of Ely's Harbour and be led up to a shipwreck, where five minutes is spent feeding the fish, then sped around the Royal Naval Dockyard and into the Great Sound, where you can have some free play. The rates (per ski) are $90 for a single, $105 for a double, and $115 for a triple. As these tours are very popular, we recommend you call and reserve a ski at least 24 hours in advance.

Windjammer Water Sports
Building 41, The Royal Naval Dockyard
• (441) 234-1343

Windjammer is well named (after a kind of sailing ship dating back to 1899) since it offers a whole host of sailing activities, as well as

Anglers vacationing in Bermuda have broken many sportfishing records.

motor boat and Jet Ski rentals. You can hire a 17- foot O'Day sail boat that has a small cabin and can take up to four people. It offers, staff promise, a very dry ride. Cost? For two hours (minimum length of hire) $65, for four hours $90 and for eight hours $135. You can also hire a Sunfish for $25 for the first hour and $10 per hour thereafter. How about a Laser? You can hire one for $35 for the first hour and $15 an hour thereafter. All the prices we have so far quoted in this listing are per boat. Ocean kayaks are also on hand: singles cost $15 for the first hour and $10 an hour thereon; doubles cost $20 for the first hour and after that $10 per hour. Sunrise kayak safaris are very popular. Offered every Monday and Saturday at 8 AM, they give you the opportunity to paddle to the *Vixen* wreck, snorkel around it and feed the fish. These escorted tours (a minimum of 4 people and a maximum of 13 can participate) start at Cambridge Beaches (see Cottage Colonies Chapter) and last 90 minutes. They cost $38 per person, with the cost including all snorkeling equipment.

You can't sail but would like to? Staff are happy to offer one on one or one on one couple lessons for $60 an hour. Perhaps windsurfing is more your line. Windjammer has the largest selection of Mistral boards and sails. Boards can be long or short depending on whether you want high wind or light air windsurfing. The cost is $35 for the first hour and $10 an hour from thereon. Windsurfing one-hour lessons are also available and run at $60 per person for beginners and $75 per person for the advanced.

But if sailing or windsurfing is not for you then rent out one of Windjammer's 15-foot motor boats complete with bimini, cooler, ice, map and safety equipment. After receiving instruction and orientation, you can tool out to the Great Sound, around the Royal Naval Dockyard and into Hamilton Harbour. Cost is $40 per boat for the first hour and $20 an hour thereafter. In addition you pay $30 for a full tank of gas. Feel like fishing? No problem — for 24 hours you can rent fishing equipment for $10. If speed is your thing, then escorted Jet Ski tours may be for you. You'll be supplied with goggles and, when necessary, with wet suits, plus, of course, the Jet Ski. A CPR trained guide, well versed on these machines,

will accompany you for a 90-minute tour, which, weather permitting, takes you to the *Vixen* and to the reef for snorkeling. These Jet Ski safaris can be an excellent way of checking out local homes and architecture. You can ride into Riddell's Bay, along the North Shore and into Fairylands and understand more about traditional Bermudian roofs, for example, or welcoming arms steps. There is a maximum of five Jet Skis per tour. Cost is $95 for one person and $135 for two (on a double seater Jet Ski.) If you're really feeling adventurous, then you might like a three-hour, round-the-island, snorkeling safari. This excursion is for single Jet Skis only and is available on request. Call for reservations and rates.

Waterskiing and Parasailing

We have put these sports in a separate category so that you'll more easily find the few centers in Bermuda that offer them. Remember how we mentioned our trinity of sky, sea and land in this chapter's introduction? Parasail and you'll experience it all in one ride! But bear in mind that times of sessions are subject to weather conditions. A beautiful sunny day without a breath of wind may make parasailing impossible. The operators will advise you about the possibilities, or lack thereof, when you make your reservation. For waterskiing, wear swimming gear, but for parasailing wear ordinary comfortable clothes. You won't land in water.

St. George's Parish

St. George's Parasail Water Sports Ltd.
Somers Wharf, Water St.,
Town of St. George
• **(441) 297-1542**

Jamal Harte will take you out in his boat a few feet from the wharf in St. George's Harbour. He will then make sure you're sitting safely in a harness attached to a parachute. A few minutes later you'll be up in the sky, literally higher than a kite. For eight minutes Jamal will cruise round the harbour so that you can enjoy viewing our old town from on high. Don't worry that you'll end up in the water; you'll land on the boat. If you'd rather have company, you can take a tandem ride — two harnesses are attached to one parachute.

The cost for the fun is $50 per adult. Children ages 5 to 12 cost $35 per person. The center is open from 9 AM to 6 PM, and the boat leaves every half-hour. You should reserve about two to three hours in advance. In addition, Jamal offers banana boat and big tube rides at $30 per adult for 15 minutes; kids pay $25 for the same length of time. St. George's Parasail is open from May 1 to October 30.

Hamilton Parish

Blue Hole Water Sports
11 Blue Hole Hill, Bailey's Bay
• (441) 293-2915

Michael Stevens (owner and manager) and Sean Correia will be happy to let you skim the waters of Grotto Bay or Castle Harbour on skis. In fact, they'll give you instruction in all types of waterski-type activities, including wakeboarding, which they say is the fastest-growing sport on the island. One hour will cost you $95, 30 minutes is $60, and 15 minutes is $40. Waterskiing is available from April 1 to October 31. See the Sailboat, Personal Watercraft and Motorboat Rentals section in this chapter for other activities at Blue Hole.

Sandys Parish

Bermuda Waterski Centre
Robinson's Marina, Somerset Bridge
• (441) 234-3354

Kent Richardson is a champion waterskier and accomplished triathlon athlete. Yet he has lots of patience for beginners. He'll take you out into Ely's Harbour and teach you the intri-

cacies of balance. The ultimate skiing experience, Kent says, is using one ski only, and he'll show you that too. One hour of fun will cost you $100, 30 minutes is $60, and 15 minutes is $30. The Waterski Centre operates from May 1 to the end of September. However, Kent will take tourists out during the winter months, subject to weather and demand.

Skyrider Bermuda Ltd.
Water Sports Center,
Royal Naval Dockyard • (441) 234-3019

Parasail here and you'll definitely ride the sky. But you'll go for a boat ride on the western end of Bermuda first. Then you'll sit in a chair made for two, take off and for eight minutes achieve a higher level of consciousness as you float above the island. You'll come back to earth on the boat. The cost is $80 per adult couple. Kids are welcome, provided they are accompanied by an adult. Younger than 13, they pay $32. If you just want to ride in the boat, it will cost you $32 as well. Try to reserve a day ahead. Skyrider operates from March to the end of November, weather permitting.

Deep-Sea and Reef Fishing and Charter Boats

Come fish in Bermuda and take part in our traditions and folklore. Many of our anglers, you see, were born with the sport in their blood. Their fathers (and sometimes their mothers) fished before them, and their grandfathers before that.

Louis S. Mowbray, former curator of the Bermuda Aquarium, once defined a fisherman as a "liar." We wouldn't dream of agreeing with him, preferring instead to define one as a "great story teller." You want an Insider's view of Bermuda's past and present? Talk to the men and women who fish. They will tell you

---

INSIDERS' TIP

Spiny sea urchins are important to our ecosystem; they help clean the moss from our reefs. However, step on them and they don't like it. Their sharp spines will penetrate your skin and are difficult to remove. A general rule is: Don't put your foot in it.

tales that just don't appear in any brochure. Are they true? Who cares? As Nathaniel Hawthorne put it, "Nobody has any conscience about adding to the improbabilities of a marvelous tale."

Storytellers they may be, and you can take their tales with a grain of salt if you like. However, where the sea is concerned, they are the experts. Going to them (rather than a "friend of a friend") when getting the right information regarding our seas is crucial. That way you will be better assured of a rewarding and safe fishing experience.

Licenses, Safety, Conservation Rules and Regulations

So you want to go fishing? Your first question is probably going to be, "Do I need a fishing license?" The pleasantly simple answer is no. When you go out on a charter boat you are covered by the captain's license. Every charter boat we list is skippered by an experienced, licensed captain. Their boats are inspected and re-licensed annually by the Bermuda government.

All boats are equipped with lifesaving equipment (in accordance with U.S. Coast Guard lifesaving regulations), ship-to-shore telephones, toilet facilities and up-to-date fishing equipment, which includes fighting chairs, outriggers, and all the necessary tackle and bait. As we have already explained, we now have strict fishing regulations to protect our marine environment. You may not spear fish within 1 mile of any shore, you may not spear one while using an aqualung, and you may not use a spear gun at any time.

Our skippers will explain where you may or may not fish, based on government regulations. For example, from May 1 to August 31 three ocean areas off the southwest, east and north shores of Bermuda are protected because they are breeding grounds for grouper. Captains will also explain size restrictions on catching fish. You can't, for instance, catch and keep a black rockfish that's less than 30 inches. The fish (and mammals) that can't be caught at all include whales, porpoises, dolphins, gag groupers (fine scale), Nassau groupers, red groupers, deer and green hamlets, mutton hamlets and tiger rockfish.

So what fish can you catch? Look to the next two sections.

Reef Fishing

Reef fishing, by the way, does not mean actually fishing on the reef. It means you won't go outside the reef line to where the continental shelf drops.

If sea sickness is likely to be a problem for you, then reef fishing may be a better option than deep-sea fishing. Inside the reef line the waters are usually more protected and less turbulent. Fish you are likely to catch include Bermuda chub, gray and yellow tail snappers, barracuda, porgies, hinds, amberjack, bonefish and assorted bottom fish. Light tackle is used.

Deep-Sea Fishing

Captains on deep-sea trips will take you out about 10 miles offshore, depending on the weather and where they think there might be some good strikes. As soon as you go outside the reef line, you can feel the Atlantic swell — enjoyable for those of us with good sea legs.

Expect to find blackfin and yellowfin tuna, wahoo, shark, barracuda and dolphin. (Don't worry. We promise we're not referring to the Flipper sort of dolphin; we're just not that nasty. We mean dolphin as in mahi mahi or the dorado.) Marlin? Yep, we have those too — both blue marlin and white marlin.

Here we must mention the important matter of the tag-and-release policy. On the whole, you will be encouraged to release the fish that are not good to eat. Of course, if you bring in a fish that is likely to break a record of some sort, the skipper will probably be understanding about it. If you want a fish mounted, most captains can help you arrange it through agents here or abroad. (Ask about costs, since they depend on the color and size of the fish.) However, most mounted fish are artificial, their construction based on the estimated measurements of the fish you catch. Hence, it's often possible to keep the fish, so to speak, yet let it go. The government promotes the release policy by presenting certificates of release to anglers who have let fish go. These certificates are presented to you by the skipper.

As for the fish that are good for eating, catch policies are at the captain's discretion. You should ask about them when you reserve your trip. Typically, the skipper will clean and prepare fillets that you can eat that night. Captains tend to avoid giving out enough fish to sell.

Rates and Reservations

The rates we quote in the individual listings are (on the whole) per boat, not per person. Where there are exceptions to this, we will explain in the individual listings. Generally, captains will take out groups of six who share the cost. They will also take out fewer people if those guests agree to pay the whole charter price.

The rate includes all equipment, but it usually does not include drinks, food or a gratuity. (Gratuities are gratefully received but not mandatory.) Typically, guests bring their own lunch and drinks, although sometimes drinks are included in the rate. Often the captain prefers to negotiate times and prices with one person who represents the group. That way there's less confusion. Groups often come from conventions or are made up of people who are staying in the same hotel. You can

reserve through your guest accommodation or one of the booking offices listed in this chapter, or, of course, you can call the captain direct. It's best to talk to him about arrangements anyway. Rates are subject to change. Some captains, but not all, fish year-round, weather permitting. We will tell you if they only operate during specified seasons.

In the summer months be sure to bring a decent hat and lots of suntan or sunblock lotion. That sea breeze may feel cool, but it won't stop you from burning in the sun. Wear comfortable clothing, including rubber-soled shoes with a good grip: You don't want to slip if you have to move quickly on the deck or bridge. Bring lunch and plenty of bottled water. Some captains allow alcohol, usually beer; remember that this can increase dehydration. If you're prone to sea sickness, alcohol's not a good idea.

And now to the listings, which are given in east-to-west geographical order, parish by parish. Note that we use the boat name in each header. A captain is known by his boat, right?

St. George's Parish

Barong
14 Jacob's Point Rd., St. David's
• (441) 297-0715

This boat belongs to Captain Peter Olander and his wife, Jeannie. The captain goes deep-sea fishing only. He usually departs from Ordnance Island, St. George's, or Marriott Castle Harbour at 6:30 AM. "The fish," Jeannie says, "bite early." A half-day costs $660 for up to five hours; that rate is for six people. Per person, the rate is $140. A full day for six people costs $840. No per-person rates are available for a whole day's fishing. All prices include free water, soda and beer. Catch policy? You'll get to keep enough to eat. A 24-hour cancellation policy applies; Captain Olander will take your credit card number when you make reservations. Weather permitting, he fishes year-round.

INSIDERS' TIP

Be careful of the Portuguese man-of-war jellyfish. Their tentacles can extend 50 meters, and they can badly sting you.

Hamilton Parish

Striker 1
3 Aubrey Rd • (441) 293-4390

Captain Clifton Lambert owns a 34-foot Canyon Runner, specially equipped for all types of fishing. He will pick you up at Albuoys Point in Hamilton anywhere between 7 and 8:30 AM for either a half or a whole day's fishing (he specializes in both reef and deep-sea fishing). "I like catching yellow finned tuna," he says, "but they do give you sore arms!" A half-day costs $650 per boat while a whole day costs $875. Call him to arrange times for afternoon trips. A 24-hour cancellation policy applies.

Pembroke Parish

Gringo
9 Old House Ln., Spanish Point
• (441) 295-3500

Captain Joey Dawson's 35-foot Bruno, *Gringo*, carries the whole range of tackle for deep-sea fishing. For a half-day (four hours), he charges $600, and it's $750 for a full-day, eight-hour trip. He usually departs between 7 and 8 AM from the dock nearest to your accommodation. Sodas are included, but bring your own lunch.

Dawson concentrates on deep-sea fishing, aiming particularly for wahoo and tuna. Usually, he'll take you out to the Banks and the North Shore. Catch policy? He will always give guests what they can eat. As for marlin, the captain is a supporter of the tag-and-release policy. Dawson's season runs from April 1 to October 31. Credit cards are not accepted; you'll need to pay with cash or travelers' checks.

Eureka
11 Abri Ln., Spanish Point
• (441) 296-5414

The 65-foot *Eureka* is owned by Captain Allen DeSilva (see subsequent listing for *Mako 4*) but skippered by Captain David Soares. Soares takes the boat out deep-sea fishing from 8 AM to noon, Tuesday through Saturday. In the afternoons he goes reef fishing from 1 to 5 PM. On deep-sea trips, Soares goes outside the reef line by the North Channel in search of grouper, snapper, barracuda and shark. For reef fishing he stays closer to shore, where the water is calm and protected.

Rates are per person, rather than per boat. In both mornings and afternoons, adults and teens pay $60 a person; children younger than 12 pay half price. On Sundays only you can have a full-day, deep-sea trip from 7:30 AM to 4:30 PM for $100 a person. Passengers may keep the fish they catch. All departures leave from Albuoy's Point in Hamilton. Summer season runs from April 1 to October 31. However, depending on the weather, the *Eureka* will go out during November and March. Call for those rates and for info about private charters.

Mako 4
11 Abri Ln. Spanish Point
• (441) 234-8626, (441) 295-0835

Captain Allen DeSilva will take you deep-sea fishing in his 53-foot Jim Smith sportsfishing boat, which he says is "the largest and fastest charter boat on the island." Yes, DeSilva will be sure to give you enough of the day's catch to eat, but when it comes to marlin, he favors the tag-and-release policy. By the way, a couple of years ago the captain broke a Bermuda record by bringing in a 1,352-pound blue marlin.

A half-day on the *Mako 4* (7:30 AM to noon or 1 to 5 PM) costs $700. A full day (7:30 AM to 5 PM) costs $1,000. Sodas, beer and water are included in the price. DeSilva has a seven-day cancellation policy and requires a 30 percent advance deposit. The season runs from April 1 to October 31. You can go out every day of the week, subject to demand and weather.

Princess
8 Tulo Ln., Spanish Point
• (441) 295-2370

Captain David DeSilva, son of Captain Allen DeSilva, has private charter or per-person rates for half- and full-day deep-sea fishing trips on the *Princess*. Most likely, David DeSilva will take you to the Argus or Challenger Banks in search of wahoo, tuna and blue and white marlin. He'll let you have enough of the day's catch to eat and will depart from any location you choose.

Half-day rates are $650 for a regular party of six, $110 per person. In the morning, the boat leaves at 7:30 or 8 AM (whichever you prefer) and returns at 11:30 AM; in the afternoon, you leave at 1 PM and return at 5 PM. Full-day rates are $875 for six people or $150 per person. Departure is at 7:30 or 8:30 AM, and you will return eight hours later. Sodas are included in all prices. DeSilva has a 48-hour cancellation policy and will need a credit-card number when you reserve. His season starts April 1 and runs through November 30.

Tango
8 Tulo Ln., Spanish Point
• **(441) 295-2370**

Captain David DeSilva's specialty is reef fishing. With the *Tango*, he'll depart from anywhere you choose in Hamilton and take you to a reef line on his 42-foot custom-built boat. Where you go depends on where DeSilva thinks the fish are. He'll probably take you off the South Shore or to the northwestern side of the island. The pick of the catch goes to his guests. "That gives them incentive to catch fish," DeSilva says. His personal favorite fish is yellowtail snapper: "Fry it, stew it, boil it …it's always white and flaky."

DeSilva offers a full-day, eight-hour trip for $875; a half-day (four hours) will cost you $650. Departure times are mutually agreed upon. If possible, reserve with a credit card before you arrive in Bermuda. If you cancel within 24 hours of your scheduled trip, it'll cost you 50 percent of the rate.

Lobster Reef
16 Mariners' Lane Spanish Point
• **(441) 292-0518**

Captain Pace specializes in deep-sea fishing and has a strict tag-and-release policy for marlin. Actually, a marlin is his favorite fish to catch while a rockfish is his favorite to eat. He'll pick you up from your hotel dock and take you beyond the reef in his 42-foot Sportsfisherman boat. Mornings he'll meet you at 8 AM and afternoons at 1 AM. Both half-day trips last four hours and cost $650. A whole day's fishing costs $900.

Southampton Parish

Lady Gina
18 Coral Acres Dr.
• **(441) 238-2655**

Captain Allan Virgil concentrates mostly on deep-sea fishing. *Lady Gina*, a 35-foot Bertram Sportsfisherman boat, therefore is equipped with Pan international rods, state-of-the-art reels and the latest trolling tackle. It's also air-conditioned. Departure location? It's at your convenience. If your group is staying at a hotel, Virgil will pick you up there or at the nearest dock.

As for catch policy, you will be allowed to take what you can eat that night. Where marlin are concerned, the captain encourages the tag-and-release policy whenever possible. However, if you want the catch of your life mounted, he'll be happy to arrange it for you. By the way, you might like to know that under Virgil's jurisdiction, a boy unexpectedly celebrated his 15th birthday in 1996 by bringing in a 792-pound blue marlin. A full day of fishing costs $875; a half-day is $650. Sodas are available for $1 each. Departure time is usually 8:30 AM, but it's open to negotiation.

Sandys Parish

Jamie C
5 Sound View Dr.
• **(441) 234-3081**

Captain Sinclair Lambe and his 35-foot Main Coaster *Jamie C* will take you reef or deep-sea fishing. Robinson's Marina in Sandys is his preferred departure point. He'll pick you up in Hamilton, but he reminds you that it will deplete your fishing time. Lambe follows the tag-and-release policy for marlins.

Half-day deep-sea fishing trips are from 7 to 11 AM and costs $650. Half-day reef fishing jaunts are out from 12:30 to 5:30 PM and cost $550. There's no full-day reef fishing option, but for $900 you can deep-sea fish for eight hours (7 AM to 4 PM). Lambe enforces a 24-hour cancellation policy.

Bermuda has become a
Cinderella with both
slippers polished,
annually luring more
than 1,000 wave-
dancing yachts to its
sheltered harbors, inlets
and bays.

Yachting and Marinas

Legend has it that after St. Brendan and 17 other seafaring monks hoisted sails over their currach (a boat made of tanned oxhide stretched over a wooden frame then slathered with fat to preserve the hide) and took a seven-year traipse around the Atlantic in the mid-6th century, they may have sailed into one of Bermuda's coves. To those who find an intriguing nugget of possibility in such a tale, St. Brendan and crew may then arguably be considered Bermuda's first visiting yachtsmen.

Almost 15 centuries later, the exploits of the Irish monk notwithstanding, Bermuda has become a Cinderella with both slippers polished, annually luring more than 1,000 wave-dancing yachts to its sheltered harbors, inlets and bays. Yet, every so often yacht skippers miss us completely and have to tack around and try again.

Although on a clear day Bermuda's low green hills can be seen 25 miles out, visibility can be slashed to less than 5 miles when the skies are gray, cloudy or hazy. On clear nights though, Gibb's Hill Lighthouse, erected between 1844 and 1846 and reputed to be one of the oldest iron lighthouses in the world, provides a clear beacon (500,000 candlepower) for craft up to 40 miles away. And speaking of beacons, North Rock Beacon, sited about 10 miles offshore on the island's most northerly reef, flashes a much dimmer light. Bermuda's other lighthouse, St. David's Lighthouse, is at the island's easternmost tip. Built of Bermuda stone, its white light of about 30,000 candle-power is visible from 23 miles and produced by a prism-reflected electric bulb of 1,500 watts. Emergency generators kick in if electricity fails.

As You Near Bermuda

When en route to the island, particularly if sailing June through November, keep alert for sudden tropical storms and hurricanes that can blow up from the southeast. Equally important, North Atlantic gales can strike with little warning between December and April, so maintain a keen eye on your barometer.

Bermuda Harbour Radio (which is also the Rescue Coordinating Centre; see more just below) must be contacted on your approach and given an ETA. A continuous listening watch is kept on 2182 Khz USB (Upper Side Band) and on marine VHF Channel 16, which is the call and distress channel that should not be used unless contacting Harbour Radio or another vessel. Once initial vessel-to-vessel contact is made, move to a working frequency or indicated channel. Do not use the channel for general communication. Also, channels 10 and 12 are reserved for government tenders, tugs and branch pilots; they are not for casual boaters or yacht captains. Bermuda Harbour Radio and the Rescue Coordinating Centre can also help with matters related to customs, immigration, health and berthing.

Remember that St. George's is the port of entry for all visiting yachts, and all yacht captains and passengers must clear customs and immigration before traveling about the island (by land or sea). If you are in doubt about regulations or are unfamiliar with entering St. George's after dark, lie off until sunup. Once in St. George's Harbour, you'll find a 24-hour clearance facility located on Ordnance Island (near the *Deliverance* replica). And don't forget that illegal drugs (including marijuana), guns, plant and vegetable matter are forbidden. A valid passport is essential for all visiting yacht passengers who are not from the United States. U. S. citizens can use a photo I. D.

There are a few other things of which you must be aware. If you intend to visit for more than a week and live onboard your boat, health regulations must be complied with, and the Department of Marine and Ports, (441) 295-6575, should be notified. And if Fido or Garfield is among shipboard companions, a general health certificate, issued by a licensed veterinarian no more than 10 days prior to arrival, is needed. Animals without relevant documents will be refused entry.

A word about bridge openings: The Swing Bridge, spanning the entrance between Ferry Reach and Castle Harbour, is opened on demand between 7:30 AM and 7 PM daily from April 1 to September 30, and from 7:30 AM to 5 PM daily from October 1 to March 31. If sailing from St. George's to Hamilton — a trip that can take up to two hours — going through the Swing Bridge can knock more than 30 minutes from your journey.

A publication that should prove helpful is *The Bermuda Yachting Guide,* and we advise that you get your hands on one if you are interested in bringing your craft to the island. It is published by the Bermuda Maritime Museum Association, P.O. Box MA 273, Mangrove Bay MABX, Bermuda. The organization may be reached by phone at (441) 234-1333. The North American distributor for the publication is Bluewater Books & Charts, 1481 S.E. 17th Street Causeway, Fort Lauderdale, FL 33316. The guide provides, among many other things, a list of places where proper charts can be purchased in the States. It is also a fine reference to the many anchorages in Bermuda and the easiest way to reach them.

We have listed a couple of boatyards and marinas (and be advised that a marina in Bermuda is not quite the same as in the United States). Facilities vary, and berthing may not be available. Occasionally, free docking for a couple of days can be had in St. George, the old town priding itself on having catered to seafarers for almost four centuries.

And don't worry about that Bermuda Triangle business. We don't, and St. Brendan didn't.

Bermuda Harbour Radio
Fort George Signal Station, St. George's • (441) 297-1010

The Rescue Coordinating Center for the Bermuda area, Bermuda Harbour Radio keeps a continuous listening watch on the international distress frequencies 2182 kHz, 500 kHz, Channel 16 VHF, channel 70 VHF (MMSI number 003100001) and digital selective call frequencies 2187.5 kHz. It broadcasts warnings related to maritime safety which include weather information by wireless, voice and Navtex. Round-the-clock contact with US Coast Guard and air-sea rescue centers in North America, the Caribbean and Europe is constant. For more information their web site can be visited at www.rccbermuda.bm

Boatyards and Marinas

St. George's Parish

St. George's Boatyard Ltd.
**25 Wellington Slip Rd.,
Town of St. George • (441) 297-0877**

Once inside St. George's Harbour, you'll find St. George's Boatyard to the west. It does a great deal of everything. A full-service facility that offers a do-it-yourself option, its services range from the hauling of up to 40 tons on a travel lift to carpentry, sandblasting, spray-painting and fiberglass repairs. There are showers and bathroom facilities, and 110— and 220-volt power supplies. At its Esso ma-

---

INSIDERS' TIP

If you want to get in a little fishing and are unfamiliar with the best spots, tune to Channel 06 when in local waters. This is the channel used by most Bermudian anglers, and you might pick up info on what fish are biting and where to drop your line.

rine station, duty-free fuel is available to yachts in transit — maximum draft 7 feet at low tide. Other on-site services include welding and electrical and engine repair.

Captain Smokes Marina
Godet & Young, McCallans Wharf, 13 Wellington St., Town of St.George
• **(441) 297-1940**

The welcome mat is spread out here where a number of convenient services are on hand, among them fresh water supplies, 110 and 220 electrical hookups and showers. The yachtsman or woman can transmit a fax, send or receive FedEx or UPS packages and make long distance telephone calls (phone cards are cheaper and available).

If your vessel or group of vessels can use the 500-gallon minimum, you may refuel from a duty-free Esso truck. Remember too that it is important to conserve fresh water; Bermuda, unlike other destinations, relies almost solely on rainwater for its potable supply.

Mills Creek Marine
17 Mills Creek Road, Pembroke
• **(441) 292-6094**

Nestled next to one of the island's most sheltered creeks, this full service boatyard offers complete services — travelift. fiberglass repairs, awlgripping, rigging, and handling electrical and refrigeration problems. Contact them if you need moorings or a shipwright.

Offshore Yachting & Maintenance
Red Hole, 83 Harbour Road, Paget
• **(441) 236-9464**

Located near the Royal Hamilton Amateur Dingy Club, this boatyard provides expert marine service for all of your possible boat repair requirements. Haulage, insurance repairs and yacht brokerage along with refits are available.

Sandys Parish
Somerset Village

This area, so favored by Sir George Somers (see our History chapter) that it became known as "Somers' seate," is a rural village of small farms, quiet parks and nature reserves, open spaces, wind-beaten coastlines

and several businesses including a couple of banks, restaurants, supermarkets, pharmacies and a family bakery. Composed of four islands — Watford, Boaz and Ireland Island North and South — it is best known for the Royal Naval Dockyard, where once-dilapidated 19th-century fortifications have been resurrected into major visitor attractions.

The Dockyard has two breakwater-protected basins of 4 to 5 fathoms. The north breakwater is a fine deep-water harbor. The Department of Marine and Ports uses a portion of the area known as the North Basin for maintaining its tenders, tugs and ferries. Its northwest corner has slipways for hauling craft with a draught up to 6 feet.

Dockyard Marina
9 Dockyard Ter., Royal Naval Dockyard, Ireland Island • **(441) 234-0300**

This marina is within the confines of the century-old Dockyard breakwater, at the intersection of the North, South and Dundonald shipping channels. The deep-water port allows the marina to easily accommodate vessels alongside one of their convenient berths. Whether your stay is a couple of days or several months, water, dockside electricity, fuel, ice, newspapers and clubhouse facilities are available on a daily, weekly, monthly or yearly basis. Call ahead for price information.

West End Yachts Ltd.
Royal Naval Dockyard, Ireland Island
• **(441) 234-1303**

With old naval buildings forming a backdrop, this full-service boatyard has no problem providing a comprehensive range of services — long- and short-term storage, haulouts and launch, full rigging facilities, spraypainting and refinishing among them. With 7,000 square feet of workshops, the staff prides itself on being able to handle any repairs.

Yacht Clubs

The two we mention below have the "royal" designation. The granting of what is known as a "royal warrant" is an ancient tradition. In 1155, Henry II granted a royal charter to the Weaver's Company in Britain. Only a few more than 800 royal warrants remain outstanding. Most have been granted by the present Queen Elizabeth II, the others by the Queen Mother, the Duke of Edinburgh and the Prince of Wales. Only about two dozen warrant holders — among them the Royal Bermuda Yacht Club listed below — have held the distinction continuously since Queen Victoria's reign, which lasted from 1837 to 1901.

Royal Bermuda Yacht Club
Albuoy's Pt., Hamilton
• **(441) 295-2214**

Fifty years ago a local writer, in describing this club, noted that "Neither fortune nor fame will necessarily qualify you for membership in the Royal Bermuda Yacht Club." The writer was right, this is a very private club.

Lying on Albuoy's Point in the city and commanding a fine view of Hamilton Harbour, the club was founded in 1844 when Samuel Triscott — who became a noted regatta organizer — and 29 others gathered under a calabash tree at Walsingham in Smiths Parish to form the Bermuda Yacht Club. It received its royal designation from Queen Victoria in 1845 and is one of the world's oldest yacht clubs, listed 12th in order of founding.

The RBYC has a breakwater-type dock with members' vessels inside and space available alongside the outer wall or stern-to; they have mooring buoys in a line parallel to the dock about 75 feet off. This is a popular place to dock since it is in the heart of Hamilton.

Berthing, available to non-members, is stern-to, and maximum ship size is 80 feet. The cost without electricity is $1.50 per foot per night; with electricity, it's $1.75. Visiting yacht captains should tie up and enter the club to register so that an account can be opened in the boat's name. This will allow the crew to enjoy club services. The club does request that someone always remain onboard during the night for security reasons.

Royal Hamilton Amateur Dinghy Club
Mangroville, Paget
• **(441) 236-2250, (441) 236-8372**

Dinghy racing, which became increasingly popular with sailing aficionados from the mid-1800s onward, was a motivating factor behind the formation of the Hamilton Amateur Dinghy Club (HADC) in the spring of 1882. Then, a small group of students from Charles E. Clay's school on Angle Street (what is now called "back of town") met above Gosling Brothers' Ltd., on Front Street in Hamilton. In a tiny room, they laid the groundwork for today's thriving club.

In 1883, following a visit to the island by Princess Louise, Marchioness of Lorne and the wife of Canada's governor general, the club applied to the princess for her patronage. The application was granted, and the club was able to append the title "royal." However, members received a shock in 1890, when Queen Victoria abrogated patronage by relatives and children (such as had been granted by Louise) and assumed sole authority for conferring the honor. The club's royal designation was rescinded. Not until 1953 did Queen Elizabeth II approve the reintroduction of royal to the club's name.

The RHADC sits on the rim of Red Hole, a bay at the eastern end of Hamilton Harbour. Its dock is large enough to provide space for visiting yachts. Although Red Hole is dotted by local craft of every type, you may be able to secure a private mooring. Contact the club's dockmaster for information on services and costs. The RHADC, along with the RBYC and

www.insiders.com
See this and many other
Insiders' Guide®
destinations online.
Visit us today!

INSIDERS' TIP

When approaching Bermuda be aware that reefs can come up on you quickly; do not ignore your depth sounder. If faced with a serious but not life-threatening situation, use the urgent "Pan Pan" signal rather than the "Mayday" signal.

Photo: GIS

The perfect way to spend an afternoon in Bermuda.

The Bermuda Dinghy, an Eccentric Bermudian Legend

The local dollar coin is stamped with its picture, it is part of the logo of the Royal Hamilton Amateur Dinghy Club, and it is one of the most eccentric little boats you will ever encounter. Not only will it threaten to dump you into the sea, odds are that if you sail it often enough, you will end up overboard.

Fourteen feet long with a 25- to 43-foot mast carrying between 300 and 1,400 square feet of sail, the Bermuda fitted dinghy occupies a sailing niche all its own. Racing them and winning is a challenge, and we're not just talking about having the swiftest craft. Victory may also depend on how efficiently the bailer (one of six crew members) shovels water out of the boat as it spills in, and whether or not the skipper (as has happened) orders a couple of crew members over the side. Winning in these competitions will not be compromised by excess weight.

This is probably the only class that allows boats to finish with fewer crew members than they began with. One story tells of a winning boat rolling over and sinking after crossing the finishing line, putting the skipper into the harbor in which his crew had already been dumped.

These little rascals are susceptible to capsizing at the smallest wave, but dinghies have sunk during a race, been frantically raised, bailed, re-rigged and gone on to compete in later races that same day - and even winning! The boats offer a unique way of challenging wind, sea and competition.

The evolution of local dinghy races - the racing season is from May 24 to mid-September - can be traced to 1853 and the first one-masted open boat race in St. George's. The competitors raced small family boats (12-foot keels or less) generally used as transportation between St. David's and St. George's; there was no connecting bridge or road in those days.

These everyday transport boats were converted temporarily for racing. Often "fitted" with shifting ballast - a couple of sandbags or pieces of lead with rope through them - and built of Bermuda cedar, the fittings became more elaborate as dinghy races became increasingly popular within the sailing community.

As the Bermuda fitted dinghy evolved, one of its features became the iron fin, known to have been used in 1870 and possibly before; another feature was the introduction of temporary decking to reduce the amount of water shipped when racing. Hull lines improved, and once into the 20th century, various designs were explored. The Bermuda Maritime Museum at the Dockyard (see our Attractions chapter) has on display a fully rigged champion dinghy.

Photo: Panatel VDS Ltd

Sunday dinghy boat races are a sailor's dream and exciting to watch.

the St. George's Boat Club, organizes a number of races throughout the year.

Yacht Racing

Bermuda has always been wedded to the sea, its love affair with sailing having spawned a racing calendar filled with competitions between all boat classes.

International racing spans more than a century here, with one of the earliest competitions held in 1849 when the American yacht *Brenda*, owned by George W. Collimore of Boston, was matched against the Bermudian-owned *Pearl* in the Great Sound. The *Pearl* won by 55 seconds.

Races organized by various clubs are held in the Great Sound almost every weekend, and specific class series are held throughout the year. These include tornados, dinghies, lasers, Etchells International one-designs and others. The Snipe Class is very active throughout the summer months.

The Bermuda Sailing Association is the governing body for yacht racing in Bermuda and is recognized by the Bermuda government and the International Yacht Racing Union (IYRU) based in London. The association's membership is comprised of the island's sailing clubs and individuals who participate in sailing activities.

Bermuda fitted dinghy racing is usually in full swing throughout June, July and August. These boats (see this chapter's Close-up) have been called bizarre. They are only 14 feet long but can cost more than $100,000 to build. Race venues are at Mangrove Bay, Hamilton Harbour and St. George's.

Newport-Bermuda Yacht Race

First held in 1906, when three boats competed for the Sir Thomas Lipton Cup (which was won by Tamerlane), this biennial race is often called the "Thrash to the Onion Patch." As one of the major events on the racing calendar, this high-powered competition attracts more than 100 participants. Several classes — yachts, sloops, cutters, ketches and yawls — are represented. The race begins in Newport, with craft leaving on the third Friday in June. Depending on weather conditions, the winner usually crosses the finish line just off

St. David's Lighthouse late the following Tuesday or early on Wednesday.

Organizers — the Royal Bermuda Yacht Club, the New York Yacht Club and the Cruising Club of America — faced with dwindling interest, in 1990 changed the then-existing handicap system, replacing it with IMS (International Measurement System) rules. The event's reputation as a leading racing competition had been curtailed in 1970 with the introduction of the MHS handicap system that favored cruising-type yachts over the sleeker racing rigs. The IMS permits two racing divisions — cruising and spinnaker — with the spinnaker division competing for the St. David's Lighthouse Trophy. The introduction of the IMS rules revitalized the event, attracting a record 281 requests for entry. A total of 180 were selected.

Some 188 yachts registered for the 1998 race, although by the time of the starting-gun, around two dozen boats had dropped out. However, race organizers were happy with the final number of starters, the high entry due in no small measure to a more aggressive marketing campaign that included race notices sent to almost every IMS skipper around the world. In raising the media profile of the race, boats were required to radio their positions twice daily to the *Rainbow*, a motor vessel sailing with the race fleet.

Marion-Bermuda Cruising Yacht Race

This event is a more sedate affair compared to the Newport-Bermuda. First sailed in 1977 after getting the thumbs-up from Coles Diel, then-commodore of the RHADC, the four- to five-day race from Buzzard's Bay in Marion, Massachusetts, is held on alternate years to the Newport. This is an offshore event for cruising yacht skippers carrying an amateur crew, a limited number of sails and no spinnakers. Sponsored by the RHADC, the Beverly Yacht Club and the Blue Water Sailing Club, the Marion-Bermuda attracts more than 100 entries, with the finish line just off St. David's Lighthouse.

A number of changes have been announced for the June 18, 1999 Marion to Bermuda crossing. The implementation of the AMERICAP handicapping system will be continued, as will a website providing information. Both features were new to the 1998 Newport-Bermuda race.

Additionally, Ocean Spray, the leading juice-drink company, has this year put up a trophy (which the winning club will hold until the next race) for the yacht club or sailing organization whose three-member team has the best corrected combined time.

Yacht Charters

There are more than a dozen yachts from which to choose for that daytime or sunset cruise through Bermuda's placid waters. All are skippered by experienced, licensed captains. Weather permitting, most sail throughout the year, but a few only ply the waters between April and November. All yachts offer restroom facilities, and some have separate changing rooms.

Most charter yacht operations can be found in the phone book, and yacht and motor craft information can be found at the Bermuda Department of Tourism at Global House, 43 Church Street, Hamilton. In this section, we provide a couple of fine charter companies to get you started. More cruising options are listed in the Snorkeling and Sightseeing Motor Cruises section of our Watersports chapter.

Charter rates depend on the length of cruise (usually three to eight hours) and number of persons. Once you have decided on checking out a few, call ahead to get quotes; you'll find there is not a great deal of difference between operations. Most have amenities that include beer, wine and soft drinks, with food available on request. Reservations are required. Some of the charter yachts depart from a fixed location; others may be willing to make pickup arrangements that suit the client. Make certain you get all the pertinent details.

Sailing Charters

Allegro Charters
• (441) 235-3481

Got a yen to cast off the landlubber life and see Bermuda from the sea? Allegro Charters and Captain Richard McGlynn operate two sailing vessels, *Allegro* and *Artemis*, each of which will take you into that relaxed and carefree nirvana you only dreamed about before Bermuda and its tranquil waters seduced.

A three-hour cruise on the *Allegro* will cost $35 per person; a six-hour cruise is $50 per person, with a maximum of eight people. Boats depart year-round from Barr's Bay Park in Hamilton (near the Royal Bermuda Yacht Club), and overnight trips for couples can be arranged.

The *Artemis*, a 41 foot Robert Perry sloop, can take up to 20 people. A three-hour cruise costs $50 per person; a six-hour jaunt is $90 per person. You can also indulge yourself in an *Artemis* weekend escape, in which you will be pampered and catered to for two nights and three days. The charge is $650 per person, and it is all-inclusive.

Or you can choose from a flexible sailing schedule. For the *Allegro* it's $200 for a half-day and $350 for a full day; on the *Artemis*, you'll pay $400 per half-day and $600 for the full day. All charters include soda, bottled water and beer. Snorkel gear is also included if you wish to slip beneath the waters to enjoy the beauty of an undersea world you will be thrilled to experience.

Sail Bermuda Yacht Charters
• (441) 236-9613

Departing from Albuoy's Point in Hamilton at 10 AM and 2 PM Monday through Sunday, Alibi Captain Bobby Zuill will take you on a "getaway half-day sail" — a relaxing, tranquil

---

INSIDERS' TIP

Clearances under local bridges are as follows: Swing Bridge in St. George's, 9 feet; Flatts Bridge in Hamilton Parish, 8 feet; Somerset Bridge, 11 feet 9 inches; Longbird Bridge (at the causeway), St. George's, 6 feet 6 inches; Watford Bridge in Sandys, 20 feet.

three-hour waltz through Hamilton Harbour, the islands of the Great Sound and toward the west end of the island. All you'll need will be a bathing suit and towel — and your camera, of course!

But it's not all just great sailing. A brief stop is made so you can swim in the enticing waters, and if you don't have your own, snorkeling gear is provided. A complimentary rum swizzle, Dark 'n' Stormy (if you haven't already learned, they're made with local black rum and ginger beer) or soda will quench your thirst, though you will be charged for additional beverages.

You will also have the option of choosing the Sunset Sail, which is a 90-minute "fantasy" sail that departs about an hour before sunset. Experience it. For further information and rates, call the captain.

Salt Kettle Yacht Charters Ltd
Salt Kettle, Paget
• **(441) 235-1929 or (441) 236-1837**

For cruising Bermuda's gentle bays and coves in comfort, you can choose this company's luxury 55-foot sloop *Bright Star* that holds up to 26 people, or its 35-foot flybridge motor cruiser *Magic Carpet* with an 18-person capacity. The *Bright Star* is spacious and comfortable and you could opt for, among others,

a 2-hour cocktail cruise around Hamilton Harbour and the Great Sound. The *Magic Carpet* offers a splendid way to explore the island's many coves and inlets. Snorkel on outer reefs and wrecks, or have a catered dinner-cruise for a special occasion. Contact David Ashton for further information and rates.

Motor Charters

Pembroke Parish

Town & Country Yacht Charters
Three Market Ln.
• **(441) 292-6050, (441) 236-0127**

For those who want the luxury of cruising in plush comfort and style, the *Lady Tamara* or *Lady Erica* should fulfill your fondest desires. Within these "Lady" boats you'll find wall-to-wall carpeting, excellent bar facilities and food. Fully air-conditioned, the 100-foot *Lady Tamara* is superb for fashion shows, receptions, weddings and theme or post-conference parties. *Lady Erica*, though smaller at 60 feet, has all the luxuries of her larger sister, with comfortable sofa seating and teak interior paneling. It is ideal for intimate VIP parties. For booking information and rates, contact Nigel Prescott.

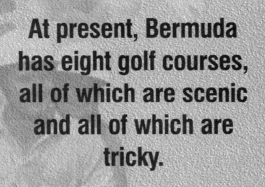

At present, Bermuda has eight golf courses, all of which are scenic and all of which are tricky.

Golf

William Wordsworth once described a game of golf as "a day spent in a round of strenuous idleness." Where Bermuda's golf courses are concerned, many golfers would argue that the word "idleness" just does not apply. "Strenuous," on the other hand, most certainly does.

At present, Bermuda has eight golf courses, all of which are scenic and all of which are tricky. Indeed, it's the very fact that they are scenic that presents special challenges to the most experienced of golfers. Proximity to the ocean means that water is frequently very much part of the play and can be a real hazard. A shot over a cliff and the sea, for example, calls for nerves of steel. In addition, where there's ocean, there's also wind. Sea breezes on the courses make for some interesting situations.

When is the best time of year to play golf in Bermuda? We recommend October to March since during those months, the courses are at their most lush. True, it might rain more, but remember that for golf courses, rain is almost always good news. It makes fairways even fairer. Furthermore, from November on, hotel rates tend to be reduced, and tee times are more readily available.

And there's the matter of tournaments. One week during October, January, February and March is given to tournaments that appeal to golfers of all ages and ability. You'll find specific information about tournaments in the Spectator Sports chapter. Be aware here, though, that visitors are welcome to watch and even participate.

If you are visiting during the summer months, sunset golf (in the late afternoon until dark) might appeal to those who fear the heat or prefer to walk. While gas carts are mandatory during the day at some courses, you are typically allowed to hoof it in the evening. It also tends to be cheaper.

How do you reserve tee times? You can call the clubhouse directly, or, if you are stay-

ing in a hotel, you can ask the staff there to make your bookings for you. Where the three public, government-owned courses are concerned, you can simply call the automated (441) 295-6000 number to make reservations or cancellations and to receive information about course features.

In this chapter we alert you to the idiosyncrasies of Bermuda's golf courses. We will also, of course, tell you about fees and facilities. Should you go à la cart or not? We'll tell you that too. And in golf, as you know, if you ain't got that swing it does mean a thing. That's where the golf pros come in. Private lessons are available at nearly all courses, and we'll give you rates in the individual listings. First, we offer some information on how golf came to Bermuda, and why our golf courses are important to our environment.

History

As any Scot will tell you, golf is always identified as Scottish in origin. Did the Scots bring the game to Bermuda? It's possible, if Scots were officers here in the British Army. According to *The Royal Gazette*'s Bermuda Online service, golf started in Bermuda when "well-heeled British Army officers brought their golf clubs with them to while away the time during their assignments in Bermuda. They hacked away all over the place." In 1457, King James II of Scotland banned the game of golf in his country because he felt it interfered with time that should more properly be spent on archery practice. Presumably, governors of Bermuda were not so worried about their officers' marksmanship.

By 1905, there were apparently two golf courses here, neither of which is in existence today. But the story of golf in Bermuda officially started with the rise of tourism after World War I. Riddells Bay Golf and Country Club, Bermuda's oldest, opened in 1922. Meanwhile, the Furness Withy Shipping Line (see our History and Resort Hotels chapters) developed two of our private courses: the Mid Ocean, which opened in 1922, and the Castle Harbour, which opened in 1931.

As tourism increased, so did the number of golf courses, which proved popular with locals and visitors alike. Today, there are three public and five private courses, but many hotels and cottage colonies can make arrangements for guests to play the private layouts since three open days are generally available for non-club members. At the moment, another private golf course has been promised to us. It will be situated on what was formerly the US Naval Annex in Southampton Parish (now renamed Morgan's Point), and it will probably open in the summer of 1999. Designed by Jack Nicklaus, it will be an 18-hole, par 72 course, and rumor has it that the Golden Bear will model it after his favorite Pebble Beach golf course in California. Seven-thousand yards long, it will be Bermuda's first full championship course. It will also be the first completely irrigated course on the island. Plans are in the making for a luxurious clubhouse and a championship practice range.

For the Birdies

Today, Bermuda claims to have more acreage per square mile dedicated to golf than any other country. Whether this is true or not, it is definite that golf courses take up about 17 percent of our open space. Given that we have a total of just 21.6 square miles of land, our open spaces are obviously very important to us, and Bermuda is becoming more and more environmentally aware.

In the past, golf courses were not altogether friendly to the environment. For starters, they had a definite aversion to land crabs. What's wrong with land crabs? Well, besides having the curious habit of walking sideways, land crabs also like to make holes. Granted, holes are what a golf course is supposed to be about — nine are fine; 18 are even better

— but the crabs were considerably more generous than that, pockmarking island courses. The result was that heavy pesticides were used to control them. The trouble with that solution was that the bird population suffered too.

In the mid-1970s, Dr. David Wingate, conservation officer at the Department of Agriculture, Fisheries and Parks and president of the Bermuda Audubon Society, hit on the brilliant idea of bringing in some pairs of yellow-crowned night herons from the Tampa Bay Nature Reserve in Florida. He believed these birds had been prevalent in Bermuda at the time of the first settlers in 1609 and had suffered the same fate as the cahows (see our Flora and Fauna chapter). Yellow-crowned night herons live on shellfish, and Wingate nurtured them on small pieces of — yes, you guessed it — land crab, which they took to immediately. Today, these herons roam the mowed areas of Bermuda's golf courses and do golfers a favor. The herons thrive, the land crabs no longer have a holier-than-thou attitude, and pesticides are not as heavily used.

In the meantime, other birds also enjoy the golfing habitat. Bluebirds in particular are also happy at the courses (no cats are around to threaten them), and they help out by eating worms and caterpillars, cockroaches and crickets. Check each course for bluebird nesting boxes. Look out for that streak of blue, and remember there's more than one way to appreciate a birdie.

Bermuda Courses

And now for the listings, which, as usual, we will present east to west, parish by parish, subset by subset and thereafter in alphabetical order. A word about the parish designations: Mid Ocean and Castle Harbour golf courses are arguably in both St. George's and Hamilton Parish. You see, golf knows no boundaries, and neither does Tucker's Town, that select area of land where both golf courses are definitely located. See our History chapter for more information about Tucker's Town. In the meantime, we have decided to be arbitrary about the parish issue.

St. George's Parish

The Mid Ocean Club
1 Mid Ocean Dr., Tucker's Town
• (441) 293-0330

Having hosted the Merrill Lynch Shoot-Out Series for two years, and the Gillette for another two, The Mid Ocean is definitely Bermuda's most exclusive private golf club. The Furness and Withy Line wanted it that way right from the start. They bought land and beaches in Tucker's Town to lure the American rich and the famous who wanted luxurious seclusion. The owners financed this beautiful course as well as what was originally known as the Castle Harbour Hotel and the Castle Harbour Golf Club. Charles Blair McDonald, a titan of American golf, designed the course in 1922. Nine years later, Robert Trent Jones revised it. Many a famous politician has played here, including US Presidents Dwight Eisenhower, John F. Kennedy, Richard Nixon, George Bush and Jimmy Carter. Golfing British prime ministers have included Winston Churchill, Harold MacMillan and Edward Heath. You might like to know that the legendary Babe Ruth also played here. At the fifth hole he managed to put two balls in the lake. Enough said. One can't be brilliant at everything.

Select though this club is, it is possible to enjoy a round here. Mondays, Wednesdays and Fridays are open days for non-club members. If you want to play on other days, introduction by a member is required, but many resort hotels and cottage colonies have club memberships. If you are a guest, they will be happy to make arrangements for you to play at Mid Ocean. (See our Resort Hotels and Cottage Colonies chapters for more information.)

So what is this illustrious par 71 course like? Comprising 6,547 yards, it offers some extremely interesting water challenges. Four holes are near lakes and ponds, and the ocean comes into play as well. The signature hole is No. 5. Its dramatic, elevated tee forces you to drive your ball at least 200 yards over a lake

before playing your second shot to a green that is well-protected by bunkers. There are surely lots of balls in that lake, likely including those two that Babe Ruth dropped. You'll be relieved to know that at the 9th hole, by Harrington Sound, a half way house offering cool drinks and snacks awaits you. No. 18 hugs the ocean and gives you great views. Mid Ocean can be tame on a nice day, but watch out for those ocean winds. On the opening hole, southwest winds can affect your play, and on the 17th hole in particular, wind plays a key role in your club selection.

Bear in mind that this is the only course in Bermuda where caddies still assist you. Carts are available, but walking the course is recommended. On average, the round takes about four hours and 15 minutes. Be sure to look out for the birds, as about 30 bluebirds have set up home at Mid Ocean. In addition, you may well see some great cranes, of the wading bird variety. And don't worry about summer brown out: Most tees and all of the greens are irrigated.

The clubhouse, pink and white and trimmed with cedar in true Bermudian style, looks down on the 18th green and is surrounded by the glorious South Shore. There you can enjoy a well-earned drink in one of two bars or dinner in the main dining room. You can munch on lunch too. Locker rooms and a well-stocked golf shop are available. In addition to the course, Mid Ocean has a driving range and two putting greens. Greens fees are $160, and carts are $40. Caddies work for $25 per bag, and, as we explained, are preferred. If you need lessons to cope with that tricky 5th hole, they cost $60 an hour. No half-hour lessons are available. By the way, Tuesday mornings from 7:30 to 9:30 AM are set aside for lady golfers. See the map on page xv.

St. George's Golf Club
1 Park Rd. • (441) 297-8067

This 4043-yard, 18-hole course is Bermuda's newest. Designed by Robert Trent Jones as a par 62, it ranges along hillsides and overlooks the St. George's shoreline and Fort St. Catherine. Most of the holes are par 3s, with six par 4s just less than 400 yards on the shorter side of the course. Wind is an important factor in your game here and can demand careful club selection. Depending on the weather, on a couple of par 3s you might need anything from a 9-iron to a driver to reach the green. Watch out for the 14th hole. It's a dogleg next to Coot Pond, opposite Tobacco Bay. You have the difficult choice between playing into the dogleg or going for the green. That's why it's more familiarly known as the "Oh no hole." Fairways are generally narrow and challenging.

Daily greens fees are $43. Play after 3 PM, and they're reduced to $21. Gas carts (mandatory on weekends and public holidays) cost $34, and pull carts are $7. A full set of clubs rents for $18; golf shoes for $6. You need lessons? No problem. Kim Swan will help you out at $40 for a half-hour. The clubhouse has a bar and restaurant where you can relax after your game, and there's a pro shop. Do not be misled by the word Club, by the way. Because the Bermuda government owns this course, no membership is necessary. See the map on page xv.

Hamilton Parish

Castle Harbour Golf Club
6 Paynters Rd. • (441) 293-2040

Castle Harbour Golf Club's course dates back to 1927 when Charles Banks, close friend of Charles Blair McDonald, started to design it for the Furness Withy Line. Unfortunately, he died in 1929, two years before it was completed, so he never got to see the full glory of his work. Later, Robert Trent Jones added modifications. Gently undulating through the contours of hills, valleys and fields, this 6,440-yard, par 71 course is renowned for its stunning panoramic views of the open Atlantic, Castle Harbour Bay and Harrington Sound. At the very first of the 18 holes, the dizzying blue

view of sea and reefs could well distract you, so be careful. From there on, up-and-down fairways, together with unpredictable sea winds, make for interesting situations. So do blind holes. The finishing hole, a par 3, runs 234 yards along the harbor side to a well-targeted green that is protected by a large pond. Marriott's Castle Harbour Resort acts as a back drop. There, by the way, you can enjoy refreshments at The View bar and restaurant. The clubhouse has lockers and facilities. Castle Harbour was the venue for the 1984 American zone qualifying competition for the World Cup.

If you are a guest at Marriott's Castle Harbour Resort, greens fees are $100 a round. Otherwise, they are $120. Gas carts are mandatory here and cost $23 per person. Golf clubs are available for rent for $28, and golf shoes are $8. Need professional help? A half-hour lesson costs $45. Double that fee for a full hour. See the map on page xv.

Devonshire Parish

Ocean View Golf Course
2 Barkers Hill • (441) 295-9093

Originally a membership club, Ocean View is now a Bermuda government facility. In the 1990s, it has added a brand-new clubhouse (with a bar and restaurant), conference rooms, a well-stocked pro shop and lockers. It also has a driving range. As its name suggests, this course does overlook the ocean — the North Shore. A nine-hole, par 35 course that is just under 3,000 yards, Ocean View is not as easy as it might look. Rolling hills make for challenges. The signature hole is No. 9, where a pond (very threatening indeed) is stuck in the middle of the fairway, 162 yards from the white tees. The course finishes with a blind, uphill dogleg. But when you get to the last

Photo: GIS

Be careful; the vistas may drive you to distraction!

green, you'll be rewarded with a stunning view of the ocean. You might even see a cruise ship glide by.

Greens fees are $32 for the whole day or $25 for nine holes. If sunset golf in the evening is for you, the fees go down to $16. Check for exact times. Gas carts (mandatory only on weekends and public holidays) cost $18 per person for 18 holes or $9 for nine. Pull carts cost $6. Club rentals are available for $20 per set; golf shoes for $6. Dwayne Pearman is on hand to offer playing lessons. His fee is $40 for a half-hour. See map on page xv.

Paget Parish

Horizons and Cottages Golf Course
33 South Rd. • (441) 236-0048

You may have already come across Horizons and Cottages in our Cottage Colonies chapter. If not, refer there for a detailed description of the property. Guests naturally get first preference, but this nine-hole mashie course is also open to members of the public. You might think a par 3 course of 1000 yards

is nothing to be frightened of, but *Golf Digest* described it last year as "a thousand yards of pure poison."

Given that the longest hole, No. 4, is about 125 yards and the shortest are 75 yards (there are two or three of those), you can see why no carts are necessary. Not many golf clubs are necessary either. In fact, one Insider plays Horizons and Cottages with nothing more than a 5-iron. The 9th hole is the tightest and is the most picturesque point of the course. You hit back to the Main House and toward Garland's Cottage. Bluebirds, by the way, don't always think the grass is greener somewhere else. Six families have nested at just one green.

Guests pay $4 greens fees and have preferred tee times. Otherwise, the fees are $20 per person during the week and $25 per person during weekends and public holidays. It is generally not much trouble for a non-guest to play at Horizons. Junior players who aren't guests can play for $10 Monday through Friday. Weekends and public holidays in the summer season they pay $12.50. No carts or shoes are available for rent, but you can rent clubs (three of them) for $2.50 a set. Horizons does not accept credit cards. See map page xiv.

Riddells Bay Golf and Country Club
24 Riddles Bay Rd.
• **(441) 238-1060, (441) 238-3225**

Described by Bermudian golfers as "a real gem" and "the course you must play," this is Bermuda's oldest course. It was born, so to speak, in 1922, but right now, in 1997, it is about to undergo a facelift. The clubhouse will be completely remodeled.

Meandering along Riddells Bay's peninsula, which measures just 600 yards at its widest, the 5,668 yards of this par 70, 18-hole course offer scenic delights and plenty of challenges, including one pond and three ocean holes. As pro Darron Swan put it, "What we don't have in length we make up in beauty." So do take the time to appreciate the serenity of this setting, and notice the dark, mysterious roots of the mangroves that hug the water's edge. Winds from the sea are again an important factor, so that, ironically, shooting's no breeze. The 8th hole, a dogleg right, is the one to watch out for. If you're accurate, you shoot in to a green that's surrounded by water and a pond. If you're not, never mind: You've just added to the Great Sound's Grand Golf Ball Collection. From this hole you can see the benevolent gaze of Gibbs Hill Lighthouse — maybe it can cast light on the subject. Carts are not compulsory here. Play takes from three-and-a-half to four hours.

This is a private club, but tee times are set aside for tourists every weekday as follows: Monday and Wednesday, 8 AM to 2:30 PM; Tuesday, 9:30 AM to 2:30 PM; Thursday, 2 to 2:30 PM; and Friday from 10:30 AM to 2 PM. Weekdays, greens fees are $55 a person for up to 18 holes. Weekends and public holidays, it's $75. Club members play at a reduced rate. Gas carts are available at $40 each, and pull carts are $7. Shoes will cost you $5. Darron will be happy to give you an hour's lesson for $70 or a half-hour one for $40. See map page xiv.

Southampton Parish

Port Royal Golf Course
Middle Rd. • (441) 234-0974

Port Royal, a par 71 and one of Bermuda's three public 18-hole courses, has been described as the flagship of golf courses in Bermuda. Another of Robert Trent Jones' creations, its 6,565 yards roll along the natural terrain of Southampton's cliffs overlooking the South Shore. It goes without saying, then, that you'll take in the greens of the water as well as those of the golf course. Elevated tees and holes with distinctive characteristics make Port Royal a challenging course to even the most experienced golfers.

The par 4 No. 1 is a 432-yard dogleg right with water in front of a heavily bunkered green. The par 3 16th is definitely the signature hole. Yes, it's beautiful, but it's also lethal. Depending on the weather, you'll use a pitching wedge or a 3-wood to shoot over cliff and ocean. Is there Spanish treasure sunk in the waters below? Possibly. But, depend on it, there's definitely a generous collection of golf balls from Port Royal. If you're in any danger of forgetting your experience at No. 16, you can buy a memento poster of the hole for just $2. And after you've survived the 16th, look out for the recently restored lake at the 17th. It's a great place to spot egrets. No. 18 is also interesting. It will literally uplift you (it's an uphill climb) all the way to the clubhouse, where you can collapse in the bar or restaurant for some much-needed sustenance. Play should take no more than four-and-a-half hours. By the way, Port Royal has "golf rangers" on hand to help you maintain proper pace of play. They recommend that players should take 15 minutes or less per hole.

Weekday greens fees are $70; weekends and public holidays, they are $80. Avoid weekends altogether if possible, as this course gets very busy. If you have no choice, book early for Saturday or Sunday to avoid disappointment. After 3 PM, you can play sunset golf for $30 Monday through Friday, and for $40 on weekends and public holidays. You will see some glorious sunsets from this course. It's at the western end of the island, remember. Gas carts (mandatory only on weekends and public holidays) cost $36 per cart. Pull carts are $9; golf shoes are $12. You can rent clubs for $25. Need practice for that tricky 16th? Frankie Rabain offers lessons — call the clubhouse for details and rates. Port Royal's practice greens and driving range will also help you get up to par. See map page xiv.

Southampton Princess Golf Course
101 South Rd. • (441) 239-6952

This 18-hole, par 3 course surrounds the Southampton Princess hotel, which was once described by *Golfweek* as a "vast, beached pink cruise ship . . . sitting atop a bluff near the Gibbs Hill Lighthouse." For more information about this luxury liner of an accommodation, check the Resort Hotels chapter. In the meantime, know that this course is an ideal introduction to Bermuda's more challenging full-length courses.

Here, 2,684 yards are neatly sculpted out of steep terrain, so any mountaineering skills you may have will prove helpful. The vertical drop on the first two holes is at least 200 feet, and the rise along the 178 yards of No. 4 makes for an uphill driving experience. Elevated tees, cunningly placed bunkers and a few water holes (three, to be exact) mean that you may need every club in your bag. Mountaineers may climb mountains "because they are there," but they also climb for the views. Get to the 16th hole that sits in a cup fringed with oleander, and you'll see the backdrop of Gibbs Hill Lighthouse and the blue of the ocean. Get to No. 18, and you can speed your way to the 19th: the clubhouse's fully licensed bar and restaurant. Play takes about two hours, leaving you plenty of time to enjoy Bermuda's other attractions. Incidentally, because of the hotel's irrigation system, the course always looks lush, even in the midst of summer.

For 18 holes, hotel guests pay $37 greens fees; other visitors pay $42. Gas carts are mandatory at most times and cost an additional $17 per person for guests and $18 for visitors. When available, pull carts cost $6 and so do golf shoes. Check out Wayne Lima for lessons at $80 an hour. Half-hour sessions are $40. See the map on page xiv.

Golf Instruction

The Bermuda Golf Academy
10 Industrial Park Rd.
• (441) 238-8800

We have to get academic about this listing. We include it in this chapter because it offers a wonderful opportunity for adults and kids to practice and improve their game. Opened in 1996, The Bermuda Golf Academy features a 320-yard driving range with 40 practice bays. Don't worry if the rain pours down or the sun blazes too fiercely — 25 of them are covered. In addition, 8 target greens are placed from 75 to 230 yards out, and a sand trap, located beside the range, allows you some out-of-bunker practice.

Floodlit at night, the facility will let you play until 10:30 PM. At present, after-dark golf is unavailable anywhere else in Bermuda. The facility opens at 9 AM. Need lessons as well as practice? Three professional golfers are on hand to help you out. If you're not photophobic, they'll even video your play. That way you can see yourself in action and receive professional analysis. Hour-long lessons per person are $60, and half-hour ones are $35. For two persons, lessons are $75 an hour or $45 for half an hour. You can rent two clubs for $2. During the day, a basket of balls costs $4; after sunset, it costs $5. Monday through Friday children can get a basket for $3.50. Weekends and nights they pay $4. Seniors get these rates too.

The driving range proved so popular that in 1997 the academy added an 18-hole minigolf course, suitable for the whole family. Featuring pagodas, waterfalls and brilliantly blue waterways, the course takes about 45 minutes to complete. How do you negotiate the 16th hole? You shoot a ball over a drawbridge. On weekdays adults older than 16 play for $7, and on weekends and public holidays it's $8. Children play any day of the week for $6. If they don't like miniature golf, send them to the jungle gym while you're doing your thing. When you're all through, you can relax over snacks and drinks at the licensed restaurant, appropriately named The Wedge and Divot. You'll find it in the clubhouse. See map page xiv.

The most recent international register shows 11,443 companies registered here, with 327 having a strong physical presence.

International Business

Overview

A flock of private jets nesting at Bermuda International Airport on almost any given day is commonplace in this country where, once you scratch the surface, you'll find a world apart from pink-white sandy beaches, startling blue-green waters, and charming moped rides along winding country roads.

From its earliest days when a 17th century tobacco industry propped up a virgin economy (between 1612 and 1687 Bermuda and Virginia secured a monopoly on the tobacco trade until the industry in Bermuda crashed), and ship-building enabled local inhabitants roam the Atlantic and Caribbean in search of trade — and privateering plunder — the business of Bermuda has always been the pursuit of happiness in the form of profit.

The island's colonization was financed by a coterie of London businessmen who in 1612 sold their ownership of the isles to the newly-formed Bermuda Company. This mid-Atlantic archipelago remained in private hands until 1684 when the Bermuda Company folded and its charter was taken over by the British Crown.

Today, the local economy is no longer dependent on venturesome seamen braving capricious oceans and seas, but on the exquisite seduction of visitors and international corporations, many of which are Fortune 500 entities. The most recent international register shows 11,443 companies registered here, with 327 having a strong physical presence.

The success of this international business sector has spurred growth of the local economy, in 1997/1998 buoying Bermuda's Gross Domestic Product (GDP) by 6.6 percent. This performance exceeded that of most major industrialized countries, a fact pointed out by Bermuda's Finance Minister, the Hon. Eugene Cox, in a speech to the local Chamber of Commerce in December 1998.

By any yardstick the local economy is thriving. Inflation, as measured by the Consumer Price Index (CPI), fell to two percent during the first nine months of 1998. However, this economic success had not been without price. Commercial buildings have modified the shape of the traditional skyline. Vanished are many buildings that were reminders of a gentler era. In their place, Bermuda's version of skyscrapers — the tallest of which is eight stories — houses hundreds of companies that contribute nearly $750 million annually to the island's coffers, making the international business sector the dominant economic engine.

But what has contributed to this explosive growth that has allowed this tiny, fishhook-shaped isle to merge with the wider world at an exhilarating pace?

The island's regulatory environment, much of its evolution arising from the mid-1930s and the incorporation of Elbon Ltd., has made attracting top corporate players in the global economy possible, and indeed preferable for the companies involved.

The insurance tide rolled ashore around 1947, and over the half-century since, has grown in volume to make Bermuda the world's leading insurance and reinsurance center. And, of course, the island's political stability has featured greatly in achieving this global niche.

Expansion throughout the 80s witnessed an unprecedented explosion of office space within the city of Hamilton. By 1990 it had more than doubled (leaping from 1.04 million square feet to 2.12 million, representing about 95 percent of all office space) as international business leapfrogged into the financial lead, surpassing tourism.

While the 327 international companies physically present amount to only 3.3 percent of the total number on the international register, their involvement in the local community is wide-ranging. But more on this later. Overall, international companies employ 2,667 people. Fifty-seven percent or 1,528 of these employees are Bermudian.

Professor Brian Archer's most recent (1997) Report on International Companies, released in 1999, shows that these global giants spent $743.3 million in 1997, an increase in expenditures of $112 million or 17.7 percent over 1996. During 1997 they spent $340.5 million on salaries and benefits, $159.4 million in professional and bank fees, $186.7 million to firms for goods and services such as office rentals, communications and utilities, and a further $56.6 million in taxes.

These corporations engage in activities of varying descriptions — commodity trading in petroleum, chemical, and forest products, raw minerals, precious metals, to dealings in other commodities and stocks. Others are international sales corporations for finished goods. Some are formed locally to license patents, trademarks, copyrights and computer software systems internationally. Bermuda-based companies are also formed for the purpose of owning, managing or chartering ships. A ship owned by a Bermuda-registered company qualifies for British registry, and there are more than 600 shipping companies on the local register.

Growth in the number of collective investment schemes is healthy, with 1,068 regis-

tered at the end of the second quarter of 1998, a 13 percent increase over a 12 month period. The total net asset value of the collective investment schemes registered in Bermuda reached $21.1 billion at the end of the second quarter of 1998.

With more than 900 collective institutional investment schemes, the island has attracted fund management groups like Fidelity, Jupiter Asset Management, and ED&f Man. However, Bermuda is not generally considered a retail fund center, despite continuing expansion in this area.

Similarly, there has been a surge of healthcare formations and incorporations of captives with insurance company parents.

Insurance and Reinsurance

The first reinsurance company to operate here was American International Reinsurance Company in 1948. And although the formation of the Bermuda Marine Assurance Company had taken place more than a century earlier to insure cargo en route from Bermuda to Philadelphia aboard the sailing ship 'Liberty', only within the last twenty years has the insurance industry become a strategic-planning Pit Bull in the international business kennel. It is the leader with 1,487 domiciled here, most of them captives.

A captive insurance company, according to the Captive Insurance Company Directory, is "a closely held insurance company whose insurance business is primarily supplied by and controlled by its owners, and in which the original insureds are the principal beneficiaries."

This captive insurance whirlwind swept across the Atlantic in the early 60s. It was a

Photo: GIS

In the growing market of convention business, Bermuda is ideally suited, based on our proximity to the U.S. mainland and our modern telecommunications systems.

development put on the local table by Fred Reiss, the founder of Bermuda's first captive insurance company — International Risk Management. He brought concepts that found, at first, ground that needed to be watered and fertilized before those notions took root.

After an uphill effort with the Bermuda Government, and after a number of feasibility studies, local authorities were eventually convinced to allow him introduce the first Bermuda-based captive insurer. Reiss had foreseen the beneficial economic results captive insurance would bring the industry and Bermuda if the thrust were given a nod and a handshake.

The nod was given, the handshake was firm, and today Bermuda enjoys prosperity from the presence of all insurance and reinsurance companies (OICs) domiciled on its shores.

In 1960 less than ten OICs transacted business from Bermuda. In 1970 there were 120. And a decade later this had climbed to 753 with $2.8 billion in net premiums. In 1996 these companies wrote nearly $20 billion in premium income according to the Bermuda Government's 1997 Annual Economic Review. The asset base of these companies exceeds $100 billion.

The global insurance industry has seen a significant change in its role and competitive structure over the last two decades. Banks and financial service companies presented competitive threats with their offering of insurance products targeted at defined sectors of their customer base. Consequently, direct sales challenges have changed the way insurance business is conducted, and the growth of the Internet and e-commerce has caused the industry to rethink many of its traditional approaches to new-product launches and customer service. Investment in new technology has been a separating marker between the traditional and current thrusts now driven by Information Technology (IT).

By keeping on the cusp of changing trends, and through the use of IT as a strategic business development tool, the industry has carved a competitive advantage.

The Bermuda insurance market has taken the lead role on the global stage with an increasing presence through market expansion and acquisition. The demand for superior technology and telecommunications continues as these companies tailor their delivery systems to meet the diverse needs of the geographical markets in which they operate.

Regulation of International Companies

As Bermuda became host to international companies, insurance companies in the early years were essentially self-regulating. But by 1971 the government recognized the need for strong and defined regulation if the island was to develop respect as a reputable insurance center. In 1978 the final draft of the Insurance Act was presented and passed through the local legislature.

This Act formed the basis for today's government supervision of both domestic and international insurance companies. Administered by the Registrar of Companies assisted by an advisory committee of personnel from within the insurance industry, the Act was later modified by Insurance Amendment Acts of 1983 and 1985.

Although the Act requires certain levels of minimum and paid-up capital for companies conducting long-term business, there is no need for them to publicly disclose their accounts. However, annual statutory financial statements must be submitted to the Registrar of Companies. Flexible and effective legislation accommodates an innovative industry that has developed structures, concepts and approaches to maximize profits.

The regulation of international companies encompasses two stages. During a company's application for incorporation in Bermuda, government authorities work closely with private sector professionals to screen applicants. Impeccable financial references are crucial before the company can proceed through the regulatory process. In the case of OICs, the Insurers Admissions Committee must be satisfied with the company's capital base and the reputation and competence of key personnel.

The second stage, through the Compa-nies Act, gives the Finance Minister authority to appoint an inspector to investigate the affairs of any exempted company registered in Bermuda. The use of the term 'exempt' derives from Bermuda's laws. Translated, this means that such companies are exempt from local laws that require limited companies in Bermuda to have a minimum 60 percent Bermudian ownership. And, unlike local companies, they are exempt from Exchange Control regulations and liability for stamp duties on executed documents.

However, companies in the exempt category can transact business from Bermuda, but not in Bermuda. They are limited to using the island solely as a base for their overseas business. Quite often these corporations are subsidiaries of companies based in countries like the United States, Canada, the UK and Hong Kong.

Much of the business transacted by these companies include private investments, trusts, aviation and shipping. Among these firms are Bacardi International Ltd, American International, Esso, Shell, and Transworld Oil.

Although the overwhelming majority of locally-based international companies are exempt, about 10 percent are permit companies. Such companies are allowed non-Bermudian majority ownership, and can transact business locally. Sun Life Insurance of Canada is one example of this.

Why Bermuda?

In the late 70s and throughout the 80s insurance companies in Bermuda proliferated. Globally, the industry suffered from a number of man-made and natural crises. Property, workers' compensation and liability insurance became expensive, and in some countries, completely unavailable. Catastrophes in many instances had a devastating financial impact.

INSIDERS' TIP

The Archer Report is a study prepared for the Ministry of Finance by Professor Brian Archer at the University of Surrey, England. It analyses the Bermuda economy and its export earnings.

Photo: GIS

Hamilton's majestic City Hall was designed by architect
Wil Onions to resemble an oversized Bermuda cottage.

Disasters — among them the Lockerbie bombing, hurricanes Andrew and Hugo, and a 1986 San Francisco earthquake that measured 5.3 to 5.6 on the Richter Scale — took a severe toll. And insurance giant Lloyds of London in the UK came into disrepute when investors lost money or withdrew from the market. From 1988 to 1992 their losses exceeded $12 billion.

Consequently, many international industrial corporations started up offshore captive insurance subsidiaries and chose Bermuda as a desirable place from which to operate. Robert Stewart, author of 'Bermuda, an Economy Which Works', states that: "Regulation in Bermuda is geared toward business and the reputation and solvency of those who provide the insurance cover." As well, domiciled insurance companies in Bermuda are able to insure against punitive damages, something not generally the case in many American states where regulation varies from state to state and tends to be directed more toward the consumer.

The partnership between the Bermuda government and international business allows easy communication between both. In January 1999, two months after the 9 November 1998 election victory of the Progressive Labour Party (PLP), the new Premier, the Hon. Jennifer M. Smith, in addressing the International Companies Division (ICD) of the local Chamber of Commerce, stated: "We know that other jurisdictions have some complex and sometimes unnecessary regulatory bodies which makes doing business in those locations difficult. We aim to keep ours business-friendly while maintaining the proper regulatory controls that will enhance our reputation as a first-class jurisdiction for the conduct of international business." She added that as a sign of the PLP's commitment to this sector, tax exemptions for exempted companies had been extended an extra four years from 2016 to 2020.

Other government initiatives include speeding up the processing of work-permit applications, allowing companies to set up more quickly. Part of this process will be tied to recent amendments to the Companies Act that streamline incorporations.

Not surprisingly, given Bermuda's positioning in the international business arena, a record number of delegates attended the 1999 World

Insurance Forum, with 600 delegates converging for this fourth Forum held at the Southampton Princess hotel. With attendance up ten percent over the 1996 forum, investment analyst Paine Webber described Bermuda as a domicile of choice from which to operate as the island continues to lead the world in attracting new captive insurers. Last year new captive licenses totaled 305 worldwide, with strong growth centered here.

Rating agency Standard and Poor (S&P) has confirmed the island's double A stable foreign currency rating, highlighting Bermuda's drive to maintain a low tax offshore center for financial services, keep its debt low, and maintain fiscal prudence. In addition, S&P confirmed: "Many firms are drawn to Bermuda because of its relatively light regulatory environment and might even remain even if the tax advantages were diminished."

Bermuda's clean image is undeniably one of its greatest assets. There have been no major financial scandals. "Security and creativity are the twin engines for our industry's growth," said Registrar of Companies, Kymn Astwood, earlier this year.

Bermuda and the OECD

Despite its enviable reputation, and careful monitoring of companies seeking to become registered here, the Organization (sometimes called the Convention) for Economic Cooperation and Development (OECD) in the latter part of 1998 expressed concerns about financial transactions carried out by Dependent Territories and Crown Dependencies.

Bermuda, a Dependent Territory, is considered part of the United Kingdom for OECD purposes, with the Bermuda Stock Exchange as much a part of the OECD as are the London, Luxembourg, and Dublin Stock Exchanges. However, in outlining the OECD's position and Bermuda's place within its parameters, the Bermuda International Business Association has stated: "When the UK ratified the Convention it did not specify what territorial application should be given. As uncertainty developed over the convention's scope in respect of the UK's Dependent Territories and Crown Dependencies, the UK decided to clarify the situation. On 29 July 1990 it formally transmitted a Declaration to the Government of France, Depositary State of the OECD Convention, in which it confirmed that the convention applied to the Channel Islands, the Isle of Man, Gibraltar and Bermuda. Bermuda and Gibraltar are, therefore, the only UK Dependent Territories to which the convention applies."

The OECD, composed of some 30 member countries, provides member governments a setting in which to discuss and develop social and economic policies that seek solutions to common problems. Exchanges lead to agreements for establishing legally-binding codes for free flow of capital services, and crack downs on bribery and money-laundering through a Financial Action Task Force on money laundering (FATF). The anti-tax haven thrust is led by the OECD, the European Union, and G7, which involves the world's top economic and industrial countries.

To allay suspicions or considerations that Bermuda may be among those countries with dubious regulatory practices, the local government has embarked on a review of OECD, European Union, and Tax Treaty positions. Legal counsel has been engaged to represent Bermuda in the UK and Europe. The point to be made is that Bermuda already has significant and effective regulations in place to combat money laundering. The government emphasis is on showing that the island is not a dodgy financial jurisdiction.

In February 1999, the Premier and Minister of Finance met with OECD representatives in Paris to present Bermuda's case. With this spotlight on offshore jurisdictions, the United Nations also is focusing on so-called tax havens with the intent of drawing up a league table of internationally approved offshore centers.

"We would expect to be on any approved list — right at the top," the Finance Minister, the Hon. Eugene Cox, has stated. "We are doing all we can to protect Bermuda's reputation as a place of business which has regulation in place which will meet any standards."

The Third Engine

Often forgotten as one looks at international business, is the impact of foreign investment income, now vaunted as Bermuda's third economic engine. Even as Bermuda has welcomed international business, Bermudian investors continue to stretch overseas in the quest for profit.

The key factor behind the growth of foreign income earnings was the reduction some five years ago of a ten-percent tax on currency exported for investment overseas. The reduction — to one-quarter percent — had an immediate effect. In 1994 receipts from foreign income were $77 million. The following year, receipts bounded to $117 million. And last year reached $131 million, expected to increase through 1999.

The virtual eradication of exchange controls has enabled private individuals diversity and expand their overseas investment portfolios. Prior to the change, local investors sank their money in real estate, local shares, and deposit companies.

International Company Impact on Housing

While the local economy waltzes to the tune of three-quarters of a billion dollars annually derived from the international sector, the housing market has been greatly impacted by this presence. And even as the international community has created jobs for Bermudians, available housing in the rental market has contracted for many Bermudian renters.

A quarterly report of the Bermuda Housing Corporation (BHC) released late summer 1998, pointed out that Bermudians are often discriminated against by landlords who prefer to rent to foreign personnel.

The report noted that: "Bermuda has a two-tier rental market, with demand arising on the one hand from foreign workers, and from Bermudian renters on the other hand. In some cases the foreign workers' rent is subsidized by their employers, especially in the booming international business sector. The low-income Bermudian renter finds it hard to compete in this market."

The core reason for this development lies in the upscale rents that are obtained for prime rental properties, both commercial and domestic. In real terms, centrally-located office space rents for upwards of $50 per square foot, and house rentals often run in the $10,000 to $12,000 per month range (often higher) for key senior executives.

International Business and Community Initiatives

While companies register here to maximize profits, they frequently want to contribute to the local community, showing themselves to be responsible corporate citizens. Companies within and outside the insurance world support education and various community concerns and charities.

In 1995, for example, Corange Limited commemorated its 25th anniversary and interest in life-science research by donating $1 million to Bermuda College. In 1997 Orbis Investment Management pledged $500,000 for educational purposes and youth development. To date, the ICD has donated in excess of $3 million in ICEA awards and scholarships for students pursuing business-related studies. Fidelity donated more than $5 million to the Bermuda Underwater Exploration Institute (see Attractions).

In the US there are about seven charities for every 10,000 people; in Bermuda there are almost 50 charities for the same number of people. Donations from various international firms are healthy, with several companies offering free advisory services and establishing in-house programs whereby company employees commit to volunteer community work.

Some companies, including ACE and XL, have instituted their own charity foundations. Many key international business personnel sit on local boards of charity and scholarship committees. Several charities benefiting are health-related (see Healthcare).

Buoyed by the success of the inaugural 1997 Bermuda International Business Exposition, in 1998 some 50 booths showcased the international business industry. From mid-morning to 6 PM, Hamilton's City Hall parking lot was the venue for these participating-company booths that attracted several thousand people.

Officially opened by the Premier and the mayor of Hamilton, the Expo featured some of the leading Bermuda-based international companies. Various live performances throughout the day by local groups included among others, the Bermuda Youth Orchestra Jazz Ensemble. With a grand finale by the Warner Gombeys (see Arts and Culture), the event was a success as international company representatives met with parents and students and discussed various career possibilities in this sector. Leading up to this event, International Business Week was launched, and comprised a radio quiz, contests, and an open forum with industry representatives.

From various sports related endeavors to the Arts, a number of international businesses have become an integral part of the local business, charity, education, and art world.

One might arguably conclude that Bermuda has come full circle. In the beginning, a consortium of London traders invested in the island's colonization with the full intent of reaping commercial profit. Today, international businesses have invested in Bermuda as the curtain goes up the next millennium. And both Bermuda and these corporations are benefiting from a rewarding economic symbiosis.

Some house names you may notice while exploring our island can be seen as wry reminders of the price we have to pay. "At Last," "Dream's End," "Last Penny" and the more smug "Sitting Pretty" are examples.

Real Estate

Where prices are concerned, we might be forgiven for thinking real estate in Bermuda is actually unreal — or perhaps surreal is more to the point. Given that we have only about 21 square miles of land that is densely populated, it's inevitable that buying property here is very expensive. In fact, some house names you may notice while exploring our island can be seen as wry reminders of the price we have to pay. "At Last," "Dream's End," "Last Penny" and the more smug "Sitting Pretty" are examples.

But if property is expensive for Bermudians, it's even more so for foreigners. Because of our limited land and number of houses, we have to restrict non-Bermudian property ownership and property speculation. Is it possible for non-Bermudians to buy property? Yes. In this chapter we'll tell you how and what nonresidents may buy. We will explain the different rules and regulations that apply when buying a house as opposed to a condominium. But because most non-Bermudians residing here rent rather than purchase, we'll also focus on the rental market for long-term and holiday rentals. Prices and rents depend on location, so we'll mention the more exclusive neighborhoods as well.

It's more common than not that people wanting to buy or rent operate through a real estate agency.

So we'll tell you what you can generally expect from agents and/or sales representatives. At the end of the chapter, we'll give a sampling of some agencies with details of their specializations.

Buying a House

OK, you're not Bermudian, and you want to buy a house here. The first thing any real estate representative will tell you is that your choice is restricted to houses that have a minimum Annual Rentable Value (ARV) of $43,800. Sounds reasonable? The bad news is that the ARV at present bears no true relation to the market price. In effect, your starting price to buy will be about $1.5 million. For that you can expect a substantial detached house of 4,000 to 5,000 square feet, probably with a pool on a half-acre or more of land. Your location will most likely be in one of the following exclusive areas: Tucker's Town; South Road, Paget or South Road, Southampton; Harbour Road, Paget; Knapton Hill, Smiths; or Fairy Lands and Point Shares, Pembroke. Some agents say that buying such a house right now for $1.5 million would be a steal. Market prices can be anywhere from $2 million to $5 million and occasionally have been known to hit $17 million.

Once you've chosen your house, you apply (through your real estate agent) to the Bermuda government for a license. You pay an application fee of $442, which is refunded if your application is successful. However, the license fee itself is 22 percent of the purchase price (doing the quick math, that's more than $300,000 for a $1.5 million home). It's a one-time fee, but if you sell the house to a non-Bermudian, then that buyer will have to pay it as well. And if you in turn buy another house, you pay another license fee.

You should also know that, as a non-Bermudian, you may own just one property at a time. Under exceptional circumstances you may have permission to acquire a second property, but that permission is conditional on selling the first one within 12 months. If you want to rent your house to a tenant, you must receive permission from the Minister of the Department of Immigration, who will rarely allow you to rent it out for longer than 12 months. Rent it to a non-Bermudian, and you pay a levy of 5 percent of the monthly rent.

You may be wondering how many non-Bermudians do buy houses in Bermuda. Well, at the moment the stock of houses available to them is about 292. Generally people who buy these properties do so because they want to retire here or because of tax laws in their own countries. The previous trend of buying holiday homes is apparently now on the decline. As you can see, buying a house in Bermuda is an extremely costly endeavor. A cheaper option is to buy a condominium.

Buying a Condominium

Condo living is a relatively recent phenomenon in Bermuda. When housing became a key issue during the '70s, the Bermuda government saw condos as a good way of meeting the housing demand without using too much land. And so the first condo complexes started to appear. Right now we have a variety all over Bermuda. Non-Bermudians can buy them, but again, they are restricted to condos in higher price brackets, with a minimum ARV of $15,300. In effect, the starting price is $350,000, but more luxurious units can go as high as $1 million. As with a house, you must apply for a license (the application fee is the same), which will cost you 15 percent of the purchase price. The rule about acquiring a second property also applies. Condominiums available to non-Bermudians include South-down Farm in Southampton; Mizzentops,

Warwick; Inwood, Paget; St. James' Court, Flatts; and Grosvenor Apartments, Pembroke.

So what do you get for your money? Typically, you will have two to three bedrooms, a combined living/dining room area (sometimes, but not always, with fireplace), a well-equipped kitchen and two bathrooms. Of course, one advantage to condo living is that you don't have to constantly worry about external maintenance. In return for a monthly maintenance fee (the cost ranges from $300 to $500 a month), your water tank, roof and external walls are kept in good repair and the grounds are cared for by gardeners. Technically, grounds are communal, but sometimes tenants are allowed to create their own garden; if gardening is important to you, check the rules before buying. With the more expensive condos, you'll usually find additional communal amenities such as tennis courts and swimming pools. Policies regarding pets differ, but usually you're allowed cats, small pets such as birds and gerbils and, in some cases, dogs.

Long-term Rentals

Most non-Bermudians who come here for employment rent rather than buy housing. Typically, they rent through real estate agencies that readily help them find suitable accommodations. There are no restrictions on what non-Bermudians can rent. However, there is currently a heavy demand for rental properties, and the result has been sky-high rental rates. Studio or one-bedroom apartments cost between $1,000 and $1,500 a month. Two-bedroom apartments or houses average between $1,800 and $2,500. Three-bedroom houses generally start at $3,500, but houses at that price are hard to find at the moment; you're more likely to find one at $4,000 to $5,000. Executive rentals — properties ideal for entertaining — are even higher, with a $7,000 monthly rent likely.

Location, of course, has a huge impact on

INSIDERS' TIP

When in St. George's, if you find you've run out of or forgotten bus tickets or lost your token, you can purchase tokens at St. George's Liquors, immediately next to the bus stop on York Street.

rent. Take a three- or four-bedroom house in Tucker's Town, for example. Let's say it has two or three bathrooms, a living room, dining room and a den, along with a patio, swimming pool and a water view. What would that cost? Take a deep breath. We're talking $16,000 a month. Again, condominiums can be a more affordable option if you want that second bathroom and bedroom. Monthly rents start at $2,500 and go up to $4,500 and higher for the more luxurious ones in the central parishes.

When you agree to rent a property, you usually sign a one-year lease that gives you an option for renewal. However, three-year leases are sometimes available. You can break your lease (giving two to three months' notice) only if your work permit is pulled or you have to leave Bermuda. For an unfurnished property, the deposit is usually 50 percent of one month's rent. For a furnished one, you'll put one month's rent up front.

In addition to rent, you'll be responsible for costs of electricity, gas, telephone, cable television, utilities and pest control. You'll also be responsible for minor maintenance such as hinges, locks, fastenings and tap washers. Rent an accommodation for more than two years, and you should plan to repaint the interior. There may be additional costs, depending on the landlord. You could, for example, be required to pay part or all of the land tax on the property, and if you rent a condo, the owner could require you to pay part or all of the monthly maintenance fee as well.

Location

As we've already mentioned, some locations are exclusive. Tucker's Town, for example, is definitely the Land of Multimillionaires — particularly those who want ocean views, privacy and luxury. Point Shares and Fairylands are next on the exclusive list. If the most exclusive areas are not for you, you may want to know the advantages of one parish over another.

Perhaps the first consideration is whether to commute or not. If you work in Hamilton, for example, how long do you want to drive? Live in St. George's, St. David's or Sandys, and you're 45 minutes to an hour away from work. Our rush-hour traffic picks up from 8 to 9:30 AM and 5 to 6:30 PM. If you're from a larger country (and let's face it, countries don't get much smaller than Bermuda), an hour commute might be no big thing. Yet strangely enough, the longer you stay in Bermuda, the farther apart distances seem. Sometimes a trip from Hamilton to St. George's (they are about 15 miles apart) can feel like a major excursion.

That fact makes the central parishes — Devonshire, Smiths and Paget — the most popular places to live. In turn, that means you may well find more reasonable rents on the eastern or western ends of the island. While we're on the subject of commuting, get this: Many people living in the eastern parishes would not dream of moving to the western ones. Why? Because of the sun. We're serious. Travel from the east, and you don't get dazzled going to work or coming home from the city. Travel from the west and that "Busy old fool, unruly Sun" is in your eyes.

Those of us who live in Paget, Warwick or Southampton enjoy easy access to several grocery stores and to the South Shore beaches. We probably wouldn't move to St. George's or St. David's because of the noise of aircraft coming into the airport. On the other hand, those who do live on the eastern end would argue that since the base has closed, there's much less air traffic, and that after a while you don't even notice it. They have their own beaches as well. What about Somerset in Sandys Parish? Ah, that's God's country, innit?

Real Estate Agents

Strictly speaking, a real estate office in Bermuda has just one agent. Other personnel dealing directly with sales or rentals are technically "representatives," but they are often loosely referred to as agents. Nomenclature doesn't really matter, since they are required to be licensed in real estate. That means they have passed a tough exam covering mathematics and law, as they pertain to real estate, plus land tax and evaluations.

Why Go to an Agency?

Moving to a new country is always a challenge. You have to contend with different laws and practices and often with a whole new set of cultural attitudes. Bermuda's real estate agents know this, and they offer a range of services designed to help your move go smoothly. Throughout the complicated and lengthy procedure of buying or renting a home or condo here, agents can provide you with information about property evaluation, legal aspects and government requirements. They will also advise you how to sign up for telephone service, electricity and/or gas and cable.

A few agents who deal in executive rentals share those high-end listings along with new information about suitable properties that are available. Deal with these agencies, and you often will be shown a property long before it is advertised in the papers. In fact, chances are the property will already be gone by the time it's advertised (yes, you read that correctly). Since there's heavy demand for executive rentals at the moment, you can see that it's wise to use an agency. In our listings, we'll tell you which ones focus on upscale rentals and which ones focus on house sales.

Who is the agency working for? In America there are buyers' agents and sellers' agents and some who wear both hats. Disclosure regarding where an agent's commission comes from has been a big issue. Where sales are concerned in Bermuda, the agent charges the seller a commission, which is a set percentage of the purchase price. So agents here are working for the seller rather than the buyer. Where rentals are concerned, the property owner pays the agent either a finder's fee (consisting of half a month's rent for every year of the lease) or a management fee (10 percent of the rent). A management fee applies when the agent undertakes responsibility for the property regarding maintenance and tenants.

Real Estate Agency Listings

Pembroke Parish

Bermuda Realty Company Ltd.
LPG Building, 34 Bermudiana Rd.,
Hamilton • (441) 296-2600

This company opened in 1994, but it resulted from a merger between the real estate operations of L. P. Gutteridge and the real estate operations of the Bank of Bermuda Ltd. Bermuda Home Limited is the parent company. At present it has 10 sales representatives, including the manager and five rental representatives. It offers full services, including sales to Bermudians and non-Bermudians, rentals and executive relocation, appraisals, evaluations and estate settlements.

C.R.E. Properties Ltd.
Washington Mall (upper level), Church St.,
Hamilton • (441) 295-5487

You want to rent a cottage or house in Bermuda for a vacation? Beverly Sgobba, owner and president of C.R.E., will not only arrange it, but will also organize domestic help for you. Give her your credit card number, and she will (for no service charge) get you one week's groceries and, if you like, a rented bike. Utility services will be waiting for you when you arrive. If you need a fax machine or

Photo: GIS

Bermuda's waterfront real estate is highly sought after worldwide
and the ultimate in prestige.

some other item, she rents it on your behalf from a rental agency.

Rent varies, but a two-bedroom, beachfront cottage runs about $400 a night. You pay 20 to 25 percent of a week's stay as a deposit. Mrs. Sgobba will organize utility bills for you (renters get free electricity the first week but pay after that), deduct the amounts due from your deposit and send you the remaining balance about six weeks after you return from vacation. Mrs. Sgobba also specializes in sales (to Bermudians and non-Bermudians) and long-term executive rentals. She serves on the executive committee of the Real Estate Division of the Bermuda Chamber of Commerce.

Dorchester Realty Ltd.
Chevron House, 11 Church St., Hamilton • (441) 295-5252

Dorchester's history goes back to 1918. Not that it was called Dorchester in those days. The firm was originated by Meyer M. Malloy, possibly the first real estate agency on the island. Today Dorchester has five representatives and concentrates mostly on local sales. It has been particularly involved with the Boaz Island Development (condominiums available

to local purchasers) and handles about 300 rentals.

Executive Relocation Ltd.
International Centre, 26 Bermudiana Rd., Hamilton • (441) 232-0059

Iris Deveney-Doughty, assisted by her staff of two, specializes in helping executives and their families relocate to Bermuda. She can assist with buying a car, finding child care, booking a driving test and starting bank accounts. She takes charge of customs clearance and helps with pets coming into Bermuda and finding domestic help. Iris also makes sure the utilities are running and is always available to advise on schools, shopping and social organizations. She offers a relocation package that includes all these non-real estate services for a one-time payment. "There's no cut off time," she says. "I've helped executives move several times over to different houses in Bermuda."

Typically, companies pay for her relocation services. To protect their confidentiality, Iris prefers not to publish prices; call her directly for information on cost. In addition, she helps executives find housing for purchase or

rent, but this is a separate activity from the relocation package. Her firm comes under the Hope Bowker Bermuda Real Estate umbrella (see subsequent listing).

Hope Bowker Bermuda Real Estate
International Centre, 26 Bermudiana Rd, Hamilton • (441) 295-9191

Hope Bowker's real estate experience goes back to 1974. In 1981 she established her present firm, and in 1984 she chaired the executive committee of the Real Estate Division of the Bermuda Chamber of Commerce. She still serves on that committee. Ms. Bowker specializes in sales and rentals to both overseas and local residents. She says her clients come from "across the board," but they certainly include those who want to rent or buy properties in the upscale range.

Jones and Waddington
20 Brunswick St., Hamilton • (441) 292-1793

One of Bermuda's busiest real estate agencies, Jones and Waddington opened in 1977. As Mr. Arthur Jones, joint owner and chartered surveyer puts it, "We set the trends in Bermuda. And we contribute to the modernizing of real estate practices." The other owner

is Mr. Ian Waddington. The firm specializes in rentals for commercial as well as for residential purposes and in house purchases for both overseas and local clients. It also offers worldwide relocation services. "We try to cover the market," Mr. Jones explained. In addition to dealing with real estate management, the firm also offer land surveying, planning, evaluation and appraisal services. Three agents run the rental department, eight run sales, and three surveyors run the land surveying department.

Kitson and Company Ltd.
Kitson Bldg., 5 Reid St., Hamilton • (441) 295-2525

Kitson started in 1947, which means it's the oldest Bermuda real estate firm retaining its original name. Along with owner Kirk Kitson, there are seven agents who concentrate on selling and renting Bermuda's finer homes to overseas as well as local purchasers. Kitson also deals with short-term holiday rentals. Rents for these range from $360 a night to $1,000 a night for a luxurious house in Tucker's Town. In addition, this agency offers house management for property owners who do not want to rent out their houses while away. For $200 a month, Kitson will check the properties, pay utility bills and even work out pension contributions and payroll for housekeeping staff still working while their employers are away.

Thomas B. Moss Real Estate Ltd.
Walker Arcade, Reid St., Hamilton
• (441) 292-6294

Thomas Moss and his wife, Deanna, work together with two other representatives in this small company. They provide personal service for people requiring rented houses in the middle-of-the-road price range. (They tend not to deal with studios.) Established some 16 years ago, the company also deals with sales for "the average middle class family" and offers property management services.

The Property Group
Sherwood, 66 Pitt's Bay Rd., Hamilton
• (441) 292-6890

Cris Waldes-Dapena is president and owner of this company. She also serves as chair for the executive committee of the Bermuda Chamber of Commerce's Real Estate Division. Three rental experts and six full-time representatives work together as resident property specialists. In addition, The Property Group has two part-time representatives. The firm specializes in providing executive rentals in the highest price range and in selling houses in the middle to top price range.

Rego Ltd.
The Stables, Reid St. E. • (441) 292-3921

Established in 1949, Rego has 13 representatives that specialize in selling more expensive properties to overseas purchasers. However, they do work with a more general market as well. Similarly, they specialize in the

more upscale executive rentals but will help with the midrange ones. In addition, Rego handles property management.

Sinclair Realty Limited
2 Reid St., Hamilton • (441) 296-0278

This agency was founded in 1988. In 1995 it became the exclusive Bermuda affiliate of Christie's Great Estates, the real estate arm of the famous international auction house. Sinclair Realty therefore works internationally in tandem with 350 affiliate real estate offices, 10,000 sales associates and Christie's offices in 38 countries, including the US, the UK, Switzerland, Hong Kong, Australia and South Africa. With its three agents, Sinclair is known as a "boutique" agency that is committed to the sale, purchase and rental of Bermuda's premium properties, including houses, estates, condominiums and land. It specializes in sales to international clients but it also carries out sales of choice properties in the Bermudian market. As John Sinclair, Managing Broker, says, "Servicing the luxury market requires high sensitivity to a number of variables. The driving force behind Sinclair Realty's success is its passionate approach and attention to detail in coordinating these variables to a seamless, successful conclusion."

John W. Swan Ltd.
26 Victoria St., Hamilton • (441) 295-4255

With more than 30 years in business, this firm caters to a broad section of the market. Its six sales and three rentals representatives share the company motto: "Where service begins and satisfaction never ends." As well as sales and rentals, John W. Swan also offers appraisals and renovation services.

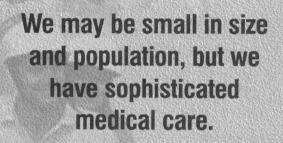

We may be small in size and population, but we have sophisticated medical care.

Healthcare

Some people unfamiliar with Bermuda are under the illusion that we dress in grass skirts, that we live in huts and that our medical services are unutterably primitive. Well, we've yet to see anyone in a grass skirt, and our houses are hurricane proof, thank you very much. So what about our healthcare? We may be small in size and population, but we have sophisticated medical care. In this chapter we'll tell you about our hospitals, support groups and other health-related services. We'll also discuss hospital funding and medical insurance policies for residents and overseas visitors.

Hospitals

We have two hospitals in Bermuda, one dealing with general health, the other focusing on mental health. Both are maintained by the Bermuda Hospitals Board, a government-appointed entity headed by an executive director. Both hospitals are funded mostly from fees and from the Bermuda government's Employment Tax. This tax is payable partly by every local employee and partly by every employer throughout Bermuda. (See the Healthcare Costs section in this chapter for more information about health costs.) The Hospital Auxiliary, a volunteer organization, also contributes enormously to the hospitals' finances. Check their listing below for more information.

General Care Facilities

Paget Parish

King Edward VII Memorial Hospital
Point Finger Rd. • (441) 236-2345

This is our one general hospital, and it has consistently received high ratings for quality of treatment and services from the Canadian Council on Health Services Accreditation. At present it has 324 beds in private, semi-private and public wards. It's well-equipped with modern facilities and technology that includes a dialysis unit (see subsequent information on this unit), a vein clinic and an up-to-date intensive-care unit. In November 1998 a new surgical wing opened. It houses new operating theatres, induction rooms and an endoscopic suite. King Edward VII also offers diagnostic services such as a pathology laboratory, a hematology laboratory, ECG and EEG and diagnostic imaging such as X-rays, CAT scans and ultrasound. Therapeutic services available include dietary treatment, medical social work, occupational therapy and physiotherapy. The Bermuda branch of the Red Cross operates The Blood Donors' Centre within the hospital. (Call (441) 236-5067 if you're interested in donating blood. Donors are always needed.) The hospital has one small hyperbaric chamber but is hoping to have a new and larger one by the end of 1999. Hyperbaric therapy services will start when the chamber arrives.

What specialists do we have? King Edward has physicians and surgeons specializing in anesthesiology, diabetes, gerontology, internal medicine, obstetrics, gynecology, ophthalmology, orthopedics, pediatrics, pathology, psychiatry, radiology, surgery, urology and preventive medicine. Although cornea and ossicle transplants are conducted, no other transplants are available. Angioplasty and coronary bypass surgery are not possible here either. For surgery and treatments unavailable here, patients tend to be admitted to hospitals on the Eastern Seaboard of the United States or in Canada. King Edward VII has an excellent relationship with air ambulance companies, so air ambulance transport is always possible in emergency situations.

The emergency department is, of course, staffed 24 hours a day and has a fast-track system for patients who have had minor traffic accidents. A separate doctor is on hand for dealing with "road rash" (the local term for those relatively minor, but painful, scrapes and bruises). In addition, emergency has a triage system by which a nurse assesses which patients need immediate attention. The hospital runs its own ambulance service and has six well-equipped ambulances staffed with trained emergency medical technicians. Visiting hours in the wards are from noon to 8 PM.

The Dialysis Unit

We are extremely fortunate to have a hemodialysis unit, and we are proud to tell you that no resident in need in Bermuda is denied dialysis. Situated opposite the King Edward VII Memorial Hospital entrance on Point Finger Road, the unit houses 20 artificial kidney machines. At present, the unit treats 60 people on an outpatient basis.

Before October 1978, when the unit first opened, Bermudians suffering from end-stage kidney failure often spent months on kidney machines in North America while awaiting transplant surgery. Since dialyzing can take four to five hours at a time, three times a week, they could not easily return to Bermuda. So you can see how important our dialysis unit is to us. And yes, it is possible for overseas visitors suffering from kidney failure to use the facility. Call the hospital to ask if space is available; demand can be high. Usually the winter season is not so heavily booked. Be aware the unit will not accept overseas patients who have Hepatitis B or are HIV-positive. (That restriction does not apply to residents, however.) Bermudians living abroad and wanting to return for a vacation are given priority. The cost is $681 a session, and you can pay with credit card or personal check.

Hospital Costs and Payments for Overseas Visitors

In general, you'll have to pay up front for medical costs incurred here, even if you're covered by a health insurance company in your own country. You can pay with personal checks, cash or credit cards. Eventually, you can submit receipts to your insurance company for reimbursement.

Bermuda's hospitals, however, will accept Blue Cross and Blue Shield insurance for people who may need inpatient services while visiting Bermuda. Inpatient daily rates for non-residents are now $1,031 for public ward accommodation, $1,232 for semi-private accommodation, and $1,485 for private accommodation. Patients can rent televisions and telephones. Outpatient costs and how they relate to insurance carriers are complex. Call the hospitals directly for more information and be aware that all costs are subject to change.

The Hospital Auxiliary
King Edward VII Memorial Hospital, Point Finger Rd.
• **(441) 236-2345, (441) 236-2488**

This organization was once known as the Women's Auxiliary. It started up in 1953, at a time when the government was not providing King Edward VII Memorial Hospital much money. A group of ladies got together to raise funds through activities, such as charity teas, fetes, white elephants and other events. Even-

www.insiders.com
See this and many other **Insiders' Guide®** destinations online.
Visit us today!

INSIDERS' TIP

So you're a breast-feeding mother on vacation, and your breast pump breaks down? Call the Nurses' Practice at (441) 232-0264, and they will sell you one, or you can also rent one. The practice is at 8 South Road, Smiths Parish, and Liz Bowden and Rita Stevens offer group and individual educational sessions on all aspects of pregnancy. In addition, they hold newborn baby clinics on Wednesdays and Friday mornings to discuss issues with new parents concerning allergies, baby development, nutrition and breast feeding. Overseas visitors are welcome.

tually, the women became known as Pink Ladies, because they wear pink uniforms. These days we have Pink Men as well; although they are willing to wear pink shirts, they prefer to be called Pink Panthers. So now you know.

Today the Hospital Auxiliary has 600 members and 378 active volunteers. Inactive members pay $30 a year in dues; active ones pay $10. Active members save the hospital an estimated $1 million a year through volunteer work. They take charge of the front desk at the hospital's entrance, which means they answer visitor and telephone inquiries. They visit patients to bring a mobile library and hospitality cart and to take care of their flowers.

Perhaps most importantly, they operate the coffee shop and gift shop in the foyer. Open from 9:30 AM to 3:45 PM Monday through Friday and 9 AM to 1:30 PM Saturday, the coffee shop offers breakfast, lunch and afternoon snacks. It's quite a social center — people don't just eat there when they come to visit inpatients; they make a point of coming there especially for a meal. (There's no smoking, by the way, in the coffee shop.) The gift shop (same hours of operation as the coffee shop) has items that make for unusual presents, especially at Christmas, when it's famous for ornaments and Advent calendars.

The auxiliary also runs a thrift shop, affectionately known as the Barn, opposite St. Brendan's Hospital (see subsequent listing). People can drop off clothes, books and other items they no longer want anytime between 9 AM and noon Monday through Saturday. Volunteers sort and price the goods and put them on sale every Thursday and Saturday from 9 AM to noon. These combined operations generate $250,000 a year for King Edward VII Memorial Hospital. If you come to Bermuda to live and have some spare time, the auxiliary is a great place to lend your services (active volunteers put in a minimum of 2.5 hours a week). A junior contingent, consisting of about 90 Candy Stripers, also offers volunteer help.

Yet another group within the Hospital Auxiliary is of interest to overseas visitors. The Overseas Family Health Service is dedicated to offering basic sympathy and support to visitors who become ill on vacation or whose relatives need medical help. Volunteers assist with shopping, finding accommodations near the hospital for relatives and obtaining access to telephones for calls abroad. The service also makes sure your baggage is secure.

Agape House
Point Finger Rd. • (441) 293-2025

Just behind the King Edward VII Memorial Hospital, this very gracious ninteenth-century house is Bermuda's one hospice. Containing 12 beds and several communal areas such as dining and sitting areas, Agape House is dedicated to offering terminally ill patients unconditional care. The staff focuses on making patients physically, emotionally and spiritually comfortable for as long as there is life. They also offer outpatients day treatment such as infusions and transfusions. The King Edward VII Memorial Hospital board funds trained nurses and a resident doctor. Friends of Hospice is a charity that raises additional funds for Agape House. The charity also organizes volunteers who offer meal service, read and talk to patients and give general support. By the way, 24-hour visiting is available.

Mental Health Facilities

Devonshire Parish

St. Brendan's Hospital
44 Devon Spring Rd. • (441) 236-3770

St. Brendan's is accredited by the Canadian Council on Health Services Accreditation. It's a 162-bed psychiatric facility caring for acutely disturbed inpatients and outpatients. Programs include the In-Patient Psychiatric

INSIDERS' TIP

Need a physician, dentist or optometrist? If you're on vacation, hotel managers can often recommend doctors that are available. Otherwise, check the Yellow Pages in the Bermuda phone book for listings. We have no referral service in Bermuda.

Programme, the Learning Disability Programme, Community Mental Health Services and the Montrose Substance Abuse Programme (see following listing).

Outpatient services include 24-hour crisis intervention plus individual and group psychotherapy. The staff also works with community group homes and child and adolescent services. The hospital provides consulting and educational services to government and community agencies such as courts, prisons, nursing homes and the Health Department. The staff at St. Brendan's is happy to assist overseas visitors who need treatment or whose prescriptions need renewal. Visiting hours are noon to 8 PM.

Substance Abuse Support Groups

OK, holidays ought to be fun and restful, but as we all know, they can be stressful, particularly for people recovering from an addiction to alcohol or other substances. Since alcohol is highly visible and available in most of our supermarkets and hotels, we feel it's important to mention our support groups, where overseas visitors are warmly welcomed. In fact, they typically are overwhelmed by the friendliness and support they receive from group members. Meetings here tend to be smaller than those abroad.

Our National Drug Commission distributes in our post offices and hotels a quarterly calendar of support group meetings held throughout the island. You can call the numbers below, and you will probably get a recorded message telling you the meeting venues and times for the week. Leave a telephone number, and a member will be sure to call you back. They are used to receiving calls from all over the world. Support group numbers are

Alcoholics Anonymous, (441) 236-8293; Al-Anon, (441) 236-8606; Narcotics Anonymous, (441) 293-0999.

Montrose Substance Abuse Centre
44 Devon Spring Rd.
• (441) 236-3770

This outpatient center is attached to St. Brendan's and shares the same telephone number. Patients arrive at Montrose through referrals or self-referrals. Two nurses and three qualified substance abuse counselors offer three-week education programs and treatment to help beat substance addiction. Programs include films, together with individual and group counseling. Counselors give follow-up support for at least a year to each patient completing the program. Overseas visitors are welcome if they can stay for a three-week period.

Public Health Clinics

The Ministry of Health operates a number of day health clinics all over the island, primarily for women and children. The doctors, nurses and health personnel offer a variety of services including family planning, prenatal and antenatal care, inoculations, treatment and advice on sexually transmitted diseases, and dental clinics. In addition, should visitors or residents have cuts and bruises as a result of a minor traffic accident, clinic nurses can help them out.

Treatment is free. Though there's a charge for medications, it is at a much lower rate than usual. Antibiotics, for example, cost $5 a prescription. Baby clinics are for children up to 5 years old who need weight-monitoring, nutritional assistance, immunizations and treatment for common ailments. Overseas visitors are welcome to take their children should they become ill on holiday.

INSIDERS' TIP

As well as operating the Blood Donors' Centre at King Edward VII Memorial Hospital, the Bermuda Red Cross also has a hospital equipment rental service. Items include wheelchairs, walkers, commodes and crutches. Interested in first aid and CPR training? A ten-hour training course spread over three weeks costs $35, books included. Call (441) 236-8253 for information.

Here we list the clinics east to west, parish by parish. The Hamilton Health Centre is the only one open daily. If you call one of the others on a day it is closed, leave a message, and a nurse will get back to you.

St. George's Parish

St. George Health Centre
1 Old Military Rd., Town of St. George • (441) 297-8200

This clinic opens every Monday from 9 to 11:30 AM to deal with general health problems. Friday afternoons from 2 to 4 PM there is a baby clinic.

Pembroke Parish

Hamilton Health Centre
67 Victoria St., Hamilton • (441) 236-0224

Open daily from 8:30 AM to 12:30 PM and from 1:45 to 4 PM, Hamilton Health Centre offers all the services we mentioned in our introduction to this section. Thursday afternoons are known as "travel clinic." That's because patients can get all inoculations necessary for traveling abroad. The tetanus, diphtheria and polio inoculations are free. Others, depending on the type required, cost between $10 and $53. The clinic gives treatment to the indigent and will see any adult or child.

Warwick Parish

Warwick Health Centre
Middle Rd. • (441) 236-0649

A baby clinic is open every Monday afternoon from 2 to 4 PM.

Sandys Parish

Somerset Health Centre
55 Mangrove Bay Rd. • (441) 234-0202

This public health clinic offers blood screening, family planning and healthcare for women every Tuesday morning from 9 to 11:30 AM. Friday afternoons from 2 to 4 PM, there's a baby clinic.

Healthcare Costs

Because Bermuda is a British dependent territory, overseas visitors sometimes assume that we have a national health plan. This is not true. All medical and dental practitioners, other than those working in the public health clinics, are in private practice.

So how do we pay for the care we receive? We have to confess that this insurance issue is very complex. There are, for example, no standard rates for health insurance because these are negotiated directly between employers and their insurers based on the number of employees in the workplace. Work in Bermuda, and your employer has partial legal responsibility for your health coverage and that of your non-working spouse and children. If you and your spouse are both working here, then either one employer or the other will provide the coverage for children. But be aware that health plans differ from workplace to workplace. Some may cover major medical, dentistry and optometry, as well as doctors' visits. You should discuss health plans carefully with your employer.

How much comes out of your salary for coverage? Again, this is difficult to answer. Generally the employer will pay half, and you will pay half. However, it's safe to say that between 8 and 10 percent of your salary is

INSIDERS' TIP

P.A.L.S. (Patients Assistance League and Service) is a registered charity dedicated to enabling cancer patients to stay at home. Qualified nurses make home visits and help with dressings, medications and nutritional supplements. Overseas visitors suffering from cancer are welcome to call (441) 236-7257 for help. The organization is centered at 21 Point Finger Road, Paget Parish. Donations are greatly appreciated.

Herbal and Old-fashioned Remedies

So you've got a fever? These days chances are you'd think of a visit to the doctor and the pharmacy. But up until 50 years ago, the chances are you would have visited your garden instead. Match-me-if-you-can leaves (see Flora and Fauna chapter) rolled and soaked in bay rum were the answer to aspirin. Applied to the forehead, wrists and soles of feet, they would help reduce the fever and alleviate headaches. What about a cough?

Boiled down Father John's leaves with elder bush and cedar berries added apparently made an effective cough syrup. Where pneumonia is concerned, Bermudian senior citizens still swear by the Bermuda onion. Many a story is told of a small child's life being saved, thanks to a poultice of fried onions. And a juice created from sliced

onion sprinkled with brown sugar helped to relieve whooping cough. They also swear by drinking green paw paw juice to lower high blood pressure. For general fatigue, rue soaked in brandy made an excellent pick-me-up. As for babies' teething problems, poppies used to be the answer. People would pick the purple flowers, put them in a bottle and add brown sugar. Then they'd set the bottle by the window until the sugar melted. Rubbing the juice on the baby's gums meant peace at last. But Bermuda's Health Department didn't approve of this particular remedy because it was a form of opium. In the 1930s officials put an end to the practice by using kerosene to kill off the poppies.

Where did herbal remedies in Bermuda come from? Early settlers probably brought knowledge culled from herbal books and from oral accounts handed down in their families from generation to generation. In fact, they may have brought the knowledge before they brought the herbs. We know from Lefroy's *Memorials of the Discovery and Early Settlement of the Bermudas or Somers Islands* that in 1616 the Bermuda Company sent herbs including fennel, cumin, basil and marjoram to Governor Daniel Tucker. As Jill Collett points out in *Bermuda: Her Plants and Gardens 1609-1850*, the same remedies recommended in herbal books written abroad were used here. However, when a remedy was not grown here then an alternative local or imported plant was used. For example, in England, sage, or *salvia officinalis,* was used as a toothbrush and gargle. In Bermuda, a different sage, lantana, served the same purpose. Collett also points out that many of the herbs imported became "escapes" — that is, they eventually grew wild in Bermuda. Fennel is the obvious example, as today it grows like a weed. Collett cites the words of William Coles, a seventeenth century English gardener, who wrote that fennel was used for "those that are grown fat, to abate their unwieldiness and cause them to grow more gaunt and lank." But in Bermuda, she says, fennel was used as an eye wash and was recommended for kidney ailments.

Aloes were also medicinally important. In the early nineteenth century, a mill in Flatts Village was used to extract the juice, which was good for colds and dysentery. Applied externally, aloe also prevented gangrene. Today, of course, we use it for burns and in shampoo. Other remedies she quotes from an article written in 1957 by Mrs. Vaughan Pugh for the *Bermuda Historical Quarterly*: Rosemary boiled with molasses, and shark oil boiled with aloe and honey were two cough medicines. And according to Pugh, cedar dust acted as a drying agent for newborn babies' navels.

One of Pugh's recipes makes sense of E. A. McCallan's remark in *Life on Old St. David's Bermuda*: "Some home cures were of such a nature that I refrain from

— continued on next page

mentioning them." Pugh's cure for asthma was: "Swallow live cockroaches. Their struggles with their legs break the web. Take live hog lice, twelve at a time; take a dozen for six days." William Zuill, in his *Bermuda Sampler,* quotes an article from the August 9, 1831, issue of *The Royal Gazette* entitled "Beneficent Uses of Cockroaches." Here is what it says:

"These troublesome, destructive and offensive vermin, have happily been found to form an article of incalculable value in the Materia Medica of the modern date; having been recently used with singular success in the cure of Lock Jaw, when every other supposed remedy had been perseveringly tried. The application of Cockroaches, as a medicated plaster, have proved of the greatest efficacy in removing external inflammation; in promoting suppuration in the most obstinate tumours . . ."

How was the plaster made up? We are told that "The Cock Roach, having the head, wings and legs removed, must be prepared with fresh cold hog's lard or other sweet, soft grease; and in that form applied in all cases to the parts affected . . . ."

Herbal remedies are definitely making a comeback, but fortunately so far no one's recommending a return to creepy crawly concoctions. Injections against tetanus are infinitely preferable.

deducted to cover medical insurance, pension and government taxes. But note that your employer coverage does not cover any relative other than your non-working spouse or children. Should your parents come to visit, for example, any healthcare costs they incur are not covered.

Blood Laboratories

Quinton Butterfield owns and manages four labs for blood and urine testing. All the laboratories offer a range of chemistry, hematology, microbiology, urine and serology tests. Examples of tests include blood count, HIV, pregnancy, thyroid, cardiac enzyme and stomach ulcer testing.

Patients usually come with laboratory forms from their doctors. Overseas visitors are welcome, and forms from doctors abroad are honored. Four technicians are on hand to provide fast customer service. You'll get a pregnancy test result in 20 minutes. Others come back in 24 hours, though HIV test results take about a week because they are handled in batches.

Butterfield also provides profiles for many health and life insurance companies. Depending on the requirements, blood is either sent abroad for testing or is tested at the Bermuda laboratory. Single tests cost about $40. On average clients requiring a group of tests pay up to $250. Overseas clients pay directly and submit receipts to their insurance companies abroad.

Laboratory locations and operating hours follow. In St. George's Parish, East End Medical Laboratory, 1 Clarence Street, Town of St. George, (441) 297-2502, is open Tuesday and Thursday from 8:30 to 10:30 AM. In Pembroke Parish, Central Diagnostics, 53 Union Street, Hamilton, (441) 292-9940, is open 8:30 AM to 6 PM Monday through Thursday and 8:30 AM to 1:30 PM on Friday. Also in Hamilton, City Laboratory, 17 Parliament Street, (441) 296-6313, is open 9 AM to 2 PM Monday through Thursday and 9 AM to 1 PM on Friday. And in Sandys Parish, Sandys' Medical Lab, 32 Somerset Road, (441) 234-3295, is open from 8:30 to 10:00 AM Monday, Wednesday and Friday.

Bermuda's emphasis on education has created a professional class that makes our country one of the best educated per capita in the world.

Education and Child Care

Education

Among the many sights that intrigue first-time visitors to Bermuda are thousands of schoolchildren in crisp uniforms. From the time a child enters primary school at the compulsory age of 5, until leaving secondary school at the minimum age of 16, uniforms are mandatory with each school identified by its own color skirt, jacket, trousers and tie.

The Ministry of Education governs our public school system, which includes one senior secondary school, five middle schools and 18 primary schools. The school year lasts nearly 10 months beginning in early September, with breaks at Easter, Christmas and during summer.

Bermuda's emphasis on education has created a professional class that makes our country one of the best educated per capita in the world. According to the latest census, nearly 10 percent of Bermudians older than age 16 hold a post-secondary degree.

Some families still choose to send their children to boarding schools in America, Canada or the U.K., but there are almost 6,500 students in Bermuda's public and private schools. There, high school graduates are prepared for further studies at the Bermuda College or institutions abroad. The United States, Canada and England are students' main choices for post-secondary study.

Public Schools

Bermuda approached the '90s cognizant that glaring deficiencies in the public school system could not be ignored. In 1988 educators, parents and business leaders came together to form an Education Planning Team mandated with examining where we were in terms of public education, where we had to go and the best way to get there. Far-reaching recommendations came out of frank and open discussions.

What emerged was the imperative of initiating a total restructuring of the existing education system. An active and more viable relationship between the community, schools, and both the domestic and international business sectors was deemed critical.

Among the many points of concern at the time were an apparent lack of suitable preparation of students for the workplace, a higher dropout rate for boys, and inadequate dissemination of the technical skills necessary for Bermudian students to compete in a rapidly advancing communications infrastructure.

The essence of the restructuring decision included the development of new curricula, the integration of students with special needs into regular classrooms, and the establishment of ongoing professional development for teachers. But the more contentious issue in the $124.5 million plan was the focus on the introduction of middle schools and senior secondary schools as key components of a re-vamped system.

A 1991 *Royal Gazette* poll revealed that while 72 percent of respondents supported restructuring, almost as many were against the establishment of a senior secondary school, believing that a school with 1,000 or more students would exacerbate problems such as drug use among school children.

One of the keys critical to the long-term success of revamping local education — an exercise that is not expected to be completed until 2002 — is the participation of the business community. Business involvement has emerged as a part of establishing what Bermuda College's vice president of academic affairs has called "significant linkages" between educational institutions and the business sector. Pivotal to these linkages is the development of curricula that respond directly to the needs of business both now and in the next millennium.

An example of the relevance of this hand-in-hand approach is seen in the successful two-year insurance studies program begun in 1995 in response to insurance industry requests. Significantly, with Bermuda now established as a prominent international insurance center (see our International Business chapter), this program places graduating students squarely on the rung for entry and advancement in this sector.

An education sub-committee of the Bermuda Insurance Institute has reached out to introduce students to the insurance industry. In August 1998, a networking cocktail party held at the Bermuda Underwater Exploration Institute (BUEI) saw actuaries, underwriters, brokers and accountants discuss their careers and companies with interested students.

These eager young people were also brought up-to-date on scholarships offered by the Bermuda Foundation for Insurance Studies. (See the Bermuda Foundation for Insurance Studies in this chapter.) Cooperative programs involving tourism and other industries are being encouraged.

The importance attached to the school/business relationship has resulted in some companies introducing an adopt-a-school program. Several businesses have become active partners. Adoption programs involve work shadowing, in which young students visit corporate offices to gain firsthand experience of the business environment. Whenever possible, corporate staff members visit classrooms. Other aspects include summer job programs. An ethic of excellence is promoted.

The Ministry of Education also oversees a Business Education Partnership, designed to bring students together with key persons in an industry in which they show particular interest. A business Institute of Directors has developed a Young Enterprise program that provides students with practical experience in understanding how to establish and manage companies.

Several initiatives, in the form of scholarships, grants and awards, number in the dozens and cover several disciplines, with benefits ranging from hundreds to several thousand dollars.

In 1998, the law firm Conyers Dill & Pearman continued to offer its Award for Legal Education to an outstanding young Bermudian pursuing a legal career. The $12,000 award covers the first academic year and is renewable for a further three years subject to the chosen recipient's scholastic progress.

Another top firm, Appleby, Spurling & Kempe (AS&K), has a Legal Education Scholarship program that has entered its third decade. The 1998 recipient, Michelle Correia, won the scholarship, which is worth $12,500 a year for three years. Bursary awards of $6,000 were also donated to each of three other law students, with two others each receiving bursaries of $3,000.

The commitment of Bermuda's legal, governmental, banking and international business community to developing a well-educated and trained professional workforce is apparent, and for some firms, long-standing.

Both the Bank of Butterfield and the Bank of Bermuda have for many years offered scholarships to qualifying Bermudian students. In 1998, the Bank of Bermuda distributed more than $250,000 to a dozen students.

Among the many government-sponsored grants is the Environmental Education grant promoted by the Department of Agriculture and Fisheries. This grant encourages the study of ecology, conservation, agriculture, horticulture, and related subjects. Worth $5,000 and applicable for one academic year, it is awarded to a Bermuda resident attending an accredited college or university in the U.S.

Another helpful government initiative was the 1998 reduction — from 22.25 percent to 5 percent — of customs duties on portable computers for student use. However, there is a caveat: Students wanting to take advantage of the reduction must attend a school that has a program where laptops are integrated into the curriculum. However, this stipulation may change. The Ministry of Education, which advises the Collector of Customs to apply the new duty rate, must certify the program.

Some charitable organizations also play major roles. Last year, Youth Net, a charity that helps keep young people on track toward a rewarding future, continued a mentorship program begun in 1995. This program pairs public school students with volunteer adult mentors willing to commit a minimum of an hour a week with a student for a full academic year. So far, more than 60 students have been paired, but the need for mentors is growing and expected to double.

Millions have been allocated for renovations to existing buildings, with $6.2 million spent in 1997. More computers will be introduced into classrooms as we approach the year 2000, and changing teaching methods will see staff organized into interdisciplinary teaching teams focusing on core subjects.

A key initiative within the public school system was the introduction in January 1997 of a reading recovery program. Developed out of the research of Dr. Marie Clay at the University of New Zealand, this early-intervention program, designed for children who have spent just a year in school, targets the lowest achievers. Children experiencing reading and writing difficulties are caught before the problem escalates.

By the end of summer 1998 around 18 teachers had qualified to administer the program, with others undergoing training.

Following the November 9, 1998, elections, which saw the Progressive Labour Party (PLP) elected as the new government (see History chapter), a number of proposals have been brought to the fore, among them a thrust to set national academic standards, with schools accountable for meeting these standards; a curriculum and assessment system will be put in place.

These and other programs have priority, coming under the Education portfolio held by the Premier, Ms. Jennifer Smith, who sees certain education changes as necessary for Bermuda's children. Part of her aim is to introduce representative elected school boards to take the place of appointed boards. These new school boards will include parents, teachers, neighborhood business representatives and residents.

A formal approach to teaching moral and character values will be incorporated within a multi-cultural syllabus.

Middle Schools and Senior Secondary Schools

Introduced in 1997, the middle school changeover will be completed by 1998-99. The restructured Bermudian educational system will consist of six years of primary schooling (including kindergarten; kids typically begin school in Bermuda at age 5), three at middle school and four at the senior level.

While the middle school concept is not new to North America, it represents a new direction for Bermuda. With visual arts, music, dance and theater as additional subjects to enhance the core curriculum, and with business studies, technological education and computer-related instruction, students will be exposed to a wide range of subjects and activities not available under the former system.

This concept has required a different set of teaching approaches and skills. As a result, the Ministry of Education initiated a variety of workshops and training programs for teachers leading up to September 1997 when the five middle schools (former secondary schools that were revamped and renovated) welcomed students to a newly structured educational environment. The average class size in these schools is 24, but the pupil-teacher ratio (when all professional staff is included) hovers at roughly 13-to-1.

CedarBridge Academy (see this chapter's Close-up) is the island's first senior secondary school, with the Berkeley Institute expected to become the second in 1999. Both are structured to receive students from the middle schools and immerse them in a four-year program. Career guidance and other student support services are integral components.

The government's desire to answer questions and allay community fears regarding the overall educational direction resulted in the Ministry of Education turning to two advertising agencies for their public relations expertise. The ad campaign centered on middle schools in 1997, with a series of newspaper advertisements and some radio exposure. Part of the motivation for this new approach was in response to an education audit by a team led by an Iowa State University professor. Among the findings was that communication to the public on the intentions, results and potential benefits of the restructuring had been inadequate.

Private Schools

Private schooling in Bermuda has always been regarded as superior to that of the public schools. When government announced plans to restructure the public system, some of the proposed changes resulted in an avalanche of applications to the island's six private schools, most of which are modeled on the British system. In fact, total enrollment has seen a 10 percent flight of student enrollment from public schools to private. However, all offer the type of education that allows students to enter either North American or United Kingdom universities.

Unlike the BSSC (Bermuda Secondary School Certificate) exam taken by public school students, graduates at the private schools take the GCSE (General Certificate in Secondary Education), a British exam providing those who pass with a recognized qualification in the United States, Canada or the United Kingdom. The student then can choose to enter 11th or 12th grade at a U.S. preparatory school or take an associate degree at the

Bermuda College. Note that the island's Roman Catholic and Seventh-day Adventist schools operate on a U.S.-type grading system.

Although at one time most private schools had a majority of white students on the rolls (and some were exclusively for whites), today that has changed. One or two schools have a fairly even racial ratio.

Pembroke Parish

Bermuda High School for Girls
27 Richmond Rd.
• **(441) 295-6153**

This is Bermuda's only all-girls school. Founded in 1894 by Mrs. Grosvenor Tucker and other prominent citizens, today it is a general academic school for grades 1 through 12. It is an affiliated member of the National Association of Independent Schools as well as a member of the European Council of International Schools. A student body of 634 (77 percent white, 23 percent black) enjoys an 8-acre campus, with the BHS modeled on Britain's prestigious Cheltenham Ladies' College.

Students here take the GCSE (General Certificate of Secondary Education) exams at age 16. These British exams provide students with a qualification accepted not only in the UK, but also in the United States and Canada. The student body is 71.5 percent Bermudian. Some 90 percent of graduates go on to university and college, with many attending Bermuda College.

Saltus Grammar School
St. John's Rd.
• **(441) 292-6177**

Founded in 1888 as a boys' grammar school, Saltus became coeducational in 1992. Today, with enrollment approaching 1,000 students, it is considered the premier private school in Bermuda and has an international reputation. A member of the National Association of Independent Schools in North America, Saltus has, within the past decade, changed from an institution populated by white males to one that is reflective of the wider community. Current student enrollment is more than

CedarBridge Academy Begins a New Era in Bermudian Education

On September 15, 1997, CedarBridge Academy in Devonshire Parish, the first of two planned public senior secondary schools, welcomed its first 1,200 students. Costing $60 million, it is Bermuda's latest and most modern educational institution.

As one of the key pieces in the island's restructuring program for its public school system, the thrust at CedarBridge is toward more project-based learning with a direct focus on skill acquisition. The Berkeley Institute entered 1999 as the second senior secondary school, joining CedarBridge. By 2000, the current Bermuda Secondary School Certificate (BSSC) will be replaced.

CedarBridge, the largest of the island's schools, has a state-of-the-art library, more than 260 computers (with plans to install more), a sick bay and electronic security. Wheelchair-accessible, the school is divided into three zones — central, north and south — with 32 main classrooms and tutorial rooms located in the south. Specialized subjects are taught in the northern zone where science labs, two music rooms, a design and technology area, fitness rooms and computer labs are housed. The gymnasium, cafeteria, business studies and trades classrooms are also in the northern zone. One of the school's finest features is the central zone's 640-seat Ruth Seaton James Auditorium, named in honor of a prominent local educator. It is Bermuda's largest and best-equipped auditorium.

While every emphasis is being placed on the maturation of students, staff development is currently at the top of the priority list. Out of the $1 million set aside in 1997 to finance professional development throughout the entire public school system, $250,000 was earmarked specifically for CedarBridge and its 77-member teaching staff.

— continued on next page

Photo: GIS

Cedar Bridge Academy represents a new era of education in Bermuda.

Initial responses from a survey conducted in 1991 showed that a majority of the community opposed the building of a "mega-school" in Prospect. When it was completed in 1997 and opened to accept registrations, an avalanche of applications poured in from students, several of them transferring from the private school system.

However, despite some teething problems in Bermuda's so-called "mega-school," CedarBridge students are quickly showing their talents in a number of areas, particularly the arts.

35 percent female and 21 percent black. Seventy-four percent of students are Bermudian; 26 percent are from the international community.

The school's curriculum allows entry into both the European and American academic streams, with 95 percent of graduates entering universities in the United States, Canada and the UK. Favored universities include Dartmouth in the UK; Yale, Brown and MIT in the United States; and McGill in Canada.

In 1997 Toshiba and Microsoft invited Saltus to join 42 other schools in North America and Australia as one of the pioneers in a "Learning through Laptops" program. By 2000 (perhaps before), every Saltus student will have a laptop, at a projected total cost of $1.3 million.

A graduated payment plan and the school's student aid program helped parents obtain the computers which cost around $1,800 each. Government's reduction of customs duties on these computers has proven helpful.

Beginning with students in the Junior and Senior 2 classes, the first laptops were issued in 1998; they are now compulsory student equipment and are connected to the school's computer network. Log-on capability without wires is facilitated through hand-held radio-frequency monitors installed in class and study rooms.

Mount Saint Agnes Academy
99 Dundonald St. W., Hamilton
• (441) 292-4134

This academy, now operated by the Hamilton Roman Catholic Diocese and assisted by a board of governors, was founded in 1890 by the Sisters of St. Vincent De Paul

(Halifax) who owned and operated the school until 1975.

An independent, fee-paying Roman Catholic school catering to students from kindergarten to grade 12, the student body is made up of 550 youngsters aged 5 to 18, most of whom are Bermudian. The remainder are children of non-Bermudian workers, mostly from America, Canada and Britain. Enrollment preference is given to Roman Catholics, but the school does accept students from other denominations. Non-Catholics comprise more than 25 percent of the student population.

Course work follows North American guidelines, and the school is accredited for the purposes of college entry after graduation. This facilitates ease of transfer between Bermuda and North America. Students from Britain find the curriculum at each grade level comparable to what they have experienced at home.

Warwick Parish

Montessori Academy
45 Middle Rd. • (441) 236-9797

Located at Tivoli in Warwick in a magnificent hilltop property, the Bermuda's Montessori school was founded in September 1991, when the academy was opened. Although it began small, by September 1991 the academy opened its doors to 66 students ages 3 through 10. Today, with more than 125 students, there is an expectation that the school will include a middle school level in 1998.

Though relatively new to Bermuda, the Montessori method of education has been used successfully throughout the world since

Dr. Maria Montessori opened her first school in Italy in 1907. The Montessori Academy encourages students to learn at their own pace in an environment that is less traditional and not so rigidly structured. Eight to 10 percent of the students have varying degrees of learning disorders, but the school's multisensory approach to teaching and learning brings out their potential. Students at Montessori take the California Achievement Tests, with results that often surpass those of children at other schools.

Warwick Academy
117 Middle Rd. • (441) 236-1917

This school is not only the oldest in Bermuda — many believe it is the oldest in the New World, dating back to 1662 when it was established by the Bermuda Company. The academy joined the public school system in 1960 after almost 300 years as a private primary and secondary school. In 1990, however, it reverted to private status after being designated for conversion to a middle school as part of the government's restructuring program. The school's board believed it could better serve the community as a private school.

Student enrollment approaches 600 and final exams are for the GCSE. Eighty-five to 90 percent of graduates either enter the Bermuda College or go to universities or colleges in North America or the United Kingdom. Once an all-white private school, Warwick Academy's current enrollment is 60 percent black, and the boy-girl ratio is 57 percent to 43 percent. The school's music program is considered one of the best on the island, and the musical potential of students is deliberately encouraged.

Southampton Parish

Bermuda Institute
Middle Rd. • (441) 238-1566

Founded and run under the auspices of the Seventh-day Adventist Church, the Bermuda Institute operates on the standard U.S. grading system. It offers a Christian-focused education aimed at not only bringing out students' best academic efforts, but also developing social, physical and spiritual qualities. It endeavors to integrate faith with learning.

Serving a student body of 508, the institute has a special-needs program that involves a teacher working with students who have some difficulty with academics. Bermuda Institute students who graduate after grade 12 with a high school diploma, transcripts and high Scholastic Aptitude Test scores are able to move on either to Bermuda College or to schools overseas. Eighty-eight percent of graduates go on to universities or colleges in the United States, the West Indies or the United Kingdom.

Higher Education

Bermuda College
1 College Dr.
• (441) 236-9000

Less than 2 miles from Hamilton, nestled in the heart of Paget, the Bermuda College has emerged as a school deserving consideration by students seeking higher education. However, this was not always so, and the struggle to gain acceptance as a quality school of advanced learning did not come quickly.

The college as it exists today is the result of an amalgamation of the Bermuda Technical Institute (established in 1956), the Bermuda Hotel and Catering College (established in 1965) and the Academic Sixth Form Center (established in 1967). The hotel and catering college began as a domestic science school in the 1930s. The technical institute was established to fill the void left by the closure of the Royal Naval Dockyard, which for many decades had provided young males with training in the trades. The Academic Sixth Form Center had been the springboard for high school graduates preparing to go abroad to university.

The Bermuda College Act of 1974 resulted in the college's establishment, and since its inception the institution has undergone a continuing physical, administrative and curriculum expansion. Including the more than $2 million spent to purchase the property on which its campus is located, more than $40 million has been spent on the school's devel-

Bermuda's schoolchildren get a solid academic grounding in public and private schools.

opment. Today Bermuda College serves an annual average of 500 full-time students. The college, governed by a 12-member board, has overcome a somewhat negative image held by the general public and students. Its academic, technical, hotel and business training is regarded as comparable to the level offered at North American institutions of equal size.

Although it does not have university status, Bermuda College's links with overseas universities and colleges allow graduates to transfer credits if they wish to enter a four-year degree program. Currently the college offers 10 associate degree programs and 15 certificate-level courses.

In summer 1998, as part of its educational expansion, the college signed an agreement with the University of Plymouth in England to allow Bermuda College students — provided they have maintained at least a 2.75 grade point average — to transfer credits to that university after they complete 62 semester hours. This will enable them to enter the third year of an honors degree. Transfer agreements prior to last summer had generally focused on Canadian universities such as Acadia and Dalhousie. Bermuda College students now have access to Northeastern University in Boston for that institution's engineering programs.

Throughout 1998, links with some 10 universities in the U.S., Canada and the United Kingdom were also established.

If the plans that are currently underway bear fruit, the Bermuda College will become a four-year institution. According to Vice-president Dr. Donald Peters, the college wants to grant degrees in international business, insurance, information technology, hotel administration, and liberal arts.

The continuing education arm of the college, the Faculty of Adult and Continuing Education, has formed viable links with a number of local organizations. Marketing its own brochure for each of the spring, summer and fall terms, this department serves an average of 3,200 adult students annually.

Private Sector Initiatives

Seniors Learning Centre
Bermuda College
• **(441) 239-4029**

With more than 9 percent of Bermuda's population aged 65 and older, the Seniors Learning Centre, formed in 1990, has seen its membership mushroom from 11 at inception to almost 600 today.

The center is affiliated with the overseas Elderhostel Institute network that organizes institutes of learning for retirees in Canada and the United States.

"Our motto, 'Better Living Through Learning', goes for our minds as well as our bodies," says President, Rita Basist. Curriculum Committee Chairman, Bertram Guishard, arranges a number of varied classes throughout the year. From lectures on Bermuda history, and instruction on financial planning, to arts & crafts activities, conversational Spanish, line dancing, the physical benefits of Tai Chi, and more, members – a few of whom are in their 90s – keep mentally and physically active.

"We not only put on educational courses, but we have theatre outings, visits to the Bermuda Underwater Institute, or even trips to Nonsuch Island, among many other things," says Guishard.

Joining fee is $20, and life membership is $120. Those who do not wish to become life members pay annual dues of $10.

Bermuda Foundation for Insurance Studies (BFIS)
Cedarpark Centre, 48 Cedar Avenue
City of Hamilton
• (441) 295-1266

This registered charity was formed in 1996 to develop, coordinate and direct educational funding and training for Bermudian students pursuing insurance-related careers. Four scholarships are available for those entering a four-year program leading to a baccalaureate in Business Administration with an insurance focus. The first two years are spent at the Bermuda College where a 3.0 grade point average or above must be maintained. The remaining two years must be at an approved overseas college or university.

The Foundation also enables those students seeking internships to find places within the insurance industry during their summer break.

BFIS fosters several programs to further insurance studies both here and abroad. One program for Bermuda College graduates with an Associate degree in Business Administration, allows entry into the New York-based College of Insurance, and leads to a Bachelor of Business Administration degree.

Webster University (Bermuda) Campus
15 Gorham Road, City of Hamilton
• (441) 293-6343

Founded in Missouri in 1915, and with some 72 campuses located throughout the US, Europe and Asia, Webster has had a campus in Bermuda since 1981. It offers postgraduate education — Master of Arts degrees in Management, International Business, and Master of Business Administration (MBA) — to the local community.

"Our faculty are comprised of full time professors from the main campus, and qualified local and overseas adjunct instructors who bring both academic qualifications and real world experience to the classroom," says local director, Helen Pearman Ziral.

Designed to suit the needs of working professionals, Webster's programs have been successfully completed by more than 500 Bermudian residents.

Bermuda Biological Station for Research
17 Biological Station Ln.,
Town of St. George
• (441) 297-1880

The BBSR is an independent, nonprofit research institution founded in 1903. Though located in Bermuda, it is incorporated in New York State.

The BBSR is engaged in numerous research and educational initiatives, among them the Risk Prediction Initiative, a program within the Atlantic Global Change Institute of BBSR. Its goal is to form a bridge between the international scientific and business communities.

The station's educational outreach programs are varied and dedicated to encouraging secondary and undergraduate students to pursue science careers. It sponsors a number of university-level courses, plus graduate and undergraduate internships. Grants supporting various scientific research projects are also available through BBSR.

While the initial reason for its establishment was to provide a base for overseas scientists engaged in research, a strong locally based research group is now in place. Resident programs cover four principal areas: marine biology and ecology, global geosciences, molecular biology and Bermuda environmental quality.

Those interested in examining published research papers on BBSR's work on Bermuda will find them in the station's E. L. Mark Library, which contains more than 20,000 volumes and 200 up-to-date scientific journals and abstracts covering the four key disciplines. Special publications and general books on Bermuda's natural history and geography are also found at the library.

Among the current and popular activities supported and promoted at the BBSR is the JASON Project, founded in 1989 by Dr. Robert Ballard following his discovery of the wreck of the *Titanic*. Thousands of interested school children wrote and expressed such an interest in his discovery that Ballard and a team of associates developed the project. It aims at providing a vehicle for both teachers and students to take part in various global explorations through the use of advanced interactive telecommunications.

Since 1993 BBSR has acted as the Preliminary Interactive Network Site for Bermuda's school children and the general public when JASON explored two sites along Mexico's Baja California peninsula. Since then, JASON has visited Belize, Hawaii and Southern Florida. In 1998 the project will focus on Bermuda itself.

Also in 1998, BBSR launched a new holiday concept for divers. This vacation lets divers explore not only Bermuda's coral reefs — the island is the most northern area in the world where colonies of reef-building coral are found — and its numerous shipwrecks, but to dive with two top scientists and audit lectures about marine life.

These dive holidays, organized through September, October and November, cost just under $2,000.

Throughout last year the station put on a lecture series embracing a variety of topics related to its International Year of the Ocean Symposium. Dr. John Woods from Imperial University in London; Dr. John Farrington of Woods Hole Oceanographic Institution; Dr. James Yoder from University of Rhode Island; and Dr. Anthony Knap, BBSR director, discussed new technologies as they examined potential threats to the ocean environment.

Bermuda Underwater Exploration Institute
40 Crow Lane, City of Hamilton
• (441) 292-7219

With an obvious focus on things marine, the institute last year held a slate of public lectures in its Tradewinds Auditorium. This exciting series included "Whales & Dolphins," presented by Greg Stone, associate director at the New England Aquarium. Stone has on occasion worked with Bermuda diver, Teddy Tucker, who along with Robert Canton in 1955 discovered and brought to the surface a significant treasure from the *San Pedro*, wrecked northwest of Bermuda in 1595.

Also presented in 1998 were slide-accompanied lectures by avid mountain climber and sea kayak adventurer, Dr. Olaf Malver. Other presentations included: "The Coral Reefs of Bermuda & Florida," by Dr. Robbie Smith, resident Bermudian scientist at BBSR; and "*The Mary Rose*, its history and the museum," by Dr. Margaret Rule, maritime archaeologist and head archaeologist of King Henry VIII's warship *Mary Rose*, which sank near the Isle of Wight in 1545.

Many of these lectures were followed by a buffet supper laid on by La Coquille (see Restaurant chapter) and held in the main lobby. Lecture tickets for non-members of BUEI were between $7.50 and $10 (see Attractions for more on BUEI).

Continuing Education

Community Education Development Program
72 Middle Rd., Warwick Parish
• (441) 236-0829

This public education program was begun in 1980 to deliver a wide range of educational, recreational, social and cultural programs to various individuals, community organizations and groups.

With an initial enrollment of 428 students at the Warwick Community Education School, the program was extended three years later to St. George's Community School. That same year the Community Education Development Program (CEDP) became a permanent aspect of the educational landscape.

Co-sponsored by the Ministry of Community and Cultural Affairs and the Ministry of Education, it is now affiliated with the International Community Education Association (ICEA), a non-governmental association for people working in local communities. Founded in 1974 in the United States, ICEA is a worldwide organization with members in more than 80 countries.

CEDP has grown tremendously since 1980, with an average of 108 courses offered during each of the spring, summer and fall terms. Several centers on the island make the program highly accessible, with certified, experienced instructors delivering training. Along with the Warwick location, other CDEP centers are at Sandys Community School (register at Sandys Middle School, 21 Scott's Hill Road, (441) 234-1346, and St. George's Community School, (441) 297-0007).

Low tuition has proven an incentive for participation. Tuition ranges from $40 to $100, with the majority of courses costing less than $60. Golden Agers (those 60 years and older) may register free if minimum requirements for enrollment have been met. (The exceptions are computer classes and those classes having an enrollment limit.) Be advised that materials do cost extra.

Academic, technical, computer and college preparatory courses are offered, plus others on do-it-yourself subjects, personal development, language, music, dance and fitness. At the end of each course participants are awarded a certificate of participation. The level of course work often serves as a bridge to more advanced education.

Although offered on a non-credit basis, these courses allow individuals of all ages to explore new fields, sharpen professional skills and enrich their personal lives through friendships and contacts made during the various semesters. Not only do Bermudians register for the course work, but non-Bermudians comprise 25 percent of those enrolled. The overall atmosphere stimulates cross-cultural friendships.

Since the inception of the CEDP, there have been more than 50,000 registrations. High en- rollment has enabled costs to be minimized. Seventy-five percent of participants are repeat students often taking two or more courses each semester. Many businesses sponsor employees to take accounting, management, supervisory or computer courses. Senior citizens and children have not been ignored. Scores of seniors take advantage of the opportunity to stay mentally and physically active as do numbers of children placed by parents in the Holiday Fun Camp Program, which is active over the Easter, midterm and Christmas holidays.

CEDP's goals for 1998 include developing additional community programs, among them the establishment of a central Community School Resource Center at the new CedarBridge Academy.

Adult Education School — CSC
16 Dundonald St., City of Hamilton
• (441) 292-5809

The Adult Education School (AES), on the corner of Brunswick and Dundonald streets, was founded in 1958 by Mrs. Merle Swan Williams to offer persons 16 and over a second chance at obtaining an education. The focus was on equipping them to earn a GED.

Having faced and overcome various financial problems during the nearly four decades since its establishment, the school has emerged as a strong educational provider. Its young graduates often go on to earn placements in institutions overseas. By the end of 1997, the majority of the 100 students were between 16 and 20 years of age. But it is anticipated that this may change in the future, as the school's focus may return to the scholastic development of the mature student.

Government-aided, the school has full- and part-time teachers for day classes and volunteer tutors during the evening. The school closes during the summer.

Child Care

Bermuda's child-care facilities are many, varied, and of exceptionally high quality. Nursery school regulations formulated in 1984 do not recognize separations between nurseries, preschools and day-care centers. Both public

and private preschools are geared toward preparing youngsters for the transition to the elementary school environment and its demands.

Government preschools focus on curricula aimed at merging playtime activities with learning, and social and emotional needs are considered equally important as physical development. Head Start, the now-familiar U.S. program that developed out of a need to provide help for disadvantaged children, has proven valuable in Bermuda's schools. With a government preschool in each parish, each school registers 4-year-olds from that parish every February for a September induction. Information on government preschools can be obtained by calling the Ministry of Education's Child and Family Services at (441) 236-0224.

In general, however, curricula vary depending on whether the preschool is public or private. Many of the private schools are fundamentally traditional in their approach to study, emphasizing the "three Rs." Some private schools place additional value on religious training, while others put less focus on teaching social skills.

A perusal of the number of child-care facilities in Bermuda — and this includes nurseries, day-care centers, preschools and after-school care — yields more than 40 establishments, with many of them offering a full range of programs and services including holiday camps, computer instruction and transportation services. New regulations related to childcare are currently being developed. If legislated, these would become included in a Children's Act rather than in the Public Health Act, where they are at present.

In mid-summer 1998, then Social Services Minister Wayne Furbert announced a government subsidy of $50 per child per week for parents with children attending licensed daycare facilities. With as many as 60 percent of Bermuda's pre-schoolers having working mothers, the initiative was introduced "to ease the financial burden on the modern family," the Minister said.

Almost 400 children qualified for this financial aid package that is linked to total household income. The subsidy is expected to cost the government upwards of $1 million annually.

Child Development Program
37 Tynes Bay House, Palmetto Rd.,
Devonshire Parish
• **(441) 295-0746, (441) 236-0224 ext. 205**

Under the Ministry of Health, Social Services and Housing, this government program, directly administered by the Department of

Child and Family Services, provides support for families with preschool children. Services are offered when children reach the age of 2, although a referral basis can lead to quicker access.

A major program feature is an assessment and evaluation aspect, applied to all children between 24 and 30 months of age. Staff members visit the home and, through various monitored tests with specific materials, evaluate how the child is developing and share their findings with the parents. Depending on the information gleaned from these tests, another assessment may be indicated, with one of four home visitation programs offered. These programs zero in on educational enrichment by encouraging verbal interaction between parent and child, behavior management that is positive for the child, the child's language development and the initiation of structured learning for those children shown to be lagging in developmental aspects.

Other features available to all parents include a parent library, parent discussion groups, a newsletter and developmental information booklets.

The Featherbed Alley Print Shop — a quaint attraction tucked away on Featherbed Alley (what else?) in the Town of St George — was the birthplace of Bermuda's first newspaper, the *Bermuda Gazette*, edited and printed by Joseph Stockdale. The paper rolled off the press on 17 January 1784.

Media and Communications

Occasionally a beachcomber finds a letter in a bottle that has washed ashore. This bit of "sea mail" is generally thrown overboard by a crewman on a passing freighter, or a visitor leaving the island by cruise ship or private yacht. For most of us, keeping current with local and foreign news is important, and bottles washed ashore are a gentle curiosity. With virtually every home and apartment in Bermuda connected to cable, and with satellite dishes and the internet, the island's links to the outside world have made it easy to follow global events. Our daily, *The Royal Gazette*, enjoys a circulation approaching 16,000, with the front, editorial and obituary pages the first perused.

The Featherbed Alley Print Shop — a quaint attraction tucked away on Featherbed Alley (what else?) in the Town of St George — was the birthplace of Bermuda's first newspaper, the *Bermuda Gazette*, edited and printed by Joseph Stockdale. The paper rolled off the press on 17 January 1784, and on 1 March the same year reported that snow fell in Bermuda the previous night. Considering Bermuda's location, the "snow" probably consisted of little more than light flurries that lasted for a few minutes. But we might be wrong. (Incidentally, Bermuda's first postal service also began in 1784.)

After Stockdale died in 1803, his three daughters assumed control as publishers. And 13 years later, when the 1,616th issue was published, they relinquished direct control.

The Bermuda Library, just off the city of Hamilton's Queen Street, and adjacent to Perot's post office (see Let's Explain Bermuda chapter for more on this, the island's oldest post office), has a comfortable reading lounge. Newspapers from the United States, Britain, Canada and the Caribbean are available daily, though they must remain in the library, which is open Monday to Friday from 9:30 AM to 6 PM and on Saturday from 9:30 AM to 5 PM. For those seeking a wider range of foreign newspapers and magazines, there is a comprehensive selection in the Phoenix Centre on Reid Street, across from the library.

The Bermuda Broadcasting Company, DeFontes Broadcasting, and Bermuda Cablevision provide 54 local and overseas television channels. Included among them is an overseas Portuguese cable channel of interest to 9 percent of our local population. The island's eight AM and FM radio stations offer a wide choice of music and talk formats.

Deregulation in certain areas of Bermuda's telecommunications services within the past 18 months has sparked intense competition between telephone service providers. Many issues are being thrashed out during this period of extraordinary growth and rapid telecommunications change. The cost of overseas phone calls may decrease, and the lowering

---

INSIDERS' TIP

Headed for a day in the great outdoors of Bermuda? Any transistor radio will receive Bermuda broadcasts. Both radio companies offer local and international programming 24 hours a day.

of rates for interconnection between competing firms on the island has spawned a great deal of contention. Local broadcasters will see a relaxation of various regulations related to radio and television programming, particularly regarding political broadcasts. Following the Progressive Labour Party's (PLP) 9 November 1998 victory, a new nine-member Telecommunications Commission is overseeing the thrust to ensure the local communications industry marches in tandem (and even leads in certain areas, such as e-commerce) with worldwide trends and advances.

www.insiders.com

See this and many other
Insiders' Guide
destinations online.

Visit us today!

Newspapers

Usually you can find major American and Canadian daily newspapers at the larger hotels and leading pharmacies on the afternoon of the day of publication. A very small but delightful place where discussion of the topic of the day is commonplace is Twice Told Tales, 34 Parliament Street, Hamilton, (441) 296-1995. This second-hand bookstore is found directly across from the magistrate's court. Insiders sometimes gather here simply to read, sip cappuccino and debate current-events.

Dailies

The Royal Gazette
2 Par-la-Ville Rd., Hamilton
• (441) 295-5881

Bermuda's only daily newspaper, *The Royal Gazette* was established in 1828. Donald McPhee Lee of Halifax, Nova Scotia, became the King's Printer and the publisher of the *Royal Gazette* in 1828. Delayed by a harrowing sea journey to Bermuda, McPhee Lee did not publish the first two issues of *The Royal Gazette*. However, his brother, David Ross Lee, printed the January 8 and 15, 1828, issues. Donald arrived in time to print the third issue for January 22, 1828, and put out the paper every week for 60 years. The January 30, 1883, issue was his last; he died 11 days after its publication.

The paper remained a weekly or biweekly publication until January 1, 1921, when it merged with *The Colonist* to become a daily newspaper — *The Royal Gazette and the Colonist Daily*. In 1946 the title was shortened to *The Royal Gazette*. For the better part of two decades, starting the next year, the *Gazette* also published a Sunday edition, but in 1963 that was discontinued. Today it is published every day except Sunday.

The Royal Gazette is an award-winning paper that is wide-ranging in coverage of local and international topics. Letters to the editor provide intimate glimpses into community concerns, debates and arguments. In addition to its own editorial staff, the paper relies on wire services for up-to-the-minute information.

Just under 16,000 papers are printed daily and circulated island-wide. Papers are delivered door-to-door and sold at grocery and local parish stores, drugstores, eateries, gas stations and hotels. Subscriptions are available.

Weeklies

Mid-Ocean News
2 Par-la-Ville Rd., Hamilton
• (441) 295-5881

Readers picked up the first edition of the *Mid-Ocean* on August 16, 1911. S. S. Toddings, who since 1869 had been the successful editor and owner of *The Colonist*, founded the new paper. Published in Hamilton, it began as a four-page paper issued on Wednesday and Saturday.

Mid-Ocean News had various production schedules and incarnations from the early

---

INSIDERS' TIP

Cable Channel 11, the "Bermuda Weather Station," offers a three-day forecast, updated several times throughout the day.

1900s to the late '60s. It was a biweekly, then a triweekly, briefly a daily, then the government paper from 1951 to 1959. In 1968 it began publishing on Friday and continues to do so today.

The Mid-Ocean News Company was incorporated in 1947, and bought by The Bermuda Press (Holdings) Ltd. in 1962. While it is owned by the same company that publishes *The Royal Gazette*, *Mid-Ocean News* retains editorial independence and offers readers a different brand of local news than its sister organization. With sales of 13,000 to 14,000 per week, the *Mid-Ocean News* covers hard news, sports and entertainment, and offers reviews. Its columnists often provide intriguing insights as their topics cover technology, gardening, finance, business profiles, health, politics, social comment and art reviews.

The paper, circulated Fridays, provides a weekly bulletin of the previous week's top local news stories and lists Bermuda nightlife and entertainment options.

Exclusive interviews with government dignitaries and notable figures in both the private and corporate sectors of the community are common. Especially appreciated for its in-depth reporting and witty columnists, it is the only newspaper regularly providing color photographs on its front page.

Bermuda Sun
41 Victoria St., Hamilton
• (441) 295-3902

Bermuda Sun appeared at newsstands on May 11, 1964. Covering local events and issues, the *Sun* is generally thought of as less of an establishment newspaper than *The Royal Gazette* or *Mid-Ocean News*. However, it is not an "alternative weekly" but a mainstream newspaper with significant business and investment sections, a large section of local religious news and entertainment, sports and general and political news.

Bermuda Sun publishes legal advertising

in Bermuda and has a contract to publish official government notices. The paper is published on Fridays, and weekly circulation is 12,500, entirely generated by street sales. A second, Wednesday edition was launched in 1998. There is no home delivery, though overseas mail subscriptions are available.

Monthly and Twice Monthly

SALT
Suite 748, 48 Par-la-Ville Rd.,
Hamilton HM 11 • (441) 295-5884

SALT is a free, tabloid-sized, monthly entertainment newspaper printed by Salt Kettle Publishing Limited. Launched in April 1998, and with a circulation of 7,000, it can generally be found in most bars, coffee shops, galleries and restaurants. Primarily, local artists and musicians are featured. There is a comprehensive listing of clubs, restaurants, and galleries. The best way to contact them is through their mailing address or telephone number listed above.

The Workers Voice
48 Union Square, Hamilton
• (441) 292-0044

The Workers Voice began as a tabloid in 1973 following several years of appearing as a mimeographed four-page newsletter produced by a staff of two. It was decided after two years of printing about 200 copies an issue, to expand the size of the paper and widen the number of outlets. In 1993, restructuring saw the paper's pages expanded to 12 magazine-sized pages. With a current distribution of just over 1,000, the paper appears every two weeks. With copy produced by regular columnists and members of the Bermuda Industrial Union staff, content usually focuses on trade union matters. However, community-related articles and political comments are often featured.

INSIDERS' TIP

Every Friday, *Bermuda Sun* and *Mid-Ocean News* publish complete weekly cable TV guides. The *Mid-Ocean News* guide is inserted in the paper, but the *Bermuda Sun* listings must be purchased separately.

Magazines

RG Magazine
2 Par-la-Ville Rd., Hamilton
• **(441) 295-5881**

RG Magazine, first published in January 1993 by Crown Communications, is a free publication usually circulated the last Thursday of every month as part of *The Royal Gazette*. *RG* has carved a positive niche within the island's print media and has a favorable relationship with its readership. The most widely distributed magazine in Bermuda, the news- and lifestyles-based periodical focuses on topical issues, homes and gardens, food and travel and is filled with splendid full-color photographs. *RG* also provides a detailed calendar of events and has monthly columnists and book reviews.

The magazine, published by Crown Communications, a division of The Royal Gazette Ltd., also publishes *The Bottom Line Magazine* (see subsequent listing). A variety of special event, publicity and sports magazines for events such as the Gillette Tour Challenge Championship and the Samuel L. Jackson Golf Tournament are regularly printed. Crown's offices are in the same building as those of *The Royal Gazette* and *Mid-Ocean News* newspapers.

The Bottom Line Magazine
2 Par-la-Ville Rd., Hamilton
• **(441) 295-5881**

The Bottom Line rolled off the presses in 1991. Published quarterly, it is a general, in-depth business and economics magazine covering current news and information about the island and its largest and fastest-growing sectors — risk and insurance management and international business (see our International Business chapter). Each April issue ties in with the annual RIMS (Risk and Insurance Management Society) Conference. An additional 2,500 issues are printed at that time, bolstering the usual 6,500 magazines normally published each quarter.

Bermudian Magazine
P.O. Box HM 283, Hamilton
• **(441) 295-0695**

Bermudian Magazine is the island's oldest monthly publication, its first edition coming out February 10, 1930. Since then, the editorial focus has centered on showcasing Bermuda's history, society, personalities, arts, architecture, homes and gardens and local lifestyles. Beautifully designed, it offers full-color features, essays, profiles and anecdotes. Published by the Bermudian Publishing Company, *Bermudian Magazine* is available at local newsstands for $4. Local subscriptions are $34, and overseas mailings are $40.

Bermudian Business
P.O. Box HM 283, Hamilton
• **(441) 295-0695**

Bermudian Business, also published by Bermudian Publishing Company, is a quarterly magazine with a strong emphasis on the island's growing international business sector. It offers readers in-depth features and analyses of the Bermuda insurance market, banking, investments, trusts, technology and financial services sectors. The annual Bermudian Business/Deloitte and Touche Insurance Survey, published in the spring edition, is well-read both here and in overseas markets. At local newsstands the magazine sells for $4.25. Subscriptions are $13 yearly in Bermuda, $30 a year in North America, $38 in the U.K. and Europe and $48 for all other regions.

This Week in Bermuda
P.O. Box HM 283, Hamilton
• **(441) 295-0695**

This Week in Bermuda is a free publication that celebrated its 50th birthday in 1997. *This Week* provides visitors with updated weekly listings of cultural, business and sporting events as well as comprehensive information about the island's history, shopping, restaurants, nightlife, boating and watersports and public attractions. You can pick up *This Week*, published by Bermudian Publishing Company, at the Visitors Service Bureau in the Bermuda International Airport, at the Royal Naval Dockyard and in major hotels and guest houses throughout the island. Copies are also made available for conventions and groups and can be obtained by advance order.

Bermuda Magazine
5 Butterfield Pl., 67 Front St., Hamilton
• (441) 292-7279

Described as the magazine that tells the world about Bermuda, *Bermuda Magazine* is a general interest magazine that covers the island's history, culture, art, society and any number of other subjects that help keep visitors in touch with their "home away from home." Its editorial mood is light and breezy. Subscribers here and abroad appreciate its insights into the island's idiosyncrasies as well as its fresh, sometimes playful and irreverent approach to local issues. Published quarterly by Bermuda Marketing Ltd., *Bermuda Magazine* is available by subscription for $19.95 in the U.S. (where it's mailed from) and $27.95 elsewhere.

Preview Magazine
P.O. Box 3273, Hamilton
• (441) 295-4155

Now in its 40th year, *Preview* is a tightly-packed complimentary magazine that provides up-to-date information for Bermuda's visitors. Regular sections include Bermuda Weekly Calendar of Events, Bermuda Business Perspective, Sightseeing, At the Galleries, Wining & Dining, and Shopping. Nautical-related information is also included, as are some small, helpful maps highlighting Bermuda's parishes and several areas. The magazine is available

from all Visitor Service Bureaus, hotels, guest houses, and many shops, restaurants and visitor attractions. Submissions from readers are welcomed.

Radio

It may surprise you, but on our petite island there are eight radio stations. They are evenly distributed between each of our two broadcast companies.

ZFB 1230 AM
ZBM-2 1340 AM
ZBM 89.1 FM
Power 95 FM
P.O. Box HM 452, Hamilton
• (441) 295-2828

The Bermuda Broadcasting Company operates two AM and two FM radio stations. ZBM-2 1340 AM broadcasts two talk format programs for mature listeners and airs international sporting events. ZFB 1230 AM offers religious programming and gospel music and three days per week airs the show "Sixty Something," designed to inform those in their golden years in Bermuda. The show runs from 10 AM to noon Monday, Tuesday and Thursday.

ZBM 89.1 FM plays easy listening music for those who enjoy the mellow tunes. Power 95 FM, launched in 1992, rocks Bermuda with the latest music of today's generation. Diverse, it is current but reminiscent and, most importantly, downright funky.

VSB-1 1450 AM
VSB-2 1280 AM
VSB-3 1160 AM
VSB 106.1 FM (Mix 106)
94 Reid St., Hamilton
• (441) 295-1450

DeFontes Broadcasting Co. Ltd. currently operates three AM radio channels and one FM station. VSB-1 1450 AM plays country-western music 24 hours a day. VSB-2 1280 AM

INSIDERS' TIP

Bermuda's first radio station went on the air on February 10, 1930. Thomas J. Wadson broadcast from his shop in Hamilton using the call letters TJW.

offers nondenominational religious programing. VSB-3 1160 AM features BBC World Service news and current events programing. VSB FM 106.1 is Bermuda's only station that plays an adult contemporary mix of tunes.

Television

Local Broadcast Stations

Bermuda Broadcasting Co. Ltd.
P.O. Box HM 452, Hamilton
• **(441) 295-2828**

In 1997 Bermuda Broadcasting Company celebrated its 50th anniversary, and it continues to provide the island with two of its local commercial television stations. ZFB-TV Channel 7 (cable channel 2) is the Bermuda affiliate of the ABC network in the United States. ZBM-TV Channel 9 (cable channel 3) is the Bermuda affiliate of America's CBS network.

Bermuda Broadcasting Company also produces local programs apart from daily news broadcasts and special events. The company also offered award-winning coverage of Bermuda's unprecedented 1994 run in the World Cup, delivering live satellite coverage as Bermuda competed in Canada, Jamaica, Haiti and El Salvador.

DeFontes Broadcasting (Television), Ltd.
94 Reid St., Hamilton
• **(441) 295-1450**

DeFontes Broadcasting became a competitor in the television-viewer stakes in June 1991 when it launched from studios in the heart of Bermuda at Barkers Hill in Devonshire Parish. VSB-TV Channel 11 (cable channel 4) offers a mix of programming from Cable News Network, Channel America Network and NBC, of which it became an affiliate in October 1993.

VSB-TV has established itself as a leader in local programming by offering viewers an award-winning news broadcast with comprehensive weather and sports at 7 PM Monday through Friday, and in-depth late news coverage at midnight. Other programs include "Tourism in Focus," produced by our Department of Tourism; the "Curious Cook," a monthly cooking show; and "Inside Bermuda," a talk show focusing on the events and personalities of Bermuda.

Cable Television

Bermuda Cablevision Ltd.
19 Laffan St., Hamilton
• **(441) 292-5544**

Bermuda Cablevision holds the island's cable reins. It is the only local cable subscription service and is hooked-up to some 13,000 households and hotel properties in Bermuda. Through various packages, more than 50 channels are accessible 24 hours a day from the U.S., Canada, the U.K. and Portugal.

Closed-Circuit

The Bermuda Channel
5 Butterfield Pl., 67 Front St., Hamilton
• **(441) 292-7279**

The Bermuda Channel, an informational videotape service, is offered via closed-circuit TV to 70 percent of the island's major resorts and hotel rooms. Produced by Bermuda Marketing Ltd., this colorful, picturesque video is filled with information about Bermuda history, culture, sightseeing, sports, transportation, restaurants, shopping and much more. Updated annually, tapes can be purchased from Bermuda Marketing Ltd. for $24.95.

Internet Services

Logic Communications Ltd.
Richmond House, 12 Par-la-Ville Rd., Hamilton • (441) 296-9600

Logic Communications, formerly Internet Bermuda Ltd., was Bermuda's first Internet service provider. With more than 4,000 dial-up

INSIDERS' TIP

The Royal Gazette carries next-day stock reports.

and 1,500 corporate customers, Logic has experienced phenomenal acceptance among Bermuda's 60,000 residents. They began operations in January 1994. In 1995, Logic completed an agreement with Netscape Communications Corporation to become its master value-added reseller (VAR) for all of the Caribbean, establishing itself as a leading Internet provider. For dial-up customers, Logic offers more than just basic connectivity and e-mail. Personal web pages, help desk and several community websites are a few of their other services. The principal website address (http://www.logic.bm) is Logic's magazine-style site that offers information to tourists and locals alike. Current events are highlighted on the home page, where the local weather is updated three times daily.

Logic provides temporary dial-up accounts for the business traveler. In addition to dial-up connections, Logic offers a wide range of corporate services that include dedicated-line connections to the Internet, website design and hosting, Internet/Intranet, security consultation and low-cost international faxing service.

North Rock Communications Ltd.
7 Washington Ln., P.O. Box HM 1661, Hamilton • (441) 296-2700

In December 1997, North Rock Communications went online to become the island's second service provider. One surprise announcement, however, involved North Rock NetTV — a set-top device that allows users to surf the web, send e-mail and chat in newsgroups, all without owning a computer.

In conjunction with the global roaming network iPass, North Rock announced it will offer local-call Internet and e-mail access from more than 1,460 locations in more than 150 countries. Internet users can visit North Rock's website (http://www.northrock.bm) for more information and updates.

Telephone Services

Bermuda Telephone Company Limited (BTC)
31 Victoria Street, Hamilton
• (441) 295-1001

For more than a century the Bermuda Tele-

phone Company has provided telephone and communication services to and from the island. Its first telephone exchange opened on 18 July 1887, and today the company is considered a world-class communications organization. With several hundred employees, BTC handles the bulk of local telephone calls combined with an average 35,000 overseas calls placed each workday. In tandem with continuing expansion of the island's international business sector, the company has geared up to meet challenges as it strives to keep abreast of sophisticated telecommunications demands.

Cable & Wireless Plc
20 Church Street West, Hamilton
• (441) 297-7000

This company has had a presence in Bermuda since 1907 when, following the development of wireless, Bermuda became a key link in the wireless network between London and Canada. Direct services were quickly established with New York and the West Indies. And telephone services from Bermuda to a number of European and African countries followed. Today, international phone calls can be made from any touch tone phone using their Prepaid World Calling Cards (in denominations of $10, $25 and $50) available at a number of locations throughout Bermuda. Overseas phone booths, cable and fax services are available at their main office opposite City Hall in Hamilton.

TeleBermuda International Ltd.
Mintflower Place, 8 Par-la-Ville Road, Hamilton • (441) 296-9000

Through its digital fibre-optic connections, TeleBermuda connects Bermuda to the world. Direct dial, fax, calling cards, and digital international leased circuits are services provided. Their Customer Care center (open from 10 AM to 5 PM weekdays and 10 AM to 2 PM Saturdays) is in the Emporium Building on Front Street in Hamilton. There you can buy Prepaid Global Calling Cards (in denominations of $10, $25 and $50) which can be used in Bermuda, the US, Canada and the UK. For more information call (441) 292-7853.

It is likely you will have no problem finding a place that fits your religious framework. As you tour the island you will notice the number of churches dotting each parish, their pastel colors as striking as domestic dwellings.

Worship

Just a couple of decades ago it was said Bermuda had more churches, and bars, per square mile than any other spot on earth. Sin and salvation were neatly juxtaposed, often within the proverbial stone's throw of each other. But although the number of bars has declined and many have been replaced by fancier pubs and restaurants, the number of churches has grown. Some 30 different faiths have generated more than 105 places of worship, with Sabbath and Sunday claiming steadfast adherents.

The island's most recent census revealed that Anglicans, Catholics and African Methodist Episcopalians (AME) comprise just over one half of the population. Other denominations with significant congregations include Seventh Day Adventist, Methodist, and Presbyterian. However, Church of God and Pentecostal denominations reflect the largest increase of new members, each recording a 39 percent rise.

It is likely you will have no problem finding a place that fits your religious framework. As you tour the island you will notice the number of churches dotting each parish, their pastel colors as striking as domestic dwellings. Although today Bermuda embraces most of the world's faiths, this tolerance did not always exist.

History

From the outset of the island's colonization, the Anglican religion was the official and established faith — and God help those who dared to follow any other religion. The early settlers were required to take an oath that demanded they stand by the Church of England and maintain it against all "Atheists, Papists, Anabaptists, Brownists, and all other heretiques and sectaries whatsoever." (Brownists were the followers of Puritan separatist, Robert Browne (1550-1633), who preached against the discipline of the Anglican church. He would later become reconciled with the Church of England after a three-year exile in Holland.)

The Virginia Company in London, those businessmen who invested in Bermuda as a commercial enterprise, had very early on instructed the governor and local council to be vigilant against "all factious and seditious preaching, teaching and disputing, as well in private, as publicke." And although Presbyterian adherents were among the early colonists — we'll discuss more on them further on — Anglicans dominated the religious landscape.

St. Peter's Church in St. George's, which was first built of cedar in 1612 by Governor Richard Moore, is the oldest Anglican Church in continuous use in the Western Hemisphere. It stands on the site of what is believed to be the most ancient Anglo-Saxon church site in the New World. It was also here where the first General Assembly (the equivalent today would be Bermuda's Parliament) held its initial meeting on 1 August 1620. (See Attractions chapter.)

Although Anglicanism was Bermuda's official faith, Presbyterianism dates from 1612. On the Middle Road in Warwick, across from the Belmont Hotel golf course, is Christ Church (Church of Scotland). It is said to not only be the oldest Presbyterian Church in the British colonies, but also in the Western world. The present building, which has been added to over the years, was erected in 1719. The church still uses an exquisite mahogany pulpit that was built prior to the abolition of slavery by a slave named James Williams.

The compatibility, or lack thereof, of slavery with Christianity presented knotty problems for Bermudian whites, the majority of whom preferred to keep the scriptures at arm's length from the slave population. Many professed uncertainty as to whether a slave possessed a soul, and if he or she did, Christianity would render that slave unfit for servitude. Baptism was soundly discouraged. Although slaves were generally allowed to bury their dead in existing churchyards, the burial plots for slaves were distinctly separate from the rest of the churchyard. In addition, the burial service was always conducted by a black person.

This distinction is clearly evident at St. Peter's Church where the burial plot for slaves lies just west of the church. In his book *Bermuda in the Old Empire*, late historian Henry C. Wilkinson notes that: "A twentieth-century descendant of these slaves has remarked, half quizzically and half ironically, concerning the chances of his forebears: 'So far was the internment to the westward, it was not expected the dead would ever see the dawn of Resurrection Day'."

Marriage for slaves, which included significant numbers of Native Americans shipped to Bermuda following brutal wars and skirmishes in the colonies in America, followed a ceremony no doubt familiar to black American slaves: that of jumping three times over a broomstick held at a convenient height by selected principals. A church wedding was unheard of.

However, slavery notwithstanding in all its particular and peculiar aspects in Bermuda, whatever transpired in the "Mother Country" usually had some affect on the island populace. Storm clouds of religious dissent, beginning toward the middle of the seventeenth century, crossed the Atlantic to hover ominously over Bermuda's struggling community. Puritans in England, who dominated the first three parliaments of Charles I, challenged Catholic elements of Anglican hierarchy and liturgy and broke with uniformity, adopting the motto, "The Bible, the whole Bible, and nothing but the Bible".

www.insiders.com
See this and many other
Insiders' Guide
destinations online.
Visit us today!

Charles' pressure on Presbyterian Scotland to accept the Anglican *Book of Common Prayer* led to the Bishop's War (1639-1640), and his insistence on forcing conformity between Puritans and Catholics helped fan the flames for civil war.

Inevitably, Bermudian society became increasingly polarized, the situation approaching volatility. A small Puritan band formed, holding meetings in a mill at Mill's Creek in Pembroke. (The mill no longer exists.) Following the British Privy Council's statement that some "nonconformist" ministers — a term originally applied to Church of England members who did not conform with its rituals — were coming to Bermuda to "nourish and preserve their factious and schismaticali humours," the seeds for a Puritan exodus from Bermuda took root.

William Sayle, who served a first term as governor in 1641, a second in 1643, and who composed a triumvirate with Stephen Paynter and William Wilkinson in 1644, became a firm supporter of the local Puritans who welcomed the endorsement of the British New Model Army. The army's declaration that the inhabitants of Bermuda "shall, without any molestation or trouble, have and enjoy the liberty of their consciences in matters of God's worship" failed to influence local royalists who had no patience with the homegrown "roundheads" (a name that originally referred to the short haircuts of the apprentices who demonstrated against Charles I at Westminster in 1640).

By 1647, religious wrangling proved too much for Bermuda's Puritans, who determined to depart Bermuda and form their own society in Eleuthera.

Eleuthera — a Greek word meaning freedom — is a long, narrow island perched on the edge of the Atlantic, on the eastern rim of the Bahamas. It would ultimately become home to these Puritan Bermudians who would

INSIDERS' TIP

A detailed listing of churches can be found in the Yellow Pages of the Bermuda telephone directory or by consulting the social desk at your hotel.

be the first to colonize the Bahamas more than 100 years after the Lucayan Indians were transported from that area by the Spanish.

Early in 1648 approximately 70 local settlers led by Sayle, and accompanied by some Puritan "strangers", a handful of slaves, and a free African, set sail to carve a new life in the Caribbean.

Just off the northern end of Eleuthera lies the Devil's Backbone, a barrier of treacherous reefs that sent the Puritans' ship *William* to a watery grave. Having suffered one fatality (believed to be the African) in the wreck, the bedraggled Puritans struggled ashore. Less than 200 yards inland they found a cave. Within its cathedral-like atmosphere, they chiseled a crude pulpit out of rock. Eventually named Preacher's Cave, it became both a church and the seat of government.

In June 1992, the bones of a woman and child were unearthed in this cave, along with pottery shards, clay pipes, and animal bones. The young woman, estimated to have been in her early twenties, had been buried in a shroud and placed in a wooden casket. Brass pins that had fastened the shroud lay close by. The child, believed under 2 years of age, had been interred in a shroud.

American archaeologist, Robert S. Carr, who directed the excavation, described the discovery as "comparable to finding the remains of the Pilgrims in North America. They have something of the drama about them, akin to discoveries at Pitcairn Island. This discovery is significant not only to Bermuda, but also to the Bahamas. It will replace a lost page of our New World history."

Any number of circumstances affected Bermuda's religious life. In 1660, two Quakers, the first of that sect to arrive in Bermuda, traveled throughout the island and were successful in attracting many followers. Despite these followers, their reception was far from warm, and they experienced considerable persecution. Eventually they packed their bags and, like the Puritans, bid the island adieu. By the end of the seventeenth century, the Presbyterians had become a dominant group, but this did not last. By 1720, the Anglican Church had solidly revived and remains the preeminent denomination today.

As Bermuda struggled through those early centuries to establish a sound economy — and this was often by almost any means necessary — many church leaders were not immune to recognizing an opportunity for a personal financial growth.

In his 1924 book *Bermuda Past and Present*, Walter B. Hayward relates a story associated with St. Ann's Church, situated near Church Bay in Southampton. This church, occupying its present site since the island's early settlement, had its nave erected in stone in 1717, and has been said to possess Bermuda's "Holy Grail" — a silver chalice hallmarked 1603-04.

During the eighteenth century, Bermudian "wreckers" would place lights on the reefs to deceive passing ships and lure them to their doom. These wreckers would then row out in whaleboats or sail out in gigs to plunder these "lame ducks" of whatever booty could be transported safely back to the mainland.

"Many an unfortunate skipper," writes Hayward, managed to "save ship and cargo only to lose both in satisfying the claims of wreckers." According to Hayward, the church rector was preaching fervently one stormy Sunday when a man entered St. Ann's and whispered to several members of the congregation who then promptly reached for their hats. It did not take the rector long to notice signs of uneasiness, and he demanded of the man his reason for disturbing the service. "Parson," came the answer, "there's a ship on the southwest breakers."

Hayward continues: "Sabbath piety, as the rector knew, must disappear under the circumstances, and he remarked impressively, 'The congregation will remain seated until I take off my surplice, and then, boys, we'll all start fair.'" Apparently religious matters were one thing, while secular profit was quite another.

Throughout the eighteenth century as white ministers and missionaries arrived and preached, blacks were barred from the churches. In July 1800, Methodist missionary John Stephenson was jailed in St. George's for six months and fined for "preaching the gospel of Jesus Christ to African blacks and captive Negroes." While in prison, Stephenson continued to preach to slaves through his cell window.

Many delightful churches sprang up throughout the parishes in the eighteenth century. Yet, in his book *America*, published in 1795, W. Winterbotham noted that "A regard for religion is not the characteristic of Bermudians; they seldom go to church, except to attend a funeral or get their children baptized, or hear a stranger." However, this may have been a somewhat harsh judgment.

Some of the island's most historic churches were built during the nineteenth century, among them the Cobb's Hill Wesleyan Methodist Church. From the 1800s onwards, no doubt influenced by the Stephenson episode, slaves began organizing their own prayer meetings, despite various efforts to discourage such development. And it was the growth of one such prayer group, the Warwick Methodist Society, that led to the construction of the chapel at Cobb's Hill.

Built by slaves prior to Emancipation, this chapel lies near the boundary between Paget and Warwick parishes. Its construction was spearheaded by Edward Fraser, a slave who could read and write and who worked as a shoemaker and an assistant in a shipping business. Once done with their daily tasks, male and female slaves worked on holidays and at night, carrying stone from nearby quarries in their determination to build their own place of worship.

Aided by Chief Justice James C. Esten, Fraser had been able to cut through a great deal of red tape in purchasing the property. On 17 November 1827, the one-room chapel, fitted with cedar pews, was dedicated. It has since been added to, and some members of today's congregation are direct descendants of those first builders. Fraser, who became a minister, was sent by the Methodists to the West Indies and spent the rest of his life serving as a missionary in Antigua, the British Virgin Islands, Dominica and Jamaica.

The Cobb's Hill chapel paved the way for other churches composed of predominantly black congregations. In May 1885, Bermuda's first African Methodist Episcopal (AME) Church, St. John, on Wilkerson Avenue in Bailey's Bay, was dedicated.

In the city of Hamilton, the Bermuda Cathedral, with its Gothic and Middle English architecture, is a striking landmark. Constituted by an 1894 act of the Bermuda Legislature, the cathedral cost more than 50,000 pounds sterling to build (roughly equivalent to a quarter-million dollars). It is constructed of local limestone, granite columns from Scotland, Caen stone from France, Bedford Buff Indiana limestone, as well as stone from Nova Scotia. One of the city's main attractions, the cathedral is often a venue for varied musical events. The church tower is 143 feet tall and open for tours year-round. Visitors who climb the 155 steps obtain an unparalleled view of Hamilton as it retreats from the harbor.

Many churches in Bermuda chronicle genealogical history, with church records enabling many Bermudians to trace their ancestry back many decades and more. It is not uncommon to find generations of one family having belonged to a particular parish church for centuries. Often you'll find plaques, stained-glass windows, hymnals and other religious items given to churches in memorial of deceased family members.

Bermudians can be rather expressive musically during worship, and some churches may have more than one choir singing during services. Each year there is a concert in the city's Victoria Park showcasing local gospel choirs and singers from around the island. Sacred music recitals are also sponsored by several churches throughout the year.

A Melting Pot of Faiths

In this chapter, rather than give you individual listings of churches by parish, we thought it appropriate to give an overview of the denominations represented.

Various nationalities and ethnic groups have brought new dimensions to Bermuda's religious diversity. Although, as we've pointed out earlier, the latest census shows significant numbers of our population belong to the Anglican, Catholic and AME churches, you will find many other religions. Some of these you might be surprised to find on so tiny an island. We have Muslims, Rastafarians, Jehovah's Witnesses, members of the Ausar Auset Society, the Ethiopian Orthodox Church, practitioners of Baha'I, and the Unity Foundation of Truth.

Although there are no synagogues or a

resident rabbi in Bermuda, the Jewish Community has lay leaders who conduct a Shabbat service on the first Friday of every month at the Unity Foundation of Truth on Reid Street. Torah study is on a Sunday, usually in the middle of the month, and is generally held at someone's home. For special holiday services, a visiting rabbi conducts worship. We have some East Indians that are Hindu, but you'll currently find no temples here. Most of the Hindus perform family worship in their homes.

The conventional mainstream churches on the island include the Anglican (Church of England), AME, Baptist, Roman Catholic, Methodist, Presbyterian, Lutheran, the Bermuda Division of the Salvation Army and the Seventh-Day Adventist. There are also a number of churches, perhaps with smaller congregations, which have established sound reputations within the community. They include the Brethren, Church of God, Church of Christ, Apostolic Faith, Church of God Prophecy, Christian Science, Church of the Nazarene, Church of Jesus Christ of Latter-day Saints, New Testament Church of God, United Holy Churches of Bermuda (Pentecostal), Worldwide Church of God, and the Evangelical Church of Bermuda which has served the community for more than 150 years.

A broad spectrum of assemblies and ministries are also represented. Some of these are the Pentecostal Assemblies of Canada (Maritime District), Pentecostal Assemblies of the West Indies, Revival Assembly of Bermuda, Living Epistle Ministries, Full Gospel Charismatic (Paget) Christian Assembly, Exousia Christian Fellowship, Touch Through Me Ministries, Hands of Love Ministry, and Cure Ministries — Christians United Reaching Everyone. Another sector of our population worships with Radnor Road Christian Fellowship or the Evangel Tabernacle (God's Deliverance Center). Both churches are nondenominational.

No matter how inclusive our listing may appear, there may be those denominations and faiths that we have missed. Still, we think you'll get the point: This is a country where freedom of religion is enjoyed and wholeheartedly embraced.

Practicing What They Preach

Throughout Bermuda's history, church congregations have been active in the community and they continue to do so today. Currently this can be observed in the crossover of ministers and pastors who are occasionally involved in the social and political arenas. A number of ministries have developed programs and services that offer emergency shelter facilities, free meals, medical screening and clothing giveaways to the needy. The Salvation Army is deeply involved in various outreach programs, including helping those with drug and alcohol problems.

Some churches also assist the Emergency Measures Organizations (EMO), a group formed 20 years ago to combine the services of government, the utilities and private agencies into one body that provides the public with information and help before or after a storm or hurricane. In addition, there are several radio and television ministries that make scripture-based family and marriage consultation available.

Through ministerial associations, there are pastoral alliances at the east and west ends of the island, and a new group is being formed for the central parishes — the Central Parishes Ministerial Fellowship. Historically, such associations have fostered fellowship, mutual understanding and support among ministers in Bermuda.

Whether you take a meditative stroll along the beach, attend Mass or visit a mosque, following your religious preferences can be a pleasant experience in Bermuda. To further acquaint yourself with worship options on our island, you will find additional information and individual church listings in the weekend newspapers — Friday in the *Mid-Oceans News* and *The Bermuda Sun*, and Saturday in the *Royal Gazette*.

Index of Advertisers

Index

Going Somewhere?

Insiders' Publishing presents these current and upcoming titles to popular destinations all over the country — and we're planning on adding many more. To order a title, go to your local bookstore or call (800) 582-2665 and we'll direct you to one.

Adirondacks

Atlanta, GA

Baltimore, MD

Bend, OR

Bermuda

Boca Raton and the Palm Beaches, FL

Boise, ID

Boulder, CO, and
Rocky Mountain National Park

Bradenton/Sarasota, FL

Branson, MO, and the
Ozark Mountains

California's Wine Country

Cape Cod, Nantucket and
Martha's Vineyard, MA

Charleston, SC

Cincinnati, OH

Civil War Sites in the Eastern Theater

Civil War Sites in the Southern Theater

Colorado's Mountains

Denver, CO

Florida Keys and Key West

Florida's Great Northwest

Golf in the Carolinas

Indianapolis, IN

The Lake Superior Region

Las Vegas, NV

Lexington, KY

Louisville, KY

Madison, WI

Maine's Mid-Coast

Maine's Southern Coast

Michigan's Traverse Bay Region

Minneapolis/St. Paul, MN

Mississippi

Monterey Peninsula

Myrtle Beach, SC

Nashville, TN

New Hampshire

New Orleans, LA

North Carolina's Central Coast
and New Bern

North Carolina's Mountains

Outer Banks of North Carolina

Phoenix, AZ

The Pocono Mountains

Relocation

Richmond, VA

Salt Lake City, UT

San Diego, CA

Santa Barbara, CA

Santa Fe, NM

Savannah, GA

Southwestern Utah

Tampa/St. Petersburg, FL

Texas Coastal Bend

Tucson, AZ

Virginia's Blue Ridge

Virginia's Chesapeake Bay

Washington, D.C.

Wichita, KS

Williamsburg, VA

Wilmington, NC

Yellowstone

THE INSIDERS' GUIDE ®

Insiders' Publishing • P.O. Box 1718 • Helena, MT 59624
Phone (406) 443-3021 • Fax (406) 443-3191 • www.insiders.com